NOVELS
for Students

Advisors

Erik France: Adjunct Instructor of English, Macomb Community College, Warren, Michigan. B.A. and M.S.L.S. from University of North Carolina, Chapel Hill; Ph.D. from Temple University.

Kate Hamill: Grade 12 English Teacher, Catonsville High School, Catonsville, Maryland.

Joseph McGeary: English Teacher, Germantown Friends School, Philadelphia, Pennsylvania. Ph.D. in English from Duke University.

Timothy Showalter: English Department Chair, Franklin High School, Reisterstown, Maryland. Certified teacher by the Maryland State Department of Education. Member of the National Council of Teachers of English.

Amy Spade Silverman: English Department Chair, Kehillah Jewish High School, Palo Alto, California. Member of National Council of Teachers of English (NCTE), Teachers and Writers, and NCTE Opinion Panel. Exam Reader, Advanced Placement Literature and Composition. Poet, published in *North American Review, Nimrod,* and *Michigan Quarterly Review,* among other publications.

Jody Stefansson: Director of Boswell Library and Study Center and Upper School Learning Specialist, Polytechnic School, Pasadena, California. Board member, Children's Literature Council of Southern California. Member of American Library Association, Association of Independent School Librarians, and Association of Educational Therapists.

Laura Jean Waters: Certified School Library Media Specialist, Wilton High School, Wilton, Connecticut. B.A. from Fordham University; M.A. from Fairfield University.

NOVELS
for Students

**Presenting Analysis, Context, and Criticism on
Commonly Studied Novels**

VOLUME 30

GALE
CENGAGE Learning

Detroit • New York • San Francisco • New Haven, Conn • Waterville, Maine • London

Novels for Students, Volume 30

Project Editor: Sara Constantakis

Rights Acquisition and Management: Leitha Etheridge-Sims, Sari Gordon, Aja Perales, Jhanay Williams

Composition: Evi Abou-El-Seoud

Manufacturing: Drew Kalasky

Imaging: John Watkins

Product Design: Pamela A. E. Galbreath, Jennifer Wahi

Content Conversion: Katrina Coach

Product Manager: Meggin Condino

For product information and technology assistance, contact us at **Gale Customer Support, 1-800-877-4253.**
For permission to use material from this text or product, submit all requests online at **www.cengage.com/permissions.**
Further permissions questions can be emailed to **permissionrequest@cengage.com**

While every effort has been made to ensure the reliability of the information presented in this publication, Gale, a part of Cengage Learning, does not guarantee the accuracy of the data contained herein. Gale accepts no payment for listing; and inclusion in the publication of any organization, agency, institution, publication, service, or individual does not imply endorsement of the editors or publisher. Errors brought to the attention of the publisher and verified to the satisfaction of the publisher will be corrected in future editions.

Gale
27500 Drake Rd.
Farmington Hills, MI, 48331-3535

ISBN-13: 978-0-7876-8687-1
ISBN-10: 0-7876-8687-5

ISSN 1094-3552

This title is also available as an e-book.
ISBN-13: 978-1-4144-4946-3
ISBN-10: 1-4144-4946-1
Contact your Gale, a part of Cengage Learning sales representative for ordering information.

11/09

Table of Contents

The Informed Dialogue: Interacting with Literature

When we pick up a book, we usually do so with the anticipation of pleasure. We hope that by entering the time and place of the novel and sharing the thoughts and actions of the characters, we will find enjoyment. Unfortunately, this is often not the case; we are disappointed. But we should ask, has the author failed us, or have we failed the author?

We establish a dialogue with the author, the book, and with ourselves when we read. Consciously and unconsciously, we ask questions: "Why did the author write this book?" "Why did the author choose that time, place, or character?" "How did the author achieve that effect?" "Why did the character act that way?" "Would I act in the same way?" The answers we receive depend upon how much information about literature in general and about that book specifically we ourselves bring to our reading.

Young children have limited life and literary experiences. Being young, children frequently do not know how to go about exploring a book, nor sometimes, even know the questions to ask of a book. The books they read help them answer questions, the author often coming right out and *telling* young readers the things they are learning or are expected to learn. The perennial classic, *The Little Engine That Could, tells* its readers that, among other things, it is good to help others and brings happiness:

"Hurray, hurray," cried the funny little clown and all the dolls and toys. "The good little boys and girls in the city will be happy because you helped us, kind, Little Blue Engine."

In picture books, messages are often blatant and simple, the dialogue between the author and reader one-sided. Young children are concerned with the end result of a book—the enjoyment gained, the lesson learned—rather than with how that result was obtained. As we grow older and read further, however, we question more. We come to expect that the world within the book will closely mirror the concerns of our world, and that the author will *show* these through the events, descriptions, and conversations within the story, rather than *telling* of them. We are now expected to do the interpreting, carry on our share of the dialogue with the book and author, and glean not only the author's message, but comprehend how that message and the overall affect of the book were achieved. Sometimes, however, we need help to do these things. *Novels for Students* provides that help.

A novel is made up of many parts interacting to create a coherent whole. In reading a novel, the more obvious features can be easily spotted—theme, characters, plot—but we may overlook the more subtle elements that greatly influence how the novel is perceived by the reader: viewpoint, mood and tone, symbolism, or the use of humor. By focusing on both the obvious and more subtle literary elements within a novel,

Novels for Students aids readers in both analyzing for message and in determining how and why that message is communicated. In the discussion on Harper Lee's *To Kill a Mockingbird* (Vol. 2), for example, the mockingbird as a symbol of innocence is dealt with, among other things, as is the importance of Lee's use of humor which "enlivens a serious plot, adds depth to the characterization, and creates a sense of familiarity and universality." The reader comes to understand the internal elements of each novel discussed—as well as the external influences that help shape it.

"The desire to write greatly," Harold Bloom of Yale University says, "is the desire to be elsewhere, in a time and place of one's own, in an originality that must compound with inheritance, with an anxiety of influence." A writer seeks to create a unique world within a story, but although it is unique, it is not disconnected from our own world. It speaks to us *because* of what the writer brings to the writing from our world: how he or she was raised and educated; his or her likes and dislikes; the events occurring in the real world at the time of the writing, and while the author was growing up. When we know what an author has brought to his or her work, we gain a greater insight into both the "originality" (the world of the book), and the things that "compound" it. This insight enables us to question that created world and find answers more readily. By informing ourselves, we are able to establish a more effective dialogue with both book and author.

Novels for Students, in addition to providing a plot summary and descriptive list of characters—to remind readers of what they have read—also explores the external influences that shaped each book. Each entry includes a discussion of the author's background, and the historical context in which the novel was written. It is vital to know, for instance, that when Ray Bradbury was writing *Fahrenheit 451* (Vol. 1), the threat of Nazi domination had recently ended in Europe, and the McCarthy hearings were taking place in Washington, D.C. This information goes far in answering the question, "Why did he write a story of oppressive government control and book burning?" Similarly, it is important to know that Harper Lee, author of *To Kill a Mockingbird,*was born and raised in Monroeville, Alabama, and that her father was a lawyer. Readers can now see why she chose the south as a setting for her novel—it is the place with which she was most familiar—and start to comprehend her characters and their actions.

Novels for Students helps readers find the answers they seek when they establish a dialogue with a particular novel. It also aids in the posing of questions by providing the opinions and interpretations of various critics and reviewers, broadening that dialogue. Some reviewers of *To Kill A Mockingbird,* for example, "faulted the novel's climax as melodramatic." This statement leads readers to ask, "Is it, indeed, melodramatic?" "If not, why did some reviewers see it as such?" "If it is, why did Lee choose to make it melodramatic?" "Is melodrama ever justified?" By being spurred to ask these questions, readers not only learn more about the book and its writer, but about the nature of writing itself.

The literature included for discussion in *Novels for Students* has been chosen because it has something vital to say to us. *Of Mice and Men, Catch-22, The Joy Luck Club, My Antonia, A Separate Peace* and the other novels here speak of life and modern sensibility. In addition to their individual, specific messages of prejudice, power, love or hate, living and dying, however, they and all great literature also share a common intent. They force us to *think*—about life, literature, and about others, not just about ourselves. They pry us from the narrow confines of our minds and thrust us outward to confront the world of books and the larger, real world we all share. *Novels for Students* helps us in this confrontation by providing the means of enriching our conversation with literature and the world, by creating an *informed* dialogue, one that brings true pleasure to the personal act of reading.

Sources

Harold Bloom, *The Western Canon, The Books and School of the Ages,* Riverhead Books, 1994.

Watty Piper, *The Little Engine That Could,* Platt & Munk, 1930.

Anne Devereaux Jordan
Senior Editor, TALL (Teaching and Learning Literature)

Introduction

Purpose of the Book

The purpose of *Novels for Students* (*NfS*) is to provide readers with a guide to understanding, enjoying, and studying novels by giving them easy access to information about the work. Part of Gale's "For Students" Literature line, *NfS* is specifically designed to meet the curricular needs of high school and undergraduate college students and their teachers, as well as the interests of general readers and researchers considering specific novels. While each volume contains entries on "classic" novels frequently studied in classrooms, there are also entries containing hard-to-find information on contemporary novels, including works by multicultural, international, and women novelists.

The information covered in each entry includes an introduction to the novel and the novel's author; a plot summary, to help readers unravel and understand the events in a novel; descriptions of important characters, including explanation of a given character's role in the novel as well as discussion about that character's relationship to other characters in the novel; analysis of important themes in the novel; and an explanation of important literary techniques and movements as they are demonstrated in the novel.

In addition to this material, which helps the readers analyze the novel itself, students are also provided with important information on the lit-erary and historical background informing each work. This includes a historical context essay, a box comparing the time or place the novel was written to modern Western culture, a critical essay, and excerpts from critical essays on the novel. A unique feature of *NfS* is a specially commissioned critical essay on each novel, targeted toward the student reader.

To further aid the student in studying and enjoying each novel, information on media adaptations is provided (if available), as well as reading suggestions for works of fiction and nonfiction on similar themes and topics. Classroom aids include ideas for research papers and lists of critical sources that provide additional material on the novel.

Selection Criteria

The titles for each volume of *NfS* are selected by surveying numerous sources on notable literary works and analyzing course curricula for various schools, school districts, and states. Some of the sources surveyed include: high school and undergraduate literature anthologies and textbooks; lists of award-winners, and recommended titles, including the Young Adult Library Services Association (YALSA) list of best books for young adults.

Input solicited from our expert advisory board—consisting of educators and librarians—guides us to maintain a mix of "classic" and contemporary literary works, a mix of challenging and engaging works (including genre titles that are commonly studied) appropriate for different age levels, and a mix of international, multicultural and women authors. These advisors also consult on each volume's entry list, advising on which titles are most studied, most appropriate, and meet the broadest interests across secondary (grades 7–12) curricula and undergraduate literature studies.

How Each Entry Is Organized

Each entry, or chapter, in *NfS* focuses on one novel. Each entry heading lists the full name of the novel, the author's name, and the date of the novel's publication. The following elements are contained in each entry:

Introduction: a brief overview of the novel which provides information about its first appearance, its literary standing, any controversies surrounding the work, and major conflicts or themes within the work.

Author Biography: this section includes basic facts about the author's life, and focuses on events and times in the author's life that inspired the novel in question.

Plot Summary: a factual description of the major events in the novel. Lengthy summaries are broken down with subheads.

Characters: an alphabetical listing of major characters in the novel. Each character name is followed by a brief to an extensive description of the character's role in the novel, as well as discussion of the character's actions, relationships, and possible motivation.

Characters are listed alphabetically by last name. If a character is unnamed—for instance, the narrator in *Invisible Man*—the character is listed as "The Narrator" and alphabetized as "Narrator." If a character's first name is the only one given, the name will appear alphabetically by that name.

Variant names are also included for each character. Thus, the full name "Jean Louise Finch" would head the listing for the narrator of *To Kill a Mockingbird*, but listed in a separate cross-reference would be the nickname "Scout Finch."

Themes: a thorough overview of how the major topics, themes, and issues are addressed within the novel. Each theme discussed appears in a separate subhead and is easily accessed through the boldface entries in the Subject/Theme Index.

Style: this section addresses important style elements of the novel, such as setting, point of view, and narration; important literary devices used, such as imagery, foreshadowing, symbolism; and, if applicable, genres to which the work might have belonged, such as Gothicism or Romanticism. Literary terms are explained within the entry but can also be found in the Glossary.

Historical Context: this section outlines the social, political, and cultural climate *in which the author lived and the novel was created.* This section may include descriptions of related historical events, pertinent aspects of daily life in the culture, and the artistic and literary sensibilities of the time in which the work was written. If the novel is a historical work, information regarding the time in which the novel is set is also included. Each section is broken down with helpful subheads.

Critical Overview: this section provides background on the critical reputation of the novel, including bannings or any other public controversies surrounding the work. For older works, this section includes a history of how the novel was first received and how perceptions of it may have changed over the years; for more recent novels, direct quotes from early reviews may also be included.

Criticism: an essay commissioned by *NfS* which specifically deals with the novel and is written specifically for the student audience, as well as excerpts from previously published criticism on the work (if available).

Sources: an alphabetical list of critical material used in compiling the entry, with full bibliographical information.

Further Reading: an alphabetical list of other critical sources which may prove useful for the student. It includes full bibliographical information and a brief annotation.

In addition, each entry contains the following highlighted sections, set apart from the main text as sidebars:

Media Adaptations: if available, a list of important film and television adaptations of the novel, including source information. The list also includes stage adaptations, audio recordings, musical adaptations, etc.

Topics for Further Study: a list of potential study questions or research topics dealing with the novel. This section includes questions related to other disciplines the student may be studying, such as American history, world history, science, math, government, business, geography, economics, psychology, etc.

Compare and Contrast: an "at-a-glance" comparison of the cultural and historical differences between the author's time and culture and late twentieth century or early twenty-first century Western culture. This box includes pertinent parallels between the major scientific, political, and cultural movements of the time or place the novel was written, the time or place the novel was set (if a historical work), and modern Western culture. Works written after the mid-1970s may not have this box.

What Do I Read Next?: a list of works that might complement the featured novel or serve as a contrast to it. This includes works by the same author and others, works of fiction and non-fiction, and works from various genres, cultures, and eras.

Other Features

NfS includes "The Informed Dialogue: Interacting with Literature," a foreword by Anne Devereaux Jordan, Senior Editor for *Teaching and Learning Literature* (*TALL*), and a founder of the Children's Literature Association. This essay provides an enlightening look at how readers interact with literature and how *Novels for Students* can help teachers show students how to enrich their own reading experiences.

A Cumulative Author/Title Index lists the authors and titles covered in each volume of the *NfS* series.

A Cumulative Nationality/Ethnicity Index breaks down the authors and titles covered in each volume of the *NfS* series by nationality and ethnicity.

A Subject/Theme Index, specific to each volume, provides easy reference for users who may be studying a particular subject or theme rather than a single work. Significant subjects, from events to broad themes, are included.

Each entry may include illustrations, including photo of the author, stills from film adaptations, maps, and/or photos of key historical events, if available.

Citing Novels for Students

When writing papers, students who quote directly from any volume of *Novels for Students* may use the following general forms. These examples are based on MLA style; teachers may request that

students adhere to a different style, so the following examples may be adapted as needed.

When citing text from *NfS* that is not attributed to a particular author (i.e., the Themes, Style, Historical Context sections, etc.), the following format should be used in the bibliography section:

> "*Night.*" *Novels for Students.* Ed. Marie Rose Napierkowski. Vol. 4. Detroit: Gale, 1998. 234–35.

When quoting the specially commissioned essay from *NfS* (usually the first piece under the "Criticism" subhead), the following format should be used:

> Miller, Tyrus. Critical Essay on "*Winesburg, Ohio.*" *Novels for Students.* Ed. Marie Rose Napierkowski. Vol. 4. Detroit: Gale, 1998. 335–39.

When quoting a journal or newspaper essay that is reprinted in a volume of *NfS*, the following form may be used:

> Malak, Amin. "Margaret Atwood's *The Handmaid's Tale* and the Dystopian Tradition." *Canadian Literature* 112 (Spring 1987): 9–16. Excerpted and reprinted in *Novels for Students.* Vol. 4. Ed. Marie Rose Napierkowski. Detroit: Gale, 1998. 133–36.

When quoting material reprinted from a book that appears in a volume of *NfS*, the following form may be used:

> Adams, Timothy Dow. "Richard Wright: 'Wearing the Mask.'" In *Telling Lies in Modern American Autobiography.* University of North Carolina Press, 1990. 69–83. Excerpted and reprinted in *Novels for Students.* Vol. 1. Ed. Diane Telgen. Detroit: Gale, 1997. 59–61.

We Welcome Your Suggestions

The editorial staff of *Novels for Students* welcomes your comments and ideas. Readers who wish to suggest novels to appear in future volumes, or who have other suggestions, are cordially invited to contact the editor. You may contact the editor via e-mail at: **ForStudentsEditors@cengage.com.** Or write to the editor at:

Editor, *Novels for Students*
Gale
27500 Drake Road
Farmington Hills, MI 48331-3535

Literary Chronology

1660: Daniel Defoe is born in London, England.

1722: Daniel Defoe's *A Journal of the Plague Year* is published.

1731: Daniel Defoe dies of a stroke in on April 24, in London, England.

1812: Charles Dickens is born on February 7, in Landport, near Portsmouth, England.

1828: Jules Verne is born on February 8, in Nantes, France.

1840: Thomas Hardy is born on June 2, in Dorset, England.

1852–53: Charles Dickens's *Bleak House* is published.

1870: Charles Dickens dies of a stroke on June 9, at Gadshill, near Rochester, England.

1873: Jules Verne's *Around the World in Eighty Days* is published.

1890: Agatha Christie is born on September 15, in Devon, England.

1895: Thomas Hardy's *Jude the Obscure* is published.

1900: Antoine de Saint-Exupéry is born on June 29, in Lyon, France.

1905: Jules Verne dies of diabetes on March 24, in Amiens, France.

1906: Richard Llewellyn is born Richard Herbert Vivian Lloyd on December 8, in Hendon, England.

1906: T. H. White is born on May 29, in Bombay, India.

1919: J. D. Salinger is born on January 1, in New York, New York.

1920: E. R. Braithwaite is born in Georgetown, British Guiana.

1928: Thomas Hardy dies on January 11, in England, after contracting pleurisy.

1936: Agatha Christie's *The A.B.C. Murders* is published.

1937: Walter Dean Myers is born on August 12, in Martinsburg, West Virginia.

1939: Jane Yolen is born on February 11, in New York, New York.

1939: Richard Llewellyn's *How Green Was My Valley* is published.

1943: Antoine de Saint-Exupéry's *The Little Prince* is first published in French and is published in English later the same year.

1944: Antoine de Saint-Exupéry vanishes on a flight mission begun from a base in Corsica on July 29. He is presumed to have been shot down over Nazi-occupied Southern France.

1955: Gish Jen is born Lillian Jen on August 12, in Long Island, New York.

1958: T. H. White's *The Once and Future King* is published.

1959: E. R. Braithwaite's *To Sir, With Love* is published.

1961: J.D. Salinger's Franny and Zooey (initially published as two separate short stories in 1955 and 1957, respectively) is published.

1963: Ann Patchett is born on December 2, in Los Angeles, California.

1964: T. H. White dies on January 17, in Athens, Greece.

1976: Agatha Christie dies on January 12, in Cholsey, England.

1983: Richard Llewellyn dies of a heart attack on November 30, in Dublin, Ireland.

1988: Walter Dean Myers's *Fallen Angels* is published.

1991: Gish Jen's *Typical American* is published.

1992: Jane Yolen's *Briar Rose* is published.

2001: Ann Patchett's *Bel Canto* is published.

Acknowledgments

The editors wish to thank the copyright holders of the excerpted criticism included in this volume and the permissions managers of many book and magazine publishing companies for assisting us in securing reproduction rights. We are also grateful to the staffs of the Detroit Public Library, the Library of Congress, the University of Detroit Mercy Library, Wayne State University Purdy/Kresge Library Complex, and the University of Michigan Libraries for making their resources available to us. Following is a list of the copyright holders who have granted us permission to reproduce material in this volume of *NfS*. Every effort has been made to trace copyright, but if omissions have been made, please let us know.

COPYRIGHTED EXCERPTS IN *NfS*, VOLUME 30, WERE REPRODUCED FROM THE FOLLOWING PERIODICALS:

America, v. 169, July 31, 1993. Copyright © 1993 www.americamagazine.org. All rights reserved. Reproduced by permission of America Press. For subscription information, visit www.americamagazine.org.—*Belles Lettres*, v. 7, winter, 1991-92. Reproduced by permission.—*The Book Report*, v. 12, May/June, 1993. Copyright © 1993 by Linworth Publishing, Inc., Worthington, Ohio. Reproduced by permission.—*Booklist*, May 15, 2006. Copyright © 2006 by the American Library Association. Reproduced by permission.—*Children's Literature*, v. 33, 2005. Copyright

© 2005 by Hollins University. All rights reserved. Reproduced by permission of Johns Hopkins University.—*Chronicle of Higher Education*, v. 51, February 11, 2005. Copyright © 2005 by *The Chronicle of Higher Education*. This article may not be published, reposted, or redistributed without express permission from *The Chronicle*.—*Critique*, v. 47, winter, 2006. Copyright © 2006 by Helen Dwight Reid Educational Foundation. Reproduced with permission of the Helen Dwight Reid Educational Foundation, published by Heldref Publications, 1319 18th Street, NW, Washington, DC 20036-1802.—*Detroit Free Press*, July 6, 2001. Copyright © 2001 Detroit Free Press Inc. Reproduced by permission of the *Detroit Free Press*.—*The English Journal*, v. 95, July, 2003. Copyright © 2003 by the National Council of Teachers of English. Reproduced by permission of the publisher.—*Explicator*, v. 57, spring, 1999; v. 60, fall, 2001; v. 60, winter, 2002; v. 64, fall, 2005. Copyright © 1999, 2001, 2002, 2005 by Helen Dwight Reid Educational Foundation. All reproduced with permission of the Helen Dwight Reid Educational Foundation, published by Heldref Publications, 1319 18th Street, NW, Washington, DC 20036-1802.—*FORUM*, v. 47, 2005 for "Alex Bloom, Pioneer of Radical State Education" by Michael Fielding. Reproduced by permission of the author.—*Guardian*, June 29, 2002 for "The Virtues of Imprisonment" by John Mullan. Reproduced by permission of the author.—*Horn Book Magazine*, v. 84, September/October,

2008. Copyright © 2008 by The Horn Book, Inc., Boston, MA, www.hbook.com. All rights reserved. Reproduced by permission.—***Insight on the News***, v. 11, February 6, 1995. Copyright © 1995 News World Communications, Inc. All rights reserved. Reproduced with permission of *Insight*.—***Kenyon Review***, v. 24, spring, 1962. Copyright © 1962, renewed 1990 by Kenyon College. All rights reserved. Reproduced by permission.—***The Lion and the Unicorn***, v. 23, 1999. Copyright © 1999 The Johns Hopkins University Press. All rights reserved. Reproduced by permission.—***Modern Language Quarterly***, v. 48, September, 1987. Copyright © 1987 Duke University Press. All rights reserved. Used by permission of the publisher.—***Mosaic***, v. 27, June, 1994. Copyright © *Mosaic* 1994. Acknowledgment of previous publication is herewith made.—***Narrative***, v. 14, May, 2006. Copyright © 2006 by the Ohio State University Press. All rights reserved. Reproduced by permission.—***New Statesman***, v. 130, July 30, 2001. Copyright © 2001 New Statesman, Ltd. Reproduced by permission.—***Notes and Queries***, v. 55, March, 2008 for "Marrying One's Ward and 'Bleak House'" by Jill Durey. Copyright © 2008 Oxford University Press. Reproduced by permission of the publisher and the author.—***Publishers Weekly***, v. 239, July 20, 1992; v. 246, March 22, 1999. Copyright © 1992, 1999 by Reed Publishing USA. Both reproduced from *Publishers Weekly*, published by the Bowker Magazine Group of Cahners Publishing Co., a division of Reed Publishing USA, by permission.—***The Reading Teacher***, v. 54, February, 2001. Copyright © 2001 International Reading Association. Reproduced by permission of the International Reading Association.—***School Library Journal***, v. 34, June/July, 1988; v. 39, April, 1993; May 15, 2008. Copyright © 1988, 1993, 2008. All reproduced from *School Library Journal*, a Cahners/R. R. Bowker Publication, by permission.—***Signal***, January, 1973. Copyright © 1973 The Thimble Press. Reproduced by permission of The Thimble Press, Lockwood, Station Road, South Woodchester, Glos., GL5 5EQ, England.—***Times Literary Supplement***, July 27, 2001. Copyright © 2001 by The Times Supplements Limited. Reproduced from *The Times Literary Supplement* by permission.—***Western Folklore***, v. 43, July, 1984. Copyright © 1984 Western States Folklore Society. Reproduced by permission.—***Wisconsin Studies in Contemporary Literature***, v. 3, winter, 1962. Copyright © 1962, renewed 1990 by the Board of Regents of the University of Wisconsin System. Reproduced by permission.—***The Women's Review of Books***, v. 8, July, 1991. Reproduced by permission.—***World Literature Today***, v. 76, spring, 2002; v. 81, May/June, 2007. Copyright © 2002, 2007 by *World Literature Today*. Both reproduced by permission of the publisher.—***The Yearbook of English Studies***, v. 24, 1994 for "Eat a Bowl of Tea: Asian America in the Novels of Gish Jen, Cynthia Kadohata, Kim Ronyoung, Jessica Hagedorn, and Tran Van Dinh" by A. Robert Lee. Reproduced by permission of the author.

COPYRIGHTED EXCERPTS IN *NfS*, VOLUME 30, WERE REPRODUCED FROM THE FOLLOWING BOOKS:

Frazier, Tom. From "Coal Mining, Literature, and the Naturalistic Motif," in ***Caverns of Night: Coal Mines in Art, Literature, and Film***. Edited by William B. Thesing. University of South Carolina Press, 2000. Copyright © 2000 University of South Carolina. Reproduced by permission.—King, Bruce. From ***The Internationalization of English Literature***. Oxford University Press, 2004. Copyright © Bruce King 2004. All rights reserved. Reproduced by permission of Oxford University Press.

Contributors

Bryan Aubrey: Aubrey holds a Ph.D. in English. Entries on *Bleak House, Fallen Angels*, and *Typical American*. Original essays on *Bleak House, Fallen Angels*, and *Typical American*.

Catherine Dominic: Dominic is a novelist and a freelance writer and editor. Entries on *A Journal of the Plague Year* and *To Sir, With Love*. Original essays on *A Journal of the Plague Year* and *To Sir, With Love*.

Sheldon Goldfarb: Goldfarb is a specialist in Victorian literature who has published academic books as well as a novel for young adults set in Victorian times. Entry on *How Green Was My Valley*. Original essay on *How Green Was My Valley*.

Joyce Hart: Hart is a published author and freelance writer. Entries on *The A.B.C. Murders* and *Briar Rose*. Original essays on *The A.B.C. Murders* and *Briar Rose*.

Neil Heims: Heims is a freelance writer and the author or editor of over two dozen books on literary subjects. Entry on *Jude the Obscure*. Original essay on *Jude the Obscure*.

Diane Andrews Henningfeld: Henningfeld is a professor emerita of English who holds a Ph.D. in medieval literature. Entry on *The Once and Future King*. Original essay on *The Once and Future King* .

Claire Robinson: Robinson has a master's degree in English. She is a teacher of English literature and a freelance writer and editor. Entry on *The Little Prince*. Original essay on *The Little Prince*.

Bradley A. Skeen: Skeen is a classics professor. Entry on *Around the World in Eighty Days*. Original essay on *Around the World in Eighty Days*.

Leah Tieger: Tieger is a freelance writer and editor. Entries on *Bel Canto* and *Franny and Zooey*. Original essays on *Bel Canto* and *Franny and Zooey*.

The A.B.C. Murders

AGATHA CHRISTIE

1936

The A.B.C. Murders, first published in 1936, is considered one of Agatha Christie's more popular novels. The story features Inspector Hercule Poirot, a famed Belgian detective who lives in London and has an ego almost as big as his reputation. As the story opens in 1935 London, readers find Poirot perplexed by an anonymous letter sent to mock his reputation. The writer of the letter tells Poirot where he will commit a murder and taunts Poirot to find him before he accomplishes the feat. Poirot gets there too late to prevent the murder and while sorting through the clues receives a second letter, in which the anonymous writer announces that a new murder is to be carried out. Poirot rushes to prevent the second murder, but again he is too late. So the sequence continues as the murderer keeps producing new victims, from Mrs. Ascher in Andover to Miss Barnard in Bexhill and on down the alphabetical line.

Readers follow Poirot through his investigations as Christie builds up the tension. The path to the climax runs along a twisting plotline that turns as sharply as a narrow mountain road. Finally, Poirot announces his stunning conclusion, and readers find that the character who seemed most guilty is not the killer at all. Not until the closing chapters does Poirot explain who the real culprit is, a total surprise to the other characters of the story as well as to the reading audience. A new hardcover edition of this novel was published in 2006.

Agatha Christie (*AP Images*)

AUTHOR BIOGRAPHY

One of the world's best-known murder-mystery writers, Agatha Christie began her life in Torquay, in Devon, England, on September 15, 1890. She was born Agatha Mary Clarissa Miller to Frederick Alvah Miller, a well-to-do American stockbroker, and Clarissa Boehmer, who was the daughter of a British army captain. Christie had two older siblings, her sister, Madge, and her brother, Monty.

The author married Colonel Archibald Christie in 1914, when she was twenty-four. Five years later, in 1919, she gave birth to her only child, Rosaline. In 1926, Christie's husband told her that he was leaving her for another woman. Christie disappeared for a week and a half, and rumors spread that she wanted the police to think that her husband had murdered her to punish him for leaving. Christie remarried in 1930 to an archaeologist, Sir Max Mallowan, who was fourteen years her junior. She traveled throughout the Middle East with Mallowan, which contributed to the settings of several of her novels, such as *Murder on the Orient Express* (1934).

Christie's writing was prolific over the next decade, during which time she developed two major characters for her murder mysteries, Inspector Hercule Poirot and Miss Jane Marple. Poirot made his first appearance in Christie's first novel and was long featured by the author, acting as the main character in almost fifty novels and short stories. Miss Marple was a later creation, making her first appearance in 1930 in *The Murder at the Vicarage*. Miss Marple appeared in fewer than twenty of Christie's stories.

Christie's mystery novels have sold in the billions, but she wrote in other genres as well, penning short stories; stage, radio, and television scripts; three collections of poems; and two nonfiction books, including an autobiography. She also wrote six romance novels under the pseudonym Mary Westmacott. Many of her works were adapted by other authors into plays, television shows, and movies. Video games based on her novels have also become available in the past several years. In 2004, Japanese animation artists created a television series based on Christie's leading characters, called *Agatha Christie's Great Detectives Poirot and Marple*.

In 1971, five years before she died, Christie was named a dame of the British Empire, the female equivalent of being knighted. Christie died on January 12, 1976, at Winterbrook House in Cholsey Parish, and she is buried in St. Mary's Churchyard there. She was eighty-five.

PLOT SUMMARY

Chapters 1–7

Christie's *The A.B.C. Murders* opens in London in 1935. Inspector Hercule Poirot's friend Captain Hastings is visiting. Poirot has recently received an anonymous letter. The letter writer has named a deed that he will perform in Andover on the twenty-first of the month and has challenged Poirot to discover it. The writer also mocks Poirot in the letter, suggesting that the inspector thinks too highly of himself.

The next chapter introduces Alexander Bonaparte Cust. The reader, at this point, knows nothing about Cust. He and his everyday actions are described, but no comment is made about how he fits into the story.

On the twenty-first of the month, there is indeed an incident in Andover. Mrs. Ascher has

MEDIA ADAPTATIONS

- Christie's *The A.B.C. Murders* was made into a movie in 1965 titled *The Alphabet Murders*. David Pursall and Jack Seddon wrote the script, Frank Tashlin directed, and Tony Randall played the role of Hercule Poirot.

- In "The A.B.C. Murders" was a 1992 television adaptation made as part of the series *Agatha Christie: Poirot*.

- An audio CD of *The A.B.C. Murders* was made by Audio Renaissance in 2003, with Hugh Fraser reading the text.

- In 2008, Awe Productions published a computer game titled *Agatha Christie: The A.B.C. Murders*. In this game, players help Inspector Poirot find the murderer.

been murdered. Chief Inspector Japp of Scotland Yard appears at Poirot's door to make the announcement. Although Japp also knew of the anonymous letter that Poirot received, he was unable to stop the crime as he had too little information to act on.

Upon arrival in Andover, Poirot checks in with the local police and gathers information about Alice Ascher, the murder victim, and any possible suspects. Mrs. Ascher's husband is among the list of names. Franz Ascher is an unemployed alcoholic who often threatened Mrs. Ascher if she refused to give him money. However, Mr. Ascher has an alibi. Meanwhile, Poirot learns of a train schedule, known locally as the A.B.C. railway guide, that has been left at the scene of the crime.

Poirot and Hastings travel to Overton to question Mary Drower, Mrs. Ascher's niece. Mary is a housemaid and often visited her aunt; Mary had also lived with her aunt after her own mother died. She tells Poirot that Mr. Ascher is not the type who would have killed his wife. He threatened his wife, but Mrs. Ascher always said she could handle him. Mary has no idea who might have killed her aunt.

Chapters 8–14

The second letter arrives at the beginning of chapter 8. In the letter, the anonymous writer tells Poirot that with the murder of Mrs. Ascher, the murderer has scored the first point. Then the murderer states that the next murder will occur in Bexhill-on-the-Sea on the twenty-fifth. After reading this latest letter, Hastings and Poirot realize, because of the alphabetical progression, that they have a serial killer on their hands.

Scotland Yard officials call a meeting. In attendance are Poirot and Hastings as well as Inspector Japp; Inspector Glen, from Andover; a psychologist, Dr. Thompson; and a relatively young inspector who is new to the force, a man named Crome. During their discussion, Poirot suggests that the next victim's last name will probably begin with the letter *B*. The police accept this as a possibility and plan to keep a lookout for suspicious strangers in Bexhill.

On the morning of the twenty-fifth, news of a murder in Bexhill-on-the-Sea is delivered to Poirot. A young woman by the name of Elizabeth Barnard has been strangled. Her body was discovered on the beach, and an A.B.C. train schedule was found under her body.

In Bexhill-on-the-Sea, Poirot and Hastings interview Miss Merrion, who owns the Ginger Cat Café, where Elizabeth Barnard worked as a waitress. They also talk to Miss Higley, one of Elizabeth's coworkers. Poirot does not gain much insight into Elizabeth's life and character from these two women, so he, Hastings, and Inspector Crome pay a visit to Elizabeth's parents. There they learn that Elizabeth is survived by an older sister, Megan, and a boyfriend named Donald Fraser. As the other officers are inspecting Elizabeth's bedroom, Hastings lags behind, and as he does so, Megan comes through the front door. When Poirot notices Megan and Hastings going into the kitchen, he joins them. As they all introduce one another, Poirot and Hastings are surprised to hear Megan refer to her sister as "an unmitigated little ass!"

Megan further explains that her sister was a terrible flirt. Megan had tried to counsel Elizabeth, telling her she would be a fool to lose Donald. Donald and Elizabeth had recently had, as Megan says, "flaming big rows," or big arguments. At one point in an argument, Donald even told Elizabeth that she made him mad enough to kill. Megan also says that her sister had been seeing a married man.

Donald shows up, and Poirot questions him. Donald confesses that he had tried to spy on Elizabeth the previous night. He had waited for her after work, hoping to see her take a bus to the next town. When she did not show, he went to the next town and walked around looking for her. He never found her, though he was sure that she was meeting another man.

Back in London, Scotland Yard receives a description of a tall, middle-aged man wearing glasses with whom Elizabeth was seen on the night of her murder. There is a discussion about whether the inspectors should give the story about the letters to the newspapers. They are concerned about the publicity, which the murderer might actually be seeking. So they decide to wait and see if Poirot receives a third letter.

In chapter 14 the third letter arrives. In this next letter, the murderer makes fun of Poirot, telling him that he is not as great an inspector as he might have thought. Then the letter provides the town and the date for the third murder, namely, Churston and the thirtieth of the present month. But Poirot realizes that that day is the thirtieth. The previous letters provided warnings a few days before the actual events. Poirot and Hastings note that the letter is addressed improperly, which has delayed its delivery. Hastings thinks the mistake might have been made purposefully, to allow the murderer more time, but Inspector Crome does not buy this assumption. Crome believes serial killers follow strict sets of rules that they establish for themselves. As the inspectors head for Churston, news comes that a Sir Carmichael Clarke has been found dead.

Chapters 15–21

In chapter 15, Poirot discovers that it was Clarke's younger brother, Franklin, who found Carmichael's body. The victim's head was bashed in, similar to the fatal blow that Mrs. Ascher received in the first murder. An A.B.C. train schedule was found on the body. When Franklin comments that he does not understand the motives of a serial killer, Inspector Crome attempts to explain the psychology of such a person: "There is a desire to assert one's personality, to make a splash in the public eye—in fact, to be a somebody instead of a nonentity." After Franklin hears this, he turns to Poirot to verify this assumption, which does not go over well with Inspector Crome. Crome feels he is competing with Poirot for authority. Poirot notices Crome's annoyance but chooses to ignore

it. Poirot tells Franklin of the serial-killer type, "he belongs to the class of person who is usually passed over and ignored or even laughed at!"

Miss Thora Grey, Carmichael Clarke's secretary, is introduced to the inspectors. She is questioned, and then the inspectors survey the crime scene. Later, during a conversation with Hastings, Franklin comments that he does not trust Crome and is more sure of Poirot being the one who will crack the mystery.

Chapter 16 is devoted to Alexander Bonaparte Cust, who upon coming out from a movie buys a newspaper and reads about the murder in Churston. A young stranger strikes up a conversation with Cust. Having noticed that Cust's hands are shaking, the young man asks if Cust is suffering aftereffects of having been in the war. Cust tells him that this is the case. He gets such bad headaches, he often does not remember what he has done.

Franklin Clarke visits Poirot in London. Franklin suggests that a group be formed, to include Megan Barnard, Donald Fraser, Thora Grey, Mary Drower, and himself. The group should meet with and take direction from Poirot. If they work in a group, Franklin says, they might have a better chance of catching the murderer. Poirot agrees. Poirot assigns each person a task after he receives the next letter, which reveals that the next incident will take place in Doncaster on the eleventh of September.

Thora Grey, under further questioning by Poirot, remembers that a stranger selling nylon stockings had come to the house on the day that Carmichael was killed. Poirot remembers that the Barnards had had a similar visitor. And a pair of new stockings had also been bought by Mrs. Ascher's neighbor on the day that Ascher was murdered. This provides Poirot with a new clue.

Chapters 22–28

Chapter 22 returns to Cust. Mrs. Marbury, Cust's landlady, notices that Cust is not feeling well. She suggests that Cust stay in his room. Cust insists that he must go, as he has some business to take care of. He is heading for Doncaster.

Poirot, Hastings, and the group that Franklin Clarke formed all head for Doncaster. Hastings is concerned that despite their having received fair warning of the next murder, they will not be able to pick out the stranger responsible in the midst of the big crowds that have gathered for a horse race.

Chapter 24 is set in a movie theater in Doncaster, where the fourth murder takes place. Afterward, the officials find an A.B.C. railroad guide under the seat of the victim. Cust was in the same movie theater. Upon arriving at his hotel room, Cust notices he has blood on his sleeve. When he puts his hand in his pocket, he pulls out a bloody knife. When a housemaid, Mary Stroud, enters, she sees a bowl of bloody water in which Cust has washed off the blood. After she leaves, Cust hurries out and rushes to catch a train.

Poirot finds out that the murderer might have made a mistake, as the victim's name in this case begins with an *E* rather than a *D*. Then a witness comes in, a man whose name is Roger Downes. Since Mr. Downes's name begins with a *D*, the local police believe he may have been the targeted victim. As soon as Downes leaves, the woman from the hotel where Cust had stayed comes in. She describes Cust as a short man who is slightly stooped over. The police go to the room where Cust stayed and find a suitcase stuffed with small boxes of stockings.

Tom Hartigan, a friend of Lily Marbury, the daughter of Cust's landlady, has become suspicious of how Cust always seems to be traveling during each of the A.B.C. murders. So he goes to Inspector Crome and relates that he thinks Cust might be the murderer. Since the description that Tom provides of Cust matches the description Mary Stroud gave of the man who stayed at the hotel in Doncaster, Crome decides to interview Cust.

When Tom meets Lily for lunch, he tells her about his visit with Crome. For some unexplained reason, Lily excuses herself momentarily and makes a phone call to Cust, informing him that officials from Scotland Yard are planning to visit him. Even Cust does not understand why Lily called and told him this. However, he quickly packs a suitcase and leaves.

Chapters 29–35

Scotland Yard officials search Cust's room and discover boxes of stockings, stationery that matches the paper used for the letters sent to Poirot, and A.B.C. railways guides, as well as the knife that Cust found in his pocket after leaving the movie theater. Despite this evidence, Poirot is not convinced that Cust is the murderer. Poirot says that one thing is missing, and that is a motive.

Chapter 30 is told from Cust's perspective. Cust is in Andover, where the first murder occurred. There is no reason given for his being there. He is hungry and broke. As he walks down

the street, he finds himself in front of the police station, where he collapses.

Discussions of Cust's trial and sentencing engage Poirot and other officials in the next chapter. Poirot has doubts that Cust is the murderer. The story of a Mr. Strange, who comes forward and gives Cust an alibi for the night that Elizabeth Barnard was killed, makes Poirot even more uneasy. Poirot decides to call a meeting of Franklin Clarke, Thora Grey, Mary Drower, Megan Barnard, and Donald Fraser. Poirot asks each person one question and makes them swear to tell the truth. From their answers, Poirot finds what he is looking for, though he does not share that information with anyone.

The next day, Poirot visits Cust in jail. Cust believes that everyone is against him. He swears that he is innocent. But at the end of the conversation, Poirot suggests that Cust is the murderer and Cust replies affirmatively. However, when Poirot suggests that Cust does not know why he killed those people, Cust again agrees. Poirot concludes that Cust is very unsure of himself and very open to suggestion.

Poirot again meets with the group. He recounts the events of the crimes and expresses his concern that the clues he has do not match the personality of Cust. For one, Poirot relates that Elizabeth Barnard was supposedly lured to the beach by a man who was charismatic, which Cust is not. He then declares his conclusion that there was only one murder that had a true motive, and all the other murders were committed to provide a cover-up. The main murder, Poirot announces, was that of Carmichael Clarke. Clarke's wife was about to die, Poirot points out. Meanwhile, Carmichael had insinuated in a letter that he might be interested in Thora Grey. This possibility of a wedding taking place had alarmed Franklin Clarke, Carmichael's brother. If Carmichael were to remarry, Franklin would not then inherit his brother's wealth. Poirot's conclusion is that Franklin murdered Carmichael so that he could gain access to his brother's money. Franklin killed the other people as well to cover up his brother's murder.

CHARACTERS

Alice Ascher

Alice is the first victim of the A.B.C. murderer. She was the owner of a small tobacco shop in Andover. She was the wife of Franz and tolerated her husband's constant pleas for financial assistance.

Elizabeth Barnard

Elizabeth Barnard is the second murder victim. She lived in Bexhill-on-the Sea. She was a young, flirtatious woman who worked at the Ginger Cat Café. Elizabeth was about to be engaged to Donald Fraser. She was very manipulative, especially with men; she liked their attention. Poirot assumes that whoever killed Elizabeth was flirting with her before he murdered her.

Megan Barnard

Megan is Elizabeth's older sister. Megan lives in London and was not at the Barnard home when Elizabeth was murdered. However, she arrives there shortly afterward and gives Poirot details about her sister's personality. Megan later joins a group of interested parties to help Poirot solve the crimes. In the end Poirot insinuates that Megan might be a better woman for Donald Fraser, formerly Elizabeth's boyfriend, to pursue. Megan's nature and personality, Poirot states, are superior to Elizabeth's. Megan is very intelligent and more grounded.

Sir Carmichael Clarke

Carmichael is the third murder victim, a retired physician and a wealthy man. With his wealth, Carmichael started a hobby of collecting valuable artifacts from the Far East. His collection grew so large that he erected a special building just to house it. He also hired a secretary, Thora Grey, to help keep track of his possessions. Carmichael was married to a woman who was dying of cancer. As Poirot investigates Carmichael's murder, he discovers a letter in which Carmichael suggests that he might have intended to ask Thora Grey to marry him after the death of his wife.

Franklin Clarke

Franklin is the younger brother of Carmichael. Franklin is the person who comes up with the idea of forming a group of interested parties to help Poirot solve the crimes. Franklin keeps a very cool head throughout the story, despite the fact that it was he who planned and executed the murders, as well as framing Cust as the murderer. In the end, Poirot discovers that the murderer was indeed Franklin, who feared he would have lost his brother's wealth had Carmichael married Thora Grey.

Lady Clarke

Lady Clarke is the wife of Sir Carmichael Clarke. She is dying with cancer. Lady Clarke is jealous of Thora Grey, hinting that Thora was after her husband and his money.

Inspector Crome

Crome is a young investigator at Scotland Yard. Hastings describes Crome as a "silent, superior type" and "several shades too pleased with himself." Crome's superiority is especially aroused around Poirot, as he believes that he is more intelligent and better educated than Poirot. Hastings says, "His manner to Poirot was a shade patronizing. He deferred to him as a younger man to an older one," but he did so too self-consciously. Crome is also prone to bragging, making sure everyone knows how much success he has had in solving crimes. There is a sense, throughout the story, that Crome is competing with Poirot. He does not look into the evidence as deeply as Poirot and thus arrests the wrong man.

Alexander Bonaparte Cust

Cust is described as the type of man who is easy to forget. He is stooped and often shabby looking. He has almost constant headaches and occasional epileptic fits, which make him question his own actions. Poirot describes Cust as being very gullible and willing to adopt another person's opinion of him. He is a confused man who often contradicts himself, saying at one moment that there is a conspiracy to make him appear guilty of murder; however, when Poirot suggests that Cust definitely did kill, Cust gives in, though he claims to not know how or why he did it. Christie sets the story up to make Cust look guilty.

Mary Drower

Mary Drower is Mrs. Ascher's niece. She takes part in the group that comes together to help Poirot. She is not looked upon as a possible suspect. She is quiet and quite honest.

Donald Fraser

Donald was Elizabeth Barnard's boyfriend. He and Elizabeth were close to becoming engaged, but Donald was jealous of Elizabeth's need to see other men. After her death, he confesses to Poirot that he has dreams that he was the one who killed Elizabeth. Donald looks as if he might have had a motive to kill Elizabeth but did not have any motive for the other murders.

Thora Grey

Thora Grey is Carmichael Clarke's secretary. Poirot sums Thora up as a conniving woman who was after Carmichael's money. Lady Clarke is herself suspicious of Thora, believing that upon her death, Thora was planning to get Carmichael to marry her. In the end, Thora claims to be thoroughly insulted by Poirot's suggestion that though she was not involved in the murder, she was after Carmichael's money.

Tom Hartigan

Tom, a friend of Cust's landlady's daughter, grows increasingly suspicious of Cust's comings and goings, which coincide with each of the alphabet murders. Finally, after the fourth murder, Tom goes to Scotland Yard and tells Inspector Crome that he might know who the murderer is.

Captain Hastings

Captain Hastings is a friend of Poirot's who enjoys the challenge of helping the inspector solve mysteries. There is no doubt that Poirot is the mastermind in this duo, with Hastings acting as Poirot's sidekick. Hastings narrates most of the story but otherwise is mostly quiet, following Poirot and asking occasional questions.

Miss Higley

Miss Higley is an employee at the Ginger Cat Café, where Elizabeth Barnard worked as a waitress. Poirot discovers that Miss Higley knows next to nothing about Elizabeth and quickly dismisses her as a potential witness or suspect.

Chief Inspector Japp

Though Inspector Japp appears in many of Christie's books, his role in this novel is very small. His presence is acknowledged in a few scenes when Poirot is in the midst of Scotland Yard officials, but Japp has very little to say and provides scant influence.

Lily Marbury

Lily is the daughter of Cust's landlady. Lily has trouble believing that Cust is the murderer. When Lily's boyfriend, Tom Hartigan, goes to Scotland Yard to turn in Cust, Lily secretly telephones Cust to warn him. Her actions are never explained.

Miss Merrion

Miss Merrion owns the Ginger Cat Café, where Elizabeth Barnard worked as a waitress. Poirot questions her about Elizabeth, but Miss Merrion offers only minimal information and no clues.

Hercule Poirot

Hercule Poirot is one of Christie's most enduring characters, appearing in many of the author's stories. In each story Poirot's history is expanded, adding to the verisimilitude, or realistic portrayal, of the character. Poirot is originally from Belgium and often uses French sayings. He is a well-respected retired detective and lives comfortably in London. In *The A.B.C. Murders*, Poirot is personally taken aback by the letters that he receives and wonders if some madman is targeting him because he is a foreigner. Poirot is also somewhat offended by the young Scotland Yard inspector Crome, who tends to look down on Poirot because he is growing old.

Poirot is known for his high intelligence and his methodical exploration of crimes. Most officials at Scotland Yard admire Poirot's experience and success. Poirot's strength as a detective is mostly based on his belief in a logical methodology. He is good at detecting clues that other inspectors overlook. When he comes upon these clues, he often keeps them to himself, allowing them to accumulate like pieces of a puzzle until he can see the whole picture. He drops small hints along the way, especially to Hastings, but he does not divulge his thoughts until he is confident in his conclusions, which happens at the end of the story. The clues that he collects are not just material objects, such as weapons; he is also good at understanding motives and psychological aspects of suspects, such as their personalities and personal needs. An example of this is when Poirot realizes that the description of Cust does not match with his idea of a man who could lure Elizabeth Barnard (the second murder victim) to the beach through flirtation.

Mr. Strange

Mr. Strange is a man who comes forward late in the story and provides Cust with an alibi for the night that Elizabeth Barnard was murdered. Strange claims that he met Cust at a hotel and engaged him in a game of dominoes, which lasted past midnight, thus preventing Cust from being at the scene of the crime. Strange's story, plus Poirot's lingering doubts about Cust having a motive for the murders, as well as Cust's displaying no knowledge of the letters that Poirot received, motivate Poirot to question that Cust is guilty.

Mary Stroud

Mary Stroud is a young woman who works in the hotel where Cust stays during the fourth murder.

TOPICS FOR FURTHER STUDY

- Read Christie's *Murder on the Orient Express.* Pay special attention to the group of people that Christie sequesters in a special room. In most of her murder mysteries, Christie brings a group of suspects together as the protagonist attempts to solve a crime. Compare the group in *The A.B.C. Murders* with the one in *Murder on the Orient Express.* How are they similar? How do they differ? How does each help Poirot solve the crime? Write a report on your findings.

- Christie does not provide a court scene for either Cust's or Franklin Clarke's trial. Pretend you are the lawyer for one of these men and prepare a closing statement for your case. How would you defend your client? Think about the evidence the prosecution might have against the accused man. How could you weaken your opponent's arguments? If the story does not provide enough clues, you can make them up, but they must fit within the confines of the storyline. Present your statement to your classmates, addressing them as the jury.

- There have been several portraits made of Inspector Poirot, as artists have imagined what he might have looked like. What are your impressions of the character? Research past images of Poirot and then create one of your own. What do you think Poirot might look like if he were living in twenty-first century London? Use a medium of your choice, then present your portrait to the class, explaining why you chose to emphasize particular characteristics.

- Gather the psychological traits of a serial killer as Christie presents them in this novel. Then research how modern psychologists describe mass murderers. How do the descriptions compare? What do psychologists say about the motives of a mass murderer? Are there personality traits that are consistent from one mass murderer to another? Present your findings to your class in an oral report.

- Research the history of Belgium. Why do some of the people in Belgium speak French? What other languages are spoken there? When was Belgium created? What were the circumstances? What is the present-day political environment like? There are rumors that Belgium will be redrawing its boundaries. Why is this happening? What special status does Belgium hold in the European Union? Write a report on your findings.

She walks into Cust's room and sees the bloody water sitting in a bowl, where Cust has tried to rinse out the sleeve of his jacket. Mary is able to provide a description of Cust.

Dr. Thompson

Dr. Thompson works with Scotland Yard and is referred to as an "alienist," a medical professional who is recognized by a court of law as an expert in determining the mental competence of a person who has been charged with a crime. When Poirot and Crome discuss the possible motives of the A.B.C. murderer, they often turn to Dr. Thompson to confirm their conclusions.

THEMES

Power

There are two power struggles going on in *The A.B.C. Murders.* The first is between Poirot and the murderer, through the anonymous letters. The second is between Poirot and Inspector Crome, the younger Scotland Yard official. In some ways, the struggles are very similar. Both the murderer and Crome want to knock Poirot off his pedestal as the greatly praised and successful detective. The murderer wants to astonish and mock Poirot as he goes about committing murders that the inspector cannot, at first, solve or stop. In his anonymous letters, the murderer baits Poirot,

Tony Randall as Hercule Poirot and Margaret Rutherford as Miss Jane Marple (an uncredited role) in the 1965 film The Alphabet Murders *(AP Images)*

giving him a few skimpy clues to the murders he is about to commit but not offering enough for Poirot to find him. He taunts Poirot to hurry up and find him so that the next murder will not be pulled off. Of course, Poirot is too late to stop the murders from happening because the clues are too thin. This provides an opportunity for the murderer to criticize Poirot and claim that he has power over Poirot; in other words, the murderer is seeking to prove that Poirot is not as good as has been claimed.

Inspector Crome also has power issues with Poirot. These issues come from a more positive angle but nonetheless are not constructive. Crome's issues are professionally related, as he has ambition to outdo Poirot—just as the murderer has, but on the right side of the law. As such, Crome brags about his accomplishments. He attempts to contradict the hypotheses that Poirot develops. He smirks at Poirot when the older inspector comes to conclusions that do not agree with his own. He is also pained when those around him snub his presence and authority and turn to Poirot for answers.

Poirot appears to become more flustered with the murderer's challenge than he does with Crome's. Poirot obviously feels more confident when challenged by Crome than when challenged by the murderer. This is due in part to the veil of secrecy that the murderer maintains in hiding his identity. There are many unknown facts that Poirot cannot address until he finally deduces who the murderer is. With Crome's power challenge, on the other hand, Poirot knows that the younger inspector still has a lot to learn.

Greed

Most of Christie's mystery novels deliver a moral at the end; her stories are not just puzzles that must be solved. In *The A.B.C. Murders*, one of the morals relates to greed. Being too greedy can lead some people into trouble, the story suggests. In this instance, the greed is that of Franklin Clarke and Thora Grey.

Franklin's greed is what led him to kill his brother. Franklin was not financially in trouble;

he did not really need more money to live a good life. Franklin's greed was based on the fact that he wanted to be more like his brother. He wanted to have as much money as Carmichael. He became fearful that he would lose his chance of claiming all his brother's money when he realized that Thora was just as greedy as he was.

Christie does not offer very much history for Thora, but the fact that she was working as Carmichael's secretary suggests that she did not have any personal wealth. She was a working woman, reliant on the salary that Carmichael provided. But Thora saw a chance to earn more. She figured that if she could get Carmichael to marry her after the death of Lady Clarke, she could thus inherit Carmichael's wealth. She was like Franklin in that way. She was not satisfied with what she had, though she led a comfortable life.

In the end, Christie punishes both of these greedy characters. Franklin is sent to jail, and Thora is humiliated by Poirot, who sends her away fully scorned.

Manipulation

Several of the characters in this story manipulate others. Some do this for good, while others are more evil. The murderer, Franklin Clarke, manipulates Poirot through the anonymous letters that he sends. He not only makes Poirot edgy about the murders he is threatening to commit but also throws Poirot's confidence off kilter. Poirot begins to wonder if the letter writer dislikes him because he is Belgian. The murderer more than likely insinuates this to both taunt Poirot and throw the inspector off his trail.

Poirot also manipulates people. He knows that if he puts people at ease, they will open up and reveal more about themselves. Poirot does this with Cust in particular. Sensing that Cust is very open to suggestion, Poirot states that Cust must be the murderer, even though Poirot does not believe this. He does it merely to see for himself whether Cust can be easily manipulated. Franklin manipulated Cust even more, making him believe that he was acting as a legitimate salesman of a stocking company. Thora Grey also manipulated, or at least attempted to manipulate, Carmichael Clarke into marrying her. And Inspector Crome attempts to manipulate those around him into believing that he is a better investigator than Poirot.

STYLE

Simple Language and Dialogue

Christie uses language and concepts that anyone can easily understand. The language is so simple that the book could be classified as a young adult novel despite the fact that it was written for an adult audience. The vocabulary requires no dictionary, which makes the reading of the novel very comfortable and fast paced.

In addition, there are very few descriptive passages. Christie offers little information about how her characters look, what the landscape is like, what the atmosphere is, or any other sensory details. Her aim is to tell the story in as few words as possible. She devotes most of her literary energies to what the characters say. Hastings narrates what he sees happening around him and fills in details about what might have happened that the reader was not privy to, but most of the story is told through dialogue among the characters. The dialogue, along with the reader's desire to solve the case along with Inspector Poirot, pushes the narrative forward. There is little time to ponder what the characters might be thinking or feeling. Although some descriptive passages slow the pace a little in the beginning of the story, such passages all but disappear as the story progresses. Thus, by virtue of Christie's use of simplistic language and minimal description, her stories can often be read in a few sittings.

Murder-Mystery Novel

Although the themes and some of the characters change from story to story, most of Christie's novels follow the conventions of the murder mystery. Murder mysteries often open with a murder, which occurs very early in the story. The protagonist, in this case Hercule Poirot, then investigates the crime. Many murder-mystery detectives have a sidekick, and Poirot's partner is Captain Hastings. The sidekick often bumbles his way through the investigation for the most part but also offers potentially important clues to solving the crime. Announcing the identity of the murderer is the privilege of the protagonist. His or her conclusions are often startling and will not be known until the last chapters.

One style convention of many murder mysteries, and of Christie's in particular, is misdirection, or diverting the audience from seeing the solution to the mystery. In *The A.B.C. Murders*, Christie uses a red herring; that is, she casts

COMPARE & CONTRAST

- **1930s:** Immigrants from other parts of Europe flock to England as Nazis come into power and threaten the lives of Jews. Immigrants compete with British citizens for scarce jobs.

  Today: Pressure mounts against Muslim immigrants in England as terrorism by militants increases.

- **1930s:** Crime rates are very low in Great Britain. The prison population stands at 11,000, causing the government to close down a number of prisons.

  Today: In 2008, the United Kingdom has more prisoners than the government can house. There are 82,000 inmates, and police officials are estimating that this number will continue

to rise. For this reason, Justice Secretary Jack Straw asks courts to consider sending fewer people to prison.

- **1930s:** There are no serial killers in Great Britain in this decade, but Albert Fish is finally arrested, tried, and executed in 1936 as a serial killer in the United States. Police believe he may have killed one hundred children. Fish, however, claims that he killed more.

  Today: In 2000, the physician Harold Shipman, known as Britain's worst serial killer, is convicted of killing fifteen of his female patients. Upon further investigation, it is decided that the number of victims was at least 215.

suspicion on a character who is not actually the murderer, in this case Alexander Bonaparte Cust (whose initials are A.B.C.). Cust's remarks about having headaches and not remembering what he has done make him look very suspicious, as do his constant movements in and out of the same towns where the murders take place. Christie goes out of her way to bring up these details and then leaves a lot of space for readers to come to their own conclusions. In this way, until the very end, Cust looks like the murderer. The only task that remains is for Poirot or Scotland Yard officials to find him. Christie intentionally leads every character but Poirot astray. Because everyone else incorrectly assumes that Cust is the criminal, Christie builds up Poirot's status as a mastermind. Poirot is the only one who does not fall for the author's red herring and therefore stands out as the hero.

HISTORICAL CONTEXT

Great Britain in the 1930s

Much of *The A.B.C. Murders* is set among upper-class British society, but not everyone in

1930s Britain was enjoying a comfortable life. For one thing, the economic disaster referred to as the Great Depression in the United States also was affecting the economy in Britain. Unemployment, for example, was experienced by almost three million people in 1933. Industries that had once provided many British people with jobs, such as those making steel, building ships, and mining coal, were crushed under the unfavorable economic conditions. In addition, due to the invasion of German forces across Europe, Britain had to face increased immigration; many people who feared for their lives under Adolf Hitler's rule, especially European Jews, sought asylum in Britain. However, because of the economic pressures that the British people were experiencing, more stringent immigration laws were set up to help protect the decreasing number of jobs for British citizens. Immigrants then had to have jobs lined up before being allowed to enter the country. The combination of the shortage of jobs and the increased immigration could account for Christie's inclusion of comments in this novel concerning dislike of foreigners that Poirot often suspects are aimed at him.

Magnifying glass (Image copyright Denis Selivanov, 2009. Used under license from Shutterstock.com.)

Sir Arthur Conan Doyle

While Agatha Christie was considered the best murder mystery author of the 1930s, it was Sir Arthur Conan Doyle (1859–1930) who made the crime novel popular in the prior generation. Christie is known to have studied Doyle's works in mastering the form of the mystery novel. There are some similarities between Doyle and Christie in the ways they formulated their stories. This is especially true regarding their main characters. Where Christie had Inspector Poirot with his sidekick Captain Hastings, Doyle had Sherlock Holmes and his sidekick Dr. Watson. Watson often narrates Doyle's stories, just as Hastings narrates Christie's novels. Like Poirot, Holmes is exceptionally intelligent. Like Hastings, Dr. Watson is often silent and merely acts as an assistant.

Scotland Yard

Scotland Yard is the headquarters for London's metropolitan police force, which has been in service since 1829. There are questions about the origin of the name, but according to an article in *Smithsonian Magazine*, there is an actual Scotland Yard, a space of land that used to be the site of an old Scottish palace.

Sir Robert Peel, Home Secretary in Britain, was handed the job of organizing the first police force that was associated with Scotland Yard, which included 20 inspectors, 88 sergeants, and 895 constables. This new police force replaced officers who were once called watchmen. Several of the first police recruits, however, were dismissed for showing up drunk. As a matter of fact, in the first six months, according to the U.K. metropolitan police Web site, 51 percent of recruits were let go for this reason.

The new police force did not go over well with the general public. Ordinary citizens were used to taking matters into their own hands. An organized police force appeared, at first, to be intrusive in citizens' lives, so initially there was a lot of resistance to the uniformed officers patrolling London streets. The public complained that having law enforcers in their midst usurped their freedoms. Once, two officers were killed while on duty, and the courts ruled that these were justifiable homicides. Eventually, though, the public came to understand that the police were working in their favor. This was partly due to the famed novelist Charles Dickens, who took a liking to a Scotland Yard constable and used him as a favorable model in his novels.

Scotland Yard gained renown through some spectacular cases, such as the search for the serial killer called Jack the Ripper in the late nineteenth century. Though the murders finally ended, Scotland Yard never found the murderer. Furthering the reputation of Scotland Yard were stories written by Sir Arthur Conan Doyle, whose detective Sherlock Holmes often works closely with the Yard's inspectors, as does Inspector Poirot in Christie's fiction. Officers of Scotland Yard also are often pictured in British media protecting London's royal family.

Belgian Influence

Some critics have questioned why Christie made Hercule Poirot Belgian. Some have pointed out that there was a large immigration of Belgians into Britain during World War I. This was caused by the invasion of Belgium by German forces looking for another route into France. Britain welcomed the 250,000 immigrants and wounded soldiers, helping them find homes and otherwise settle into the countryside. However, there was an understanding that after the end of the war, the Belgians would return to their country. Most of the Belgians did go back home, but many stayed in Britain. Since *The A.B.C. Murders* is set after World War I, the character Poirot is understood to be one of the Belgians who stayed on. Poirot makes a few statements in this novel about the dislike that some people in Britain had toward foreigners. This might reflect the fact that the British assumed all Belgians would leave and were disappointed when some did not.

CRITICAL OVERVIEW

So popular were Christie's many crime mysteries, especially those that contained Inspector Poirot, that when Christie finally decided to end her character's life in her novel *Curtain* (1975), the *New York Times* published Poirot's obituary. Thomas Lask, the obituary writer, relates his surprise that Christie's novels have continued to maintain such a large audience over the years: "Her hold on her audience is remarkable in a way because the kind of fiction she writes is, well, not exactly contemporary." However, Lask quotes another *New York Times* reviewer, Anthony Boucher, who once wrote of Christie, "Few writers are producing the pure puzzle novel and no one on either side of the Atlantic does it better."

Another reviewer, Marty S. Knepper, writing for *Armchair Detective*, calls Christie the "Mistress of Mystery." Knepper, analyzing Christie's stories for aspects of feminism, states that "Christie's more famous novels, especially the ones written in the 1930s, perpetrate a number of anti-feminist ideas about women." However, Knepper also finds that "only a writer with a healthy respect for women's abilities and a knowledge of real women could create the diversity of female characters Christie does. Her women characters display competence in many fields, are not all defined solely in relation to men, and often are direct contradictions to certain sexist 'truisms' about the female sex." Knepper also praises Christie's ability to portray female characters that seem real: "Christie's depiction of the various problems women face in their lives reveals her astuteness as a psychologist and an observer of human nature."

Writing for the *Claremont Quarterly*, Stewart H. Benedict refers to Christie as "the world's best-selling authoress" and a "literary godmother." Benedict adds that "Miss Christie's prestige among her fellow mystery writers is towering." In an attempt to explain Christie's popularity, another reviewer, M. Vipond, for the *International Fiction Review*, states that Christie "gave her readers exactly what they anticipated, yet added just enough that was intriguingly new to keep them stimulated and absorbed. Her characters are recognizable and familiar individuals through whom escape and adventure can be enjoyable without being frightening." Vipond adds, "She did not delve very deeply into the souls of her characters, but in examining large numbers of them, and from various angles, she revealed just a few of the contradictions and complexities of real life."

Earl F. Bargainnier, in his book *The Gentle Art of Murder: The Detective Fiction of Agatha Christie*, also postulates as to why Christie's readers have remained so faithful. One reason is that despite the fact that she followed the forms and conventions of the mystery novel, she did so while

WHAT DO I READ NEXT?

- *And Then There Were None* (1940) is one of Christie's most acclaimed works. In this novel, ten people are invited to an island, where they are told upon arrival that their hosts have been delayed. The ten guests are then given copies of stories of how ten other people died. One by one, the guests meet their own deaths in manners similar to the deaths in the stories they have received.

- In 1926, Christie wrote what many fans consider one of her best Inspector Poirot mysteries, *The Murder of Roger Ackroyd*. The book caught contemporary readers off guard with its surprise ending.

- *Murder on the Orient Express* (1934) is another of Christie's most famous Poirot mysteries. It was first published in the United States with the alternative title *Murder in the Calais Coach* and in 1974 was adapted into a celebrated film. The movie retained the original title and starred the British actor Albert Finney as Poirot. In this story, Poirot investigates a murder that takes place while he is on a train to Istanbul.

- Christie's short story "Witness for the Prosecution," published in the collection *The Hound of Death* (1933), was later adapted to the stage and then into a film that won several Academy Awards. The story takes place in the courtroom, as the main character attempts to defend a man accused of murder. The plot twists make this an intriguing story as well as a thriller.

- A more contemporary murder mystery is Karen MacInerney's *Murder on the Rocks* (2006), set on an island off the shores of Maine. The novel pits real estate developers against those who want to protect the pristine natural environment of Cranberry Island. When the focused real estate developer turns up dead, all eyes turn to Natalie, the woman whose voice was the loudest in her attempts to preserve the island.

- Jon P. Bloch's *Best Murder of the Year* (2004) is popular among mystery fans. In this story, Rick Domino is a gossip columnist living in Los Angeles. While he is covering the Academy Awards, his friend goes missing. Domino finds his friend murdered, but when the police show up, Domino is the one who looks guilty, standing with a gun in his hand and a dead body at his feet. Domino has to solve the mystery to save his own life.

- *An Autobiography* (1977), by Agatha Christie, is a personal account published shortly after the author's death. Christie recounts many details of her life, with a special emphasis on her relationship with her mother.

- Before Agatha Christie, Sir Arthur Conan Doyle was one of the public's most favorite crime/mystery writers. In the 1986 compilation *Sherlock Holmes: The Complete Novels and Stories*, Vol. 1, readers will find Doyle's *A Study in Scarlet*, the first story in which Sherlock Holmes appears, and *The Sign of Four*, another of Doyle's early novels. Also included in this collection are many of Doyle's short stories featuring Sherlock Holmes as the protagonist.

---

finding "numberless variations." Bargainnier states that she was "a superb storyteller," explaining that "she fulfills readers' expectations of what her fiction will be, by staying within the boundaries of her genre, while surprising them with new twists and turns of plot and characterization." Another positive trait is that Christie "demands no specialized knowledge of her readers but, at the same time, makes them want to join a process of discovery of the truth." Bargainnier also notes that Christie's books are generally optimistic: "Her lack of violent action, her belief that human beings can solve their problems, and her strict morality are comforting to readers."

Charles Osborne, in his book *The Life and Crimes of Agatha Christie*, devotes particular attention to *The A.B.C. Murders*. He writes that the plot of that novel "is positively brilliant in its imagination and originality, and its characters are splendidly brought to life in what is one of Agatha Christie's masterpieces."

CRITICISM

Joyce Hart

Hart is a published author and freelance writer. In the following essay, she examines the women in The A.B.C. Murders *from a feminist perspective.*

Christie has been praised for creating female characters that are progressive models of women, especially considering the time in which Christie herself lived. She empowered many of her characters with a sense of independence in a world that did not always reflect such modern sensibilities. Her novel *The A.B.C. Murders* was written in the 1930s, after the first wave of feminism but long before the second wave, which would more expressly secure women's rights. Women of the 1930s still lacked many rights in terms of politics, economics, and social benefits. Yet many of Christie's women speak their minds and create lives that are independent of men. The critic Marty S. Knepper has supported this notion but has also stated that some of Christie's female characters in her more popular novels, including *The A.B.C. Murders*, are mere stereotypes. Yet, while their independence is somewhat limited, several of Christie's female characters in *The A.B.C. Murders* stand out as models for more fully liberated women still to come.

The main female characters in Christie's novel are presented in three two-women partnerships. These groupings are Alice Ascher and her niece Mary; Elizabeth Barnard and her sister, Megan; and Lady Clarke and Thora Grey. It does not appear that Christie created the groupings for any specific reason, but in each pair there are two women who are related either through bloodlines or close experience, and they offer interesting contrasts with and reflections of one another. Some of the women appear stronger than others. Some are more independent. Others reflect old classifications of the woman's role in society, while their

> BECAUSE SHE PUT UP WITH, AND EXCUSED, HER HUSBAND'S ABUSIVE NATURE, ONE MIGHT THINK OF ALICE AS AN OLD-FASHIONED COWERING AND LONG-SUFFERING WOMAN. HOWEVER, ALICE FOUND HER WAY IN THE WORLD IN SPITE OF HER HUSBAND. SHE SAW THROUGH HIS THREATS AND SENSED HIS WEAKNESSES."

counterparts are advancing the model of what it means to be a more fully actualized woman.

Taking the female pairs as they appear in the story, first are Alice Ascher and her niece Mary. Alice is described, in the beginning of the novel, as having been old and poor. Yet Alice is portrayed as one of the strongest and most independent women in the story. She worked hard all her life, never bore a child, and put up with an abusive and alcoholic husband. Though she ran away from her husband twice, he followed her. Though he continued to threaten her with physical abuse, Alice refused to divorce him. Because she put up with, and excused, her husband's abusive nature, one might think of Alice as an old-fashioned cowering and long-suffering woman. However, Alice found her way in the world in spite of her husband. She saw through his threats and sensed his weaknesses. She tolerated him because she honored her marriage vows. Underneath her tolerance, though, was a very independent and fearless woman.

Alice worked most of her life as a housemaid, keeping other people's houses clean. Shortly after marrying, she discovered her husband's great flaws. He had a weakness for alcohol and could not hold onto a job. So not only did Alice have to work hard enough for both of them, while her husband continually demanded money to pay for his drinks, she also had to overcome her husband's lack of social graces. It was because of her husband that Alice's employment security was threatened; no one wanted to have to put up with him. So Alice would move to a new town so that her husband would not find her. But he always did. In the end, she got lucky, inheriting a small amount of money from one of her employers. With a smart wit, Alice invested in a small business, one that would see her through, though meagerly, to the end of her days. Alice was an entrepreneur, an independent woman who was not in need of a man. If Alice had one weakness, it was for her husband; she could not fully abandon him. But she was a free spirit and as modern as any feminist.

Alice's niece, Mary, followed in Alice's footsteps. Alice raised the young woman since she was eleven, and Mary proved devoted to her aunt. Like Alice, Mary is a compassionate woman, and she remained in the country so that she could be near her aunt. However, once Alice is murdered, Mary decides that the country life is not for her, and she moves to London to get a job. Though Mary, like Alice, makes a living as a maid, a line of work that allows little freedom, she is strong enough to not confine herself to that role. Even if she does have to take a job as a maid in London, the new atmosphere, she tells Poirot, will open up new opportunities for her. Readers are not told what those opportunities are. Mary might go on to pursue an education, a new job, or a husband. Christie offers few details about Mary, but readers do know that despite her seemingly quiet and shy nature, she is strong enough to strike out in a new direction, overcoming the tragedy of losing the only family member she had left. She does not bemoan the sorrows that have plagued her life. She moves on in search of ways to better her life.

Elizabeth and Megan Barnard represent two different types of women. Elizabeth used her physical charms to lure men. She was fairly superficial and did not do much to better herself, to expand her mind, or to challenge herself in any way. She held a job but not one that offered a future. The money she earned was spent on clothes. Her future goal was to be married. In the meantime, she spent all her energy on gaining the attention of men. She lived off this attention, frivolously dressing herself like a mannequin to gain men's approval. As Christie portrays her, Elizabeth was a two-dimensional figure, like a model walking along a runway, smiling at her audience without true emotion. She is both a throwback to an older type of a woman as well as a cautionary figure of women to come— women with no sense of feminist liberation no matter what age they live in. Elizabeth was manipulative and shallow, always in need of men in her life to make herself feel whole.

Elizabeth's sister, Megan, is stronger. She moved away from home and took a job in London. She often counseled her sister and tried to show Elizabeth that what she was doing with her life was superficial. Megan is clear minded enough to see that women can do so much more than just entice men. She knows that excitement gained from men is a fleeting pleasure. Megan's inner life is deeper than was her sister's. Megan does not pretend. She does not flinch from truth, even in front of the police or Inspector Poirot. She speaks her mind. At one point she sees through Poirot's games as he tries to unmask the murderer, and she challenges him. Poirot praises Megan for her intelligence and insight. Megan is not shy in exposing her intelligence.

The last pair in the trio is the weakest of all. These two are Lady Clarke, who is withering away from cancer, and Thora Grey, who is scheming to capitalize on Lady Clarke's fate. Though few details are provided, readers can assume that Lady Clarke is a pampered woman. She married a doctor, who went on to amass a fortune. They lived in a huge house, and in the end, Lady Clarke was given a private nurse to take care of all her needs. Though Lady Clarke probably had every financial benefit throughout her life, she suffers not only from cancer but from jealousy. In some ways, she has every right to be jealous. However, jealousy is a sign of weakness. Lady Clarke does not trust her husband and does not have enough confidence to believe in herself. She has not built a strong enough relationship with her husband, and she feels him slipping away. Not only does she lack confidence, but also she lacks power. Christie portrays Lady Clarke as a fading shadow, a role of women that is vanishing. Of all the women in this novel, Lady Clarke is the most lacking from a feminist perspective.

Finally there is Thora Grey, a Swedish beauty who attracts not only the Clarke brothers' attention but also Poirot's. Thora plays a slightly diminutive role, that of a secretary. Her job is to take care of Carmichael's business details. Within a certain realm, she exerts some initiative, but that realm is very limited. She is very dependent on Carmichael. He has the money. He buys the objects and ships them home; Thora merely keeps track of them. However, by some very limited definition, Thora is ambitious. She wants to be the next Lady Clarke. She waits patiently for Lady Clarke to die. Then, by all insinuations, she will make her move and marry herself into the life that Lady Clarke will leave behind. She knows what she wants and how to get it, which could be considered a positive and empowering trait. Her ambitions, though, like those of Elizabeth Barnard, are

Alphabet (Image copyright Alan Merrigan, 2009. Used under license from Shutterstock.com.)

> OF ALL THE AUTHORS OF THE TRUE WHODUNIT, AGATHA CHRISTIE, AS IS EVIDENCED BY HER POPULARITY IN VOLUME AND OVER TIME, HAS HAD THE GREATEST SUCCESS IN SATISFYING HER READERSHIP. THE KEY TO THIS SUCCESS LIES IN THE NON-ARBITRARINESS OF MOST OF HER SOLUTIONS."

very superficial. Her goal is to be taken care of. She is active, but her activity is basically underhanded. Christie leaves the interpretation and judgment of Thora for her audience to make. Thora, then, combines both feminist and antifeminist qualities.

Christie could have made all her female characters either maids or pampered women, but she chose to give her women more depth. She was, after all, an enterprising woman herself. Later in her life, Christie replaced Poirot as her favored protagonist with a female sleuth, Miss Marple. In this particular novel, with Poirot still at the helm, Christie nonetheless presents a full range of female characters. Some are more independent than others. Some think for themselves and are not afraid to expose their intelligence or challenge the men around them. They are women of Christie's time, possessing feminist values of the author's generation as well as hints of the feminism to come.

Source: Joyce Hart, Critical Essay on *The A.B.C. Murders*, in *Novels for Students*, Gale, Cengage Learning, 2010.

Eliot A. Singer

In the following excerpt, Singer discusses the use and effectiveness of block elements, or obstructions between images and their referents, in Christie's works, including The A.B.C. Murders.

> To my utter amazement and, I must admit, somewhat to my disgust, Poirot began suddenly to shake with laughter. He shook and he shook. Something was evidently causing him the most exquisite mirth.

> "What the devil are you laughing at?" I said sharply.

> "Oh! Oh! Oh!" gasped Poirot. "It is nothing. It is that I think of a riddle I hear the other day. I will tell it to you. What is it that has two legs, feathers, and barks like a dog?"

> "A chicken, of course," I said wearily. "I knew that in the nursery."

> "You are too well informed, Hastings. You should say, 'I do not know.' And then me, I say, 'A chicken,' and then you say, 'But a chicken does not bark like a dog,' and I say, 'Ah! I just put that in to make it more difficult.' Supposing, Hastings, that there we have the explanation..."

In calling attention to a shared enigmatic quality, the analogy *whodunit* to *riddle* is such a commonplace that it is almost more a synonym than a cliche. Yet analogy is never a substitute for analysis, and the very obviousness of this equation has seemed to mask the extent to which the riddle can provide real clues to the structure of the whodunit. Many traditional speech genres present distillations of fundamental literary devices. In more complex literary constructions, even in a popular culture form like the mystery, the combination of such devices often covers up the simplicity of the devices themselves. Thus, by carefully considering the construction of folkloric forms, it often becomes possible to uncover devices that are essential to literature but concealed in it. This essay suggests that by taking seriously the notion of the whodunit as riddle, that is by applying those devices utilized in riddling strategies to this type of mystery, it becomes both possible and necessary to reconsider the basic nature of whodunit construction.

Riddling is a form of social interaction that involves an asymmetric power relationship. The poser of the enigma maintains the right to impose a pre-determined solution. Alternative solutions, even if cleverer than that of the poser, are automatically rejected as incorrect. Likewise, in the whodunit, the writer is the authoritative source. The murderer is whomever the author, not the reader, chooses it to be. But this asymmetry is not institutionalized; it is a product of choice within the social interaction itself. The hearer or reader also retains a degree of power, albeit of a higher logical type. He or she may interrupt, walk away, throw a book into the fire, ruin the author's livelihood by refusing to buy another, or hypothetically, even murder the perpetrator for a particularly annoying solution. The poser of the enigma is omnipotent at the whim of the posee, and that whim lasts only so long as the solutions are satisfying. The aesthetics of the mystery is that of rationality rather than of morality or sentiment; as Roger Caillois has said, "What the reader demands is that [someone] with believable human motives pull off a crime that seems to defy reason but that reason can eventually uncover." Thus, a satisfactory solution to a mystery must be acceptable as *rationally* superior to those alternatives that the reader has conceived.

The dominant conception among both critics and other readers is that reading a whodunit is an almost pure hermeneutic exercise in which bits of conflicting information are given the reader to enable him or her to arrive at a solution through systematic analysis. (This is why the genre is a favored paradigm for much recent reader-centered literary theory.) In Kermode's words, "The narrative is ideally required to provide, by various enigmatic clues, all the evidence concerning the true character of [the murder] that the investigator and the reader require to reconstruct [it]." The reader and the story detective, then, are expected to follow the same hermeneutic procedure, sorting through true and false clues and eschewing "red herrings" in order to discover a coherent pattern.

Riddle scholars often refer to solutions as being "arbitrary," and as any experienced reader can attest, in reading a whodunit, it is almost always possible to conceive of several rational solutions that account for at least the most crucial disparate clues. Most whodunits suggest numerous incorrect solutions in the course of the telling, and while these are rejected because of incongruous elements, it takes little imagination to by-pass these incongruities. As parodies like the film *Sleuth* imply by giving and then dismissing alternative solutions without even bothering to falsify them, in many whodunits the reason why a subsequent solution takes precedence over an earlier one has to do with its temporal

placement, not its superior logic; the final solution is merely the last one. Such solutions are indeed arbitrary. But whodunits whose murderers are arbitrary choices no better than the reader's suspects do not provide satisfactory reading experiences, and their authors cannot expect to achieve consistent popularity unless, like Dorothy Sayers or Peter Dickinson, their writing is satisfying for reasons other than the mystery.

Of all the authors of the true whodunit, Agatha Christie, as is evidenced by her popularity in volume and over time, has had the greatest success in satisfying her readership. The key to this success lies in the non-arbitrariness of most of her solutions. Contrary to the common practice of whodunit writers, which, as Haycraft points out, goes back to Poe, Agatha Christie's murderers are not "*the least likely*." Nor are they taken at random from the list of suspects. Rather, more often than not, they are *the most likely*—husbands, wives, lovers, relatives, or others with clear cut motives of gain or vengeance—that is, murderers much like those in real life. As Miss Marple explains in *The Moving Finger*, "Most crimes, you see, are so absurdly simple...Quite sane and straightforward—and quite understandable—in an unpleasant way of course."

Given the straightforwardness of her murders, why then are Agatha Christie's whodunits so difficult to solve? The answer lies in the reader's mistaken presumption that the mystery is complex and that the texts are hermeneutically structured to enable a reader to imitate the detective or alter-ego in sorting through clues to discover a pattern. Agatha Christie's hermeneutic, however, is a negating one, one that takes a relatively simple murder and through the reading process controverts the reader's reason. To quote again that source of wisdom, Miss Marple, "The greatest thing in these cases is to keep an absolutely open mind." What Dame Agatha consciously and insidiously does is *close the reader's mind*. The clues themselves, then, become insignificant, and the solution lies not in untangling their pattern, but in discovering the mechanism by which the reader's mind is closed.

A riddle is enigmatic because there is an obstruction between the image it presents and the referent the riddlee is supposed to guess. In riddling scholarship this obstruction, following Petsch, is usually called *the block element*. Roger Abrahams has elaborated upon this concept by delineating four different, though not always distinct, block elements (or riddling strategies): *too little information, too much information, contradiction,* and *false gestalt.* A close examination of the construction of Agatha Christie's whodunits shows that, at one time or another, she makes use of each of these block elements to detour the reader from the solution.

While most Agatha Christie mysteries utilize a multiplicity of riddling strategies, it is usually possible to single out one block element as dominant. The 1939 Hercule Poirot novel, *Sad Cypress,* for instance, is unsolvable because there is *too little information.* In this story a poisoning takes place in the presence of two women, one of whom, as the reader learns at the outset, is on trial for murder, and hence may be presumed innocent (despite *Witness for the Prosecution*). The other woman, Nurse Hopkins, not only has the opportunity to commit the murder, but having "misplaced" the precise poison used, has the means as well. Moreover, she is seen urging the murdered girl to make a will leaving everything (which turns out to be a considerable legacy not a pittance) to her aunt in Australia. The block occurs because Nurse Hopkins has no apparent motive. There is too little information to connect Nurse Hopkins to the inheritance since the only hint the reader receives is an aside that the unseen aunt is a nurse. The crucial fact, that Nurse Hopkins and the Australian aunt are one and the same, is revealed only in a Perry Mason-style ending.

For a satisfying reading experience, as Van Dine insists, "The reader must have an equal opportunity with the detective for solving the mystery. All clues must be plainly stated and described." And since a reader cannot reason out a solution for which there is too little information, but can only guess at it, this mystery riddling strategy is the least fair. It is one, however, to which Christie rarely resorts, and in *Sad Cypress* even the slightest hint would make it trivial to arrive at the solution. (For other writers, Conan Doyle, for instance, giving too little information is essential—Holmes is forever sending off telegrams or utilizing arcane knowledge.)

A more reasonable block element is the opposite one, *too much information.* There is a sense in which all "red herrings" are too much information, extraneous facts that lead the reader astray. With writers like Chandler and Hammett, as Jameson points out, entire subplots filled with gangland murders are too much information, which is irrelevant to the enigma of the central murder. Agatha

Christie, too, uses many "red herrings"—the embezzling lawyer in *Death on the Nile,* or the imposter archaeologist in *Murder at the Vicarage* are examples—but they are usually introduced late in the text, and are easily identifiable by the attentive reader. Sometimes, however, too much information becomes the dominant strategy for misleading the reader. In *Funerals Are Fatal,* for example, Aunt Cora, who is known for her tendency to state awkward and embarrassing truths, blurts out at her brother's funeral, "But he was murdered wasn't he?" When she in turn is murdered, the police and reader alike assume that her death is a result of knowledge about that of her brother. This awkward "truth," however, turns out to be extraneous information; the brother, in fact, had died an innocent death, and the murderer of Aunt Cora is the only person it could be, her companion and legatee, Miss Gilchrist, who had impersonated the victim in order to produce the misdirecting clue.

An even more elaborate use of *too much information* is *The A.B.C. Murders.* In this novel there are three murders for which the only apparent connection is that the victims' first and last initials coincide with the first letter of the town where the murders take place in alphabetical order. This coincidence, along with other clues such as the presence of the British train time table known as the ABC, insists that an alphabetical pattern be deciphered. The block element is that there is no pattern, or, rather, that the pattern is the murderer's artifice. The real victim is the third one, Sir Carmichael Clarke of Churston (the only wealthy victim), and the murderer is simply his avaricious brother, Frank, who committed the other murders to establish a false pattern to throw the police, and of course the reader, off the scent. A similar block element is used in *A Pocket Full of Rye* in which the elaborate pattern coinciding with the nursery rhyme is the fabrication of the murderer, the black sheep son of the victim.

Perhaps even more basic to the whodunit than the "red herring" is the block element *contradiction.* Locked rooms, iron clad alibis, falsified times of death, letters from the already dead, and other contradictory clues of time, place, and manner usually must be explained away before a murder can be deciphered. But such empirical contradictions, favorites of writers as diverse as Poe, Conan Doyle, and John Dickson Carr, should not bother the experienced reader, and are usually only used by Christie as secondary devices. (One exception is *Murder in Mesopotamia* where the principle block involves figuring out how "Dr. Lardner could murder his wife from the roof without leaving it," a murder which is easily accomplished by the dropping of a heavy quern attached to a rope.)

More subtle are contradictions in character, murderous stratagems that seem implausible because they require more physical strength or more intelligence than a given character would seem to possess. In *The Hollow*, for instance, the philandering murdered husband's wife is found standing over the body with a gun in her hand, but is easily cleared since this gun turns out not to be the murder weapon. The contradiction occurs because to throw initial suspicion on oneself in order to be eliminated as a suspect is a stratagem that requires more imagination and intelligence than the wife, "poor Gerda," who is consistently portrayed as a simpleton, would seem to possess. But she is not so simple as all that, as the attentive reader should remember from when early in the book she muses, "It was amusing to know more than they thought you knew. To be able to do a thing, but not let anyone know that you could do it."

An even better illustration of contradiction occurs in one of Christie's classics, *And Then There Were None*. In this book one fact totally contradicts all others, rendering any solution impossible. All of the suspects are dead, and the last to die could not have committed suicide. The reader, of course, assumes that the dead must remain dead, so when Justice Hargrave (the notorious "hanging judge" and the only character not guilty of the death of an innocent, except perhaps in his official capacity, and therefore the most obvious suspect in these execution style killings) becomes the sixth victim, he is immediately presumed innocent. But the reader learns of his death through the statement of Dr. Armstrong, "He's been shot." As Agatha Christie insists time and again, information and interpretation provided by characters is often accidentally or deliberately false. The reader, however, is usually too little wary of prevarication. One can recognize that Dame Agatha in her last pronouncement is speaking to the reader as well as to Hastings when Poirot says, "But perhaps, after all, you have suspected the truth? Perhaps when you read this, you already know. But somehow I do not think so . . . No, you are too trusting . . . You have too beautiful a nature." That which is the product of a character's

discourse is not necessarily true, and so the once and future murdered Justice Hargrave may reasonably rise from the dead to stalk his final victims.

Sklovskij, in an early Russian formalist study, has pointed to the false gestalt as a general analogy for the whodunit. "These mysteries at first present false solutions . . . ," he writes, as in the Russian folk riddle, "'It hangs dangling. Everybody grabs for it.' The solution: 'A towel.'" This analogy is, however, a little broad, and the notion of false gestalt is better limited to those texts that allow not only for alternative solutions, but for general misconceptions. (It should be noted that, while for the riddle false gestalt involves instantaneous recognition of a solution, usually an obscene one, which turns out to be false, for the whodunit this block element is not distinct but is a result of too much information or of a contradiction that leads the reader into forming a false picture of the whole circumstances of the murder, not just of its details.) One such false gestalt occurs in *The Body in the Library* where the reader assumes that the body is who it is supposed to be. This gestalt is reconstituted only when the witness who identifies the body is shown to be an accomplice. Another false gestalt that Christie induces is a misconception as to victim. In *Peril at End House* the reader assumes that, unlike Hastings who tends to jump to conclusions, Poirot is infallible, and therefore, he or she follows the detective in believing that quiet Maggie Buckley has been mistakenly done in instead of her lively cousin, Nick, whose potential assassination Poirot has cleverly deduced. In *The Mirror Cracked*, when a harmless busybody, Mrs. Badcock, is killed by an overdose, Dame Agatha hits the reader over the head with an epigraph from Tennyson, "the mirror crack'd from side to side; 'The doom has come upon me' cried the lady of Shallot," repeated, in slightly altered form, by a reliable witness to describe the actress Marina Gregg's reaction upon learning that the busybody is the probable cause of her unhappy infertility. Yet characters and readers alike are led astray because the rest of the novel provokes the false gestalt that the murder is a mistake, that the intended victim is the jaded actress, herself, for whose death there would be many possible suspects. In both cases the reader, like Poirot, fails to consider "K," "a person who should have been included in the original list, but who was overlooked." One need only remember that corpses are usually not those of mistaken victims to realize that it is the assumed targets, Nick Buckley and Marina Gregg, who are actually the guilty parties.

(*The Caribbean Murders*, in which there really is a mistaken murder, albeit late in the book, is, I believe, one of Christie's failures.) . . .

Source: Eliot A. Singer, "The Whodunit as Riddle: Block Elements in Agatha Christie," in *Western Folklore*, Vol. 43, No. 3, July 1984, pp. 157–71.

Schechter, Harold, *Deranged: The Shocking True Story of America's Most Fiendish Killer*, Pocket Books, 1990.

Thorpe, Andrew, *Britain in the 1930s: A Deceptive Decade*, Wiley-Blackwell, 1992.

Vipond, M., "Agatha Christie's Women," in *International Fiction Review*, Vol. 8, No. 2, Summer 1981, pp. 119–23.

SOURCES

Bargainnier, Earl F., *The Gentle Art of Murder: The Detective Fiction of Agatha Christie*, Bowling Green University Popular Press, 1980, pp. 199, 201, 203–204.

Barnard, Robert, *A Talent to Deceive: An Appreciation of Agatha Christie*, Dodd, Mead, 1980.

Barrett, David, and Gavin Cordon, "Prison Population Exceeds Capacity for the First Time," in *Independent* (London), February 23, 2008, http://www.independent.co.uk (accessed November 7, 2008).

Benedict, Stewart H., "Agatha Christie and Murder Most Unsportsmanlike," in *Claremont Quarterly*, Vol. 9, No. 2, Winter 1962, pp. 37–42.

Blumberg, Jess, "A Brief History of Scotland Yard," in *Smithsonian*, September 28, 2007, http://www.smithsonianmag.com/history-archaeology/brief-scotland.html (accessed November 7, 2008).

Carr, John Dickson, *The Life of Sir Arthur Conan Doyle*, DaCapo Press, 2003.

Christie, Agatha, *The A.B.C. Murders*, Bantam Books, 1983.

Feinman, Jeffrey, *The Mysterious World of Agatha Christie*, Award Books, 1975.

"Harold Shipman Found Dead in Cell," in *BBC News*, January 13, 2004, http://news.bbc.co.uk (accessed January 12, 2009).

Keating, H. R. F., ed., *Agatha Christie: First Lady of Crime*, Holt, Rinehart and Winston, 1977.

Knepper, Marty S., "Agatha Christie—Feminist," in *Armchair Detective*, Vol. 16, No. 4, Winter 1983, pp. 398–406.

Lask, Thomas, "Hercule Poirot Is Dead; Famed Belgian Detective," in *New York Times*, August 6, 1975, p. 73.

Metropolitan Police, http://www.met.police.uk (accessed November 7, 2008).

Osborne, Charles, *The Life and Crimes of Agatha Christie*, Collins, 1982, p. 88.

Robyns, Gwen, *The Mystery of Agatha Christie: An Intimate Biography of the Duchess of Death*, Penguin, 1989.

FURTHER READING

Dommermuth-Costa, Carol, *Agatha Christie: Writer of Mystery*, Lerner Publications, 1997.
    This biography of Christie is written in easy-to-read language for young adults.

Hart, Anne, *The Life and Times of Hercule Poirot*, Putnam, 1990.
    Having studied all of Poirot's appearances in Christie's books, Hart gathered the biographical information that Christie supplied and created an imaginary biography for Poirot. From his birth to his imagined death, Hart provides a unique account of one of Christie's most lovable and eccentric characters.

Hurdle, Judith Diana, *The Getaway Guide to Agatha Christie's England*, RDR Books, 1999.
    Hurdle takes her readers on a tour of England as Christie might have enjoyed it. Included in this book are hotels and shops that both Christie and her characters visited. Readers also enjoy a visit to Devon, where Christie grew up. This book can be used either as a travel guide or as a visual glimpse into Christie's life and environment.

Rowland, Susan, *From Agatha Christie to Ruth Rendell: British Women Writers in Detective and Crime Fiction*, Palgrave, 2001.
    Included in this study are the works of Christie and Rendell as well as Dorothy L. Sayers, Margery Allingham, Ngaio Marsh, P. D. James, and many others. The book presents students with an overview of the authors' works, their lives, and the critical debates surrounding them.

Zemboy, James, *The Detective Novels of Agatha Christie: A Reader's Guide*, McFarland, 2008.
    Zemboy offers detailed information about sixty-six of Christie's novels, including comments on the geographical location and historical setting of each book. He discusses current events, fashions, and fads that are relative to the stories. Plot summaries and character lists are also provided.

Around the World in Eighty Days

JULES VERNE

1872–1873

Titled *Le tour du monde en quatre-vingts jours* in the original French, *Around the World in Eighty Days* is perhaps the best known of Jules Verne's novels, especially through its film adaptations. Verne authored one of the first literary "franchises," with his works marketed to maximum profit through the use of the new mass media, and *Around the World in Eighty Days* first appeared in serial form in the French newspaper (owned by Verne's book publisher) *Le Temps* (*The Times*). The first installment was published on December 22, 1872, which is also the dramatic date of the closing of the novel. This led to the misconception that the story was reporting actual events. In any case, journalists lost no time in replicating the voyage around the world as the basis of popular news stories and continued to do so through the twentieth century, most recently in Michael Palin's 1988 British Broadcasting Corporation (BBC) series, as the idea of such a journey became part of modern mythology.

Around the World in Eighty Days is somewhat unusual among Verne's work, or at least among his works that are best known today. Verne helped to create the genre of science fiction, and many of his novels either concern a voyage of fantastic scientific discovery (*Cinq semaines en ballon* [*Five Weeks in a Balloon*], 1863; *De la Terre à la Lune* [*From the Earth to the Moon*], 1865) or imagine the ramifications of technology that did not yet exist but seemed likely to be developed in the near future (*Vingt mille lieues sous les mers* [*Twenty Thousand Leagues under*

Jules Verne

the Sea], 1869–70). *Around the World in Eighty Days*, however, deals only with exploiting existing technology, especially railways and steamships, to its limits. The novel celebrates the nineteenth-century idea of progress, the concept that life was being constantly improved by new technological advances. For the details of the plot, Verne drew on a series of newspaper articles and journalistic books touting that, according to the schedules of transportation companies, a voyage around the world in eighty days should be possible, so the book's premise is not fantastic as much as enthusiastic about what technology had already achieved.

AUTHOR BIOGRAPHY

Jules Gabriel Verne was born on February 8, 1828, in the city of Nantes, a prosperous port on the Atlantic coast of France. His father was a successful lawyer, and Verne received a classical education at Saint Donatien College (a Catholic boarding school). In 1847 Verne began to study law in Paris (completing his degree by 1849), but he also began to write for the theater, and it was this second career that increasingly interested him. In 1852 there was a definitive break with his family when Verne refused to take over his father's law firm in Nantes. Verne was eventually forced to work as a stockbroker to support himself and the new family he acquired in 1857 when he married Honorine de Viane, a widow with two children.

In 1862 Verne began to work with the publisher Pierre-Jules Hetzel. By 1864 Verne was writing novels full-time and had become an unprecedented literary success. His works, beginning with *Cinq semaines en ballon* (*Five Weeks in a Balloon*, 1863), were serialized in Hetzel's magazines and then republished in book form. Hetzel created a special series for Verne's novels, Voyages extraordinaires. In part because of Hetzel's marketing genius, all of Verne's books were financial successes. His novels were always tales of fantastic adventure, and while most merely took place in exotic locales, many engaged directly with the fact that technology and industry were changing the conditions of life in France (and in western Europe and the United States) at an ever-increasing rate. They frequently dealt with technological developments or discoveries that had not yet occurred (or at least had not yet been fully exploited) but which seemed inevitable. These included such ideas as aerial warfare (*Robur-le-conquérant* [*Robur the Conqueror*], 1886) and manned exploration of the moon (*De la Terre à la Lune* [*From the Earth to the Moon*], 1865). Others reinterpreted traditional mythological themes, such as the existence of an underworld below the surface of the earth, in a scientific style (*Voyage au centre de la Terre* [*Journey to the Center of the Earth*], 1864).

Around the World in Eighty Days (1872–73), on the other hand, was drawn from journalistic promotion that such a journey, unthinkable in Verne's youth, had become possible because the world had been linked together by a network of steamships and railways. Far from being a prediction of future achievement, it was a celebration of the technological progress that the nineteenth century had already witnessed. The optimistic tone of the novel was well received in France, a nation that had just had its confidence badly shaken through defeat in the Franco-Prussian War (1870–71). Verne and Hetzel badly needed a new financial success after the loss of income occasioned by the war and a nearly four-year cessation in publishing. As Verne's first new book after this period, *Around the World in Eighty Days* did not disappoint, becoming one of the pair's most successful enterprises, especially owing to sales in England, where the nationality of the protagonist Phileas Fogg contributed to its popularity.

Verne thus resumed his career as author of one of the most popular literary franchises in the world, publishing novels until 1897 (*Le sphinx des glaces* [*An Antarctic Mystery: The Sphinx of the Ice Fields*]). Verne published sixty-four novels in all in his lifetime. After Verne's death, Michel Verne completed several of his father's unfinished manuscripts, also published by Hetzel's company through 1919. In 1888 Verne was elected to the city council in Amiens, and he enjoyed a minor career in local politics. Verne died on March 24, 1905, of a sudden onset of diabetes (then untreatable) in his adopted home in Amiens.

PLOT SUMMARY

Chapters 1–4

Verne begins *Around the World in Eighty Days* with descriptions of his two main characters, the mysterious gentleman Phileas Fogg and his newly hired manservant Passepartout. Fogg is said to keep to a mechanically precise daily schedule, being occupied each day with going to and from the Reform Club (a prestigious association that catered to the British elite), where he took his meals, read several newspapers, and played the card game whist in the evening before returning home. One evening, Fogg overhears two bits of news that will drive the plot of the novel. The first is that the Bank of England was robbed of fifty-five thousand pounds, and the police are watching all ports of exit from the country for the thief, on the premise that he will flee, and have even sent detectives off to transportation hubs around the world to watch for him. A reward of two thousand pounds and five percent of any money recovered has been offered to these officers. One of Fogg's whist partners suggests that the thief will not be caught because the world is too large to search. Fogg takes exception to this and insists that it is being made smaller by the new steam transportation network.

Another acquaintance introduces the other point, a newspaper article suggesting that, with the unification of the railway network in India, a

MEDIA ADAPTATIONS

- *Around the World in Eighty Days* (1874) is a stage play by Verne and Adolphe d'Ennery based on working drafts of the novel; a special-effects extravaganza, it was frequently produced in Paris through the 1950s.

- In 1919 a German satirical version of *Around the World in Eighty Days* was directed by Richard Oswald. All prints of this film have been lost, however.

- An Academy Award-winning film of *Around the World in Eighty Days* was directed in 1956 by Michael Anderson, starring David Niven; it was produced by the Michael Todd Company and released by United Artists.

- In 1963 the novel was again satirized in *The Three Stooges Go Around the World in a Daze*, directed by Norman Maurer for Columbia Pictures and starring Moe Howard, Larry Fine, and Joe DeRita.

- In 1989 a television miniseries of *Around the World in Eighty Days*, directed by Buzz Kulik and staring Pierce Brosnan, Eric Idle, and Peter Ustinov, was syndicated to various European television networks.

- Also produced in 1989, Michael Palin's BBC documentary *Around the World in Eighty Days* retraced the route of the journey in the book.

- In 2001 the playwright Mark Brown staged a new adaptation of *Around the World in Eighty Days*.

- In 2004 a loose adaptation of *Around the World in Eighty Days* was directed by Frank Coraci for Walt Disney Pictures and starred Jackie Chan.

journey around the world could be completed in eighty days. Fogg takes up this notion and eventually proposes to undertake such a journey. Wagers are quickly made with several club members over whether he can complete the journey. These bets amount to twenty thousand pounds (a sum equal to at least two million dollars in today's money), half of Fogg's total fortune. Fogg leaves immediately with an incredulous Passepartout on the overnight train-boat service heading for Dover (the regular service between London and Paris on which passengers traveled on a train, switched to a boat across the English Channel, and finally transferred to a second train to reach the opposite city, all on a single ticket).

The introductory chapters foreshadow a motif that is occasionally alluded to throughout the work and which accounts for the final turn of the plot. Fogg asks Passepartout the time, and when the manservant replies that it is 11:22 Fogg tells him that his watch is four minutes slow. Passepartout denies that this is possible since his is a very good watch, of which he is notably proud, that does not lose time. However, four minutes is the difference between the true local times of London and Paris, where the watch was presumably originally set. Periodically throughout the novel, the fact is mentioned that Passepartout keeps his watch on London time (as he thinks) and so becomes increasingly out of synch with the local time as the journey proceeds. The narrator does not call undue attention to these otherwise puzzling references, but an attentive reader would realize that the difference in times would amount to a day upon the completion of the west-to-east circumnavigation of the globe.

Chapters 5–9

Once the journey begins, the novel digresses from the course of Fogg's travel. The narrator describes instead how Fogg's wager and his journey become a popular subject in the newspapers, leading to bookies taking wagers on whether he will succeed or not. However, all this comes to an end when Detective Fix, the police officer posted at Suez, Egypt, sends home (via telegraph) a request for a warrant to arrest Fogg on the suspicion that he is the robber of the Bank of England and that his journey and wager are an elaborate ruse to cover his escape. The narrative of the journey picks up at the Suez Canal, a vital link in the modern infrastructure that makes the journey possible, cutting several thousand miles off the route, which otherwise would have had to pass around Africa. Fix cannot receive his warrant in time, however, because Fogg is traveling at the maximum possible speed, so no courier carrying the document can hope to catch up with him. Consequently, Fix joins Fogg aboard his steamer and follows him on his course, hoping to find some way to delay him so that he can receive the written authority to

make the arrest. In the meantime, Fix befriends Passepartout in order to pump him for information about Fogg, all of which he misinterprets to confirm his suspicions that Fogg is the thief.

Chapters 10–13

While Fogg is still aboard ship in the Indian Ocean he makes the acquaintance of Sir Francis Cromarty, an officer in the Indian Army with whom he begins to play whist. Once they reach Bombay, India, Fogg and his servant continue by train across the subcontinent, accompanied still by Sir Francis, who is going to join his regiment, and shadowed by Fix. They eventually discover that the rail connection has not, as reported, been completed yet and that they have to cross a mountain using local transport. Fogg buys an elephant at a ruinous price (calculating that he might have to spend as much as the twenty-thousand-pound wager to keep on schedule) and hires a local Parsee, or Parsi, *mahout* (elephant driver) to take them on to the railhead at Allahabad.

This route cuts through the lands of an independent Indian prince. There were several such rulers in British India who maintained essential autonomy within the British Raj. The territory is wild and overgrown with jungle, and the ruler still supports the ancient Hindu rite of *suttee*, whereby a widow throws herself onto her husband's funeral pyre. *Thugees* (bandits supposedly organized into a cultic association under the goddess Kali) are also still operating in the prince's lands. Reaching a site where a suttee will be taking place, Fogg learns from his mahout that the widow in question is the orphaned daughter of a wealthy Parsi family who was forced to marry an aged Hindu nobleman. Observing the preparations for the suttee from hiding, they see that she is no willing participant but will be thrown on the fire against her will. After trying throughout the night without success to find some way of rescuing the Parsi widow from her armed guards, Fogg is ready to simply rush them as she is placed on the fire, an action that would probably not only fail to save her but also get himself killed. This rash impulse redeems him in the eyes of Sir Francis, who wondered if the cold and mechanical Fogg was capable of human feeling. However, Passepartout instead simply leaps up onto the burning pyre and carries the girl off, making use of his circus and firefighting experience. The guards and priests are momentarily struck by superstitious fear, believing that Passepartout, who could not be seen clearly through the flames, was the dead husband come back to life, allowing Fogg and his companions, including the Parsi widow known as Mrs. Aouda, to escape.

Chapters 14–19

Fogg, Passepartout, and Mrs. Aouda continue by train, and Fogg promises to take the rescued woman to Hong Kong, where she believes a relative of hers lives. Once they reach Calcutta, Fix tries to delay them by encouraging prosecution of Passepartout for an earlier unwitting act of desecration. Fogg resolves this by posting and immediately forfeiting a two-thousand-pound bail, and they depart without further trouble. Aboard a ship for Singapore, Fogg and Mrs. Aouda begin their strange courtship, she acting with gratitude for his having saved her life, he acting with cold, calculating respect and exact correctness. The narrator describes the relations between them in terms of astronomical science, as if Mrs. Aouda is disturbing Fogg's orbit around the planet just as Neptune disturbs the orbit of Uranus, which allowed for the deduction of its existence before it was telescopically observed. After a brief stopover in Singapore, their ship steams on for Hong Kong. Passepartout encounters Fix again and forms the theory that he must be a private detective hired by Fogg's bettors at the Reform Club to monitor his progress.

In Hong Kong, Fogg learns that Mrs. Aouda's wealthy relative moved to Europe two years previously. Fogg then offers to conduct her to England. In an attempt to delay Fogg, Fix confesses his purpose to Passepartout, trying to enlist his aid but without success. Fix therefore separates Passepartout from his master and forces the two of them to make their way separately to Japan, with Fogg's trip on a privately chartered ship (on which he takes Mrs. Aouda and Fix, who still claims merely to be a fellow traveler) costing a fortune.

Chapters 20–24

Once in Yokohama, Japan, Passepartout decides that he must continue to press on along the route of Fogg's journey, in hopes of eventually meeting up with him. He happens to notice that a circus troupe is about to leave for San Francisco and joins them, on the basis of his experience as a circus acrobat. Participating in the troupe's final performance in Yokohama, Passepartout causes a human pyramid of acrobats to collapse when he spots Fogg in the audience and rushes out of his position to rejoin his master. Having learned that his servant had arrived on the scheduled steamer from Hong Kong, Fogg had set about looking for him, and "chance or a sort of premonition led him" to the circus.

The passage by steamship from Yokohama to San Francisco is uneventful, except in two respects. Fix's long-sought warrant had finally reached him in Japan, but it is now useless since they are outside of British territory. Fix thus determines that since Fogg evidently really does intend to return to England, all he can do is wait to arrest him there. Accordingly, he determines to now do everything he can to help speed Fogg toward British soil. He even convinces Passepartout of his intent to do this, discouraging the manservant from revealing Fix's true identity to Fogg. The other matter involves the narrator calling attention to the travelers' crossing of the international dateline in the middle of the Pacific Ocean on November 23. Passepartout notices that his watch again seems to agree with the ship's chronometers (when in fact it is exactly twelve hours off). Passepartout recalls Fix's earlier attempts to explain geography and time zones to him, producing a piece of comic diversion:

> "What a load of nonsense this scoundrel talked about the meridians, the sun and the moon!" Passepartout repeated. "Huh! If people like that had their way we'd have some clever sorts of clocks and watches around! I knew for sure that one day or the other the sun would make up its mind to set itself by my watch."

Chapters 25–30

Once in San Francisco, Fogg and his companions are caught up in a riot that arises out of political campaigning. Fogg and Fix are personally assaulted by a ruffian named Colonel Stamp W. Proctor. Fogg resolves to return to America after completing his journey in order to fight a duel with this individual; as he cannot be detained by the matter just then, he and his companions board the train for New York. Passepartout discovers that Proctor is in fact also on the train, so he, Fix, and Mrs. Aouda try to prevent a meeting between the two men by keeping Fogg in his cabin playing whist. But the two inevitably meet and determine to fight for their honor. The railway employees and passengers obligingly put an entire car of the train at their disposal for this purpose, but just as they are pacing off for their duel, a Sioux war band attacks the train, and Fix and Proctor both turn their efforts to fighting the boarders. Since some Sioux warriors incapacitated the engineer and firemen, the train is running out of control at high speed. Passepartout saves the day, however, by using his acrobatic skills to crawl underneath the length of the train and decouple the cars from the engine, causing the train to come to rest just in front of a U.S. Army fort, whose soldiers drive off the attackers. Proctor is severely wounded in the attack, ending the matter of the duel. The Sioux, however, kidnaps some passengers, including Passepartout. Fogg goes with a troop of cavalry to rescue his servant, and he succeeds, but not before the train departs. When he returns, the narrator for the first time descriptively shows the growing affection between Fogg and Mrs. Aouda: "As for Mrs Aouda, she had taken the gentleman's hand and was squeezing it between her own, unable to speak."

Chapters 31–34

Fix finds a way for Fogg and his companions to continue, namely, by sailing over the frozen prairie on a sledge powered by sails like those on a racing yacht. In this way they proceed to Omaha, where they immediately board a train leaving for Chicago, to make a connection for New York. They arrive there, however, forty-five minutes after the steamer on which they have planned to sail left port. By his usual strategy of overpaying and bribery, of both the captain-owner and the crew, Fogg diverts a merchant ship bound for the French port of Bordeaux to Liverpool, England. However, the ship is not loaded with enough coal to cross the Atlantic Ocean at full steam the entire way, so Fogg is obliged to buy the ship from its captain for sixty thousand dollars and proceed to burn its wooden superstructure for fuel. This brings the total cost of the trip up to very nearly twenty thousand pounds, as Fogg had expected. But they only get as far as Ireland, where Fogg determines to take one of the fast sloops that carry mail from transatlantic steamers to Liverpool. Transferring to one of these, Fogg calculates, should give them sufficient time for him to win the wager.

As soon as they land in Liverpool, Fix finally arrests Fogg. Yet it turns out that the real thief was arrested three days previously in Scotland, which Fix, isolated aboard ship, had not known. The difficulties in getting Fogg released delay him just long enough to make returning to London to win the bet impossible. When Fogg steps out of his jail cell, he loses his temper for the only time in his life and strikes Fix down. Fogg's last effort of commissioning a special train makes no difference; the narrator assures the reader, "He had lost."

Chapters 35–37

Fogg returns to his house in Savile Row with Passepartout and Mrs. Aouda. His wager lost, the remainder of his fortune spent on the journey, Fogg is ruined, and his companions fear he might kill himself. Toward the evening of the next day, after Fogg has made an accounting of the few assets he has left, he meets with Mrs. Aouda, who surprises him by proposing marriage, which he can only accept.

With news of the real thief's capture, Fogg's wager became a popular item in the newspapers again, and public betting grew heavier than before. Naturally, there is a large crowd outside the Reform Club waiting for his return at the deadline of 8:45 p.m. on December 22. That very evening, while attempting to engage a priest to perform Fogg and Aouda's marriage, Passepartout discovers that the day Fogg thought was the twenty-third is really the twenty-second, as Fogg's calculation of the date was a day off. The wager began because so many newspaper and magazine articles had deduced from railway and steamship schedules that a journey around the world would take eighty days. While that might have been literally true in the sense of taking 1,920 hours, as far as the calendar was concerned the trip would take either seventy-nine (if traveling east-west) or eighty-one days (if traveling west-east) relative to the point of origin, because it would involve crossing the international dateline, which lies at 180 degrees longitude in the middle of the Pacific Ocean. Realizing that he has gained a day, Fogg proves able to go to the Reform Club and win his wager.

CHARACTERS

Mrs. Aouda

Mrs. Aouda is the daughter of a wealthy Parsi merchant whose death left her destitute, forcing her to marry a Hindu nobleman. As she is introduced into the story, he has just died, and she is in a drugged stupor about to be thrown onto her husband's funeral pyre against her will. Verne's initial description casts her as exotic—her garb is a rather fantastic version of traditional Hindu clothing—but is simultaneously meant to make her familiar to his readers, especially where she has "skin as white as a European's." Fogg's Parsi mahout adds more details of her life: "She was an Indian lady famous for her beauty, a Parsee by race and the daughter of a wealthy family of Bombay merchants. She had received a thoroughly English upbringing in the city and from her manners and schooling she could have been taken for a

European." As the journey progresses Fogg takes her on to Hong Kong, where she believes she has a relative, but, since he has moved to Europe, Fogg resolves to take her to England with him. She is naturally grateful to Fogg for his role in saving her life and gradually finds herself falling in love with him, as she becomes impressed with his qualities of duty and honor and his ability to meet even the most difficult situations with effective action.

Brigadier General Sir Francis Cromarty

Sir Francis meets Fogg aboard ship between Suez and Bombay, and the two frequently play whist during the voyage. They continue to journey together on the trans-Indian railway since Sir Francis is going to join his regiment at Benares (modern Varanasi). He acts to a limited degree as a local guide to Fogg, advising him about how to negotiate the gap in the rail network and in the affair of rescuing Mrs. Aouda.

Inspector Detective Fix

Fix is dehumanized from the beginning by the fact that Verne never mentions his first name. The narrator's initial description marks Fix as unpleasant and deceptive: He is "a small, skinny man, quite intelligent-looking but nervous, with an almost-permanent frown on his face. His long eyelashes concealed a piercing gaze, but one that he could soften at will." He cannot arrest Fogg without a warrant from England, and since Fogg is traveling as fast as possible away from England, the warrant will never reach him; Fix therefore uses every kind of trickery he can devise to delay Fogg's journey. Probably this is the origin of his name, since "fix" can mean illicit interference in a sporting event or wager. During the second half of the journey, when it is in Fix's interest to speed Fogg along on his return to England so as to arrest him there, Fix seems to fall under the spell of Fogg's cold, calculating bravery and become a true follower of him in the same way as Passepartout and Mrs. Aouda. During the episode of Passepartout's kidnapping, Fix voluntarily stays behind to look after Mrs. Aouda. But when he imagines that Fogg is slipping out of his grasp, Fix reverts to his single-minded intent to arrest the suspect: "His true nature reasserted itself." He then does in fact arrest Fogg as soon as they return to England.

Phileas Fogg

Fogg is the central character of *Around the World in Eighty Days*. He undertakes the journey to which the title refers in order to resolve a wager about whether it is possible to complete such a trip or not. The name Phileas is an ancient Greek word meaning "beloved." Given the French custom of naming children for Christian saints, Verne most likely conceived of his character as named after St. Phileas, an Egyptian monk who was martyred during the persecution of the Roman emperor Maximian in 307. While the name is obscure in French, it is essentially nonexistent in English (perhaps the reason Verne chose it, as would be characteristic of his sense of humor), and it is sometimes replaced in translations and adaptations by "Phineas," an unusual but not unknown English name.

Verne initially describes his main character as "the enigmatic figure of Phileas Fogg, about whom nothing was known except that he was the most courteous of men and one of the most handsome gentlemen in English high society." Verne goes on to immediately inform the reader of a great deal about Fogg. He is a lawyer (and hence bears the title of esquire), though he does not practice law. He is tremendously rich, though he has no apparent business interests. He was admitted to the prestigious social circle of the Reform Club (whose members included many of the most important men in Britain) on his bankers' recommendation that a man of his wealth ought to belong. If he has family connections of any kind, no one knows anything about them. In fact, Fogg seems to have suddenly appeared in London society a few years before the novel opens in 1872 and to have done nothing except walk from his house to his club and back with the greatest regularity, following the same timetable each day, "with such mathematical precision that it fuelled other people's imagination." In addition, he seems to know more about geography than anyone else in London (though it could not be proved that he had ever traveled extensively); eventually he is able to navigate across the Atlantic. His only pastime is the card game of whist. He gambles on the game and most often wins, but he donates that money and much more to charity, playing rather to test his skill against that of his opponents.

In the second chapter Verne begins fleshing out his description of Fogg: "The gentleman gave the impression of something perfectly calibrated and finely balanced, like a chronometer made by a master craftsman." Throughout the novel, Fogg's virtues are always presented as mechanical or mathematical—virtues of the new age of progress through machinery, industry, and science. In contrast, Verne bestows on Fogg other characteristics meant to humanize him. For instance he gives his gambling winnings to charity, and on the night of his departure he gives twenty guineas—at least a thousand dollars today—to a woman begging on the street. His other selfless act is his rescue of Mrs. Aouda. In this case, while he says that he undertakes the effort only because he has the time, he is, before Passepartout's intervention, ready to throw his life away in a last-second vain effort to take her to safety. It is principally gratitude for her rescue that endears Fogg to Mrs. Aouda and leads to their eventual marriage. Fogg is presented as characteristically English in his sense of duty. He repeatedly, for instance, spends thousands of pounds to rescue Passepartout from some trouble or other he has gotten himself into, often at the risk of completing his journey on time, because he feels responsible for him.

Jean Passepartout

Passepartout is Fogg's manservant, newly hired at the outset of the novel. We do not know his actual surname, *passe-partout* being the French word for passport at the time, a nickname he says "I earned by my natural ability to get myself out of tricky situations." Because of the precise minute-by-minute schedule that Fogg insists Passepartout keep, we see the details of the job of the manservant in more detail than in most literature of that era. He had, for example, to awaken Fogg, prepare his breakfast, prepare his shaving equipment (including heating a bowl of water, since there was no hot tap water then), help him dress and prepare his hair, and so on, throughout the day. By way of a résumé, Passepartout tells Fogg about his work history, including stints as a circus acrobat and a fireman, foreshadowing his later exploits in the novel. As an ironic foreshadowing, he tells Fogg, "When I learnt that Mr Phileas Fogg was the most precise and most stay-at-home person in the United Kingdom, I came to sir's house in the hope of being able to lead a quiet life and put behind me everything associated with Passepartout, even the name."

Throughout the novel Passepartout's eyes, rather than Fogg's, are those of the tourist, taking in the local scenery for the reader. He also provides comic relief of a slapstick type. His work history, established in the first chapter, was contrived to uniquely suit him for each of the plot points that depend on him. Verne describes him as "a good chap with a friendly face and prominent lips that were made for eating, drinking and kissing." He is sensual and physical to the same degree that Fogg is cold and mechanical. He enjoys the local color,

foodstuffs, and liquors that have no interest for his master. He is above all good natured and loyal to Fogg.

Colonel Stamp W. Proctor

This "enormous fellow with a red goatee beard, a ruddy complexion and broad shoulders" leads a gang that assaults Fogg's party during a political riot in San Francisco. Fogg determines to return after completing his journey to fight a duel with Proctor over the matter, but Proctor later encounters Fogg on the cross-country train and insults him again by belligerently taunting him about his judgment in playing whist. This leads to an immediate duel between the two; when it is broken up by a Sioux attack on the train, Proctor fights bravely and is severely wounded.

THEMES

Tourism

The most obvious theme presented in *Around the World in Eighty Days* is travel. Indeed, the purpose of the novel is to demonstrate that travel of unprecedented scope and speed has become a reality, that anyone can travel within a few weeks to exotic places on the far side of the world that seem more like places of the imagination. Progress has allowed fantasies of faraway cities to be replaced by real experience. Verne treats Fogg's fantastic journey from an experiential viewpoint as an ordinary tourist trip. This supports the idea that human progress is making the world smaller and safer—indeed, is conquering it. But Verne did not base Fogg's travels on his own experience. Many local details of the novel's various episodes, and especially Verne's minute concentration on the transportation network, were probably based on another nineteenth-century genre of travel writing, the touristic handbook such as the Baedeker's. This series of red handbooks, familiar to every traveler in the nineteenth and early twentieth centuries, included a separate volume for every destination of any importance throughout Europe, North America, and most of Africa and Asia. They provided not only detailed information on railway and maritime transportation but also lists of hotels and restaurants, complete with menus and prices, as well as detailed descriptions of local attractions. A man like Phileas Fogg, who was never known to have traveled, could thus have nevertheless gained the highly detailed knowledge of geography

TOPICS FOR FURTHER STUDY

- Paul Theroux is a great American travel writer. Read any of his travel books, such as *The Great Railway Bazaar*, *The Old Patagonian Express*, or *Dark Star Safari*, and give a presentation to your class comparing his experiences in the late twentieth century to those of Fogg and Passepartout in *Around the World in Eighty Days*.

- Prepare a map showing the route of Fogg's journey around the world with small illustrations of interesting scenes from the novel at the places on the map where they happened.

- *Around the World in Eighty Days* celebrates a vision of unlimited progress, the idea that the world has become better and will only continue to become better through the advancement of technology. Has the history of the twentieth century borne out this proposition? Or has technology caused more problems than it has solved? Organize a class debate on this question.

- Watch the 1956 film version of *Around the World in Eighty Days*. Then prepare a class presentation on the similarities to and differences from the novel. Be sure to show clips from the film that illustrate your points.

he was famous for in the Reform Club simply by reading these guidebooks. Verne most likely followed the same procedure to learn the details central to his travel novel, which in most other works of fiction would have served as mere background.

The Baedeker's handbooks certainly provided the kind of colorful details with which Verne ornaments *Around the World in Eighty Days*. Verne's narrative moves from point to point around the globe: "Paris, Brindisi, Suez, Bombay, Calcutta, Singapore, Hong Kong, Yokohama, San Francisco, New York, Liverpool and London." In just the same way one could leap from volume to volume in a library of Baedeker's guides, such as might be owned by a gentleman's club. (Oddly, for eastern North America, where Verne had travelled

personally, all local details are absent from the narrative.) The encounter with India in the novel, for instance, begins with precise statements of its area in square miles and its population. Next comes a precise description of the main rail lines with the mountains they pass over and the principal stops. Bombay consists of points of touristic interest: libraries, marketplaces, the seat of government, mosques, churches, temples, synagogues, and the local ancient ruins. The local ethnic cuisine is sampled, and local color is described: a Parsi festival featuring Indian dancing girls. Passepartout gets into trouble because he enters an Indian temple for purely touristic enjoyment, without removing his shoes first—precisely the kind of customary detail he could have read in a Baedeker's if he had taken the time to do so. To advance to the next destination, Verne faithfully follows the map of the railway lines and describes the type of train in service on them. He proceeds in the same manner for each stop and each leg of the journey, thus giving a grand summary of the nineteenth-century tourist experience.

Science and Technology

Verne is generally, if somewhat simplistically, known as a science fiction writer, so it is no surprise that science plays a large part in *Around the World in Eighty Days*. Perhaps the main theme of the work is that the technology created by modern science is completely transforming the world, most notably making transportation many orders of magnitude faster and more dependable and making the extraordinary journey of the work's title possible. Not merely is the world being changed, but furthermore its change is heading, like Fogg, on a definite path at the highest possible speed toward a final goal, scientific utopia. All of the technological advances that represented progress in the nineteenth century were tied together in travel. The steam engine, iron rails, and steam-powered steel-hulled ships combined to represent the highest point of industrialism. The transportation network itself had become global in scale, providing the main elements of the novel's plot as well as its title. Moreover, unlike, for instance, the equally rapid advances being made in the sophistication of military weapons, transportation and travel were viewed as an unalloyed good for common people that would serve to link the world together. Fogg symbolizes the new modern man who is shaped by science and the new technology; while not lacking in human virtues, he acts with the efficiency of a machine, and even his innermost

*David Niven as Cantinflas in the 1956 film
version of* Around the World in Eighty Days
(The Kobal Collection. Reproduced by permission.)

emotions, such as with his falling in love with
Mrs. Aouda, are described in metaphors based
on the science of celestial mechanics.

Verne reveals a number of aspects of nineteenth-
century progress in the novel, through both the
story and his telling of it. The unification of the
world through travel was being accomplished in
one particular way, colonialism, by which the rest
of the world was being linked to Europe and made
over in Europe's image. Civilization was proving
triumphant and would tame the rest of the world.
Thus in India Fogg passes through the city of
Monghyr, an industrial center that is like the Brit-
ish cities of Manchester or Birmingham trans-
ported to the East. The native peoples are judged
according to pseudoscientific racial categories
popularly accepted in the nineteenth century.
Mrs. Aouda is the most acceptable non-European
because of her constantly mentioned whiteness, in
contrast to the natives of the Andaman Islands
(between India and Southeast Asia): "The savage
inhabitants of the island . . . stand at the very bot-
tom of the human scale." Far from being a vision-
ary, Verne was as locked into the popular beliefs

and traditions of his time as anyone else, and
Around the World in Eighty Days reflects the sci-
ence and beliefs of that time.

STYLE

Orientalism

Orientalism in one of its senses is a constructed
way of viewing cultures outside of Europe or the
United States connected to the political and eco-
nomic relationships of colonialism that dominated
interactions between the West and the rest of the
world in the nineteenth century. Orientalism denies
the real identities of African, Asian, or American
Indian cultures and recasts them as an exotic,
romantic "other." Many of Verne's novels take
place in exotic settings and exhibit an orientalist
attitude toward the strange and foreign, treating it
as a mysterious and exotic departure from the
everyday world of the European reader while at
the same time making the setting comprehensible
by using the familiar stereotypes by which the read-
ing public comprehends the exotic.

To a large extent the crux of *Around the World
in Eighty Days* is the railway spanning the Indian
Subcontinent, the report on the completion of
which impels Fogg on his journey and the unreality
of which presents the chief obstacle to his journey.
In the space between the two rail heads in India,
Fogg and his companions plunge into a fictitious,
romantic world. It is a world different than the one
reported in the newspapers and so to Fogg a world
that is unreal. Given that railroads tend to follow
roads, it is unlikely that such a gap would have
been crossed by any means other that a horse-
drawn wagon or coach, but Fogg rides an elephant,
perhaps because that is a popular cliché the reading
public would have had about "exotic" India. The
adventure he has in this fictive space involves the
cult of the *thugees* and the rite of *suttee*, both
elements of Indian culture that the British had, by
and large, suppressed by 1872. The *thugees* were an
organized system of criminal gangs that robbed
and murdered travelers and looked to the Hindu
goddess Kali to protect them in their dangerous
work. But Verne adopts a more fantastic and
romantic interpretation of their activities well
known from the popular press, that their murders
were a cultic act of worship to Kali. The suttee, in
turn, was the Hindu custom of a widow commit-
ting suicide by throwing herself onto the funeral
pyre of her husband as a final act of devotion.

Verne heightens the dramatic sense of the act by presenting not a Hindu but a Parsi woman (Mrs. Aouda) forced to undergo this ritual against her will but rescued at the last moment. In fact, the suttee and the thugees existed (albeit a half century or so before Verne's novel is set) at opposite ends of the social structure of Indian society, yet Verne chooses to tie them together, making the thugees responsible for carrying out the suttee of their victim. There is nothing to truly connect them in reality except their alien and romantic character.

The setting of this portion of the novel is the last mountain fastness of fanatical Hinduism where the British have not established their authority (which, seemingly improbably, is nevertheless the area where the British are building the unifying link in the Indian rail network), surrounded by jungle inhabited by cheetahs, leopards, and other "flesh-eating animals," and where Fogg eats a meal of bananas, a fruit then wholly unknown in Europe. The suttee is to be carried out by "a group of elderly fakirs . . . working themselves up into a furious frenzy. Their bodies were streaked with bright yellow markings and covered with cross-shaped incisions from which blood was oozing. . . . Behind them [were] a few Hindu priests, in the full splendour of their oriental costumes." Although used here to represent the epitome of "otherness," the image seems to be drawn from the Hebrew Bible (1 Kings 18), a founding document of Western culture, with its prophets of Baal, who induced religious ecstasy in themselves by cutting their skin with knives. Verne is thus drawing on stereotypical images of the other rather than describing real Indian institutions. Mrs. Aouda, on the other hand, forms a link between this exotic world and the West. Fogg and his companions rescue her from the depths of the Orient. She is an Indian, but a Parsi, a member of a monotheistic religion like Christianity or Judaism. She is also described as being European in appearance, that is, "white," and educated so that she speaks and acts like an aristocratic British woman. She forms the link to the oriental world that Fogg is able to take with him back to Britain and eventually join with in marriage. In this way Fogg overcomes the other and makes it Western, thus fulfilling the positive self-perception of colonialism in replacing exotic culture with European culture.

Encyclopedic Literature

Verne's publisher Hetzel insisted that Verne's volumes in the Extraordinary Voyages series contain a large amount of educational material about the newly burgeoning Victorian science and technology as a selling point to persuade parents to buy the books for their children. The idea was that reading these books would help prepare children for the technical professions of the future unfamiliar to the parents. On the other hand, Verne himself had not done much traveling outside of western Europe and the eastern United States. Both of these factors conditioned the nearly wholesale incorporation into *Around the World in Eighty Days* and his other novels of material closely based on almanacs, encyclopedias, and other reference works. *Around the World in Eighty Days* contains countless passages that Verne appears to have adapted from such technical literature with very little alteration. This is evident, for instance, in his comments on naval architecture:

> The ships of the P&O line which sail the China Seas have a serious design fault. The ratio between their draught when laden and their depth has been wrongly calculated and as a result they lack stability in heavy seas. . . . These ships are therefore far inferior—if not by their engines and their steam apparatus, then at least in their design—to the sorts of ships used by the French mail service, such as the *Impératrice* and the *Cambodge*. Whereas, according to the engineers' calculations, the latter can take on board a weight of water equal to their own weight before sinking, the P&O ships, the *Golconda*, the *Korea* and lastly the *Rangoon*, could not take on board a sixth of their weight without going down.

These details must have come from reading of the technical literature produced by the various firms involved. Another kind of literature, perhaps a travel book, would have supplied this kind of detail, explaining the geography and limnology of the great Salt Lake in Utah:

> The Great Salt Lake, which is about seventy miles long and thirty-five miles wide, is situated at about 3,800 feet above sea level. . . . It has a high salt content, since its waters hold in solution a quarter of their weight in solid matter. Its specific gravity is 1,170 compared to 1,000 for distilled water. . . . However, the idea that the density of its waters is too great for anyone to dive into it is untrue.

In this way Verne's writing contains many qualities of a compilation or anthology of technical and scientific literature, which in his era formed popular subjects of fascination in the way that computer science does in contemporary literature, as for instance in the novels of Michael Crichton or William Gibson.

COMPARE & CONTRAST

- **1872:** Verne's novel *Around the World in Eighty Days* suggests that a journey around the world using regularly scheduled commercial transportation (railroads and steamships) can be accomplished in eighty days. Fifteen years later, the American journalist Nellie Bly beats Verne's fictional record, traveling the world in just over seventy-two days.

  Today: A journey around the world using regularly scheduled commercial transportation (airliners) would take as little as forty-five hours.

- **1872:** The Parsi community in India is open in its embrace of British culture, expanding demographically, financially, and culturally.

  Today: The Parsi community is shrinking, with one of the lowest birth rates in the world, and is deeply divided between members who wish to preserve old conservative traditions and others who are leaving the community through intermarriage with other groups.

- **1872:** Steam and steel technology symbolize the cutting edge of human progress.

  Today: In the popular imagination, computer technology now symbolizes human progress.

HISTORICAL CONTEXT

Mass-Market Publishing

Verne was part of one of the earliest mass-market publishing empires, that of Pierre-Jules Hetzel (1814–1886). Hetzel in some measure created Verne's phenomenal publishing success through the integrated use of magazine, newspaper, and book publishing. He created an entire series of Verne's books, titled "Voyages extraordinaires" ("Extraordinary Voyages"), in order to promote completist collecting. Verne's novels were regularly serialized in a newspaper or magazine owned by Hetzel and then published in book form at the end of the year, making them available as Christmas presents. Each book was published simultaneously in three different formats with three different prices, ranging from cheap paperbacks to elaborately illustrated hardbacks.

Around the World in Eighty Days was the single greatest success in this series, especially for Verne. In addition to his usual collaboration with Hetzel, Verne coauthored a highly successful and long-running play that relied on elaborate special effects to simulate the exotic events of the novel, such as the burning pyre from which Passepartout rescues Mrs. Aouda, as well as the motion of the various trains and ships that figure so largely in the story. Verne personally made more money from this stage enterprise than he did from almost all his book royalties combined; it was in some sense the nineteenth-century equivalent of selling film rights. Most of the transportation firms mentioned in the books were real companies. As the serialized chapters became more and more popular (a process reflected, or predicted, in the novel itself as newspaper readers in England become more and more interested in Fogg's wager and journey), several railroad and steamship companies offered to pay Verne to make sure their services were mentioned by name. Verne claimed that as a gentleman he had to turn down such offers, but whether this is true or not, it was perhaps the earliest demonstration of the principle of product placement, the now ubiquitous practice by which companies pay to have their products featured in popular narratives.

Parsis and Westernization

Mrs. Aouda, the woman that Fogg and his companions rescue from the *suttee* (the ritual of a Hindu wife burning herself to death on her husband's funeral pyre), is a Parsi. The Parsis (now less commonly spelled "Parsees") are the descendants of Iranians who fled their homeland in the eighth to tenth centuries in the face of the Arab

An illustration from the box of a late 19th-century parlor game based on the novel (The Art Archive / Private Collection / Marc Charmet)

conquest. A main reason that they fled was to preserve their traditional religion rather than convert to Islam. Their religion was Zoroastrianism, named after their prophet Zoroaster, who lived in the mid-second millennium BCE. He was the first prophetic figure to found an entirely new religion, preaching that his followers should worship God (Ahura Mazda in the Iranian language) and his semidivine helpers while fighting against the evil principle that exists in the world (Angra Mainyu or Ahriman). History, in the Parsi view, is leading to a definite end when Zoroaster will be reborn and herald the final victory of God over evil together with the dissolution of the physical world and the judgment of the dead as to whether they had followed God or the evil principle.

By the nineteenth century, the Parsi population in India was concentrated in Bombay (modern Mumbai), where they formed a large and prosperous mercantile middle class, amounting to more than 100,000 people, or a fifth of the city's population. Because it brought tremendous advantages in business, the Parsis rapidly adopted British-style education and produced a disproportionate number of leading Indian physicians, lawyers, teachers, journalists, and other professionals, as well as businessmen. Praising them for their adoption of modernity, Verne states that the Parsis are "the most hard-working, civilized, intelligent and austere of the Indians and are the race to which the wealthy native merchants of Bombay currently belong." By the mid-1850s, upper-class Parsi girls were also beginning to receive Western educations (at least through a grammar-school or high-school level), which helps explain Aouda's degree of anglicization and easy interaction with her British rescuer and eventual husband. Despite any religious scruples, Parsis also formed an extensive trading community throughout the British Empire, and Fogg and his companions begin to encounter them as far west as Aden, in Arabia.

Parsis had to overcome their own particular obstacles to accommodate their integration with the modern world. Like Jews, they were hampered in this by purity laws that had functioned adequately in the tribal existence of their ancestors thousands of years ago but which made interaction with the modern world difficult. In particular, Parsis considered fire to be a sacred manifestation of God on earth and maintained perpetually burning fires in their temples; they considered the harnessing of fire for any purpose (such as warfare) other than cooking or illumination to be blasphemous. For this reason, the steam engine was viewed as unclean and something that Parsis could not come into contact with. As a result, Parsis, again like Jews, split into traditionalist and reforming factions. At the same time, educated Parsis became leaders in the scientific study of their own religious literature (the Avesta, attributed to Zoroaster, and a few later works). The conflict between tradition and modernity in regard to the Parsi religion led to the doctrine that a separate tradition taught by "secret masters" revealed that in fact nothing in the Avesta was incompatible with modernity. The interaction of Parsis holding such beliefs with Western occultists helped lead to the formation of interfaith spirituality known today in the United States and Europe as "New Age." The deep Parsi religious belief that the purpose of human existence is to fight evil was put into action in the nineteenth century by a number of charitable organizations funded by wealthy Parsis, providing a complete social safety net of subsistence, medical care, and education for even the poorest members of the Parsi community. Accordingly, Verne's narrative condition that Aouda, though the daughter of a wealthy Bombay Parsi merchant, was abandoned by the community when she was orphaned and forced to marry a Hindu prince is far-fetched as a historical probability.

CRITICAL OVERVIEW

Verne has enjoyed a renaissance in the opinion of French critics in the last generation, but in the English-speaking world he is still often not taken as a serious author. In fact, Verne is often classed as children's literature. It is true that Hetzel serialized many of Verne's most strongly scientific pieces in his magazines intended for juvenile audiences because those stories were in part considered didactic, that is, teaching about science. However, Verne did not aim his work at children, nor were they mainly taken as such in France. Verne's reputation as a juvenile author in the English-speaking world

depends mainly on the purposes and faults of his translators. Translations (frequently anonymous) of Verne are often made explicitly for children, and in those cases the text is likely to be either summarized or radically altered, ironically leaving out the most scientific and technical elements of the books. *Around the World in Eighty Days* is certainly not children's literature, but it has suffered from misdirected marketing to younger audiences often enough. A notable example is the 2004 Disney film adaptation of the story, which was heavily marketed to children, abandoned any effort at scientific or dramatic plausibility, and seemed to take place in some sort of steam-punk fantasy world rather than the reality of 1872 where Verne set his book.

A reappraisal of Verne's oeuvre began in the 1960s among French critics and has slowly made its way into the English-speaking world. Arthur B. Evans's seminal (for English criticism of Verne) *Jules Verne Rediscovered: Didacticism and the Scientific Novel* points out that what is often misunderstood as science fiction in Verne is his praise of the positivist tendency in nineteenth-century thought and its extrapolation. This positivism is apparent in the scrupulously realist *Around the World in Eighty Days* in that the speed of modern transportation seems, in the book's ending, to even create time itself. Evans points out that Verne's writing style, especially in the presentation of human character, is "consistently condemned by critics as 'superficial,' 'wooden,' and 'nonliterary.'" And this is nowhere more true than in the flat characterizations spelled out at the beginning of the novel for Fogg and Passepartout. But Evans defends Verne's stylistic choice on the ground that it is modeled on the presentation of facts in scientific literature. Communicated by Andrew Martin in *The Knowledge of Ignorance: From Genesis to Jules Verne* is the basic insight of French scholarship that Verne is a champion of the shift from the biblical paradigm, wherein knowledge led to humanity's fall in the garden of Eden, to a modern paradigm wherein knowledge for its own sake brings salvation; in Verne's literature, logic and engineering replace lyricism.

William Butcher has done the most of any scholar writing in English to provide a context for *Around the World in Eighty Days* based on the new wave of French Verne scholarship. In the introduction to his translation of the work, he characterizes its author as highly experimental and far ahead of his time. Butcher finds Verne's overarching themes in the novel to be space and time themselves. He sees the leap in the narrative from Paris to Suez to be an internalization in Verne's style of the instantaneous communication made possible by the telegraph. Butcher praises the ending of the novel, which symmetrically returns to its origin in the Reform Club via flashback cut off by Fogg's entry as an unexpected *deus ex machina* (literally, "a god from a machine," a character or device introduced to resolve a plot that otherwise cannot be resolved) to win the bet. Finally, Butcher argues that the narrator of the book is highly unusual because he seems to labor under many of the misapprehensions of the characters: the narrator informs the reader, inaccurately, that the railway crossing India has been completed, that the image of Passepartout rescuing Mrs. Aouda from the burning pyre is the dead Indian prince come back to life, and that the wager has been lost. For Butcher, this makes the novel uniquely modern in that the reader can find no definite framework of truth.

Among other studies of Verne, Timothy Unwin, in his *Verne: "Le tour du monde en quatre-vingts jours"* (which uses the original French in its title but which is written in English), follows in Butcher's footsteps, drawing on French scholarship to situate *Around the World in Eighty Days* as a link between traditional linear novels and modern works of introspection and experimentation. Curiously, even Verne scholars can show a lack of familiarity with *Around the World in Eighty Days*. For instance, in *Jules Verne: An Exploratory Biography*, Herbert R. Lottman refers to Mrs. Aouda as being Hindu.

CRITICISM

Bradley A. Skeen

Skeen is a classics professor. In this essay, he considers Around the World in Eighty Days *with respect to the concept of progress.*

Around the World in Eighty Days is a celebration of the nineteenth-century idea of progress. J. B. Bury wrote the history *The Idea of Progress: An Inquiry into Its Origin and Growth* in 1920, at the very end of the concept's unlimited sway over the Western imagination. He describes it as nothing less than "the animating and controlling idea of western civilisation." This belief was occasioned by the tremendous economic growth created by the Industrial Revolution, when steam-

WHAT DO I READ NEXT?

- *The Jules Verne Encyclopedia*, by Brian Taves and Stephen Michaluk, Jr. (1996), provides a wide variety of information, focusing on the history of publication, translations, and adaptations of Verne's works.

- The Web site of Zvi Har'El's Jules Verne Collection (http://jv.gilead.org.il) provides a wide spectrum of resources, including online texts of Verne's works, scans of the original illustrations of many of Verne's books, scholarly articles about Verne, a discussion forum, and much more.

- Emmanuel J. Mikel's 1991 translation of *Twenty Thousand Leagues under the Sea* (1869–70) presents a full and careful rendition of Verne's second best-known novel, complete with introduction and notes.

- *Paris in the Twentieth Century* was Verne's second novel, written in 1863 but rejected by his publisher Hetzel and so not published until 1994. Translated by Richard Howard in 1996, the work presents a grim dystopian future where technology has destroyed traditional culture and suggests an entirely different path that Verne might have taken without Hetzel's guidance.

- H. G. Wells was in some sense Verne's rival as a "science fiction" author, though Verne disliked the comparison since he saw himself dealing with scientific reality while Wells pursued more fantastic subjects. The original 1898 text of Wells's famous *War of the Worlds* was edited and annotated by Leon Stover in 2001.

powered (later electrical-powered) machinery replaced handwork as the main means of production. The economist John Maynard Keynes, writing around the same time as Bury in *The Economic Consequences of the Peace* (1919), chronicles the nineteenth-century economic prosperity that was ended by World War I. The transformation of society by the Industrial Revolution meant that food became cheaper and easier to obtain. The threat of famine was thus removed from Western culture, a new level of security that seemed little short of miraculous. The nature of society was changed beyond all recognition, as many people left lives as agricultural workers in the countryside to live in large cities and work tending machinery. Intellectuals and politicians in the nineteenth century conceived of these changes as entirely good and beneficial. Although there were no clear connections with them, nearly every American ideal, such as liberty, democracy, charity, and justice, was linked to scientific and industrial progress. The belief in progress became the guiding star of culture in the same way that religion had been in the Middle Ages. Progress could only lead to the creation of a utopia, a fully realized paradise on earth. As Bury puts it, "The hope of an ultimate happy state on this planet to be enjoyed by future generations . . . has replaced, as a social power, the hope of felicity in another world" after death. Keynes also described the new prosperity brought about by industrial progress in terms of a mythical paradise. Indeed, the idea that the world is ever progressing toward the ultimate degree of human happiness derives from the Christian idea that history is inevitably moving toward a definite end in the return of Jesus and the resolution of the world into a paradise. Marxist thought about the inevitability of a socialist utopia had the same origin in Christian thought. Although the technological developments that sparked the Industrial Revolution were mostly made in England, once they were adopted in France (a few years before Verne's birth), French thinkers took the lead in developing an ideology of progress. Bury advises his readers, "The preponderance of France's part in developing the idea [of progress] is an outstanding feature of its history."

Verne superficially seems to be an unreserved supporter of the idea of progress with his predictions of the limitless development of technology, and certainly that is the most obvious reading of *Around the World in Eighty Days*. However, Verne does sometimes express reservations. In *Les cinq cents millions de la bégum* (*The Begum's Fortune*), Verne envisions two parallel paths of progress coming to fruition in two different cities. One is a utopian paradise of prosperity and freedom, but the other is a dystopia, a society in which everything has turned out for the worse. There, society is organized to curtail personal freedom, and technology is used to create weapons of mass

destruction. One of Verne's most noteworthy works was the second novel he wrote, *Paris au XXᵉ siècle* (*Paris in the Twentieth Century*). Written in 1863, it was not published until 1994 because Verne's publisher, Hetzel, considered it too pessimistic to gain a wide audience. It is set in the year 1960 and presents a French society wholly devoted to economic concerns, where culture has been transformed into a commercial commodity and all sense of tradition has been lost. (The work also prefigures the use of computers in business and of the Internet, though since mechanical computers had been described as early as the 1760s and had been used to produce logarithmic tables as early as 1855, Verne was hardly predicting them.) As Keynes points out, such pessimistic fears for the future did not become mainstream until World War I made their possibility all too obvious.

Verne himself lived through two of the most decisive moments in the history of the idea of progress. As Bury points out, the Revolution of 1848 in France was aimed at reforming the French government to become a servant of progress, behind the belief that its "movement cannot be arrested or diverted; that it is useless to struggle against it; that men, whatever they may do, cannot deflect the clock-like motion regulated by . . . Providence." The theorists and politicians of that movement held that progress was inescapable because it was part of human nature. It was at this time that progress came not merely to be viewed as an inevitable process but also to be described in terms of the mechanical devices whose constant invention seemed to be driving it. The process of progress was like clockwork, and progress itself became a sort of railway journey leading to the station of the glorious future. Perhaps the ultimate celebration of progress was the Great Exhibition held at the Crystal Palace in London in 1851, the first world's fair. In the inaugural speech of the exhibition, Prince Albert of England (as quoted by Bury) explained how the railway would serve as a literal engine of progress:

> Nobody who has paid any attention to the peculiar features of our present era will doubt for a moment that we are living at a period of most wonderful transition, which tends rapidly to accomplish that great end to which indeed all history points—*the realisation of the unity of mankind....* The distances which separated the different nations and parts of the globe are rapidly vanishing before the achievements of modern invention, and we can traverse them with incredible ease;...thought is communicated with the rapidity, and even by the power, of lightning.

Whether or not history points in that, or indeed in any, direction, this speech does point toward the ever-increasing interest of the popular press during the following twenty years in the technological conquest of distance, as railways and steamships crossed distances in hours that formerly would have taken days. Especially after the British rail network in India spanned the entire subcontinent in 1870, the fact that the world could be circled in as little as eighty days—compared to the famous circumnavigation of the globe by the explorer James Cooke a century earlier, which consumed nearly four years (1782–85)—became nearly commonplace in newspapers and other popular literature. Keynes argues that the ability to move freely and rapidly anywhere in the world, without specialized knowledge or connections, without custom or political barriers at borders, aided only by money, which could be drawn from international bank branches around the world, seemed like one of the great marvels of the age. As Verne says, "In the past it took at best six months to go from New York to San Francisco. Now it takes seven days." That is the miracle of progress for him.

It was natural enough, therefore, for Verne to fix on the idea of such a voyage in *Around the World in Eighty Days* as an expression of the idea of progress. The more general idea expressed by Prince Albert was that improvements in transport and communications would bring the world together and, as strangers became well known, promote the exchange of ideas and peaceful relations, but Verne's novel takes quite another direction. The fact that the journey itself is possible becomes the goal of progress. Verne's traveler, Phileas Fogg, seems to travel because he wants to test what progress has made possible. Although Verne largely presents Fogg as an unresolved mystery, Fogg embodies progress in himself:

> Phileas Fogg was a person of mathematical preciseness, someone who was never rushed but always ready, always economical in his movements. He never took an unnecessary stride and always chose the shortest route. He never allowed himself to be distracted. He was careful never to make a superfluous gesture. He had never been known to be upset or disturbed. He was the least hurried person in the world, but he always arrived on time.

Moreover, Fogg does precisely the same thing at the same time everyday. Fogg's life is like the clockwork machinery that made the industrial realization of progress possible, and he moves through the world unerringly and unhaltingly toward his goal, just as progress was believed to do.

Fogg embodies modernity within himself. Noting Fogg's complete imperviousness to fatigue, Sir Francis calls him "a man of iron!" But Passepartout corrects him and says his master is "a man of steel." The distinction could not be more significant. In Greek mythology, the Iron Age is an era representing the decline of mankind after the end of the Golden Age. In archaeology, the Iron Age is the relatively primitive time before the expansion of the Greek and Roman empires. Steel, on the other hand, is a modern industrial product, the symbol of the age of progress. Fogg's actions and plans are not only mathematical but also scientific: "He was not travelling, he was tracing a circle. He was matter in orbit around the globe, following the laws of physics." Just as the idea of progress originally descended from myth, Fogg's actions are often described in mythological terms. Fogg is "an incarnation of the god of punctuality," or he is like Zeus riding on the storm: "Land and sea seemed at his...command. Steamers and railways obeyed him. Wind and steam united to further his progress." In exotic India, Verne drives home the point that progress has become the new mythology of the age: "But what could Brahma, Shiva and Vishnu be thinking of the now 'Britannicized' India that they looked on from above as a steamboat shrilly chugged past, disturbing the holy waters of the Ganges." Steam, rather than the breath of the gods, became for Verne the animating force of modernity and progress.

Source: Bradley A. Skeen, Critical Essay on *Around the World in Eighty Days*, in *Novels for Students*, Gale, Cengage Learning, 2010.

Michael Tournier

In the following essay, Tournier explores the hero's struggle in Around the World in Eighty Days.

Jules Verne publishes *Around the World in Eighty Days* in 1873. He is forty-one years old and already familiar with notoriety, thanks notably to his novel *Twenty Thousand Leagues Under the Sea*, which appeared four years earlier.

The field of his themes and inventions seems limitless and without real cohesion. The dirigible balloon and the submarine, the sledge and the steam locomotive, the desert island and the raging fire at the center of the earth—all inventions and natural elements are fair game. Yet there is a curious obsession that we recognize in diverse forms in many of his books. This obsession is a loathing of inclement weather and the happiness of a sheltered life. More than one of his tales could bear as an epigraph this curious principle: to live happily we must live buried away. This is true for *Twenty Thousand Leagues Under the Sea*. Because the effect of the worst storms dissipates at depths of greater than twenty meters, the principal advantage of being undersea is always navigating in absolutely calm water. Underground mines are similar. In *Underground City*, or *The Child of the Cavern* (1877)—one of the strangest and most beautiful novels of the nineteenth century—Jules Verne describes the tranquil happiness of a population living three hundred meters below the surface of the earth. There are fields, lakes, forests, animals; all are enveloped in a perpetually unchanging atmosphere, and the passage of seasons and sudden jumps in temperature are unknown. Oddly, in both cases, dear Jules Verne forgets what is for man the fundamental problem of light. How can he neglect the fact that in the sea, as in the depths of the earth, darkness reigns where no source of artificial light reaches?

In *Around the World in Eighty Days* the problem of inclement weather is central. The hero Phileas Fogg is a studious man. His vigorously regular habits revolve around his library, composed principally of boat and train schedules. From his bookish, a priori knowledge, Fogg deduces that one should be able to go round the world in eighty days. If he leaves to travel, it will only be to verify the truth of this deduction and, in short, to test abstract knowledge against concrete experience. This problem, above all philosophical, is also the subject of Cervantes's *Don Quixote*: the courageous, naïve knight Quixote, fed on a diet of chivalric tales, will travel through the world turning his literary daydreams into real deeds.

Now, Fogg's theoretical boat and train schedules meet an imposing obstacle: accidents of meteorology, storms, winds, snow, fog, so many causes for delay. Again we recognize Jules Verne's loathing of inclement weather. His novel is about the struggle of chronology (Time) against meteorology (Weather) and the triumph of Time, like the victory of reason against the absurd. In passing we note this amusing detail: Jules Verne chose to name his hero Fogg (le brouillard) and to endow the valet Passepartout with a virtue of the greatest importance, the resourcefulness (la débrouillardise) which will win his master victory.

The struggle and victory of the a priori against the a posteriori—here, in a word, is the subject of this tale of extraordinary adventures and travels. Strange paradox! But Verne did not stop there. His tale closes with a dramatic flourish right out of Kant's *Critique of Pure Reason*. The German philosopher explains to us that, in effect, time and space, even reduced to their most purely theoretical dimensions, nevertheless remain sensible intuitions that cannot be reduced to concepts of pure reason. We must experience time and space with our eyes and muscles; no abstract construction will replace this. And he gives us a striking example of his proposition: "If the whole world consisted entirely of a single glove, the glove would still have to be a right glove or a left glove, and this is something that pure reason will never make out."

Fogg has such an experience himself on the last page of the novel. He has just journeyed round the world, and now finds himself back in London. But his travel log clearly shows: he traveled for eighty-one days, and so he has lost his wager and is ruined. He will confess his defeat at the Reform Club, then commit suicide. At this moment the affable Passepartout intervenes. It is Sunday, the 21st of December. The term for the eighty days was Saturday, the 20th of December. Passepartout goes out to inform the Reverend Samuel Wilson of Fogg's approaching marriage to the charming Mme Aouda, whom he saved from the pyre. He returns breathless and wildly disheveled. It is not Sunday, it is Saturday! The Reverend is not at home. But the journey round the world was completed in eighty days, and the wager is won!

The thing is that Fogg traveled from west to east, against the movement of the sun, and he thereby gained twenty-four hours. He must go immediately to the Reform Club to announce his success. The ending illustrates a paradox first formulated by Kant, but experienced by all air travelers today: jet lag. Never was Jules Verne a more profound philosopher or a more prophetic fantasist.

Source: Michael Tournier, "Jules Verne and *Around the World in Eighty Days*,", translated by Julia Abramson, in *World Literature Today*, Vol. 76, No. 2, Spring 2002, p. 106.

Marie Belloc Lowndes

In the following excerpt from an interview originally published under the name Marie A. Belloc in Strand *magazine in February 1895, Verne and his wife discuss the author's literary career; the origins of some of his works, including* Around the World in Eighty Days; *and his writing process.*

. . . Jules Verne, in his personal appearance, does not fulfil the popular idea of a great author. Rather does he give one the impression of being a cultured country gentleman, and this notwithstanding the fact that he always dresses in the sombre black affected by most Frenchmen belonging to the professional classes. His coat is decorated with the tiny red button denoting that the wearer possesses the high distinction of being an officer of the Legion of Honour. As he sat talking he did not look his seventy-eight years, and, indeed, appeared but little changed since the large portrait, hanging opposite that of his wife, was painted some twenty odd years ago.

M. Verne is singularly modest about his work, and showed no desire to talk about either his books or himself. Had it not been for the kindly assistance of his wife, whose pride in her husband's genius is delightful to witness, I should have found it difficult to persuade him to give me any particulars about his literary career or his methods of work.

"I cannot remember the time," he observed, in answer to a question, "when I did not write, or intend to be an author; and as you will soon see, many things conspired to that end. You know, I am a Breton by birth—my native town being Nantes—but my father was a Parisian by education and taste, devoted to literature, and, although he was too modest to make any effort to popularise his work, a fine poet. Perhaps this is why I myself began my literary career by writing poetry which—for I followed the example of most budding French litterateurs—took the form of a five-act tragedy," he concluded, with a half-sigh, half-smile.

"My first piece of work, however," he added after a pause, "was a little comedy written in collaboration with Dumas *fils*, who was, and has remained, one of my best friends. Our play was called *Pailles Rompues*, and was acted at the Gymnase Theatre in Paris; but, although I much enjoyed

> I HAD ALWAYS BEEN DEVOTED TO THE STUDY OF GEOGRAPHY, MUCH AS SOME PEOPLE DELIGHT IN HISTORY AND HISTORICAL RESEARCH. I REALLY THINK THAT MY LOVE FOR MAPS AND THE GREAT EXPLORERS OF THE WORLD LED TO MY COMPOSING THE FIRST OF MY LONG SERIES OF GEOGRAPHICAL STORIES."

light dramatic work, I did not find that it brought me anything in the way of substance or fortune.

"And yet," he continued slowly, "I have never lost my love for the stage and everything connected with theatrical life. One of the keenest joys my story-writing has brought me has been the successful staging of some of my novels, notably *Michel Strogoff*.

"I have often been asked what first gave me the idea of writing what, for the want of a better name, may be styled scientific romances.

"Well, I had always been devoted to the study of geography, much as some people delight in history and historical research. I really think that my love for maps and the great explorers of the world led to my composing the first of my long series of geographical stories.

"When writing my first book, *Five Weeks in a Balloon*, I chose Africa as the scene of action for the simple reason that less was, and is, known about that continent than any other; and it struck me that the most ingenious way in which this portion of the world's surface could be explored would be from a balloon. I thoroughly enjoyed writing the story and, even more, I may add, the researches which it made necessary; for then, as now, I always tried to make even the wildest of my romances as realistic and true to life as possible.

"Once the story was finished, I sent the manuscript to the well-known Paris publisher, M. Hetzel. He read the tale, was interested by it, and made me an offer which I accepted. I may tell you that this excellent man and his son became, and have remained, my very good friends, and the firm are about to publish my seventieth novel."

"Then you passed no anxious moments waiting on fame?" I asked. "Did your first book become immediately popular, both at home and abroad?"

"Yes," he answered modestly. "*Five Weeks in a Balloon* has remained to this day one of the most read of my stories, but you must remember that I was already a man of thirty-five when this book was published, and had been married for some eight years," he concluded, turning to Mme Verne with a charming air of old-fashioned gallantry.

"Your love of geography did not prevent your possessing a strong bent for science?"

"Well, I do not in any way pose as a scientist, but I esteem myself fortunate as having been born in an age of remarkable discoveries, and perhaps still more wonderful inventions."

"You are doubtless aware," interposed Mme Verne proudly, "that many apparently impossible scientific phenomena in my husband's romances have come true?"

"Tut, tut," cried M. Verne, deprecatingly, "that is a mere coincidence, and is doubtless owing to the fact that even when inventing scientific phenomena I always try and make everything seem as true and simple as possible. As to the accuracy of my descriptions, I owe that in a great measure to the fact that, even before I began writing stories, I always took numerous notes out of every book, newspaper, magazine or scientific report that I came across. These notes were, and are, all classified according to the subject with which they dealt, and I need hardly point out to you how invaluable much of this material has been to me.

"I subscribe to over twenty newspapers," he continued, "and I am an assiduous reader of every scientific publication; even apart from my work I keenly enjoy reading or hearing about any new discovery or experiment in the worlds of science, astronomy, meteorology, or physiology."

"And do you find that this miscellaneous reading suggests to you any new ideas for stories, or do you depend for your plots wholly on your own imagination?"

"It is impossible to say what suggests the skeleton of a story; sometimes one thing, sometimes another. I have often carried an idea in my brain for years before I had occasion to work it out on paper, but I always make a note when anything of the kind occurs to me. Of course, I can distinctly trace the beginnings of some of my books: *Around the World in Eighty Days* was the result of reading a tourist advertisement in a newspaper. The paragraph which caught my attention mentioned the fact that nowadays it would be quite possible for a man to travel round the world in eighty days, and it immediately flashed into my mind that the traveller, profiting by a difference of meridian, could be made to either gain or lose a day during that period of time. It was this initial thought that really made the whole point of the story. You will, perhaps, remember that my hero, Phineas Fogg, owing to this circumstance arrived home in time to win his wager, instead of, as he imagined, a day too late."

"Talking of Phineas Fogg, monsieur: unlike most French writers, you seem to enjoy making your heroes of English or foreign extraction."

"Yes, I consider that members of the English-speaking race make excellent heroes, especially where a story of adventure, or scientific pioneering work, is about to be described. I thoroughly admire the pluck and go-ahead qualities of the nation which has planted the Union Jack on so great a portion of the earth's surface."

"Your stories also differ from those of almost all your fellow-authors," I ventured to observe, "inasmuch that in them the fair sex plays so small a part."

An approving glance from my kindly hostess showed me that she agreed with the truth of my observation.

"I deny that *in toto*," cried M. Verne with some heat. "Look at *Mistress Branican*, and the charming young girls in some of my stories. Whenever there is any necessity for the feminine element to be introduced you will always find it there." Then, smiling: "Love is an all-absorbing passion, and leaves room for little else in the human breast; my heroes need all their wits about them, and the presence of a charming young lady might now and then sadly interfere with what they have to do. Again, I have always wished to so write my stories that they might be placed without the least hesitation in the hands of all young people, and I have scrupulously avoided any scene which, say, a boy would not like to think his sister would read."

"Before daylight wanes, would you not like to come upstairs and see my husband's workroom and study?" asked my hostess; "there we can continue our conversation."

And so, with Mme Verne leading the way, we went once more through the light, airy hall, where a door opened straight on to the quaint winding staircase, which leads up and up till are reached the cosy set of rooms where M. Verne passes the greater part of his life, and from where have issued many of his most enchanting books. As we went along the passage, I noticed some large maps—dumb testimonies of their owner's delight in geography and love of accurate information—hanging on the wall.

"It is here," remarked Mme Verne, throwing open the door of what proved to be a tiny, cell-like bed-chamber, "that my husband does his actual writing each morning. You must know that he gets up at five, and by lunch-time, that is, eleven o'clock, his actual writing, proof-correcting, and so on, are over for the day; but one cannot burn the candle at both ends, and each evening he is generally sound asleep by eight or half-past eight o'clock."

The plain wooden desk-table is situated in front of the one large window, and opposite the little camp bed; between the pauses of his work on winter mornings M. Verne, by glancing up, is able to see the dawn breaking over the beautiful spire of Amiens Cathedral. The tiny room is bare of all ornamentation, save for two busts of Molière and Shakespeare and a few pictures, including a water-colour of my host's yacht, the *St. Michel*, a splendid little boat in which he and his wife spent, some years ago, many of the happiest hours of their long dual life.

Opening out of the bedroom is a fine large apartment, Jules Verne's library. The room is lined with book-cases, and in the middle a large table groans under a carefully sorted mass of newspapers, reviews, and scientific reports, to say nothing of a representative collection of French and English periodical literature. A number of cardboard pigeon-holes, occupying however wonderfully little space, contain the twenty odd thousand notes garnered by the author during his long life.

"Tell me what are a man's books, and I will tell you what manner of man he is," makes an excellent paraphrase of a good old saying, and might well be applied to Jules Verne. His library is strictly for use, not show, and well-worn copies of such intellectual friends as Homer, Virgil, Montaigne and Shakespeare, shabby, but how dear to their owner; editions of Fenimore Cooper, Dickens and Scott show hard and constant usage; and there also, in newer dress, many of the better-known English novels have found their way.

"These books will show you," observed M. Verne genially, "how sincere is my affection for Great Britain. All my life I have delighted in the works of Sir Walter Scott, and during a never-to-be-forgotten tour in the British Isles, my happiest days were spent in Scotland. I still see, as in a vision, beautiful, picturesque Edinburgh, with its Heart of Midlothian, and many entrancing memories; the Highlands, world-forgotten Iona, and the wild Hebrides. Of course, to one familiar with the works of Scott, there is scarce a district of his native land lacking some association connected with the writer and his immortal work."

"And how did London impress you?"

"Well, I consider myself a regular devotee of the Thames. I think the great river is the most striking feature of that extraordinary city."

"I should like to ask you your opinion of some of our boys' books and stories of adventure. Of course, you know England has led the van in regard to such literature."

"Yes indeed, notably with that classic, beloved alike by old and young, *Robinson Crusoe*; and yet perhaps I shall shock you by admitting that I myself prefer the dear old *Swiss Family Robinson*. People forget that Crusoe and his man Friday were but an episode in a seven-volumed story. To my mind the book's great merit is that it was apparently the first romance of the kind ever perpetrated. We have all written 'Robinsons'," he added, laughing; "but it is a moot question if any of them would have seen the light had it not been for their famous prototype."

"And where do you place other English writers of adventure?"

"Unhappily, I can read only those works which have been translated into French. I never tire of Fenimore Cooper; certain of his romances deserve true immortality, and will I trust be remembered long after the so-called literary giants of a later age are forgotten. Then again, I thoroughly enjoy Captain Marryat's breezy romances. Owing to my unfortunate inability to read English, I am not so familiar as I should like to be with Mayne Reid and Robert Louis Stevenson; still, I was greatly delighted with the latter's *Treasure Island*, of which I possess a translation. It seemed to me, when I read it, to possess extraordinary freshness of style and enormous power. I have not mentioned," he continued, "the English writer whom I consider the master of them all, namely, Charles Dickens," and the face of the King of

Storytellers lit up with youthful enthusiasm. "I consider that the author of *Nicholas Nickleby*, *David Copperfield* and *The Cricket on the Hearth* possesses pathos, humour, incident, plot and descriptive power, any one of which might have made the reputation of a less gifted mortal; but here, again, is one of those whose fame may smoulder but will never die."

Whilst her husband was concluding these remarks, Mme Verne drew my attention to a large bookcase filled with rows of apparently freshly bound and little-read books. "Here," she observed, "are various French, German, Portuguese, Dutch, Swedish and Russian editions of M. Verne's books, including a Japanese and Arab translation of *Around the World in Eighty Days*," and my kindly hostess took down and opened the strange vellum-bound pages wherein each little Arab who runs may read of the adventures of Phineas Fogg, Esq.

"My husband," she added, "has never re-read a chapter of a single one of his stories. When the last proofs are corrected his interest in them ceases and this, although he has sometimes been thinking over a plot, and inventing situations figuring in a story, during years of his life."

"And what, monsieur, are your methods of work?" I inquired. "I suppose you can have no objection to giving away your recipe?"

"I cannot see," he answered good-humouredly, "what interest the public can find in such things; but I will initiate you into the secrets of my literary kitchen, though I do not know that I would recommend anybody else to proceed on the same plan; for I always think that each of us works in his or her own way, and instinctively knows what method is best. Well, I start by making a draft of what is going to be my new story. I never begin a book without knowing what the beginning, the middle, and the end will be. Hitherto I have always been fortunate enough to have not one, but half-a-dozen definite schemes floating in my mind. If I ever find myself hard up for a subject, I shall consider that it is time for me to give up work. After having completed my preliminary draft, I draw up a plan of the chapters, and then begin the actual writing of the first rough copy in pencil, leaving a half-page margin for corrections and emendations; I then read the whole, and go over all I have already done in ink. I consider that my real labour begins with my first set of proofs, for I not only correct something in every sentence, but I rewrite whole chapters. I do not seem to have a grip of my subject till I see my work in print; fortunately, my kind publisher allows me every latitude as regards corrections, and I often

have as many as eight or nine revises. I envy, but do not attempt to emulate, the example of those who from the time they write Chapter I to the word *Finis*, never see reason to alter or add a single word."

"This method of composition must greatly retard your work?"

"I do not find it so. Thanks to my habits of regularity, I invariably produce two completed novels a year. I am also always in advance of my work; in fact, I am now writing a story which properly belongs to my working year 1897; in other words, I have five manuscripts ready for the printers. Of course," he added thoughtfully, "this has not been achieved without sacrifice. I soon found real hard work and a constant, steady rate of production incompatible with the pleasures of society. When we were younger, my wife and myself lived in Paris, and enjoyed the world and its manifold interests to the full. During the last twelve years I have become a townsman of Amiens; my wife is an Amienoise by birth. It was here that I first made her acquaintance, fifty-three years ago, and little by little all my affections and interests have centred in the town. Some of my friends will even tell you that I am far prouder of being a town councillor of Amiens than of my literary reputation. I do not deny that I thoroughly enjoy taking my share in municipal government."

"Then have you never followed the example of so many of your own personages and travelled, as you easily might have done, here, there and everywhere?"

"Yes, indeed; I am passionately fond of travelling, and at one time spent a considerable portion of each year on my yacht, the *St. Michel*. Indeed, I may say I am devoted to the sea, and I can imagine nothing more ideal than a sailor's life; but with age came a strong love of peace and quietude, and," added the veteran novelist, half sadly, "I now journey only in imagination." . . .

Source: Marie Belloc Lowndes, "Jules Verne at Home: Edited with an Introduction by Lance Salway," in *Signal*, No. 10, January 1973, pp. 3–13; originally published in *Strand*, February 1895.

SOURCES

Boyce, Mary, *Zoroastrians: Their Religious Beliefs and Practices*, Routledge & Kegan Paul, 1985, pp. 196–215.

Burton, Richard Francis, *Of No Country: An Anthology of the Works of Sir Richard Burton*, edited by Frank McLynn, Scribner, 1990.

Bury, J. B., *The Idea of Progress: An Inquiry into Its Origin and Growth*, Macmillan, 1920, pp. vii–xi, 316, 330.

Butcher, William, "Introduction," in *Around the World in Eighty Days*, translated by William Butcher, Oxford University Press, 2008, pp. vii–xxxi.

Evans, Arthur B., *Jules Verne Rediscovered: Didacticism and the Scientific Novel*, Greenwood Press, 1988, p. 54.

Gallagher, Edward J., Judith A. Mistichelli, and John A. Van Eerde, *Jules Verne: A Primary and Secondary Bibliography*, G. K. Hall, 1980.

Keynes, John Maynard, *The Economic Consequences of the Peace*, Harcourt, Brace and Howe, 1920, pp. 9–12.

Lottman, Herbert R., *Jules Verne: An Exploratory Biography*, St. Martin's Press, 1996, pp. 162–64.

Martin, Andrew, *The Knowledge of Ignorance: From Genesis to Jules Verne*, Cambridge University Press, 1985.

Rivers, Christopher, *Face Value: Physiognomical Thought and the Legible Body in Marivaux, Lavater, Balzac, Gautier, and Zola*, University of Wisconsin Press, 1994.

Said, Edward, *Culture and Imperialism*, Vintage Books, 1994, pp. 93–116.

Swedin, Eric G., and David L. Ferro, *Computers: The Life Story of a Technology*, Greenwood Press, 2005, pp. 1–24.

Unwin, Timothy, *Verne: "Le tour du monde en quatre-vingts jours,"* University of Glasgow, 1992.

Verne, Jules, *Around the World in Eighty Days*, translated by Michael Glencross, Penguin, 2004.

FURTHER READING

Bly, Nellie, *Around the World in Seventy-Two Days*, Pictorial Weeklies, 1890.
> This book by the pioneering female reporter Nellie Bly capitalized on the popularity of Verne's novel. Her articles about her real travels in 1889 were also published in newspapers and then collected in book form. The text of the book is available online at http://digital.library.upenn.edu/women/bly/world/world.html through the digital library at the University of Pennsylvania.

Butcher, William, *Verne's Journey to the Centre of the Self: Space and Time in the Voyages Extraordinaires*, St. Martin's Press, 1991.
> This is a seminal English-language critical study of Verne's oeuvre as a whole.

Gildea, Robert, *Children of the Revolution: The French, 1799–1914*, Harvard University Press, 2008.
> This is a recent standard survey of French history and culture covering the entirety of Verne's lifetime. It provides a useful background for understanding Verne within his own society.

Hinnells, John R., *Persian Mythology*, Hamlyn, 1973.
> This work, intended in part for younger readers, gives a basic introduction to the beliefs and history of the Parsi religion.

Bel Canto

ANN PATCHETT
2001

Ann Patchett's fourth novel, *Bel Canto*, portrays the relationships that develop over a four-and-a-half month hostage situation. Notably, the novel is based on a similar hostage situation that occurred in Lima, Peru, from 1996 to 1997. The novel takes this real-life occurrence and transforms it into an examination of humanity—of how love, friendship, and hope can flourish in even the most unlikely of circumstances. The novel's themes additionally explore issues of class and privilege. Although several of the young terrorists are as kind, talented, and gifted as their captives, their disparate station in life has led them to widely diverse destinies. The power of art is also considered through one of the novel's main characters, an opera singer named Roxane. Patchett's humanizing look at political violence in a world increasingly susceptible to terrorist acts adds to the book's relevance today. Indeed, given the book's rich thematic depth, it has served as an ideal novel for students of literature.

Published in 2001 to great critical and popular acclaim, *Bel Canto* is widely available in several paperback editions.

AUTHOR BIOGRAPHY

Ann Patchett was born December 2, 1963, in Los Angeles, California. Her father, Frank Patchett, was a police captain, and her mother, Jeanne Ray

Ann Patchett (*AP Images*)

Patchett, worked as a nurse. The family moved to Nashville, Tennessee, when Patchett was six years old. Patchett attended Sarah Lawrence College, earning her bachelor of arts degree in 1984. After graduating, she worked as an editorial assistant for the Ecco Press. She then attended the University of Iowa and was awarded her master of fine arts degree in 1987. By this time, Patchett had already begun to receive awards and recognition for her essays and short stories. That recognition also led Patchett to several fellowships and academic positions. She was a residential fellow at Yaddo and the Millay Colony for the Arts in 1989 and the writer in residence at Allegheny College from 1989 to 1990. In 1992, she served as a visiting assistant professor at Murray State University. That same year, Patchett's first novel, *The Patron Saint of Liars*, was published.

Patchett's second novel, *Taft*, followed in 1994, the same year she was awarded a Guggenheim fellowship. *The Magician's Assistant*, Patchett's third novel, was next released to great acclaim in 1997. The book was nominated for England's prestigious Orange Prize. Also in 1997, Patchett served as the Tennessee Williams fellow in Creative Writing at the University of the South. Published in 2001, *Bel Canto* cemented Patchett's position as an author worthy of great renown. The book was an international bestseller, garnering the Orange Prize and the PEN/Faulkner Award, as well as a nomination for the National Book Critics Circle Award.

Taking a break from fiction, Patchett published the memoir *Truth and Beauty: A Friendship*, in 2004. The memoir won the Alex Award, the *Chicago Tribune* Heartland Prize, and the Harold D. Vursell Memorial Award. Patchett also served as the guest editor of the 2006 edition of *The Best American Short Stories*. The following year, Patchett's fifth novel, *Run*, was published. Her short stories and essays have appeared in numerous anthologies and periodicals, and her work continues to attract critical praise. As of 2008, Patchett was living in Nashville with her second husband, internist Karl VanDevender.

PLOT SUMMARY

Chapter One
In an unnamed poor country presumably in Latin America, a lavish birthday party is being thrown for Katsumi Hosokawa, the chairman of a large technology company in Japan. The country's government is throwing the party for Hosokawa because it hopes that he will open a factory there. Hosokawa, however, has no such plans, but he agrees to attend the party because his favorite opera singer, Roxane Coss, will be performing for him. Dignitaries and their wives gather at the vice president's mansion. As Roxane finishes her last song, the lights go out. At first everyone thinks the outage is part of the act, but as the darkness lingers, most think it is caused by the country's poor infrastructure. French ambassador Simon Thibault, however, notices that the lights are on in the kitchen. He realizes something is wrong, so he grabs his wife and heads for the exit. Before the couple is able to leave, several armed men storm into the room. The lights go on and the partygoers see that they are surrounded.

The vice president, Ruben Iglesias, thinks of President Masuda and how he cancelled his plans to attend the party at the last minute. Though Masuda is said to be attending to state matters pertaining to Israel, he actually stayed home to watch his favorite soap opera. Unfortunately, the armed men have arrived to kidnap the president, and they do not believe Ruben when he tells the men that Masuda is not there. One of the terrorists pistol-whips Ruben and orders the party-goers to lie on the ground as they search for Masuda.

After the terrorists have vainly searched for Masuda, they ask Ruben where he is. Ruben tells them the truth. The terrorists had planned to kidnap Masuda and leave the building in under ten minutes. Now, too much time has passed, and they can hear the sirens approaching. The failed kidnapping has now become a hostage situation.

Chapter Two

Hosokawa feels responsible for the situation; he knows that he agreed to attend the party without good intentions. He feels especially awful about putting Roxane in harm's way. By morning, the captors are taking small groups of hostages from the rooms. Many fear the worst, but it soon becomes clear that the hostages are being taken to use the restroom. A Red Cross worker named Joachim Messner knocks on the door. The terrorists gather round it and send Ruben to greet him. Unfortunately, Messner does not speak Spanish; he was in the country on vacation when he was called to help in the standoff. The terrorists check Messner for weapons and allow him to enter. Hosokawa's translator, Gen Watanabe, is called upon to facilitate Messner's opening negotiations with the terrorists. Unable to elicit any compromises, Messner leaves and promises to return shortly.

Over eighteen hours have gone by since the standoff began, and the terrorists have not slept. No one has eaten and everyone is restless. There are over two hundred hostages, but there are only eighteen captors. Thus, when Messner returns, the terrorists agree to release the women and two Catholic priests. They also agree to release the household staff, party staff, and anyone who is ill. One of the terrorist leaders, General Alfredo, gives Messner a list of demands. The hostages are being separated from those who are to be released when the younger of the two priests, Father Arguedas, asks to be allowed to stay with the hostages.

Chapter Three

The women are exiting through the front door when General Hector, another of the terrorist leaders, pulls Roxane aside. He does so partly because he is enamored with her voice (which he overheard while waiting to storm the building) and partly because he believes she will be a valuable hostage. Roxane's accompanist has grown increasingly ill during the standoff, but he refuses to leave Roxane's side. When he loses consciousness, Roxane goes through the accompanist's pockets and finds an empty vial of insulin. She realizes the man has gone into a diabetic coma. Roxane asks the terrorists to contact Messner and request insulin, but it is too late and the accompanist soon dies.

The terrorists consider shooting the corpse to make it look like a murder and bolster their position in the negotiations. Roxane blocks his body and says they will have to shoot her first. The terrorists let the matter drop and inform Messner of what has transpired. Messner returns with food for everyone and to retrieve the accompanist's body. He is angry that Roxane has not been released along with the rest of the women. Hosokawa again wonders if he is responsible; he feels accountable for the accompanist's death. He asks Gen to give Roxane his condolences. Roxane and Hosokawa begin a conversation via Gen's translations, and they all sit together eating.

Soon after, Gen is called away to aid the terrorists. He translates for them as they take down the names and ranks of each hostage. After determining which hostages are the most valuable bargaining tools, the terrorists release all who are deemed unimportant. They also give Messner another list of demands and state that they will not negotiate further until those demands are met. Thirty hostages and Father Arguedas remain.

Chapter Four

A week has passed. Both captives and captors sit idle in a state of constant boredom. Hosokawa has begun keeping a notebook of Spanish words in the hopes that he might begin to communicate with the other hostages. It has become clear that, aside from the generals, most of the terrorists are teenagers. Things have also relaxed a bit, and the captives are able to move somewhat more freely throughout the mansion's main floor. Some of the younger terrorists have even begun to speak to the hostages. Ruben gives one of the boys a pair of shoes from his own closet.

The younger soldiers wander about in awe of the mansion's finery. They stare at the television, and though they know what it is, they have never seen one work. When Simon suddenly turns it on for them, they nearly kill him during their initial shock.

As time goes by, it is revealed that two of the young terrorists are actually girls in disguise, Beatriz and Carmen. The captives are surprised to learn that Roxane is not the only woman in their midst. Notably, many of the hostages are enamored with Roxane, mostly because they love her voice, but they do not speak to her for fear of bothering her.

After another week has gone by, Roxane begins to ask the others if anyone can play the piano. Though she does not want to sing for the terrorists, she must begin to sing in order to stay in practice. Tetsuya Kato, one of Hosokawa's employees, is an accomplished pianist. He plays for Roxane as the hostages and captors gather to listen.

Chapter Five
Gen translates the conversations between Roxane and Kato as they begin to practice together. Messner continues to arrive daily. He, too, is enamored with Roxane. With the help of Father Arguedas, he arranges to have sheet music delivered to Roxane and Kato. When Messner arrives with the scores, General Alfredo tries to stop him. Roxane sings and threatens never to sing for the terrorists again if the scores are not given to her. Realizing that this could cause an insurrection, General Alfredo acquiesces. Roxane then sits with Hosokawa to read the music, their hands occasionally touching as they read.

Meanwhile, Kato plays the piano and Carmen prays "that God would look on them and see the beauty of their existence and leave them alone." Later that night, Carmen wakes Gen and asks him to secretly teach her English, to read and write, and to speak better Spanish. Gen, who is falling for Carmen, agrees.

Chapter Six
Now that Roxane is singing again, it is as if the terrorists have lost power over the hostages. Carmen has befriended Roxane, but Beatriz prefers to play dice with the other soldiers. Roxane sings and practices daily. When she does "no one gave a single thought to their death," a thought that, given the circumstances, is constantly looming. Ironically, Hosokawa realizes that he is happy for the first time in his life. Music had always made him happy, but "the difference was that now the music was a person."

While Gen is looking for Carmen, Victor Fyodorov, one of the Russian hostages, asks Gen to translate for him so he can speak to Roxane. Gen agrees and the two men decide to meet later.

Now that more than two weeks have passed, the Red Cross has stopped sending sandwiches and started sending groceries. Gen enlists the soldiers to help with the cooking because they have all of the knives. In return for this favor, Gen promises that Hosokawa will play chess with General Benjamin. Gen and Carmen also plan to meet secretly in the china closet to begin her lessons.

Chapter Seven
Another week has passed. Father Arguedas has begun to conduct mass for anyone who is interested. One morning, after Roxane has finished singing, Hosokawa leads her away by the arm. Carmen tells Gen that Roxane is in love with Hosokawa, and Gen is surprised because he had noticed the reverse. Gen is also in love, albeit with Carmen; he has not told her of his feelings. Instead, they continue to meet each night in the china closet and practice grammar.

Carmen beckons for Gen to follow her into the bathroom, but before he can enter, Fyodorov tells Gen that he is ready to speak with Roxane. He even insists on waiting for Gen outside the bathroom.

In the bathroom, Carmen tells Gen that no one will be going home, that the mansion is their home now. She and Gen kiss, but they are interrupted by Fyodorov's knocking. Gen is forced to join the Russian, and they find Roxane in the kitchen. Through Gen, Fyodorov tells Roxane that he is in love with her and that he does not expect her to love him in return. He only wants to give her his love like "a gift." Having done so, he happily leaves the kitchen, leaving Gen and Roxane in embarrassed silence.

Chapter Eight
The standoff has now gone on for three months. The boundaries between captive and captor have begun to blur. One day, as Hosokawa and General Benjamin are playing chess, Messner arrives and tells General Benjamin (via Gen) that the government is unlikely to meet their demands. The general responds that he does not care; he says he can wait, and he hands Messner a list of additional demands.

Roxane, who is the only hostage granted a private bedroom, tries to think of a way to sneak Hosokawa into her room. Roxane has fallen in love with him; given the circumstances, she thinks their love was fated to be. Although she is embarrassed to share her feelings with Gen, she asks him to tell Hosokawa of her plans.

Beatriz comes to Father Arguedas to give confession. As penance, Father Arguedas tells Beatriz to be kind to others for the rest of the day. Later, Carmen and Gen meet in secret and Gen asks Carmen to sneak Hosokawa up to Roxane's room. Carmen is afraid of what will happen to her if the generals find out, but she agrees anyway.

At two in the morning, Carmen leads Hosokawa up the servant's staircase. They pass through the nursery to reach the hallway adjoining Roxane's room. Though the nursery is usually empty, Beatriz is sleeping there, shirking her night watch duties. Beatriz wakes and points her rifle at Carmen and Hosokawa. Carmen explains what she is doing, and Beatriz remembers the priest's instructions; she lets them pass and promises not to tell. Carmen takes Hosokawa to Roxane's room before returning to Gen in the china closet.

Carmen leads Gen out to the back porch, an area forbidden to the hostages. Gen has not been outside in three months. They spend the night together outside, and no one finds out about Gen and Carmen or Roxane and Hosokawa that night.

Chapter Nine

The next morning, Roxane sleeps in and misses her usual practice. One of the young soldiers, Cesar, sings in her stead. His voice and gestures perfectly mimic Roxane's. The hostages and terrorists are shocked by his talent, as is Roxane, who overhears him and realizes that Cesar could become a star with the proper training. When Roxane comes down the stairs, Cesar is embarrassed and runs into the garden. She begs to be allowed into the garden to speak to him, and to everyone's surprise, General Benjamin decides that all of the hostages should be allowed a day in the garden.

He orders the soldiers to ready their guns and escort the hostages outside. Many do not understand what is happening and are afraid they are going to be killed. Gen translates and everyone happily goes outside. Roxane coaxes Cesar out of the tree he has climbed, and they plan to begin singing lessons later that day.

Ruben, Father Arguedas, and Oscar Mendoza (another hostage) are weeding the yard as Ishmael, a young soldier Ruben has befriended, stands guard. All three men have grown fond of Ishmael, and Ruben offers to adopt him while

Oscar offers to give the boy a job after the hostage situation has ended. Father Arguedas thinks it is inappropriate to talk like this. He knows their situation will probably end badly, and he feels that to pretend it might be otherwise is a form of madness.

Chapter Ten

The hostages have been held for four and a half months now, and they are regularly allowed into the garden. Messner enters with a heightened sense of urgency and tells Gen that they must get the terrorists to negotiate. He says they must surrender today. The generals do not notice Messner's mood and try to dismiss him, but he refuses to leave. Messner tells Gen that the government is tired of the negotiations and they will not allow him to come much longer. He tells them they must surrender. Although Messner knows it is an empty threat, the terrorists say they will begin killing people. Messner tells them that this would not change the situation's outcome. The generals refuse to surrender and leave the room.

Gen realizes that all the terrorists he has grown to know, including Carmen, will be arrested or killed in the end. He also realizes that, despite the impossibility, he wants all of them to escape. Gen, however, soon forgets his worry, as does everyone else. The only people who do not forget are Messner and Simon Thibault, who desperately misses his wife.

Cesar's singing lessons have progressed, and now he is almost as skilled as Roxane. Everyone listens to his lessons before going outside to garden or play soccer. Roxane and Cesar linger at the piano, and Hosokawa goes to the kitchen to make Roxane some tea. A masked uniformed man enters the room and Roxane screams. She ducks under the piano as Cesar is shot. Roxane drags him under the piano and covers his body, but she knows it is too late. Suddenly there are uniformed men and gunshots everywhere, storming into the house and garden.

All of the generals and some of the young soldiers, including Ishmael, are already dead. Beatriz freezes, drops her weapon, and raises her hands in the air, but she, too, is shot. Gen wants to call for Carmen but she is nowhere to be found. He does not know that she was in the kitchen with Hosokawa. When they heard Roxane scream, they ran into the living room and both were shot.

Epilogue

Roxane and Gen are married in a church in Lucca, France. Simon Thibault and his wife, Edith, attend the ceremony. Gen and Simon talk about how the newspapers did not report that two of the soldiers were female. Gen says, "It's almost as if they never existed." Gen tells Simon that he loves Roxane, that "when I hear Roxane sing I am still able to think well of the world. . . . I don't think I would last a day without that now." Simon thinks that "Gen and Roxane had married for love, the love of each other and the love of all the people they remembered."

CHARACTERS

Accompanist

The accompanist is the pianist who travels with Roxane Coss to perform at Mr. Hosokawa's birthday celebration. At the end of Roxane's performance, he kisses her just as the lights go out and just before the terrorists storm in. Everyone assumes that he and Roxane are lovers, an assumption bolstered by the accompanist's refusal to leave Roxane's side, even at the cost of his own freedom and, ultimately, his own life. Roxane later reveals that while the accompanist was in love with her, she did not return his sentiments. His death is all the more pointless given this insight. This may be why he is the only character in the novel who is not given a name.

General Alfredo

General Alfredo is one of the terrorist leaders. He is one of the more brutal of the three generals, and he suffers from insomnia. He is also the most matter-of-fact about their situation. He is an experienced soldier who has seen many battles and taken many bullets. Two of his fingers are missing, having been shot off during one such incident. He is also the general who pistol-whips Ruben Iglesias when he learns that President Masuda is not at the party. Additionally, General Alfredo unsuccessfully attempts to withhold the musical scores from Roxane. He relents only when he realizes that her refusal to sing may cause an insurrection.

Father Arguedas

Father Arguedas is a young and devout Catholic priest from a poor parish. He is at the party only because one of the church's rich benefactors, aware of the priest's love of opera, secures him an invitation as a gift. Father Arguedas chooses to stay to minister to the hostages despite being granted his freedom. This is in contrast to the rich priest, who chooses to leave. Father Arguedas cares for the accompanist and administers last rites over his body; he also inspires Beatriz to be more kind. Toward the end of the novel, the priest worries about Ruben and Oscar's promises to the young soldier Ishmael. Perhaps because of his own poverty, he is one of the few hostages who realizes that the burgeoning friendships between captives and captors are destined to end badly.

Beatriz

Beatriz is one of the two female soldiers. Unlike Carmen, however, Beatriz is masculine in both her looks and her behavior, preferring to gamble and socialize with the boys. She seems to be one of the soldiers who is least affected by the art and finery around her, although she loves watching the television and is intrigued by the priest and religion. She gives her first confession, and on the advice of Father Arguedas, she genuinely tries to be kinder to others afterwards. This effort leads her to overlook Hosokawa's clandestine liaisons with Roxane, as well as Carmen's involvement in the affair. When the mansion is stormed and her compatriots are shot, Beatriz thinks only of trying to survive; she drops her weapon and raises her hands in surrender, but she is shot and killed nevertheless.

General Benjamin

General Benjamin is the most reasonable and civil of the terrorist leaders. He suffers from a case of shingles but denies himself medicine or treatment for it. A former schoolteacher, General Benjamin became a soldier after his brother was taken as a political prisoner. He often plays chess with Hosokawa and is the general who first allows the hostages into the garden.

Carmen

Carmen is one of the two female soldiers. She is very shy and enamored with the art and opportunity surrounding her. She watches over Roxane and guards her bedroom, and she is also fascinated with Gen's ability to speak multiple languages. Carmen wishes to better herself, and she thinks that by learning to speak English, to read and to write, she will have more opportunities after the hostage situation has ended. It is this desire to better herself that gives Carmen the courage to approach Gen, even though it puts both her and him at risk. Carmen and Gen fall in love and begin an affair, and she often helps Roxane and Hosokawa despite what the generals might do to her should they find out.

Carmen knows that the terrorist leaders have no real exit plans, and this is why she tells Gen that the mansion is their home now. Some part of her realizes that this is impossible, but she fears losing all that she has come to love. Carmen rushes from the kitchen with Hosokawa when they hear Roxane scream, and she is shot and killed alongside Hosokawa before Gen even knows that the building is being stormed.

Cesar

Cesar is one of the young soldiers who reveals that he is as smart and talented as his captives. Cesar finds that he is enamored with the music around him, especially Roxane's singing. Privately, he finds that he can mimic her singing quite accurately, and when Roxane sleeps in one morning, he sings in her stead. Although he is embarrassed when he sees Roxane watching him, he agrees to begin lessons with her. Roxane intends to turn Cesar into an opera star when the hostage situation has ended, but he is shot and killed during the government's siege on the mansion.

Roxane Coss

Roxane Coss is the famous opera singer brought to perform at Hosokawa's birthday party. The government uses her presence to entice Hosokawa to build a factory in the country. Roxane defies the terrorists on several occasions; she attempts to escape out the front door, refuses to allow them to shoot her accompanist, and refuses to sing unless she is given her sheet music. She and Hosokawa fall in love, and in their growing happiness, they ignore the doom inherent in their situation. It is through this willed ignorance that Roxane believes she can turn the young terrorist Cesar into an opera star. Roxane even tries to protect Cesar, blocking his body with her own.

Victor Fyodorov

Victor Fyodorov is one of the Russian dignitaries who attends Hosokawa's party. Like many of the other hostages, he is enamored with Roxane. Unlike the other hostages, he reveals his love to her. He explains that his love for her is similar to his childhood love of art and that she has come to personify that love. In this way, he is similar to the accompanist. Yet Fyodorov makes no demands on Roxane; he gives her his love like

"a gift" that he does not expect returned. In this way, he is unlike the accompanist.

General Hector

General Hector, another of the terrorist leaders, is missing an arm, presumably from battle. He is one of the more brutal terrorist leaders, as he pulls Roxane aside when the women are leaving the mansion. When Roxane attempts to leave anyhow, he grabs her by the hair. He is also the general who suggests that they shoot the accompanist's corpse.

Katsumi Hosokawa

Katsumi Hosokawa is a Japanese businessman who loves opera. It is this love that brings him to see Roxane Coss perform. Because he attends the party in his honor under false pretenses, Hosokawa feels that he is personally responsible for the ensuing hostage situation. Yet as the hostage situation progresses, he forgets about his family in Japan and about his responsibilities as a corporate executive. Even before his affair with Roxane begins, Hosokawa realizes that, as impossible as it may seem, he has never been happier in his life.

Like Roxane and many of the other hostages, Hosokawa loses sight of his life before the party and of the standoff's likely outcome. When Carmen teaches Hosokawa to sneak around the mansion, he could easily escape, but he does not want to. In fact, the thought never even occurs to him. Ironically, Hosokawa's lack of decision in this instance ultimately costs him his life. He is the only hostage killed when the mansion is stormed.

Ruben Iglesias

Ruben Iglesias is the vice president of the unnamed country in which the story is set. He is also the party's host. When the terrorists enter the mansion in search of President Masuda, Ruben steps forward and informs them that the president is not at the party. When he admits that the president chose to stay home to watch his favorite soap opera, General Alfredo hits him over the head with a pistol. The injury heals slowly over the course of the standoff, and it is completely healed by the story's end. The wound becomes a symbol of the relationships that grow between captors and captives; as it disappears, so does the line between hostage and terrorist.

Ruben continues to act as the party's host long into the hostage crises. He cleans the mansion, cooks the food, and weeds the garden. Ruben takes pleasure in caring for the mansion and his guests, tasks that were once relegated to the household staff. Ruben also grows fond of one of the young soldiers, Ishmael. Like Roxane's unrealistic plans to present Cesar to the world as an opera singer, Ruben plans to adopt Ishmael as his son. Ruben has also forgotten that such dreams are impossible n their circumstances.

Ishmael
Ishmael is a young soldier who becomes a favorite of the hostages. Ruben promises to adopt him when the standoff ends, and Oscar Mendoza promises to give him a job. Just as Carmen learns grammar from Gen and Cesar learns to sing from Roxane, Ishmael learns to play chess by watching Hosokawa and General Benjamin. Just as Carmen and Cesar are killed, so is Ishmael.

Tetsuya Kato
Tetsuya Kato is one of Hosokawa's employees. Yet he also secretly practices piano every morning before going to work. This talent comes in handy after Roxane's accompanist dies. Like Hosokawa, Kato is happiest during the standoff. He feels as if he is fulfilling his purpose as a musician, rather than working as a business executive. He, too, does not miss his family or his old life.

President Masuda
President Masuda is the Japanese head of state in an unnamed Latin American country (an oddity that goes unexplained in the novel). Notably, the terrorists at first believe that Hosokawa is Masuda because he is also Japanese. Masuda is not at the party because he is said to be dealing with state matters related to Israel and thus cannot attend at the last minute. In reality, he stays home to watch his favorite soap opera. This fateful decision leads to the hostage situation.

Oscar Mendoza
Oscar Mendoza is one of the hostages who becomes fond of Ishmael. He unrealistically promises to give the boy a job after the standoff has ended.

Joachim Messner
Joachim Messner is a Red Cross worker who happens to be vacationing in the country when the standoff begins. This is why he is called in as the hostage negotiator, despite his inability to speak Spanish. Although the terrorists initially agree to release several of the hostages, they do so mostly to pare the group down to a more manageable number rather than as a sign of goodwill toward negotiations. Messner is little more than an errand boy who brings food and leaves with increasingly unreasonable lists of the terrorists' demands. Little credence is given to Messner's anger at the accompanist's death and at the terrorists for retaining Roxane as a hostage. As the standoff nears its inevitable conclusion, little credence is paid to his increased sense of urgency. The terrorists literally ignore his statements that a solution must be reached. Messner's marked urgency and attempts to distance himself from the other hostages are clear (but ignored) signs that a siege is imminent.

Edith Thibault
Edith Thibault is one of the women at the party who is released on the first day of the standoff. She is forced to leave her husband, Simon, behind. At the end of the book, she and Simon attend Roxane's and Gen's wedding.

Simon Thibault
Simon Thibault is a French ambassador who attends the party and is kept as a hostage. When his wife is released, she leaves him her scarf, and Simon carries it around throughout the standoff like a security blanket. Simon loves his wife dearly, and he misses her so much that (unlike the other hostages) he never forgets the reality of his situation.

Gen Watanabe
Gen Watanabe travels to the party as Hosokawa's translator. Able to translate in several languages, Gen is instrumental during the standoff, aiding communications between the terrorists and Messner, as well as for the other hostages (especially Roxane and Hosokawa). Gen begins to teach Carmen grammar in secret, and the two eventually begin an affair. He is shocked and dismayed by Carmen's statement that they and all the other hostages will live together in the mansion forever, but he does not truly realize the implications of that statement. Gen is one of the few people who notices Messner's changing attitudes as the siege nears. Yet he again overlooks the implications. Gen is too happy with his newfound love to focus on the ugly truths around him.

THEMES

Class and Privilege
The narrative opens as a world-famous opera singer finishes a performance for a room filled with well-dressed ambassadors and dignitaries.

TOPICS FOR FURTHER STUDY

- Recall a time when you and a stranger or someone you did not like were forced to spend time together. What were the circumstances, and how did your relationship develop or change? Recount your experience in a brief narrative.

- Attend an opera or listen to a recording of an opera. Then prepare an oral report in which you discuss your reactions to the music. Why do you think the characters in *Bel Canto* were so affected by Roxane's singing?

- Write an alternate ending to *Bel Canto*. Do more hostages die or do more survive? What happens to the terrorists? Include an epilogue that addresses what has happened to the surviving characters.

- Do you think that Roxane and Gen should have married? Do you believe that they truly love one another, or do you agree with Simon Thibault's assessment of their relationship? Why do you think the two married? Write an essay on the topic.

The party is being held at the vice president's mansion, and the scene is the quintessential picture of wealth, privilege, and political power. By contrast, when the soldiers storm the building, they are barely in uniform. Their clothes are threadbare and their shoes are falling apart. One of the generals is missing an arm, one is missing two fingers, and another is suffering from an untreated case of shingles. The great divide separating the wealthy from the poor is highly evident. That divide becomes even more evident when Carmen's brilliant mind, Ishmael's talent for chess, and Cesar's ability to sing are all revealed. If not for the young soldiers' poor start in life, each could easily have achieved the exalted status of their captives.

Although the case is not stated explicitly, it is clear that this stark imbalance of power is what has caused the hostage situation in the first place. Indeed, General Benjamin would never have become a soldier if not for his brother being arrested as a political prisoner. Carmen, Ishmael, Cesar, and several of the young soldiers would not have enlisted had they been afforded better opportunities.

Love, Hope, and Friendship

Although it would seem that the hostage situation is a dire ordeal, it becomes an opportunity for love and friendship. People who would never have come together for more than a few moments in normal circumstances suddenly find themselves friends and lovers. Roxane and Hosokawa do not even speak the same language, yet their love for one another transcends this barrier. Both Roxane and Hosokawa are aware that their love would be impossible if not for the standoff that fostered it. Because of this, both feel as if their love was fated, and they are almost grateful for the standoff's occurrence. This is evidenced by the fact that, toward the end of the standoff, Hosokawa could easily escape and chooses not to (in fact, he does not even consider the possibility). Gen and Carmen feel similarly. Additionally, Victor Fyodorov's love for Roxane would never have come to be. That unrequited love, which Fyodorov gives as "a gift" to Roxane, sustains Fyodorov throughout the standoff, a fact he admits to Roxane and for which he expresses his gratitude.

The friendships fostered between Ishmael and Ruben, Carmen and Hosokawa, Hosokawa and General Benjamin, and Roxane and Cesar would also have been impossible in any other circumstance. The standoff, seemingly an evil and negative thing, ironically brings much beauty into the lives of both captives and captors. Perhaps this is why so many choose to ignore the doom inherent in their situation. Many blindly hope for a peaceful resolution that is all but impossible. This blind hope manifests itself in Roxane's plans for Cesar and Ruben's plans for Ishmael, as well as in Carmen's belief that everyone will live together in the mansion forever. That hope, perhaps more than any of the other myriad emotions brought forth during the standoff, sustains captor and captive alike.

The Power of Art

While the standoff may provide an opportunity for unlikely affairs and friendships to develop, it is often the power and beauty of art that acts as a vehicle for those relationships. The party (and thus the standoff) would not have occurred if not for Hosokawa's love of opera. The same can be said of Roxane and Hosokawa's relationship; music had

Hostages sitting on the floor (© *Photos 12 | Alamy*)

always made Hosokawa happy, but "now the music was a person." Similarly, Fyodorov admits that his love for Roxane is based on his childhood love of art and beauty. Kato is also the happiest he has ever been during the standoff, and this is solely because he is able to play the piano for Roxane and everyone else. Even Carmen and Gen's relationship is based on art. Carmen approaches Gen because she is taken by his mastery of language, a mastery she wishes to achieve for herself. The same is also true of Ishmael and Cesar; their exposure to the arts (in the form of chess and music, respectively) inspires them to aspire to beauty. Even more powerful is the fact that music acts as a balm for the hostages and terrorists throughout the novel. Nearly all of them forget the direness of their situation when Roxane sings.

STYLE

Foreshadowing

The narrative in *Bel Canto* is filled with foreshadowing, a literary device used to hint at events

that will take place later in the story. The inauspicious power outage and Simon's growing awareness that something is wrong is one such example. The love between Roxane and Hosokawa is also foreshadowed by their interactions as well as Carmen's observation that Roxane is in love with Hosokawa. This, coupled with Gen's observation of the reverse, makes the relationship seem as fated as Roxane and Hosokawa believe it to be. The revelation that Carmen is a girl is also foreshadowed, predominantly by the hostages' observations that she is quite delicate and pretty for a boy. The greatest aspect of foreshadowing in the novel, of course, relates to the standoff's likely end. Though the characters often ignore their despair, it resurfaces again and again. Messner's changing attitude as negotiations continue is also a significant form of foreshadowing. Yet another form is the whispered rumors that the government is building a tunnel under the house. To this end, the heavy use of foreshadowing at every turn underscores the fact that the characters' impending doom is not only undeniable but also inevitable.

Juxtaposition

Many of the book's themes are established and underscored through the use of juxtaposition, relating different ideas or objects to one another in order to compare or contrast those objects or ideas. Indeed, the themes of class and privilege are made evident via the contrast between the poor soldiers and their wealthy hostages. The beauty and power of art is heightened by its pairing with the constant threat of violence during the standoff. As one of the only characters who never forgets the stark reality of the situation, Simon acts as a foil (contrast) for those who have grown complacent. His undying love for his wife and his longing to be with her, when juxtaposed with the relationships between Gen and Carmen and Roxane and Hosokawa, further underscore the untenable nature of the standoff. Smaller instances of juxtaposition include General Benjamin's humane treatment of the hostages (as opposed to the inhumane acts of the other generals). Another such example is the rich priest's decision to act in his best interest and accept his freedom, whereas Father Arguedas, a poor parish priest, chooses to stay and minister to the hostages.

Omniscient Third-Person Narrator

Bel Canto is told by an omniscient third-person narrator, a narrator who is not a specific character in the story, who is able to portray the thoughts of all the characters, and who is otherwise all-seeing and all-knowing. In *Bel Canto*, the omniscient narrator allows the reader a glimpse into the hearts and minds of the novel's large cast of characters. More than any other narrative device, it gives the reader the feeling of being a fly on the wall during the standoff. It also alerts the reader to the standoff's finale, as well as to several of the characters' willful ignorance of it. In this sense, the narrative's most powerful effect is that it gives the reader the feeling of watching an impending accident without the ability to alert those in danger. Yet at the same time, the device also distances the reader from the immediacy of the situation. Indeed, if the novel were told from a first-person point of view (often by a specific character participating in the story or by a narrator speaking as "I," and therefore unable to know the thoughts of the other characters or have knowledge of action taking place outside of their immediate experience), the reader would identify closely with the narrator, resulting in a more visceral experience of the standoff. The third-person narration, by contrast, makes the reader more conscious of the act of story-telling.

HISTORICAL CONTEXT

Stockholm Syndrome

Stockholm syndrome refers to the phenomena that occurs when captives identify with their captors (or when the abused identify with their abusers). It is clear that many of the hostages in *Bel Canto* suffer from this syndrome. Key examples are Roxane's relationship with Cesar and Hosokawa's relationship with Carmen. Both Roxane and Hosokawa attempt to protect their captors from their rescuers. Notably, the attempt costs Hosokawa his life. Gen's relationship with Carmen and Ruben and Oscar's fondness for Ishmael are also examples of Stockholm syndrome.

The term *Stockholm syndrome* was derived from a hostage situation in Stockholm, Sweden. On August 23, 1973, an escaped prisoner entered a bank and held three women and one man hostage. The escaped prisoner demanded that another prisoner be released, and that convict also became a part of the standoff (which lasted for over five days). When the hostages were rescued, they expressed sympathy for their captors and fear of the police who rescued them. Indeed, two of the women later became engaged to their captors. The syndrome is also referred to as the psychological phenomenon of transference or as the common sense syndrome or survival identification syndrome.

Notably, Stockholm syndrome is believed to be more prevalent than is actually the case. Yet with one minor exception, all of the key contributing factors are present in *Bel Canto*. These factors include a victim's fear of a rescuer, a victim's identification with the perpetrator, and the perpetrator's identification with the victim. All three elements are present in the novel. Additional contributing factors include the length of time that has passed during the hostage situation (the longer the standoff, the more likely the syndrome is to develop), continued contact between captive and captor (for example, the hostages are not segregated from the hostage takers), and captors who treat their captives humanely. If one were to overlook Ruben's injury at the beginning of the standoff, then all three of these elements are also present in the novel. The most significant source of Stockholm syndrome is the captives' and captors' identical fear of being injured by police. This too, is present in *Bel Canto*.

1996–97 Hostage Situation in Peru

The story in *Bel Canto* is loosely based on a four-and-a-half month hostage crisis that took place at

Lady singing opera *(Patrick Riviere / Getty Images)*

the Japanese embassy in Lima, Peru. Over the course of the standoff, there were reports that soccer games, large pizza orders, and chess matches took place. On December 17, 1996, fourteen Tupac Amaru rebels took four hundred diplomatic party-goers at the Japanese embassy hostage, releasing all but seventy-two hostages over the next seventy-two hours. The rebels reportedly targeted the embassy as a protest over the policies of Alberto Fujimori, the descendant of Japanese immigrants and then-president of Peru. On April 22, 1997, fifteen Peruvian soldiers stormed the embassy wearing ski masks; they rescued all but one of the hostages and killed all the rebels. Notably, the hostage who died was Peruvian, not Japanese. The hostage also reportedly died of a heart attack. Several of the hostages were injured, and two of the soldiers were killed.

The siege was planned over the course of two weeks, following the construction of several tunnels under the embassy. The tunnels were used to gather intelligence about the locations of the hostages and terrorists, as well as their daily routines.

Indeed, most of the rebels were killed when a tunnel under the soccer field was filled with explosives and detonated. Three years after the siege, both Fuji-mori and his intelligence officer, Vladimiro Montesinos, resigned amid unrelated allegations of bribery. Later, it was alleged that Peruvian troops shot the Tupac Amaru even after they had surrendered. The bodies of the rebels were exhumed in March 2001, and three were found to have been executed. Montesinos, who headed the 1997 siege, has since been charged with ordering their deaths.

CRITICAL OVERVIEW

Both critical and popular response to *Bel Canto* has been filled with praise and approbation. The book won several prestigious awards and nominations and was an international bestseller. Of Patchett's five novels, *Bel Canto* is considered her best work by far. According to *New York* magazine writer Daniel Mendelsohn, "*Bel Canto* is an unexpected transformation in Patchett's writing." Mendelsohn explained that "the author has taken what could have been a variation on the *Lord of the Flies* scenario (a descent into primitive chaos after the onset of lawlessness) and fashions instead a 'Lord of the Butterflies,' a dreamlike fable in which the impulses toward beauty and love are shown to be as irrepressible as the instincts for violence and destruction." Yet it was this very aspect that perturbed some critics. One such reviewer, *Los Angeles Times Book Review* contributor Jonathan Levi, stated that "the danger of *Bel Canto* . . . is in the message that with the right soundtrack, with the right singer singing the right music, all battlefields can become utopias." Complaining about Patchett's use of a real crisis to evoke this sentiment, Levi remarked: "In a more fictionalized context, Patchett's philosophy could be filed under reactionary claptrap and forgotten. But there is something particularly irresponsible about copying political history—and even worse, recent political history—for purely romantic purposes."

Regardless of this dissenting voice, nearly all of the book's reviews were positive and celebratory. For instance, *New York Times* contributor Janet Maslin called *Bel Canto* "a novel that begins with a kiss and absolutely deserves one." She went on to describe the novel as an "elegantly alluring book . . . that works both as a paean to art and beauty and a subtly sly comedy of manners." Seconding this opinion in the London *Guardian*, Alex

Clark noted that "the novel's sensibilities extend from the sly wit of observational humour to subtle, mournful insights into the nature of yearning and desire. Like the blueprint of operatic performance that she has imported, Patchett slides from strutting camp to high tragedy, minute social comedy to sublime romanticism." Clark was also impressed by Patchett's mastery over so large a cast of characters. He declared that "Patchett's stereotypical foreigners evoke humour rather than glibness," adding that "in the becalmed sections of her narrative, Patchett has the space and capacity to animate each of these lives and more, and the deftness to tuck them neatly into the story as a whole."

CRITICISM

Leah Tieger

Leah Tieger is a freelance writer and editor. In the following essay, she critiques Bel Canto *as a meditation on the power of art.*

Though the plot in *Bel Canto* is straightforward, the novel's themes are many, and what appears to be a simple story of diplomats taken hostage is instead a lengthy meditation on the power of art. Indeed, though it is difficult to overlook the daily minutiae of the lives and relationships of the captives and their captors, these relationships ultimately pale in comparison to the art that surrounds and sustains them. Notably, this is the case even in the characters' own eyes. Furthermore, while the book's many themes are all significant in their own right, only the power of art is fully explored. For instance, the terrorists' impending doom is clear from the very beginning of the novel; the narrator states from the start that they will not survive. Yet, their deaths seem unimportant and remain otherwise overlooked, perhaps because of their very inevitability. The political implications behind the standoff are rarely mentioned, and thus the novel barely addresses the human causes of political violence. Patchett also avoids addressing the implications of Stockholm syndrome; the phrase is not mentioned once in the book, nor is it even alluded to. Though love and friendship do occur, their implications remain largely unexplored except through the vehicle of art.

This latter point is best explored through the example of Victor Fyodorov. Fyodorov fully admits that his love for Roxane stems from his childhood love of art. He tells Roxane of a book of impressionist paintings that belonged to his

WHAT DO I READ NEXT?

- First published in 1954, William Golding's *Lord of the Flies* brings together a group of strangers under disastrous circumstances, as is the case in *Bel Canto*. However, the relationships formed in *Lord of the Flies* bear wildly different results.

- Patchett's first novel, *The Patron Saint of Liars* (1992), is perhaps her second most popular book (after *Bel Canto*). Told from several points of view, *The Patron Saint of Liars* tells the tale of a married woman who leaves her husband and moves into a home for unwed mothers. There, she secretly gives birth to their daughter.

- At the beginning of *Bel Canto*, Roxane sings an aria from *Rusalka*. The famous opera, with a score by Antonin Dvorak and libretto by Jaroslav Kvapil, was first performed in 1901.

- David Farber's 2005 book, *Taken Hostage: The Iran Hostage Crisis and America's First Encounter with Radical Islam*, is an excellent nonfiction account of a lengthy hostage crisis. Farber explores the 444-day standoff that occurred when Islamist militants invaded the American Embassy in Iran, holding fifty-two American diplomats hostage.

grandmother, and of how it inspired this love: "I could have had one life but instead I had another because of this book. . . . What a miracle is that? I was taught to love beautiful things." Fyodorov goes on to explain that this love grew to include not just paintings but all art forms until "I came to realize that what I had seen in the paintings I could see in the fields or a river. I could see it in people." Indeed, Fyodorov's love for Roxane is not only "a gift" but also a product of his love of art. This latter love is, in Fyodorov's own words, the thing that makes him "specifically qualified" to love Roxane. This qualification, that one must love art in order to love another, is not limited to Fyodorov. Indeed, it is what draws Hosokawa to Roxane (it

> THOUGH IT IS DIFFICULT TO OVERLOOK THE DAILY MINUTIAE OF THE LIVES AND RELATIONSHIPS OF THE CAPTIVES AND THEIR CAPTORS, THESE RELATIONSHIPS ULTIMATELY PALE IN COMPARISON TO THE ART THAT SURROUNDS AND SUSTAINS THEM."

is what draws everyone to Roxane), and it is also what draws Carmen to Gen.

Carmen is in awe of Gen's mastery of the art of language, an ability she wishes to learn for herself. This is what first draws the couple together. Yet the aptly and operatically named Carmen is also fully aware of the miracle of art that surrounds her. She is in love not only with Gen, language, and the opportunities they present but also with the music that emanates from Roxane. Indeed, Carmen sleeps outside Roxane's room and watches over her as if to protect her. Carmen is also enamored with the mansion and its finery. Her desire to stay in the house is tantamount; she thinks: "Yes, the Generals wanted something better for the people, but weren't they the people? Would it be the worst thing in the world if nothing happened at all, if they all stayed together in this generous house?" It is this desire that causes Carmen to pray "that God would look on them and see the beauty of their existence and leave them alone."

The irony here, of course, is that the fruition of Gen's and Roxane's abilities, as well as the comforts and splendor of the mansion, are all predicated on the very power structure that Carmen and her fellow soldiers have set out to destroy. This is an irony that Patchett barely touches upon, if at all. To do so would be to undermine her treatise on art's redeeming qualities. Art may redeem the individual, but its very creation is predicated on the subjugation of others. Furthermore, while art may make the passage of the standoff more bearable, even enjoyable for some of the characters, the underlying threat of violence both undermines and bolsters that beauty. For instance, the experience of art is heightened within the confines of the standoff. The assembled politicos and executives would never have taken the time to appreciate the art and finery around them if not for the enforced stillness of the standoff itself. The same is true of

the terrorists, who would never have had access to the music and finery around them in the first place. Yet, though art may act as a balm, it is powerless to save them. And, it would seem, that powerlessness in the face of death is tantamount. Many of the captors and captives are aware, however unwillingly, that their all-too-brief idyll will come to a violent end. Carmen knows that the terrorist leaders have no real exit plans, and this is why she tells Gen that the mansion is their home now. Some part of her realizes that this is impossible, but she fears losing all that she has come to love, so she chooses instead to believe in a fantasy. Carmen nevertheless knows that when the hostage situation ends, all that she has gained—love, art, friendship, and education—will be lost.

Father Arguedas is also well aware of this fact. The one hostage who has chosen to be there of his free will, he is also the only hostage without wealth or power. When Ruben offers to adopt Ishmael and when Oscar offers the boy a job, the priest feels "something cold and startling move through his heart. The men should not be talking to Ishmael this way. They were forgetting the circumstances." Father Arguedas fears for the future. He, like Carmen, knows that "the only way things could work out would be for everything to stay exactly as it was, for no one to speak of the future as if speaking of it could bring it on." Yet, the priest is the only hostage who fully envisions his future. Earlier in the standoff, in pursuit of musical scores for Roxane, Arguedas is allowed to call a fellow priest. When the two men are on the phone, Arguedas "knew then for sure that he would survive this. That there would come a day when... they would shamelessly recount the pleasure of this exact moment. He would have to live if only to have that cup of coffee with his friend."

Simon Thibault is yet another proverbial canary in the gold mine. "Except for Messner, whose job it was to remember," Simon is the only person who thinks of the outside world, of a life outside of the mansion; "even in his sleep [he] thought of nothing but his wife." His love for his wife also allows Simon to understand the inanity of the love the others have for Roxane. It is a symbolic love only. Early in the novel, Simon, newly separated from his wife, looks on as Roxane weeps over the accompanist's corpse. The accompanist's love is "the kind of love that offers its life so easily, so stupidly," and this "is always the love that is not returned." Indeed, "Simon Thibault would never die in a foolish gesture for Edith. On the contrary, he would take every cowardly resource available to him to ensure that their lives were spent together." If this statement can be taken at face value, what can be said of Hosokawa's love for Roxane? During the final siege of the mansion, he is killed as he steps in front of Carmen to protect her.

It is not to be argued that the art and song surrounding the hapless standoff is a powerful thing. It causes the characters to fall in love, to form alliances and friendships, to recognize their similarities rather than their differences. But it is also the power of art that blinds them to the harsh disparities that exist between captor and captive—despite the bonds of love and humanity that may exist between them. Both captors and captives alike are nearly drowned in art, lulled into complacency and into a willful ignorance of the fate that awaits them.

Source: Leah Tieger, Critical Essay on *Bel Canto*, in *Novels for Students*, Gale, Cengage Learning, 2010.

Nancy Posey

In the following review, Posey discusses the motifs of music and communication in Patchett's Bel Canto.

A synopsis of the plot of Ann Patchett's *Bel Canto* might lead a reader to expect a suspense thriller, the typical summer read. Patchett's fourth novel, recipient of the 2001 PEN/Faulkner Award, opens in an unnamed poor country, where guests of several nations come together for a performance by acclaimed lyric soprano Roxane Coss in celebration of the birthday of Japanese industrialist Katsumi Hosokawa. Coss has agreed to appear as a coincidence of good timing and a handsome fee; Hosokawa is drawn there by Coss, but he feels that his presence may be misleading: he has no intention of building a plant in that country. The opportunity to hear the soprano's pure voice in the intimate setting of the vice-presidential mansion has been his real incentive.

As Coss finishes singing and applause breaks out, however, the lights are extinguished and terrorist soldiers rush in, taking the guests as hostages. Mishandled on both sides, the hostage situation stagnates, and the real story begins as a day drags into months, characters emerge, and relationships develop. Most of the terrorist soldiers are practically children; a couple are females. Their captives, strangers to one another, are separated by language barriers.

While the plot impels the reader to keep turning pages, the real beauty of Patchett's story lies in the role that music and language play in the lives of her characters. While Coss and Hosokawa are unquestionably central to the story, Patchett gathers an impressive ensemble cast. The crucial link between them is Gen Watanabe, Hosokawa's translator, whose gift for language allows him alone to serve as a liaison between captives and captors; similarly, once she resumes singing, Roxane's music speaks to everyone.

Hosokawa has loved opera since his first introduction to it on his eleventh birthday, but with his busy life, he has to steal time, at best thirty minutes a day, to enjoy it. In fact, he remembers as one of the best times of his life a short bout with food poisoning that afforded him the luxury of listening to Handel's *Alcina* over and over for three days. Now, suddenly, all he has is time.

The story unfolds almost exclusively in the single setting of the vice-president's home. The characters' isolation is reinforced by a veil of fog that obscures their awareness of the world outside the palace windows. Like the survivors of *Lord of the Flies*, Patchett's hostages and their captors begin to establish a routine. Unlike *Lord of the Flies*, however, the guests and the soldiers do not divide into clear lines of good and evil; in fact, those lines soon begin to blur.

Once they realize that their situation is not going to be resolved quickly or easily, the characters settle in, establish lines of authority, and, most importantly, open up lines of communication. Watanabe, because of his prodigious gift for language, becomes a pivotal figure in the palace. Upon first working with Watanabe, Hosokawa notes that everything Gen touches becomes a smooth surface. Gen's voice, he realizes, though not musical, affects him as music does. Only Gen can communicate with everyone—the Russians, the French, the English, and the Spanish speakers. His gift of language even leads one of the young soldiers to seek his help in learning to read.

As time passes, lines between the captives and captors blur, and what evolves is no Stockholm Syndrome, where hostages develop sympathy for the terrorist cause, but rather a microcosm of the larger world outside the palace's fog-shrouded windows. As Gen is pressed into service as a translator and more, Roxane also channels her gift of music to her companions. Gradually other characters display individual gifts and provide resources that make the endless days bearable. For example, to the surprise of everyone, one of Hosokawa's employees proves himself an able accompanist.

Young Father Arguedas, stubbornly remaining behind when offered release, not only provides spiritual comfort, but also obtains sheet music for the soprano from his parish. In another instance, the young soldier Cesar reveals his natural operatic voice.

The appeal of this story reaches far beyond the imagination of music lovers alone. Among the party-goers that first night are devoted opera fans, as well as those who despise opera, characters who have never heard Coss's name but who, by the novel's end, weep openly in the presence of her music. Patchett artfully draws readers into the temporary, artificial world she creates, a world where music plays and time seems to stand still—just before the real world rushes inside. For a time, the music stops.

The inevitable rescue catches the soldiers, their hostages, and the reader off guard in this story, where unlikely alliances develop, familial bonds form, and love grows. Patchett's epilogue, the only part of the narrative set outside vice-president Iglesias's home, offers a bittersweet ending reminiscent of Charles Frazier's *Cold Mountain*. Readers may find themselves, as I did, turning to reread the ending one more time—just to be sure.

Source: Nancy Posey, Review of *Bel Canto*, in *English Journal*, Vol. 92, No. 6, July 2003, pp. 92–93.

John Mullan

In the following essay, Mullan investigates the role of confinement in Bel Canto.

Ann Patchett begins *Bel Canto* by sealing in her characters. In some unspecified Latin American country, insurgents have stormed the vice-president's mansion during a diplomatic party, believing that they will capture the President himself. Unfortunately for the guerrillas, he has stayed home to watch his favourite soap opera, and they are left with a miscellaneous collection of hostages from various nations. Surrounded by the unseen forces of the state, waiting for some final crisis, captors and captured while away the days that follow.

Confinement is enforced as a matter of the novel's plot, but is also a formal device. It is what enables the novelist to bring together characters in otherwise unlikely combinations and to pursue surprising relationships. A Japanese translator and a female terrorist slowly fall for each other during grammar lessons. An American diva, who was the star performer at the party, becomes involved with the opera-mad president of an electronics company who has long worshipped her from afar.

Confinement is a familiar principle of much drama. In plays, characters have to be brought together and kept on stage. All the parties and reunions we know from modern drama are ways of confining characters in each other's company. Such restriction is important to novelists too. How can a novelist segregate his or her cast from the world around so that their interactions might be plotted, their personalities known?

Patchett traps a small world of characters, almost all from different countries, speaking different languages. Most of the novel's comedy comes from the odd national differences between their experiences of a shared ordeal. Her situation is carefully contrived (and, of course, risks seeming a contrivance). Yet the principle of fiction is often some arranged restriction. "3 or 4 Families in a country Village is the very thing to work on" was Jane Austen's advice to a would-be novelist. The mock-modesty of the suggestion contains a hard truth about how her own novels work. In her country villages her characters cannot escape each other; they are forced together.

It is no accident that what is often thought to be the first novel, Daniel Defoe's *Robinson Crusoe*, is a tale of confinement. Only hemmed in by the sea, driven back on his physical and spiritual resources, can Crusoe come to know himself, and know God's will. The two great works of the next pioneer of 18th-century fiction, Samuel Richardson, are also stories of confinement. The heroines of *Pamela* and *Clarissa* spend much of their time imprisoned, scribbling the endless letters that form their narratives.

Readers will be able to think of all the ways in which great novelists have confined their characters, whether in villages or prisons, on ships or on islands (Joseph Conrad specialised in both of the last two of these). It is also an arrangement much used in popular fiction. Gothic novels began by locking their heroines in ancient buildings, setting their imaginations feverishly to work with every creak and whisper. The device became something like art in the work of Poe or in Stoker's *Dracula*, and is alive and well in horror fiction to this day.

Think, too, of whodunnits and thrillers. For the former, there is the country house, the cruise boat on the Nile, or—from Wilkie Collins onwards—whatever can limit and specify a collection of suspects. For the latter, there are trains and ships and planes. When I was a boy, my favourite was Alistair MacLean, who specialised in groups of desperate men cut off in Arctic outposts (*Ice Station Zebra*, *Bear Island*) with a traitor or two among them.

Patchett's novel, however, uses the convention to deny all thrills. Some political plot is going on, but the reader is hardly allowed to know more of this than the captives. The siege is more like a weird idyll, in which time is to be filled by talking, dreaming, playing and, for a lucky few, romancing. The novel is interested in what happens to people when the once urgent-seeming plots of their lives are suspended. What then animates them? What do they actually care about? You can only find out by keeping them captive.

Source: John Mullan, "The Virtues of Imprisonment," in *Guardian*, June 29, 2002, p. 32.

Marta Salij

In the following review, Salij praises Bel Canto *as a "provocative and enchanting" book about the transformative power of art.*

What is the point of the arts, anyway? Are literature and music mere frills that might make life sweeter, but do no more? Or are they essential?

Bel Canto, the fourth novel from Ann Patchett, presents a world in which opera, standing in here for all the arts, is absolutely central to the characters' very survival. Music becomes the means by which the characters become understood to each other—and to themselves. And, once understood, they become transformed into their highest, best selves.

That may seem fabulous, and *Bel Canto* has its fable-like elements. But Patchett doesn't push the fantastic too much. Rather, she seems interested in translation in all its definitions and in just what it is that art can do.

Bel Canto was inspired by a terrorist act, the 1996 takeover of the Japanese embassy in Lima, Peru, by the organization Tupac Amaru. That takeover started when rebels stormed a cocktail party, and lasted for several months, until the guerrillas were all killed or captured.

In *Bel Canto*, the Latin American country is unnamed, though like the Peru of 1996, it has a president of Japanese parentage. The country is poor and very much wants foreign investment, so it woos the chairman of the Japanese Nansei Corp., hoping he will build a factory there. Katsumi Hosokawa has no such intentions and has resisted the

> MUSIC BECOMES THE MEANS BY WHICH THE CHARACTERS BECOME UNDERSTOOD TO EACH OTHER—AND TO THEMSELVES. AND, ONCE UNDERSTOOD, THEY BECOME TRANSFORMED INTO THEIR HIGHEST, BEST SELVES."

politicians' advances so far, but then they tempt him with a birthday party at which they promise the American lyric soprano Roxane Coss will sing. They have figured out that the workaholic Hosokawa has one passion, opera, embodied in one singer, Coss.

Hosokawa accepts the invitation, and he is gathered at the vice president's mansion with nearly a hundred politicians, diplomats and businessmen when 18 terrorists stream through the air-conditioning ducts. They are there for the president, they shout. They want freedom "for the people," or failing that, for some comrades held in prison.

But President Matsuda isn't at the party. He's at home, watching his favorite soap opera, "The Story of Maria," on television. It's the episode in which Maria might escape her kidnappers, and he can't be expected to miss that.

That's the first hint this will be a novel about the mesmerizing power of art, though to put the president in the thrall of a soap opera may sound as though it's a setup for satire. To Patchett's credit she doesn't make too much comedy out of the parallels—Hosokawa and opera, Matsuda and soap opera; Hosokawa and Roxane, Matsuda and Maria—leaving them untouched to demonstrate that devotion can come on many levels.

The terrorists are utterly befuddled upon being confronted with dozens of hostages, none of whom they want. They dither until the next day, when a Swiss Red Cross volunteer named Joachim Messner calmly appears at their door and suggests that they free all the women, who consist of wives (apparently there are no women among the diplomats' ranks) and Coss. The terrorists agree, but then shake off their confusion for an instant to insist that Coss stay. She is, after all, their one celebrity and so their one bargaining chip.

What happens next is a standoff that is both a touch fantastic and yet deeply alluring. The terrorists shoot no one and seem not very eager to shoot anyone. The hostages attempt no escapes and seem not very eager to attempt any escapes. Each day Messner appears with the same old demands from the government, which he never presses on the rebels, and leaves each day with the same old demands from the terrorists, which he never presses on the government. Food and toilet paper get quietly replenished, as if the vice president's mansion had been turned into a four-star spa and all the inhabitants were on a long-needed sabbatical.

Even the weather contributes to the fairy tale. For weeks the city is beset by a foggy drizzle that never quite turns into rain, muting the sounds of the government's bullhorns outside and enwombing the rebels and the hostages within the walls of the vice president's garden. It becomes quite cozy there, every need met, listening to Coss sing aria after aria day after day.

Is it any wonder that, in this fantasy world, love and friendship bloom? More than one of the hostages falls in love with Coss; she eventually falls in love with one of them. Love blossoms between Hosokawa's shy young translator, Gen, and an even shier terrorist, the beautiful teenager Carmen. The hostages, who are French, Dutch, Japanese, German, Italian, Russian and American and who seldom speak each others' languages, become friends with each other.

The hostages even befriend the terrorists, such as when the vice president offers antibiotics to the shingles-afflicted terrorist leader. (Even more remarkable, those are the antibiotics the vice president got to treat a cut sustained when a terrorist struck him on the face, during the bad first day of the capture.)

How is it possible that the differences among all these people are bridged?

Patchett sets up several translators—bridge-builders—among her cast. First is the amazing Gen, who is fluent in an incredible number of languages and blessed with the empathy to translate hundreds of conversations each day. Gen is an obvious bridge, but he soon comes to believe that his language skills are not what are bringing the hostages and rebels together.

Second is Messner, who is appointed to bring the siege to a peaceful conclusion. But his willingness and hard work are not enough, signaled by his name ("messing up?") and by his insistence on neutrality (a dig at the Swiss?).

So the answer must come from Roxane Coss—whose name rhymes with and reminds us of "Red Cross"—who speaks a language everyone in the room is ready to hear: music. It's in the figure of Coss that Patchett's fantasy elements get the clearest expression. Coss' singing is not merely charismatic; like Circe's, it has the power to make every man who hears her fall in love, even those who have never heard opera before. (A charming scene, which Patchett rightly avoids playing for comedy, has one of the Russians declaring his sudden mad love for Coss through Gen's patient translation.)

Her singing emboldens Carmen to ask Gen to teach her to read. It empowers another one of the young terrorists, Cesar, to sing himself and to discover that he has a great gift. It teaches the vice president to put aside his political ambitions to vow to become a more doting father.

Her singing even makes the terrorists put down their guns during a tense moment, when she launches into "O mio babbino caro," the show-stopping aria from Puccini's "Gianni Schicchi." Opera fans make big claims about their beloved art, but few would say singing can stop bullets.

There are other fabulous threads to the story—Gen is a genius, Carmen is a Venus, a captive priest is a saint—and they are heightened by the contrast with Patchett's matter-of-fact style, which is more news bulletin than fairy tale. The matter-of-factness helps with the epilogue, which tries to explain what happened after the inevitable moment when the government finally became fed up with the rebels and burst into the mansion. The epilogue is not as successful as the rest of the novel; some readers will think that Patchett misjudged some of her key characters' motivations.

Others will see that the epilogue aptly captures the disappointment when a fantasy collides with the outside world. After all, not even a fantasy as delightful as *Bel Canto* can last forever.

But while it does last, Patchett's novel is a provocative and enchanting look at the power art has to suspend real life and to create a better world, one in which the differences between people can be erased and the barriers to our best selves can be hurdled.

Source: Marta Salij, Review of *Bel Canto*, in *Detroit Free Press*, July 6, 2001.

Margaret Stead

In the following review, Stead discusses the plot of Patchett's Bel Canto *and refers to the ending as a happy one.*

Virginia Woolf said that the most difficult thing in writing fiction was getting her characters from one room to the next. In choosing to base her novel on the 1997 siege of the Japanese embassy in Peru, Ann Patchett has found a way to simplify the "mechanics" of fiction, creating a realistic setting in which to explore the interaction between an unlikely cast of characters. The result is a variant of a time-honoured tradition: the mismatched group of people locked away together in an isolated country house.

Bel Canto is set in a tiny, poverty-stricken, unnamed Latin American country which (unsurprisingly) has a local-born Japanese president. This "host country" (as it is referred to) invites an American diva, Roxanne Coss, to come and sing at a soirée hosted by the vice president. The aim is to lure a potential investor, a Japanese businessman called Katsumi Hosokawa—an opera fanatic who adores Coss's voice—to visit. A group of rebels storms the residence, intending to capture the president, but when they find that he is not there (he is at home watching his favourite soap opera), they are forced to take hostages. Among the colourful, multinational group captured are the diva; the besotted Mr Hosokawa; the amiable vice president; and Gen, Mr Hosokawa's polyglot interpreter, through whose eyes much of the drama unfolds. Gen's facility for languages means that he becomes the conduit for communication between the rebels and the hostages, a Red Cross negotiator and the rebels, and even between the hostages themselves.

As in the siege of the Japanese embassy in Peru, the crisis drags on for months without loss of life, and slowly the barriers between captors and hostages break down. The diva decides that she must continue to exercise her voice. Sheet music is brought in from the outside world (all of the diva's demands, unlike the rebels', are met), and each morning all in the house, rebels and hostages alike, listen to her sing. *Bel Canto* is in part about how we interact outside the borders of language and culture, and for the hostages, music becomes the main means of communication, the diva the icon they worship.

For many of the hostages, the siege is a time of great happiness, captivity liberating them from their normal lives. The vice president finds that he has a real talent for housekeeping, Mr Hosokawa finds love in the arms of his diva, and Gen exchanges lessons in Spanish for lessons in love with one of the rebels, who is fittingly named Carmen. This development of the characters, the way in which each deals with the situation, is charmingly, often humorously portrayed in a narrative that moves effortlessly between the protagonists.

Apart from the generals who lead them, the rebels are little more than children, unsophisticated, amazed to find themselves in a dreamlike palace. They delight in trying on the vice president's clothes, and watching television. Bonds are formed—Roxanne begins to teach one boy to sing, the vice president promises to adopt another as his son "when this is all over"—but the fate of the rebels is preordained, and the looming tragedy is underlined in the novel not only by its similarities to the 1997 crisis, but equally through its references to opera. This makes the violent conclusion no less shocking.

A somewhat puzzling epilogue aims at creating symmetry—or simply a happy ending for two of the hostages—but seems rather to lessen the impact of the climactic scene inside the residence. *Bel Canto* explores how quickly we adapt to new surroundings and make them our own, our capacity for change, how each of us may have depths and strengths that remain untapped except in times of crisis. The novel plays with the characters' perceptions of reality—yet it is both deliberately surreal and at the same time dependent upon a real-life event, perhaps in order to allow the reader to accept its narrative framework. Ultimately, something about this marrying of the real and the fantastical jars, as though the obvious reference to the real is too heavy a burden for such a delicate exploration of ideas.

Source: Margaret Stead, "A Diva among the Hostages," in *Times Literary Supplement*, No. 5130, July 27, 2001, p. 21.

Ruth Scurr

In the following essay, Scurr criticizes Bel Canto, *calling it "uneven."*

The point of departure for Ann Patchett's new novel is the raid, in December 1996, on the Japanese embassy in Lima, Peru, which lasted for more than four months and during which one hostage and 14 rebels were killed. *Bel Canto*, like *La Traviata*, opens on a wonderful party. In the unnamed capital of an underdeveloped country, the vice-president is hosting a birthday party for a Japanese industrialist. Mr Hosokawa has been seduced into attending the party, held in his honour, by the promise of a private performance from the world-famous soprano Roxane Coss. As the last notes of the aria from Dvorak's Rusalka settle on a rapt and prestigious international audience, the lights go out and another uninvited audience, ragged and gun-toting, bursts from underground and takes the whole party hostage.

This is a promising basis for a novel: a canny way to combine the austere desert island scenario with high culture, and a neat means of imposing the classical dramatic constraints on action, character and setting. Patchett is an astute and amusing observer of bourgeois shock, immediately dividing the female hostages into two groups: those who expect to survive and are careful not to crease their gowns as they lie down on the drawing-room floor, and those quicker to anticipate death or worse and abandon their sartorial preoccupations. She continues to divide and subdivide the group by temperament, nationality, religion and intellect, but soon the problem faced by the terrorists becomes Patchett's own: there are simply too many of these people and some of them must go.

For their part, the terrorists only meant to take a single hostage, President Masuda, who should have been at the party but wasn't, because it clashed with his favourite soap opera. They are a splinter organisation of impoverished outlaws, aiming to overthrow the government in the name of the people; most of them adolescents following a doughty old general, painfully disfigured by shingles. When General Alfredo collapses in an armchair, his face covered in blisters, sighing with relief because most of the hostages have been released and the remaining 40 will be much more manageable, Patchett's own relief is also audible. She gives very fleeting attention to the problem of establishing discipline and routine in such peculiar circumstances, noting that "a week after Mr Hosokawa's birthday party ended seems as good a place as any" to rejoin the story. And she homes in on the love interest that emerges, in true operatic style, between two couples: Hosokawa and Coss (sharing only the language of music); and Hosokawa's fantastically skilled translator, Gen, and a girl terrorist called Carmen.

The best parts of this uneven novel are the most hammed-up and comically implausible. They offer a novelistic celebration of opera, where no one ever held wild improbability against a charming libretto. In the necessary absence of music and singing, farce comes out on top. There is an excellent scene in the kitchen where a French hostage settles down to preparing coq sans vin, directing a line-up of terrorists wielding confiscated kitchen knives. But many of the more passionate and romantic scenes seem wooden and affected. "Her knees touched his legs. If he took even half a step back he would be on the commode." The beleaguered General Alfredo is far from convincing when he insists, "We are an army, not a conservatory." All around, people burst into song as they rediscover the importance of music. As a result, the community of prisoners and guards acquires a surprisingly anodyne, ad hoc identity as the weeks pass, making the predictable (and authorially predicted) bloody ending all the more baffling. It's like gunmen breaking into the Big Brother house and murdering the inmates: horribly silly.

Source: Ruth Scurr, Review of *Bel Canto*, in *New Statesman*, Vol. 130, No. 4548, July 30, 2001, pp. 3–5.

SOURCES

"About," in *Ann Patchett Home Page*, http://www.ann patchett.com/about.html (accessed December 2, 2008).

"Ann Patchett Biography (1963–)," in *Biography.com* (accessed December 2, 2008).

Clark, Alex, "Danger Arias," in the *Guardian* (London), July 14, 2001.

Fuselier, G. D., "Placing the Stockholm Syndrome in Perspective," *FBI Law Enforcement Bulletin*, July 1999, pp. 22–5.

Levi, Jonathan, "Tin Ear," in the *Los Angeles Times Book Review*, July 8, 2001, p. 4.

Maslin, Janet, "Uninvited Guests Wearing You Down? Listen to Opera," in the *New York Times*, May 31, 2001.

Medelsohn, Daniel, "Ransom Notes," in *New York* magazine, June 11, 2001.

Patchett, Ann, *Truth and Beauty: A Friendship*, Harper-Collins, 2004.

Stead, Margaret, "A Diva among the Hostages," in *Times Literary Supplement*, July 27, 2001, p. 21.

"Troops Storm Embassy in Peru," in *BBC: On This Day*, http://news.bbc.co.uk/onthisday (accessed December 2, 2008).

FURTHER READING

Chaliand, Gerard, and Arnaud Blin, eds., *The History of Terrorism: From Antiquity to al Qaeda*, University of California Press, 2007.

This book places today's terrorist acts and hostage crises in historical context with other acts of terrorism over time. The volume also sheds political insight on the motivating factors behind terrorism.

Graham, Dee L. R., Edna I. Rawlings, and Roberta K. Rigsby, *Loving to Survive: Sexual Terror, Men's Violence, and Women's Lives*, New York University Press, 1994.

Stockholm syndrome occurs not only in hostage situations but also in cases of domestic violence. This book provides an in-depth look at the latter phenomena.

Lewis, Richard L., and Susan Ingalls Lewis, *The Power of Art*, 2nd ed., Wadsworth, 2008.

Whereas *Bel Canto* is a fictional exploration of art's power, this book is a nonfiction exploration of the same theme. The book examines art history and its cultural, political, and social influence.

Wilder, Thornton, *The Bridge of San Luis Rey*, A&C Boni, 1928.

This classic Pulitzer Prize–winning novel set in Peru contains a similar narrative style to that found in *Bel Canto*.

Bleak House

CHARLES DICKENS

1852–1853

Bleak House, a novel by Charles Dickens, was first published in installments from 1852 to 1853. It was extremely popular with readers, with each part selling about thirty-five thousand copies. In 1853, it was bound into one volume and published in America by Harper. Many modern critics consider it to be Dickens's finest novel. *Bleak House* has several plotlines. One is a legal case regarding the settlement of a will that has dragged on for more years than anyone can remember and shows no sign of being settled. A second is an unfolding mystery and detective story surrounding the aristocratic Lady Dedlock and an anonymous copier of law documents. A third is the story of Esther Summerson, told by Esther in the first person as she lives at Bleak House in the care of her guardian. The plotlines all intersect and give Dickens many opportunities for satire that attacks the failure of England's social institutions to perform the tasks they are designed to do. He takes aim at the long delays of the legal system, the inability of Parliament to address the needs of the poor, the misguided efforts of philanthropists who do not understand the real needs of people, and the unsanitary, disease-ridden conditions in England's capital city. *Bleak House* treats a broad swath of English society, from aristocratic houses to the slums and many points in between. It contains a typical Dickensian gallery of memorable characters, both noble and ignoble, and ample amounts of comedy and tragedy.

Charles Dickens (*The Library of Congress.*)

AUTHOR BIOGRAPHY

One of England's greatest novelists, Charles Dickens was born in Landport, near Portsmouth, Hampshire, on February 7, 1812, the second of eight children of John Dickens and Elizabeth Barrow. John Dickens was a clerk in the Navy Pay Office. When Dickens was twelve, his father got into financial difficulties and was imprisoned for debt in Marshalsea Prison. The young Dickens was sent to work for several months in a shoe-blacking warehouse, thus interrupting his education and giving him a lifelong sympathy for the plight of child laborers. Several years later, Dickens became a solicitor's clerk and then a court reporter. In 1832, he was a reporter for an evening newspaper, and he later became a reporter for the *Morning Chronicle*.

Dickens's first short story was published in a magazine in 1833, and in 1836 he published his descriptions of London life, *Sketches by Boz*, which were inspired by his journalistic work. In that year he also became the editor of a new magazine, *Bentley's Miscellany*, and married Catherine Hogarth, the daughter of the editor of the *Evening Chronicle*. They had ten children but separated in 1858.

Dickens's first novel was *The Pickwick Papers* (1836–37), which, like most of his fiction, was published in installments in magazines. The success of this novel encouraged Dickens to continue, and within the next few years he wrote *Oliver Twist* (1837–39), *Nicholas Nickleby* (1838–39), *The Old Curiosity Shop* (1840–41), and *Barnaby Rudge* (1841). His work was enormously popular in both England and the United States, and he embarked on his first trip to the United States and Canada in 1842, speaking out in favor of the abolition of slavery. *American Notes* (1842) and *Martin Chuzzlewit* (1843–44) were the direct result of his American tour.

During the 1840s and 1850s, Dickens continued to publish at a prodigious rate. *A Christmas Carol* (1843), *Dombey and Son* (1846–48), *David Copperfield* (1849–50), *Bleak House* (1852–53), *Hard Times* (1854), *Little Dorrit* (1855–57), and *A Tale of Two Cities* (1859) all appeared during this period. Dickens was also the editor of *Household Words*, a magazine he founded in 1850. When that magazine ceased publication in 1859, he became editor of a new magazine, *All the Year Round*.

Dickens continued to enjoy great popularity, and in the 1850s and 1860s he traveled around England, Scotland, and Ireland giving highly successful public readings from his novels. He also gave a reading in Paris in 1863 and went on a reading tour of the east coast of the United States for four months from 1867 to 1868.

During the 1860s, Dickens was frequently in poor health, but he continued to take on new work and reading engagements. *Great Expectations* (1860–61) and *Our Mutual Friend* (1864–65) were the products of the final decade of his life. In 1870, Dickens was working on *The Mystery of Edwin Drood*, which had begun publication but remained unfinished, when he had a stroke. He died at the age of fifty-eight, at Gadshill, near Rochester, Kent, on June 9, 1870.

PLOT SUMMARY

Chapters I–VI

Bleak House begins on a foggy day in London, probably in the 1840s. The fog is at its densest at the Court of Chancery, where legal cases drag on for years without resolution. In particular, the case of Jarndyce and Jarndyce has gone on for generations and is so complex that not even the

MEDIA ADAPTATIONS

- *Bleak House* was adapted for television, starring Gillian Anderson, Alun Armstrong, and Charlie Brooks, and issued on DVD in 2006 by BBC Warner. Running time is 465 minutes. This was a very successful adaptation. It is split up into half-hour episodes, each one ending with a cliffhanger.

- An earlier adaptation, starring Diana Rigg, Denholm Elliott, Philip Franks, T. P. McKenna, and Brian Deacon, and directed by Ross Devenish, was made in 1985 by BBC Warner and was released on DVD in 2005. Running time is 418 minutes.

- Several versions have been released on audio CDs. In 2007, Blackstone Audio released an unabridged edition.

- In 2003, Universal released an audiobook version read by Terje Rypdal.

- In 2003, Penguin Audiobooks released a version with Beatie Edney and Ronald Pickup as narrators.

- A 1986 version, read by Sir John Gielgud, is available on audiocassette, published by Newman Communications.

lawyers understand it. It is legendary for its length and its costs, both human and monetary. This day, two young people who are wards of the court in the Jarndyce case are applying to live with their cousin, John Jarndyce.

Chapter II takes place in the London home of Lady Dedlock and her husband, Sir Leicester Dedlock. They receive a visit from their lawyer, Mr. Tulkinghorn, about the Jarndyce suit, in which Lady Dedlock has an interest. She is startled by the handwriting in one of the documents the lawyer shows her.

Chapter III introduces Esther Summerson, who tells of her deprived early life when she was raised by her aunt, Miss Barbary, in Windsor. After Miss Barbary dies when Esther is fourteen,

Esther is told that Mr. John Jarndyce wants to provide for her education and is now her guardian. Esther teaches school for six years in Reading. Then she goes to London, where she meets the two wards in the Jarndyce case, Ada Clare and Richard Carstone. They all are sent to live with John Jarndyce at Bleak House in Hertfordshire.

In chapter IV, before they go to Bleak House, they stay the night with Mrs. Jellyby, a philanthropist who devotes herself to the betterment of Africa, neglecting her husband and seven children. The following day (chapter V) the three young people visit the Krook Rag and Bottle Warehouse near the Chancery. The owner, Krook, tells them that one of the suitors in the Jarndyce case, Tom Jarndyce, shot himself out of frustration because the case had dragged on so long. Later (chapter VI), the young people go to Bleak House, where they meet their guardian and cousin, Jarndyce. At dinner they meet Harold Skimpole, a charming, childlike man who expects others to look after him. Later that night, Skimpole is saved from being arrested for debt by Esther and Richard, who pay the debt for him.

Chapters VII–XII

In chapter VII, the narrative turns to the Dedlocks' estate in Chesney Wold, Lincolnshire. The old housekeeper, Mrs. Rouncewell, is there with her grandson, who has taken a fancy to Rosa, one of the maids. Mr. Guppy, a junior law clerk from London, arrives with a friend, wanting to take a tour of the house. He is fascinated when he sees a portrait of Lady Dedlock. Her face is familiar to him, but he does not know why.

In chapter VIII, Jarndyce explains the Chancery suit to Esther. It began with a will made by one of the rich Jarndyces. The dispute is over how the trusts named in the will are to be administered. Jarndyce explains the misery the case has inflicted on everyone. Esther is entrusted with the management of the house. One day Mrs. Pardiggle, a do-gooder like Mrs. Jellyby, visits Bleak House with her five young sons, whom she compels to donate their weekly allowances to worthy causes. Esther and Ada accompany Mrs. Pardiggle to the house of a poor brickmaker, where she lectures the family.

Richard and Ada fall in love (chapter IX), and Jarndyce is visited by an old friend, the quarrelsome but kind Lawrence Boythorn, who is in a dispute with Sir Leicester about a right-of-way between their properties. Guppy arrives with papers for

Boythorn. Alone with Esther, he proposes to her, but she rejects his proposal immediately.

In chapter X, Mr. Tulkinghorn goes to the law-stationer's shop near Chancery Lane run by Mr. and Mrs. Snagsby. Tulkinghorn wants to know the name of the law copier who copied the Jarndyce document he carries with him. Snagsby tells him that the clerk's name is Nemo. Tulkinghorn visits Nemo at his lodgings at Krook's but finds him dead from an opium overdose. An inquest takes place in chapter XI. No one knows much about Nemo, and the verdict is accidental death. In chapter XII, the Dedlocks return from Paris and are visited by Tulkinghorn. Tulkinghorn informs Lady Dedlock that the writer of the document she inquired about is dead. This news distresses her. She and Tulkinghorn are suspicious of each other.

Chapters XIII–XVIII

Richard needs to find an occupation. He impulsively decides to become a surgeon and is apprenticed to Bayham Badger in Chelsea. Love-sick Guppy makes a nuisance of himself by following Esther around, and Ada tells Esther that she and Richard are in love. Jarndyce says they must wait until Richard is established in a profession.

In chapter XIV, Esther and Ada meet Caddy, Mrs. Jellyby's oldest child, who is planning to elope and marry a dancing teacher, Prince Turveydrop. Esther meets Prince and his vain father at the dance academy and then with Jarndyce visits one of the lodgers at Krook's, the eccentric Miss Flite. Esther also encounters a young doctor, Mr. Woodcourt.

Chapter XV follows Jarndyce as he tries to help the orphaned children of Neckett, the sheriff's officer who had tried to arrest Skimpole for debt and who has just died. The oldest child, thirteen-year-old Charley, is looking after the others so they will not be sent to the orphanage.

In chapter XVI, an unnamed woman in a veil (clearly Lady Dedlock) goes to the slum district in London known as Tom-all-Alone's. There she seeks out Jo, a boy who knew Nemo, the dead law copyist. She gets Jo to take her to where Nemo lived, died, and was buried.

Esther narrates chapter XVII. Unsuited to becoming a doctor, Richard goes into law instead so he can follow the Jarndyce case. Jarndyce tells Esther what he knows about her origins; he does not know who her parents are. Woodcourt informs

them he is to become a ship's surgeon and will be away for a long time.

In chapter XVIII, the residents of Bleak House visit Boythorn, and at church, Esther sees Lady Dedlock for the first time. The aristocratic woman reminds Esther of her aunt and her childhood, but she does not know why. Later, on the Dedlock estate, Lady Dedlock is introduced to Esther and looks quickly away as if in dislike.

Chapters XIX–XXIV

Mr. and Mrs. Snagsby entertain Mr. Chadband, a minister, and his wife for tea. A constable brings in Jo, who is suspected of stealing. Jo says a lady gave him the money. Guppy questions the boy, wanting to put the pieces of the puzzle together. He also hears Mrs. Chadband speak of her time as housekeeper for Miss Barbary, Esther's aunt.

In chapter XX, Guppy wants to spy on Krook and arranges for his friend Jobling to lodge in the room formerly occupied by Nemo.

Chapter XXI is devoted to the humorless Smallweed family. The grandfather is a moneylender. An old soldier, Mr. George, who has borrowed money, visits. Smallweed threatens him with unpleasant consequences should he be late in repaying it. George mentions that Smallwood and his moneylending associates tricked his friend, Captain Hawdon.

In chapter XXII, Tulkinghorn is investigating a connection between Lady Dedlock and Nemo. He sends Inspector Bucket and Mr. Snagsby to the slums to find the boy, Jo. When they return to Tulkinghorn with Jo, a veiled lady is there. Jo at first identifies her as the lady who gave him the money, but then when he sees her hand and hears her voice, he says it is not her. The lady is Lady Dedlock's maid, Hortense, whose clothes Lady Dedlock had borrowed.

Chapter XXIII returns to Esther's narration. Richard is in debt and is foolishly putting his faith in the Jarndyce suit. He wants to join the army. Esther visits Caddy Jellyby and helps her tell Prince's father that she and Prince are engaged. Mr. Turveydrop at first opposes the engagement but then gives the couple his blessing.

In chapter XXIV, Richard is given an army commission and is to serve in Ireland. Jarndyce asks him to break off his engagement to Ada, since he is not showing much responsibility. This leads to an estrangement between Richard and Jarndyce. The Jarndyce case drags on, and the slowness of the law claims another victim, a Mr. Gridley, who has been in a long battle with Chancery.

Chapters XXV–XXX

Mrs. Snagsby notices a change in her husband, who has been asked by Bucket to keep the incident involving Jo secret. Mrs. Snagsby suspects her husband has been up to no good, even thinking that Jo must be his son.

Chapter XXVI shows Mr. George at the shooting gallery he owns, with his assistant, Phil. Smallweed arrives and asks about Captain Hawdon, George's friend, saying that he does not believe Hawdon is dead. He adds that a lawyer friend of his (Tulkinghorn) would pay George to produce a letter with Hawdon's handwriting on it. Smallweed and George go to Tulkinghorn's chamber (chapter XXVII), where Tulkinghorn asks George for the handwriting sample. George refuses, and also insists that Hawdon is dead. George visits his friends the Bagnets for advice and returns to Tulkinghorn, still refusing to hand over the requested sample.

In chapter XXVIII, the Dedlocks receive Mrs. Rouncewell's son, an ironmaster who is standing for Parliament. Mr. Rouncewell asks permission for his son Watt to marry the Dedlocks' maid, Rosa. Sir Leicester, conscious that the ironmaster is his social inferior, says they will allow the girl to make up her own mind.

In chapter XXIX, Guppy visits Lady Dedlock and mentions the resemblance between Lady Dedlock and Esther. His aim is to find out about the circumstances of Esther's birth because he wants to marry her. He has found out that Esther's name was Esther Hawdon, not Summerson. Explaining further, Guppy says that the dead Nemo was Captain Hawdon and that he knows Lady Dedlock went to visit his grave. He adds that Hawdon left a collection of letters, which Guppy can bring to her if she wishes. Lady Dedlock is stunned by this news. Esther is her child. Her sister, Miss Barbary, had told her the baby had died but had secretly taken her and raised her.

In chapter XXX, Esther receives a visit from Mr. Woodcourt's mother, who says her son is restricted in his choice of a wife because of the distinguished family he comes from, thus discouraging Esther from having hopes of marrying him. Esther attends Caddy's wedding.

Chapters XXXI–XXXVI

Esther and her new maid, Charley, get called to a cottage in St. Albans, where they find Jo. The sick boy was found on the street. Esther takes him home, and Jarndyce agrees that he should stay the night. However, in the morning, Jo has vanished. Charley gets sick with smallpox, caught from Jo, and she infects Esther. Charley recovers, but Esther goes blind.

Chapter XXXII returns to Guppy. Krook has agreed to show Hawdon's letters to him and Weevle (the name used by Jobling). When they go to Krook's room, all they find are charred clothes and ashes. Krook has literally gone up in smoke, a case of spontaneous combustion.

In chapter XXXIII, Guppy wants Weevle to stay on at Krook's so he can get his hands on all of Krook's papers. But Smallweed turns up and announces that Krook was Mrs. Smallweed's brother. He takes possession of the shop. Guppy has to tell Lady Dedlock that he cannot, after all, produce the letters he promised her, because they perished with Krook.

In the next chapter, Smallweed demands from George payment of a debt, for which George's friend Mr. Bagnet is a cosigner. George and Bagnet ask Smallweed for more time, but Smallweed just sends them to his lawyer, Tulkinghorn. George gets out of the bad situation when he agrees to show Tulkinghorn a letter from Captain Hawdon.

Chapter XXXV returns to Esther's narrative. She recovers her sight but her face is scarred. She learns from Jarndyce that Richard has turned hostile to him. Miss Flite comes to visit and tells Esther her story. All her family have been ruined by the Jarndyce lawsuit. Miss Flite also informs Esther that Woodcourt was in a shipwreck and became a hero by saving others.

In chapter XXXVI, Esther and Charley stay at Boythorn's house. Esther meets Lady Dedlock, who admits she is Esther's mother. She says she did not know Esther had survived. She tells Esther that this is the only time they are to meet and that Esther must keep her secret. Esther forgives her.

Chapters XXXVII–XLII

Richard, still hoping to get rich from the Jarndyce case, visits Esther. He thinks Jarndyce is working against his interests. Esther tries to reason with him, to no avail.

In chapter XXXVIII, Esther visits Caddy Turveydrop, who is now happily married. They visit Guppy, who thinks Esther is coming round to accepting his proposal. But when she raises her veil and he sees her disfigured face, he wants to escape any commitment to her. She asks him to cease his pursuit into her affairs, and he agrees.

In the next chapter, Richard visits his lawyer, Vholes, who says that progress is being made in the Jarndyce case. He also says that Jarndyce is working against Richard's interests, which is what Richard wants to hear. Guppy and Jobling go to the shop formerly owned by Krook to collect Jobling's belongings. The Smallweeds are there, going through Krook's possessions, and Tulkinghorn is there also, secretly seeking the missing letters from Lady Dedlock to Hawdon.

Chapter XL tells of the general election in England. Sir Leicester loses control of two parliamentary seats he had controlled to the opposition party, which is supported by Mr. Rouncewell and his son. Tulkinghorn tells a story in the presence of Lady Dedlock that is clearly Lady Dedlock's own, although he disguises the details. Now Lady Dedlock knows that Tulkinghorn knows about her past.

In chapter XLI, Lady Dedlock confronts Tulkinghorn, saying that she is willing to sign any document that would help her husband. She plans to leave Chesney Wold that night. Tulkinghorn tells her not to. For the time being, he intends to keep her secret because he is mindful of the honor of Sir Leicester and the family reputation.

Tulkinghorn returns to London (chapter XLII), where he is confronted by an angry Hortense, the French maid who has been fired by Lady Dedlock. Tulkinghorn has been using her to ensnare Lady Dedlock. Hortense demands that the lawyer either find her new employment or use her to destroy Lady Dedlock.

Chapters XLIII–XLVIII

Esther, Ada, and Mr. Jarndyce ask Skimpole not to take money from Richard. Sir Leicester invites the Bleak House residents to visit Chesney Wold, which makes Esther realize she must confess her secret about her mother to her guardian to prevent such a situation arising. When he hears Esther's story, Jarndyce is kind to her.

In chapter XLIV, Esther and Jarndyce discuss Lady Dedlock's precarious situation, with Tulkinghorn and Hortense wanting to bring her down. Jarndyce writes a letter to Esther, asking her to marry him. She does not reply for two weeks, at which point she accepts his proposal, putting her feelings for Woodcourt to rest.

In chapter XLV, Vholes, Richard's lawyer, visits Bleak House and says that Richard is in debt and will lose his army commission. Esther visits Richard at his barracks in Deal, Kent. Richard says it is too late, but anyway, he does not like being a soldier. He is obsessed with the Chancery suit. As Esther leaves, she encounters Woodcourt and asks him to befriend Richard in London.

The next two chapters (XLVI and XLVII) focus on the fate of the poor boy, Jo. Woodcourt encounters Jo in the slum of Tom-all-Alone's. Jo is still sick, and Woodcourt arranges for George at the shooting gallery to take him in. George tells Woodcourt that Tulkinghorn has a hold over him and may evict him from the gallery. Jo feels guilty because he made Esther sick, and he hopes he can be forgiven. Despite Woodcourt's efforts, Jo dies.

In chapter XLVIII, Lady Dedlock tells Rosa, her maid, that she is sending her away so that she can be with the young man who is courting her. When Lady Dedlock tells her husband of her intentions, Tulkinghorn is there also. Then in private, Tulkinghorn tells Lady Dedlock he will expose her secret because she has broken their agreement by trying to protect Rosa from the shame of being associated with her. Later, Tulkinghorn is shot dead in his own house.

Chapters XLIX–LIV

At a birthday party for Mrs. Bagnet, George and Inspector Bucket are in attendance. After a pleasant evening, Bucket and George leave together, and Bucket arrests George for the murder of Tulkinghorn.

Chapter L returns to Esther's narrative. Esther tries to help Caddy, who is unwell and has also given birth to a handicapped child. Woodcourt restores Caddy to health. Esther explains to Ada and Caddy that she is engaged to her guardian. Ada seems to withdraw from Esther after hearing this news.

Woodcourt fulfills his promise to befriend Richard (chapter LI). Ada confesses to Esther that she and Richard have been married for two months and she will henceforth be living with him. Esther is happy for them but sad that she will no longer have Ada living with her at Bleak House.

In chapter LII, Woodcourt, Esther, Mr. Jarndyce, and later the Bagnets visit George in prison. They all believe he is innocent, but he refuses to hire a lawyer. George tells Esther that on the night of the murder, he saw a woman who resembled Esther, dressed in black, coming down the stairs at Tulkinghorn's house. Mrs. Bagnet sets off to find George's mother.

Chapters LIII and LIV show Inspector Bucket at work, solving the murder case. He has been receiving anonymous letters accusing Lady Dedlock of being the murderess. He tells Sir Leicester the case is almost complete, and he questions Mercury, a footman at the Dedlock townhouse, about when Lady Dedlock went out for a walk on the night of the murder. Bucket tells Sir Leicester about Lady Dedlock's past, including her lover, her child, and her visit to Hawdon's grave. Smallweed arrives, wanting to be paid for the letters from Lady Dedlock to Hawdon that he had found at Krook's and passed on to Tulkinghorn. Bucket then brings in the murderer, Hortense, Lady Dedlock's former maid. Hortense had been lodging at the Buckets' home, and the inspector and his wife collected evidence against her. Sir Leicester is shocked and has a stroke.

Chapters LV–LX

In prison, George is reunited with his mother. Mrs. Rouncewell goes to Lady Dedlock with an anonymous letter accusing Lady Dedlock of the murder. She asks her to help George. Guppy informs Lady Dedlock that her letters to Hawdon have been found. Feeling the net closing in on her, Lady Dedlock writes to her husband, denying the murder but confessing her shame. She leaves the house in the night.

In chapter LVI, the stricken Sir Leicester is nursed by Mrs. Rouncewell. He writes on a slate that he forgives his wife. In Lady Dedlock's room, Bucket finds Esther's handkerchief. This gives him the clue he needs, and he and Esther set off in search of Lady Dedlock. The chase continues in chapter LVII, during a severe snowstorm. In St. Albans, they find that Lady Dedlock was at the house of Jenny, the brickmaker's wife, but left on foot. As the day wears on, Bucket begins to lose hope. Then he thinks he knows what happened, and he and Esther turn back toward London.

In chapter LVIII, Sir Leicester waits, hoping for his wife's return and explaining to everyone that nothing has changed between him and his wife. He still loves her and has no complaint against her.

Esther's narrative continues in chapter LIX. Bucket and Esther reach London and go to the Snagsbys, where they are given a note left by Lady Dedlock when she stopped there to rest. The note says she knows she will die in the streets. Guster, the maid, says that Lady Dedlock asked her for directions to the pauper cemetery (where Nemo was buried). Bucket and Esther, as well as Woodcourt, walk to the cemetery, where they find Lady Dedlock lying dead.

In chapter LX, Esther becomes ill following her mother's death but recovers under Woodcourt's supervision. Woodcourt accepts a position in Yorkshire, arranged for him by Jarndyce. Richard becomes more ill and is still obsessed with the Jarndyce case. His wife Ada is pregnant.

Chapters LXI–LXVII

Esther tells Skimpole not to visit Richard and Ada because he uses their money. Skimpole agrees. Woodcourt walks Esther home and tells her he loves her, but for Esther, honored though she is, it is too late. She is already committed to Jarndyce.

In chapter LXII, Esther and Jarndyce agree to marry next month. Bucket arrives with Smallweed, who has found a will relevant to the Jarndyce case, and it is dated later than the other wills. It favors Richard and Ada. Jarndyce takes the will to a lawyer, Kenge, who says it will settle the case.

Chapter LXIII tells of George's trip to the industrial north, where he visits his brother at one of the latter's iron factories. They have not seen each other for years, and it is a joyful reunion. George is now settled at Chesney Wold, his boyhood home, with his long-lost mother, Mrs. Rouncewell.

In Esther's narrative (chapter LXIV), Esther inspects the house in Yorkshire that Jarndyce has prepared for Woodcourt. It is called Bleak House. Jarndyce tells Esther that he knows she would be happier marrying Woodcourt, and that is what he desires for her. Back in London, Guppy, now a lawyer, makes another marriage proposal to Esther, which Jarndyce rejects on her behalf.

In chapter LXV, the Jarndyce case is finally settled. No one gains anything except the lawyers because all the money is eaten up in costs. The stricken Richard is reconciled to Jarndyce. He acknowledges his mistake and talks about starting over, but he dies as he embraces Ada.

Chapter LXVI reveals that Lady Dedlock is buried in the family vault. The much weakened Sir Leicester is attended by George, Mrs. Rouncewell, and his cousin Volumnia. The Dedlock family is in its final decline.

In the final chapter, Esther reveals that she has been married to Woodcourt for seven years and they have two daughters. Ada has a son, Richard, and they both live with Jarndyce. Woodcourt is respected and loved by the local people, and Esther is also admired.

CHARACTERS

Bayham Badger

A cousin of Kenge's, Bayham Badger is a surgeon in Chelsea to whom Richard Carstone is apprenticed.

Mrs. Bayham Badger

Mrs. Badger has been married twice before, and she speaks often and with admiration of her former husbands, Captain Swosser and Professor Dingo.

Matthew Bagnet

Bagnet owns a music shop and is an old friend of Mr. George. He defers to his wife in all things. Bagnet is cosigner for a loan George receives from Smallwood and at one point fears he may have to go to prison for debt.

Mrs. Bagnet

Mrs. Bagnet is Matthew's wife. She is described as "strong, busy, active, honest-faced," and it is her intelligence and efficiency that keep the Bagnet household running smoothly. Her husband relies on her.

Bagnet Children

The Bagnet children, Woolwich, Quebec, and Malta, are named after the places where they were born.

Miss Barbary

Miss Barbary is Esther's aunt. She is an unsmiling, highly religious woman who raises Esther in secrecy after telling her sister Honaria (Lady Dedlock) that the baby, born out of wedlock, is dead. Miss Barbary was once in love with Lawrence Boythorn but she abruptly broke off their relationship in order to raise Esther. She tells

Esther it would have been better had she never been born.

Mrs. Blinder

Mrs. Blinder is a good-natured old woman who runs a boardinghouse in Bell Yard where Tom Gridley and the Neckett family live. She takes a kindly interest in the welfare of the children.

Lawrence Boythorn

Boythorn is an old friend of John Jarndyce from their school days together. He is a man of violent and extreme opinions, which he always expresses with great force. He is involved in a long-running dispute with his neighbor, Sir Leicester, about a right-of-way between their properties. Despite his fiery temper, however, Boythorn is an amiable, kind, and harmless man, and Esther, Ada, and Richard like him. Boythorn is a bachelor, having been disappointed in love by Miss Barbary.

Inspector Bucket

Inspector Bucket is the detective who solves the Tulkinghorn murder, relying on careful police work and his own instincts. He is a courteous man who understands human nature and often has a certain sympathy for those he has to arrest.

Mrs. Bucket

Mrs. Bucket is enlisted by her husband to help solve the murder by watching Hortense's every move when she stays as a lodger at their house.

Richard Carstone

Richard Carstone is a nineteen-year-old orphan and one of the wards in the Jarndyce case. As a young man he is generous, cheerful, and carefree. He quickly falls in love with Ada Clare when they live together at Bleak House under the guardianship of John Jarndyce. However, Richard does not find his way in life. He decides on impulse to train as a surgeon but quickly gets bored by it. Then he wants to become a lawyer, but only because this can help him get deeply involved in the Chancery suit, which he is convinced is going to make him rich. He starts to get into debt, leaves the law, and joins the army, but he still goes on accumulating debt. He marries Ada, but it is too late to repair his fortunes. He dies a young man after hearing that he will not after all acquire any money from the suit.

Mr. Chadband

Mr. Chadband is a pompous minister who speaks in high-flown rhetorical language that many regard as nonsense. He singles out the poor boy Jo and tells him he is living in a state of darkness and sin, and that is why he is miserable.

Mrs. Rachel Chadband

Mrs. Chadband, Mr. Chadband's wife, used to be Miss Barbary's housekeeper, and therefore she knows the secret of Esther's origins. She is a severe, mostly silent woman.

Ada Clare

Ada Clare is a seventeen-year-old ward of the court in the Jarndyce case, and she is sent to Bleak House to live with her cousin, John Jarndyce, who serves as her guardian. She and her fellow ward Richard Carstone soon fall in love, and she also forms the closest of friendships with Esther. Ada secretly marries Richard when he comes of age, and she gives birth to his son after his death. Ada is sweet, innocent, and affectionate.

Coavinses

See Mr. Neckett

Lady Dedlock

Lady Dedlock is Sir Leicester's wife. She is twenty years younger than he, and in middle age she is still beautiful, although she has a proud, haughty demeanor. She is also bored with her life and travels between the family estate in Lincolnshire and their townhouse in London without much purpose. She and Sir Leicester have no children. Lady Dedlock has some unstated interest in the Jarndyce case, and she also guards a secret—that she had an illegitimate child with Captain Hawdon before she met Sir Leicester. Piece by piece, the secret comes out, beginning when she reacts noticeably when she sees Hawdon's handwriting on a legal document that Tulkinghorn shows her. When she meets Esther by chance and discovers that Esther is her daughter, she drops her cold manner and embraces Esther with great emotion. She also shows kindness to her maid, Rosa, perhaps seeing her as a substitute daughter. But when her enemy, the lawyer Tulkinghorn, threatens to expose her secret, the net closes in on her. After she realizes that she may also be accused of murdering Tulkinghorn, she leaves a note for her husband and runs away, dying in the snow at the gates of the London cemetery where Hawdon lies.

Sir Leicester Dedlock

Sir Leicester married his much younger wife out of love, and he continues to love her and treat her with great respect throughout their marriage. Even when he discovers his wife's guilty past, he forgives her completely. Sir Leicester is an aristocrat of the old school. He is proud of his family heritage and believes himself to be an important man. He is very disturbed at the social changes going on in England and is shocked when the two parliamentary seats he is used to controlling are won by the opposition party.

Volumnia Dedlock

Volumnia is Sir Leicester Dedlock's sixty-year-old cousin. A single woman, she lives modestly in Bath on an allowance from Sir Leicester, visiting him at Chesney Wold from time to time. After Sir Leicester's stroke, she nurses him, and she becomes his heir.

Miss Flite

Miss Flite is an eccentric old woman who hopes to gain something from the Jarndyce case. Every day she waits at Chancery for a judgment. In her lodgings at Krook's, she keeps about twenty birds in cages, saying she will release them when the judgment comes.

Mr. George

Mr. George is a fifty-year-old former soldier who runs a shooting gallery. He trains Richard Carstone. A good-hearted man, he takes in those down on their luck, such as his assistant Phil and the boy Jo. He owes money to Smallweed and is afraid he may be evicted. Mr. George is arrested for the murder of Tulkinghorn, but his innocence is soon established. He is reunited with his mother, Mrs. Rouncewell, and his brother.

Mr. Gridley

Mr. Gridley is a man who is made very angry by a long delay in his legal case at the Court of Chancery. He becomes so belligerent about it that he is cited for contempt of court. He takes refuge at George's shooting gallery, where he dies.

Mr. William Guppy

Mr. Guppy is an ambitious and cunning law clerk at Kenge and Carboy's. He takes a fancy to Esther and proposes to her, but she is not the slightest bit interested. Guppy manages to find out about Lady Dedlock's secret, although he fails in his goal of finding the letters she sent to Hawdon. After he has qualified as a lawyer, he proposes a second time to Esther but is once again turned down.

Guster

Guster is the maid in the Snagsby household. She is clumsy and excitable, given to having fits.

Captain Hawdon

See Nemo

Mademoiselle Hortense

The Frenchwoman Hortense is Lady Dedlock's maid. When Lady Dedlock dismisses her and favors Rosa instead, Hortense is angry and bitter. When Tulkinghorn refuses to help her, she murders him.

John Jarndyce

John Jarndyce is the guardian of his cousins Ada Clare and Richard Carstone, and also of Esther. Jarndyce is a single man of about sixty, and he is always kind and courteous, careful to do the right thing. He is well off financially and offers help to the less fortunate whenever he can, but in a quiet way that is the opposite of the kind of philanthropy offered by loud individuals such as Mrs. Pardiggle and Mrs. Jellyby. Jarndyce appoints Esther as the housekeeper of Bleak House, and although he is old enough to be her father, he entertains thoughts of marrying her. When he finally gets around to asking her, she accepts, but Jarndyce, magnanimous and thoughtful to the last, realizes that she will be much happier with Woodcourt and arranges for that marriage to take place.

Tom Jarndyce

Tom Jarndyce was John Jarndyce's great uncle. Frustrated at waiting for a judgment in the Jarndyce case, he shot himself. John Jarndyce inherited Bleak House from him.

Caddy Jellyby

Caddy Jellyby is Mrs. Jellyby's oldest daughter. Her mother uses her as a secretary for her philanthropic projects, depriving her of a normal education. She is befriended by Esther, and she marries Prince Turveydrop, ending up managing his dancing academy. She gives birth to a deaf and dumb baby.

Mr. Jellyby

Mr. Jellyby is Mrs. Jellyby's long-suffering husband. A mild-mannered, largely silent man, he goes bankrupt but receives little support from his wife.

Mrs. Jellyby

Mrs. Jellyby is a busy do-gooder who is obsessed with helping the African population of Borrioboola-Gha. She is far more interested in the Africans than she is in her own family, and she neglects her husband and seven children, including her oldest daughter, Caddy.

Peepy Jellyby

Peepy is the youngest Jellyby child. Like all the others, he is neglected by his mother.

Jenny

Jenny is the wife of a brickmaker in St. Albans. When Esther visits her cottage with Mrs. Pardiggle, Jenny is holding her dead baby. Later, Jenny tries to help Jo. When Lady Dedlock runs away from her home, she stops at Jenny's and changes clothes with her in order to elude pursuit.

Jo

Jo is a boy who ekes out a meager living sweeping a crossing in London. He lives in the slum of Tom-all-Alone's. Most of the time Jo is close to starving; Mr. Snagsby and Nemo take pity on him and are kind to him. After Jo shows Lady Dedlock where Nemo is buried, he attracts the attention of Tulkinghorn and Bucket. Jo catches smallpox, which he passes on to Charley and Esther after they take him to Bleak House. Jo dies at George's shooting gallery, where he has found refuge.

Mr. Kenge

Mr. Kenge is a member of the law firm Kenge and Carboy's, which handles John Jarndyce's affairs. He is called Conversation Kenge because he loves the sound of his own voice.

Mr. Krook

Mr. Krook owns a rag-and-bottle shop that buys up all kinds of junk, including collections of old law documents. The illiterate Krook is an odd, rather sordid old man, "short, cadaverous and withered." His neighbors call him the Lord Chancellor and his shop the Court of Chancery because everything in it is going to ruin. Krook dies when, soaked in alcohol, he spontaneously combusts.

Liz

Liz is a brickmaker's wife and friend of Jenny.

Lord High Chancellor
The Lord High Chancellor presides over the Court of Chancery.

Mercury
Mercury is the footman in the London townhouse of the Dedlocks.

Mr. Neckett
Mr. Neckett, nicknamed Coavinses by Skimpole, is a sheriff's officer who arrests people for debt, including Skimpole. Because of Neckett's occupation, he is unloved. When he dies he leaves three orphans, including Charley.

Charley Neckett
Charley Neckett is the oldest of the three Neckett children. Esther takes her on as a maid. Charley catches smallpox but recovers.

Nemo
Nemo was an army officer, and George served under his command. Captain Hawdon, as he was known in the army, is widely believed to be dead, but in fact, ruined by moneylenders and addicted to opium, he ekes out a living as a law writer who calls himself Nemo. He dies of an overdose of opium, and only gradually does his real identity as Hawdon emerge. He had a love affair with Lady Dedlock before her marriage to Sir Leicester, and this resulted in the birth of Esther.

Mrs. Pardiggle
Mrs. Pardiggle is a tireless woman who likes to think that she is helping the poor when she visits them and gives them lectures, trying to convert them to her religion. She forces her children to donate their allowances to charitable causes, which they bitterly resent.

Rosa
Rosa is a maid at the Dedlock mansion. Lady Dedlock likes her and appoints her as her personal maid in place of Hortense. Rosa is courted by Watt Rouncewell.

George Rouncewell
See Mr. George

Mr. Rouncewell
Mr. Rouncewell is the successful son of Mrs. Rouncewell. About fifty years old, he is an ironmaster and has been invited to stand for Parliament. He has a confident manner and is not intimidated when he calls on the aristocratic Dedlocks to inform them that his son Watt wishes to marry Rosa.

Mrs. Rouncewell
Mrs. Rouncewell has been housekeeper to the Dedlock family at Chesney Wold for fifty years.

Watt Rouncewell
Watt, Mr. Rouncewell's son, wants to marry Rosa the maid.

Harold Skimpole
Harold Skimpole is a man of about sixty who lives at Bleak House. Skimpole takes pride in describing himself as a child who has no knowledge of financial matters or any sense of responsibility. Because he is charming and entertaining, Skimpole always finds others to support him and pay his bills. Jarndyce, for example, indulges Skimpole's irresponsibility, allowing him to take advantage of his friend's generous spirit. Skimpole is a bad influence on Richard Carstone, and eventually Esther has to tell him to stay away from Richard.

Bart Smallweed
Bart Smallweed is the fifteen-year-old grandson of the Smallweeds. He is a law clerk at Kenge and Carboy.

Judy Smallweed
Judy Smallweed is Bart's twin. She is learning how to make artificial flowers.

Mr. Smallweed
Mr. Smallweed is an old, crippled moneylender. His body is helpless but his mind is sharp, and he takes pleasure in ruining those he lends money to. He traps numerous people, including Hawdon and Mr. George. He is described as "a mere clothes-bag with a black skull-cap on the top of it."

Mrs. Smallweed
Mrs. Smallweed is Mr. Smallweed's wife. He throws pillows at her whenever she mentions the subject of money, which is frequently.

Mr. Snagsby
Mr. Snagsby is the timid owner of the law-stationer's shop in Cook's Court. He is dominated by his shrewish wife.

Mrs. Snagsby
Mrs. Snagsby is the bossy, sharp-tongued wife of Mr. Snagsby. She has a jealous nature and is

suspicious when her husband gets caught up in the Lady Dedlock mystery.

Phil Squod

Phil Squod is Mr. George's assistant at the shooting gallery. He used to be a tinker and met with many accidents, as a result of which he is deformed and cannot walk straight.

Esther Summerson

Esther is one of the two narrators of the story. She is raised by her aunt, Miss Barbary, knowing nothing of her parents. Miss Barbary prevents her from mixing with other children, telling her that she is different from them. In spite of her deprived and lonely childhood, however, Esther grows up to be a compassionate, wise, and affectionate young woman, always kind and considerate to others. After her aunt dies, she becomes a schoolteacher and then housekeeper at Bleak House, a position assigned to her by her guardian, John Jarndyce. Esther eventually discovers that she is the daughter of Lady Dedlock. She catches smallpox as a result of helping Jo, and she is disfigured by the disease. However, this does not prevent her from being courted by Allan Woodcourt, whom she marries. She and Woodcourt settle in a house in Yorkshire that is also called Bleak House.

Mr. Tulkinghorn

Mr. Tulkinghorn is the Dedlocks' lawyer. He is the keeper of all the family secrets, and his loyalty is to Sir Leicester rather than to Lady Dedlock. Tulkinghorn is an austere, detached, remote figure who shows no emotions. He enjoys being in a position of power over others. He is described as "An Oyster of the old school, whom nobody can open."

Mr. Turveydrop

Mr. Turveydrop is Prince's father. He is a vain old man who prides himself on being a model of deportment.

Prince Turveydrop

Prince Turveydrop is a young man who teaches dance. He marries Caddy Jellyby and is a good husband, but his health is poor and he eventually goes lame.

Mr. Vholes

Mr. Vholes is Richard Carstone's lawyer. He is an unpleasant character whose only real purpose is to continue to extract money from Richard.

Mr. Woodcourt

Allan Woodcourt is a doctor, a man of integrity who tries to help the poor, even though he finds it hard to make a living by doing so. He becomes a ship's surgeon in an attempt to improve his financial situation and then becomes a hero when he saves many people after a shipwreck. He marries Esther.

Mrs. Woodcourt

Mrs. Woodcourt is proud of the distinguished Welsh family from whom her son is descended, and at first she opposes a marriage between Allan and Esther because she thinks Esther is not of sufficiently high rank.

THEMES

Love versus Greed and Self-Interest

For the most part, the characters who embody love and compassion for their fellow humans overcome obstacles and flourish. They are contrasted with those who exist merely to advance their own interests in a greedy fashion, ignoring the needs of others. Esther, for example, is a model of self-effacing goodness, aware of her debt to her guardian and always trying her best, quietly and tactfully, to promote harmony and love. For some readers, Esther may seem too good to be true, a perception that prompted George Orwell to comment facetiously, "it is important to teach boys that women like Esther Summerson don't exist," but Dickens intends her to be a shining light, an example of how simple goodness can triumph in a world full of snares. Esther's eventual husband, Woodcourt, is another example of selflessness; he works to alleviate the suffering of the poor even though he knows he will never get rich by doing so. Mr. George is another example of integrity and compassion; he takes on the deformed Phil Squod as his assistant, thus giving a chance to a man who would otherwise be in desperate straits. He is also willing to take in the unfortunate Jo.

Of the other characters, Ada is unwavering in her selfless devotion to Richard, even though Richard does little to deserve it, and she eventually finds happiness (one presumes) raising her young son and living with her cousin John Jarndyce. Jarndyce of course is another character whose behavior is impeccable. He always thinks of the welfare of others before his own, and he is willing to make a huge personal sacrifice, renouncing his claim on

TOPICS FOR FURTHER STUDY

- One of the most noticeable aspects of *Bleak House* is the vast gap between rich and poor in London. Research the same phenomenon in today's American cities. Why is there such a large gap between rich and poor? What institutions or programs are there to help the poor, and how successful are they? Should the income gap in the United States be reduced or left as it is? If it should be reduced, how can that best be accomplished? Write an essay in which you explore this topic.

- Research traditional beliefs about marriage, the family, and illegitimate births in Western societies. How and why have traditional attitudes changed over the last forty years or so? Are these changes desirable or regrettable? Do children from single-parent families fare as well as those from more traditional family structures? Discuss the topic in an essay.

- Dickens is famous for creating memorable characters. Reread some of his character descriptions in *Bleak House*, such as Mr. Chadband, Inspector Bucket, Boythorn, or any other character who appeals to you. Note the satirical, humorous elements that go into each portrait. Then imagine that you are a modern Dickens and write a paragraph or two in which you describe a character of your own choice. Remember that Dickens, like almost all novelists, often based his characters on real-life people he knew.

- Read Dickens's preface to *Bleak House*, in which he defends the reality of spontaneous human combustion (the fate he gives Krook in the novel). Research spontaneous human combustion on the Internet. Is it a genuine phenomenon or a myth? Give a class presentation on the subject, beginning with the account Dickens gives of Krook's death. Does Dickens's account match other reports of spontaneous human combustion? Can the phenomenon be scientifically proven? If it cannot, what other explanations can be offered for the many stories and examples that testify to it?

Esther because he knows she will be happier with Woodcourt.

Set against these examples of those who are capable of extending themselves beyond their selfish desires are those for whom narrow self-interest and a lack of compassion are the dominating features of their personalities. Many of them have a stake in a corrupt social system, whether financial or legal. Mr. Tulkinghorn, a single man who lives alone and has no family ties, uses his powerful position as a lawyer to exert control over others, regardless of the suffering this may cause. He lives with a closed heart, and his death goes unmourned. Mr. Vholes, Richard Carstone's lawyer, is another example of greed and self-interest. Like Tulkinghorn, he is a serious, self-contained man; he does not reach out to others at a personal level. His only concern is to fulfill the "one great principle of the English law... to make business for itself" at the expense of his clients. Like others in his profession, Vholes has no regard for morality, for what is right or wrong, but only for what is to his advantage or disadvantage. He may be, in the eyes of society, a "respectable" man, but he is in truth far from it. Not only does his name give his nature away (a vole is a small rodent), but the language with which he is described suggests that he is less than human and has a spooky, ghostlike presence. When Esther meets Vholes, for example, she notes the stark difference between him and her guardian. Whereas Jarndyce speaks openly, Vholes appears to hold in what he has to say in "a cold-blooded, gasping, fish-like manner," and when Vholes leaves, Esther remarks that he "put his dead glove, which scarcely seemed to have any hand in it, on my fingers... and took his long thin shadow away.... chilling the seed in the ground as it glided along." These descriptions make it clear that Vholes and others like him are scarcely members of the human community. The same applies to the moneylender Smallweed, who is described as resembling a "species of spider" that draws victims into its web, and also, along with the others in his family, as bearing a "likeness to old monkeys." Like his father before him, Smallweed (whose name also gives him away) worships the god of "Compound Interest." He knows how to make money grow, but nothing of what it means to nourish human life.

Families, Orphans, and Abandonment

The ideal presented in the novel is that of the loving family, like the one that Esther finally establishes with Woodcourt and that can also be seen in the Bagnets and, after they have overcome difficulties, the Turveydrops. Many of the families presented are dysfunctional (the Jellybys, the Pardiggles, the Smallweeds) or scattered (the Rouncewells), but Dickens holds up as an ideal the reconciliation and reunion among those who have lost their family connections. Mr. George, for example, is reunited with his mother and his brother after many years of absence, and he finally returns to the house he lived in as a boy to be with his mother. Esther, who thought she was an orphan and was raised in isolation, discovers and is reconciled with her mother. Even though that story ends in tragedy, for Esther finally to meet and forgive her mother is a vital part of her journey of self-discovery and gives her the opportunity to heal some of the wounds of the past.

As Esther's story shows, more characters than not live outside the love and comfort that a family can provide. The shadow cast by those who have in one way or another been abandoned by family or marginalized by society is a long one. These characters are outsiders, struggling to survive as best they can. There is the poor boy Jo, dependent on the kindness of strangers; Miss Flite, whose family has been ruined by the Jarndyce suit and who lives alone at Krook's; Krook himself, origins unknown; Phil Squod, rescued from destitution by George; and Guster, rescued from the workhouse by the Snagsbys. Nemo (Hawdon) is caught in the trap of the moneylenders and lives a shadowy, solitary, anonymous existence; the orphan Charley and her two siblings find their way only through the help of others; and Mr. Gridley is another solitary figure who has lost his family and is driven to distraction and death by a protracted lawsuit. Jarndyce too is alone, although he makes the

This house, No. 58 Linclon's Inn Fields, was introduced by Dickens as Bleak House in the novel.
(Hulton Archive / Getty Images)

best of his loneliness through a generous, magnanimous nature.

Of course, having an intact family is no guarantee of love and comfort. Caddy and Peepy Jellyby are virtual orphans even within their own family, so great is their neglect by their mother. Even Ada and Richard, orphans who would appear to be lucky in having the wealthy Jarndyce as their guardian, are made poor by Chancery, which cannot give them their just inheritance. They are orphaned once by death and then again by the legal system.

Given this polarity between the nurturing ideal in a family and the thousand forms in which it breaks down, Dickens appears to put his faith in simple goodness of character that calls some to take care of those who otherwise would be tossed on society's scrap heap. The many who elude this fragile safety net are the nameless multitudes who live and die in urban slums like Tom-all-Alone's, the name itself an apt metaphor for what lies outside the bonds of loving hearth and secure home.

STYLE

Symbolism

Dickens uses symbolism, a device in which concrete objects are used to represent abstract concepts, in a variety of ways in this novel. He uses the weather, for example, not only to create mood and atmosphere but in a symbolic sense also. The first chapter begins with a long description of the fog in London on a November day. Fog creeps in everywhere, on the river and the marshes, and in the streets, where the stores must light up two hours before darkness falls. The fog is densest around London's legal district: "at the very heart of the fog, sits the Lord High Chancellor in his High Court of Chancery." This august official should be sitting "with a foggy glory round his head." Clearly, fog is a symbol, one might almost say metaphor, for the Court, in which nothing can be seen clearly. People stumble through Chancery without sight of their goal; they wander around, lost and confused.

In chapter II, Dickens also uses the weather to characterize the condition of the Dedlock estate, and the Dedlock family, in Lincolnshire. It has been raining for days. The entire scene is redolent of dreariness and decay. The river is "stagnant," the church in the park is "mouldy," and "there is a general smell and taste as of the ancient Dedlocks in their graves." The dreariness reflects Lady Dedlock's boredom, and the sense of decay suggests that the fortunes of the family are on their way down. The snowstorm in which Lady Dedlock dies is another symbolic use of the weather. Esther describes how, as she and Bucket search for the runaway woman, "The sleet fell all that day unceasingly, a thick mist came on early, and it never rose or lightened for a moment."

Other symbolic elements include the birds that Miss Flite keeps in cages, which symbolize not only the suitors who are in effect imprisoned by the Jarndyce case but also the various qualities, both good and bad, that the case brings into play. This is shown by the symbolic names she gives the birds (according to Krook in chapter XIII), which include "Hope, Joy, Youth," as well as "Ruin, Despair, Madness, Death," and "Folly, Words, Wigs."

There is a symbolic element also in the description of the environment in which Tulkinghorn lives. On the ceiling of Tulkinghorn's chambers is painted a male figure in a Roman helmet pointing his finger downward. The narrator calls the figure Allegory. Further reference is made to Allegory in chapters XXII and XLII. In the latter, the narrator comments that the room is too dark, even though lit by candles, for Tulkinghorn to see the figure. But after he has had his fateful encounter with Hortense, which will lead to his murder, "now and then, as he throws his head back in his chair, [he catches] sight of the pertinacious Roman pointing from the ceiling." The figure of Allegory, always pointing at the lawyer, is both accuser and prophet of the lawyer's ultimate fate; respectable citizen he may appear to be, but the way he uses his powerful position to manipulate and torment others brings about his inevitable fate. In chapter XLVIII, the narrator draws attention to Allegory pointing down at the corpse of the murdered man.

Finally, Krook's rag-and-bottle shop is a symbolic equivalent of the real nature of the Court of Chancery. Useless stuff accumulates in the shop but nothing ever seems to get sold (just like Chancery in which documents accumulate but there rarely seem to be any judgments). Ironically, although law books and parchment scrolls lie around, Krook is unable to understand any of them because he cannot read. (The lawyers in Chancery can read but they might as well not be able to for all the sense they make.) Krook explains that neighbors have nicknamed him Lord Chancellor and call his shop Chancery because everything in it is "wasting away and going to rack and ruin." Chancery may occupy a fine building, but the dirty, crowded mess that is Krook's shop reveals the true essence of the all-powerful court.

Double Narrative

The novel has two alternating narrators. The first is an almost omniscient narrator who speaks in the third-person voice (using "he" or "she" instead of "I") in the present tense, sometimes called the historic present. This narrator knows about all the events and characters in the story, including their innermost thoughts; he is also what is called an intrusive narrator, in the sense that, as M. H. Abrams puts it, he "comments on his characters, evaluating their actions and motives and expressing his views about human life in general." This is the narrator who adopts a number of different tones throughout the book. He can be sarcastic and ironic (as in his descriptions of Chancery), angry (as in his observations about the life of the poor), and satirical, or lightly mocking (as in his portraits of characters such as Mrs. Jellyby or

COMPARE & CONTRAST

- **1850s:** It takes nearly three days to get from Paris to London and then to Lincolnshire in eastern England. Travelers use a horse and carriage, and cross the English Channel by boat.

  Today: Traveling from Paris to London, via the Channel Tunnel, takes only two and a half hours by train, and the drive to Lincolnshire takes only another few hours. By air, it takes one hour to get from Paris to London.

- **1850s:** There is a social stigma attached to having an illegitimate child, a child born out of wedlock. Such children are often given up for adoption.

  Today: The stigma attached to having a child born out of wedlock has largely disappeared,

  as has the term *illegitimate* in regard to such a child. In the United Kingdom in 2003, 42 percent of children born are born out of wedlock.

- **1850s:** Thousands of poor children in London die young. They live in dirty, cramped conditions, often without heat or adequate food. Only ten years earlier, in 1839, half of all funerals in London were for children under ten years old.

  Today: Although few children in London die of hunger, preventable disease, or neglect, over half a million children in London live in poverty. This represents 41 percent of the total number of children in London.

Mr. Chadband, to name only two). His voice is impersonal; he surveys the scene and makes judgments about it, noting in particular the failures of society's institutions.

In contrast, Esther Summerson tells her story in the first-person voice (using "I"), employing the past tense. This means that she describes only what she personally observes or experiences or hears about from others. Esther's voice is quite different from that of the third-person narrator. Her narrative is marked by her own growing awareness of herself and the world around her. She gradually gets to know about the injustices that the other narrator is always aware of. Her personal voice expresses innocence, faith, goodness, hope, and also common sense, good judgment, and shrewd observation.

HISTORICAL CONTEXT

The Court of Chancery

In Dickens's day, the Court of Chancery was different from the Courts of Common Law. The latter dealt with crimes such as murder and

theft, the former with matters such as legacies and trusts. The Court of Chancery was presided over by the Lord Chancellor, the highest legal officer in England. Chancery cases were decided by a judge, not a jury. Cases could drag on for a very long time. Once a case about a disputed will (as in *Bleak House*) was initiated, all property in the case was taken over by the court and was held to ensure that all expenses were met. A long case could mean that the value of the inheritance, once the case was decided, was greatly reduced (to nothing at all in the fictional case of Jarndyce and Jarndyce). Long delays in Chancery were a talking point of the day. In June 1852, for example, the magazine *Punch* discussed a case in which a question of whether an old lady who had died in 1827, twenty-five years earlier ("which is nothing in the age of a Chancery suit"), had made a "power of appointment" in her will. This simple question had involved no fewer than sixteen lawyers, arguing either that she had or had not. Dickens himself was involved in Chancery in 1844 when he sued some publishers for copyright infringement. The ruling was in his favor, but his costs amounted to more than he

The one-time home of Charles Dickens, located in Kent in southeast England. It was named Bleak House after the novel. (Ben Stansall / AFP / Getty Images)

was able to collect in damages, which contributed to his sour feelings about Chancery proceedings.

Dickens based his tale of Jarndyce and Jarndyce, as he explained in his preface to the novel, on several actual cases, including the Dry case, which began in 1834 and was still continuing, with no sign of a settlement, in 1853, by which time it had already cost more than seventy thousand pounds and involved up to forty lawyers. Dickens also cited a case that had begun in the previous century and was still not resolved but had cost more than twice as much as the Dry case. Bearing these cases in mind, although the Jarndyce and Jarndyce case might seem extreme, scholars are in general agreement that Dickens's portrayal of how the Chancery court operated at the time was accurate.

The British Parliament passed legislation in 1852 that reformed the Court of Chancery. Further reforms followed in 1858 and 1862.

Landowners and Industrialists

The penultimate, or second-to-last, chapter in *Bleak House* shows the decline of the Dedlocks, one of England's great landowning families. The silence at Chesney Wold can be taken at least in part as a metaphor for some of the changes going on in English society during this period. In essence, these upheavals resulted in the strengthening of manufacturing interests at the expense of those of landowners. This was in part a result of the Great Reform Act of 1832, which tripled the number of men allowed to vote in England. The act gave more parliamentary representation to cities, which had grown larger as a result of the Industrial Revolution. This meant that more of the growing middle classes had the opportunity to vote. In 1846, the repeal of the Corn Laws (import tariffs on corn, or grain, that benefited English landowners) was, according to historian George Macauley Trevelyan in his *History of England*, "the first signal victory of the middle classes over the gentry, and of the industrial over the agricultural interest."

This is the background for chapter XL in *Bleak House*. Sir Leicester Dedlock bemoans the emerging political power of industrialists such as

Mr. Rouncewell. He is shocked that Mr. Rouncewell, a man of common birth, has been invited to stand for Parliament and has been campaigning against him. In this respect, Sir Leicester appears to have been very much a man of his own time. According to Trevelyan, after the Great Reform Act, and continuing into the 1860s, "the presence on the benches of the House of Commons of persons of middle-class origin ... was tolerated as a curiosity or resented as an impertinence by the Whig and Tory squires around them." Sir Leicester is equally shocked when he hears the news that such middle-class upstarts have made gains in the general election of 1852.

The beginning of chapter XL also has contemporary references. Dickens's fictional names Coodle and Doodle represent two great figures in English politics who cannot agree on a government until they realize that the nation is endangered by their disputes. This refers to the instability of the government in 1851 and 1852 and of the party system that produced it. That Coodle and Doodle finally reach agreement is likely a reference to the formation of a coalition government under Lord Aberdeen in 1853. But Dickens was obviously not impressed by this compromise and attacked the prevalence of bribery in the political process. He presents a picture of "Britannia being much occupied in pocketing Doodle in the form of sovereigns, and swallowing Doodle in the form of beer, and in swearing herself black in the face that she does neither." He was not alone in bringing attention to these abuses. In 1852, the town of St. Albans, which figures prominently in *Bleak House*, was disenfranchised, that is, taken off the election rolls, by act of Parliament because of bribery and corruption. The Corrupt Practices at Elections Act, also passed in 1852, further focused attention on the issue of political bribery.

CRITICAL OVERVIEW

Reviews of *Bleak House* after the publication of the final installment in 1853 were mixed. Some reviewers found it too full of unsympathetic characters and lacking in humor, although characters such as Jo and Inspector Bucket were widely admired. Some special interests were offended by Dickens's satires of various social groups: politically, Conservatives objected to the portrayal of Sir Leicester Dedlock, while Liberals and feminists took issue with the presentation of Mrs. Jellyby. The satirical portrait of Chadband, the pompous preacher, also aroused indignation in some religious circles. Among literary critics, George Brimley, in *Spectator*, criticized the novel for a lacking a coherent plot. He comments, "The series of incidents which form the outward life of the actors and talkers has no close and necessary connexion"; he adds that the Chancery suit "has positively not the smallest influence on the character of any one person concerned; nor has it any interest of itself." A much more positive view was taken by Dickens's friend, John Forster, in his unsigned review in *Examiner*. Forster writes that the novel "touches and amuses us, but it is destined to draw tears and smiles also from our children's children." Forster had particular praise for the characters Mrs. Jellyby, Boythorn, Skimpole, and Chadband, as part of "that crowd of fresh and ever real creations that will live while the language continues."

From the 1850s to the 1870s, *Bleak House* was regarded by many critics as falling far short of Dickens's best work, but this is a view that modern critics have not shared. In fact, over the last half century, the standing of the novel has steadily increased. In 1964, Geoffrey Tillotson called the novel "the finest literary work the nineteenth century produced in England," as quoted by Elliot L. Gilbert in the introduction to *Critical Essays on Charles Dickens's "Bleak House."* Gilbert offers an explanation of why *Bleak House* has recently attracted as much or more critical attention than any other work by Dickens. He suggests that in the novel, the "freshness and spontaneity" of Dickens's early works combine with the "deliberate structuring and complex thematic development" of the later books in "a perfect balance." In the introduction to a Modern Critical Interpretations edition of the novel, renowned critic Harold Bloom praises the character of Esther as "the most mysteriously complex and profound personage" in the novel and comments that "there is now something close to critical agreement that *Bleak House* is Dickens's most complex and memorable single achievement."

CRITICISM

Bryan Aubrey

Aubrey holds a Ph.D. in English. In this essay on Bleak House, *he discusses Dickens's interest in the "Condition of England" question and his concern for the unsanitary conditions in which the poor lived.*

WHAT DO I READ NEXT?

- Dickens's novel *Hard Times* (first published in 1854 and available in several modern editions) is one of Dickens's shorter novels. It is set in the fictional northern industrial city of Coketown and includes Dickens's satire of the English educational system, which emphasizes the learning of facts and discourages the development of the imagination. Dickens also targets the utilitarians, who see everything in terms of facts, figures, and statistics, and calls for an improvement in working conditions in factories.

- *Vanity Fair: A Novel Without a Hero* by William Makepeace Thackeray was first published in serial form between 1847 and 1848. One of the great Victorian novels, it is set a generation earlier than *Bleak House*, in early nineteenth-century England, and is a satire on the hypocrisy of English society. A modern edition was published in 2003 in the Penguin Classics series.

- *North and South* by Elizabeth Gaskell was first published in *Household Words*, the magazine edited by Dickens, in weekly installments from 1854 to 1855. The novel, which is considered to be Gaskell's best, describes the life of a young woman who moves from a prosperous but boring life in southern England to the industrial north. She learns there about the hardships endured by factory workers and also develops a romantic interest in a mill owner. The novel conveys much about industrial conditions in England in the mid-nineteenth century as well as relations between men and women at the time.

- *Dickens: A Biography* (1988) by Fred Kaplan is well regarded for its meticulous research and fair-minded judgments. It is also highly readable and was named as a notable book of the year by the *New York Times*. In a swift-moving narrative, Kaplan brings out some of the contradictions and conflicts in Dickens's personality as he describes the novelist's successful career, his wide circle of friends, and his unhappy marriage.

Dickens's purpose in writing *Bleak House* was not merely to tell an entertaining story with a gallery of fascinating characters. He was a man with a social conscience, and he felt keenly the injustices and the perils of English society. In particular, he wanted in this novel to draw attention to the wide gap between rich and poor and the appalling unsanitary conditions in which the latter lived. As such, *Bleak House* is, at least in part, an investigation of what was often known as the Condition of England question, a phrase that had its origin in Thomas Carlyle's examination of the lives of the English working classes during the Industrial Revolution, *The Condition of England*, published in 1839. Also relevant is the political novel *Sybil: Or the Two Nations* by Benjamin Disraeli, who went on to become Britain's prime minister in 1868 and again from 1874 to 1880. The two nations Disraeli refers to are the rich and the poor, and in the novel

he describes the poverty of the working classes, contrasting it with life in the great country houses and other places patronized by the aristocracy. His character Stephen Morley, a journalist, expresses the central thesis: "Two nations; between whom there is no intercourse and no sympathy; who are as ignorant of each other's habits, thoughts, and feelings, as if they were dwellers in different zones or inhabitants of different planets."

From the material comforts the Dedlocks enjoy at Chesney Wold and in London, and which are also in evidence in the comfortable life led by Jarndyce in Bleak House, to the slums of Tom-all-Alone's, Dickens gives his own impression of the Condition of England and his understanding of the "two nations." Are there indeed two separate nations in the one kingdom of England? He poses the question directly in chapter XVI, when he asks what possible connection can there be between the aristocratic Dedlocks and Jo, the poor crossing sweeper boy who lives in Tom-all-Alone's? Esther feels this division keenly also. When the do-gooder Mrs. Pardiggle takes her and Ada to visit the poor brickmaker's family, Esther, feeling unable to be of much assistance, observes that "between us and these people there was an iron barrier," and she has no idea about how that barrier might be removed.

Certainly, Dickens, through his third-person narrator, has little faith in the ability of Britain's political institutions to address the dire situation of the poor, which he sees as inseparable from the problem of poor sanitation in the slums. In chapter XLVI, he derides all the "mighty speechmaking ... both in and out of Parliament," as a result of which Tom (his shorthand for the people who live in Tom-all-Alone's) will "be reclaimed according to somebody's theory but nobody's practice."

In fact, following the Royal Commission on the Sanitary State of Large Towns, which met from 1843 to 1845, much legislation had been passed in the 1840s, including the Public Health Act of 1848, designed to improve urban sanitation. But as *Bleak House* shows, it continued to be an issue into the 1850s and beyond. According to Dickens's biographer Peter Ackroyd, not until the establishment of the Metropolitan Board of Works in 1855 and the creation of new sewers in the mid-1860s "was there any proper attempt to create a healthy or decent environment in what was then the greatest city in the world."

In addition to the filthy conditions in slums like Tom-all-Alone's, Dickens also brings attention to the health hazards that emanate from the overcrowded cemeteries where paupers are buried. The body of Nemo, for example, is taken to a small churchyard, "pestiferous and obscene, whence malignant diseases are communicated"

to the living. Bringing attention once more to the idea of "two nations," the narrator regards this as "a shameful testimony to future ages, how civilisation and barbarism walked this boastful island together. "

In her book, *The Companion to* Bleak House, Susan Shatto gives some grim details about these London cemeteries:

> Bodies recently buried were disinterred to make room for later ones, mass graves were left open to save the gravediggers work, and coffins were crammed against each other, the topmost within a foot or two of the surface. Such conditions caused a pestilent stench which pervaded the grounds and gave rise to sickness as it spread to adjacent houses and streets.

Dickens was not alone in his outrage about such burial grounds for people who could not afford to pay for a proper funeral. As Shatto notes, during the 1830s and 1840s there was a movement for reform that eventually resulted in the passage of the Metropolitan Interment Act, which sought to improve the conditions under which London's dead were buried.

Although Dickens's anger in his description of the pauper cemetery and the Tom-all-Alone's slum is obvious, he deliberately spares his reader the full disgusting details, believing such details would repel them rather than arouse their compassion. Instead, he gives his reader the pathetic, appealing character of Jo the crossing sweeper, who is made to stand for the many thousands of anonymous poor in London. Crossing sweepers were ubiquitous in London at the time, responsible for keeping major street intersections free of mud and other obstructions so that people could cross streets without getting dirty. They earned very little but could get tips from regular passersby. Needless to say, it was not an easy life, as can be gleaned from the pages of Henry Mayhew's contemporary study, *London Labour and the London Poor*, first published in 1851–52, in which he gives quite a long account of the street sweepers and the lives they led. Mayhew's opinion was that the sweepers, who "constitute a large class of the Metropolitan poor," were "private scavengers," pursuing an occupation that they resorted to "as an excuse for begging; and, indeed, as many expressed it to me, 'it was the last chance left of obtaining an honest crust.'" Mayhew tells the stories of a number of street-sweeper boys who resemble Dickens's Jo.

What Dickens emphasizes about Jo is his total ignorance. He is presented as a member of the one nation (the poor) that has no connection, materially or culturally, to the other (the rich). At the inquest on Nemo's death, for example, when Jo is brought before the coroner, his evidence is considered inadmissible because he is so ignorant of everything that society regards as essential; he knows his name, but that is about all. He does not know that everyone has two names, or that Jo is an abbreviation. He cannot spell his name since he never went to school. He has no father, mother, or friends. His habitual response when asked a question is that he "don't know nothink." In chapter XVI, the narrator spends several paragraphs musing about how the world of London might appear to the illiterate Jo:

> It must be very puzzling to see the good company going to the churches on Sundays, with their books in their hands, and to think (for perhaps Jo *does* think, at odd times) what does it all mean, and if it means anything to anybody, how comes it that it means nothing to me?

The narrator imagines that Jo must feel that he is scarcely human, since he was not even accepted as a witness, and feel that he belongs more with the horses, dogs, and cattle that he sees going by than in any human society. He is truly from a different world. Later, when Woodcourt tries to find shelter for Jo, he considers the strange fact that it is easier to dispose of an unowned dog than this homeless poor boy.

Such are the "two nations" that live side by side in mid-nineteenth-century London but are entirely separate from each other. But are they really separate? Dickens makes it plain, in a way calculated to alarm the "rich" nation, that the two are more interrelated than might be thought, because the air that carries disease knows no boundaries of place or class:

> There is not a drop of Tom's corrupted blood but propagates infection and contagion somewhere.... There is not an atom of Tom's slime, not a cubic inch of any pestilential gas in which he lives, not one obscenity or degradation about him, not an ignorance, not a wickedness, not a brutality of his committing, but shall work its retribution, through every order of society, up to the proudest of the proud, and to the highest of the high.

The point is made forcefully when the smallpox Jo catches jumps from one "nation" to another when it first infects Charley and then Esther, who is left permanently scarred by the disease. Smallpox was only one of the infectious diseases to which Londoners, rich and poor alike, were

subject. As Ackroyd points out, in November and December 1847, half a million people caught typhus fever, almost one in four of the population. The two nations, so distinguished from each other in so many ways, became one in sickness, fever, and death.

In the face of this stark reality, perhaps the most touching of the many appeals that Dickens, through his narrator, makes for ways in which a positive bridge can be made between rich and poor is his description of poor infants who, in their purity and innocence, resemble the Christ child. Mr. Snagsby is touched by such a perception when he gazes down on the three-week-old baby of Liz, the wife of a poor brickmaker, and is reminded, as he sees the baby in the light of the candle he holds, "of another infant, encircled with light, that he has seen in pictures." Esther has a similar perception as she looks down on the dead baby of Jenny, another poor woman, and "seemed to see a halo shine around the child." This might be regarded as sentimental, but Dickens was in earnest. There are countless biblical allusions scattered throughout the novel, and although a Christian moral is never made explicit, Dickens suggests that to recognize the likeness of the divine in even the most humble and small of God's creatures is to inspire a compassion that will reach out beyond artificial barriers and create a more humane society, a society in which the divine likeness is not smothered by poverty, abuse, or shame.

Source: Bryan Aubrey, Critical Essay on *Bleak House*, in *Novels for Students*, Gale, Cengage Learning, 2010.

Jill Durey

In the following essay, Durey discusses John Jarndyce's relationship with Esther in Bleak House *in the context of nineteenth-century marriage norms.*

John Jarndyce's proposal of marriage to his ward Esther in *Bleak House* (1852–3) by Charles Dickens (1812–70) comes as a shock. The age difference between them is nearly forty years, and their social roles are that of guardian and ward. Although, seemingly, they are not linked by blood or marriage, there is a hint that the tight web of close family connections goes beyond John Jarndyce, Ada Clare and Richard Carstone, the three cousins in the Jarndyce and Jarndyce Chancery case, which is popularly thought to have been based on a real-life case that resulted in the disputed property being eaten up entirely by legal

> **NOT QUITE A HUNDRED YEARS AFTER THIS BOOK, WHEN FORMALIZED MARRIAGE HAD BECOME THE NORM, DICKENS'S INTRODUCTION OF A POSSIBLE MARRIAGE BETWEEN GUARDIAN AND WARD WAS DECIDEDLY *RISQUÉ*."**

costs. Since the fictional Chancery suit has already been in progress for more than a couple of decades, the family connections have widened considerably and an interested onlooker informs the two young cousins, Ada and Richard, that, together with their surnames, the names of Barbary and Dedlock are also interconnected, but he fails to explain how.

It is not until Esther's parentage is established that it becomes evident that John Jarndyce is actually related by blood to two of his wards and by marriage to one of them, although he himself had been unaware of the precise nature of his connection to Esther when he chose her as his bride. He knew that he was distantly related to the Dedlock family, but had not known until Esther told him well after their secret betrothal that she was Lady Dedlock's illegitimate daughter, so guardian and ward are related by marriage. Although not close enough to be within the Church's forbidden degrees of relationship, their kinship ties are significant. Lady Dedlock's surname before marriage was Barbary and it was Miss Barbary, her sister, who cared for Esther as a child, having told her real mother that the infant had died. Barbary is the other name in the Jarndyce and Jarndyce case, so Esther, too, is distantly implicated in the legal battle. But the real significance in her ties to John Jarndyce lies in her position as his ward.

John Jarndyce had applied successfully through the Chancery court to be the guardian of his distant young cousins, Ada Clare and Richard Carstone, so that they would not become divided as a consequence of the legal dispute. To provide them with a loving sanctuary he brings his other young ward—a little older than the two cousins—to his home. He is therefore in *loco parentis* of all three wards. The court even deliberates on the propriety of this. As Esther seems not to be 'related to any party in the cause', the court approves it.

Since its approval tacitly acknowledges Jarndyce's role as parent in his adopted family, it would not have approved of his marrying either of his female wards and its disapproval would have derived from that of the Church.

The Church frowned upon marriages between guardians and their adoptees, for these were regarded as spiritual ties, whereby the assumption of the parental role by the guardian should not be infringed by a more intimate relationship. Such an infringement could blur the implicit moral code of conduct undertaken by the guardian, whose role it was to act as protector to his ward, for it could lead to an ascending and descending relationship which the Church utterly condemned.

It was the ascendant-descendant relations within the extended family that were deemed forbidden in Chapters 18–20 of Leviticus in the Bible. These relations embraced consanguineous ones, which refer to connections made through blood as well as affinal ones, which refer to connections made through marriage—a sister-in-law, for instance. Also prohibited was any sexual relationship within the nuclear family between blood relatives and half-blood relatives as well as between those in direct line across the generations, for example grandparents and grandchildren or father and daughter-in-law, for these 'have wrought confusion'. Nor were liaisons between children and their aunts and uncles permitted, whether or not they were aunts and uncles by blood or through marriage, 'for they are … near kin … '. The inference to be drawn, since the taboos applied to both blood and non-blood relationships, was that such unions, referred to as 'abominations' which 'defile' the perpetrators, upset the equilibrium of social relations. It was the status within the family that determined the prohibition, since such relations threatened the harmony and stability of family dynamics.

In the centuries intervening between the prohibitions in Leviticus and Dickens's writing of *Bleak House*, the Church had reviewed its attitude many times. By the eleventh century the prohibitions 'had been extended' to 'spiritual kin', but the banning of marriage between guardian and ward had been established as early as the sixth century in Byzantium. Yet the early part of the eighteenth century had witnessed behaviour that even today might seem out of control. Prior to the Marriage Act of 1753 marriages were often not formalized. Three years after this Marriage Act there was still sufficient debate about family relationships to prompt John Fry to write *The Case of Marriages between Near Kindred* (1756), in which he explained why the marriage of ascending-descending relations would harm the very fabric of the family. He said that parents and children had 'such *relative Duties* which they owe one another, as makes it *unfit* for them to be joined together in Marriage', for God ordered people, 'with Relation to Marriage, *to leave Father and Mother',* which meant that Marriages between *Parents and their Children were prohibited'*. Grandparents and grandchildren, too, shared these 'natural Duties', but also had an *'Inequality of Age',* which acted 'as another *moral Impediment* of Marriage'. These kinds of marriages were prevented through 'the Modesty of Nature', which makes 'Restraints' through 'Duty and Reverence'. These duties were also shared by mothers-in-law and fathers-in-law as well as by spiritual relatives like 'appointed Guardians, with those that are left under their Care'. For this reason they 'are to be looked on as *effectually* barred from marrying one another', for 'at least as long as they are so under their Care, and till their Trust is legally discharged'.

Not quite a hundred years after this book, when formalized marriage had become the norm, Dickens's introduction of a possible marriage between guardian and ward was decidedly *risqué.* His many attempts to cloak this relationship in respectability would have appealed to the Victorian sense of decorum at the same time as adding tantalizing spice to the narrative. Esther's initial description of John Jarndyce as 'handsome, lively and iron-grey', who appears 'nearer sixty than fifty', but is 'silvered, upright, hearty and robust', while being 'fatherly' in the way he kissed his young wards, encapsulates the ambivalence of the guardian's position. He is an attractive elderly man acting as father to three young people, including two young girls nearing marriageable age. His letter of proposal, later in the narrative after Esther has fallen in love with a young doctor compelled to work overseas, is 'not a love letter' and stresses his 'ripe age' and 'silvered head'. There is also Esther's assumption that her guardian is marrying her out of pity now that she is scarred from smallpox, so a kind of propriety is hinted at in what is portrayed as a passionless match. Resolved to marry him, Esther notes that her guardian is 'just as usual; quite as frank, as open, and free', with 'not the least constraint in his manner', and so the mask of respectability is maintained. At least he does not appear as

a seedy old man. Her guardian's subsequent generosity in purchasing another 'Bleak House' in Yorkshire so that she can marry the young doctor she loves once he has returned to England and declared his love for her, restores rectitude, yet indicates Jarndyce's continued protection, not only by dint of his owning Esther's marital home but also by endowing it with the name of his own.

Having extricated himself from a suspect match in a way that makes him look benign, John Jarndyce could possibly be contemplating another with obvious advantages. After her own future marriage is set and the beautiful Ada is about to be widowed with a child to support, Esther herself speculates that their guardian would 'cherish her [Ada] if she were left alone', for she observes him 'as he gently passed his hand over her golden hair, and put a lock of it to his lips'.

Even allowing for this being a death bed scene and a highly charged moment, John Jarndyce's kissing of his ward's celebrated golden hair has a frisson that is quite unfatherly, and the tie between guardian and ward no longer appears simply spiritual. As a married woman, Ada had already left her guardian's protection. Yet, despite this being a period of social upheaval whereby old traditions were giving way to new ideas, the Church was unlikely to smile on such a match.

Source: Jill Durey, "Marrying One's Ward and *Bleak House,*" in *Notes and Queries*, Vol. 55, No. 1, March 2008, pp. 39–41.

Emily Steinlight

In the following excerpt, Steinlight examines the advertisements that appeared in the 1852–53 serial publications of Bleak House, *arguing that they may inform readings of the text.*

. . . In March of 1852, Bradbury & Evans began publishing *Bleak House* in nineteen monthly installments, or "numbers," concluding in September of 1853. Each of these numbers was printed separately in a short, unbound volume in paper covers, with illustrations by Hablôt Knight Browne preceding the text. Each four-chapter installment of the novel, consisting of thirty-two pages of uninterrupted text, is also preceded by an advertising section that constitutes just less than half of the entire volume. A large percentage of the ads are publishers' notices for a simply enormous quantity of recent or forthcoming books (including a cloth-bound Dickens anthology known as the "Cheap Edition," as well as Dickens's *Child's History of*

> **MUCH AS THE DICKENS NOVEL SOLICITS ITS READER THROUGH VARIOUS FORMS OF RHETORIC, APPEALING TO THAT PROJECTED READER'S PRESUMED COMMON HUMANITY AND SYMPATHY, THE ADVERTISEMENT HAILS THAT SAME READER AS THE GENERALIZED SUBJECT OF CONSUMPTION."**

England). Not surprisingly, many of these are novels—some long forgotten and virtually impossible to find today, alongside other major novels by the author and his best-known contemporaries, including Thackeray, Trollope, Gaskell, and Bulwer-Lytton. Also advertised are several major American novels, including Hawthorne's *Blithedale Romance* and an upcoming serial edition of *Uncle Tom's Cabin*.

The publishers' pages also offer an astonishingly diverse assortment of new and forthcoming non-fiction books, ranging in subject from Thomas Carlyle's *Life of John Sterling*, to Edward P. Thompson (the naturalist)'s *Passion of Animals* and a *Sketch of the History of Monkeys*, as well as botanists' studies of plant life in India and China, and various ethnographic studies of Mexico, Peru, Canada, Russia, Egypt and elsewhere. There are accounts of Arctic explorations, a *Narrative of a Mission to Central Africa*, a memoir entitled *Settlers and Convicts; or, Recollections of Sixteen Years Labour in the Backwoods of Australia* (whose author is listed only as "an emigrant mechanic"), and a rather different fictional memoir entitled *Confessions of an Etonian*. Also featured are various philosophical studies and a wide array of religious pamphlets and publications, including *Fourteen Sermons on the Resurrection, Atheism Considered Theologically and Politically,* and Jeremy Taylor's *Rules and Exercises of Holy Dying*. There is a large selection of historical and contemporary biography, a considerable number of writings on the emergence of the steam engine, various treatises and personal reflections on labor, and numerous volumes of ancient and modern history. There are also numerous fiction and poetry anthologies, including a collection of *Ballads for the Times* and a volume of *Specimens of Old Indian*

Poetry. Several ads announce a series of "Indestructible Books for Children" and list multiple other children's titles, including *The Doll and Her Friends*; *The Mine; or, Subterranean Wonders; an Account of the Operations of the Miner, and the Products of his Labour*; and *The Life and Perambulations of a Mouse*. There are also illustrated books intended for adults; the first serial number of *Master Humphrey's Clock* (in which *The Old Curiosity Shop* began publication as one of the "Personal Adventures of Master Humphrey") includes a large ad for a series called *Heads of the People: being Picture of the English*. These books consist of a number of etchings, accompanied by "Literary Descriptions" (from writers including Thackeray, Leigh Hunt, Captain Glascock, an unnamed MP, and others), representing "British Faces and British Manners—British Virtues and British Vices—British Liberality and British Prejudice ... delineated with the pencil and the pen of truth" and, the publishers claim, "destined to become a part of the country's literature" because they offer "Pictures of HUMAN LIFE; not dreamt of by the fashionable novelmonger ... but LIFE AS IT IS." (Printed in the front matter of a novel, such a claim certainly has interesting implications.)

Several publishers' advertisements offer maps, guides, and reference books, from the Eighth Edition of the *Encyclopedia Britannica*, to a *London Directory and Court Guide for 1853* ("containing upwards of 120,000 names and addresses"), to a handsome *Illustrated Catalogue of the Great Industrial Exhibition of 1851*, to *The Illustrated Temperance Almanack*, to *A Military Manual of Field Operations*, to a *Dictionary of Domestic Medicine and Household Surgery*, to a *Practical Manual of Photography*. A number of professional and popular science texts are also featured, including an anatomical study of *The Hand: Its Mechanisms and Endowments*, and a great many more general books on physics and chemistry. In addition, there are various guides and books of personal advice— some on investment and finance, others dealing with such questions as *How to See the British Museum in Four Visits*, still others with *How to Print, and When to Publish: Practical Advice to Writers*. Also included, of course, are multitudes of "domestic guides" (tendered largely—though not exclusively—to women, for also listed are such titles as *The Working Man's Friend and Family Instructor*). The majority of these domestic guides are books of advice on matrimony, motherhood, housewifery, "family worship," gardening, and cooking (including a work entitled *What*

Shall We Have for Dinner?, whose author claims the perfectly Dickensian name of "Lady Maria Clutterbuck").

In addition to this dizzying array of ads for publishers, bookstores, libraries, newspapers and magazines, there are assorted offerings of wigs (including Ross and Son's "Invisible Ventilating Heads of Hair"), Macassar oil, "bear's grease," and other hair treatments, watches, pipes, and an array of gloves and ladies' bonnets. There are "new feeding bottles for infants"—and for their mothers, "Amesbury's Patent Body Supports," which provide "a substitute for stays" and "guard the Spine and Chest against Deformity." The body of the reader (female or male) is the concern of much of advertising discourse. As the ads variously suggest, this body might be cared for by several different types of commodities: protected from the elements by "alpaca umbrellas" and the "Versatio, or reversible coat"; nourished and delighted by a wide selection of food items; clothed in the "Gorget Patent Self Adjusting Shirt"; beautified by a range of cosmetics and products that minister to its unfortunate bouts of "Redness and Subcutaneous Eruptions"; and cured by a diverse array of specific and generally salubrious home-remedies, including the ubiquitous "Parr's Life-Pills," "Ali-Ahmed's Healing Plaister," "Dr. Locock's Pulmonic Wafers" and "Female Wafers," various gout and rheumatic pills, lozenges, botanical extracts, tonics and elixirs, and even "Pulvermacher's Patent Portable Hydro-Electric Chain, for personal use."

The reader's other desires and needs might be served by a daguerreotype portrait gallery, iron bedsteads, "Gutta Percha lining for boxes" (in an ad specifically addressed "To Emigrants, especially such as are proceeding to the Gold Diggings"), fire-proof safes, steel pens, "improved adhesive envelopes," all manner of ink and writing paper, the services of several confirmed expert handwriting-analysts, various financial and legal services, and mutual life insurance. Yet, amidst all other products and services (other than books, of course), the overcoat is perhaps most pervasively advertised. The inside front cover of No. 1 of *Bleak House* features an ad for "Edmiston's Pocket Siphonia, or waterproof overcoat," citing, as was the convention, the highly laudatory "opinions of the press" on the quality of the raincoat. (Also listed in the inventory of articles for sale are the mysterious "newly invented swimming gloves," which are, the makers attest, "of great propelling power.")

What is perhaps most interesting in this advertisement, however, is the emphatic statement in bold capitals "NOTICE.—NAME & ADDRESS STAMPED INSIDE. NONE OTHERS ARE GENUINE." In a great many ads printed in these volumes, this rhetoric of authenticity (the injunction to "accept no imitations") is repeated and underscored. Much like the literary property of the author, the intellectual property represented by the commodity is defended in the form of stamps and seals, personal signatures and patent-protected "proprietary processes": "Prepared only by ROBERT BARKER," asserts an ad for a medicine for infants, "CAUTION.—Observe the name of 'ATKINSON & BARKER,' on the Government Stamp." On the same page, just below, Joseph Gillott ("Metallic Pen Maker to the Queen") concludes a third-person description of his merchandise with the statement, "Each pen bears the impress of his name as a guarantee of quality... with Label outside, and fac-simile of his signature." At times, the discourse of advertising must repudiate the competing claims and discredit the authenticity of a fraudulent imitator: "CAUTION.—E. Moses & Son have no connection with any other house, in or out of London, except the following. . . ." Here, the ad is not merely an appeal to the consumer but a claim to creative and productive agency: the name of the patented product or system, like the name of a novel author, serves as a kind of signature. . . .

Though the text of Dickens's *Bleak House* is for all intents and purposes still the text of *Bleak House* with or without these ads, there is something in them that begs not to be ignored. Throughout the novel, the narrative is structured around a set of uncertainties with regard to matters of legality, property, inheritance, family lineage, and legitimacy that follow from various modes of copying and reproduction. These processes seem always to produce disastrous effects and insoluble problems of subjective agency. The relationship between copying or mechanical reproduction (both in the advertisements and in the literary text itself) and these commercial invocations of uniqueness and authenticity is striking. Indeed, some of the advertisements for the services of copyists, law stationers and lithographers, as well as actual printing machines and copying presses, resonate so much with the narrative of *Bleak House* that the effect is almost uncanny. (One of the ads that appears in various forms in every number of *Bleak House* is for "Waterlow's Patent Improved Autographic

Press, or portable printing machine ... by means of which every person may become his own printer"; given Dickens's concerns about the piracy of his works overseas, particularly by American printers, and his involvement in the campaign for "International Copyright Law" in the United States, these advertisements for personal printing presses may be of interest.)

While it may quite simply be worthy of attention that images and voices of consumer culture appear and speak before, after, within, alongside, and even *to* this literary text that was itself a best-seller long before it was a classic, I would go further; I would argue that these ads are not merely curiosities for the historical imagination but companion texts that claim a definite relationship to the novel. In order to demonstrate this relationship, we need look no further than the inside back cover of No. 1: a full-page advertisement for winter overcoats, under the rubric "ANTI-BLEAK HOUSE." This billing (prepared by the clothier E. Moses of Aldgate for the first published number of the novel, prior to its publication) is followed by a long paragraph of ad copy that luridly describes the bitterness and gloom of a cold house.

The ads of E. Moses & Son, which appear on the inside back cover of each installment of *Bleak House*, often serve as vivid reminders to later readers of the simple fact of the passage of time throughout the course of the novel's serialized publication, with alternating references to "April Showers," "May Flowers," upcoming Parliamentary elections and various other political and cultural events of the day. Though the ad copy is frequently written in florid, novelistic prose, in a style of hack-"literariness" that Raymond Williams would describe as "commercial purple" (174), I think it is likely that the copy under the title of "ANTI-BLEAK HOUSE" in this particular advertisement is meant as an actual literary pastiche, recognizably rendered in the narrative style of those long, sensationally descriptive passages of a Dickens novel:

> A BLEAK HOUSE that is indeed, where the north winds meet to howl an ignoble concert, and bitter blasts mourn like tortured spirits of rebels, who, though prisoners, are unsubdued; where the whirlwind and the hurricane vow their vengeance; and the walls and timbers creak resistance, and like wounded gladiators, rise again boldly to defy the antagonist. Woe to the inhabitant of the Bleak House if he is not

> armed with the weapons of an OVERCOAT and a SUIT of FASHIONABLE and substantial Clothing, such as can only be obtained at E. MOSES & SON's Establishments, Aldgate and Minories, New Oxford-street, and Hart-street, London; or 36, Fargate, Sheffield, or 19, Bridge-street, Bradford, Yorkshire....

These inspired ads from the clothier, which appear in virtually every Dickens novel, are widely varied in genre, including quasi-journalistic reportage and commentary, brief fictional narratives, sketches and personal reflections, and a number of lengthy doggerel poems printed in both the "Martin Chuzzlewit Advertiser" and the "Dombey and Son Advertiser"). In *Bleak House*, the ads specifically refer to the novel itself on several subsequent occasions. At the end of No. 4, there appears another ad in this series entitled "A Suit in Chancery and a Suit out of Chancery," written in a similar style, the central conceit being an obvious pun on a "suit" of clothes and the seemingly interminable lawsuit in *Bleak House*'s infamous Court of Chancery:

> Now the difference between a Suit in Chancery and a Suit out of Chancery is just this:—in the former a man is every moment *tormented, worried, plagued, twisted, sharpened,* and *threatened,* until his very visage becomes like a Chancery Suit—quite a supernatural affair, But a Suit out of Chancery, especially a Suit of Summer Dress from the Establishment of E. MOSES & SON is *light, brilliant, heartcheering,* and *brainreviving;* brushing up one's spirits with the most gratifying assurances of *comfort* and PLEASURE. But a Suit in Chancery is a very different matter, with this precious portion if a gentleman has property he is in a fair way for losing it; if he has a good suit he may wear it out in expectation, and possibly may find it difficult to get another. On the other hand, a Suit out of Chancery, from E. MOSES & SON's, is the best portion of a gentleman's estate, maintained at the least expense, exceeding the most sanguine expectations—the very essence of all novel and fascinating styles.

Here, the text of the ad not only makes reference to the subject matter of the novel; it also offers a similar treatment of what we might call the hypostasized general subject of the Victorian novel's narrative. Much as the Dickens novel solicits its reader through various forms of rhetoric, appealing to that projected reader's presumed common humanity and sympathy, the advertisement hails that same reader as the generalized subject of consumption. Its appeal is not merely a transparent command to buy a product; supplementing the novel, the ad employs a language of affect in order to arouse a sympathetic response. In proto-Dickensian rhetoric, the "Suit out of Chancery" is produced not as the fulfillment of a simple need, but as the expression of desire. Its properties are not simply material; it is also "*brilliant, heartcheering,* and *brainreviving,*" and, not unlike the novel itself, it seduces the reader with promises of "*comfort* and *pleasure.*" Like Marx's hypothetical coat in the first chapter of *Capital,* the hypothetical suit of E. Moses & Son appears as a kind of inhuman specter of commodity fetishism, which stands as the "material embodiment of value" (*Capital* 141) and confronts its equivalent form (finding recognition, in spite of "its buttoned-up appearance" as "a splendid kindred soul, the soul of value"), and speaks "the language of commodities" (143). This language, which produces the commodity as a subject capable of entering into social relations with other commodities and with the consumer, also works to inspire sentiment and sympathy in concert with the work of the novel itself.

At the end of the last serial part of *Bleak House* (the doubly published numbers 19 and 20), virtually guaranteed by its spot on the inside back cover of the last installment of the novel to be the last thing one will read, the final serial ad appears, entitled "THE CLOSING OF THE STORY":

> WHEN an Author has nearly spun out the thread of his narrative, his descriptions have connected him and the public so long that they have arrived at a *pretty good understanding,* and possibly the Author thinks it is time to look out for some fresh subject to keep up the communication.

> The *good understanding* between E. MOSES & SON and the world's public, is the best basis on which Business communications can be established. The interest excited by their NOVEL Styles of ATTIRE cannot be excelled, and the comfort enjoyed in the choicest ARTICLES of DRESS has originated and long continued an intimate Business acquaintance with them, their friends, and their public. . . .

The numerous puns on "novel" (and here, "articles" as well) are a peculiar trope in this series of ads, many of which play on the suggestion of an analogy between Dickens's literary work and the work of the name-brand clothier on the basis of both quality and popular recognition. In this regard, it may be useful to consider the phenomenon of Dickens's authorship specifically as a commercial phenomenon. In these ads—even in the ones that specifically allude to "legal expectations" and to the "suit in Chancery" that figures in the literary text—the use of Dickens and of his novels

relies upon a relatively superficial awareness of the substance of the texts themselves. Though E. Moses (or perhaps his son), like many of his friends, customers and fellow Londoners, probably did read *Bleak House,* he might just as easily have drawn upon the mass-cultural 'buzz' surrounding the novel without actually reading it. Merely by virtue of living in London from 1852 to 1853, one could hardly have escaped some discussion of this best-selling serial and would probably be sufficiently familiar with the story at least to make allusion to its most salient figures. As Wicke suggests (with credit to Orwell's essay on reading Dickens), "While Tolstoy, for example, must be *read* to be known, there is another possible road to Dickens. Dickens is a phenomenon of mass culture, a writer who is present at the creation of advertising as a system, and whose work and personal career participate in shaping that system" (18). One can know Dickens without necessarily *reading* Dickens. Or perhaps, to put it differently, reading means something broader than we might tend to think. . . .

Source: Emily Steinlight, "'ANTI-BLEAK HOUSE': Advertising and Victorian Novel," in *Narrative,* Vol. 14, No. 2, May 2006, pp. 132–62.

Myron C. Noonkester

In the following essay, Noonkester discusses the classical allusions in Bleak House.

It is well known that family circumstances limited the formal education undertaken by Charles Dickens. George Gissing went so far as to remark of Dickens that "with the classics he had no acquaintance." If Gissing's statement is taken to indicate that Dickens was not the type of author who could effortlessly lace his works with classical references, it is no doubt correct. In view of classical allusions that inhabit Dickens's writings, however, Gissing's characterization is debatable. One such allusion occurs in *Bleak House,* chapter 68, when Dickens describes conditions at the townhouse of Sir Leicester and Lady Honoria Dedlock after Lady Dedlock's departure.

Sir Leicester is a dull, but honorable and hopeful, Lincolnshire baronet. His young wife Honoria is enveloped in uncertainty. Her combination of distance and familiarity invites rumor-mongering, and she does carry a secret. She had, prior to her marriage to Sir Leicester, borne a child by Captain Hawdon. Her assumption that her child and its father are dead sustains her haughtiness in the face of such unsavory conduct. But Lady

Dedlock's discovery that her child, Dickensian narrator Esther Summerson, is not dead prompts a wavering, propitiatory flight into regions of death. Her flight culminates when she perishes, justice epitomized, in the cemetery near Hawdon's grave.

It is the accompanying milieu that saves this episode from the overwrought effects of its own melodrama. Before Lady Dedlock's secret sadness resolves itself, the prevalence of gossip heralds doom for the house of Dedlock. Because gossip can insinuate what it cannot prove, it provides a motif for action in the novel. It is a form of testimony, and though its skewed depositions are not necessarily reliable in a legal or factual sense, its presence portends dissonance and distress. The gap between what is reputed and what is manifest is wide, and Dickens fills it with classical allusion. He does so through an implied contrast between an English cemetery scene and the imagery of the greatest Latin poem.

When Lady Dedlock departs, word spreads that Sir Leicester has been "sadly used," and Dickens's narrative traces the trajectory of rumor in the case. "Rumour, busy overmuch, however, will not," Dickens writes, "go down into Lincolnshire. It persists in flitting and chattering about town." "Town" in this case includes opportunities for "Rumour" to spread, and it makes its way, "flitting" and "chattering" through jeweler's and mercer's shops. Subsequently, gossip again goes 'round its circuit, which is of merely urban capacities, without rural purchase: "Thus rumour thrives in the capital, and will not go down into Lincolnshire." Lady Dedlock has gone into Lincolnshire, where rumor will not travel. Rumor, meanwhile, "knows that that poor unfortunate man, Sir Leicester, has been sadly used. It hears, my dear child, all sorts of shocking things. It makes the world of five miles round, quite merry." The radius of rumor, a circulating commodity managed like so many jewels or groceries, is thus established, as is its content. Some retailers of gossip make so bold as to report that Sir Leicester will make "application for a bill of divorce" before the House of Lords. Under these conditions, not to be party to this rumor is to be relegated to social nullity as an "unknown."

No doubt, the narrative sweep of rumor rests on a formidable imagination. But it also alludes to a once-familiar classical source. Lines 173 and 174 of Virgil's *Aeneid*, book 4, contain similar terminology: "At once Rumour runs through Libya's great cities—Rumour the swiftest of all evils. Speed lends her strength, and she wins vigour as she goes; small at first through fear, soon she mounts up to heaven, and walks the ground with head hidden in the clouds." Classical reference allows Dickens to play on the theme of the city and the country by treating the different conditions that obtained at the Dedlocks' country seat, Chesney Wold in Lincolnshire, and in their capital haunts. It also informs certain themes of the novel, retaining effectiveness even in the culminating scene, in which Lady Dedlock stumbles her way to her dead lover's grave.

The alliterative parallel between Virgil's Libya (which in the ancient world usually referred to all of Africa) and Dickens's Lincolnshire is more evocative than precise. Yet, there is a close parallel in the qualification that rumor in *Bleak House* prefers, as in Virgil, to remain in cities, thriving in "the capital." Use of this allusion as a figurative device is also appropriate because it foreshadows Lady Dedlock's eventual frenzied stroll to cemetery precincts. There she will die, and there her character acts in conformity with allusive "Rumour." Eventually, Lady Dedlock becomes, like "Rumour," a streaking shaft of guilt. Dickens's remark that "If she could be translated to Heaven tomorrow, she might be expected to ascend without any rapture" parallels Virgil's treatment of rumor: "soon she mounts up to heaven, and walks the ground with head hidden in the clouds." The circulation of rumor defines by undermining Lady Dedlock's reputation. It is as if the substance that sustains the rumor ultimately chases life from her.

It seems unlikely that Dickens's allusion to the *Aeneid* was designed to achieve an arcane effect similar to the indulgences of self-consciously modern writers. In any event, identification of Dickens's use of this device establishes a minimum standard for his familiarity with classical poetry. Such habits may have arisen from early preparation. The narrator in "Our School," who may have reflected Dickens's own experience, comments that he has indeed advanced apace in classical studies: "We were old enough to be put into Virgil when we went there." One might, of course, consider Virgil (like Shakespeare, whom Dickens also connected with "Rumour") part of the fund of common knowledge for nineteenth-century readers and therefore of little account as an indicator of classical education. But the sophistication of the Virgilian allusion employed by Dickens in *Bleak House* suggests that Gissing's remark was, to use Dickens's own words, "more conventional than fair."

Source: Myron C. Noonkester, "Dickens's *Bleak House*," in *Explicator*, Vol. 64, No. 1, Fall 2005, pp. 42–44.

SOURCES

Abrams, M. H., *A Glossary of Literary Terms*, 4th ed., Holt, Rinehart and Winston, 1981, p. 143.

Ackroyd, Peter, *Dickens*, Mandarin, 1991, pp. 405–406.

Allen, Tim, "15 May 2006: International Day of Families: The Family in the EU25 Seen Through Figures," in *Europa*, May 12, 2006, http://europa.eu (accessed October 11, 2008).

Bloom, Harold, "Introduction," in *Charles Dickens's "Bleak House,"Modern Critical Interpretations*, edited by Harold Bloom, Chelsea House, 1987, pp. 5, 6.

Brimley, George, Review of *Bleak House*, in *Dickens: The Critical Heritage*, edited by Philip Collins, Routledge and Kegan Paul, 1971, p. 283; originally published in *Spectator*, September 24, 1853, pp. 923–25.

"A Chancery Bone of Contention," in *Charles Dickens, "Bleak House,"* Norton Critical Edition, edited by George Ford and Sylvère Monod, W. W. Norton, 1977, p. 924; originally published in *Punch*, Vol. 22, June 1852, p. 255.

Dickens, Charles, *Bleak House*, Oxford Illustrated Dickens, Oxford University Press, 1996.

Disraeli, Benjamin, *Sybil: Or the Two Nations*, Penguin Books, 1985, p. 96; originally published 1845.

Forster, John, Review of *Bleak House*, in *Dickens: The Critical Heritage*, edited by Philip Collins, Routledge and Kegan Paul, 1971, pp, 290, 292; originally published in *Examiner*, October 8, 1853, pp. 643–45.

Gilbert, Elliot L., "Introduction," in *Critical Essays on Charles Dickens's "Bleak House,"* G. K. Hall, 1989, p. 1.

London Child Poverty Commission Web site, http://213.86.122.139 (accessed October 11, 2008).

Mayhew, Henry, *London Labour and the London Poor*, selections and introduction by Victor Neuberg, Penguin Books, 1985, p. 257.

Orwell, George, *The Collected Essays, Journalism and Letters of George Orwell*, edited by Sonia Orwell and Ian Angus, Vol. 1, Penguin Books, 1970, p. 50.

Shatto, Susan, *The Companion to "Bleak House,"* Unwin Hyman, 1988, p. 114.

Trevelyan, George Macauley, *History of England*, Longmans, Green, 1929, pp. 644, 646.

FURTHER READING

Hawthorn, Jeremy, *Bleak House*, Macmillan, 1987. Hawthorn describes the range of critical approaches to *Bleak House*: as an anatomy of society, in terms of narrative and form, feminist responses, and studies of character. In the second part of the book, Hawthorn discusses the experience readers go through as they read the novel.

Korg, Jacob, ed., *Twentieth Century Interpretations of* Bleak House: *A Collection of Critical Essays*, Prentice-Hall, 1968. This selection of essays contains some of the best studies of *Bleak House* from the 1950s and 1960s. The essay by J. Hillis Miller in particular is now regarded as a classic piece of criticism.

Leapman, Michael, *The World for a Shilling: How the Great Exhibition of 1851 Shaped a Nation*, Headline Book Publishing, 2002. The Great Exhibition, aimed at showing off Victorian industrial technology and design, was held in London in 1851. It was visited by six million people, a quarter of the population of Britain. Leapman shows how the exhibition was planned and created and how it excited the imagination of the British public. His account reveals much about the confidence, optimism, and inventiveness of the early Victorian era, the period in which *Bleak House* is set.

Paterson, Michael, *Voices from Dickens' London*, 2nd ed., David & Charles PLC, 2007. This work offers a glimpse into all aspects of nineteenth-century London through the accounts of residents of and visitors to the city in letters, diaries, and newspapers, as well as some of Dickens's own writings. The book reveals how difficult and even brutal life was for the majority of people in this huge city at a time of great growth and change.

Briar Rose

JANE YOLEN

1992

Jane Yolen's *Briar Rose*, first published in 1992, uses the fairy tale of Briar Rose (also called Sleeping Beauty) to tell the story of the Holocaust, the extermination of millions of people, mostly Jewish, during World War II. Through the eyes of a young woman, readers travel to Poland with the protagonist, Rebecca Berlin, called Becca, who attempts to sort through the mysteries of her grandmother's past. For some unexplained reason, her grandmother, called Gemma, has recited the story of Briar Rose to her grandchildren all through their lives. Gemma tells her grandchildren that she is the princess who was put under a wicked sleeping spell, but she does not fully understand why she believes this. On her deathbed, Gemma pleads with Becca to figure out the significance of this fairy tale—to find the castle that she vaguely remembers and the prince who saved her life.

At the heart of this novel is a young woman's deep appreciation, respect, and love for her grandmother. She fulfills her grandmother's last request and in the process encounters the story of the brutalities of the Holocaust. She hears of her grandmother's courage, her grandfather's love, and the scars that the Holocaust has left on the Polish people, Becca's ancestors.

Yolen has stated on many occasions that this book was written for an adult audience. However, since the story uses the fairy-tale theme, it is often classified as a young-adult novel. One of the

Jane Yolen (Reproduced by permission of Jane Yolen)

topics that Yolen discusses in this story is the roundup by the Nazis of people accused or suspected of being homosexuals. Homosexuals, like Jewish people, were sent to camps where they were killed. Because it treats this topic, some have deemed the book unsuitable for young readers. On the other hand, the book has also been widely praised. *Briar Rose* won the 1993 Mythopoeic Fantasy Award, was one of the American Library Association's Outstanding Books for 1993, and was nominated for the 1992 Nebula Award.

AUTHOR BIOGRAPHY

Jane Yolen, author or editor of almost three hundred books, was born on February 11, 1939, in New York City, to Isabel Berlin, a social worker, and Will Hyatt Yolen, a journalist. As her family often moved when she was a child, she was subsequently raised in California, Virginia, and Connecticut. Yolen attended Smith College, in Northampton, Massachusetts, where she won

several poetry awards and attained a bachelor's degree in 1960. Two years later, in 1962, she married David Stemple, a computer scientist who taught at the University of Massachusetts Amherst. In 1976, Yolen went back to school and completed her master's degree in education at Amherst.

Yolen's long and prolific publishing history began with her children's book *Pirates in Petticoats* (1963). Her writing since then has remained mostly in the field of children's literature, but she has also written poetry, short stories, and novels. Some of her more famous works include *The Devil's Arithmetic* (1988), which was a finalist for the Nebula Award; *Owl Moon* (1987), which won the 1988 Caldecott Medal; and *Wizard's Hall* (1991). Yolen has also published several fictional series, including *The Pit Dragon Trilogy* (1982–1987), *Tartan Magic* (1999), and *The Young Merlin Trilogy* (1996–2004). She published *Briar Rose* in 1992.

Turning to nonfiction as well as to an adult audience, Yolen published a book of essays on the importance of writing fantasies for children in her *Touch Magic* (2007). Another book geared to adults is Yolen's *Take Joy: A Book for Writers* (2003), in which she discusses her craft and the pleasure she receives from writing.

In 2006, after forty-four years of marriage, Yolen's husband died of cancer. Yolen has three adult children. She continues to write and spends her time between her home in western Massachusetts and another one in Scotland.

PLOT SUMMARY

Home
Chapters 1–5

Yolen's novel *Briar Rose* begins with three sisters, Rebecca (called Becca), Shana, and Sylvia Berlin, on their way to visit their grandmother. Gemma, as they call her, is living in a nursing home; her health is deteriorating fast. While Shana and Sylvia have just arrived from out of state, Becca, the youngest of the three, lives in the Boston area and has tended to her grandmother faithfully. Though she is mournful, Becca continues to find merit in her grandmother, unlike her sisters, who mock Gemma's failing mental health.

When the other sisters are gone, Gemma tells Becca that the story she has been telling her and her sisters all these past years, about Sleeping Beauty,

MEDIA ADAPTATIONS

- Recorded Books produced both audiotape and CD versions of Yolen's *Briar Rose*, narrated by Linda Stephens (1988).

is real. She, Gemma, was the princess, and there was a real prince who saved her. There is a real castle somewhere, Gemma also says, and she makes Becca promise to find it.

Throughout the novel, Yolen alternates chapters, presenting one in flashback and the next in the present time. In the flashbacks, Gemma tells her grandchildren the tale of Briar Rose, about a king and queen who, upon the birth of their one and only child, throw a party and invite everyone in the kingdom except for an evil witch. The evil witch appears anyway, however, and curses the little princess. She will one day prick her finger on a spindle, and a spell will be cast, putting her and everyone in the castle and in the village to sleep. A good witch, upon hearing this curse, promises that a prince will arrive one day and kiss the sleeping girl, who will then awake. In the other chapters, readers follow Becca in her search for her grandmother's past.

After Gemma's funeral, Eve Berlin, Becca's mother, shows the family a small wooden box that she has discovered among Gemma's things. Inside the box are several photographs, documents, and a man's ring, with the initials JMP and the date 1928 inscribed on it. On the documents are several names that were used by Gemma. One of them is Gitl Mandlestein. As the family looks over the documents, they are confused by all the unanswered questions of Gemma's life.

Chapters 6–10

In chapter 6, Becca goes to work at the *Advocate*, an alternative weekly newspaper. There she sits with Stan, the editor. Stan becomes interested in the story about Gemma and encourages Becca to treat it as she would any other news story, telling her to use her journalistic skills. Becca then rereads

the documents that Gemma has left behind. One is a newspaper story from a small newspaper in Oswego, New York. She calls the newspaper and discovers that a refugee camp had been built in Oswego during the war.

From another document, Becca finds the name of a town in Poland from where Gemma came. But someone has scratched through the handwriting, so it is difficult to read. Also on this form, Gemma had written an alternative name she had been called: Księżniczkaz. Becca learns that the Polish name translates as "Princess."

Chapters 11–15

Chapter 11 is one of the chapters in which Gemma is telling the story of Briar Rose. In this later flashback, the sisters are older and are not listening as intensely as they used to. They bicker among themselves and do not take Gemma so seriously.

Stan drops by Becca's home to look over the documents, and he offers to drive Becca to Oswego. The next day, Becca and Stan meet with Samantha, who has invited three old-timers from the town to come to her house. They are Randolph Feist, a retired high-school teacher; Marge Pierce, who was a high-school student in the 1940s when the local fort was used as a refugee camp; and Harvey Goldman, who was a Jewish refugee who had lived at the camp. When Harvey sees the photographs of Gemma, he immediately recognizes both himself in the photo and Gemma, whom he calls Księżniczkaz. He says they called her Princess because of her manner, which was somewhat aristocratic. He also remembered that she had a baby girl. "She was like something out of a fairy book," Harvey says. He also tells Becca that her grandmother acted "as if a curse had been placed on her."

The next day, Stan suggests that they enlarge the name of the town on the form that has been scratched through. With this clue, Becca calls Harvey in Oswego, who says the name might be Kulmhof. He tells her that Kulmhof (whose original Polish name is Chelmno) was the worst camp of all, located in "the darkest regions of hell." He adds that it would have been impossible for Gemma to have come from there, as no woman was ever known to have escaped.

Chapters 16–20

Becca decides to go to Warsaw, Poland, where she meets Magda Bronski, who will act as her interpreter. On their way to Chelmno, they go through Lublin, where there once was another concentration camp—Majdanek. It is here that Magda tells Becca about a school trip she once took. Her teacher wanted her students to know about the real history of Poland, not the one told to them by their parents, many of whom avoided stories about the extermination of Jews.

Chapters 21–24

As they drive toward Chelmno, Magda reads that the concentration camp there was even worse than the one at Majdanek. Becca tells Magda that she is already aware that no one ever escaped from Chelmno. Once they arrive, they find no one who will talk to them. One old woman tells them to go find the priest, as he will answer their questions.

Father Stashu, unlike the others, is not unwilling to talk about the past. As they walk through town, he shows Becca and Magda the old building that once housed the Jewish prisoners. Father Stashu says it was once called Schloss, German for "castle." Becca is shaken by this information, realizing that this must be the castle that Gemma kept mentioning. Later he gives them the name of Josef Potocki, a man who might be able to fill in more details.

Becca and Magda return to Bydgoszcz, where they meet with Josef. When Becca shows him the photographs she has of Gemma, Josef begins to sob. On his handkerchief are the initials JMP, the same initials as on the man's ring that was in Gemma's box. Becca asks if Josef is her grandfather. Josef laughs; he is homosexual. He tells Becca that the ring is his, and he knew Gemma and Becca's grandfather. He will tell them more if they come to his house the next day.

Castle
Chapters 25–30

Josef continues his story, explaining how he was arrested by the Nazis because he was homosexual and how he escaped from prison. He had no plan once he got out and merely ran until he could run no more. He was found by a small Polish partisan group that was intent on fighting the Germans. They were all killed, however, in a failed attack on German soldiers; Josef was the only one who got away.

After that, Josef wandered back to his family home. There, he found that his stepfather had been killed as a traitor. Germans had taken over his house, and Josef's mother had become a mistress to one of the German officers. His old nursemaid

helped him find food and fresh clothing. The next morning in the woods, Josef awakened to find himself surrounded by another group of Polish partisans, and he joined them. There was a young man who went by the name of Avenger. He was Jewish, and while he was away at medical school, his family was burned alive.

Josef continues his story in chapter 29, focusing his attention on Chelmno. No one knew much about the prison camp there, but they had heard rumors that no one ever escaped. This did not stop them from trying to free the people. Josef, the only non-Jew in the group, decided to go into Chelmno and talk to the local Poles. While there, Josef discovered that the prisoners were taken by van loads to the woods. No one knew what happened to them there, so the group of partisans decided to find the place where the vans went. They watched from the edge of the woods as trucks entered an open field and dumped dead bodies into a mass grave.

After the vans were gone, Josef and Avenger sneaked over to the open graves and peered in. Avenger thought he saw someone move. He jumped in and retrieved a young woman who was still breathing. By the time he hoisted her up to Josef, her breathing had stopped. Josef and Avenger took turns resuscitating her. When she was breathing on her own, Avenger carried her back to the woods.

The next day, after a long sleep, the woman told them that she had no memories, except for remnants of a fairy tale. When she related the fairy tale, the men called her Princess, because the story was that of Briar Rose. After regaining her strength, she became a member of the partisan group. Josef tells Becca that her Gemma was very courageous. After she had been with them for a while, Avenger asked her to marry him, and she agreed; he then told her his real name, Aron Mandlestein.

Josef heard the other men planning to return to Chelmno. They knew that their chances of releasing any more prisoners were very small, but they felt that they had to do something as long as they knew there were people suffering there. They went to conduct a ceremonial cleansing in the river; the men went first, then Gemma went down to the water. While she was in the river, gunshots were heard. Josef, who was only hit in the leg, fell into the river and insisted that Gemma be quiet. Then they floated downriver as far as they could. Gemma helped Josef walk through the woods for several days, looking for the rest of the partisan group. Josef was suffering from a raging fever. After they found their group and Josef recuperated, Emma told him that she was pregnant. Josef gave her his passport and his father's ring, hoping these would help her get out of the country. That was the last time he saw her.

Home Again
Chapters 31–33

Becca says good-bye to Josef and then to Magda. Before leaving, she tells Josef that she does not think that Gemma remembered much about what happened to her. Becca believes that all Gemma retained of her past was wrapped up in the fairy-tale that she kept telling over and over again. Both Josef and Magda say that this was for the best.

When Becca arrives home, she finds Stan waiting at the airport; he had asked her parents' permission to pick her up. Becca and Stan tease each other about being a part of a fairy-tale of their own, and eventually Stan kisses her as a prince might kiss a princess. They talk about the possibility of their living happily ever after.

CHARACTERS

Avenger

Though the role he plays is relatively short, Avenger, whose real name is Aron Mandlestein, is a pivotal character. He was, as it turns out, Becca's grandfather, a person she never met. Avenger was the young Jewish man in the last group of partisans that Josef encountered in the woods. Avenger was studying to become a doctor when he came home and found that his whole family had been slaughtered by a group of Nazis. He was the one who jumped into the mass grave of Jewish prisoners and pulled out the young Gemma, who was barely alive. He helped Josef resuscitate her and then fell in love with her. The two were married in the woods and remained partisans until Avenger's death. Avenger was killed as he and some of his group tried to rescue more Jews. Though he did not know it, he was the father of Gemma's baby, who became Becca's mother.

Eve Berlin

Eve is Gemma's only child and Becca's mother. She plays a very minor role in the story; she knows almost nothing about her mother's past. However, it is Eve who finds the wooden box that contains the photographs and papers that Becca uses as tools to recover Gemma's history.

Jerrod Berlin

Jerrod is Eve's husband and Becca's father. Though his role in the story is limited, his love for Becca and his curiosity fuel the protagonist. Jerrod is a surgeon and is very gentle with Becca, teasing her at times but obviously approving of who she is and what she is doing with her life. Jerrod encourages Becca to follow her instincts, though he is concerned about her traveling alone to Poland.

Rebecca Berlin

Rebecca, or Becca, is the youngest of the three Berlin sisters and the protagonist of the story. She remains close to her grandmother despite Gemma's deteriorating mental health. Unlike her sisters, Becca remains living at home and so is near enough to visit Gemma in the nursing home every day.

Gemma chooses the devoted Becca as the one to seek out the details of her past. She pleads with Becca to go find the castle where she once lived and to discover who her grandfather is. Having promised to do so, Becca bucks all the challenges before her and eventually goes to Poland to confront the ghosts of Gemma's life.

Becca is portrayed as a compassionate, devoted, and courageous young woman. She is committed to the promise she has made. In spite of her courage, she is also shy, especially when it comes to her feelings for Stan, the editor at the newspaper where she works. She is well loved by her parents, especially her father. She is tolerated by her sisters, who do not seem to understand her and her way of life.

Shana Berlin

Shana is Becca's sister and is married to an orthodontist named Howie. Shana and Howie have two girls, Susan and Sarah, and are obviously not happily married. They fight a lot while staying at the Berlin home after Gemma dies. Like her sister Sylvia, Shana is not as attached to Gemma as Becca is.

Sylvia Berlin

Sylvia is Becca's older sister. She is married to Mike and has one son named Benjamin. Sylvia is not very involved in Gemma's life and thinks Becca has gone too far when she decides to go to Poland.

Magda Bronski

Magda Bronski is a young college student who offers a bit of comic relief for the most serious and dramatic part of the story. She speaks in broken English, which gives Becca, as well as the readers, a chance to find humor amidst the tragic events that Becca is about to uncover.

Magda is completely compassionate about Becca's quest to find her grandmother's story. Unlike many other Polish residents, Magda has not been afraid to dig into her country's bloody past. She tells Becca that one of her favorite teachers was fired after she took a group of students to the remains of an old concentration camp not far from the city in which she lived. The teacher wanted her students to face their cultural history instead of trying to pretend it never happened. After that experience, Magda became more active politically in an attempt to further her teacher's goals.

Randolph Feist

Feist was a high-school teacher in Oswego, New York, during the war. He took a group of students to the camp so that they could meet the refugees and put faces to all the rumors that were swirling through the town about the Jewish people who had fled Europe.

Harvey Goldman

Harvey was a refugee at the camp in Oswego. When he sees the photographs that Becca has, he recognizes Gemma, though he knows very little about her. He does tell Becca that they used to call her grandmother "Princess" because of the way she carried herself. She always looked confident and had little need of those around her. Harvey refers to Gemma as Księżniczkaz, the Polish word for "Princess."

Holtz-Wadel

Holtz-Wadel plays a very minor role in this story. He was the leader of the group of partisans of which Avenger and Josef were members. It was Holtz-Wadel's idea that the group try to save Jewish prisoners from Chelmno. He died with the rest of the group when they were gunned down outside the extermination camp.

Aron Mandlestein

See Avenger

Josef Potocki

Josef lives in Poland and is Becca's link to her grandmother's past. Josef retells his story to her and defines his relationship with Gemma. He was, at one time, incarcerated by the Nazis for being homosexual. After escaping the prison, he allied himself with several groups of partisans in succession. He was with one of the groups when he and Avenger rescued Gemma from near death.

When the time came for Gemma to leave Poland, Josef gave her his passport and his father's ring, hoping that these things would help her escape. He is both saddened and happy to see Becca, whom he claims is the image of her grandmother. Recalling his story is painful for Josef, but he does so for love of Gemma and Avenger. It is through Josef that readers hear a more personalized story about Holocaust experiences.

Henrik R.

Henrik found Josef after he escaped from the prison camp Sachenhausen. Henrik was the leader of a small Polish partisan group who wanted to end the German occupation of their country any way they could.

Samantha

Samantha lives in Oswego, New York. She is an old friend of Stan's. Samantha invites over some old-time residents of the town so that Becca can ask them questions about the refugee camp that used to be there.

Stan

Stan is Becca's boss as head editor at the newspaper called the *Advocate*. Becca obviously has a crush on Stan, as she gets nervous whenever he comes near her. He is thirty-five years old and has blue eyes and dark hair, which Becca says looks like he cuts it on his own.

Stan becomes interested in Gemma's mysterious past and encourages Becca to investigate as she would any other story for the newspaper. He drives Becca to Oswego, New York, to help her find details about the refugee camp that Gemma was sent to when she first came to the United States. He also agrees to give Becca time off to travel to Poland and asks if she would write a story about her ventures for the paper. When Becca comes home from Poland, it is Stan who is waiting at the airport to pick her up even though Becca was expecting her parents. The story ends by insinuating that Stan and Becca are beginning a closer relationship.

Father Stashu

Father Stashu is the priest who lives in Chelmno, where Gemma was once held hostage in an extermination camp. He is willing to talk to Becca and Magda about the past. He is the one who tells Becca that the building where the prisoners were held was called Schloss, which is German for "castle." He also puts Becca in touch with Josef Potocki, who will fill in all the details about how Gemma was saved and about whom she eventually fell in love with and married.

THEMES

Prejudice and Its Effects

A large portion of Yolen's novel *Briar Rose* is based on the theme of ethnic hatred or prejudice, particularly the hatred of Jews during World War II. The experience that Becca's grandmother had at the hands of the Nazis was wiped from her memory. This was a result of perhaps both the gas that she inhaled when the Nazis attempted to kill her and the trauma she suffered, which would have led her to suppress all her thoughts about the event. Gemma's life was saved, but she continually repeats the story of Briar Rose as if she is attempting to understand her past and the memories that have disappeared. Though it is not made entirely clear, it appears that Gemma's mind cannot break through the emotional barriers that block her from remembering. She repeats the story knowing that it has something to do with her, but she is not certain in what way. Her dying wish is that Becca investigate what she herself is unable to uncover. Although Gemma suffered no physical scars, the psychological ones stay with her until her death. In fulfilling her grandmother's last request, Becca is also affected by the Nazi prejudice. She must conjure up enough courage and determination to go back to Poland and search out the castle and the reasons why so many people called Gemma a princess.

Another personal narrative that shows the effects of prejudice is seen in the character of Josef Potocki. He suffers imprisonment and torture because he is homosexual. Once he escapes, he joins a group of people who also suffer from severe prejudice, a group of Polish Jews. Though Josef is not Jewish, he understands their plight

TOPICS FOR FURTHER STUDY

- Draw a map of all the places that are mentioned during Becca's trip to Poland. Research these places and write a brief description of the history, culture, and geography of each town that is listed on your map. Use the map as a visual display as you read your report to your class.

- The Holocaust has been represented many times in film and literature. Why do you think Yolen used a fairy tale as the basis for her Holocaust narrative? What is the overall effect of this framework, and how does it differ from other Holocaust representations you may have encountered? Prepare a speech in which you defend or criticize Yolen's decision to portray the Holocaust through the vehicle of a fairy tale.

- Find a copy of the story of Briar Rose as written by the Brothers Grimm. How does the Grimm story differ from the version that is told by Gemma in Yolen's novel? What are the similarities between the fairy tale and Gemma's experience during the Holocaust? Which story is more compelling? Why? Write an essay on the topic.

- Pretend that you are Becca and that you have been assigned to write a newspaper article about your journey. Take all the information you have gained from the novel and turn it into a one-thousand-word news article. Do not forget to include a headline.

and works with the partisans to help free Jewish prisoners.

The Polish people in general also suffered. This is first seen through the character of Magda, who lives in Poland. Her education was slanted in that no mention was made of the Nazi atrocities. When a teacher took Magda to an old concentration camp and a memorial to the Jewish people who died there, that teacher was subsequently fired. Magda says that people do not

Children in a concentration camp

want to remember what happened because it is too overwhelming. The priest from Chelmno notes that Polish people were affected in another way. Father Stashu says that some Polish people were left filled with guilt for not having helped the Jewish prisoners and for their own ethnic hatred. More people died in concentration camps in Poland than in any other country. So the country of Poland is also ever reminded of this horrid past by the presence of the ruins of the camps, the memorials to the dead, and the tourists who flock to Poland to pay their respect to the dead.

Courage

Courage is a theme that is voiced by Josef when he tells Becca the story of her grandmother. He tells Becca that her grandmother, though she had little skill as a partisan agent, nevertheless had courage. After Gemma fully recovered from the gassing, she wielded a knife and a gun as she worked with the partisans in their attempts to foil the Nazis.

Becca is also courageous, though this is never explicitly stated. She is able to rise above the lack of support from her sisters to attempt to solve the mysteries of her grandmother's life. Despite her parents' fears, Becca travels to Poland with scant clues as to where she is to go and what she is to do next. When she meets Josef Potocki, she must overcome her fear of confronting him, knowing that he most likely will tell her a horrible story about her grandmother's past. When she returns home, despite her shyness and insecurities toward Stan, Becca is able to face him and is even a bit forward in defining their budding relationship.

Though Josef denies that he ever acted courageously, he demonstrated valor in the face of several potentially debilitating events. He escaped the Nazi prison. He sneaked into his family home even though it had been taken over by Nazis. He joined several plots to stop the German soldiers, despite his sensing that the plots were doomed. Josef also went into Chelmno and talked to local villagers to gain information about the Nazis, knowing that if anyone suspected him of being

Jewish or being homosexual, his life would be cut short. As he and Avenger watched the bodies of Jewish prisoners being amassed in a huge grave, Josef again demonstrated courage by rescuing Gemma. Even in retelling his stories to Becca, Josef exhibits courage. No one else is willing to talk to her about the past. Yet Josef opens up the psychological doors to his memories, having to relive all the details as he recounts them.

Love

The energy that drives Becca throughout this story is based on love. Of the three sisters, Becca loves her grandmother the most. She is the one who most enjoys hearing the story of Briar Rose, no matter how many times her grandmother repeats it. Becca is also the most faithful of the three women when Gemma's mental health deteriorates and she must be placed in a nursing home. Becca visits her grandmother faithfully and is forgiving of Gemma's lapses into unconsciousness.

Despite her sisters' ridicule and her parents' hesitation, Becca demonstrates her love for Gemma even after her grandmother's death. Becca has made a promise to answer Gemma's questions about her past, and she refuses to break that promise. She takes time off work and devotes her skills and her emotional strength to sorting through the clues that Gemma has left behind. Becca then wanders into very unfamiliar territory that is also somewhat threatening as she travels to a foreign land and digs into a history that most people want to leave buried. She does all of this because of her deep love for her grandmother.

Other expressions of love come from Becca's father. He is very supportive of Becca, understands her passions, and helps her in her search as much as he can. He is very gentle with her and insinuates, through his attention, that he favors her over his other daughters. Even though he teases Becca when Stan starts coming around, he does this with love for his daughter. Stan also demonstrates a budding love that begins as the story is closing.

STYLE

Flashback

Throughout *Briar Rose*, the author uses flashbacks to add depth to the story. A flashback is a transition from the present time of a novel to a period in the past. In Yolen's story, the character

of Gemma, who is confused about her past, often repeats the story of Briar Rose during flashbacks. She retells the fairy tale not only to entertain her grandchildren but also because it connects her to her past. In the flashbacks that Yolen presents as Gemma tells her stories, Gemma may be understood to also be experiencing personal flashbacks.

The present time of the novel consists of the events that unravel in Becca's life as a young adult. The flashbacks that take readers back to when Becca was a child thus also help to establish Becca's connection to her grandmother. Becca, no matter how young or how old, is very much devoted to her grandmother. Rather than stating this as a fact, Yolen demonstrates as much through the flashback scenes. While her sisters are distracted by other things in their lives, Becca is always very present, both physically and mentally, when her grandmother tells the fairy tale. She encourages her grandmother to repeat the story, and she invites friends over to the house and asks her grandmother to tell them the fairy tale. She helps Gemma by filling in portions of the story that her grandmother has missed. And she asks the most questions. Making clear the transitions, Yolen sets off the flashback chapters in a different print form. Whereas the rest of the novel is printed in standard roman characters, the flashback sections are set in italics. Italics are often used in novels to distinguish thoughts or memories from events and dialogue of the present.

Josef's story is told in flashback, and Yolen sets off that particular section of the novel in a special way. She does not use italics but instead has Josef tell the story from a third-person point of view. So instead of Josef using the pronoun *I* as he communicates the events in his past life, he uses the pronoun *he*, as if he were telling someone else's story. Yolen might have done this to highlight this particular flashback, or she might have done it to give Josef a sense of objectivity about the horrid things he is obliged to remember.

Alternating Chapters

In the course of the novel, Yolen alternates chapter types, telling Becca's present-day story in one chapter and then going into flashback in the next chapter to give readers a glimpse into the relationship between the young Becca and her grandmother. The reason for this could be that Yolen wanted to show how much Becca loved her grandmother. However, these divisions are relevant in another sense.

As readers discover as the story progresses, Gemma lived almost two separate lives. As a young woman, she lived in Poland and suffered through the Holocaust during World War II. Before the war ended, she made it out of Poland and came to the United States. There she started a new life, with a different name. There was a disconnect between those two aspects of her life. Gemma's daughter (Becca's mother) knew nothing of her mother's past. Gemma had never mentioned the circumstances of how she became pregnant, whether she was married, or whether the unnamed man was still alive. Not until Becca's mother found the small wooden chest containing documents that offered clues did members of the family gain greater insight into Gemma's past.

By alternating chapter types, then, Yolen sets up a physical division that mirrors the split in Gemma's two lives. There is the Gemma who tells fairy tales to her grandchildren in America on one side. On the other is Becca trying to resolve the puzzle of Gemma's fractured life back in Poland.

Minimal Description

Yolen devotes very little writing to descriptions of what landscapes or people look like. There are mentions of Gemma's and Becca's red hair, of Stan's nose, and of a few pieces of clothing that Becca's sisters wear. In Poland, a field of grass and a river are mentioned, but very little else is. Most of the narrative is focused, rather, on pushing the story forward. Readers follow behind Becca as she digs for clues about her grandmother. They go with her to Oswego to visit refugees from the past. Then they arrive in Poland and go on tour with Becca and Magda. And yet, readers are not given definitive descriptions of what Becca or Magda look like. They know more about how the characters feel than about what they wear. Without extensive description to follow, the reader is thus removed from the physical aspects of the characters and settings and made more aware of the emotional characteristics of the story.

HISTORICAL CONTEXT

The Holocaust

A holocaust is a mass destruction and loss of life. Between 1933 and 1945, while Germany was under the regime of a totalitarian dictatorship based on the ideology of National Socialism, also referred to as Nazism, such a mass destruction of life, referred to as the Holocaust, was carried out against people of Jewish descent. The leader of Germany during this time was Adolf Hitler. One of the main tenets of Nazism was anti-Semitism, or hatred of Jewish people.

Three months after Hitler was elected, the first concentration camp was opened at Oranienburg, outside of Berlin. Jews, as well as political dissenters, were the first people who were arrested. They were not given the benefit of a trial. They usually had little idea about why they were arrested or how long they would remain in jail. At first, many prisoners were held until their families could afford to pay a ransom. While they were held, the prisoners were often subjected to beatings and other tortures.

The concentration camp system quickly expanded into other parts of Germany. The major camps included Dachau, near Munich; Buchenwald, near Weimar; and Sachsenhausen, north of Berlin. These later camps were more organized, with Heinrich Himmler at the helm as police president of Munich. He was also head of the German secret police squad, the Schutzstaffel (SS). Himmler would later be called the father of the concentration camps, as his system of incarceration became the model for future camps.

Prisoners in the early camps were usually put to work. They labored for long hours and were poorly fed, and the environments in which they lived were unsanitary. As a result, the prisoners rapidly lost weight and got sick, and a large percentage of them died. If any prisoner disobeyed an order, he was beaten, whipped, or sent to solitary confinement, often in spaces that allowed only enough room to stand.

Over time, the discrimination against Jewish people increased in intensity. In 1935, Germany passed the racist Nuremberg Laws, which deprived German Jews of any rights of citizenship. These laws also forbade Jews to marry non-Jews. Jewish stores were boycotted. Health insurance was denied, and Jews could not enlist in the German army. By 1937, Jews were banned from professions such as teaching, medicine, and accounting.

Germany invaded Austria in 1938, and the Mauthausen concentration camp was established there near Linz. There were over 200,000 Jews living in Austria, and everyone who was of Jewish descent and over the age of fifteen was forced to register with the government. They registered their names, their wealth, and their properties and businesses. This information was used by German

COMPARE
&
CONTRAST

- **1940s:** The military dictator Adolf Hitler orders German troops to take control of Poland, Norway, the Netherlands, France, Denmark, and Belgium, killing millions of Jews in the process.

  1990s: Saddam Hussein, the Iraqi military dictator, launches an attack on Kuwait while his people go in need of medical supplies.

  Today: The military dictator Kim Jong-il builds nuclear weapons while millions of North Koreans suffer from starvation.

- **1940s:** European Jewish immigrants to the United States total 150,000 before World War II has ended. Another 140,000 arrive shortly after the war.

  1990s: U.S. residents born in Poland, both Jewish and non-Jewish, total almost 400,000, the lowest number in forty years. However, more foreign-born U.S. residents are from Poland than any other Eastern European country.

  Today: For the first time, European immigrants do not make up the largest group becoming citizens of the United States; Latin American and Asian immigrants now lead in this category.

- **1940s:** Nearly six million Jewish people die during the Holocaust. They are purposefully killed because of their ethnicity, an act known as genocide.

  1990s: In a clash between Bosnia, Yugoslavia, and Croatia, nearly 100,000 people are killed. Bosnian Serbs engage in genocide, massacring Bosnian Muslims and sending them to concentration camps.

  Today: Possibly 300,000 people die in a conflict in Darfur, a region in western Sudan. A combination of tribal and religious conflicts as well as extreme drought are said to be the causes behind this devastation, which is considered genocide.

---

officials soon afterward, easing the process of identifying and then transporting Jewish people to concentration camps as well as confiscating their possessions.

In 1939, Nazi German forces entered Czechoslovakia. By then, Jews were being forced to turn over all the gold and silver they owned. Also that year, Germany invaded Poland, where three million Jews lived, the largest Jewish population in Europe. The Polish army was easily defeated, and Germany created new laws against Jews. At this point all Jewish people were forbidden to be outside at night. They also could not own radios and were forced to wear a yellow star pinned to their clothes at all times for easy identification. Jews were also forced to move into designated and concentrated areas called ghettos, which were walled-off sections in many major cities. The first ghetto to be built was located in Lodz. Other large ghettos were built in Warsaw, Lvov, and Kraków, all in Poland. The living conditions in ghettos were severely impoverished, and Jewish people were threatened with death if they were caught trying to leave. The next stage in the genocide was to send the massive Jewish populations to concentration or extermination camps. Thus, Poland became the largest area for the annihilation of Jews. First the Jewish people in Poland were exterminated in massive numbers, and later Jews from other German-controlled areas were brought to the gas chambers in Poland. One by one the ghettos were emptied as the Jews were transported from the ghettos to the Polish death camps at Lublin, Kulmhof (Chelmno), Treblinka, Sobibor, Bełżec, and Auschwitz.

The Folktale of Briar Rose
The story of Briar Rose (or Sleeping Beauty) can be traced back at least to the fourteenth century.

Illustration of the fairy tale "Sleeping Beauty" (© Lebrecht Music and Arts Photo Library / Alamy)

Variations of this story can be found in many different cultures, including Chinese, Arabic, French, Italian, German, and English, to name a few. For recent generations in the United States, the form of the story with which most people are familiar is that of Walt Disney's animated movie *Sleeping Beauty*. One of the older versions of this story comes from Germany: the Brothers Grimm's fairy tale called "Little Briar-Rose." Both Disney's and the Brothers Grimm's stories tell of a beautiful young princess who is cursed by a jealous villager (or witch). Because she was not invited to the festivities surrounding the young princess's birth, the old woman vows that the princess will die on her fifteenth birthday after pricking her finger on a spindle. The only thing that saves the princess's life is a promise made by a friendly woman (or a good witch) that the princess's deep sleep will last only one hundred years. She will then be awakened by a kiss from a handsome prince.

Over the course of the sleeping curse, a huge briar of roses grows thickly around the castle. Though many hear of the legend of the sleeping princess, no one is able to repel the tangle of thorns to gain entrance into the castle. One day a prince comes along just as the hundred-year curse is ending. He is not deterred by the stories of previous men dying in their attempts to save the princess. As he climbs, the briars part, allowing him safe passage. Once inside, he finds the princess and kisses her, thus waking her from her long sleep. They are married and live happily ever after.

CRITICAL OVERVIEW

Many reviewers, such as Stephanie Zvirin for *Booklist*, begin their critiques of Yolen's works with a mention of the author's successes, awards, writing skills, and prolific output. Yolen has, after all, written almost three hundred books for young children, young adults, and adult readers, and her storytelling talents are consistently praised. Zvirin highlights Yolen's "strong voice," while a reviewer for *Publishers Weekly* comments that "only a writer as good as Yolen" could have so aptly brought the fairy-tale scheme together with the atrocities of the Holocaust.

Since Yolen's novel delves into so serious a subject as the Holocaust, other critics who have studied *Briar Rose* treat Yolen's ability to write as a given. They are more interested in analyzing the material that the author tackles and shapes into a story form. Adrienne Kertzer, writing for the *Lion and the Unicorn*, calls Yolen's novel "daring." Kertzer finds that even with the mature subject matter, Yolen successfully "respects the narrative expectations of young adult fiction." Kertzer concludes that although some aspects of the novel would be "absurd" in the real world, as a piece of fantasy or as a fairy tale, *Briar Rose* "makes perfect sense."

Tina L. Hanlon, writing for *Children's Literature*, also refers to the fairy-tale aspect of Yolen's novel. Hanlon notes that Yolen "weaves traditional motifs into the fabric of her tales so persistently and intricately that we recognize familiar patterns even as we are startled and delighted by amazing original ones." Hanlon emphasizes that, despite the author's comment that no woman has ever escaped Chelmno alive, "Yolen has written a fantasy of escape." That is, as the creator of the narrator, Yolen states a narrative truth, then contradicts it in allowing one woman to survive the death camp at Chelmno. As such, "Yolen has imagined one who rejoined the living by embracing the dreams of love and renewal that in fairy tales always triumph over evil." Hanlon adds that in *Briar Rose*, "the characters' bad dreams are overshadowed by the knowledge that the dead have a future when people retell the past and by the moving story of a survivor who escaped to save her baby and nurtured two generations of strong women." Hanlon also points out the disparity in public reaction to the book; while *Briar Rose* "has won awards for fantasy and young adult literature," some have publicly condemned the book as being inappropriate for young-adult readers.

CRITICISM

Joyce Hart

Hart is a published author and freelance writer. In the following essay, she examines the elements of the mythological hero's journey in Briar Rose.

The most obvious story structure in Yolen's *Briar Rose* is that of the fairy tale. Segments of the children's story Briar Rose are interspersed throughout the novel. The fairy tale is so entrenched in the story that another less noticeable structure can be easily overlooked. This is the framework that

> THE HERO IS CONFRONTED BY THESE GUARDIANS, WHO TEST HER TO DETERMINE THE STRENGTH OF HER COURAGE AND CONVICTION. IF THE HERO PASSES THE TEST, SHE WILL BE ALLOWED IN."

the scholar Joseph Campbell, in his book *The Hero with the Thousand Faces* (1968), refers to as the mythological journey of the hero. While Josef Potocki insists that his personal tale from World War II is "a story of survivors, not heroes," the many heroes in Yolen's novel are quite obvious once readers start looking for them. There is the Avenger, who rescues and then falls in love with Gemma. There is also Josef, who fights against the Nazis, saves Gemma, and then courageously recalls in detail the horrible events of his past for Becca's sake. However, the most prominent, as well as most unsung, hero of this story is Becca, the protagonist of the novel.

After devoting most of his life to the study of myths, Campbell found that many of the ancient stories involve a special journey. These mythological journeys of heroes contain specific stages. At the most basic level, these stages include the call to adventure, the road of trials, and the return. The mythical story about the hero often involves a threat, either to an individual, a family, or a whole community. A special, sometimes anointed, person is chosen to take a journey in order to prevent the disaster. The chosen one is not normally thought of as heroic, but despite his or her flaws, the challenge is accepted. The journey is not typically an easy one but rather is fraught with danger. In the end, the unsuspecting hero wins some kind of prize and returns home with it, thus freeing those who were under threat. This structure has been used not only in countless myths but in contemporary stories as well. Readers might recognize the hero's journey in films such as George Lucas's *Star Wars* series. Lucas has often made known his gratitude to Campbell for making the framework of the hero's journey so accessible.

Yolen's novel follows this structure. The call to adventure that starts Becca on her hero's journey

WHAT DO I READ NEXT?

- *The Devil's Arithmetic* (1988) is another of Yolen's books that focuses on the Holocaust. In this story, twelve-year-old Hannah is tired of hearing her grandfather's stories about the horrors inflicted on his family by German Nazis. One day, however, during a Jewish festival, Hannah finds herself transported back in time to 1940s Poland. Hannah has been captured by the Nazis and is about to be put to death. Through this story, Yolen emphasizes the importance of remembering the Holocaust in hopes that such a vast atrocity will never happen again.

- Yolen is best known for her extensive catalog of young-adult and adult fiction. In her essay collection *Touch Magic: Fantasy, Faerie and Folklore in the Literature of Childhood* (1981), she discusses her love of folklore, explaining the power of fairy tales and how they impact the lives of not only children but also adults.

- In *Favorite Folktales from Around the World* (1986), Yolen has collected some of her favorite stories. There are 160 tales in this collection, coming from Eskimo, Irish, Native American, African, and Chinese cultures, among others. Topics in these tales include the distinction between true and false love, the lives of shape-shifters and unsuspected heroes, death, and ways to fool the devil. Yolen provides background material for each section, helping readers to understand the history surrounding the stories as well as the underlying literary factors.

- Robin McKinley's *Rose Daughter* (1998) retells the fairy tale Beauty and the Beast in a more emotional rendering with darker tones. McKinley's version provides more background information on the beast and a more complex young woman in the beauty.

- The British author Angela Carter wrote several literary interpretations of fairy tales for adult audiences. In many of her stories, she stresses the principles of feminism, presenting the female protagonist as a source of power rather than one who always has to be rescued by a male. Her collection *Burning Your Boats: The Collected Short Stories* (1995) includes "The Bloody Chamber" and "Black Venus."

---

comes from her grandmother. Gemma pleads with Becca to find the castle of her fragmented memories. In this case the threat associated with the call to adventure is not physical; it is psychological. Gemma knows that there was a sleeping princess, a castle, a prince, and a kiss in her past. Through all of her adult life, Gemma sensed that the story of Briar Rose had something to do with her, but she was never able to put her finger on how this was so. Her last wish is that Becca answer this question. In order for Gemma to die in peace, she needs to hear that Becca will take on this challenge, a trial Gemma herself was never strong enough to face. Becca, in her love for her grandmother, accepts the hero's call.

As soon as Becca agrees to take on the challenge, she embarks on the road of trials, the second stage of the journey. First come the taunts that Becca receives from her sisters, who do not have the same passion for their grandmother that Becca has. They therefore do not understand why Becca feels so committed to honoring Gemma's dying request, which to them seems absurd. Becca is able to overcome her sisters' objections fairly easily. Then comes the gift. This takes the form of the wooden box that Becca's mother discovers, which holds clues that Becca must decipher. Although the documents and photographs in the box offer clues, they also represent the first serious stumbling blocks along the hero's path. What do they mean? At first these clues seem unrelated to one another. They also contradict many details that the family thought they knew about Gemma. For example, they discover that the matriarch of the family had multiple names. They also wonder if the man in the photo is Gemma's husband, as well as why Gemma never told them anything about the man who made her pregnant. Was Gemma ever married? And to whom does the man's ring found in the box belong? These are just some of the questions and challenges that Becca must confront.

Slowly but surely, Becca gathers additional information from relatively local sources. Some of the details help to clarify Gemma's past, but the really important questions, such as where the castle that Gemma talked about was and who the prince who saved her was, can only be answered if Becca leaves the safety of her home and travels to a foreign environment. Thus, the second and more challenging part of her journey begins.

Becca flies to Poland, a country she has never before visited. She knows this is where Gemma had lived, but she is not sure what her grandmother's circumstances were. Was Gemma a real princess living in a real castle? This question stems from the fairy tale Becca heard throughout her youth. Contrary to that fantasy, though, is the dark, morbid reality that Becca soon discovers. As Becca travels through Poland with her interpreter, Magda, she digs deeper into Poland's nightmarish history. The road of trials, like those in other myths, becomes more threatening. The hero is more strongly challenged. Though Becca is rebuked by some of the Polish people who refuse to reveal the secrets from the past, she finds keys along the way that open progressively larger doors. The old woman in Chelmno, who at first shuns Becca, comes back and offers a hint. She tells Becca to go visit the priest. As it turns out, the priest is relatively new to Chelmno and is therefore unburdened by any guilt over the past and offers more clues. Because Becca has refused to give in to the threats of some of the villagers, she is rewarded.

The villagers' threats, then, act like the mythological guardians at the gates. In myths, powerful sentinels may stand at the entrance to a place that the hero is attempting to enter. The hero is confronted by these guardians, who test her to determine the strength of her courage and conviction. If the hero passes the test, she will be allowed in. Thus, Becca proves her determination and rebukes those who threaten to keep their secrets to themselves. She finds the priest, who then opens up the next gate, which leads to Josef Potocki.

Behind the gates lies the prize—the true story of Gemma's sleeping curse, castle, and prince.

Facing the prize itself becomes a sort of final trial for Becca. The story that she hears from Josef turns out to be much more brutal than the fairy tale of Briar Rose. Gemma was not some beautiful princess who had a father and mother who were king and queen. The castle, under Nazi control, represented not a flowery environment but rather one that smelled of suffering and blood. The prince did not kiss Gemma back to life but rather resuscitated her after she had been deliberately gassed. In hearing this difficult tale, Becca gains the satisfaction of solving the mysteries of her grandmother's past and fulfilling her commitment to Gemma's death wish. At the same time, though, the telling of the truth has made Josef suffer and has not brought Becca's grandmother back.

The last phase of the hero's journey is the return home. The prize that Becca brings with her is a fuller and more realistic account of the Berlin family's history. Becca's mother, Eve, learns the identity of her father. Eve also finds out that her mother had very committed friends who saved her life. Though they now sadly know how much Gemma suffered, they also understand her to have been a very courageous woman. This means that not only is the family history more complete but also there is a reason for the family to be very proud of the past. On a more personal level, the reward for Becca upon her hero's return is the promise of her own fairy tale: She has a "prince" waiting at the airport to welcome her home.

Source: Joyce Hart, Critical Essay on *Briar Rose*, in *Novels for Students*, Gale, Cengage Learning, 2010.

Kenneth Kidd

In the following excerpt, Kidd uses Briar Rose *to support his claim that "for better and for worse, psychoanalysis and children's literature have been mutually enabling."*

Since the early 1990s, children's books about trauma, especially the trauma(s) of the Holocaust, have proliferated, as well as scholarly treatments of those books. Despite the difficulties of representing the Holocaust, or perhaps because of them, there seems to be consensus now that children's literature is the most rather than the least appropriate literary forum for trauma work. Subjects previously thought too upsetting for children are now deemed appropriate and even necessary. Thus, in "A New Algorithm of Evil: Children's Literature in a Post-Holocaust World," Elizabeth

Neuschwanstein Castle in Germany, which inspired the "Sleeping Beauty" image of castles (Image copyright Dainis Derics, 2009. Used under license from Shutterstock.com.)

R. Baer emphasizes the urgency of "a children's literature of atrocity," recommending what she calls "confrontational" texts, and proposing "a set of [four] criteria by which to measure the usefulness and effectiveness of children's texts in confronting the Holocaust sufficiently" (384). "A" is now for Auschwitz, and "H" for Holocaust (if sometimes for Hiroshima). And "B" is still for book, though no longer necessarily the Bible. Baer sees as exemplary texts like Roberto Innocenti's picture book *Rose Blanche* (1985), Seymour Rossel's nonfiction history *The Holocaust* (1981), and Jane Yolen's novel *The Devil's Arithmetic* (1988). Such books emphasize their protagonists' direct experiences of the Holocaust, experiences that extend to and presumably interpellate the child reader outside the story.

How to explain this shift away from the idea that young readers should be protected from evil and toward the conviction that they should be exposed to it, perhaps even endangered by it? It's almost as if we now expect reading about trauma to be traumatic itself—as if we think children can't otherwise comprehend atrocity. Just how new is this faith in exposure, experience, and confrontation, and how do we assess its significance with respect to contemporary children's literature and trauma studies?

Many people believe that the Holocaust fundamentally changed the way we think about memory and narrative, as well as about human nature. Presumably the exposure model became necessary because we no longer have the luxury of denying the existence of or postponing the child's confrontation with evil. Certainly the Holocaust helped make the often entangled projects of literature and psychoanalysis especially ever more anxious and serious. Adorno's infamous declaration that "[to] write poetry after Auschwitz is barbaric" was received more as a call to narrative arms than a moratorium; Holocaust scholars have long insisted that Adorno was speaking

> IT'S ALMOST AS IF WE NOW EXPECT READING
> ABOUT TRAUMA TO BE TRAUMATIC ITSELF—AS IF WE
> THINK CHILDREN CAN'T OTHERWISE COMPREHEND
> ATROCITY."

poetically and not literally, saying we *must* write poetry after Auschwitz, just as we must put psychoanalysis to good use. Even so, the Holocaust has only recently become a coherent narrative project in literary, psychological, and theoretical discourse. Lawrence L. Langer's foundational study *The Holocaust and the Literary Imagination* was published in 1975, and is one of the earliest long critical treatments of the "literature of atrocity." If Western culture has only lately come to terms with the Holocaust, those terms are largely literary and psychological, beginning with Holocaust memoirs and diaries, then historical analyses, and finally fictionalized treatments alongside academic trauma theory.

Only now can Baer insist that there's such a thing as "sufficient" confrontation with the Holocaust. Not everyone would agree; one of the counter-tropes of Holocaust narrative is that confrontation is impossible or always insufficient, that such faith in literature is foolish, even unethical. In any case, the Holocaust has arrived as a legitimate subject, and has ushered in the wider sense that trauma writing can be children's literature. It's not surprising that the Holocaust has functioned as a sort of primal scene of children's trauma literature, through which a children's literature of atrocity has been authorized within the last decade, asserted around both the power and limitations of narrative.

The psychoanalytic conceit is not accidental. The recent surge of Holocaust and trauma writing has many causes and vectors, among them the success of the progressive social movements of the 1960s and 1970s, and the residual faith in literature as a form of identity, empathy, and community in a pluralist society. Holocaust writing would be unthinkable without the therapeutic ethos that at once nurtured this progressive culture and formed its popular and institutional corrective (in the form of Cold War psychology,

for instance). As social historians have shown, the helping professions have engendered a belief in the complexity of psychic life and interpersonal relations, a belief with both progressive and reactionary tendencies. Psychoanalysis has long been wildly popular in the US, and now has a diffuse cultural life. Thanks in part to the dissemination of psychoanalysis and the professionalization of mental health work, trauma is a key concept in our life and literature. Not surprisingly, recent academic theory privileges literature and psychoanalysis as interrelated forms of trauma "testimony."

For better and for worse, the Holocaust has become nearly coterminous with the idea of the unconscious. Like the unconscious as theorized by Freud, the Holocaust is at once history and the never-ending story, the primal scene forever relived and reconstructed. It is something that must be spoken about but that remains inaccessible. The Holocaust is simultaneously an event that we've moved beyond and one that we cannot and must not forget: this is the necessary paradox of Holocaust writing, akin to the idea of the unconscious, the central and necessary conceit of psychoanalysis. Baer points to the promotional buttons for the United States Holocaust Memorial Museum, which read "REMEMBER" and "NEVER AGAIN"; the Museum is a walking and talking cure, one that asserts the preventative as well as recuperative power of memory.

This essay, however, does not argue for the supremacy of psychoanalysis as a tool for representing and understanding trauma in and around Holocaust literature. Instead I show how, for better and for worse, psychoanalysis and children's literature have been mutually enabling, alongside and through academic trauma theory, which rewrites the "crisis" of representation in signal ways. Children's literature, of course, has been very usefully understood as therapeutic and testimonial. Certain genres seem to function much like the dream-work as Freud described it, at once acknowledging but distorting or screening trauma. Drawing upon Freud, Bruno Bettelheim famously suggested that fairy tales help children work through both painful experiences and everyday psychic trouble. And fairy tale motifs surface in other kinds of texts about war and especially the Holocaust. Thus Donald Haase, among others, examines "the fairy tale's potential as an emotional survival strategy" (361) in and around Holocaust narrative.

But because psychoanalysis and literature are so enmeshed, this kind of treatment begs the analytical question in a sense, using one discourse to discover in the other analogous procedures and truths. In the case of the fairy tale, we might also examine how fairy tales have helped articulate psychoanalytic discourse. And in the case of trauma writing overall, we might ask—as have Holocaust scholars Adrienne Kertzer and Hamida Bosmajian in recent studies—how our understanding of trauma is discursive as well as lived, shaped by cultural pressures alongside personal experiences. What if psychoanalysis *isn't*, in fact, the best treatment for trauma, but rather one of its privileged modes of presentation? Do we usually now expect children's literature to testify to trauma in psychoanalytic fashion? Why not turn instead to alternative discourses of trauma work, among them "narrative medicine" and "narrative therapy"? Or why not abandon psychological approaches altogether, in favor of sociohistorical analysis? In *An Archive of Feelings: Trauma, Sexuality, and Lesbian Public Cultures*, Ann Cvetkovich advocates what she calls "critical American Studies," which would provide "a fuller examination of racialized histories of genocide, colonization, slavery, and migration that are part of the violences of modernity, and whose multigenerational legacies require new vocabularies of trauma" (37). Is it time to leave psychoanalysis behind?...

Through the fairy tale, people tell stories about challenge and survival, hardship and hope. By the 1990s, the fairy tale was ever more entrenched in US pop-literary culture, in the form of novelizations, films, "politically correct" satires, etc. Most of these new fairy tale forms claim both psychological and historical relevance, and vis-à-vis each other. Thus in her afterword to *Briar Rose* (first published in 1992), Yolen can write, "This is a book of fiction. All the characters are made up. Happy-ever-after is a fairy tale notion, not history. I know of no woman who escaped from Chelmno alive." Yolen can repudiate the happy-ever-after scenario precisely because we now expect fairy tales to be both *not happy*—i.e., therapeutic rather than conventionally satisfying—and *history*. It's as if Yolen is suggesting that while this particular plot element isn't accurate, the novel is still true to history—that is, to deeper psychological truths.

In this novel, ostensibly a variant of "Sleeping Beauty," a young woman does escape from Chelmno alive—an unthinkable and perhaps irresponsible plot, as Adrienne Kertzer argues in *My Mother's Voice: Children, Literature, and the Holocaust*. Kertzer chastises Yolen for pandering to the naive American desire for a happy ending in Holocaust narrative. And yet Yolen clearly sees her work as legitimately historical as well as imaginative. So does her editor Terri Windling, in her introduction to the 2002 edition of *Briar Rose*. "Way back in the 1980s," writes Windling, "I was a young book editor in New York City, and Jane Yolen was one of my heroes. Not only was she, quite simply, one of the finest writers I'd ever read, but her knowledge of the world's great wealth of fairy tales was second to none. Like Jane, I was crazy about fairy tales, and so I had the notion of publishing a series of novels based on these classic stories. Thus the Fairy Tale series was born...." Windling furnishes a nutshell history of the fairy tale, pointing to its juvenilization by Disney and hinting that its legitimacy is now being restored through her series. She implies that Yolen's novel will return to the fairy tale its rightful European seriousness, against Americanizations "stripped of moral ambiguities" and narrative complexities." [*sic*] There's even an epigraph from Jack Zipes's *Spells of Enchantment*, which suggests how closely our faith in the sociological and historical significance of the fairy tale is entangled with our faith in its psychological import. Whereas Kertzer sees the novel as a typically American exercise in imaginative denial, Yolen and Windling position *Briar Rose* as a higher truth. Kertzer and Bosmajian are right to point out that such texts are problematic, even if our disappointments with as much as our praise of children's literature confirm our faith in its testimonial power....

Source: Kenneth Kidd, "'A' is for Auschwitz: Psychoanalysis, Trauma Theory, and the 'Children's Literature of Atrocity,'" in *Children's Literature*, Vol. 33, 2005, pp. 120–49.

Adrienne Kertzer

In the following excerpt, Kertzer examines how Yolen constructs a "double narrative" in Briar Rose.

The question of my title is asked by the mother of Piri Davidowitz in the penultimate sentence of Aranka Siegal's fictionalized memoir, *Upon the Head of the Goat: A Childhood in Hungary 1939–1944*. The reader never hears the answer to the mother's question; Siegal's final sentence reports that before Mr. Shuster can respond, the German guard yells and the train door clanks shut (214). The sequel, *Grace in the Wilderness: After the*

Liberation, 1945–1948, begins in Bergen-Belsen at the end of the war. Presumably Piri, having survived Auschwitz, now knows the answer to her mother's question, but the reader is never given this answer; coherent, conclusive statements are not part of the meaning of Auschwitz. That meaning is not just hidden from the reader; it is denied. If Piri cannot know for certain what Auschwitz means for her mother, in that Piri survives and her mother does not, what meaning can the reader possibly construct? The unanswered question, in effect, becomes the meaning. For the mother's unanswered question is what the reader is left with: Do you know what Auschwitz means? Auschwitz is what I cannot narrate. . . .

Unlike Yolen's earlier and more conventional *The Devil's Arithmetic*, *Briar Rose* respects the narrative expectations of young adult fiction, only to abandon those expectations in the concluding "Author's Note." In the novel, Yolen gives us the "Hope and Happy Endings" (Paterson 172–91) we have come to expect in young adult fiction; in the "Author's Note," she deliberately takes both away. The lesson that emerges in this sophisticated interplay between text and peritext is not the consoling lesson of spiritual triumph but a much harder one in the reality of historical facts. Rewriting "Briar Rose" as the fantastic story of how one woman survives the death camp, Chelmno, Yolen initially tricks us into feeling superior to conventional fairy tales, and then in the "Author's Note" makes us regret our arrogance. She gives us the heroic language Langer critiques, albeit parodied; the Polish Jewish princess is indeed kissed by a prince (some would even call him a fairy, the derogatory homosexual slang indicating Yolen's ironic distance from conventional fairy tales). The partisans are neither romantic, heroic, nor particularly brave. "Wars do not make heroes of everyone," the narrator tells us. From a realistic perspective, the novel is absurd; a woman never asks questions about her own mother's background; it is the granddaughter, the youngest daughter, who after the grandmother's death, determines to make sense of her grandmother's obsessive and peculiar retelling of "Briar Rose." Yet as a fairy tale, *Briar Rose* makes perfect sense. Who survived? The lucky. "It explains a lot. . . . It doesn't explain anything."

Because the grandmother's memories are obliterated by the gas, when she is revived, she has no memory of her past except for a fairy tale in which she, a princess in a castle, is the only one kissed awake. The partisans try to save others; one woman before she dies tells them what it is like to be gassed: "I called my daughter's name over and over and over but she did not answer. Then the van started up and that is all I can remember." In this way Yolen enters the gas chamber and tells the reader what Siegal and Matas cannot narrate. The mother remains loyal to the daughter, at least as far as she can remember; the amnesia produced by the gas allowing Yolen a way to avoid what Lanzmann's *Sonderkommando* witnesses report, parents struggling to breathe even as they were gassed, stepping on top of their own dying children.

[Claude] Lanzmann begins *Shoah* at Chelmno, and the viewers are told that only two men survived this particular death camp, one an adolescent who was often seen by the villagers rowing up the river to get feed for rabbits. This child, Simon Srebnik, is interviewed extensively as a middle-aged adult by Lanzmann. He also appears as an unnamed character in *Briar Rose* (169–70), and there are other signs that the novel is influenced by *Shoah*, for example, when Yolen says, "There may be good people [in Chelmno]. I have never heard them interviewed." Respecting Lanzmann's insistence on the obscenity of understanding, Yolen invents a fairy tale in which a female survivor is resurrected by the partisans. Srebnik tells a far bleaker story of unloading the Chelmno gas vans:

> I remember that once they were still alive. The ovens were full and the people lay on the ground. They were all moving, they were coming back to life, and when they were thrown into the ovens, they were all conscious. Alive. They could feel the fire burn them. (Lanzmann, *Shoah* 101–2)

Yolen convinces us of a different narrative, but the lesson lies elsewhere, in the final paragraph of her "Author's Note," and its blunt refusal of the story she has just told: "This is a book of fiction. All the characters are made up. Happy-ever-after is a fairy tale notion, not history. I know of no woman who escaped from Chelmno alive."

The history that makes us wish fairy tales did happen, that life were like a children's book and we all lived happily ever after, is not an easy history to read or write. If we persist in thinking that children need hope and happy endings (and I must confess that I believe that they do), then the stories we give them about the Holocaust will be shaped by those expectations, and we will need to consider narrative strategies like Yolen's that give readers a double narrative, one that simultaneously respects our need for hope and happy endings even as it teaches us a very different lesson about history. For there are those who would tell us yet another fairy tale, one in which the mass murder of millions of people did not happen. As the daughter of an Auschwitz survivor, I know that it did, and I know that we need to find ways to tell children that it did. For what Auschwitz means to me is the voice of my mother speaking, telling me not only about the gassing of her father in October 1944, but another story, of how in the summer of 1944 she was marched into a room in Birkenau, but for some reason, nothing happened. As a child, I understood this story to mean what she said that it did, an example of grotesque and sadistic Nazi humor: "They pretended it was the gas chamber to scare us," she says. "It wasn't." But was it? And what does it say about the questions raised by memoir, as well as our understanding of what Auschwitz means, that I now find the story that my mother was not gassed more incomprehensible than the fact that my grandfather was?

Source: Adrienne Kertzer, "'Do You Know What "Auschwitz" Means?' Children's Literature and the Holocaust," in *Lion and the Unicorn*, Vol. 23, No. 2, 1999, pp. 238–56.

Cathy Chauvette

In the following review, Chauvette praises Briar Rose *as a novel that deftly blends fantasy and history.*

The most satisfying series entry to date. Yolen once again demonstrates her facility in blending history and fantasy, reworking the terrors of the Holocaust that she explored so successfully in *The Devil's Arithmetic* (Viking, 1988). Throughout her childhood, Becca's grandmother tells her "Sleeping Beauty," but with some peculiar variations. As the girl grows up, she realizes that Gemma's identification with the story is a personal one; when the woman dies, she is compelled to discover its connection to her mysterious grandmother's life. The result is Becca's immersion in the fantastic allegory her grandmother has created to deal with her past. Her memories of the woman's powerful retellings of the tale make the experience real for readers as well. Yolen's wonderful gift for poetic language is evident in these sections, in both the lyrical descriptions and in the terrifying metaphors. This is a textbook example of the use of symbolism in

literature, yet Yolen's touch is so deft that the novel never lumbers under the weight of its literary freight. Highly recommended for fantasy lovers and others, and a wonderful integrated-language opportunity for history teachers.

Source: Cathy Chauvette, Review of *Briar Rose*, in *School Library Journal*, Vol. 39, No. 4, April 1993, p. 150.

Shelley Glantz

In the following review, Glantz contends that Briar Rose *"will become a classic of Holocaust literature."*

Beginning with a treatise on the history of fairy tales by the editor of The Fairy Tale Series, this unusual novel takes the reader to the realm of Sleeping Beauty in a story that successfully combines the fairy tale, the Holocaust and a contemporary character's search for her roots. Becca, a young journalist in Massachusetts, is devastated when her beloved grandmother Gemma dies. During her final months, Gemma had insisted that she was the sleeping princess, and her death bed wish is that Becca find Briar Rose's castle. Over the objections of her parents and two older sisters, Becca travels to the site of a refugee camp in New York and then on to Poland, with only a ring, photo and official documents from World War II as clues. She finds Josef Potocki, an elderly Pole who knew her grandmother and was a member of the partisans who saved her from the infamous death camp, Chelmo. Yolen has the skill to allow Josef's story to be told in his own voice, using emotional language that will mesmerize the reader. As Josef tells Becca the story of her grandmother, of the man she married and of her experiences during the Holocaust, Becca and the reader are able to understand the parallels between Gemma and Briar Rose. The format of the book cleverly leads the reader to this understanding; as Becca searches for the truth, alternating chapters reveal Becca's childhood memories of her grandmother telling the Sleeping Beauty story. Readers' appreciation of the symbols Yolen uses to express these similarities will vary based on their maturity, but all will remember this stark story and its remarkable characters. This short book will become a classic of Holocaust literature. A bibliography of fairy tale collections, adaptations and nonfiction is included. Highly Recommended.

Source: Shelley Glantz, Review of *Briar Rose*, in *Book Report*, Vol. 12, No. 1, May/June 1993, p. 45.

SOURCES

Baker, Luke, "Iraq Conflict Has Killed a Million Iraqis: Survey," in *Reuters*, January 30, 2008, http://www.reuters.com (accessed December 1, 2008).

Campbell, Joseph, *The Hero with a Thousand Faces*, Princeton University Press, 1968.

Dawidowicz, Lucy S., *The War against the Jews, 1933–1945*, Holt, Rinehart and Winston, 1975.

Gibson, Campbell J., and Emily Lennon, "Historical Census Statistics on the Foreign-Born Population of the United States: 1850–1990," Web site of the U.S. Census Bureau, February 1999, http://www.census.gov (accessed December 1, 2008).

Hanlon, Tina L., "'To Sleep, Perchance to Dream': Sleeping Beauties and Wide-Awake Plain Janes in the Stories of Jane Yolen," in *Children's Literature*, Vol. 26, 1998, pp. 140–67.

"Immigration: Polish/Russian; A Cultural Renaissance," in *Library of Congress: The Learning Page*, http://lcweb2.loc.gov/learn/features/immig/polish7.html (accessed November 20, 2008).

Jane Yolen Home Page, http://www.janeyolen.com/ (accessed November 12, 2008).

Kertzer, Adrienne, "'Do You Know What "Auschwitz" Means?' Children's Literature and the Holocaust," in *Lion and the Unicorn*, Vol. 23, No. 2, 1999, pp. 238–56.

Lukas, Richard C., *Forgotten Holocaust: The Poles under German Occupation, 1939–1944*, Hippocrene, 2001.

Piotrowski, Tadeusz, *Poland's Holocaust: Ethnic Strife, Collaboration with Occupying Forces and Genocide in the Second Republic, 1918–1947*, McFarland, 2007.

Preston, Julia, "Immigrants Becoming U.S. Citizens at High Rate," in *New York Times*, March 29, 2007, p. A18.

"Q&A: Sudan's Darfur Conflict," in *BBC News*, November 12, 2008, http://news.bbc.co.uk (accessed January 13, 2009).

Review of *Briar Rose*, in *Publishers Weekly*, Vol. 239, No. 32–33, July 20, 1992, pp. 231–32.

Salmon, Andrew, "Starvation Threatens Millions as Aid to North Korea Dries Up," in *Times Online*, August 10, 2005, http://www.timesonline.co.uk (accessed December 1, 2008).

Simons, Marlise, Lydia Polgreen, and Jeffrey Gettleman, "Arrest Is Sought of Sudan Leader in Genocide Case," in *New York Times*, July 15, 2008, http://www.nytimes.com (accessed January 13, 2009).

Stone, RoseEtta, "A Book Review and a Discussion with Jane Yolen, Author" in the *Purple Crayon*, http://www.underdown.org/yolen.htm (accessed October 19, 2008).

Yolen, Jane, *Briar Rose*, Tom Doherty Associates, 1992.

Zvirin, Stephanie, Review of *Touch Magic: Fantasy, Faerie and Folklore in the Literature of Childhood*, by Jane Yolen, in *Booklist*, Vol. 96, No. 18, May 15, 2000, p. 1708.

FURTHER READING

Axelrod, Toby, *In the Camps: Teens Who Survived the Nazi Concentration Camps*, Saddleback Educational Publishing, 2002.

> In this volume, Jewish people who as teens were sent to concentration camps and separated from their parents in the process recount their stories of cruelty and the strong will to survive. Even in the darkest of moments, these teens found hope.

Brooks, Philip, *Extraordinary Jewish Americans*, Children's Press, 1998.

> Included in this book are the real-life stories of sixty prominent Jews from the fields of science, business, sports, politics, and the arts. Topics also include Jews in Hollywood, Jewish gangsters, and the Jewish experience during the civil rights movement.

Crispin, M. Guyle, *Holocaust: A Q&A Guide to Help Young Adults Really Understand the Holocaust*, University Press of America, 2006.

> Designed to help teens grasp what happened during the Holocaust, this book starts with questions that other teens have asked. Crispin provides the answers and a time frame of the events of World War II in an easy-to-read book with many photographs to enhance the reading experience. The book offers information on how the Nazis came into power, the conditions of the Jewish ghettos, and the impact of the Holocaust.

Davies, Norman, *God's Playground: A History of Poland*, Vol. 2, *1795 to the Present*, Columbia University Press, 2005.

> Davies presents a scholarly but accessible historical study of Poland that has been well received by critics. The book fills in a gap in the history of Europe by offering an in-depth look into the events, people, and culture that have made Poland what it is today.

Friedländer, Saul, *The Years of Extermination: Nazi Germany and the Jews, 1939–1945*, HarperCollins, 2008.

> Drawing information from extensive research and the diaries of Jewish people in Europe during the Nazi reign, Friedländer presents an excellent overview of what happened to so many Jews during World War II.

Grimm, Wilhelm, and Jakob Grimm, *The Complete Grimm's Fairy Tales*, CreateSpace, 2008.

> Fairy tales are not just for children, especially the Grimm brothers' versions. Included in this collection are sixty-two stories that have deep psychological underpinnings that all adults and students can learn from.

Paulsson, Gunnar S., *Secret City: The Hidden Jews of Warsaw, 1940–1945*, Yale University Press, 2003.

> Diaries have been studied to provide the stories of some of the few Jews who were able to evade detection or get out of the ghettos in Poland. Paulsson depicts what life was like in Warsaw during World War II.

Fallen Angels

WALTER DEAN MYERS

1988

Fallen Angels is a novel for young adults by Walter Dean Myers, first published in 1988. The novel is set in Vietnam during the Vietnam War. It follows the story of Richie Perry, a seventeen-year-old African American from Harlem, New York, who spends four months fighting in Vietnam from the fall of 1967 to the beginning of 1968. The story is presented realistically, and the author's approach is an objective one. Although he touches on many of the controversial aspects of U.S. involvement in Vietnam, he does not take sides regarding whether the war was justified or not. His goal is to present it from the point of view of the young infantrymen who fought in it, the men who risked their lives doing the job they were told to do, in a war they did not always understand. As one of the few novels about the Vietnam War aimed at a young adult readership, *Fallen Angels* is both an exciting war story and a coming-of-age story. However, the reader should be cautioned that because of the author's realistic approach, *Fallen Angels* employs strong language of the kind that actual soldiers might use. There are also scenes in which the violence of war is graphically described.

AUTHOR BIOGRAPHY

Walter Dean Myers was born on August 12, 1937, in Martinsburg, West Virginia. His mother died when he was three, and he was adopted by

Walter Dean Myers (Photo by Constance Myers. Courtesy of Walter Dean Myers.)

Herbert and Florence Dean, who moved to Harlem, New York City. He started writing poems and short stories while still in school, discovering that he enjoyed being a storyteller. He also read voraciously, borrowing books from the public library. His family could not afford to send him to college, and he left high school without graduating. At the age of seventeen, he joined the U.S. Army for three years. After that, he worked in various jobs, including factories, construction, and the post office, while pursuing his hobby of writing. His career as a writer began when he won a contest for picture book writers. His story became the basis of his first book, *Where Does the Day Go?* (1969). During the 1970s, he wrote more picture books while also working in an editorial position at the Dobbs-Merrill publishing company. During this period, he also wrote his first novels for young adults, *Fast Sam, Cool Clyde, and Stuff* (1975) and *Mojo and the Russians* (1977). The success of these novels stimulated him to turn out more work at a prodigious rate. During the 1980s he published, on average, two young adult novels per year, including *Fallen Angels* in 1988, which won the prestigious Coretta

Scott King Award and was named Best Book for Young Adults by the American Library Association. *Fallen Angels* was dedicated to Myers's brother, who was killed in action in Vietnam in May 1968. Myers published another eleven young adult novels during the 1990s.

As of 2008, Myers has written more than eighty-five books, including novels, poetry, short stories, and nonfiction. In 2008, he published *Sunrise over Fallujah*, a novel about the battle for Fallujah, Iraq, in 2004. He has won numerous awards, including five Coretta Scott King Awards, two Newbery Honor awards, the Margaret A. Edwards Award, the Virginia Hamilton Award, and the Michael L. Printz Award.

Myers is married with three grown children, and he lives in Jersey City, New Jersey.

PLOT SUMMARY

Fallen Angels begins in Anchorage, Alaska, in September 1967. A group of American servicemen are waiting for their plane to be refueled before they fly to their destination, South Vietnam, where they will join U.S. forces in the Vietnam War. The story is narrated by seventeen-year-old Richie Perry, an African American soldier who has just finished basic training. He is nervous about going to Vietnam, although he is not expecting to see any combat. He has a bad knee and has been told that he will probably receive a desk assignment and then be sent home.

On his arrival in Vietnam, Richie is assigned to the Twenty-second Replacement Company. He makes friends with Peewee Gates, another black soldier, and learns from some of the other guys that there is not much fighting going on, and the war will soon be over. Richie also meets Jenkins, a frightened new recruit. Peewee boasts about how many Viet Cong (enemy fighters) he has killed, even though he has not seen any combat yet. Richie, Peewee, and Jenkins fly to the American base at Chu Lai. After a truck ride they are assigned to Alpha Company and meet another black soldier, Johnson. They are flown out by helicopter, and Richie is told by the captain they may soon go to Hawaii, because the war is almost over. In spite of his bad knee, Richie is sent on patrol, which passes without incident, but when they are back in their base area, Jenkins steps on a mine and is killed.

Richie is stunned by Jenkins's death. He hears about the interrogation of a VC (Viet Cong) and also about white phosphorous, an artillery round that burns anything it touches. They go to a village to befriend the local population, and then, after sitting around doing nothing for a while, get called out by helicopter to secure a landing zone to help Charlie Company, which is pinned down by the enemy. When they return to base, they hear that Charlie Company lost nine soldiers.

Richie does guard duty with a soldier named Lobel. They sit in a foxhole for hours talking about movies. Another day, a television crew films the men at the base and follows them as they go on patrol. They find a VC and kill him, although Richie has forgotten to load his rifle. Later they learn that the dead man was not a VC, a guerrilla fighter, but a member of the regular North Vietnamese army.

Richie learns that the official report on the incident states that three enemy soldiers were killed, instead of one. Richie knows this is incorrect. The following morning he becomes ill with acute diarrhea. The next notable incident is that Johnson and another soldier, Walowick, trade insults and get into a vicious fight. Richie writes a letter for Peewee, to Peewee's former girlfriend.

Richie gets sent out on patrol with Charlie Company, fourth platoon. They come under fire and fire back, but a tragic error has been made. They are attacking their own first platoon, which takes many casualties. Richie is distressed and cannot sleep that night.

Richie's squad goes on a pacification mission, which is a visit to a nearby village, bearing gifts, attempting to befriend the villagers. On their return, Richie receives a letter from his younger brother Kenny, and he replies immediately, sending him money so he can join a basketball league. He promises himself that he will write more often to Kenny, and to his mother.

Bad news comes in. Another company of soldiers has gone to pacify the same village, and two of them have been injured or killed. It is also known that at night the VC go to the village and terrorize it. Therefore, Richie's squad has to return to the village and lay an ambush outside it to prevent the VC from going in. During the ambush, they kill two Viet Cong. Other Viet Cong return fire, and Lieutenant Carroll is wounded. Richie's squad fires on the village, and a helicopter joins in the attack. Civilians run for their lives. The helicopter flies them to Chu Lai, where Lieutenant Carroll dies.

At the request of Sergeant Simpson, Richie writes a letter of condolence to Carroll's wife in Kansas. The men are upset by the death of their leader. Richie is summoned to headquarters to see Captain Stewart. He witnesses an aggressive interrogation of a Viet Cong prisoner, and Stewart congratulates him on the letter he wrote.

Under their new leader, Lieutenant Gearhart, Richie's squad escorts a civilian pacification team to a village. Back at the base, Richie writes to his mother, and later they all watch TV and see themselves in the film made by the TV crew that accompanied them earlier. It is nearly Christmas.

At night they get hit by a rocket attack and take casualties. There are rumors of a truce, and Richie writes to his mom that he expects to be home within a couple of months. But the war does not end; instead, the action heats up, and Richie hears the far-off sounds of artillery and explosions constantly. The Viet Cong attack major cities in South Vietnam.

Flying out by helicopter, Richie's squad goes on patrol to stop nighttime traffic between two villages. They set up an ambush, but Gearhart makes a mistake: he sets off a flare and reveals their position to the enemy. The squad comes under fire, and as they clamber onto the helicopter to get away, one of the new squad members, Turner, is wounded. He dies by the time they get back to camp.

Captain Stewart asks Richie to rewrite a letter that Gearhart has written to Turner's family. Gearhart had blamed himself for Turner's death, but Richie rewrites the letter to put Turner in a heroic light and eliminate any mention of Gearhart's culpability.

Alpha Company is sent to the first village Richie's squad visited, in order to protect it from attack by the VC. The helicopter lands under fire and they try to secure the village. However, the Viet Cong have gotten there first; there are many dead and wounded, and the huts are on fire. The VC wanted to show the villagers that the Americans could not protect them. Richie is almost killed when a VC is about to shoot him, but the gun misfires. Richie kills him. Eventually, the Americans move the survivors out and burn the entire village down.

Alpha Company then goes to the city of Tam Ky, which is frequently being attacked. Richie's squad, working with South Vietnamese troops (ARVN), goes on patrol and sets up an ambush. The ambush is not sprung, however, because there are too many VC passing through and the squad would have been wiped out.

The next patrol involves the whole of Alpha Company. The soldiers come under heavy fire and scramble up a hill. They reach the top and fire down the other side. Brew and Richie are hit, and the call goes out to go back down the hill. Richie is treated by Jamal, the medic, and airlifted out. In the helicopter, Brew dies, while Richie's wounds are minor. He spends a short time at a medical facility, where he meets up with Judy Duncan, a nurse he met on the journey to Vietnam. Then he receives orders to report back to his unit. He sits around during a week when it rains continuously, and then does guard duty.

Men from Charlie Company bring in a Vietnamese woman and two children who were crossing a paddy field. The woman is allowed to leave, and as she reaches the edge of a dike she hands one of her children to a soldier from Charlie Company. The child is carrying explosives, and the soldier is killed. The woman runs away but is shot and killed, as is her other child.

Richie's squad explores a small hill near the village of Phuoc Ha, where the enemy has been noted. They go through a wooded area and then wait for a while, after which they head back toward the rice paddy, trying to draw fire from the enemy. They draw no fire, and they dig in on the hill and then return to the paddy and regroup at the landing zone. Having decided that the hill is safe, the ARVN try to take it, followed by Charlie Company. Richie's squad follows Charlie Company. The ARVN cross the paddy field but come under fire from the hill. They take many casualties. Richie's squad is involved in heavy fighting, gains cover, and holds its position. Under pressure, the South Vietnamese and Americans decide to take the nearby village, which they surround as the Viet Cong defends it. With the help of gunships, the Americans take the village, but Sergeant Dongan is killed.

The American soldiers burn the bodies. Soon after they move out, they encounter a platoon of VC moving across an open field, and they open fire. The Viet Cong are mowed down. Richie narrowly escapes when a rocket-propelled grenade (RPG) is fired in his direction. A U.S. plane drops napalm, setting the trees on fire. Helicopters pick the U.S. forces up and take them back to base.

Their next mission is a patrol about four kilometers away, near a river, to make sure that no Viet Cong slip through. Gearhart goes with another squad, leaving Brunner as squad leader. Lobel and Walowick climb to the top of a ridge without incident but come under fire near the river. Returning fire, they kill four Viet Cong. Returning the way they came, Peewee and Richie check out the ridge again. When they reach the top, they see that a firefight has broken out below them. It is dark, and Peewee and Richie wait. They do not know the outcome of the fight. They fire on some Viet Cong, and their fire is returned. There are Viet Cong climbing the ridge, and Peewee and Richie hide in a spider hole dug by the Cong. They wait all night. In the morning, they hear Vietnamese voices again, and a Viet Cong approaches the spider hole. Peewee and Richie pull him into the hole and kill him. They make their escape, even though Peewee is wounded, and wade across the stream to the pickup zone. They find Monaco and save his life by killing a Viet Cong who had him in his sights. A helicopter picks them up, but Richie is wounded in the leg. Peewee and Richie are taken to the hospital, where they are treated for their wounds. Richie also learns that Judy Duncan has been killed. Although Richie and Peewee will recover, their wounds are serious enough for them both to be sent back to the United States.

CHARACTERS

Brew

Brew, short for Brewster, is a black soldier in Richie's squad. He is religious, prays a lot, and wants to go to theology school at Virginia Union University. He wanted to avoid the draft by going to Canada but did not have the courage to do it. Brew is killed in action while on patrol.

Brunner

Brunner is a very tall and strong blond soldier in Richie's squad who seems to have a chip on his shoulder. He is married and lives in Seattle. When Lieutenant Gearhart goes on another mission, Brunner, who has been promoted to sergeant, takes charge of the squad when it is on patrol.

Lieutenant Carroll

Lieutenant Carroll is the leader of Richie's platoon. He is a quiet, serious, religious man from

Kansas. The men respect him because he once risked his life in an effort to rescue some of his men who were trapped under enemy fire. Carroll has plans to open a bookstore with his wife, Lois, when he returns home to Kansas, but he is killed during an expedition to a Vietnamese village.

Joe Derby

Joe Derby is an injured soldier from Las Vegas whom Richie meets in a medical facility.

Sergeant Dongan

Sergeant Dongan is a first sergeant from Richmond, Indiana, who is assigned to Richie's squad as a replacement for Sergeant Simpson. He is older than the other soldiers, probably in his thirties, and a veteran of the Korean War. The men are suspicious of him at first but soon find out he is an excellent soldier. He is killed in an assault on a village.

Lieutenant Doyle

Lieutenant Doyle is an officer in Charlie Company. He is from New Jersey, and he tried to evade the draft but was caught by the FBI.

Judy Duncan

Judy Duncan is an American nurse whom Richie meets on the flight to Vietnam. He meets her again in the medical facility where he recovers from his wound. She is later transferred to a field hospital and is killed when it comes under attack.

Peewee Gates

Peewee Gates joins the squad at the same time as Richie does, and they become best friends. Peewee is an African American from Chicago who dropped out of high school. He is a tough character, not given to self-doubt, and does not allow anyone to intimidate him. He also betrays no fear of being in Vietnam. In fact, he is always wisecracking, as if he does not have a care in the world. Less reflective than Richie, Peewee just gets on with the job of soldiering. He does have a softer side, however, and he is genuinely fond of Richie and offers him comfort when it is needed. Peewee sustains a serious wound in battle and is sent home to the United States on the same plane as Richie.

Lieutenant Gearhart

Lieutenant Gearhart becomes Richie's platoon leader as a replacement for Lieutenant Carroll. In his mid-twenties, he is from Wilmington, Delaware, and is a former football player for Delaware

State. On patrol, Gearhart makes an error in sending up a flare that reveals their position to the enemy, but he later makes up for his mistake by making the correct decision not to spring an ambush because enemy numbers are too high.

Jamal

Jamal is the medic. He is nervous whenever he is caught up in any action, and on one occasion he is close to a complete breakdown. He always manages to pull himself together and do the job that is required of him.

Jenkins

Jenkins joins the squad at the same time as Richie. His father is a colonel, and at his father's urging he has taken advanced infantry training. But he is scared to be in Vietnam and has a premonition he is going to die there. He is killed shortly afterwards, when he steps on a mine near the base.

Johnson

Johnson is a tall, powerful black soldier in Richie's squad. He is from Savannah, Georgia. He has had machine-gun training, so he is given the big M-60. Johnson is a strong personality who emerges as the de facto leader of Richie's squad, even though he is only a corporal. Once, when they are moving out of a burning village, Johnson takes no notice of an instruction from Captain Stewart, and the men follow him, not Stewart. Johnson is upset by the death of Brew and refuses to accept that his comrade is gone.

An Linh

An Linh is a Vietnamese girl about seven or eight years old who lives in the village that Richie and his squad visit on a pacification mission. Richie and Lobel befriend her.

Lobel

Lobel is a Jewish member of Richie's squad who gets promoted to sergeant. His father is a movie director, and Lobel is a movie fanatic. He thinks movies are more real than real life and has ideas for how the Vietnam war could be made into a movie. He was not drafted but enlisted in the army to impress his father, but his father is opposed to the war and writes letters to his son in which he tells Lobel about the growing opposition to the war back home.

Monaco

Monaco is an Italian American soldier in Richie's squad. He played baseball and football for his high school in Bayonne, New Jersey, and he bonds well with the black soldiers. Richie and Peewee save his life by shooting a Viet Cong who would otherwise have killed Monaco.

Kenny Perry

Kenny Perry is Richie's younger brother. He is between nine and eleven years old. Richie is fond of him and writes to him often. Kenny writes back, saying he has a job at a drug store in New York.

Mabel Perry

Mabel Perry is Richie's mother. Her husband left her when her younger son, Kenny, was four, and she has been raising both sons on her own since then. She and Richie often argued, and they do not seem to communicate well with each other. When Mabel writes to Peewee, she says she does not understand why Richie joined the army. All she knows is that he did not seem happy at home.

Richie Perry

Richie Perry is the narrator of the story. He is a seventeen-year-old African American from Harlem, New York, raised in a tough neighborhood by a single mother. He has a younger brother, Kenny. Richie graduated from high school with good grades, and his dream is to attend college and write like James Baldwin, a famous black writer. But he decided to join the army because his family is poor, and he thought that he would be able to send his mother money so she could buy Kenny some clothes that would help him stay in school. Richie also wanted to get out of Harlem.

Richie excelled in basketball at high school, but he injured his knee, so he is not expecting to see combat in Vietnam. However, his medical profile takes a while to catch up with him, and he goes into battle anyway. He is, naturally enough, scared, but he learns to perform his duties well, even though on one occasion he forgets to load his rifle. He gets along well with the other squad members, especially Peewee Gates, who becomes his best buddy.

Richie has a difficult relationship with his mother, and he thinks she did not understand what he needed. In Vietnam, he thinks of her a lot and of how much he needs her. He also thinks about the usual things that a boy of his age might. He has never had a girlfriend and wishes he had one to write to now. In the months he is in Vietnam

he experiences combat on many occasions. He sees his comrades die. He is almost killed himself and is slightly wounded twice. He kills more than one enemy soldier. Faced with these extremely difficult experiences, he thinks about God and reflects seriously on war and why he is in Vietnam, but he is never able to come up with a satisfactory explanation of why the war is going on. He is relieved in the end to make it back home in one piece.

Rings

Rings is a black soldier who wears three rings on his hand. He wants to take an oath of brotherhood with the other black soldiers by mingling blood. Peewee and Richie do not take him seriously.

Father Santora

Father Santora is a Catholic chaplain. He gets the soldiers to pray with him, although he cannot promise that the prayers will protect them.

Scotty

Scotty is a soldier with Charlie Company. He is from Tacoma, Washington, and he enlisted in the army because there was nothing much else for him to do. He tells Richie that the only thing he is good at is operating an M-60 machine gun.

Sergeant Simpson

Sergeant Simpson is the sergeant of Richie's squad. He is an efficient, competent soldier, and the men trust him. He calms them down after they witness the mayhem in a Vietnamese village. He chooses to extend his tour of duty for thirty days and is promoted to master sergeant, after which he returns to the United States.

Captain Stewart

Captain Stewart is one of the senior officers with Alpha Company. All the men think he is getting more aggressive against the VC because he wants to boost the body count before his tour of duty ends so that he will be promoted to major. He eventually gets his wish and is promoted.

Nate Turner

Nate Turner is a black soldier from the South who is newly assigned to Richie's squad. He is killed on his first patrol.

Celia Vilas

Celia Vilas is an attractive nurse from Puerto Rico. Richie meets her when he is recovering from his second injury.

Walowick

Walowick is a Polish American soldier who is already in the squad when Richie joins it. He is from Galesburg, Illinois, and he likes playing chess. He wants to go to Knox College in his hometown when he returns from Vietnam, and he wants to study music because he thinks that would be easy. Richie considers Walowick to be steady as a rock as a soldier, although Walowick does lose his composure during the horrific time at the village that has been attacked by the Viet Cong.

THEMES

Confusion about the Purpose of the War

Richie often expresses puzzlement about what the war is about. When he arrives, his understanding is that the Americans are there to stop North Vietnam taking over South Vietnam. But as the days and weeks go by and he experiences combat, he finds that such easy formulations no longer satisfy him: "The real question was what I was doing, what any of us were doing, in Nam." When the visiting television crew interviews the members of the squad and asks them why they are fighting in Vietnam, almost all the soldiers give different answers, based on what they have been officially told, but they are not convinced either. They show an interest in the pacification program because "it was like the closest thing to a real answer about why [they] were in Nam." At one point, Richie says to Johnson that he assumes someone back in the United States knows what they are doing and why, implying that he is unable to figure it out for himself. He is finding out that for the infantryman in Vietnam, the main purpose is to stay alive and not be concerned about the actual purpose of the war because there are no satisfactory answers. Although the chaplain tells the men that they are "defending freedom," Richie remains unconvinced. Toward the end of his time in Vietnam, he concludes, "The war was about us killing people and about people killing us, and I couldn't see much more to it."

TOPICS FOR FURTHER STUDY

- Some analysts have compared the U.S.-led war in Iraq to the Vietnam War. Is there any truth to these comparisons? Research both wars to determine how they are similar and how they are different. Write an essay in which you explain your findings.

- Using any medium in which you feel comfortable—drawing, painting, poetry, prose, or music—create a tribute to the Vietnam veterans. Try to create something that captures the essence of the veterans and what they went through in Vietnam. Think about the qualities you want to portray—courage, heroism, endurance, or whatever other qualities you feel are appropriate.

- Research posttraumatic stress disorder (PTSD) and its occurrence in Vietnam veterans. What is this condition? When was it first discovered, and by what other names has it been known? How is it treated? Give a class presentation in which you discuss your findings.

- Locate your local Vietnam Veterans of America chapter. (Visit http://www.vva.org/witest/chapters.aspx to search for your chapter.) Inquire about locating a veteran who would be willing to talk to you, either in person or by telephone or e-mail, about his or her experiences in Vietnam or life after the war. Ask the interviewee if you may record and share the interview. Give a class presentation in which you replay or recount portions of your interview and talk about what you learned from it.

Fear

The soldiers of Richie's company live constantly with fear, knowing that on patrol or in a firefight they can be killed or wounded at any time. Fear is presented as the natural reaction to the dangers of war, not something to hide or be ashamed of. Everyone feels it, and no one tries to convince the others that he is fearless. After his first

U.S. Marines in South Vietnam (*Archive Holdings Inc. / Getty Images*)

experience of being in a firefight, Richie admits to himself, "I had stood trembling in fear and waiting, and had run in near panic for the choppers and hoped and prayed for a few minutes more of life." A short while later, as they go to reclaim a village from the VC, he confesses, "I was scared again. Wasn't there ever going to be a time when I wasn't scared?" He is not the only one. Jamal, the medic, is scared. So is Father Santora, and he is not ashamed to admit it to Richie. After a particularly fierce incident, Lieutenant Gearhart's hands are shaking so badly that he cannot light a cigarette. But what is also noticeable is that the men overcome their fear; it does not prevent them from acting bravely in battle. They do what they have to do.

Comradeship

What sustains the men during the long ordeal of war is the comradeship they build as they face common dangers and look out for one another's safety. Although the men of Richie's squad get into arguments and even fights with each other, they also form deep bonds of friendship. Johnson, in response to Sergeant Dongan's belief that Lobel may be gay, tells Richie, "A man in Nam

fighting by my side is a man fighting by my side." He does not care about anything else; what matters is the men's solidarity with one another as they go into battle together. In particular, Richie and Peewee develop a close relationship. After Richie is stunned by his killing of a VC who was about to kill him, Peewee "put his arm round my waist and told me to come on." That night when Richie cannot sleep, disturbed by what happened, Peewee comforts him. Later, Peewee wants to make sure that if anything happens to him, Richie will get an old coin that he has at home. Peewee does not have much that is valuable, but what he does own, he wants his friend to inherit. Richie also bonds deeply with Monaco. When Richie returns to the squad having recovered from his wound, Monaco is overjoyed to see him and hugs him. Richie is deeply touched by this demonstration of affection. Later, when Richie has been wounded again and is being taken into surgery, Monaco holds his hand, prompting Richie's reflection, "I had never been in love before. Maybe this what it was like, the way I felt for Monaco and Peewee and Johnson and the rest of my squad." Amidst the horror and the death, what shines out is the comradeship of men who risk all together.

STYLE

Metaphor of the Angels

The title of the novel is explained when Lieutenant Carroll offers a prayer following the death of Jenkins. He asks God to allow them to feel sorrow for "all the angel warriors that fall." He explains the next day to Richie that his father used to refer to all soldiers with that phrase because soldiers are usually no more than boys, many of them not even old enough to vote. Angels thus become a metaphor for the soldiers, implying an innocence due to their youth. The metaphor may also carry another, darker meaning. The soldiers are fallen angels in the sense that they have been forced to lose their innocence in the chaos and cruelty of war. In the Bible, Lucifer is a fallen angel; as he falls his nature changes from good to evil, so in the novel the metaphor suggests that the soldiers as fallen angels are compelled to perform acts such as killing that go against their better natures.

South Vietnam Setting

Most of the action in the novel takes place near the American naval base at Chu Lai in what was then South Vietnam. Chu Lai is located about fifty miles southeast of the city of Danang, in the northern part of the country. Chu Lai is hot and muggy, and Richie is soon dripping with perspiration. He notes that "the air in Nam was always hard to breathe; it was heavy, thicker than the air back home." Mosquitoes are a constant nuisance, as is the threat of diseases such as malaria and other, more minor irritants. Richie gets diarrhea and Walowick a bad skin rash, and the men talk of the "Nam jungle rot," which can be fatal. However, Richie also notes moments of beauty that are strangely connected to the activity of war: "Two jets streaked across the sky. Beautiful. Dark birds in a sweeping arc across a silver sky."

HISTORICAL CONTEXT

Origin and Early Stages of the Vietnam War

After World War II, communist and nationalist forces in Vietnam battled with French forces that were trying to reestablish their control over the country. The French were defeated in 1954 at the battle of Dien Bien Phu. As a result, Vietnam was divided at the 17th parallel. North Vietnam became a communist state, with the capital at Hanoi. One of the goals of North Vietnam was to reunify Vietnam, and beginning in 1956, North Vietnam aided communist Viet Cong guerrillas in South Vietnam. American involvement in Vietnam began in 1961, when President John F. Kennedy sent military advisers and helicopters to aid the South Vietnamese government. In August 1964, the United States claimed that North Vietnamese boats fired on a U.S. destroyer in international waters. This incident, that took place in the Gulf of Tonkin, led the U.S. Congress to pass the Gulf of Tonkin Resolution, which authorized President Lyndon Johnson to use military force against North Vietnam without a formal declaration of war from Congress. In February 1965, the U.S. commenced bombing of military targets in North Vietnam. In April 1965, the number of U.S. troops in South Vietnam rose to 60,000 and reached 184,300 by the end of the year. That year also marked the first major battle involving U.S. forces. It was called Operation Starlite, and it involved an attack on a Viet Cong regiment in order to preempt a VC attack on the U.S. base at Chu Lai. In Operation Starlite, about 600 Viet Cong soldiers were killed; American casualties included 45 dead and more than 200 wounded. In 1966, the number of U.S. troops in Vietnam rose again, reaching 385,000, with 60,000 stationed offshore. That year, 6,000 Americans were killed in Vietnam, and 30,000 were wounded.

The Vietnam War in 1967

During 1967, the war in Vietnam continued to escalate. American bombing campaigns in North Vietnam continued, with airbases, factories in Hanoi and Haiphong, and rail lines being targeted. However, in December 1967, Secretary of Defense Robert McNamara admitted to a Senate subcommittee that the bombing had not achieved its objective of reducing North Vietnam's ability to send supplies to its fighters in South Vietnam or damaging North Vietnam's economy. In December, there were an estimated 400,000 Viet Cong or North Vietnamese army personnel in South Vietnam. In that month, U.S. troop strength was at 475,000, the highest number yet. In November, General William C. Westmoreland, the commander of U.S. forces in Vietnam, stated that the United States was winning a war of attrition against the enemy. Enemy losses during 1967 were estimated at 13,000 per month, including those who were killed or captured and those who defected. U.S. losses included 9,352 servicemen killed. In addition, 11,135 South Vietnamese troops died.

COMPARE
&
CONTRAST

- **1960s:** The United States fights in the Vietnam War. Peace talks begin in 1968. The number of U.S. troops in Vietnam reaches its peak of 543,000 in 1969. Antiwar demonstrations peak in the same year, with 250,000 people marching in Washington D.C.

  1980s: Vietnam, now under communist rule, starts to cooperate with the United States regarding the unresolved issue of American servicemen missing in action (MIA).

  Today: Although Vietnam still has a communist government, the United States has normal diplomatic and trade relations with the country.

- **1960s:** U.S. forces drop napalm on targets in Vietnam. Napalm is a controversial, highly flammable explosive used to burn vegetation in order to clear an area. However, the dropping of napalm also results in civilians, including children, being badly burned.

  1980s: Napalm is used in at least two military conflicts. Israel uses it in Lebanon in 1982, and Argentina uses it against British forces in the 1982 Falklands War.

Today: In 2001, the U.S. military destroys its last remaining stocks of napalm. However, firebombs similar to napalm are used by U.S. jets during the Iraq War in 2003.

- **1960s:** The United States fights in Vietnam as part of a cold war strategy to contain communism. Wars involving this strategy are often considered proxy wars—wars in which two superpowers fight indirectly through the use of third parties—and are common throughout the cold war between the United States and the Soviet Union.

  1980s: The United States continues to engage in proxy wars in countries such as Nicaragua and Afghanistan in order to prevent communism from spreading.

  Today: The United States is engaged in wars in Iraq and Afghanistan. The goal is to create stable societies that will not provide a base for international terrorist networks. Terrorism succeeds communism as the primary foreign policy concern of the United States.

Twenty-four thousand Vietnamese civilians died in 1967 as a result of the war, and 76,000 were wounded. The pacification program, called Civil Operations for Revolutionary Development Support, which attempted to win support for the anti-communist cause amongst civilians in South Vietnam, was widely regarded as ineffective.

There were indications during that year that the North Vietnamese were willing to begin negotiations, but none developed. A halt to the bombing of North Vietnam was thought to be necessary for peace talks to begin, but the United States insisted that the North must reduce its military operations in the South before bombing would be halted.

Meanwhile, at home, public opinion turned against the war. In April 1967, a crowd of an estimated 125,000 people marched in protest in Washington, D.C. In September, a public opinion poll showed that a majority of Americans opposed the war. The war become even more unpopular when the draft call increased and President Johnson imposed a 6-percent surtax to pay for the war. In June 1967, a Gallup poll showed that half of respondents did not know why the United States was fighting in Vietnam. Opposition to the war also increased in the U.S. Congress.

The Later Stages of the Vietnam War

In January 1969, President Richard Nixon took office and promised to achieve a negotiated peace with North Vietnam that would preserve South Vietnamese independence. By the beginning of 1972, U.S. troop strength in Vietnam was reduced

Vietnam War Memorial in Washington, DC *(Image copyright IMDigital, 2009. Used under license from Shutterstock.com.)*

to 133,000, from a peak of more than half a million in 1969. Fighting continued, but most of it was conducted by South Vietnamese forces. In January 1973, at peace talks in Paris, a cease-fire was signed. In March of that year, the last U.S. combat soldiers left Vietnam. However, North Vietnam did not long observe the cease-fire and resumed its attacks on South Vietnamese cities. At the end of April 1975, North Vietnamese forces captured Saigon, the South Vietnamese capital, bringing the war to an end. South Vietnam no longer existed as an independent country, and Vietnam was reunited under communist rule.

CRITICAL OVERVIEW

Reviews of *Fallen Angels* were favorable. In *School Library Journal*, Maria B. Salvadore describes it as a "compelling, graphic, necessarily gruesome, and wholly plausible novel. It neither condemns nor glorifies the war but certainly causes the reader to think about the events." In *Horn*

Book, Ethel L. Heins praises the author as "a writer of skill, maturity, and judgment" and compares the book's depiction of a young soldier in the midst of war to Stephen Crane's *The Red Badge of Courage*. In the *New York Times Book Review*, Mel Watkins has high praise for the way the characters are presented. Although some are stock types that one might find in any war story, Watkins says, the author allows "his main characters to emerge as interesting, complex people rather than just stereotypical soldiers." In particular, Watkins praises the characterization of Peewee Gates, "whose humor and unique view of life act as counterpoint to the grim depiction of war's reality." After noting that the story describes the battles in realistic detail and gives full measure to the fear and anxiety experienced by the young soldiers, Watkins concludes:

> *Fallen Angels* is a candid young adult novel that engages the Vietnam experience squarely. It deals with violence and death as well as compassion and love, with deception and hypocrisy as well as honesty and virtue. It is a tale that is as thought-provoking as it is entertaining, touching and, on occasion, humorous.

WHAT DO I READ NEXT?

- *Sunrise over Fallujah* (2008) is a sequel to *Fallen Angels*. Just as the earlier novel had graphically presented the reality of the Vietnam War, *Sunrise over Fallujah* does the same for the U.S. war against Iraq, begun in 2003. The novel features Robin "Birdy" Perry, Richie Perry's nephew, as he takes part in the 2004 battle for control of the Iraqi city of Fallujah.

- In *A Life in a Year: The American Infantryman in Vietnam, 1965–1972* (1993), by James R. Ebert, more than sixty infantrymen who served in Vietnam tell their stories in their own words. The book shows just how realistic and true-to-life *Fallen Angels* is.

- *The Things They Carried* (1990), by Tim O'Brien, is a highly acclaimed book that can be read as a memoir, novel, or collection of short stories about the men who fought in Vietnam and what they carried—not only physical objects but also emotions and memories.

- *A Vietcong Memoir: An Inside Account of the Vietnam War and Its Aftermath* (1986), by Truong Nhu Tang, is a memoir by a founding member of the Viet Cong. Tang's book is both an autobiography and an account of the Vietnam War from the other side. It has been praised by reviewers for its reasonableness and its eloquence.

CRITICISM

Bryan Aubrey

Aubrey holds a Ph.D. in English. In this essay on Fallen Angels, *he discusses the novel as a coming-of-age story.*

Fallen Angels is at once a riveting adventure story about one of the most problematic wars in American history and a coming-of-age story about one particular soldier who finds himself under fire in the paddy fields and jungles of

> THUS, RICHIE LEARNS A GREAT DEAL IN HIS FOUR MONTHS OF WAR, AND THE BURDEN OF IT IS SUCH THAT WHEN THE MOMENT COMES FOR HIS RETURN TO THE UNITED STATES, HE FEELS MORE DEAD THAN ALIVE."

Vietnam. When Richie Perry signs up for the army he is seventeen years old, just out of high school and without much life experience. Growing up in Harlem, New York, in a single-parent family, Richie was a good student and excelled at basketball. His ambition was to be a writer, but his mother did not have the resources to enable him to attend college, so his ambition seems only a far-off dream. At seventeen, then, Richie is a young African American living in Harlem with no direction in his life. What is he to do? The world does not seem to offer him much. Street life in Harlem is not for him. He once witnessed some gang activity in which, he later learned, a boy was killed. Richie is too intelligent and possesses too much common sense to get caught up in that kind of thing. But what else is he to do? Like many young African Americans in similar positions, he elects to join the U.S. Army, which offers him a chance of getting away from Harlem and the life he has known. His experience in Vietnam tests him severely; he discovers the meaning of friendship and courage, he considers matters of faith and religion, and he learns about the disturbing complexities of right and wrong. He also faces the horrors of death and dying. In short, Richie has to grow up very quickly, under the most extreme circumstances. When he returns home after just over four months of duty, he has changed irrevocably from what he was before, and well he knows it.

The first thing Richie discovers when he arrives in Vietnam is his capacity for fear. This comes as a surprise to him. He comments, "I had never thought of myself as being afraid of anything. I thought I would always be a middle-of-the-road guy, not too brave, but not too scared, either." But he discovers that he is in fact scared every time he leaves the base, every time he goes on patrol or gets into a firefight. He also learns that he is not alone in his fear; when death may lurk around every tree or in every stretch of tall grass, fear is the most natural reaction a person can have. Richie throughout demonstrates an admirable ability to not blame himself for the way he feels or for the mistakes he makes. As a rookie soldier, he does not always do things right. The first time he tries to fire his rifle, nothing happens, and he later discovers that he forgot to load it. He also sets the claymores out facing the wrong direction; if not for a VC intervening and changing the way they are pointing, they could hit Richie's own men. But Richie does not torment himself with guilt about these incidents, and they do not undermine his confidence in himself. He is a young man who shows great capacity to learn from his experiences, both on the battlefield and in his interactions with other soldiers at the base.

One thing he learns is that the government that sent him to Vietnam does not always tell the truth. It becomes a standing joke amongst the men that their side exaggerates the number of enemy dead. As his friend Peewee says, "Yeah, every time we shoot one of them his cousin and his uncle die, too." Richie also notices that the war seems different when he reads about it in the U.S. military newspaper, *Stars and Stripes*. The newspaper only occasionally mentions U.S. casualties, "but the numbers didn't seem to even match the numbers I saw in the hospital unit," he states. He is learning that, as someone once said, in war, the first casualty is truth, and it is not only the enemy that lies. He also finds out that in the midst of daily acts of courage, raw ambition rears its head, too. It is a common belief amongst the men of Richie's squad that Captain Stewart is determined to win a promotion to major, and they fear that he will take unnecessary risks with their lives in order to achieve his objective.

As Richie absorbs the lesson that under the surface of things, reality may be different from how it first appears, he thinks more deeply than the others about the nature of the conflict they are in. While most the soldiers in his squad simply accept without thinking that they are the "good guys" and the VC are the "bad guys," Richie is willing to probe a little further into such easy formulations, even if such thoughts make him uncomfortable. He clearly sees the distinction the others make. They are willing to see humanity in only one side. They will grieve for their own dead, but enemy dead are regarded as barely human. In contrast, Richie has a capacity to see the humanity even in the enemy. To him, they are still people, with their own lives and their own thoughts. When he hears some VC talking, for example, he wonders, "What were they talking about? The lousy chow they got in the army? Their families?" A short while after he has killed a Viet Cong, he remembers a picture he has seen in a hut in the village, of a man with a bicycle, and he wonders whether this was the man he shot. His thoughts are not of himself but of the other man:

> I wondered what he would have said if he had killed me. Would he have said that he was trying to stop the spread of whatever the hell he thought I stood for? What did he think I stood for? What did the bullets feel like going into his face?

He shows here that he has the capacity to imagine how life might appear to those on the other side, the enemy. This is a gift that one might expect to find in a writer, which is exactly what Richie wants to be. It is less common, perhaps, to find it in an infantryman in the midst of the Vietnam War, and although Richie never for a moment shirks his duty, which involves fighting and killing the enemy, he is too intelligent not to see some of the ironies and contradictions involved in dividing people into good and bad with no shades in between. When he hears a remark by Johnson, almost meaningless in itself, that they are in Vietnam simply because some killing needed to be done, Richie thinks that "maybe the time had passed when anybody could be a good guy." He has learned in a very short time how in war, soldiers can be called upon to perform acts that put their own humanity, their moral sense, in jeopardy.

It is these very situations that cause Richie's thoughts sometimes to turn to faith and God, subjects he appears not to have given much thought to back in Harlem. As he is about to enter a danger zone, it occurs to him to say a prayer, but he does not know any. He borrows a Bible from Brew and apparently learns the Lord's Prayer. Later, the first line of that prayer pops into his mind as he waits in an ambush for the battle to begin. By the end of the novel, he has learned how to pray, in his own way, for the safety of his comrades.

Of course, learning how to pray does not mean he is no longer haunted by the dreadful sights and sounds of the battlefield. He cries for the dead Brew and keeps hearing the sound of the zipper on the body bag as it closes up over his friend's dead body. He struggles to deal with horrors like this in simple, honest language, trying to express his awareness that human life should not be like this, that humans are made for something different: "People were not supposed to be twisted bone and tubes that popped out at crazy kid's-toys angles. People were supposed to be sitting and talking and doing. Yes, doing." His words may not be eloquent, but they are deeply felt: life is for the living; death in war is a cruel waste.

Like many young men his age, Richie has some emotional insecurities, and he feels peer pressure to be a certain type of person. He has such thoughts regarding his inexperience with women, for example: "The thing was I was a virgin. I didn't tell anybody because I wasn't supposed to be a virgin." He thinks like this because he has certain ideas of what young black men, and also soldiers, are presumed to be like. But as in other areas of life, he discovers that reality and stereotypical expectation do not always go hand in hand. He also learns much about love. As he continues his train of thought about his lack of experience, he regrets that he has not "loved anything deeply." He soon discovers that love takes many forms and that the feelings he develops for his comrades, the men who risk their lives in battle with him, and who try to protect him as he tries to protect them, are also a kind of love. He develops a particular bond with Peewee, which reaches a moment of truth near the end of the novel, when the injured Peewee cannot continue to run as they try to reach safety. Peewee tells Richie to continue and leave him behind. Richie replies, "Never happen, man. I'm not leaving you, Peewee." He will save his comrade or die with him. Just as he has commented a little earlier, "we had all learned something about dying, and about trying to keep each other alive," he now experiences the selflessness of real love, and this is a deeper thing entirely than his earlier superficial regrets about never having made love to a woman.

Thus, Richie learns a great deal in his four months of war, and the burden of it is such that when the moment comes for his return to the United States, he feels more dead than alive. Along with Peewee and Monaco, he has been within an inch of death, and as he observes to Monaco, "We're all dead over here ... and just hoping that we come back to life when we get into the World again." As he sits in the airplane that will take him home, it is as if the slim metal tube is another birth canal for him, that will deliver him again to the World (the term the soldiers use to refer to the world outside the war in Vietnam). He must somehow engineer his own rebirth, knowing that he is a different man from the one who first set foot in this killing zone in a distant corner of southeast Asia.

Source: Bryan Aubrey, Critical Essay on *Fallen Angels*, in *Novels for Students*, Gale, Cengage Learning, 2010.

Walter Dean Myers

In the following essay, Myers discusses how, as a child, he escaped from the trials of his everyday life through reading.

My last two years in high school were absolutely miserable. In the junior and senior years of a highly competitive school, one's whole existence becomes the frantic preparation to enter the next highly competitive situation. Even the most casual conversations turned to SAT scores and grade point averages. What were the Ivies looking for? What extracurricular activities gave you the biggest boost toward getting into a "name" college? Where were the scholarships?

The problem for me was that my family had grown so dysfunctional (alcoholism, depression, an uncle murdered) that even a free New York City high school had become a financial and emotional burden. My grades suffered accordingly.

And so I hid from my classmates and their discussions of colleges. I stayed away from school for weeks at a time. I went to cheap flicks on 42nd Street. I took long walks around the city. But mostly I tried to lose myself in books. I would read in Central Park if I found myself there. I would read on the subways that took me from Harlem to lower New York and Brooklyn. Books and reading became my life.

Somewhere along the way I discovered a precarious balance between the intellectual intimacy of the books I read and my personal alienation from a world in which I didn't seem to belong. Shakespeare, André Gide, Honoré de Balzac (authors suggested by my English teacher) were guides to a world I couldn't see and only sensed existed. But they were excellent guides, at hand day and night, always comforting.

Sometimes, in retrospect, I am saddened by my lost school years. But at other times I wonder if that odd, isolated life with books was what I was meant to have all along. Perhaps what I saw as a turning away was really a turning toward— leading me toward a reality it has taken me a lifetime to articulate. What I wonder most now is whether my English teacher knew it as well.

Source: Walter Dean Myers, "Reading Became My Life," in *Horn Book Magazine*, Vol. 84, No. 5, September/October 2008, p. 512.

Jennifer M. Brown

In the following excerpt from an interview, Myers discusses the connection between Fallen Angels *and his 2008 novel* Sunrise over Fallujah.

In 1988, Walter Dean Myers wrote *Fallen Angels* (Scholastic), a novel narrated by Richie Perry, just out of high school and off to Vietnam. Myers, like Perry, was very young when he went to Vietnam, and he lost a brother there. Twenty years later, Myers returns to the battlefield with *Sunrise over Fallujah* (Scholastic, 2008), a story set during the current Iraq War. This novel, also narrated by a newly graduated high school senior, unfolds through the eyes of Robin "Birdy" Perry, nephew to *Fallen Angels*'s Richie. Here Myers talks about what he learned as a young man in Vietnam, what he has learned about war as a more seasoned man, and what we as a nation still have to learn.

Why did you create a blood connection between the narrators of your two novels?

I think it was my own disappointment that we're still fighting wars. When I was 17, I was going into the army, at the beginning of a war that was then controversial, and still is; my son was in the Middle East; my grandson was in the Middle East. We haven't learned anything.... There was a time when we thought the threat of nuclear war would stop all wars. I don't believe that now.

With both narrators, you maintain an air of innocence, or perhaps hope, about them. Why?

I wanted [Birdy] to discover the layers. In the Army everyone takes infantry training and learns how to use weapons and how to defend himself. Then you go "in country" and you begin to see, okay this is complex. There are [international laws governing engagement] ... It's supposed to be precise, but it isn't. What do you say to yourself [when you've just killed someone?] How does a young person handle that psychologically?

Positioning Birdy within the Civil Affairs group was inspired.

Something I hope to accomplish with the book is getting young people to think [beyond], "Oh, these are bad people, these are terrorists." ...

One of the things that struck me as I followed the After Action reports from some of the Civil Affairs units was that many of the units realized the needs of the local people. The soldiers couldn't get them the things they needed through regular military channels. They'd [write in letters or emails home], we wish we had more toothpaste or books. On the one hand, soldiers are shooting and killing people, and on the other hand, churches are sending everyday supplies to them [for the Iraqi villagers].

In both books, the narrators are told the war is "just about over." Why?

In Iraq, there was "Shock and Awe." ... The Iraqi army, as expected, laid down their arms. That part of the war was over. Mission accomplished; relatively minor loss of life from the American point of view, and not that much from the Iraqi point of view. [But] war isn't like that. War doesn't happen that way. There's a price to pay and we're still paying that price.

In this war, as opposed to even the first Gulf war, there are different rules of reporting. [Reporters] are not allowed to show coffins or wounded people.... How are young people going to understand any of this? What are they seeing? ... And how are they going to make decisions about who to vote for in November when people aren't giving them the whole picture? When they're told 4,000 people were killed in Iraq? But 20,000 more have core injuries—to the brain, to the spinal column, loss of limbs— injuries that will affect the life of the soldier forever. We'll be living with the effects of this war well into 2050.

In both [Fallen Angels] *and* Sunrise over Fallujah, *when an officer dies, the commanding officer says a prayer for the "angel warriors." Is there any significance to that prayer for you?*

When I was doing research for *Monster* (HarperCollins, 1999), I went to prisons. One thing that struck me was that none of the prisoners were born bad. They were all born good; they were born with an aura of innocence. They were, in effect, angels to me. Something happened along the way that damaged them.

With our soldiers, the thing that really gets to me is that they are kids who are 18, 19, and 20 years old—kids who are in high school, playing high school ball, and looking for first dates—and we turn them into soldiers. America has the youngest combat soldiers of all the major countries with organized armies. In many countries, you can't enter combat until you're 19 or 20. In America you can enter combat at 17. They're children, just precious young people that we're losing. Even up to 25 and 30 years old, they're still, to me, civilians who've been turned into people who can kill, will kill, and who in turn will be killed. Human beings are meant for better than that.

Source: Jennifer M. Brown, "Two Decades Later, the Angel Warriors Continue to Fall: Walter Dean Myers's *Sunrise over Fallujah*," in *School Library Journal*, May 15, 2008.

Olubunmi Ishola

In the following interview, Myers talks about art, jazz, and his collaborations with his son, Christopher Myers.

Olubunmi Ishola: Your new book, Harlem Summer, *is about a young African American boy, Mark Purvis. Mark is in a jazz band with some of his friends and becomes involved with jazz musicians and jazz poets throughout the course of the novel. Your books are known for providing a compelling perspective on hard-hitting issues faced by at-risk youth. You also seek to portray the beauty of the African American experience, requiring young adults to question their values and decisions. What message do you feel jazz has to offer at-risk youth, especially those in the African American community? What do you want young adults to question and think about as they read* Harlem Summer?

Walter Dean Myers: All art involves the interplay of discipline and creativity. In *Harlem Summer*, my young protagonist comes to realize that what he sees as a casual activity, the jazz explosion of 1920s Harlem, actually represents a seriousness and work that is belied by the joy of performance. As he sees the characters from the Harlem Renaissance pass through the office of *The Crisis*, he begins to understand that there are young people in the world very much like him but who have adopted a seriousness and maturity that he hasn't seen previously. I would like young people to realize that the different levels of life are self-generated and not dependent on race or economic status.

OI: In Harlem Summer, *many historical figures are brought to life: Countee Cullen, Langston Hughes, W.E.B. Du Bois, Jessie Fauset, Fats Waller, Queenie, Bumpy Johnson, and others are*

> "I'M MORE AND MORE INTERESTED IN THE WAYS YOUNG PEOPLE DEVELOP THEIR VALUES AND THE DIFFICULTIES THAT SO MANY INNER-CITY KIDS FACE WHEN FORCED TO MAKE ADULT DECISIONS AT AN EARLY AGE."

all connected through sixteen-year-old Mark Purvis. I know that, while growing up in Harlem, you also rubbed shoulders with many such figures. Is this book, in some way, autobiographical?

WDM: The idea of *Harlem Summer* came from stories I heard at home in Harlem. My dad worked occasionally for the notorious gangster Dutch Schultz. Schultz had, beside his numbers business and other illegal enterprises, several legitimate companies. One of them was a moving company located a few blocks from where I lived and down the street from Fats Waller. My father worked on Schultz's moving vans. My parents attended rent parties in which Fats played and regaled his audience with his humor and songs.

OI: How much research did you undertake in re-creating these characters? Was your goal to depict their personalities as historically accurate as possible, or did you take creative liberties?

WDM: I did quite a bit of research in putting this story together. I have the major black newspaper of the day, the *Amsterdam News*, on microfilm and could follow what was going on in the black world on a weekly basis through that paper. I also have all of the issues of *The Crisis*, the magazine at which my hero worked, so I knew what was being published in 1925 and by whom. I also consulted the biography of Langston Hughes, who came to my church to read and sell his books, as well as a number of books on the Harlem Renaissance.

OI: Besides young-adult novels, you've written a great deal of poetry. Here in Harlem: Poems in Many Voices, Harlem, *and* Blues Journey *are all compelling pieces that invoke a musical feeling with their words. Similarly, jazz poetry demonstrates jazz-like rhythms, tone color, or the feel of improvisation through literary style. How would you define jazz poetry? Would you call yourself a jazz poet?*

WDM: Jazz poetry tries to emulate some of the complex rhythms of jazz and uses a musical vocabulary. I don't consider myself a jazz poet, but rather a poet whose works reflect his cultural heritage. Since my heritage is both African American and European, my poetry varies accordingly and is also affected by what I'm reading at the time.

OI: What do you feel is vital about the dialogue jazz provides between the artist and audience?

WDM: Jazz is meant to be physically interactive. The musician wants his listener to respond to the music by feeling the rhythm and at least wanting to move with it. Many old-time jazz musicians considered their performances to be most successful when people got up and started dancing.

OI: To follow up the previous question, you've collaborated with your son, Christopher Myers, on Jazz *and* Blues Journey, *two books that seek to express music in words and pictures. How is that collaboration between words and art, and the dialogue it creates, similar to the dialogue between artist and audience? How does it differ?*

WDM: Most picture books are done with the writer and artist far away from each other. In these instances, it's the editor bringing the work together into one creative endeavor. This is good, but when I work with my son, Chris, we feed off each other. I'll present a text and then Chris will respond to that text with his art. He doesn't just want to illustrate my words but to contribute his own vision to the overall piece. When I see what he's done, the nuances he brings to the work, I'll often change the text to add accents to his images. Sometimes, as we discuss ideas that we might like to work on in the future (a constant conversation) I will try to build a vocabulary around his visual concepts or try to change the rhythm of my text to contrast with his style.

OI: You've called jazz "America's gift to the world"; it is probably one of the few things that can be considered an integral part of American culture. However, jazz lacks some of the popular appeal that other styles of music have. Why do you think this is so?

WDM: Music in the United States has been heavily influenced by changing media as well as production costs. The big bands of the 1940s and 1950s were too expensive by the mid-1960s. The rise of the rap artists can be attributed largely to inexpensive production costs. Getting performers into a studio or on a set for a day and producing a video that doesn't have to have high production values is relatively risk free. Getting professional classical or jazz musicians into a performance where production values are very demanding is very expensive and therefore risky.

OI: Of the different styles of jazz—ragtime, big band, bebop, modal, cool, fusion, free, etc.— which is your favorite? Who are some of your favorite jazz artists?

WDM: I first attended jazz performances during the Count Basie and Duke Ellington period, so the big band era remains a favorite. I've always loved Louis Armstrong and the pianists of the renaissance period—Fats Waller and James P. Johnson were great. I'm most recently influenced by some of the fusion stuff from the Miles Davis-Keith Jarrett hard-rock period of the 1970s. I like the challenges the music presents, and I see myself as fusing writing styles.

OI: Is there a recent book that has captured your interest?

WDM: I'm currently reading *The Psychology of Action*, by Peter Gollwitzer and John Bargh, which discusses how people make decisions to act as opposed to internal decisions of preference. I believe that not enough attention is being paid to the differences between preferences and actions as it applies to inner-city kids. I'm also reading *Grace Under Fire: Letters of Faith in Times of War*, edited by Andrew Carroll, a fascinating and uplifting book.

OI: What outside the realm of literature has drawn your attention of late?

WDM: I'm more and more interested in the ways young people develop their values and the difficulties that so many inner-city kids face when forced to make adult decisions at an early age.

OI: What current writing projects do you have underway or have planned for the near future?

WDM: I am in the middle of a book on the war in Iraq, which is filling my head and soul with its challenges. I'm also planning a book on African American dance with the same format as *Jazz*.

Source: Olubunmi Ishola, "An Interview with Walter Dean Myers," in *World Literature Today*, Vol. 81, No. 3, May/June 2007, p. 63.

Jennifer M. Brown

In the following interview, Myers describes how his hobby of collecting rare books and photographs translated into a writing career.

The first thing Walter Dean Myers does when he arrives in town for a book signing is pull out the Yellow Pages and start searching for rare-book dealers. What began as an interest in finding images of African-American life in books and photographs has developed into a burgeoning number of children's books, written by Myers himself. His hobby has come full circle and is now a vocation. And while it is Myers who is showing children the heritage of African-Americans, it was children themselves who piqued his initial interest in collecting antique photographs.

While teaching writing to Jersey City grade-schoolers in the late 1980s, Myers asked his students to bring in photos of their grandparents as children, and was moved by their reactions. "The kids loved the photographs," he recalls. "They wanted to learn why their grand parents would wear those kinds of clothes, shoes, what kind of house they lived in. The kids took to them so warmly that I thought, 'There's something here.'"

Their enthusiasm for the photographs led to the book *Brown Angels* (HarperCollins, 1993), designed like an antique photo album with Myers's original poetry place alongside photographs he had collected. To extend readers' experience of the book, Myers created a tour for the original pictures in their antique frames. The exhibit, which included some 120 pieces, opened at the Newark Public Library; from there, roughly half of the pieces toured to various cities across the country.

A HISTORY THROUGH IMAGES

Myers believes that it is important to convey the strength of African-Americans and their history through photographs. "Kids know that 'Black is beautiful' is a slogan from the 1970s," he says, "but unless they see the images, they don't believe it." The sepia-toned photographs he collected for *Brown Angels* show African-American children from the past who were loved and celebrated; as Myers says, through this album, readers can "see an adorable child nicely dressed, nicely cared for."

In *One More River to Cross: An African American Photograph Album* (Harcourt, 1995), Myers moved from presenting images of children

in the past to historical images of adults, from "black nuns to black Jews to black jockeys," Myers says. Unlike the majority of pictures showcased in *Now Is Your Time: The African-American Struggle for Freedom* (HarperCollins, 1991), which portrays more prominent African-Americans, the photos Myers collected for both *Brown Angels* and *One More River to Cross* show people who are not well known, in the midst of their everyday routines. "The value of seeing those photos," he adds, "is showing that a black person can be any old thing. Kids say they want to play in the NBA or rap because we haven't given them permission to consider anything else."

Myers's most recent book, *At Her Majesty's Request: An African Princess in Victorian England* (Scholastic, 1999), is perhaps the most direct result of his rounds with rare-book dealers, who Myers says comprise a tightly knit community. Having learned of Myers's hobby a London dealer sent him notice of a packet of letters penned by Sarah Forbes Bonetta, an African princess. One of the major stumbling blocks to his purchase of the letters was that several had been written by Queen Victoria, and Myers had to get special clearance to take them out of the country

Once he purchased the letters, Myers spent a great deal of time figuring out whether or not he could piece together the events that occurred between the lines, as it were. "Here's this fairly literate lady acting as if she has no care in the world in her letters to Mrs. Schoen [her guardian] or the Queen," Myers observes. "Yet as a young girl she was almost killed, and she knew that."

While going through his own extensive library for possible clues to Sarah's life, he serendipitously uncovered a book penned by Frederick E. Forbes, the captain who rescued the princess and brought her to Britain in 1850. And later, in one of the most interesting wrinkles of Myers's "wild goose chases," he discovered that Forbes had played a prominent role in another major event. While the author was involved in research for the movie Amistad, he discovered that Forbes was also involved in destroying the "barracoon" or internment camp where the slaves aboard the Amistad had been held, at the end of the 1841 trial (this never made it into the film, however).

His serpentine route to complete *At Her Majesty's Request* led Myers from Windsor Castle to the Internet, where he discovered a photo of the princess as part of an exhibition in

Ontario. "[It's] one of the longest books I worked on," he says. Not only was the preparation for the book lengthy, but his fascination with its subject continues. In his last trip to London, Myers solved the mystery of the hotel where Sarah spent her final days. He says, "I'll be researching her for the rest of my life." Myers is on an autographing tour for the book March 22–27 in the Washington, D.C., area as well as Dallas and Chicago.

A MORE INCLUSIVE HISTORY

In his books, Myers aims to give his readers a comprehensive picture of the past, one that includes, rather than omits, African-Americans. When he was in school, history lessons left him cold. "History books give you the standard, 'Give me liberty or give me death,'" Myers says. "In school, you're taught that this is a valuable history. By extension, what you don't learn is not valuable." Myers wants to share with readers his discoveries of blacks who fought on both sides of the Revolutionary War, for instance, or the fact that at least one-fourth of the cowboys in the Old West were either black or Hispanic.

"Kids today will say, 'We're not interested in black books,'" he says. "The reason is that so many [of them] are a history of oppression, in which blacks are portrayed as victims. Kids don't want to read that. They want to read about being triumphant."

When he was growing up, Myers wanted to be a writer, but didn't think it possible because he knew of no black writers. "[Ralph] Ellison and [James] Baldwin were just coming along, and we weren't taught about Zora Neale Hurston or the Harlem Renaissance," he recalls. Instead, he read books by Thomas Mann and Andre Gide. "I met Langston Hughes one day [in Harlem], sitting on the stoops, drinking beer, but I didn't think much of him. He didn't fit my stereotype of what serious writers should be. He wasn't writing about Venice," Myers says. "Then Baldwin wrote about my neighborhood; he gave me permission to write about my neighborhood."

Myers wants to do the same thing for today's readers. In his words, "I want to write books where a child says, 'I'm going to feel good about myself.'" Whether in the photographs of beautiful children in *Brown Angels* or through the stories and images of diverse and courageous lives, Myers wants to give children permission to become whomever they want to be.

"HOPEFULLY I LEAVE MY READER WITH QUESTIONS. IF THEY OBJECT TO THE WAY THINGS END, THAT'S OKAY. LIFE FOR MOST PEOPLE DOESN'T END WELL. JUST THE FACT THAT IT ENDS IS A BUMMER. TO AN EXTENT, YOU HAVE TO REFLECT THAT REALITY.'"

Source: Jennifer M. Brown, "Walter Dean Myers Unites Two Passions," in *Publishers Weekly*, Vol. 246, No. 12, March 22, 1999, p. 45.

Amanda Smith

In the following interview, Myers discusses his life, work, and audience and rejects the notion that he might serve as a role model to young African Americans.

"I'm not interested in building ideal families in my books. I'm more attracted to reading about poorer people, and I'm more attracted to writing about them as well."

The speaker is Walter Dean Myers, and he is more than just attracted to writing. Since his first book, *Where Does the Day Go?* (Parents Magazine Press), appeared in 1969, the author has produced almost 40 works for young readers, primarily about black children and youths. His settings range from beleaguered inner cities (Newbery Honor Book *Scorpions*, HarperCollins, 1988) to wartime Vietnam (*Fallen Angels*, Scholastic, 1988). Out within the next few months will be an autobiography of Malcolm X, entitled *By Any Means Necessary* (Scholastic), and *The Righteous Revenge of Artemis Bonner* (HarperCollins), a picaresque tale set in the Wild West. Also debuting this fall is the 18 Pine St. series (Bantam), created by Myers (which he will oversee but not write); the series deals with teen problems and is designed to appeal to black teenagers.

Myers approaches his subjects with the authority of his own experience. He was born Walter Milton Myers in 1937 in Martinsburg, W. Va., a small town with two distinctive features—a V.A. hospital and surrounding apple orchards. His mother died in childbirth when he was three, and his impoverished father gave him to a family named Dean to raise—hence his nom de plume. His interest in foster children has translated itself into fiction in such books as his *Won't Know Till I Get There* (Viking, 1982), about a caring, stable family's decision to take in a teenage boy from a troubled background.

The Deans had children of their own; the father, a "tough, caring, hardworking, good man," held two or three janitorial jobs simultaneously, to try to make ends meet. The family eventually moved to Harlem, and Myers's birth family ended up moving around the corner from them. Myers describes his Harlem youth as "a nice childhood," distinctly different from the deeply troubled lives he writes of. "I had no problems. It was home. You got Mama. You got Daddy. You have no responsibilities. It's just a wonderful life. Every adult could grab you on the street and shake you if you were doing something bad. If you threw paper on the street and a neighbor caught you, it wouldn't be unusual for one neighbor to stand there to guard the piece of paper while another went and told your mother and you had to go back down the street and pick it up. People cared for and loved those children. It was good. Warm. I loved Harlem."

He was a "bright child" who could read before he began school, but had a severe speech problem. "They say they have a name for it now, but at the time they just called it mushmouth." In his shyness he turned to books. When he reached high school age, another obstacle presented itself: he realized that his foster parents would be unable to send him to college. "My folks couldn't send me to even a free college. There were days when I didn't have clothing to wear to high school, and I just didn't go. I realized at that point that it just wasn't going to happen, and I was crushed. I was ashamed. I was hurt."

He dropped out of school, got into various kinds of trouble, "survived the army," came out and "knocked around in very low-level jobs—messenger, cable twister." (In his mid-40s, Myers eventually got a degree from Empire State College, some 15 books into his career.) He originally began to write as "an avenue of value—just anything, for the tabloids, for what were then men's magazines, outdoor stuff, some quarterlies.

"I was going to be this 'serious writer,'" he says. He heard about a contest run by the Council on Interracial Books for Children, entered and won, and in 1969, at the age of 32, his winning book was published: a picture book called *Where Does the Day Go?*, in which a man elicits children's responses as to where they think the day disappears to at night.

Meanwhile, Myers continued producing short stories aimed at the black literary market. One wound up in the hands of an editor who ran into him at a party and, thinking it was part of a larger project, asked him how the rest of the book went. "I said, 'It goes like this,' and I made it up on the spot. She offered me a contract. That was my first book for teenagers, *Fast Sam, Cool Clyde and Stuff* [Viking, 1975]." The editor was Linda Zuckerman; Myers has stayed with her as she moved from Viking to Harper to Harcourt Brace Jovanovich. Because he is so prolific, he has worked consistently with two other editors as well—George Nicholson (originally Zuckerman's boss) and Jean Feiwel.

In each case, writer and editor develop each project collaboratively. While he has a longstanding relationship with his editors, he observes that "increasingly editors are not as active, not as engaged in the literary community as they once were. They seem to be more desk-bound. Fewer publishers read the slush pile. Editors seem to be working harder in a narrower field. They don't seem to be able to call someone up and say, 'Let's develop a project.'"

Noting that the publishing industry numbers few members of most minority groups, Myers says, "If you want to open up the ethnic channels, you need to have people who are interested, who know who the writers are, who are willing to go out into the communities and find people. That's not happening. It's happening to a certain extent at HarperCollins because it is sponsoring a mentoring program [in which established writers offer themselves as conduits for young, unpublished writers into the publishing world]. You have people writing, but no one's reaching out. I've been in writing workshops [for people of color] and I've never seen an editor there. Unless you get ethnic editors, you're not going to have that."

Myers himself reaches out through his writing. He sets much of his fiction in contemporary Harlem, which is radically different from the Harlem of his youth. "You didn't have guns then," he begins. "You had the beginning of drugs—dope fiends, as we used to call people who used drugs. You had authority figures. You had segregation, which put within the black community people who were judges, teachers; middle class, upper-middle class were right there because they couldn't escape. That had a remarkably stabilizing effect.

"What you need in the school system, and the community, are people to set standards. It's tough now primarily because the poverty is all over the place. You don't have that many pockets of stability. A young man could find some kind of blue-collar work. If you were willing to work, those jobs were there. Now they're not.

"Kids see what's going on. The last people who should ever use drugs are children in the inner cities, because they see firsthand the devastation that the rest of us only see on television, glamorized. These are the kids who step over the bodies and draw potsy squares in the chalk lines of bodies."

The children Myers writes about are often at the mercy of forces beyond their control, such as a fatherless home, or are asked to handle things beyond them; in *Scorpions*, a 12-year-old boy is given a gun by a boy a few years his senior—a not uncommon experience in American inner-city life. As Myers points out, "Kids are getting mixed messages. What entertains us is sex and violence. The films that make the most money are violent films. Twelve or 13 years ago, the kinds of violence we see in films today would have been a parody.

"We sell every single thing in the world through sex—books, watches, cars, beer. And then you tell kids, You shouldn't go out there and have a sexual relationship. It's a joke. I try to give my kids values—I try to create value systems within the home and try to bring them within a certain community. But if you have people who are less articulate, less lucky, where do they get their values? From outside. This is a city in which John Gotti is a hero."

His new series, *18 Pine St.*, the address of a pizza parlor and teen hangout, deliberately provides an alternative to violence and sensationalistic sex. Under the editorship of Judy Gitenstein, Myers creates an outline for each book and supervises the writing, which is done by several other writers. *18 Pine St.* is "romance, it's good values. Kids want role models. [These are] little moral tales that I do, with enough romance to be interesting...."

Of Myers's other upcoming books, the biography *By Any Means Necessary* reflects his interest in black history; *Now Is Your Time!* (HarperCollins, 1991), his history of African Americans, won the Coretta Scott King Author Award last year. On the other hand, *The Righteous Revenge of Artemis Bonner*, with its 1880s setting and its lighter tone, extends Myers's already substantial range. "I was interested in writing something about a different era—it puts my head in a different place. Kids don't know about that era.... Many of the incidental characters were actual people. It's fun to write something about the good guy and the bad guy."

Myers finds plots "a dime a dozen, the easiest thing." He and one of his three children played ball in the park once with a boy who disappeared. "The next thing I saw, he had shot someone. That was *Scorpions*. You see something about, say, a pregnant girl, and you write something like *Sweet Illusions*, about teenage pregnancy. I don't know if anybody will want to read it, but I would like eventually to do a book on how kids get sucked into and feel about drugs. I've got more ideas than I've got time to do them."

Does Myers have trouble with the dark vision in his books? "Less now than before. And only because the people I'm dealing with usually don't have that kind of background. Most of my editors don't know anything about drugs except what they've seen on television and in the movies. It's one thing to hear about steroids; it's something else to know what kinds of pressures are brought to bear [on children to excel in athletics]. Sometimes people say [a book] is unrelentingly dreary. And yet, that life is out there. If you write about a homeless child, everybody wants you to write that everything turns out okay. It's not like that.

"Hopefully I leave my reader with questions. If they object to the way things end, that's okay. Life for most people doesn't end well. Just the fact that it ends is a bummer. To an extent, you have to reflect that reality."

Myers says he "got some flak" about the violence and language in *Fallen Angels*, his novel about day-to-day life and death in the Vietnam war. Myers is a veteran though he never went to Vietnam; but his younger brother Sonny was sent there and was killed on his first day. Myers's sadness and guilt for having been the model for Sonny's enlistment eventually found some release in writing *Fallen Angels*. The best letter he has received in response to the book came from a boy who had been enthralled by the Persian Gulf war. "He was so excited he couldn't wait until he turned 17 to join up. He read my book and changed his mind."

Myers says he doesn't see himself as an example for younger blacks. "I made a conscious decision that what I need to do is what I do—write. I need to do it as best I can. I'm not going to be a role model. I don't like the idea. I work harder than most people, and I've been lucky."

Myers found himself writing for children and teens, because, as he puts it, "It's where I found myself one day, and I said, 'Isn't this a nice place to be?' Sometimes I think if I had not gotten into this field, I would be writing novels for adults. I don't think I have even explored what I can do. I think I can do more." Given how much Myers has already accomplished, it will be interesting to see where he chooses to go from here.

Source: Amanda Smith, "Walter Dean Myers: This Award-Winning Author for Young People Tells It Like It Is," in *Publishers Weekly*, Vol. 239, No. 32–33, July 20, 1992, p. 217.

Maria B. Salvadore

In the following review, Salvadore commends Fallen Angels *for its realism.*

A riveting account of the Vietnam War from the perspective of a young black soldier. Richie Perry, a 17 year old from Harlem, arrives in Vietnam in 1967. His first-person narrative provides an immediacy to the events and characters revealed. His experiences become readers' experiences, as do his fears and his insight about this war, any war. "We spent another day lying around. It seemed to be what the war was about. Hours of boredom, seconds of terror." During one of those terrifying times, a large number of American soldiers are killed. Because they cannot be carried back, the decision is made to burn the bodies. "I was afraid of the dead guys. I saw them, arms limp, faces sometimes twisted in anguish, mostly calm, and I was afraid of them. They were me. We wore the same uniform, were the same height, had the same face. They were me, and they were dead." In the end, when Richie is wounded, he returns home. This is a compelling, graphic, necessarily gruesome, and wholly plausible novel. It neither condemns nor glorifies the war but certainly causes readers to think about the events. Other difficult issues, such as race and the condition of the Vietnamese people, are sensitively and realistically incorporated into the novel. The soldiers' language is raw, but appropriate to the characters. This is a book which should be read by both young adults and adults.

Source: Maria B. Salvadore, Review of *Fallen Angels*, in *School Library Journal*, Vol. 34, No. 10, June/July 1988, p. 118.

SOURCES

"Battlefield: Vietnam, Timeline," Public Broadcasting Service Web site, http://www.pbs.org/battlefieldvietnam/timeline/index.html (accessed November 1, 2008).

Butwell, Richard, "Vietnam War," in *The Americana Annual; An Encyclopedia of Current Events*, 1968, pp. 734–38.

Davidson, Phillip B., *Vietnam at War: The History, 1946–1975*, Oxford University Press, 1991.

Heins, Ethel L., Review of *Fallen Angels*, in *Book Review Digest*, Vol. 85, 1990, p. 1191; originally published in *Horn Book*, Vol. 64, July–August 1988, p. 503.

Jenkins, Philip, *Decade of Nightmares: The End of the Sixties and the Making of Eighties America*, Oxford University Press, 2006, p. 215.

Myers, Walter Dean, *Fallen Angels*, Scholastic, 2008.

"Napalm," in *GlobalSecurity.org*, http://www.globalsecurity.org/military/systems/munitions/napalm.htm (accessed November 3, 2008).

Salvadore, Maria B., Review of *Fallen Angels*, in *School Library Journal*, Vol. 35, June–July 1988, p. 118.

Subryan, Carmen, "Walter Dean Myers," in *Dictionary of Literary Biography*, Vol. 33, *Afro-American Fiction Writers after 1955*, edited by Thadious M. Davis and Trudier Harris, Gale Research, 1984, pp. 199–202.

"Timeline: Vietnam," in *BBC News Online*, August 6, 2008, http://news.bbc.co.uk/2/hi/asia-pacific/country_profiles/1243686.stm (accessed February 25, 2009).

Walter Dean Myers Home Page, http://www.walterdeanmyers.net (accessed November 4, 2008).

Watkins, Mel, Review of *Fallen Angels*, in *New York Times Book Review*, January 22, 1989.

FURTHER READING

Goldman, Peter, and Tony Fuller, *Charlie Company: What Vietnam Did to Us*, William Morrow, 1983.
    Two journalists tell the story of sixty-five men who belonged to the combat infantry unit called Charlie Company.

Maraniss, David, *They Marched into Sunlight: War and Peace, Vietnam and America, October 1967*, Simon & Schuster, 2003.

In this Pulitzer Prize-winning book, Maraniss tells two interconnected stories that took place during mid-October 1967: an ambush in Vietnam, in which an American battalion known as the Red Lions fought the Viet Cong in a battle north of Saigon, and an antiwar demonstration that took place at the University of Wisconsin.

Marler, Myrna Dee, *Walter Dean Myers*, Greenwood Press, 2008.

This book surveys Myers's life and work in a format suitable for young readers.

Myers, Walter Dean, *Bad Boy: A Memoir*, HarperCollins, 2001.

Myers writes entertainingly of growing up in Harlem, dropping out of high school, joining the army, and eventually finding his calling as a writer.

Franny and Zooey

J. D. SALINGER

1955–1957

J. D. Salinger's *Franny and Zooey* was first published as two separate stories in the *New Yorker*, with "Franny" appearing in the periodical in 1955 and "Zooey" appearing there in 1957. Though some critics might describe *Franny and Zooey* as two linked short stories, both episodes feature Franny Glass and both take place in almost immediate chronological order. Thus, the continuity of the two stories, as well as their connected and overarching themes, legitimizes reading *Franny and Zooey* as a full-fledged novel. Indeed, they were published as such in 1961 and since then have been reviewed and discussed as a whole. *Franny and Zooey* has become an American classic; among Salinger's work, it is second only to his foremost classic novel, *The Catcher in the Rye*. Notably, both books have remained mainstays on high school curricula and reading lists for several decades.

Franny and Zooey is not only an examination of the Glass family but also a critique of materialism and New England intellectualism. First and foremost, it is an exploration of the intersection between art and spirituality. The book, remarkably, has remained in print since its initial publication. A recent edition was released in 2001 by Back Bay Books.

AUTHOR BIOGRAPHY

J. D. Salinger was born Jerome David Salinger in New York City on January 1, 1919. His father, Sol Salinger, was a successful importer, and the

J. D. Salinger *(AP Images)*

family, including Salinger's mother, Miriam, and his older sister, Doris, enjoyed an upper-middle-class lifestyle. Salinger showed an interest in writing from a young age, neglecting his academic career in favor of this pursuit. He graduated from the Valley Forge Military Academy just outside Wayne, Pennsylvania, in 1936. He next attended New York University, where he wrote and pursued acting, for only one semester. He spent the following semester at Ursinus College in Collegeville, Pennsylvania, where he wrote for the school paper. He also briefly attended Columbia University. Salinger was drafted into the U.S. Army in April 1942. While stationed at Fort Dix in New Jersey, he completed the first draft of his best-known novel, *The Catcher in the Rye* (the book would not be published for another nine years). Next stationed overseas and trained in counterintelligence, Salinger saw action in the famed Battle of Normandy and also participated in the liberation of France. In 1945, he married a French doctor named Sylvia. Little is known about her or the marriage, and the couple divorced in 1947.

After being discharged from the army in 1945, Salinger turned down Simon & Schuster's offer to publish a collection of his short stories. He spent the next few years doing little more than socializing with other literary figures, most of whom congregated in the Greenwich Village neighborhood of Manhattan. When Salinger's first novel was finally published in 1951, it was met with immediate and widespread approbation. Salinger adamantly refused to step into the limelight as the book's author, refusing book tours and interviews and even going so far as to have his picture removed from the book's cover. Two years later, in 1953, Salinger moved to Cornish, New Hampshire. That same year, several of Salinger's short stories, previously published in periodicals, were collected and released as *Nine Stories*. The book was a brief bestseller and received good reviews, though it was not nearly as successful as *The Catcher in the Rye*. On February 17, 1955, Salinger married Claire Douglas, a student at Radcliffe. The marriage lasted for twelve years and produced two children, Margaret Ann and Matthew.

Salinger published two books during the 1960s, but the content of both publications was initially published in magazines during the 1950s. *Franny and Zooey* was released in book form in 1961, but it was first published as two separate stories in the *New Yorker*. "Franny" appeared in the periodical on January 29, 1955, and "Zooey" appeared there on May 4, 1957. *Raise High the Roof Beam, Carpenters; and Seymour: An Introduction* was published in book form in 1963. Like *Franny and Zooey*, the book consists of two lengthy short stories that were first published in the *New Yorker*. "Raise High the Roof Beam, Carpenters" appeared in the periodical on November 19, 1955, while "Seymour" was printed there on June 6, 1959. Notably, both books feature characters from the fictional Glass family. Both books also became bestsellers, though their critical reception was lackluster.

On June 19, 1965, Salinger published "Hapworth 16, 1924" in the *New Yorker* (it was later released in book form in 1997). Though Salinger has reportedly continued to write, no new publications have been released since then. The author has continued to live a reclusive life, making every effort to avoid the public eye. When an unauthorized collection of Salinger's work, *The Complete Uncollected Stories of J. D. Salinger*, was released in 1974, Salinger stepped forward to denounce it. He stepped forward again in 1986, filing suit in an attempt to stop the publication of a biography about him. The biography, Ian Hamilton's *In*

Search of J. D. Salinger was to include several of Salinger's unpublished letters. Ironically, though the biography was eventually published in 1988 without the letters, much of the contested correspondence was reprinted in newspaper articles that covered the initial court battle.

PLOT SUMMARY

Franny

It is a wintry Saturday morning and the big Yale game is to take place later that afternoon. Several male students are at the train station waiting for their girlfriends from the nearby women's colleges to arrive. Lane Coutell braves the cold and stands alone on the platform, rereading a letter from his girlfriend, Franny. In the letter, Franny sounds like a typical adoring girlfriend who loves and misses her boyfriend. It is clear that the letter is important to Lane. When the train arrives, Franny asks Lane if he received her letter, and he responds with feigned nonchalance. Lane asks Franny about the book she is holding, but she says it is nothing and puts it in her purse. She lies and tells Lane she missed him and guiltily holds his hand. It appears that Franny's letter was disingenuous.

The couple is eating lunch at Sickler's, an elite college hangout. Lane feels proud to have such a pretty girl with him. Franny notices his pride and feels guilty for noticing. Lane talks at length about a paper he wrote, though Franny seems distracted. She interrupts him to ask for his martini olive but feels bad when Lane looks affronted by the request. Though his hurt look has ruined the taste of the olive for her, she pretends to enjoy it. As Lane goes on about his paper, she accuses him of being a student who uses his brilliance to tear things apart (as opposed, supposedly, to building things up). The two squabble about this for a bit and order more martinis. Franny apologizes for her behavior and says she should have taken the semester off, that school is an "incredible farce." She apologizes again as Lane presents counterarguments against this statement. Lane will not let the matter drop, even as Franny apologizes yet again.

The two move into a discussion about what defines a true poet. Franny grows increasingly pale and repeatedly states that she does not feel well and does not want to talk about poetry. Lane persists until Franny excuses herself to go to the restroom, and then he finally begins to

MEDIA ADAPTATIONS

- An unauthorized film adaptation of *Franny and Zooey* was released as *Pari* in Iran in 1995. Through the threat of legal action, Salinger prevented the film's New York City debut during the 1998 Iranian Film Festival.

- The 2001 Wes Anderson film *The Royal Tenenbaums* features characters loosely based on the Glass family and contains some scenes reminiscent of those in *Franny and Zooey*. Written by Wes and Owen Anderson and released by American Empirical Pictures, the film starred Gene Hackman, Anjelica Huston, Ben Stiller, Gwyneth Paltrow, Luke Wilson, Owen Wilson, Bill Murray, and Danny Glover.

show concern for her well-being. After Franny has gone to the restroom, Lane sits alone at the table looking dejected. When he sees a fellow student at another table, Lane changes his expression to one of cool detachment.

In the restroom, Franny enters a stall, sits on the floor, and holds herself as she sobs loudly for several minutes. She stops suddenly and removes her book from her purse. She hugs it, puts it away, washes her face, and then walks, smiling, back to the table. Lane asks Franny if she is all right, and Franny replies that she has never felt better. They order lunch, but even Franny's plain meal (she requests a chicken sandwich) annoys Lane. He tells her that they are meeting Wally Campbell at the game. Franny cannot remember meeting Lane's friend, though Lane says they have met several times. Franny replies that Wally looks and acts like everyone else and is thus eminently forgettable. She apologizes before Lane can chastise her, but he does anyway. Franny repeats yet again that she does not feel well, that she feels like she is going insane. Lane is concerned and asks if anything has happened. Franny says she is fine.

Franny tells Lane that she quit acting because it was too much about ego (hers and everyone else's). She explains that she does not want to be like everyone else, just trying to make a name for themselves. Franny repeats that she feels like she is going crazy. Lane asks Franny about her book for the second time that day, and Franny again tries to avoid the question, but Lane persists. Franny tells him that the anonymously authored book, *The Way of the Pilgrim*, is about a man who reads about ceaseless prayer in the Bible. The man sets out to learn how to do this and meets a sage who teaches him how to use the "Jesus Prayer": "Lord Jesus Christ, have mercy on me." Lane seems to be paying more attention to his food (frogs' legs and escargot) than to Franny. He mentions his paper again and ignores Franny's recommendation that he read the book.

Franny tells Lane that the secret to constant prayer, as it is laid out in the book, is that you first repeat the prayer over and over using your lips. Eventually, the prayer becomes second nature, syncopated with a person's very heartbeat. It is at this point, according to the book, that the petitioner experiences a new spiritual awakening. The constant prayer ultimately allows a person to see God. Franny is clearly enamored with the idea, citing similar and numerous examples to be found in vastly different religions and religious texts. Lane remains unimpressed. By now, Franny is chain smoking and has not touched her sandwich. Lane dismisses the idea of spiritual awakening as a psychological phenomenon. The waiter clears their plates. Lane tells Franny he loves her, and Franny responds by excusing herself to go to the restroom. On her way there, she faints by the bar.

Franny regains consciousness on the couch in the manager's office. She says she is embarrassed but otherwise fine. She is worried about missing the game, but Lane insists on taking her back to the girls' dormitory where she is staying for the weekend. Even in the midst of his genuine concern for Franny, Lane crudely hints that it has been far too long since they have been intimate. He goes to get them a cab, and Franny, now alone, begins to move her lips as if she is repeating a silent prayer.

Zooey

Though the narrative up until this point has been in the third person, it now changes into the first person. In a roundabout way, the narrator indicates that he is Buddy Glass, writing in 1957 about events that took place in November 1955. After identifying himself and his family's objections to the way they are about to be portrayed, Buddy lapses from the first person to the third. Buddy describes his handsome little brother Zooey Glass. Zooey is twenty-five years old. He is soaking in the bathtub in the Glass family's Upper East Side Manhattan apartment, smoking and reading a four-year-old letter from Buddy. Zooey is a successful television actor and the second youngest of seven siblings, five boys and two girls. At this point, a footnote in the narrative names all of the Glass children in order of their birth. The eldest, Seymour, committed suicide in 1948 at the age of thirty-one; the second eldest, Buddy himself, is a writer in residence at a women's junior college in upstate New York. Buddy is followed by Boo Boo, a married mother of three. Next in birth order are the twins, Walt and Walker. Walt was killed in 1945 during the occupation of Japan, and Walker is a Roman Catholic priest. The twins were followed by Zooey. Following the footnote, the narrative returns to the main text with a mention of Franny, the baby of the family, eighteen years younger than Seymour. All of the precocious Glass children took part in a radio program called *It's a Wise Child*.

Buddy presents the letter Zooey is reading in its entirety. It was written on the three-year anniversary of Seymour's death. In it, Buddy writes about both the sadness and hilarity of traveling to Florida to retrieve Seymour's body. He also talks about how both he and Seymour were adults by the time Zooey and Franny were born, and how the elder brothers took it upon themselves to teach their youngest siblings everything they could about Eastern religion and philosophy. Buddy also talks about how he waited a year after Seymour's death before seeing Zooey and Franny, hoping to avoid the painful task of sharing in their grief. The letter is the first instance in which Buddy has broached the subject with either of them. Buddy next talks about Zooey's acting career in the letter, calling his little brother by his full name, Zachary Martin Glass. Buddy states that if Zooey ever does "anything at all beautiful on a stage, anything nameless and joy-making," then Buddy and his dead brother will visit Zooey backstage with flowers.

Zooey finishes reading the old and creased letter and then begins to read a script. His mother, Bessie, soon knocks on the door and asks to come in. Annoyed, Zooey puts the script down, draws the shower curtain, and invites her in. While Bessie is ostensibly entering to bring Zooey some new toothpaste, she really wants to know when he is going to talk to Franny, who has been camped out on the living room couch having a nervous breakdown for the past couple of days (ever since the big game at Yale). Zooey gives a noncommittal answer and asks Bessie to leave. Instead, Bessie sits down and says she does not know why Buddy insists on maintaining the private phone line that he and Seymour had in their old room, when Buddy does not even have a phone at his current address. (This complaint has been raging for over four years, as Buddy mentions it in his letter to Zooey.) Zooey says his mother is being stupid. She ignores him and keeps talking about the phone; she wants to get in touch with Buddy and tell him about Franny.

Zooey keeps asking Bessie to leave and she keeps ignoring him. She says that Les (Bessie's husband and the Glass children's father) is also concerned about Franny but that "he's never faced anything as long as I've known him." As if to prove her point, Bessie says that Les still listens to the radio in the vain hope that he will hear his children again (including Seymour and Walt). She says Les "lives entirely in the past." Indeed, Les's solution to Franny's emotional distress has been to offer her a tangerine. Zooey laughs. Bessie calls Franny an "overwrought little college girl that's been reading too many religious books." Like Lane and Franny, Bessie and Zooey have been intermittently bickering throughout their conversation. Both fall silent until Zooey threatens to get out of the tub whether his mother is in the room or not. Bessie leaves but says she will be back. She reminds Zooey to use the bath mat.

A few moments later, Zooey stands at the sink shaving. Bessie reenters the room. She returns to the topic of what should be done about Franny, and Zooey returns to his combative sarcasm. Bessie mentions that Lane has been calling and is concerned for Franny. Zooey says Lane is only concerned about how Franny feels about Lane, not how Franny feels in general. Bessie replies that Lane is the one who told her about Franny's religious book. Franny told Lane that she got the book from her college library, and Bessie says the library should not carry such texts. At this, Zooey becomes very upset. He tells her the book and its sequel, *The Pilgrim Continues His Way* (which Franny has also been reading), were taken from Seymour's desk in the room he shared with Buddy. The books have been there since before Seymour's

death, and Zooey is offended that Bessie did not realize this. Bessie sadly explains that she avoids going into that room. Zooey apologizes.

Several times throughout their conversation, Bessie has been comparing her male children with one another. Zooey finally gets fed up with this and tells his mother that Buddy tries to be like Seymour in so many ways that he might as well kill himself too. He also says that Buddy and Seymour turned him and Franny into "*freaks*" with their childhood indoctrination in Eastern belief systems. He tells Bessie that because of his brothers, he secretly says a prayer called "The Four Great Vows" before every meal, and that he has done so for the last fifteen years. The one time he tried to eat without saying the prayer, he nearly choked on his meal. Bessie has never even heard of the prayer. Zooey again asks his mother to leave the bathroom and she responds by saying that she wishes he would get married. Zooey laughs.

Zooey warns Bessie not to send Franny to a psychoanalyst. He reminds her of what psychoanalysis did for Seymour. He says it will drive Franny to an insane asylum or worse. He also outlines the content of the books that Franny has been reading. Bessie says this explains why Franny has been muttering to herself for the last few days. Zooey and Bessie soon begin bickering again, and Bessie again asks Zooey to talk to his sister. Zooey says he would if he had something useful to say. By now, he has finished shaving and is putting his shoes on. Bessie finally begins to leave the bathroom. As she does, she tells Zooey, "in the old radio days . . . you all used to be so sweet and loving to each other it was a joy to see." She adds, "I don't know what good it is to know so much and be smart as whips and all if it doesn't make you happy."

Franny lies sleeping on the couch in the living room. The room is excessively furnished. It is also cluttered with the memorabilia from *It's a Wise Child* that Les has collected. Zooey, now fully dressed, wakes Franny, who tells him about a dream she was having. The family cat, Bloomberg, is lying with Franny. She and Zooey discuss Zooey's new scripts. During their conversation, Zooey notices that Franny's lips are moving. Zooey critiques his scripts, but when Franny asks why he works on projects he does not like, he says, "Because I'm tired as hell of getting up furious in the morning and going to bed furious at night." He says he hates himself because he makes people feel like they do not want to do good work, only work "that will be thought good." Franny says she is ashamed that this is exactly what she did to Lane. Zooey replies, "We're freaks... [Buddy and Seymour] got us nice and early and made us into freaks with freakish standards... and we're never going to have a minute's peace, the rest of our lives." Franny pets the cat and continues to move her lips throughout the conversation. Zooey says, "I could happily lie down and die sometimes."

Franny says she would tear her fellow students apart in the same way that Zooey has described, even though she would hate herself for doing it. She tells him she could stand college if there were any acknowledgment that knowledge leads to wisdom. She states that in nearly four years of attending college, the only time she ever heard the word "wise" was in reference to a retired politician who made his fortune in the stock market. She says that knowledge has become as much a commodity as all the other "treasures" people spend their time collecting. Zooey points out that Franny is trying to do the exact same thing with the Jesus Prayer, trying to amass something "that's every...bit as ne*go*tiable as all those other more material things." He asks her, "Does the fact that it's a prayer make all the difference?" Zooey wonders if the difference for Franny is "in which side somebody lays up his treasure—this side or the other?"

Franny admits she's been asking herself this very question. She says it is this conundrum (not the prayer or college) that has led her to have a breakdown. Franny is crying. Zooey looks out the window and watches a little girl playing with her dog. He says, "There are nice things in this world...we're all such morons to get so sidetracked." Franny continues to move her lips. Zooey tells her that he does not intend to dissuade her from her prayer. He admits he once thought of doing it himself. But, he also says that he doesn't like Franny's approach. Though she is clearly in pain, her behavior has also been hurtful to their parents, and Zooey disapproves. He adds that while he agrees with Franny's dislike for the ego-infested academic world, she takes her dislike too far by making it personal. However, he admits that he is often guilty of the same thing, even though he knows better.

Lastly, Zooey tells Franny that when she was ten, she decided she no longer liked Jesus because she disagreed with his teachings, namely that man

is superior to other animals. Based on this, he concludes that Franny is "constitutionally unable to love or understand any son of God who says a human being, *any* human being...is more valuable to God than any soft, helpless Easter chick." He accuses Franny of saying the prayer to Jesus as she would like him to be, not as he was. Given this, he asks how the Jesus Prayer is going to help her. Zooey asserts that Franny's breakdown is being caused by faulty logic and that persisting in faulty logic will not make her feel any better. By now, Franny is sobbing uncontrollably. Zooey realizes that he has failed his sister. He wanders around the living room aimlessly and then apologizes. This only makes Franny cry louder, and Zooey leaves the room.

Zooey runs into Bessie in the hallway. She wants to know about his talk with Franny, but he waves her away and goes into his room. He comes out a minute later with a cigar in his mouth and a white handkerchief over his head. For the first time in seven years, he enters Seymour and Buddy's old room. Zooey closes the door behind him and begins to read the quotes posted behind the door. The quotes are taken from various religious texts, novels, and famous philosophers. Zooey then sits at Seymour's old desk for upwards of twenty minutes. He suddenly stirs, opens up one of the drawers, rifles though it, and half reads Seymour's notes about his twenty-first birthday party. Zooey puts everything back in the drawer and then sits for another thirty minutes. Afterwards, he goes over to Buddy's desk and picks up the phone. He removes the handkerchief from his head and places it over the phone's mouthpiece.

Franny and Bessie are in the living room when the phone rings. Bessie goes into her bedroom to answer it. She returns and tells Franny that Buddy is on the phone and wants to talk to her. She says he sounds like he has a cold, which Franny also notices when she gets to the phone. "Buddy" asks Franny how she's feeling and Franny starts to complain about Zooey. When "Buddy" makes a disparaging remark about Zooey, Franny realizes that she is actually on the phone with Zooey, not Buddy. Franny tells Zooey that she knows it is him, but Zooey persists in the ruse. He finally gives up and tells her that he does not really want to stop her from saying the Jesus Prayer. He does point out, though, that the prayer will mean nothing if she does not distance herself from desire. However, he says that Franny became a brilliant actress because of her earlier desire to do so. He says, "You can't just *walk out* on the results of your own hankerings.... The only thing you can do now, the only re*ligious* thing you can do, is *act*. Act for God, if you want to." He also warns her about her previous criticisms of the audience and its ignorance. Zooey tells Franny that "an artist's only concern is to shoot for some kind of perfection, and *on his own terms*, not anyone else's. You have no right to think about those things."

Franny has not been crying during the phone conversation, though she has been silently holding her face in her hands. Zooey tells Franny about a time when he was scheduled to appear on *It's a Wise Child*. Although he did not want to shine his shoes for the radio show, Seymour told him to do it for the "Fat Lady." Franny says that Seymour once told her to be funny for the Fat Lady. Zooey then asserts that "*There isn't anyone out there who isn't Seymour's Fat Lady*." Everyone at school whom she despises, even her stupid audience, are all the Fat Lady. He says, "*Don't you know who the Fat Lady really is? ...*It's Christ Himself. Christ Himself, buddy." At these words, Franny can barely hold onto the phone because she is so happy. Franny and Zooey are both silent for a moment and then Zooey says that he can't talk any longer and hangs up the phone. Franny continues to hold the phone, listening intently to the ensuing dial tone. After a while, she puts the phone down, smiles contentedly, and falls asleep on her parents' bed.

CHARACTERS

Lane Coutell

Lane Coutell is Franny's college boyfriend. He attends Yale and is a member of the intellectual and upper-middle-class elite. Lane is very conscious of social expectations and conforms to them religiously. For instance, though he loves Franny and the letter she wrote him, he responds to both with feigned nonchalance. Lane goes to great lengths not to appear vulnerable and to bolster his masculinity. He is also extremely upset by Franny's behavior while they are at Sickler's. While Lane orders such delicacies as frogs' legs and escargot, as would be expected of him in such a restaurant, Franny orders a plebeian chicken sandwich. Lane is barely able to hide his annoyance at her order, and he is even more annoyed when she leaves her meal untouched.

Lane is acutely aware of other people's perceptions of him. When Franny goes to the restroom and Lane sits looking dejected, he immediately changes his expression to one of cool detachment when he sees a fellow student.

Lane's constant preoccupation with how he is perceived makes him insensitive to Franny's clearly distressed state. He barely listens to her and prefers to talk about himself, even as Franny repeats that she does not feel well and thinks she may be going insane. Though Lane's genuine concern for Franny does surface at times, Lane constantly undermines that concern with his own selfishness. Even after Franny has fainted and he is being truly accommodating to her, he hints that it has been a long time since they have been intimate. Lane is the embodiment of all that Franny is beginning to despise.

Bessie Glass

The Glass family matriarch, Bessie is a former dancer who retains some of her former beauty. She is often to be found wearing a kimono-like housecoat with additional pockets sewn on around the Glass apartment. These pockets contain a plethora of odds and ends, as well as tools. All of the Glass children refer to her as Bessie and they often make fun of her. Buddy ridicules Bessie in his letter to Zooey, and Zooey calls her stupid in her presence on more than one occasion. Bessie has very strong opinions about her children and what is best for them; her abrasive approach to child rearing clearly upsets and annoys her children, as is the case when she barges in on Zooey in the bathroom and continuously pesters Franny to eat some chicken soup. Yet, it is also clear that Bessie loves her children and that she has their best interests at heart.

Bessie is more perceptive than her children give her credit for, as she calls Franny an "overwrought little college girl that's been reading too many religious books." She also makes a perceptive remark about Zooey's personality, one that gives him pause. Indeed, the narrator notes that Bessie is accustomed to making such statements and to the pregnant pauses they incite. Like all of the characters in the novel, Bessie constantly smokes. She is also largely responsible for the disarray and clutter of the Glass family home (she is almost a walking embodiment of that disarray). Bessie is also an archetype of maternal behavior; she alternately admonishes Zooey to use the bath mat, get married, and get a haircut.

Boo Boo Glass

The eldest female child in the Glass clan, Boo Boo is only referred to by her nickname, and her full name is never revealed. Though she is described in Buddy's footnote as a married mother of three, little else is said about her.

Buddy Glass

The second eldest of the Glass family children (and oldest surviving child), Buddy is a writer who is serving as writer in residence at an unnamed women's college in upstate New York. Buddy does not have a phone at his current residence, although he maintains the old private line that he and Seymour kept in their shared childhood room. Everyone in the family clearly looks up to Buddy and solicits his opinion. This is evidenced by Bessie's frustration at not being able to contact him during Franny's crisis, as well as by Zooey pretending to be Buddy on the phone (after his own attempts at consoling Franny have failed). The love and respect accorded to Buddy is also illustrated by the four-year-old letter from Buddy that Zooey has kept and continues to read. Bessie also compares Zooey to Buddy on several occasions.

Buddy's letter to Zooey reveals the pain of handling Seymour's suicide, as well as his acknowledgment that he avoided Franny and Zooey after the tragedy. He encourages his brother to act and act well (just as Zooey later does for Franny). Buddy also seems to be apologizing for his and Seymour's early influence on Zooey and Franny, for flooding them with so much Eastern philosophy, yet it seems that even this damaging behavior was well-intentioned.

Franny Glass

Twenty-year-old Franny Glass is the central character of the novel, though not necessarily its protagonist. The youngest of the Glass children, Franny chain smokes her way through an emotional, spiritual, and intellectual crisis. At its core, the crisis itself is largely unremarkable (i.e., it is typical for someone her age). It centers around the unbridgeable differences between one's internal values and the external values celebrated in the world at large. What is remarkable, however, is that Franny struggles to cope with this crisis, and that she turns to the Jesus Prayer for consolation. Throughout her conversations with Lane and Zooey, Franny demonstrates that she dislikes the academic world, the commoditization of culture (making culture into a product to be bought and sold), and intellectual and spiritual

conformity. She is also disgusted by the role that ego plays in all of these perceived ills. This is why she finds the theory and practice outlined in *The Way of the Pilgrim* and *The Pilgrim Continues His Way* so attractive. It is also significant that these books belonged to Seymour.

When Zooey argues with Franny about her behavior—that while her objections to academia are valid, she takes them too personally, and that the Jesus Prayer is invalid because her recognition and understanding of Jesus is insincere—Franny cries inconsolably. She also admits that the underlying reason behind her breakdown is not her distaste for the commoditization of culture but the question of whether or not her attraction to the Jesus Prayer is also a form of commoditization. Yet, in the end, it is Zooey's suggestion that Franny turn her acting into a form of prayer that begins to console her. When Zooey describes the Fat Lady as both a symbol for everyone, including the audience, and a symbol for Christ, he is conflating everyone (the audience) and Christ, indicating that they are one and the same. Through this argument Franny finally finds peace. Zooey has rationalized Franny's acting for her as a form of the Jesus Prayer itself.

Les Glass

Les Glass never appears in the novel and is only referred to a few times by Bessie and the narrator. A former vaudeville performer, Les is described as a man who does not face anything and who lives in the past, decorating his living room with memorabilia of the children's radio heyday and listening to the radio in the hopes of hearing his children (alive and dead) again. According to Bessie, Les impotently tries to console Franny by offering her a tangerine.

Seymour Glass

Though Seymour has been dead for seven years, his figure (and his suicide) still looms large. Buddy's letter to Zooey is written on the three-year anniversary of Seymour's death, and it is the first instance in which Buddy openly discusses the suicide with his younger sibling. Bessie's obliviousness to the fact the Franny has taken the religious books from Seymour's old desk is clearly upsetting to Zooey, though he relents when Bessie sadly admits that she tries to avoid Seymour's old room. Zooey avoids the room himself. He enters it for the first time since Seymour's death in order to use the phone to call

Franny. That Buddy maintains the old phone in their childhood bedroom is also a clear indication that Buddy is not entirely willing to let go of his brother. Seymour's influence on Franny and Zooey in the form of his and Buddy's instillment of Eastern values is also clearly felt. Zooey and Franny both struggle not to tear down the art and people around them, a fact that Zooey attributes to this indoctrination. Seymour's suicide and the pain it has caused are further underscored by the military death of another Glass sibling, Walt. Indeed, Walt's life and death are barely remarked upon.

Waker Glass
See Walker Glass

Walker Glass
Walker is the fifth Glass child, born just after his twin, Walt. A Roman Catholic priest currently on a mission outside the country, Walker is affectionately referred to by his family as Waker.

Walt Glass
The fourth Glass child and Walker's elder twin, Walt served in the military and was killed in 1945 in a freak explosion while stationed in occupied Japan.

Zachary Martin Glass
See Zooey Glass

Zooey Glass
Zooey can be considered the novel's protagonist, because although the action in *Franny and Zooey* revolves around Franny and her breakdown, it is Zooey's thoughts and ideas that make up much of the narrative. Zooey, like his mother and sister, is often smoking, though he prefers cigars to cigarettes. Five years older than Franny, Zooey shares many of her views, though he is far more equivocal about them. At one time he, too, considered saying the Jesus Prayer. Because of the similar worldviews that Zooey and Franny share, Zooey, of all the Glass children, is best suited to approach Franny. This is not acknowledged by the rest of the family, however, as Bessie tries to get in touch with Buddy in the hopes that he can help her. Even Zooey acknowledges this perception by pretending to be Buddy when talking to Franny on the phone. Nevertheless, although Buddy is narrating the events, he is not an active participant in them, and it is ultimately Zooey who assuages Franny's

crisis. Because he has shared her feelings and learned to cope with them, he is able to impart all that he has learned to this effect. Notably, Zooey blames Buddy and Seymour for turning him and Franny into "freaks." He says that they "got us nice and early and made us into freaks with freakish standards . . . and we're never going to have a minute's peace, the rest of our lives."

Furthermore, it is clear that Zooey has given much thought to the purpose of the Jesus Prayer, and to the nature of Jesus Christ. He is the person who takes issue with Franny's softening of Jesus to suit her needs. He says that Jesus is not as lovable as Saint Francis of Assisi, the champion of animals, but that he is the only person in the Bible who truly understood man's relationship to God. He assures her that the Jesus Prayer is meant to give the supplicant "Christ-Consciousness." These arguments lay the foundation for Zooey's statement that the figurative Fat Lady they perform for is both everyone and Christ. This latter statement is the balm that finally affords Franny some relief. It is the realization that inside everyone she despises, something holy resides nevertheless.

THEMES

Family Dynamics
The Glass family dynamics in *Franny and Zooey* largely inform the characters' interactions. Zooey's and Franny's position as the youngest of seven siblings bonds them in a singular way. It explains why Zooey is the only sibling still living at home and why Franny would choose to return there when she can longer stand being away at school. That both look up to their older sibling Buddy is also clear. Zooey keeps and reads an old letter from his brother, and Franny is willing to speak to him on the phone even in the midst of her crisis. Yet, Zooey blames both Buddy and Seymour for his and Franny's unhappiness. Notably, Zooey and Franny are both on the verge of adulthood in a family where their older siblings have moved away to pursue their own lives and careers. Though Walt was killed in the military in 1945, it is Seymour's 1948 suicide that looms large in all of the family members' lives. Both Bessie and Zooey avoid Seymour's old room, and Buddy waits three years before broaching the subject of Seymour's death with Zooey. Franny's pilgrim books, which sparked her breakdown, were taken from

TOPICS FOR FURTHER STUDY

- Do you think Franny or Zooey is the novel's protagonist? Can it be both? Write an essay in which you support your thesis, making sure to include examples from the book.

- Read another of Salinger's stories about the Glass children. Give an oral presentation in which you outline how that story affects your understanding of *Franny and Zooey*.

- Conduct a research project on Eastern philosophy and religion and share your findings with the class in a multimedia presentation. What aspects of your research can be seen in the novel?

- Write a third-person narrative about your own family. What family dynamics are revealed in your story?

Seymour's old desk. The Glass family matriarch and patriarch also shed much light on the family relationships. Where Bessie is nosy, bossy, and overbearing, Les is just the opposite. Bessie barges in on her children in the bathtub and dispenses unwanted advice. Les never faces anything and surrounds himself with memorabilia from the past, even hoping to hear his dead children's voices on a long-canceled radio show. This large sprawling family is filled with ghosts, literal and metaphorical, and it is this backdrop that sets the tone for the book's centerpiece: Franny and Zooey's philosophical discussions.

Critique of Intellectual and Cultural Conformity

While Franny and Lane eat lunch at Sickler's, she criticizes Lane for conforming to the expectations of the intellectual elite. To Franny, the critical paper that Lane is so proud of is emblematic of everything that is wrong with academia. Instead of fostering a genuine pursuit of knowledge, college has become a place of intellectual one-upmanship. A similar critique is espoused by Zooey when he says that the scripts he is working on, no matter

how good they may be, are little more than commodities. In the first chapter of the novel, Lane is acutely aware of conforming to the expectations of those around him, he pretends not to care about Franny as much as he does, to look cool in the restaurant, and to order the right food there. Even the restaurant itself was chosen for its cultural cachet. Franny is also aware of the cultural stereotypes and roles that surround her. When she meets Lane at the train station, she matches the women around her to their various colleges, and she does so based on little more than their clothing and bearing. Even the train station, the big game, and the restaurant trip are all part of a larger cultural ritual in which Franny and Lane take part.

Later, when Franny tells Zooey that the acquisition of knowledge is akin to any of the other forms of materialism that drive society, Zooey points out that the Jesus Prayer is also a form of acquisition. The only difference is that Franny seeks to amass "treasure" in the spiritual world as opposed to the physical or material world. Franny admits that it is this realization that is behind her breakdown. Thus, amidst Franny and Zooey's critiques of the society around them, both struggle to find a means of navigating that society in a blameless way. In other words, both siblings must be able to live in a world they find fault with but without finding fault with their own methods for doing so.

Clash between Art and Spirituality

This conundrum leads both Zooey and Franny to question how they can create art in a spiritually corrupt world. Both Zooey and Franny struggle with the ego inherent in making art. Since both are actors, both must also cope with the multiple egos inherent in communal art: the conflicting egos of fellow actors, scriptwriters, and directors all trying to make a name for themselves. Then, of course, there is the ever-present audience (whom Franny views as inferior and ignorant). Yet both Zooey and Franny hate themselves for believing, and for making others believe, that they don't "really want to do any good work" but only want to make work "that will be thought good." Zooey explains to Franny that he keeps acting simply because he is "tired as hell of getting up furious in the morning and going to bed furious at night." Indeed, Zooey likely persists because of Buddy's letter. In it, Buddy encourages Zooey to act and tells him that were he to do "anything at all beautiful on a stage, anything nameless and joy-making," then Buddy and his dead brother would appear to

View of Manhattan from above *(Image copyright Natalia Bratslavsky, 2009. Used under license from Shutterstock.com.)*

greet him with flowers. The letter's importance to Zooey as both a brother and an actor is clear not only in the letter's worn and oft-read appearance but also in the fact that Zooey reads it before beginning to read a new script.

Though Zooey does not paraphrase Buddy when he convinces Franny to act again, he is clearly channeling his brother's advice when he tells her that "the only re*lig*ious thing you can do, is *act*. Act for God, if you want to." Just as Buddy wishes for Zooey to achieve something "nameless and joy-making," Zooey tells Franny that "an artist's only concern is to shoot for some kind of perfection, and *on his own terms*, not anyone else's." Thus, both siblings ultimately find that rather than allowing their art to conflict with their spirituality, they not only can work together but can become one and the same thing. This idea is further underscored by Zooey's conflation of the symbolic Fat Lady into a representation of both everyone and Christ. Thus, the audience they despise is transformed into Christ, and their art is no longer a wasted effort presented to the ignorant masses but instead a gift to Christ, a performance for Christ alone.

STYLE

Diction

Though diction simply means word choice, it becomes more notable when that word choice is stylized or idiosyncratic, as is the case in *Franny and Zooey*. Part of this is due to the fact that much of the book is composed of philosophical, intellectual, or spiritual discourse. Thus, the diction takes on a more instructing, elevated, or pedantic tone, as opposed to a conversational tone. The language of Freudian psychoanalysis (i.e., words such as *ego*, *superego*, and *subconscious*) is also used fairly often. Franny's frequent use of the term *ego*—in Freudian terms, a part of the human consciousness—is one such example. Interestingly, while the Glass family members are educated and highly intelligent, they often lapse into slang or ungrammatical speech.

Point of View

The first chapter and most of the second chapter of *Franny and Zooey* is told from the omniscient third-person point of view, that is, by a narrator

COMPARE
&
CONTRAST

- **1950s:** Many secular colleges are for either men or women only, and even coeducational ("coed") colleges have strict policies regarding single-sex dormitories. Curfews are also part of college life, and students who are not in their dorms by curfew risk suspension or expulsion. This is why, in *Franny and Zooey*, a train arrives full of girls who are meeting their boyfriends and why Franny is staying in a girls' rooming house during her visit.

  Today: Far more secular colleges are coed, and many of those that are place few restrictions on dormitory life. Many dorms are also coed. Cohabiting couples are not subject to expulsion (as they were in the 1950s), and curfews are rare.

- **1950s:** Psychoanalysis, a school of psychology developed by Sigmund Freud, is gaining in popularity. It is also gaining respect and validity in intellectual, academic, and health-care communities.

  Today: While psychoanalysis is still used by some psychologists and psychiatrists, it is not held in such high esteem as it once was. Several alternative therapies exist and are often more widely used. Psychiatric drugs and cognitive therapy are two such alternatives.

- **1950s:** The American culture of commodity emerges in the 1950s. America, finally at peace after two world wars, experiences the height of economic prosperity. This prosperity leads to the rise of the middle class and its purchasing power. This in turn spurs the commoditization of culture, a trend that both Zooey and Franny lament. Much literature written during the time also laments this tendency.

  Today: While there is more awareness of the benefits and detriments of consumer culture, it continues largely unabated. In fact, much of the American economy relies upon consumer culture.

who is not a specific character in the story, is able to portray the thoughts of all the characters, or is otherwise all-seeing and all-knowing. However, the beginning of the second chapter is narrated in the first person by Buddy Glass. The first-person point of view is often told by a specific character participating in the story or by a narrator speaking as "I," who is therefore unable to know the thoughts of the other characters or have knowledge of action taking place outside their immediate experience. Buddy states that both Bessie and Franny object to how they are to be portrayed in his version of the following events. He also states that the year is 1957, though he is writing about events taking place in 1955. This jarring interruption in the narrative causes the reader to question who was narrating the first chapter. It also causes the reader to question the factual nature of the second

chapter. Indeed, though Buddy fades into the background by switching back into an omniscient third-person narration, the fact remains that Buddy is the person relating the story. However, he takes no active part in the events as they unfold. Thus, the reader must conclude that Buddy is relating secondhand information and wonder how accurate, therefore, it can it be.

HISTORICAL CONTEXT

Conformity and Consumer Culture in the 1950s

Following the economic depression that paralyzed the United States during the 1930s, relief was brought about by the military-industrial complex and American involvement in World

War II. By the war's end, the United States was well on its way to economic prosperity, which reached its peak in the 1950s. The rise of the middle class at this time was largely caused by this economic boom. Also, by the 1950s, the widespread popularity of television perpetuated cultural images in an unprecedented manner. This prosperity was also behind the growing college culture, as more and more families could afford to send their children to college. Thus, the combined factors of economic prosperity, widely available standardized education, and the constant broadcast of cultural images led to a culture largely based upon consumption and conformity. This is the culture that Franny and Zooey lament; they find themselves unable to happily take on the yoke of mindless materialism. It is why Franny cannot stand the hollow academic culture that surrounds her; she finds that knowledge itself has been reduced to just another commodity—a means to an end, that of securing a good job. Indeed, for many people this was the point of attending college during the 1950s. In such a culture, the novel suggests, people become as unremarkable and interchangeable as the prefabricated homes and other standardized factory goods that dominated the 1950s. For instance, Franny cannot remember meeting Lane's friend Wally; he looks and acts like everyone else and is thus eminently forgettable. Salinger's novel is an overt critique of the conformity and consumer culture of the 1950s.

Influence of Eastern Philosophy and Spirituality

Eastern philosophy and spirituality gained increasing popularity in the United States during the 1950s. This was partly because the exchange of information became more widespread because of the increased availability of television, film, and other media, as well as through academia. Yet the more likely (and compelling) reason behind the rising popularity of Eastern belief and practice in the 1950s is that its basic tenets were entirely antithetical to those espoused in mainstream American culture at the time. One such tenet is that material things are not only worthless but are no more than an illusion. Thus, it is impossible to place any spiritual or emotional value on belongings that are deemed inherently valueless. The Eastern religion of Buddhism, in particular, teaches its followers that desire kills the soul, especially the desire for material goods. All of these teachings and values are reflected in the novel (though

Giant buddha *(Image copyright Videowokart, 2009. Used under license from Shutterstock.com.)*

Zooey blames his and Franny's early immersion in Eastern thought for turning them into "freaks"). Notably, Eastern thought and spirituality were reflected in much of the literature produced during the 1950s. The Beat movement (a 1950s literary movement) particularly emulated Eastern philosophy and spirituality, just as it lamented the consumer culture.

CRITICAL OVERVIEW

Though *Franny and Zooey* was an immediate bestseller, it received an ambivalent critical reception at best. Indeed, while most critics found the novel to be well written and well constructed, they ultimately took issue with the book's primary message, that everyone is Christ. For instance, *New Statesman* contributor Frank Kermode points out that "if it seems strange to be saying a Jesus prayer to a lot of louts in a theater, [Franny] is to remember that they're all Christ." Kermode goes on to remark that "it is to make us accept this conclusion that Salinger has worked so deviously. And, as one of his admiring audience, I find it hard to believe he could be selling anything so simple and untrue." Joan Didion, writing in the *National Review* states that "however brilliantly rendered (and it is), however hauntingly right in the rhythm of its dialogue (and it is), *Franny and Zooey* is finally spurious, and what makes it spurious is Salinger's tendency to flatter the essential triviality within each of his readers, his predilection for giving instructions for living." Emphasizing her point, Didion goes on to call the novel a "self-help [book] . . . for the upper middle classes."

In a rare positive review printed in the *Canadian Forum*, Hilda Kirkwood applauds Salinger's "artfully deliberate accumulation of detail," adding that the "writing is unique and justly celebrated." Contrary to most critics, Kirkwood notes that "one finds oneself in considerable awe of J. D. Salinger's power to transmit so eloquently the mood of the modern intellectual dilemma and to transmute it into such intensely moving stories as *Franny and Zooey*." However, regardless of critical opinion, *Franny and Zooey* has remained in print for over forty years, and the novel is a mainstay in school curricula. Though some may take issue with the book's spiritual message, few argue that the book is entirely without value. *Franny and Zooey* remains an important work by an essential American author.

WHAT DO I READ NEXT?

- J. D. Salinger's *The Catcher in the Rye* (1951) is his best-known work to date; the book launched Salinger to international fame and remains an American classic to this day. The story is similar to *Franny and Zooey*: both books feature young protagonists who come of age through their struggle to accept the distasteful world around them.

- Lawrence Ferlinghetti's 1958 book of poetry, *A Coney Island of the Mind*, shares many of the themes of *Franny and Zooey*. The collection is also a definitive work of Beat literature.

- *Eastern Philosophy: The Greatest Thinkers and Sages from Ancient to Modern Times* (2006), by Kevin Burns, is an introduction to Eastern thought for the nonspecialist. The book is likely to shed additional light on any reading of *Franny and Zooey*.

- Another Salinger work essential to a deeper understanding of *Franny and Zooey* is the short story collection *Raise High the Roof Beam, Carpenters; and Seymour: An Introduction* (1963). The stories largely pertain to Seymour Glass, further illuminating the Glass family saga.

CRITICISM

Leah Tieger

Leah Tieger is a freelance writer and editor. In the following essay, she examines the themes in Franny and Zooey *as a means of explicating the novel's conclusion, namely that everyone is Christ. Tieger also examines Salinger's earlier attempts at articulating this theme.*

The instruction to recognize all that is Christlike in people is essentially a way of saying, "Look on the bright side" or "Look for the good in people." In a 1962 review of *Franny and Zooey* in *Wisconsin Studies in Contemporary Literature*, Carl Bode summarizes Salinger's argument thus: "There is the message, the answer to Franny's question. The false is finally just as true as the true because God is everywhere, in everything. The phoney and the genuine equally deserve our love because God manifests himself in both. All

must be good and true, if not always beautiful." Indeed, as dressed up as it is in religious or spiritual garb, the edict itself is rather simple and banal. Notably, it is this banality that incited the book's cool critical reception, yet the arguments set forth in *Franny and Zooey* are not entirely without merit. Indeed, as a social critique, the book is a success, tackling the problems of conformity, commoditization, ego, and intellectual bankruptcy. The book also artfully portrays the characters' struggles to make art in a meaningful way, one that remains untainted by worldly concerns. At the same time, when those arguments are reviewed in hindsight (that is, in light of their ultimate conclusion), even they become suspect.

For instance, when one revisits Franny's complaints regarding the conformity that surrounds her, those complaints are undermined by the idea that everyone shares an essentially identical quality, that of being imbued with Christ. Here, one can diverge to note that the word *Christ* could easily be interchanged here with other words, such as *soul, spirit,* or *inherent goodness,* for instance. Indeed, Franny tells Lane that because everyone is essentially the same, "everything everybody does is so . . . tiny and meaningless and—sad-making. And the worst part is if you go bohemian or something crazy like that, you're conforming just as much as everybody else, only in a different way." However, while Franny may lament the negative aspects of conformity, of the essential sameness of everyone, it is ultimately the positive side of that same sameness that eases her crisis. Indeed, the idea that everyone is Christ is the ultimate conformation, however unwitting. Certainly, the thought conforms everyone to the same idea, the same standard, albeit one that Franny is now able to accept.

Frany's arguments regarding her dislike for the ego are also undermined by Zooey's assertion regarding the Fat Lady, and even more so by Franny's acceptance of it. For instance, Franny explains to Lane why she quit acting: "It started embarrassing me. . . . It seemed like such poor taste. . . . I mean all the *ego.*" She goes on to tell her boyfriend, "All I know is I'm losing my mind. . . . I'm just sick of ego, ego, ego. . . . I'm sick of everybody that wants to *get* somewhere. Do something distinguished." Certainly, while Franny cannot be accused of trying to make a name for herself, one can accuse her of possessing quite a large ego in that she is able to act only for Christ. That Franny is unable to act for an audience *she* deems to be ignorant and beneath her is, to all intents and purposes, an act of ego in the extreme. Indeed, when considering the question of ego, the contradictions abound. According to Zooey, Franny is "constitutionally unable to love or understand" Jesus, yet he also, successfully, tells her, "The only thing you can do now, the only re*lig*ious thing you can do, is *act.* Act for God, if you want to." Earlier in the novel, Zooey himself indirectly accuses Franny of egomania, of allowing her distaste for the world and the people around her to get too personal. Is this also not a crime of ego, taking the world's venality as a personal affront?

Thus, the novel's assertion that everyone is Christ has been lambasted by critics. The assertion also undermines much of the novel, as it soon becomes clear that through her acceptance of it, Franny is just as guilty of the sins she finds fault with in the world around her. Nevertheless, the literary background, or provenance, of the idea has gone largely unnoticed by literary scholars. Notably, that provenance lends the idea that everyone is Christ (and the soothing effect of that idea) an added authority. Indeed, in Sherwood Anderson's 1919 American classic novel *Winesburg, Ohio,* a nearly identical assertion is made. One critic to point out the connection, *College English* contributor James E. Bryan, quotes the statement from Anderson's novel that "everyone in the world is Christ and they are all crucified." Though the statement is not as crucial to the themes in *Winesburg, Ohio* as it is in Salinger's novel, the similarity is striking. Furthermore, given the renown of Anderson's book, it is hard to imagine that Salinger had not read it. At the same time, the added clause "they are all crucified" changes the meaning of the idea to a great extent.

More notably, Bryan points out that the idea has appeared in Salinger's earlier works. He states that *Franny and Zooey* "provides a not unwelcome annotation of symbolism and underlining of theme which can often serve as a reference to the interpretations of earlier stories." Thus, the novel's redeeming value is that the contested assertion, and its underlying symbols, shed insight on much of Salinger's oeuvre. One story in particular, Bryan finds, shares not only a similar message but also similar symbols used to convey that message. That story is "Just Before the War with the Eskimos" (a 1948 *New Yorker* story that appeared in Salinger's 1953 *Nine Stories* collection). According to Bryan, the story features "Franklin Graff, a loathsome misfit, [who] is vested with certain provocative physical qualities, circumstances, and a symbolic prop, a chicken sandwich suggestive of the Eucharist, which seem to mark him a Christ in identical terms—repulsive human suffering—to the Fat Lady."

Given this insight, there are two instances in *Franny and Zooey* where chicken becomes symbolic of the Eucharist. The first is the chicken sandwich that Franny orders when having lunch with Lane at Sickler's, the same sandwich that annoys Lane by nature of its very plainness at so un-plain a restaurant. Franny does not eat the sandwich. It sits untouched as she descends deeper and deeper into her crisis. Later, after Franny has gone home, she continuously refuses her mother's offer of chicken soup. Zooey calls his mother's soup sacred, openly comparing it to the Eucharist and chastising Franny for her inability to recognize it as such. As Bryan states, "Although Franny has refused her mother's Eucharist of love, Seymour's Fat Lady finally brings the same redeeming truth home to her . . . . In 'Just Before the War with the Eskimos,' Salinger has approximated this truth through the guises of verbal irony; in 'Zooey,' he has felt constrained to have his protagonist . . .say it straight out."

Source: Leah Tieger, Critical Essay on *Franny and Zooey*, in *Novels for Students*, Gale, Cengage Learning, 2010.

Donald Greiner

In the following excerpt, Greiner explores the relationship between Salinger and American author John Updike and discusses Updike's famous review of Franny and Zooey.

In 2003, when John Updike published *The Early Stories, 1953–1975*, an 839-page collection honored with the 2004 PEN/Faulkner Award for Fiction, he included a foreword in which he recalled the development of the first two decades of his enduring and esteemed career. The germ of the career took its initial significant shape at Harvard, where Updike was an undergraduate from 1950 to 1954, and where, in 1953, he submitted to Albert Guerard's creative writing class a story titled "Ace in the Hole." On the advice of Professor Guerard, he sent the story to the *New Yorker*, which rejected it. As Updike explains in the foreword, "The next year, though, after 'Friends from Philadelphia' and some poems had been accepted by the magazine in my first post-collegiate summer, I resubmitted the story and it was accepted" (ix). Thus, although "Friends from Philadelphia" is Updike's first professional story, as it was published in the *New Yorker* for 30 October 1954, "Ace in the Hole" was written earlier and is his initial important contact with the magazine that would feature his work for the next half century.

Yet the foreword to *The Early Stories* is particularly noteworthy for confirming what initiated readers have long suspected: that J. D. Salinger's short fiction, the stories largely published in the *New Yorker* during the late 1940s and early 1950s, was so refreshingly new as to have a lasting impact on Updike when he was taking his first steps

> " THE FOREWORD TO *THE EARLY STORIES* IS PARTICULARLY NOTEWORTHY FOR CONFIRMING WHAT INITIATED READERS HAVE LONG SUSPECTED: THAT J. D. SALINGER'S SHORT FICTION . . . WAS SO REFRESHINGLY NEW AS TO HAVE A LASTING IMPACT ON UPDIKE WHEN HE WAS TAKING HIS FIRST STEPS TOWARD PERFECTING THE ART OF THE TALE."

toward perfecting the art of the tale. "Ace in the Hole" brought the two writers together. As Updike remembers:

> The story is entangled, in my memory of those heady days of the dawning literary life, with the sudden looming, in the lobby of the Algonquin, of J. D. Salinger, a glowingly handsome tall presence not yet notoriously reclusive; he shook my hand before we were taken in to lunch with our respective editors, William Shawn and Katharine White. He said, or somebody later said he said, that he had noticed and liked "Ace in the Hole." His own stories [. . .] had been revelations to me of how the form, terse and tough in the Thirties and Forties, could accommodate a more expansive postwar sense of American reality; the bottle of wine that ends "Friends from Philadelphia" owes something to the Easter chick found in the bottom of the wastebasket at the end of "Just Before the War with the Eskimos."

All did not remain cordial, however, between the established star of the *New Yorker* and the younger writer poised to share the acclaim. Salinger's fiction took an unexpected tack with the publication of "Franny" in the *New Yorker* (29 January 1955). Although the perspective of hindsight confirms that the tack was signaled in "Teddy" (*New Yorker*, 31 January 1953), the point remains that the Glass family stories were radically different from "Just Before the War with the Eskimos," just as the latter was radically different from the tales by William Faulkner, Ernest Hemingway, F. Scott Fitzgerald, and John O'Hara in the previous decades. When Salinger published *Franny and Zooey* in 1961, the editor of the *New York Times Book Review* assigned the review to Updike, who responded with an analysis of Salinger that conveyed both debt and dismay. The review has since taken on a life of its own in Salinger circles.

... Updike's review of *Franny and Zooey* was originally published in the *New York Times Book Review* for 17 September 1961. The date is significant. By 1961, it was evident to those committed to contemporary American literature, and thus to American culture, that the era of the Modernist giants was over. Ernest Hemingway (Nobel Prize winner) had killed himself on 2 July 1961. John Steinbeck's (Nobel Prize winner) major work was far behind him, although he had published *The Winter of Our Discontent* in 1961 and would follow it a year later with the enormously popular *Travels with Charley: In Search of America.* Robert Frost's career had all but ended (he died on 29 January 1963), and T. S. Eliot (Nobel Prize winner), while remaining a presence, was no longer a force. Ezra Pound had finally been released from St. Elizabeth's Hospital on 7 May 1958, but was more or less in disgrace. And, most important of all, William Faulkner (Nobel Prize winner) had published *The Mansion*, the final volume of the renowned Snopes trilogy, in 1959 and was now within a year of his death. During the tense decades of the cold war, the strength of the country's literary and cultural reputation was a national concern.

Given the impending vacuum, a significant question in 1961 was, "Who will take the places of these literary heroes?" Norman Mailer was much talked about, partly because of *The Naked and the Dead* (1948), but largely because of his determination to be famous as a public intellectual. Saul Bellow was much admired, primarily because of *The Adventures of Augie March* (1953), the first of his three National Book Award winning novels, and *Henderson the Rain King* (1959). Yet in 1961, the author generally identified as most likely to follow the great American Modernists was J. D. Salinger. Frederick L. Gwynn and Joseph L. Blotner, for example, began their 1958 book *The Fiction of J. D. Salinger* with the following observation:

> For the future historian, the most significant fact about American literary culture of the Post-War Period may be that whereas young readers of the Inter-War Period knew intimately the work of a goodly number of coeval writers (Hemingway, Fitzgerald, Dos Passos, Wolfe, Sinclair Lewis). the only Post-War fiction unanimously approved by contemporary

literate American youth consists of about five hundred pages by Jerome David Salinger.

Further, Mailer described Salinger in 1959 as "everybody's favorite," although he himself demurred (*Advertisement* 467–68). Finally, *Time* featured Salinger on the cover of the 15 September 1961 issue, complete with a banner proclaiming "A Private World of Love and Death."

Although Salinger had been publishing short stories from the time "The Young Folks" appeared in the March–April 1940 issue of the famed *Story* and had continued to publish stories in such magazines as *Kansas City Review, Cosmopolitan, Mademoiselle, Esquire, Collier,* and the *Saturday Evening Post* while serving with distinction in World War II, he later repudiated his early work by refusing to let it be collected or reprinted. More important, he even dismissed the story that led to *The Catcher in the Rye* in 1951 and that featured a prep school boy named Holden Caulfield on Christmas break. Written in 1941 with the title "Am I Banging My Head against the Wall?" and accepted by the *New Yorker*, the story was finally published in the 21 December 1946 issue as "Slight Rebellion off Madison." His breakthrough year was 1948 when he published three stories in the *New Yorker* that confirmed he was a major new talent with a singular new voice and brought him critical as well as popular recognition: "A Perfect Day for Bananafish" (31 January 1948), "Uncle Wiggily in Connecticut" (20 March 1948), and "Just Before the War with the Eskimos" (5 June 1948). He followed these short story masterpieces with the equally admired "The Laughing Man" (*New Yorker*, 19 March 1949), "Down at the Dinghy" (*Harper's*, April 1949). "For Esme—with Love and Squalor" (*New Yorker*, 8 April 1950), and "Pretty Mouth and Green My Eyes" (*New Yorker*, 14 July 1951). By the time *The Catcher in the Rye* reached the bookstores in July 1951, two years before Bellow's *Augie March*, Salinger was deemed an author to watch. When he completed this astonishing half-decade burst of creativity with "Teddy" and "De Daumier-Smith's Blue Period," the latter originally published in *Nine Stories* in April 1953, both *The Catcher in the Rye* and *Nine Stories* had become best sellers and critical successes. Salinger was unexpectedly, not to mention reluctantly, cast into the spotlight.

Updike took notice. Born in 1932 and thus thirteen years younger than Salinger, he began reading the *New Yorker* in his teens, particularly after his mother forced the family to move from the small town of Shillington, Pennsylvania, to an isolated farm near Plowville, Pennsylvania, in 1945. By the time Updike matriculated at Harvard in 1950, Salinger had published seven stories in the *New Yorker*. And by the time Updike was graduated in 1954 as an English major and as president of the Harvard *Lampoon*, he had had a literary breakthrough eerily similar to Salinger's. The *New Yorker* published "Duet, with Muffled Brake Drums," a light-verse poem, on 19 August 1954, and "Friends from Philadelphia" on 30 October 1954. Just as Salinger continued to be featured in the *New Yorker* until he famously ceased publishing altogether with "Hapworth 16, 1924" (*The New Yorker*, 19 June 1965), so Updike quickly became the new favorite of that revered magazine. While studying drawing, for example, at the Ruskin School of Drawing and Fine Art in Oxford, England, during 1954–55, he was hired by the *New Yorker* to begin writing "Talk of the Town" columns upon his return to the United States in August 1955. He remained a staff writer for the magazine, while also contributing poems and stories, until March 1957, when he resigned the salaried position to devote his time to fiction, poetry, and essays.

As of this writing, then, Updike has become the quintessential "*New Yorker* author," publishing during his more than half-century association with the journal hundreds of items in six different genres: stories, poems, essays, reviews, personal reminiscences, and commentary. He kept reading Salinger during the latter's final decade as a *published* author (one assumes that Salinger has continued writing during his forty-year retreat from literary acclaim): "Franny" (*New Yorker*, 29 January 1955), "Raise High the Roof Beam, Carpenters" (*New Yorker*, 19 November 1955), "Zooey" (*New Yorker*, 4 May 1957), "Seymour An Introduction" (*New Yorker*, 6 June 1959), and "Hapworth." By the time *Franny and Zooey* appeared to best-seller sales in 1961 (*Raise High the Roof Beam, Carpenters and Seymour An Introduction* was also a best seller in 1963), Updike was positioned to review the eagerly-awaited book written by an author whom he admired and whose pre-Glass family stories were, he readily affirmed, a "revelation," a catalyst that prompted him to envision a kind of short story refreshingly different from those written by the previous generation.

Also in 1961, what became known as "the Salinger industry" was underway. An onslaught of critical appraisals became available, led primarily

by Arthur Heiserman and James E. Miller, Jr., "J. D. Salinger: Some Crazy Cliff" (*Western Humanities Review*, Spring 1956); Charles Kaplan, "Holden and Huck: The Odysseys of Youth" (*College English*, November 1956); Ihab Hassan, "Rare Quixotic Gesture: The Fiction of J. D. Salinger" (*Western Review*, Summer 1957); Maxwell Geismar, "J. D. Salinger: The Wise Child and *The New Yorker* School of Fiction" (*American Moderns: From Rebellion to Conformity*, 1958); and Frederick L. Gwynn and Joseph L. Blotner, *The Fiction of J.D. Salinger*, 1958). Whether the industry accelerated Salinger's retreat and eventual silence is open to speculation, but the fact remains that as scholars published dozens of articles about Salinger between 1956 and 1961, as readers bought his books in the millions, and as college students knocked on his door as if completing a pilgrimage to a venerated shrine, Salinger became alarmed. Much of his alarm was based on an irony: He understood that he wrote fiction to be published; but as his books became best sellers, he became skeptical about publishers. Distrusting the paperback revolution of the 1950s as having a leveling effect on American cultural standards, he despised what he saw as an unholy alliance between publishers and professors: Paperback titles on college syllabi sell books. Little wonder that Seymour Glass, Salinger's secular holy man and author of haiku, refuses to release his poems to the world. Little wonder that Franny Glass rails against university "section men," detests English major Lane Coutell's supercilious comments about Flaubert, scorns the Professor Tuppers of the academy, and promptly suffers a nervous breakdown. For Seymour and Salinger, but not for Seymour's brother Buddy (who is, after all, both a teacher and a writer), publishing profanes art.

Given Salinger's uneasiness in 1961—he was just four years away from refusing to publish altogether—it is not surprising that Updike's review upset him. He had dedicated *Franny and Zooey* to William Shawn, editor of the *New Yorker*, "lover of the long shot, protector of the unprolific, defender of the hopelessly flamboyant, most unreasonably modest of born great artist-editors." Shawn, Salinger's "defender," was also one of Updike's editors. Even more telling was Salinger's dedication in *Raise High the Roof Beam, Carpenters and Seymour An Introduction*: "If there is an amateur reader still left in the world—or anybody who just reads and runs—I ask him or her, with untellable affection and gratitude, to split the dedication of this book four ways with my wife and children." By 1961, many professional commentators and general readers saw Salinger as the hope of American fiction and Updike as an important *New Yorker* regular; but Updike was decidedly not an "unprolific" writer, an "amateur" reader, or "anybody who just reads and runs." In the span of only two years, he had published four books: *The Carpentered Hen and Other Tame Creatures* (poems, 1958), *The Poorhouse Fair* (novel, 1959), *The Same Door* (stories, 1959), and, most important, *Rabbit, Run* (novel, 1960). The latter gave him the recognition necessary to review Salinger's blockbuster with authority, as well as put him in the public eye to stay. Two years later, he ensured his fame when the 1963 novel *The Centaur* won the National Book Award. Salinger, on the other hand, was nearing the hour of his silence . . . .

Source: Donald Greiner, "Updike and Salinger: A Literary Incident," in *Critique*, Vol. 47, No. 2, Winter 2006, pp. 115–30.

Carl Bode

In the following excerpt, Bode examines the nature of the characters, story, and style in Franny and Zooey.

The most remarkable thing about Salinger's pair of stories is how old they are. Their kind is medieval at the very least. "Franny" is a Dialogue between Body and Soul, in terms not much changed since the Middle Ages. The only notable difference is an important one, however. Body and Soul seem here so disassociated that little give and take results. Though the Soul displays a tinge of respect for the expression of its antagonist, to the Body the dialogue as dialogue hardly exists at all. This disassociation Salinger makes profound. It is a matter not only of words but of attitudes and actions. Perhaps the very extent of the cleavage is what makes the story most modern. The medieval moralist, for instance, could paint his fat burgher in lurid colors but there was something appealing in his grossness, his triple chin, the sheer gusto of his appetites. Not so in "Franny." What strikes us here is how bitterly Salinger hates the Body.

A college man named Lane Coutell waits at the station for his girl, Franny Glass, a guest at the big football weekend. When she arrives he takes her to a restaurant for drinks and lunch. During their stay at the restaurant they bicker

> **THE MOST REMARKABLE THING ABOUT SALINGER'S PAIR OF STORIES IS HOW OLD THEY ARE. THEIR KIND IS MEDIEVAL AT THE VERY LEAST. 'FRANNY' IS A DIALOGUE BETWEEN BODY AND SOUL, IN TERMS NOT MUCH CHANGED SINCE THE MIDDLE AGES."**

and Franny becomes so overwrought that she flees to the restroom. There she cries convulsively. When she rejoins Lane their dialogue, raised now, begins again. It ends when Franny leaves the table for a second time and faints.

Lane is so ordinary that Salinger does not bother to describe him. The only physical attribution is unpleasant: Lane's long fingers are his vanity. We know him, and know him well, through what he does rather than through how he looks. We know him through his actions. These are never really good, they are seldom neutral, and they are often offensive. From the start of the story Salinger takes the privilege, relished by Victorian writers but rarely used today, of criticizing what one of his characters does. "Lane himself lit a cigarette as the train pulled in. Then, like so many people, who, perhaps, ought to be issued only a very probational pass to meet trains, he tried to empty his face of all expression that might quite simply, perhaps even beautifully, reveal how he felt about the arriving person." Salinger's indignation is sharpened by his irony. His hostility is so open that the effect is overdone. After Franny's arrival and throughout the long luncheon Lane remains repellent. There are degrees—he is more so at one time than another—but he never makes much claim on the reader's regard.

But Franny we are invited to love. She looks beautiful and acts beautiful. Even when she is distraught. Just before her paroxysm of crying she presses the heels of her hands against her eyes. Salinger says, "Her extended fingers, though trembling, or because they were trembling, looked oddly graceful and pretty." When she returns to Lane's table she looks "quite stunning."

The extent of Salinger's commitment to her is shown by the frankly naive quality of his praise. There is something far from sophisticated in his descriptions of her—"quite stunning" is schoolboyish—just as there is in his descriptions of Lane's offensiveness.

She is both beautiful and good. To a degree she represents embodied Soul. But in "Franny" she is lost and trying to find her way. She has been looking around her, with more and more desperation, for the absolutes. In her search she finds it far easier to detect what she is not after than what she is. Like Holden Caulfield in *The Catcher* she can tell the phoney from the genuine, though she is never as offhand and intuitive in doing so. She is subtler but more apt to be confused. Yet she knows, for example, that the "section men," the glib graduate students who take over the literature classes in the professors' absence, are frauds when they tear down Turgenev to build up their own favorites. As the luncheon goes along she sees that Lane, who postures like them about a paper he wrote on Flaubert, is also a fake.

Her testing for the beautiful is of a piece with her testing for the true. The English department at her school includes two widely heralded poets, Manlius and Esposito. Lane is impressed. Not only are they two of the best men in the country, he says, they are poets. "They're not" is her flat answer. She tries to make clear to him what the beautiful is. It is not the much reprinted poems of Manlius or Esposito. These two leave nothing beautiful behind them. They and their sort write verses which at best "may just be some kind of terribly fascinating, syntax *droppings*—excuse the expression." These men may reach the mind but never the heart. Franny fails to make Lane understand, however, the more so because she herself remains unsure of what the beautiful is and how to find it.

She is a little clearer about the good. She says that through her Religion Survey course she has come upon a small book by a "Russian peasant, apparently," called *The Way of a Pilgrim*. He wanders about Russia looking for someone to tell him how to pray without stopping. Ultimately he meets "a starets—some sort of terribly advanced religious person" who directs him to a wonderful collection of the writings of the Church Fathers, the *Philokalia* or "The Love of Spiritual Beauty." There he finds his treasure and learns how to pray incessantly. Then he goes

about teaching others. His message, which so appeals to Franny, is that even though you start by merely praying words, if you persist the word will become the reality. The good, the beautiful, the true will grow apparent. You will, Franny explains to Lane, "purify your whole outlook and get an absolutely new conception of what everything's about."

Striving for the Pilgrim's knowledge has made Franny change. She has given up dramatics, which before meant a great deal to her. She has surrendered some of her comfortable ideas of excellence; for example, she used to think Manlius remarkable but now she writes him off as just another poor fellow. She has lost most of her illusions about Lane, leaving in their place, however, enough of a feeling of guilt to make her demonstrative. The less highly she thinks of him the more warmly she holds his hand. Just before the story opens she has written him a letter full of affection; in the course of the story she admits solemnly, "I had to strain to write it." Throughout the luncheon the strain of her search and the compulsion to apply her new standards are always present. She tries to stifle them but is only briefly successful. Twice the tension in her comes to a peak. The first time is when she leaves the table and sobs in the restroom, the second when she collapses and loses consciousness.

During the meal she tries tensely to show Lane what she is looking for. While she pleads with him—indirectly—for understanding, he sits and eats. She cannot bring herself to touch her own slight meal. Her forehead glistens with sweat, she turns pale, her hands shake. But Lane plods with workmanlike pleasure through his food. He has ordered snails, frogs' legs, and a salad. Salinger makes us watch while Lane cuts all this up and stuffs himself. As Franny sits in torment he finishes everything on his plate. Then, "thoroughly relaxed, stomach full," he dismisses all that Franny has had to say—and she excuses herself only to faint.

As the story ends, Lane intimates that he will attempt to reach her by a back stair, when she feels better, and sleep with her. Then he leaves. Franny, now lying in the restaurant manager's office, looks at the ceiling and moves her lips in the Pilgrim's prayer.

"Zooey" is the complement of *"Franny."* Much longer, it is, on balance, just barely as good. Essentially it is a theological tract, of three sections which easily fall apart but which taken together constitute the answer to the question of "Franny." They give Franny herself what she is looking for. Salinger takes care to deny that "Zooey" should be considered a tract—or as he puts it "a mystical story, or a religiously mystifying story"—and calls it a love story. It is not. Or if it is, so is the New Testament.

A better and shrewder technical term for the story is the other one he uses: a home-movie. In form and content both, "Zooey" seems homemade, family-style. The Glass family are the cast. Only three appear in the film but the rest are often invoked. The parents are Bessie and Les Glass, a pair of ex-vaudevillians. We never see Les but Bessie brilliantly plays herself through the picture. Their galaxy of children ranges from the oldest, Seymour (now dead nearly seven years but still a strong influence), to Franny, the youngest. In between come Buddy, a kept writer at an unnamed college; three other children with no direct bearing on the present story; and Zooey, described as one of the most popular leading-men in television. Nearest in age and spirit to Franny, he plays the main role. Salinger insists on the remarkable excellence of the Glass children's minds. All the children have in their time been regulars on a noted juvenile quiz show, "It's a Wise Child." There and elsewhere all have shown extraordinary powers. One of the younger boys, for instance, once got over an unhappy love affair by trying to translate the Mundaka Upanishad into classical Greek. And Franny is not only beautiful but so talented an actress that even her brothers admire her acting.

"Zooey" opens with a piece of professional posturing. Salinger puts mirrors face to face; between them the narrator preens. Buddy Glass, the older, "writing" brother tells the story. In the posturing introduction he implies that he is both the author of a long letter, which will be reproduced, and of the narrative to follow. As Salinger has him put it, "The style of the letter, I'm told, bears a considerably more than passing resemblance to the style, or written mannerisms, of this narrator, and the general reader will no doubt jump to the heady conclusion that the writer of the letter and I are one and the same person. Jump he will, and, I'm afraid, jump he should." One argument can be made for this posturing: it continues throughout the story.

It appears in the style itself. Buddy is bound to remind his readers that he knows a cliché when he sees one. Even near the climax he writes self-consciously. "This was the first time in almost seven years that Zooey had, in the ready-made dramatic idiom, 'set foot' in Seymour's and Buddy's old room." The posturing appears still more in the content of "Zooey," especially when Salinger wants to impress us with the depth of the Glass erudition. Again and again he has Zooey, in particular, pour out a fund of religious information, usually esoteric, in the matiest [*sic*] possible accents. "This is Kaliyuga, buddy," he will remark, "the Iron Age." Or he will burst out, "I feel like those dismal bastards Seymour's beloved Chuang-tzu warned everybody against." It can be argued that this is Buddy writing rather than Salinger just as it was Holden Caulfield speaking in *The Catcher*. But Zooey shows off in dialogue which Buddy is reporting and not composing. Some of this pretentiousness is clearly Salinger as Salinger anyway, as we can see from his other Glass stories. And it is this pretentiousness which is largely responsible for the mixed effect "Zooey" gives. "Seymour's beloved Chuang-tzu!"

The three sections of "Zooey" differ considerably from one another. The first, after the unnecessary introductory letter, is a delightful *tour de force*. It presents Zooey and Bessie in the Glass bathroom. While Zooey bathes and shaves, Bessie beetles her way around, worrying about Franny, who is now back home. The dialogue alternately rushes and meanders; the comedy timing is admirable. Salinger describes Zooey's and his mother's actions with loving care. The writing turns at times almost hypnotic, for Salinger can list the contents of a medicine chest and make us read every word. The effect of the dialogue and brilliant stage directions is much like that of some play by Samuel Beckett, say, *Krapp's Last Tape*.

The second section takes Zooey from the bathroom to the living room, where Franny is sleeping on a couch. After some theological backing and filling, he quizzes her on her breakdown, her praying, and her religious feelings. She becomes more and more harrowed as he goes through his maneuvers. The second section climaxes when she says, almost inaudibly, "I want to talk to Seymour." Zooey proceeds with his questions and answers, however, probing as far as he can into her mind. He continues, in fact, for another twenty pages after Franny says she wants to talk with her dead brother. It takes that long for Zooey to know that he is beaten. Then: "In an instant, he turned pale—pale with anxiety for Franny's condition, and pale, presumably, because failure had suddenly filled the room with its invariably sickening smell."

In the final section Zooey calls her on the telephone, pretending that he is Buddy—that is, the best surrogate for the dead Seymour. To answer the phone Franny returns to her childhood and to the womb. As she goes down the long hall in the apartment, she appears "to grow younger with each step." By the time she reaches her parents' bedroom door her "handsome tailored tie-silk dressing gown" looks like a small child's woolen bathrobe. She takes up the phone in the bedroom and there listens while Zooey disguised as Buddy tries to make talk and defend himself. The upturn of this discussion comes when she realizes that Zooey is speaking. Zooey, now desperate and inspired, reassures her about her praying but tells her that the phoniness of the world is none of her concern. She must keep her own standards in spite of it. She must do her best for the Fat Lady—Seymour's term in radio days for the audience, invisible, doubtless horrible, and yet completely dependent. Actually, Zooey continues with rising pitch, the Fat Lady is everyone. And he concludes with the revelation. *"Don't you know who that Fat Lady really is?"* he demands of Franny. "Ah, buddy. Ah, buddy. It's Christ Himself. Christ Himself, buddy."

Franny is overjoyed at the revelation. Peace comes to her in a moment. She gets into her parents' bed and smiles quietly just before falling asleep.

There is the message, the answer to Franny's question. The false is finally just as true as the true because God is everywhere, in everything. The phoney and the genuine equally deserve our love because God manifests himself in both. All must be good and true, if not always beautiful....

Source: Carl Bode, Review of *Franny and Zooey*, in *Wisconsin Studies in Contemporary Literature*, Vol. 3, No. 1, Winter 1962, pp. 65–71.

James E. Bryan

In the following essay, Bryan discusses the religious symbolism in Franny and Zooey.

Critics have rightly complained that J. D. Salinger's "Glass family chronicles" lack the superb poetry and economy of his *Nine Stories* period. However the garrulity of Salinger's recent narrators provides a not unwelcome annotation of symbolism and underlining of theme which can often serve as a reference to the interpretations of earlier stories.

In "Zooey," for example, the description of Zooey Glass's long war with himself (i.e., his

> IN 'JUST BEFORE THE WAR WITH THE ESKIMOS,' SALINGER HAS APPROXIMATED THIS TRUTH THROUGH THE GUISES OF VERBAL IRONY; IN 'ZOOEY' HE HAS FELT CONSTRAINED TO HAVE HIS PROTAGONIST BE ANOTHER PARCIVAL AND SAY IT STRAIGHT OUT."

ego) until he can look into a mirror and not see the self-cherished self may help to clarify the difficult "De Daumier-Smith's Blue Period." One cryptic reference early in this story, "throughout the voyage...I used our stateroom mirror to note my uncanny resemblance to El Greco," reveals the narcissism which Daumier-Smith, like Zooey, must overcome. Both young men are artists and their adolescent narcissism runs to love of the aesthetic self as well as the mirrored image. Other patent spelling-out of meanings, as in "Zooey," can throw light back on some difficult and even bizarre early symbolism; for instance the Fat Lady metaphor of "Zooey" can illuminate symbolism in "Just Before the War with the Eskimos."

In the novel-length "Zooey," Franny Glass continues her unresolved spiritual crisis of "Franny." No longer able to face the "hypocrisy" of college life, Franny has come home to suffer what brother Zooey tartly calls "a tenth-rate nervous breakdown." Zooey recalls for her a time he too was sickened by the crassitude of the world. Out of contempt for all the "morons" in their audience, Zooey had refused to shine his shoes before a "Quiz Kids" radio program on which he and older brother Seymour Glass appeared.

> "He [Seymour] said to shine them for the Fat Lady.... This terribly clear, clear picture of the Fat Lady formed in my mind. I had her sitting on this porch all day, swatting flies, with her radio going full-blast from morning till night. I figured the heat was terrible, and she probably had cancer, and—I don't know. Anyway, it seemed goddam clear why Seymour wanted me to shine my shoes when I went on the air. It made *sense*."

The depressed Franny begins to respond for the first time. She remembers that Seymour had once told her about the Fat Lady too. Then

Zooey identifies the Fat Lady: she is everyone, signifying the relationship of the one to the many (actor-audience), the awareness of the many prompting the one to become humble and grateful; and finally she is "Christ Himself," suffering, quickening the heart to sympathy, and worthy of the gift of a shoe-shine.

> "Yes. Yes. Yes. All right. Let me tell you something now, buddy....Are you listening?...I don't care where an actor acts. It can be in summer stock, it can be over a radio, it can be over *tele*vision, it can be in a goddam Broadway theatre, complete with the most fashionable, most well-fed, most sunburned-looking audience you can imagine. But I'll tell you a terrible secret—Are you listening to me? *There isn't anyone out there who isn't Seymour's Fat Lady....*There isn't anyone *any*where that isn't Seymour's Fat Lady...*don't you know who that Fat Lady really is?*...Ah, buddy. Ah, buddy. It's Christ Himself. Christ Himself, buddy."

> For joy, apparently, it was all Franny could do to hold the phone, even with both hands.

The Fat Lady as Christ may not, however, be a recent innovation in the Salinger work. In "Just Before the War with the Eskimos" Franklin Graff, a loathsome misfit, is vested with certain provocative physical qualities, circumstances, and a symbolic prop, a chicken sandwich suggestive of the Eucharist, which seem to mark him a Christ in identical terms—repulsive human suffering—to the Fat Lady of "Zooey."

Fifteen-year-old Ginnie Mannox has been "stuck" for cab fares from tennis lessons for five straight Saturdays. Thoroughly and rightfully incensed, she demands a reckoning from Salena Graff. Salena says she brings the tennis balls (her "father makes them or something"), but she consents to get the money. While waiting in the Graff apartment, Ginnie is confronted with "the funniest-looking boy, or man—it was hard to tell which he was—she had ever seen.... he looked—well, goofy."

"You Salena's brother?" asks Ginnie.

"Yeah. Christ, I'm bleedin' to death." (He has cut his finger slightly on a razor blade.)

Franklin Graff may, in banal disguise, be Salinger's bleeding Christ—in the same metaphorical aspect as the Fat Lady of "Zooey," and as an application of Jesus' averment, "Inasmuch as ye have done it unto one of the least of these my brethren, ye have done it unto me."

Franklin's appearance ("a long man...no slippers...sparse blond beard...mouth ajar") may be a caricature of an El Greco-type crucified Christ. He has an abnormal heart condition (perhaps signifying his heretical ability to love in a loveless world) and he served the war effort in an airplane factory. His time of service, thirty-seven months, recalls the Christ ministry; and airplane-making may be a startling metaphor for the Christ mission—the implementation of spiritual levitation.

Clearly one of "the least of men," Franklin seems obnoxious almost beyond pity. Toward the end of the conversation a

> ...dreamy expression came over his disorderly features. He inserted the nail of his uninjured index finger into the crevice between two front teeth and removing a food particle, turned to Ginnie. "Jeat jet?" he asked.

> "What?"

> "Jeat lunch yet?"

Presently he produces a stale chicken sandwich-half and forces it upon Ginnie.

"*Take* it, for Chrissake. I didn't poison it or anything."

Franklin *means* for Christ's sake. Again through the use of a banal echo Salinger has transfigured a mundane situation into the Holy Sacrament. The chicken sandwich is the Eucharist. This is confirmed when, leaving the apartment, Ginnie starts to dispose of the remains of the sandwich-half she had politely hidden in her coat pocket. The author then equates the chicken sandwich with a three-days-dead Easter chick—clearly representing the body of Christ.

> ...instead she put it [the sandwich] back into her pocket. A few years before, it had taken her three days to dispose of the Easter chick she had found dead...in the bottom of her wastebasket.

Ginnie has accepted the repulsive Franklin and thus Christ in more cryptic fashion than Franny Glass but with precisely the same instinct. Moreover, the spiritual Communion Ginnie was to receive at the Graff apartment is ironically foreshadowed at Ginnie's home.

> At dinner one night, for the edification of the entire Mannox family, Ginnie had conjured up a vision of dinner over at the Graffs'; it involved a perfect servant coming around to everyone's left with, instead of a glass of tomato juice, a can of tennis balls.

What appears to be burlesque can again be taken as sacramental—note the red liquid and white solid—and an even more powerful second meaning attaches itself to Ginnie's offhand allusion to "a perfect servant."

Ginnie is, of course, given a non-mystical motive for accepting Franklin: her conversation with Eric. Eric is Franklin's actor-friend who has come to take him to the Cocteau film "Beauty and the Beast" (bringing to mind the transfiguration of Franklin to Christ by Ginnie's love). He is the effete and ultra-sophisticated character much like Carl Luce in *The Catcher in the Rye* and Bob Nicholson in "Teddy."

Eric, who patronizes Franklin, is Christ's antithesis and a catalyst therefore in enabling Ginnie to recognize Franklin's gift of love. Eric considers himself "the *original* Good Samaritan" while, in fact, the support he offers is mechanical and meaningless. Ginnie sees her "righteous indignation" over the cab fares mirrored in true perspective in Eric's recital of the impositions he suffers. She forgives Salena's debt, promises to visit again, and keeps the chicken sandwich.

Perhaps as a reference to the Christ symbolism in "Just Before the War with the Eskimos," Salinger has given Franny Glass, like Ginnie Mannox, an affinity for Easter chicks. Moreover, Franny is also offered the symbolic chicken sandwich; but she must find her salvation on a more poetic plane.

Returning to Franny's story before her Fat Lady revelation, we find (in "Franny") the despondent college girl being escorted to an Ivy League football weekend by worldly Lane Coutell. Despairing of all the "ego, ego, ego" in the world, her own and everyone else's, she seeks deliverance in an incessant prayer, "Lord Jesus, have mercy on me." But Franny is as unable to find spiritual sustenance as she is to join Lane in the revelry. At a restaurant she significantly leaves untouched a chicken sandwich while Lane lustily devours frog-legs and snails (unclean things).

The sequel, "Zooey," takes up Franny's crisis several days later. Again she refuses a symbolic sustenance—this time her mother's chicken soup. The caustic Zooey chides his sister on this account:

> "You don't even have sense enough to *drink* when somebody brings you a cup of consecrated chicken soup—which is the only kind of chicken soup Bessie [Mother Glass] ever brings to anybody around this madhouse."

Franny has been seeking salvation in the most mystical terms and in world negation. Zooey thinks this futile.

> "How in *hell* are you going to recognize a legitimate holy man when you see one if you don't even know a cup of consecrated chicken soup when it's right in front of your nose.

Although Franny has refused her mother's Eucharist of love, Seymour's Fat Lady finally brings the same redeeming truth home to her—the truth, as Sherwood Anderson's Doctor Parcival put it "that everyone in the world is Christ and they are all crucified." In "Just Before the War with the Eskimos," Salinger has approximated this truth through the guises of verbal irony; in "Zooey" he has felt constrained to have his protagonist be another Parcival and say it straight out.

Source: James E. Bryan, "J. D. Salinger: The Fat Lady and the Chicken Sandwich," in *College English*, Vol. 23, No. 3, December 1961, pp. 226–29.

SOURCES

Alexander, Paul, *Salinger: A Biography*, Renaissance Books, 2000.

Bode, Carl, Review of *Franny and Zooey*, in *Wisconsin Studies in Contemporary Literature*, Winter 1962, pp. 65–71.

Bryan, James E., "J. D. Salinger: The Fat Lady and the Chicken Sandwich," in *College English*, December 1961, pp. 226–29.

Didion, Joan, "Finally (Fashionably) Spurious," in *National Review*, November 18, 1961, pp. 341–42.

Ennis, Lisa A., "Salinger, J(erome) D(avid)," in *The Scribner Encyclopedia of American Lives Thematic Series: The 1960s*, Charles Scribner's Sons, 2003.

Horowitz, Daniel, *Anxieties of Affluence: Critiques of American Consumer Culture, 1939-1979*, University of Massachusetts Press, 2005.

Kermode, Frank, "One Hand Clapping," in *New Statesman*, June 8, 1962, pp. 831–32.

Kirkwood, Hilda, Review of *Franny and Zooey*, in *Canadian Forum*, November, 1961, pp. 189–90.

Morgan, Diane, *The Best Guide to Eastern Philosophy and Religion*, St. Martin's Griffin, 2001.

Oldmeadow, Harry, *Journeys East: 20th Century Western Encounters with Eastern Religious Traditions*, World Wisdom, 2004.

Salinger, J. D., *Franny and Zooey*, Little, Brown, 1961.

Young, William H., and Nancy K. Young, *The 1950s: American Popular Culture through History*, Greenwood Press, 2004.

FURTHER READING

Anderson, Sherwood, *Winesburg, Ohio*, Signet Classics, 2005.

First published in 1919, this classic book of linked short stories is a portrait of a semirural town in middle America. Although not as central as it is in *Franny and Zooey*, a similar assertion, that everyone is Christ, is made in the collection.

Charters, Anne, *The Portable Beat Reader*, Penguin Classics, 2003.

This compilation of Beat literature is a comprehensive introduction to an important American literary movement. Although Salinger was not a Beat writer, his work was composed at the same time and espouses nearly identical themes and values.

Marling, Karal Ann, *As Seen on TV: The Visual Culture of Everyday Life in the 1950s*, Harvard University Press, 1998.

This collection of text and images attempts to document the advent of broadcast television, a phenomenon that defined the 1950s as the decade that forever altered American culture.

Salinger, Margaret A., *Dream Catcher: A Memoir*, Washington Square Press, 2001.

This memoir by Salinger's daughter offers a rare glimpse into the reclusive author's life, as well as his tenuous relationship with his children.

How Green Was My Valley

RICHARD LLEWELLYN

1939

How Green Was My Valley is Richard Llewellyn's best-known work, a bestselling novel that was first published in 1939 and was made into a popular movie in 1941. It tells the story of Huw Morgan, the son and brother of coal miners in south Wales at the end of the nineteenth and the beginning of the twentieth centuries, focusing on the destruction of his green valley by the spread of coal mining and the slag heap (a pile of waste material that is a by-product of mining).

Told as a reminiscence of happier times, the novel has a sad, sentimental tone, describing the passing away of many people in Huw's life as well as the loss of his valley's greenness. It is in part a coming-of-age tale, including a sensitive portrayal of Huw's romantic initiation. There is also some description of violence and use of mild profanity.

Although Welsh commentators have criticized the novel for inaccuracies in its portrayal of Wales, it has come to be seen as a portrayal of the essence of Welshness, but the true source of its appeal may have less to do with its specific Welsh setting than with its universal themes of loss and nostalgia.

AUTHOR BIOGRAPHY

Richard Llewellyn was the pen name of Richard Herbert Vivian Lloyd. He also went by the name Richard Dafydd Vivian Llewellyn Lloyd. Llewellyn claimed to have been born in Wales,

Richard Llewellyn (Corbis-Bettmann)

but although he was of Welsh descent, he was actually born in a suburb of London, England, on December 8, 1906. His father worked in hotel management, and Llewellyn at first followed him into that business but left to join the army in 1926, serving in India and Hong Kong. When he returned to London after six years of service, he found work as a reporter for a movie magazine and then began working in the film industry.

According to some reports, Llewellyn had been working on the manuscript of *How Green Was My Valley*, at first called *Slag*, while in India. In London, he wrote a successful play titled *Poison Pen*, from which he found encouragement to work full time on his novel. He completed the manuscript after moving to Llangollen, Wales, and published it in London in 1939, where it was an immediate success. It sold 50,000 copies in England in its first four months of publication, and in America it reached the top of the bestseller list in 1940. It won rave reviews in many locations around the world except in Wales itself, where it was criticized as not being a realistic portrayal of the coal miners. The movie based on it won five Academy Awards including best picture in 1942, and the book was translated into thirteen languages but not Welsh.

Some sources say Llewellyn based the unnamed village in the book on the south Wales mining village of Gilfach Goch. Llewellyn claimed to have worked as a coal miner in the area for research purposes, but it is not clear that this claim is true.

Llewellyn went on to write more than twenty other novels, including three sequels to *How Green Was My Valley*. None of these works matched the success of the original, though Llewellyn did win praise for *None But the Lonely Heart*, his 1943 novel about life among London criminals in the 1930s.

Published in 1960, *Up, into the Singing Mountains* (the first sequel to *How Green Was My Valley*) depicts what happens to Huw after his departure from his Welsh mining village: Huw travels to the Welsh colony in Patagonia in Argentina. In 1966 Llewellyn continued the story of Huw in Patagonia in *Down Where the Moon Is Small*. In the final sequel to *How Green Was My Valley*, *Green, Green My Valley Now* (1975), Huw returns to Wales, where he becomes involved in various movements to revive past Welsh glories.

Details of Llewellyn's life after the publication of *How Green Was My Valley* are scant, but it is known that he was in the Welsh Guards during World War II, though mostly as a non-combatant, and that he traveled widely after the war, in part to research his fiction. In addition to Patagonia, he set his later novels in such places as Israel, India, Kenya, and Brazil.

Llewellyn married Nona Theresa Sonsteby in 1952; the two divorced in 1968. In 1974 he married Susan Frances Heimann and moved with her to Dublin, Ireland, where he died on November 30, 1983.

PLOT SUMMARY

Chapter 1

How Green Was My Valley begins with the narrator, Huw Morgan, packing up and leaving his valley after having lived his whole life there. As he does this, he begins telling the story of his life, and the rest of the novel consists of this story, presented as he prepares to leave.

He begins with rough but prosperous days when his father and older brothers would come back from the coal mines, laughing and singing and tossing their pay in gold sovereigns (coins) to his mother. He also recounts extravagant Saturday dinners with ham, beef, lamb, and chicken, and the good-natured joking between his father and his mother. However, Huw hints at darker times to come, noting that his father warned him he would come to a bad end and saying that it turns out he was right.

The chapter ends with the first plot development, the meeting between Huw's oldest brother, Ivor, and the girl he is to marry, Bronwen. Huw says he fell in love with Bronwen too even though he was only a child. He ends the chapter on a characteristically sad and nostalgic note by stating all these events have passed.

Chapter 2

This chapter begins with Huw's recollection of the happy wedding of Ivor and Bronwen and includes a characteristic comment by Huw on the strange ways of memory. Huw also recounts the story of the marriage of his second brother, Ianto. Ianto marries a girl of whom his family does not exactly approve, then moves away and is not seen for years. The chapter also introduces a major plot element, the struggle for better wages at the mine, led by yet another of Huw's brothers, Davy, which results in two strikes.

Chapter 3

Huw remembers his first schoolteacher, Mrs. Tom Jenkins, and her badly injured miner husband. Mrs. Jenkins was unhappy enough about her life to question the existence of God, and Huw states that his teacher's thoughts made him think about his own life, which perhaps hurt him over the years. The chapter ends with Huw's recollections of family disagreements over whether to support a big union and Socialism.

Chapter 4

At six years old, Huw feels left out of his family's experiences. He sneaks out of the house at night to attend a union meeting, then falls in a barrel of water trying to get back into the house. His

father is waiting for him but only mildly reprimands him.

Chapter 5

Their father's moderation in union matters annoys Davy and two of Huw's other brothers, Owen and Gwilym. They leave home, which prompts Huw's mother to cry. Observing his mother crying is a disillusioning moment for Huw, because it makes her seem weak and comic to him.

This chapter includes a discussion about the destructive effect of the slag produced by mining: it is causing the valley to turn black. The chapter ends with Huw's father fetching his sons home from their boarding house because of the bad conditions there. Their mother is happy, but Huw's father feels his authority has been compromised.

Chapter 6

The union argument leads to disaster in chapter 6. Huw's mother addresses an outdoor union meeting on a wintry night, telling the men not to threaten her husband or her son Ivor, both of whom are now against the union. She succeeds in intimidating the union men, but on the way home she falls down in the snow. Huw, who is accompanying her, is barely able to save her life—he falls into the icy river and nearly dies.

Chapter 7

After his accident, Huw is bedridden for five years. His mother is also incapacitated for a while. She was pregnant and has gone into labor as a result of her fall. She gives birth to a daughter named Olwen, and Huw's sister-in-law Bronwen also gives birth to a boy named Gareth. Bronwen recovers quickly and takes over running the household, much to the chagrin of Huw's mother. When Huw's mother finally recovers, the family has a big celebration, marred only by an argument between Huw's brother Owen and the father of a girl with whom Owen has fallen in love, Marged.

Chapter 8

Owen breaks off his relationship with Marged, and she marries his brother Gwilym. However, Marged secretly still loves Owen. A new pastor, Mr. Gruffydd, begins visiting Huw and argues with a fundamentalist member of his congregation, Mr. Elias, who is upset that the minister allows festivities for Christmas.

Chapter 9

Mr. Gruffydd takes Huw to the mountains for his first outing since his accident, pushing Huw to try to recover, explaining that it is a question more of the spirit than of the body. Huw does seem to improve, but he also notices the great expansion of the slag heap, and he learns that the slag is killing the daffodils and the fish.

Chapter 10

Huw gets in trouble upon his first reappearance in chapel. He inadvertently remains behind after the service and hears the deacons denouncing a young woman for having an affair, which prompts him to confront and criticize them. His father is mortified by his young son's challenge to the authorities, but his mother supports him.

Chapter 11

Both his father and Mr. Gruffydd scold Huw for speaking out against the deacons, stating that it was brave but misguided. They tell Huw that he does not truly understand, and he should respect his elders.

Chapter 12

After his wife dies, Ianto returns home. His return is highly celebrated, but he argues with Mr. Gruffydd over the role of preachers, saying they do nothing for the socioeconomic needs of their congregations.

Chapter 13

Ianto becomes more sympathetic to preachers despite their nonrevolutionary ways. Huw spies on a woman in childbirth. His father and Bronwen later reprimand him.

Chapter 14

Mr. Elias steals the Morgans' turkeys. Mr. Gruffydd denounces the spread of thieving, warning that it will lead to the appearance of police, jails, and magistrates. He adds that the real enemy is coal, as it symbolizes money and can instill greed in the townspeople.

Chapter 15

Huw's sister Angharad is secretly seeing a local mine owner's son, Iestyn Evans. When her brothers find out, they threaten to beat up Iestyn for not asking permission first. Another sister, Ceridwen, is getting properly engaged, as is Davy. However, Marged, who has never overcome her love for Owen even though she married Gwilym, commits suicide by throwing herself in a fire.

Chapter 16

Huw goes to the National School. He does well in his entrance exams, but he fights with his fellow students and is at odds with his teacher, Mr. Jonas-Sessions. At home his father teaches him how to fight.

Chapter 17

Chapter 17 marks a special episode of vigilante justice (taking the law into one's own hands) in which the village men, led by the minister, go searching in the slums among foreigners and people of mixed blood for the rapist and murderer of a young girl. When they find him, they hand him over to the girl's family, who burns him to death. Meanwhile, Huw takes boxing lessons from trained boxers, Dai Bando and Cyfartha Lewis.

Chapter 18

Huw fights in school again and is caned by the teacher. He goes up on the mountain and has a vision of the valley being depleted of its riches.

Chapter 19

The students who mocked Huw when he first attended school are now in awe of his fighting prowess. Ceinwen Phillips, the sister of a boy he fought and beat, seems interested in him, but he is more interested in Shani Hughes. Huw's boxer friends beat up the teacher who caned him.

Chapter 20

Another strike occurs and lasts for months. Huw's father is ashamed, because the men's actions mean the women and children will go hungry. Shops close, and children die. After many months of striking, the men return to work, gaining one concession concerning a minimum wage for their work.

Chapter 21

When his teacher grabs him by the ear, Huw hits him. He has to speak to the headmaster as a result, but the headmaster is sympathetic and finds a new teacher for Huw and reassigns his old teacher to the lowest grade level. However, Mr. Gruffydd reprimands Huw for hitting an authority figure. Meanwhile, Angharad must choose between two suitors: Iestyn Evans, the rich son of the recently deceased local mine owner, and Mr. Gruffydd, the poor preacher.

Chapter 22

Huw's sister Ceridwen is getting married, and Huw gets his first suit with long trousers from the tailors, who joke in front of him in a way he does not understand; he is frustrated that no one will explain the jokes to him. Huw helps Mr. Gruffydd with carpentry.

Chapter 23

Huw's sister Angharad agrees to marry the rich dandy Iestyn, even though they squabble constantly and she really loves Mr. Gruffydd. But Mr. Gruffydd tells her he is too poor to support her and too old to be her husband.

Huw seeks answers to questions about sex and finally has them explained in a way by Mr. Gruffydd, in religious terms. Earlier he kissed his sister-in-law Bronwen in a nonbrotherly way.

Chapter 24

Huw feels like a man now that he has a suit and has developed physically, but he fears his new situation and almost wishes he was a boy again. The family gathers for the weddings of Davy and Ceridwen; at the events, there is a choir, a harpist, and even a rugby match. Ceinwen Phillips pursues Huw, who at first puts her off.

Chapter 25

The choir, led by Huw's brother Ivor, is invited to perform for the Queen.

Chapter 26

Ceinwen Phillips convinces Huw to go up the mountain to listen to nightingales. They stay for a very long time, and her family comes looking for her. Huw has to sneak off. The family continues searching, threatening a war if they find out who was with her.

Chapter 27

Ivor's choir returns from performing for the Queen at Windsor Castle. They have a large celebration; Huw's father and mother are very proud of Ivor.

Huw is eligible for a scholarship to university, but just before finishing his exams, he sees a Welsh girl being punished for speaking Welsh by his old teacher, Mr. Jonas-Sessions. Infuriated, Huw attacks the teacher and nearly kills him. He

escapes arrest but is expelled from school. His father says that he told Huw to fight.

Huw goes to apologize to his teacher, but the teacher insults him and Huw withdraws his apology. Huw can still apply to university but now decides he wants to be a coal miner like the rest of his family.

Chapter 28

Mr. Gruffydd looks old and worn. Huw wants to offer him support but is not sure how to do so. Mr. Gruffydd remarks that he has grown old without achieving anything.

Chapter 29

In chapter 29, Huw goes to work in the mines and describes what it is like inside them. He recounts the terror, the dark, the screaming wind, and the sheer joy of returning to the surface. Word comes that Angharad's husband is headed to South Africa to arrange coal for the Navy in the new war there (presumably the Boer War of 1899–1902).

Chapter 30

Huw goes up on the mountain again with Ceinwen, and the two have a romantic encounter. He later takes her to the theater, but the theater comes under attack from religious extremists who call acting sinful. Huw, along with his boxing friends, fights the extremists.

Owen marries Blodwen, the sister of Iestyn Evans, in London, and he and Gwilym go to America. The sudden marriage and departure upset their mother.

Chapter 31

Angharad returns for a visit, looking old, tired, and gray. Bronwen has a baby boy named Taliesin, and the family experiences much happiness. However, a month later, Ivor (Bronwen's husband and Huw's brother) dies in a cave-in.

Chapter 32

Huw's mother is angry over the loss of her son. She also thinks Bronwen will need a new husband, but this idea inspires jealousy in Huw, who loves Bronwen himself, though he says not in a romantic way. He does go to live with her for a while, just as a companion, but they live awkwardly together.

Chapter 33

While Davy helps plan a new strike, Ianto leaves the coal mines for the ironworks. Huw also plans to leave the mines for ironworking but talks of his preference for woodworking. Angharad incites gossip by spending time with Mr. Gruffydd while her husband is away in South Africa, and Huw and Bronwen try to deal with their difficult and ambiguous relationship.

Chapter 34

Back in the mines, Huw gets into yet another fight, this time over slighting remarks made about his sister Angharad. Fired from his job, he decides to take up carpentry.

Chapter 35

Huw is forced to go to court over his latest fight, but the charges are dismissed when the victim refuses to press them, wanting no part of court justice. At home, Huw finds out that the deacons have voted to dismiss Mr. Gruffydd, who will apparently go to Patagonia in South America.

Chapter 36

With Mr. Gruffydd departing, the chapel congregation splits in two.

Chapter 37

Huw's boxing friends take part in a prizefight for money. Huw joins them reluctantly. Despite his frequent fighting, he thinks fighting for money is wrong, especially in front of spectators, whom he calls cattle.

Huw's friend Dai wins the prizefight, but he nearly goes blind in the process. Nonetheless, Dai and Cyfartha take home enough money to buy a pub.

Chapter 38

Huw becomes a master carpenter. Looking back, he thinks he was happy sharing a house with Bronwen and her children, but at the time their odd relationship continues to cause awkwardness between them. Also, gossip prompts Huw to want to fight yet again, but Bronwen restrains him.

Chapter 39

The slag continues to bother Huw, but others, including his father, seem resigned to its expansion. Davy has to fight a court case and then decides to immigrate to New Zealand. Ianto plans to leave for Germany. Hardly anyone is left, their father observes.

Chapter 40

Another strike begins after much talk of Socialism among the union men. Huw thinks that they are turning to foreign principles, and when one of the strikers makes a slighting remark to his sister because of the family's connection to mine owners, he nearly starts another fight.

Earlier, though, he had an enjoyable experience taking Bronwen shopping. After the union meeting he has a vision of marching, singing men, lifting his spirits with a prayer.

Chapter 41

Huw and the boxers are unhappy about the strike but are also upset that Winston Churchill, the Home Secretary, has sent English soldiers to deal with the situation. A riot breaks out; a mob smashes shop windows and threatens to flood the pits. Huw and the boxers make sure the pumps keep working, helping the management.

Chapter 42

In the final chapter, the strike brings yet another tragedy to the Morgan family. Huw's father dies in a cave-in when he investigates a possible flooding in the mine, which the strikers' actions may have caused.

Huw closes the narrative by lamenting that in the thirty years since his father's death, he has failed to leave his mark on the world. Now, almost everyone in his story is gone, though not entirely gone, because they linger in his memory. He reasons that if they are truly dead, then everyone is dead. He resists making such a conclusion, though he ends his story by looking backward at his green valley, as if to say that it is gone too.

CHARACTERS

Idris Atkinson

Idris Atkinson, who lives in the poorest section of the village among the Irish and English immigrants and the mixed-blood Welsh, is found guilty of attacking a young girl by a vigilante mob and handed over to the girl's family for execution.

MEDIA ADAPTATIONS

- *How Green Was My Valley* was adapted to film and directed by John Ford in 1941. Starring Walter Pidgeon, Maureen O'Hara, and Roddy McDowall, the film won five Academy Awards including for best picture in 1942. It was produced by Twentieth Century-Fox.

- *How Green Was My Valley*, an eight-part miniseries in black and white, was produced by the British Broadcasting Corporation Television (BBC TV) in 1960. It was directed and produced by Dafydd Gruffydd and starred Eynon Evans and Rachel Thomas.

- *How Green Was My Valley* (1975–76), a six-part Masterpiece Theatre presentation, was coproduced by Twentieth Century-Fox Television and BBC TV. It was directed by Ronald Wilson and starred Stanley Baker and John Clive.

- *A Time for Singing*, a musical adaptation of the novel, was produced on Broadway for forty-one performances in 1966. The performance included music, lyrics, and a book by Gerald Freedman and John Morris.

- *How Green Was My Valley* was issued as an unabridged audiobook by Chivers Audio Books in 1992.

Dai Bando

Dai Bando is one of the boxers who teaches Huw how to fight. He nearly loses his eyesight in a prizefight.

Mr. Abishai Elias

Mr. Abishai Elias, a shopkeeper and a deacon at the chapel, thinks the pastor Mr. Gruffydd is not strict enough and becomes an enemy of the Morgan family.

Blodwen Evans

Blodwen Evans, the sister of Iestyn Evans, becomes interested in Owen Morgan and eventually marries him.

Iestyn Evans

Iestyn Evans, the son of a local mine owner, is a rich dandy who pursues and eventually marries Angharad Morgan. He and Angharad fight constantly during their engagement and are referred to as Kiss and Scratch. He goes off to South Africa during the war there (presumably the Boer War of 1899–1902).

Old Mr. Evans

Old Mr. Evans, Iestyn Evans's father, is a local mine owner who treats his men better than the large mine owners do. He dies in a mine accident.

Mr. Gruffydd

Mr. Gruffydd is the new pastor at the Morgans' chapel when Huw is bedridden. He helps Huw with his recovery, and in general, he serves as Huw's mentor. He is portrayed as sympathetic to the miners' cause, though he also believes in moderation. Mr. Gruffydd and Huw's sister Angharad Morgan fall in love, but he sends her away from him, thinking she should not marry a poor and old man like himself. However, when Angharad is unhappy in her marriage to Iestyn Evans, Mr. Gruffydd spends time with her, inciting gossip and leading the chapel deacons to dismiss him. He leaves Huw's village, apparently for Patagonia in South America.

Shani Hughes

Shani Hughes, a girl at school whom Huw likes, moves away before he gets to know her well.

Mrs. Tom Jenkins

Mrs. Tom Jenkins, the wife of an incapacitated miner, is Huw's first teacher. She is bitter over her husband's fate.

Mr. Elijah Jonas-Sessions

Mr. Elijah Jonas-Sessions, or Mr. Jonas for short, is Huw's teacher at the National School. He takes an instant dislike to Huw, apparently because Huw is from a Welsh-speaking coal mining family and Mr. Jonas looks down on the coal miners and tries to seem English rather than Welsh. When Huw witnesses Mr. Jonas-Sessions punishing a Welsh girl for speaking Welsh, he becomes infuriated and attacks the teacher, nearly killing him.

Cyfartha Lewis

Cyfartha Lewis is one of the boxers who teaches Huw how to fight.

Meillyn Lewis

Meillyn Lewis is a young woman punished by the deacons for having an affair.

Angharad Morgan

Angharad Morgan, one of Huw's sisters, is lively in her youth but becomes old and tired after making a "suitable" marriage to the heir of a mine owner instead of marrying the man she truly loves, Mr. Gruffydd.

Beth Morgan

Beth Morgan, the mother of the Morgan family, is a traditional homemaker, though she acts non-traditionally in making a threatening speech to the miners' union. She is incapacitated for a significant portion of the novel after she falls in the snow and Huw rescues her but almost dies himself. Like her husband, Beth loses control of her household, giving way to her daughter-in-law Bronwen. She also loses some of Huw's respect when he sees her crying weakly.

Bronwen Morgan

Bronwen enters the story early on as the wife of Huw's eldest brother, Ivor. As a child, Huw feels that he is in love with Bronwen. Bronwen takes over running the Morgan household when Huw's mother is unable to due to her accident, and she functions as a sort of surrogate mother to Huw. After Ivor's death, Huw moves in with Bronwen and her two children in a platonic but ambiguous relationship.

Ceridwen Morgan

Ceridwen Morgan, Huw's sister, marries in a double ceremony at the same time as her brother Davy.

Davy Morgan

Davy Morgan is the most militant of the Morgan sons. He is involved in organizing a union and gives speeches to the men. He moves out of the Morgan house after having a falling out with his father over union matters and marries in a double ceremony at the same time as his sister Ceridwen.

Gwilym Morgan

Another of Huw's brothers, the younger Gwilym marries Marged after Owen rejects her. He and Owen later leave Wales, first for London, England, and then for the United States.

Mr. Gwilym Morgan

The father of the Morgan family is a coal miner and the informal leader of his fellow coal miners in the early stages of the novel, but his leadership is challenged in the course of the story by more radical men in the developing miners' union. Some of these radicals are his own sons, especially Davy, and he loses control not only within the community as a whole but within his own household. As others become more radical, he becomes closer to management, accepting a promotion to superintendent. In the end, he tries to protect the mines from the effects of the strike, an action that costs him his life.

Huw Morgan

Huw Morgan, the narrator of the novel, is also its central figure. In some respects, *How Green Was My Valley* is a family saga and the tale of a whole community. Yet at heart it is Huw's story, the story of a young boy growing up and finding his way in life. The time frame of the narrative is left deliberately vague in the book, but Huw's father mentions that young Huw is six years old in an early chapter; his growth through adolescence to young adulthood is traced in subsequent chapters. As narrator, Huw seems to be in his early sixties, writing long after the events discussed have passed.

Huw presents himself as endearingly innocent, though he is clearly a feisty, fiery-tempered boy and young adult, ready to fight at the slightest provocation. He also becomes the family's intellectual, perhaps in part because of his several years as an invalid, during which he spends much of his time reading. In a family of coal miners, Huw is the only one who goes to secondary school and studies for examinations that will get him into college. Characteristically, his temper, along with his stubbornness, keeps him from that goal. He ultimately renounces the life of the mind, much to his father's dismay. He decides instead to follow the family trade of coal mining and, when that trade does not work out, he becomes a carpenter.

Huw rhapsodizes about carpentry and makes profound-sounding statements throughout the novel. He also speaks enthusiastically about women and love, and the novel follows him through his romantic awakening with Ceinwen Phillips and his ambiguous love for his sister-in-law Bronwen.

As the elderly narrator, Huw presents himself as a disappointed and nostalgic man, stating that he has failed to make his mark in life and expressing sadness over the disappearance of his friends and family and his valley.

Ianto Morgan

Huw's second-oldest brother, Ianto, leaves the family early in the story when he marries a woman of whom they do not fully approve, but he returns after she dies and becomes caught up in the union struggles. He later immigrates to Germany.

Ivor Morgan

Huw's oldest brother, Ivor, marries Bronwen early in the novel. He is close to his father, taking his side against the union radicals, and he leads the village choir. His major triumph is taking the choir to sing for Queen Victoria. Halfway through the story, Ivor dies in a mining accident, leaving Bronwen a widow.

Marged Morgan

Marged falls in love with Owen Morgan, but when he rejects her in the wake of her father's complaints about their relationship, she marries Owen's brother Gwilym. She never gets over Owen, however, and eventually goes mad and commits suicide by jumping into a fire.

Olwen Morgan

Olwen, Huw's youngest sister, is born after their mother's fall on the mountain. When Huw leaves the village, Olwen seems to be the only one left to say good-bye to.

Owen Morgan

Owen, another of Huw's brothers, is interested in mechanical inventions and moves first to London and then to America to pursue a business career. Early in the book, he has a relationship with a girl named Marged, but leaves her after her father makes a public complaint about them, devastating her. Much later in the story, Owen marries Blodwen Evans.

Mr. Motshill

Mr. Motshill, the headmaster at the National School, is sympathetic to Huw.

Ceinwen Phillips

Ceinwen Phillips is the sister of a boy Huw beats in a fight at school. She becomes interested in Huw and they become involved romantically, but they drift apart.

Old Twm

Old Twm is assistant to Hwfa Williams, the tailor, with whom he is always arguing.

Hwfa Williams

Hwfa Williams, the tailor, fits Huw for his first adult suit.

THEMES

Nostalgia

How Green Was My Valley is an evocation of a past that no longer exists, a time period that Huw praises as being far superior to his present time. His valley used to be green, as the title of the book states, but now it has become ravaged by a slag heap. Something has gone wrong with the world, he says; there used to be prosperity and happiness, but that has vanished. His own life has vanished, he states, without his having left a mark on the world, and all the people he knew have vanished as well. Huw's tone throughout the novel is a sad one as he remembers times gone by.

Ecology

Ahead of its time, the book deals with the destruction of the environment, showing how the green valley has become black with slag, as human greed for nature's riches has led to the destruction of flowers on the mountain and fish in the river. Huw wonders how this could have been allowed to happen, but no one else seems even to notice or justify it by asking where else the slag could be put in order to preserve the environment.

Coming of Age

How Green Was My Valley details Huw's maturity into adulthood. He develops from an innocent child into a hot-tempered adolescent who eventually learns some of the mysteries of love. Huw must also decide on a career path. Although seemingly qualified for an intellectual future, Huw is drawn to his family's life of coal mining.

Unions, Socialism, and Revolution

Much of *How Green Was My Valley* focuses on the struggles of the coal miners, some of whom are drawn to union organizing and Socialism. The book explores pro- and antiunion positions and moderation versus extremism. Some of the

TOPICS FOR FURTHER STUDY

- Research the history of Welsh nationalism. Write a paper explaining how Wales came to be controlled by England and how the Welsh have resisted or accepted English rule over the years.

- Explore the history of religious Nonconformity in Britain. What did it mean to be a Nonconformist? How were the Nonconformists connected to the Puritans of earlier ages? Give an oral presentation explaining these points and also explaining what religious groups in the United States are similar to the Nonconformists.

- Imagine what it would be like to spend several months or years bedridden. Write a short story or poem about the possible experience, including how you would occupy your time and communicate with others.

- Produce a video about Wales today and how it differs from the Wales presented in *How Green Was My Valley*. Try to incorporate the music of Welsh singers in the film.

- Organize a class debate over whether unions are positive or negative organizations. The debate might focus on the effect of strikes on the strikers, the owners, and the public. It might also include discussions of how unions are organized and regulated, and how they interact with other members of society.

- Prepare a multimedia presentation on coal mining. How was it done in the past? How is it done now? What are the effects of coal mining on human health and the environment?

characters refer to the German Socialist philosopher Karl Marx and the British Socialists Keir Hardie and Henry Hyndman. However, actual analysis of Socialist ideology rarely occurs, and the thrust of the book refutes such thinking. Strikes occur several times in the novel, and at first it seems that the workers are justified. In the climactic strike, however, the workers appear selfish and greedy, and the main effect of strikes is human suffering: children starve and shops shut down.

Welshness

In many ways, the book is a celebration of Welsh traditions, including choral singing, rugby, and Nonconformist religion. It also honors the Welsh language and the fight to preserve the language from English. The very syntax (sentence structure) of the book is part of this effort, as are the episodes at the National School in which Huw struggles against restrictions on the Welsh language. The book at times seems ethnocentric (characterized by a belief that one's own group is superior to another) in suggesting that immigrants to Wales, notably the Irish and English in the poor section of the village, have a bad effect on the community. Similarly, Mr. Morgan's rejection of Marx and other Socialists is cast in terms of their foreign status. He states that Wales is for the Welsh.

Gender Roles and Parental Control

How Green Was My Valley depicts a traditional domestic society under threat. The two maternal women in the novel, Huw's mother and Bronwen, focus almost entirely on domestic matters involved with running the household and do not work outside the home. Huw's father is the patriarch of the family and holds ultimate authority—at least until his sons revolt against his moderate politics. Afterwards, he declares that he is no longer in charge of the family, and they are all equal lodgers in the household he once ruled. Huw's mother also revolts, first by speaking at a union meeting and later by complaining that she was never taught the arithmetic that young Huw is learning. Later in the novel, Bronwen revolts against Huw's notions of male-female relations. She tells him she is not his brother's possession, and it is her decision who shares her world. Huw, however, remains caught up in romantic notions about women and the world they bring to men.

Romantic Misalliances

The novel abounds with frustrated relationships. Angharad is in love with Mr. Gruffydd, but she marries Iestyn Evans, sentencing herself to an unhappy marriage which ages her before her time. Mr. Gruffydd, who returns Angharad's feelings, loses much of his spirit after her marriage to Iestyn. After Owen rejects Marged, she

Coal miners (© *Bettmann* / *Corbis*)

marries his brother Gwilym. She never gets over Owen, and eventually goes mad and commits suicide by jumping into a fire. Huw never marries, living in the memory of his early girlfriend, Ceinwen, and in frustrated longing for his sister-in-law, Bronwen, who suffers the loss of her husband in a mine accident. Ianto also loses his wife. Derrick Price, in his article in *The Progress of Romance*, suggests that these problems reflect the breakdown of traditional life under the pressure of new forces.

STYLE

Symbolism
Symbolism is a literary device in which an object is used to represent an idea or concept. The chief symbol in the novel is the slag heap, the pile of refuse left over from coal mining. The slag heap accumulates in the valley and up the mountainside to such an extent that by the time Huw leaves the village, it is set to destroy the house in which he lives as well as other homes. Described as almost glacier-like, the slag is a slowly advancing inexorable force. Huw says the house is well built, but even it will be flattened by the advancing slag. The works of human beings are no match for the forces of nature, especially a nature that has been ravaged by human beings in the pursuit of the profits of coal mining. The slag heap can be interpreted as nature's revenge and a symbol of the defeat of human beings.

The coal pits may also be symbolic. The word "pit" is used elsewhere in the novel to mean hell, which suggests that going down into the pits is like descending into hell. When Huw finally enters the pits, he is terrified by the absolute darkness and screeching wind. Conversely, at the beginning of the novel, working in the coal pits appears to be a noble occupation.

Fire is a dual symbol in the novel. The fire consumes and kills Marged as she commits suicide, representing suffering, madness, and death. However, fire warms Huw and Ceinwen when they are on the mountain, representing comfort and security. Fire can be interpreted as either a positive or negative symbol in the book.

Syntax and Tone
Though writing in English, Llewellyn uses exotic syntax (sentence structure) to convey a sense of Welshness. The characters are all supposed to be speaking in Welsh, and Llewellyn tries to convey this fact by various constructions, notably starting a sentence or phrase with "There is." For instance: "There is clever you are," "there is heavy my mother seemed to me," and "there is pleased she was." He also uses inversion (reversing sentence components) for the same effect: "Saying nothing against Ivor I was."

Llewellyn's tone is also somewhat biblical or mystical. Huw often utters statements that appear profound, even if the subject matter is seemingly insignificant. The content is not actually philosophical, but the air of profundity, the reverential tone, creates a magical aura around the language, such that even if readers do not feel they have been transported to exotic Wales, they may at least experience a realm of fantasy or mystery.

Flashbacks and Foreshadowing
How Green Was My Valley is framed as a flashback from Huw's present to his early life, and this structure seems a completely natural complement to the book's theme of nostalgia. Huw also occasionally lets the reader know that something is coming before he presents it, thus foreshadowing to create interest and suspense. For instance, before presenting his denunciation of the deacons at chapel, Huw announces that on his first return to services he disgraced himself forever but was not sorry.

COMPARE & CONTRAST

- **1900:** Coal mining is at its peak in Wales, and slag heaps begin to take over the valleys.

  1939: After two decades of economic slump and depression, the Welsh coal mining industry is in crisis.

  Today: Coal mining has almost disappeared from Wales, and the valleys have been cleaned up and made green again as tourist locations.

- **1900:** Welsh seems to be a language in decline; many Welsh people prefer to speak English.

  1939: Efforts begin to revive the Welsh language.

  Today: Welsh can be heard in Wales on radio and television and can be seen on bilingual road signs, but English is the everyday language for most Welsh people.

- **1900:** Welsh choirs become world renowned, and Wales is known as a land of song.

  1939: With the advent of the gramophone, radio, and other leisure pursuits, Welsh choirs go into decline.

  Today: Modern Welsh people pursue a variety of leisure activities, and Welsh choirs are mostly a thing of the past.

- **1900:** Wales is ruled by England and has no independent government or local autonomy. However, a politician of Welsh descent, David Lloyd George, rises to become Prime Minister of England.

  1939: A Welsh nationalist party, Plaid Cymru, has been formed but wins little support for Welsh independence or autonomy.

  Today: The Welsh have their own National Assembly and have some autonomy within the United Kingdom.

HISTORICAL CONTEXT

South Wales Coalfield

Coal mining transformed the southeast part of Wales in the second half of the nineteenth century, particularly in the valleys of the Rhondda District in Glamorgan County. The population in the Rhondda increased from one thousand or two thousand in 1851 to 113,000 in 1901. As in the novel, a string of connected villages sprang up in the valleys, as there was not room for large towns or cities, and the amount of coal exported rose from 450,000 tons to almost thirty-seven million tons. Also, large slag heaps were created which moved and threatened towns. As late as 1966, the waste from a coal slag tip buried part of the village of Aberfan, killing more than one hundred children.

Unions and Socialism

The book's depiction of the growth of unionism reflects the actual events of the time period from the 1870s until 1910. With the growth of the coal industry, coal miners attempted to organize and affiliate with unions elsewhere. Early attempts to unionize in the 1870s failed, and the mine owners were able to impose the sliding scale system referred to in the novel, under which miners' pay fluctuated according to the price of coal. In 1898 a long strike and lockout over the sliding scale took place, much like the lengthy strike in chapter 20 of the novel. As in the novel, the strike produced much suffering and radicalized the miners, so that they turned away from moderate leaders (like Huw's father in the novel) and created the more radical South Wales Miners' Federation.

In 1910 a strike against the Cambrian Combine mining company led to riots in the town of Tonypandy, prompting Winston Churchill, the Home Secretary, to send first police and then soldiers, events depicted and referred to at the end of the novel. Within two years, radicals issued a Socialist tract, *The Miners' Next Step*,

Walter Pidgeon as Mr. Gruffydd in the 1941 film version of How Green Was My Valley *(© John Springer Collection | Corbis)*

but despite talk of Marxism and Socialism, the Welsh miners ended the strike by becoming supporters of the newly formed and relatively moderate Labour Party rather than starting a revolution.

Nonconformist Religion

The novel uses the word *chapel* rather than *church* to refer to houses of worship, reflecting the fact that the majority of the Welsh belonged to Nonconformist religious denominations. The established Church of England (the Anglicans) had churches but was a minority religion in Wales. The Nonconformists, including Baptists, Methodists, and other Protestants outside the Church of England, attended chapel. Nonconformists dominated Wales in the late nineteenth century. As a very religious, puritanical society, Wales had a chapel for every four hundred people in 1914.

Choral Singing

Simultaneous with the rise of Nonconformity and the coal industry in the late nineteenth century, the Welsh became noted for their choral singing. Most choral singing was associated with chapels, though it sometimes took place at cultural festivals known as *eisteddfodau*. Both mixed and male choirs were popular. The Treorchy Male Choir, composed primarily of coal miners, was invited to Windsor Castle to perform for Queen Victoria in 1895, much as Ivor's choir does in the novel.

Welsh Language and Nationalism

At the end of the nineteenth century, Wales was in the unusual position of having a national language (Welsh) that no more than half the population spoke. Wales had lost its independence to England centuries before, eventually becoming part of the United Kingdom. In *How Green Was My Valley*, Llewellyn implies that Welsh was suppressed by the English, who forced Welsh children to speak English at school. However, active suppression of Welsh in Wales may be less important than the influx of English immigrants, the proximity of Wales to England, and the collective belief in English as the language of the future.

In fact, attempts to revive Welsh began as early as the 1890s and continued into the twentieth century. The Welsh nationalist party, Plaid Cymru, rose during the twentieth century, ultimately winning local autonomy and a National Assembly for Wales at the end of the century.

Depression and War

Llewellyn published *How Green Was My Valley* long after the events depicted in it occurred, following two decades of economic difficulties in Wales resulting from the decline of the coalfield and one decade of a worldwide depression. Moreover, the book was published just a month after the outbreak of World War II in Europe, a time period of great difficulties.

CRITICAL OVERVIEW

Writing in 1983 in the *Dictionary of Literary Biography*, Mick Felton comments that because Llewellyn was not part of mainstream modern literature, he received little academic attention. With the appearance of some major academic studies of Welsh writing in English after 2000, the situation changed somewhat, but the academics who do write about Llewellyn tend to be critical of his work. The original reviewers of *How Green Was My Valley*, at least those outside Wales, praised the book highly. Richard Church, as reported by John Harris in his article in *Welsh Writing in English*, saw in it "the freshness of folk song and the old Celtic tales." In Wales, though the book was as popular with the public as it was elsewhere, reviewers called it "trash," according to David Smith (also known as Dai Smith) in his article in the *Anglo-Welsh Review*. Later Welsh academic critics have condemned the book for perpetuating stereotypes. Some have been more positive in their reviews than others. Although Glyn Jones calls the novel "literary hokum" in his book *The Dragon Has Two Tongues: Essays on Anglo-Welsh Writers*

and Writing and in private correspondence called it a fake, he admits that he found it absorbing to read. He praises its interesting characters, humor, and drama while also noting its use of clichés.

Smith, though conceding the novel's appeal, condemns it as "a gargantuan con-trick" similar to a "tawdry Hollywood 'B' picture," a description he removed in a later reprinting of his article. Stephen Knight criticizes the book even more. In his book *A Hundred Years of Fiction: Writing Wales in English* he sees even its popularity as a sign of the forces at work against authenticity, adding that Llewellyn's novel is "a classic example of colonized writing...making the Welsh seem quaint but willing servants of English capitalism." In an essay in *Welsh Writing in English*, Knight contrasts *How Green Was My Valley* with the more documentary, realist, and radical writings of other authors of the 1930s, criticizing Llewellyn's book for being too personalized and sentimental, in effect failing to be a Socialist novel.

Even so, *How Green Was My Valley* has some academic defenders. Whereas other academics have criticized Llewellyn for inaccuracy, Harris reports on Llewellyn's account of his research for the book, which he discarded in order to get closer to the characters in his story. For Harris, this is a candid explanation of how fiction writers work; they write imaginative stories, not documentaries. Harris goes on to praise *How Green Was My Valley* for its mythic, romantic evocation of a past golden age, the very quality that other academics condemn. Harris says that Llewellyn "taps into the elemental."

Derrick Price, in an essay in *The Progress of Romance: The Politics of Popular Fiction*, also distances himself from those who condemn *How Green Was My Valley* for inaccuracies, conservative politics, and sentimentality. Though he acknowledges the validity of some of those criticisms, he also describes the novel as "an interesting, complex, and even a key text in the body of writing about the industrial valleys of South Wales." At the same time, Price distinguishes *How Green Was My Valley* from another genre of the time period, the documentary novel; in Llewellyn's book, specific dates and place names are deliberately missing. Price states, "Instead, we are taken to a mythic past" by "an almost perfect narrator." In one of the few full-length academic articles written about the novel, Price provides a detailed examination of Huw as narrator and analyzes other aspects of the novel, including its depiction of gender relations, the symbol of the slag heap, and the pressure of new forces on old traditions. He concludes by saying that the power of the book "derives from the way in which it uses romance to take real historical struggles and return them to us as an ineluctable fall from grace of particular human beings."

In short, several reviewers have criticized *How Green Was My Valley* as a failed documentary novel, but others have praised it as a successful attempt to create something quite different from documentary realism—a timeless, universal story about the disappearance of a past golden age.

CRITICISM

Sheldon Goldfarb

Goldfarb is a specialist in Victorian literature who has published academic books as well as a novel for young adults set in Victorian times. In this essay, he examines the character of Huw in How Green Was My Valley.

Early on in *How Green Was My Valley*, the adult narrator, Huw, announces, "I am going from this house to-night to try and find out what is the matter with me and the people I know, because there is something radically wrong with us all, to be sure." It is a striking statement. Although the tone of the novel is nostalgically sad from the start and although at this point Huw has already spoken of his dissatisfaction with life, this statement seems a sweeping condemnation of all humanity. It begins, however, by Huw identifying something wrong with himself, and perhaps the key to the novel is finding out what that is.

Huw does not seem like a villain, so to search for what is wrong with him may seem misguided. He comes across first as an innocent boy wanting to find out about life, which indeed is how he still appears when, as an adult, he makes his statement condemning humanity; he is still hoping to find something out, to find out what is wrong with the world, presumably in order to set it right. This is perhaps a heroic task he sets for himself, seeming all the more so

WHAT DO I READ NEXT?

- *None But the Lonely Heart* (1943) was Llewellyn's next novel after *How Green Was My Valley*. It differs from the latter, as a tale of criminal life in London.

- *Coal: A Human History* (2003), by Barbara Freese is a popular survey of the mining and use of coal dating back to the Middle Ages and covering not just England and Wales but also the United States and China.

- *Caverns of Night: Coal Mines in Art, Literature, and Film* (2000), edited by William B. Thesing, is a collection of essays analyzing books and films about coal mining.

- *Sons and Lovers* (1913), by D. H. Lawrence, is a groundbreaking work of fiction set in an English coal mining district.

- For a Socialist novel about American coal mining, see Upton Sinclair's *King Coal* (1917).

- *Power* (1962), by Howard Fast, is a later novel about coal mining and unions in America.

- For another Welsh novel about coal mining, see *The Red Hills* (1932), by Rhys Davies.

- *Rasselas* (1759), by Samuel Johnson, is a classic tale of a young boy who has to leave a "happy valley" to discover the meaning of life.

- Joseph Conrad's tale of Africa, *Heart of Darkness* (1902), is another story about failed heroism with mythic overtones.

- For a nostalgic poem about nature and loss, see "Ode: Intimations of Immortality" by William Wordsworth, first published in *Poems, in Two Volumes* (1807).

because he makes this statement after talking about following the example of Jesus. It is as if Huw wants to bring about a revolution in human behavior similar to the one wrought by Jesus, or as if he thinks such a revolution is necessary, because there is something radically wrong with the human race.

THE TASK OF THE HERO IS TO CORRECTLY UNDERSTAND THE CHALLENGE HE FACES. HUW, FOR ALL HIS DESIRE FOR UNDERSTANDING AND HIS CLAMORING TO GRASP LIFE'S MYSTERIES, FALLS SHORT IN THIS SENSE."

If anyone can play the role of hero, it is Huw. He plays it at least once in the novel, saving his mother's life after she speaks at the union meeting and almost perishes in the snow. Huw's sacrificial heroism, which is reminiscent of Jesus, nearly costs him his own life and condemns him to five years in bed as an invalid. So Huw possesses good qualities: heroism, innocence, compassion, resourcefulness, intelligence, loyalty, devotion to family, and a strong sense of justice—perhaps too strong a sense of justice. In this trait it is possible to see something of what is wrong with Huw. The heroic yet sensitive young boy ends up failing to leave his mark, as he puts it at the end of the book, echoing Mr. Gruffydd's own concerns, as a good man who does not achieve his goals or live up to expectations. One might expect that Huw would become a writer; he does become the family's letter-writer. As Huw is educated and tells his own story, the reader perceives that a writer is speaking, that Llewellyn has created an alter ego who could have had a life of creative achievement. But this is not the path Huw follows.

His parents think he should go to college and become a lawyer or a doctor. This also seems a possibility for Huw; he has the intelligence. The headmaster at his secondary school fully expects him to win a scholarship. Huw expects it himself—and yet it does not happen, because he gets into one too many fights and is expelled from school. It is his sense of justice that betrays him perhaps. Seeing a poor young girl punished for speaking Welsh outrages him and prompts him to fight. Attacking the teacher responsible, Mr. Jonas-Sessions, seems a somewhat misguided sense of justice, in the same way that his father and Mr. Gruffydd call him "a brave boy, but misguided," when he denounces the deacons for being cruel to Meillyn Lewis.

It is striking how many fights Huw gets into in the novel. He fights with his classmates and his teacher more than once, beating him so badly he is bedridden while recovering. When he fights with a fellow mine worker over remarks the man made about Huw's sister, he is charged in court. He fights against the puritans who try to shut down the theater, and he threatens to fight the gossips who speak about him and Bronwen. He fights altogether too much.

It is true his father originally encouraged him to fight, taught him how to defend himself, and then arranged for two boxers to teach him even more about fighting. However, even his father thinks it a disgrace that Huw attacks his teacher; it is that misguided bravery again. Fighting seems a noble, traditional activity, but in Huw it becomes corrupt.

Interestingly Huw believes that prizefighting, or fighting for money, is corrupt. Huw is horrified that his boxer friends, Dai and Cyfartha, participate in a boxing match for money and sport, to entertain "cattle," as he calls the spectators. Huw believes that he fights for justice or honor but that prizefighting takes place in the modern, commercial world, turning something pure—in Huw's mind at least—into something impure. "Fight, yes," he says. "Prize-fight, no. Prostitution, it is."

Llewellyn's point, if he agrees with Huw, seems to be that something pure can be corrupted. In prizefighting, the purity of fighting is corrupted by harnessing it to modern sport and commercialism, turning something personal into a public spectacle conducted for profit. It is a turning away from the traditional context for fighting and making it into a spectacle. The same can be said in a way of Huw's fighting, though Huw's corruption is of a different sort. It is indirect, on the surface a complete rejection of the modern world and a holding tight to the old ways of fighting for honor. But he seems to hold onto tradition too tightly, or to seize on one aspect of it and forget others.

Huw might argue that in the case of his fight with his teacher, he reacted against a direct threat to traditions, a threat to the use of the Welsh language, which Mr. Jonas-Sessions would apparently like to stamp out. And this indeed is how Huw's corruption results, albeit indirectly, from the modern world, just like the corruption of his boxer friends. The modern world's threat to the traditional language, or more generally, to the old way of life, can drive someone like Huw to a one-sided, extreme embrace of certain aspects of tradition, and this one-sidedness leads him astray. A similar one-sidedness seems to be at work when Huw decides to become a coal miner like the rest of his family rather than pursue an intellectual career. This might seem like devotion to the old ways, but it is such an extreme version of devotion that it seems wrong, especially to Huw's father, who is upset that Huw will not continue with his education.

The task of the hero is to correctly understand the challenge he faces. Huw, for all his desire for understanding and his clamoring to grasp life's mysteries, falls short in this sense. His extreme devotion to fighting obstructs his path to higher education, and he continues down a path of extremism by refusing to even try to overcome this obstruction, by instead renouncing higher education entirely. He possibly sees education as part of the modern world, as the work of the English who have caused him such trouble and are a modern threat to his Welsh traditions.

Nevertheless, in rejecting education and turning first to coal mining and then to carpentry, Huw seems to swerve from the hero's path. As he would know from the Bible, Christians believe that the correct path involves properly using one's talents, not burying them. But Huw rejects his intellectual talents, in effect renouncing the heroic role he might have pursued. Now late in life, he proposes to find what has gone radically wrong with him; perhaps he will discover it. He seems already to half understand it, for he mentions that he did not make his mark in life. His carpentry work was all very well, but his intellectual talents were not utilized.

Nor does Huw make his mark in the domestic sphere. He does not marry; he does not produce children. Huw does help care for his late brother and Bronwen's children, and he is quite devoted to Bronwen, which is perhaps part of his problem. As Derrick Price notes in his article in *The Progress of Romance*, Bronwen is very much like Huw's mother. Huw in effect gives up on any chance of marriage by attaching himself to his sister-in-law in a strange relationship that in part seems romantic but is also a regression, a return to a young boy's attachment to his mother.

Huw's relationship with Bronwen apparently remains platonic. Huw's one physical relationship seems to be with Ceinwen Phillips. He describes his relationship with Ceinwen by referencing the book of Genesis in the Bible. Huw cites the story of Adam and Eve eating from the Tree of Knowledge and then being expelled from the Garden of Eden by the angel with a flaming sword. When Huw feels tortured by his relationship with Bronwen, he remembers "the curse that sent them [Adam and Eve] from the Garden," and later when talking to Bronwen about happiness, beauty, and truth, he says such things do not last, for "the Angel with a flaming sword comes to slash us out."

It is as if, for Huw, happiness resides in the Garden before the fall from God. To allow himself to pursue an adult romantic relationship with a woman and marry her would mean to lose his Garden, the preadult Garden of childhood and maternal protection. Huw lets Ceinwen disappear from his life; before that he let the other girl he was interested in, Shani, disappear too. He then clings to Bronwen in a partially childlike relationship that enables him to avoid pursuing adult relationships.

The idea of a lost paradise is in a more general way central to this novel. Huw and his father, and Llewellyn as well, lament the passing of the old world of prosperity and happiness before greed and foreign ideas and slag heaps ruined it. The book is in a very deep way about the loss of paradise, and yet the attempt to remain in paradise, in a childlike Garden of Eden, is an extreme reaction. It is a distortion or corruption brought on in part by the dangers of the modern world, the threat to paradise, which can make someone like Huw try to hold onto it too tightly and thus renounce the task of meeting the threat.

At the end of John Milton's *Paradise Lost*, a poem depicting the expulsion from the Garden of Eden, Adam and Eve venture out into the world, where they must learn to survive on their own. In *Rasselas* by Samuel Johnson, one of Huw's favorite authors, the hero similarly cannot stay in the paradisal Happy Valley forever; he must go out into the world and learn how to live; more precisely he must learn that there is no one perfect life; one must make the best of imperfection.

This is perhaps the lesson Huw should learn. Instead of fighting, he should find a way to use his intellectual talents. Rather than clinging to a childlike relationship, he should attempt to create an adult one. But one should not judge Huw too harshly. As Mr. Gruffydd says in another context, referring to the villagers' gossip and bad thoughts, "You cannot stop people from talking ... nor shall you stop them thinking. They are products of a faulty environment. And faults are what you shall expect."

In the sad world that is *How Green Was My Valley*, faults do seem to be all that one can expect. Llewellyn paints a mournful picture of a ruined paradise, a green valley turned black by the greed of men and the departure from traditional ways that results from the introduction of foreignness and modernity. But traditional ways can be abandoned even by those who seem most attached to them. When Huw defends his attack on the deacons by quoting the Bible, Mr. Gruffydd reproaches him, saying, "You know your Bible too well and life too little.... Let there be moderation in all things."

Moderation and balance are required, a combination of modern development and traditional values. Conceivably an impossible balance, *How Green Was My Valley* certainly suggests that it has not been maintained. One message of the book is that the balance cannot be maintained, that the arrival of modernity means either the destruction of traditional values or an impossible rejection of modernity, which in effect means a rejection of life. Chris Hopkins, in a 2006 commentary on the book in his study *English Fiction in the 1930s*, wonders where Huw is going at the end of the novel. Yet the more relevant question may be: What has he been doing for thirty years while everyone else has left the valley? It seems the time has passed for him to take up his challenges. Although the book ends in a mournful tone, looking back at the paradise that has been lost, it also suggests a hopeful message about the possibility of building a world beyond paradises.

Source: Sheldon Goldfarb, Critical Essay on *How Green Was My Valley*, in *Novels for Students*, Gale, Cengage Learning, 2010.

Tom Frazier
In the following excerpt, Frazier examines Llewellyn's graphic portrayal of the difficulties of life in a Welsh mining town in How Green Was My Valley.

ON THE SURFACE, THE NARRATIVE IS THE STORY OF THE LIVES OF THE VILLAGERS, PARTICULARLY THE MORGAN FAMILY, BUT ON A DEEPER, MORE SIGNIFICANT LEVEL IT IS ANOTHER CHAPTER IN THE HISTORY OF COAL MINING."

And far below, beneath his feet, the stubborn tapping of the picks continued. His comrades were all down there, and he could hear them.

Emile Zola, *Germinal*

In the too often trendy world of literature, the careful reader soon becomes cognizant of the artistic certainty that writers will search high and low for suitable and unique motifs to carry the weight of their creative efforts. At times the motifs appear to be contrived while at others the motifs arise naturally and vitalize the precept that writing is generated by the writers' and readers' backgrounds, which is central to the observations of the new historical critics.

Almost every social ingredient, whether life in the London slums or life in agricultural America, has been brought into service in the "naturalistic" literary canon. However, if one needs just one naturalistic metaphor to carry the symbolic weight of a work, coal mining more than satisfactorily fills the bill. The stark world of coal mining and the lives of those who dig the coal clearly create the verisimilitude so important to naturalistic literature. The naturalistic works that depict the real world of coal miners and coal mining show the miners trapped underground by economic forces and digging tons of coal, one shovelful at a time, to meet the day's quota while their families starve on the surface in run-down shacks or in tightly controlled company towns.

But why does coal mining stand out above other economic structures as a viable naturalistic motif? It is most likely because of the very nature of the industry. Mining seems to be the most unnatural means of attaining a livelihood from the land because in order to enjoy the economic cornucopia promised by the enterprise, individuals must dig and claw their way into the deep recesses of the earth. Today, the methods of mining are enhanced by technology, but the process remains the same. Getting to and then removing the coal dictates that the vast inner structure of a mountain or range of mountains be removed. To compensate for this removal, miners have designed man-made replacements for the extracted natural supports, first with pillars of wood and more recently with large roof bolts driven deep into the top of each mine shaft. However, natural forces beyond even the most diligent miner's control show how futile these efforts at propping up the world really are when scores of miners are killed annually as the result of mine explosions and roof falls.

A less abstract metaphorical argument is the magnitude of coal's importance to the newly emerging industrial economies in the nineteenth and early twentieth centuries. As Harry Caudill writes in *Night Comes to the Cumberlands* (1962), following the Industrial Revolution "ships, locomotives, factories and newly built electric power plants were driven by coal and millions of people warmed by its sooty flame" (71). For this reason, "in the late nineteenth and early twentieth centuries, coal was king of the industrial world" (Eller 128). The new, heavy industries required coal for power, and coal gained economic and social clout from this industrial dependence. Although coal miners often participated in work stoppages, they soon found that the omnipotent companies and company owners, in most cases, were able to push the miners' concerns aside and force the men to continue digging the coal.

The significance of coal mining as a naturalistic literary motif is even more apparent because of the breadth of its use. The coal-mining metaphor has crossed national boundaries. Wherever coal is mined as an essential segment of an area's economy, writers find the process to be a suitable vehicle for their aesthetic and philosophical biases. In fact, in *Germinal* (1885), his thirteenth Rougon-Macquart novel, Emile Zola focuses his narrative upon the inhabitants of Montsou in coal-rich northern France and the inhumane conditions under which the miners must live lives filled with "chilling resignation and despair" (Lethbridge viii).

In many instances, the lives of coal miners and the literature written about them have been governed by what Richard Taylor characterizes as "logical determinism or fatalism" (360) or to some extent group "social engineering" (Hunt 269), which was so popular with the followers of B. F. Skinner in the 1940s and 1950s. The same resignation perceived in Zola's works is just as prominent in such American coal novels as James Still's *River of Earth* (1940). At one point, Still allows one of his characters, Kell Haddix, to voice the fatalism that had been engineered in him and his fellow miners, real and fictional: "I'll kill my young'uns off before I'll let them crawl inside a mine hole.... Oh, they'll be miners I reckon. My chaps and yours'll be miners. Brought up in the camps they got no chance. No chance earthy" (200–201).

Following the failed strike that he has instigated, Zola's protagonist, Etienne Lantier, like Kell Haddix, finds similar controlling forces at work and poses the disturbing question. "Was Darwin right, was the world nothing but a battlefield where the strong ate the weak for the beauty and survival of the species?" (521). The laudable rationale for his friends' actions proves little. True, the miners felt that their indignation and rebellion were justified, but in the end might does not mean right. The economic and social forces against which they take a stand prove to be the "fittest" and remain in control, and the miners are again forced underground.

The fatalism of Kell Haddix and the epiphanic reality of Etienne Lantier clearly illuminate the coal miners' forced acceptance of lives that are beyond their control to alter. Even when miners eventually are able to gain concessions from some coal companies, they most often still find themselves at the beck and call of another outside force, a workers' organization, which continues controlling the lives of its individual members. This poststrike, defeated life is found in Richard Llewellyn's *How Green Was My Valley* (1940). Like Zola in *Germinal* in France, Llewellyn finds in coal mining in his native Wales a suitable literary vehicle because the miners' plight about which he writes is to him and to many of his readers a reality. In *How Green Was My Valley*, Llewellyn presents a graphic, naturalistic portrait of life in a Welsh mining town replete with hardships and danger. On the surface, the narrative is the story of the lives of the villagers, particularly the Morgan Family, but on a deeper, more significant level it is another chapter in the history of coal mining.

Nonetheless, Huw, one of the Morgan sons, dreams of escaping the shadows of the coal mining in his hometown through an education and a resulting better life. However, he is constantly drawn home, each time witnessing the futility of the life his family lives. For instance, Llewellyn's miners, as do those of Zola, go on a twenty-two week strike for better working conditions but are forced to return to the coal pits for even more meager wages because, regardless of their good intentions, reality dictates that they care for their families. A close reading reveals that like their mining brothers in other countries, Llewellyn's workers exist in a world against which they are powerless to act. Their lives are regulated by economic determinants that grow into deeply engineered social practices that corral generations of such miners by the fatalistic attitudes that have been fashioned for them.

The plight of the characters in *How Green Was My Valley* gained an even wider audience with the multiple Academy Award-winning 1941 John Ford film version. In fact, the set for the film *How Green Was My Valley* was so realistic and carried such an emotional import that it was used for other movies which Twentieth-Century Fox set in such countries as Norway, Scotland, and France, indicating a universality of situation and attitude of the working class depicted in the film (Halliwell 387).

English writers also wrote about the unrelenting entrapment of miners. In his Croydon-based narratives, D. H. Lawrence gives insight into the lives of those miners who stand up for their rights against the mining companies but who find their powerlessness reinforced by their failures. Lawrence adopts his life as the son of a Nottinghamshire miner as the impetus for several pieces of fiction, of special interest being the stories "Odour of Chrysanthemums" (1911), "The Miner at Home" (1912), "A Sick Collier" (1912), and "Strike Pay" (1912). Even though Lawrence's miners band together in unions in several instances, as individuals they live the same basic lives that they lived prior to their organization. Nothing changes even though they want it to. Instead of their economic well-being coming from the coal they dig, they now rely upon handouts that can be withheld at any time or for any reason by the groups which they, themselves, have created.

"A Sick Collier" tells the story of Willy and Lucy Horsepool. In the beginning, theirs is a happy story. They are newly married and have set up housekeeping in "Scargill Street, in a highly respectable six-roomed house which they had furnished between them" (75). Although Willy regularly comes home a tired, "short sturdy figure, with a face indescribably black and streaked" (76), they are able to have a relatively good life free from want. However, the workers are eventually forced into a strike that lasts for some fifteen weeks, and we are told, "They had been back just over a year when Willy had an accident in the mine, tearing his bladder" (78). While Willy is home recuperating, the miners go out on a more intense, nationwide strike. Willy can only watch the goings-on from his window.

As his pain increases, Willy's emotional and mental stability diminishes. After one extremely agonizing episode, Lucy expresses her fear: "Oh, I hope they haven't heard anything! If it gets about he's out of his mind, they'll stop his compensation" (82), indicating that even though his condition is the result of a work-related injury, both the company and the union will consider him expendable and will withdraw all support. Again, the survival of a miner is out of his own hands, a reality to which both Willy and Lucy have been conditioned by their witnessing past treatment of other miners.

More than just the physical realities of living in the coal town become apparent when Lucy notices early in the story that Willy brings a "faint indescribable odor of the pit in[to] the room, an odor of damp, exhausted air" (77), as if his body and soul exude a reminder of the control mining has over him, something that cannot be escaped or washed away. Lawrence uses this same technique of olfactory imaging in "Odour of Chrysanthemums" when he employs the clinging aroma of the title plant as a naturalistic "omen," which, like the aroma accompanying Willy, "exudes a cold, deathly smell" (Amon 99)....

Coal miners have often attempted to better their lots through organization, negotiation, and strike. However, when one looks at the coal-mining fiction, the unchanging conditions of the miners' lives are laid bare; they are caught up in a cyclical, predetermined life. Just as Zola and Llewellyn do, other mining writers show that the individual usually returns to the scene of his hard life or at least hints that there is no escape from the drudgery of the mining life....

Source: Tom Frazier, "Coal Mining, Literature, and the Naturalistic Motif: An Overview," in *Caverns of Night: Coal Mines in Art, Literature, and Film,* edited by William B. Thesing, University of South Carolina Press, 2000, pp. 199–207.

V. C. Coulter

In the following essay, Coulter uses How Green Was My Valley *to illustrate the difficulty children face in understanding abstract words like "conscience."*

...If people generally now use the word "conscience" to mean a moral monitor, then that is what the word means, whatever it may have meant to Chaucer or to Shakespeare or to Milton. This reply has the surface appearance of a scientific attitude toward language; but it disregards the fact that when the meanings in the minds of people are false to the context, there is no possibility of clear thinking. If a man believes he has "a conscience" which tells him what is right and what is wrong in any human relation, he sees no reason for doing the hard thinking required for a fuller understanding of the probable results of his action. His belief makes his decisions too easy. He resents any effort to change the direction of his thinking by calling attention to facts of which he may be unaware. Oscar Wilde had this attitude in mind when he wrote: "Conscience makes egotists of us all."

A recent court trial indicated a result of the confused thinking caused, in part at least, by the popular mystical meaning so generally attached to this word. An American citizen of some newspaper fame was convicted of being an unregistered Nazi agent. She is reported to have addressed the judge: "Your honor, one of the great fundamentals implicit in our Constitution is liberty of conscience. I felt I had a right to follow the dictates of my conscience." No one, of course, can say just how much of the system of values which led to her very numerous traitorous activities was the result of the childish thinking indicated by her statement. But it is likely that the general acceptance of that mythical meaning for the word "conscience" has done more injury to our civilization than anything she could have done as an unconvicted enemy agent.

Other people respond to these facts about the confused meanings of words and their results by asking: How did these confusions get into the minds of people? That is the intelligent and fundamental question. The answer to that question involves all the knowledge we have about the relation of language to thinking and about the ways words get meanings in the minds of people. This article gives space for only two or three suggestions.

In the first place, it is easy to understand that children get meanings for words as a result of their experiences with them in more or less vaguely recognized contexts. Since the experiences of children are necessarily limited, their first meanings for words are often inadequate and must be extended, consciously or unconsciously, through further experience and analysis. A child who has the word "tub" associated only with the family wash has difficulty understanding how Diogenes lived in a tub. For most children the word "cat" is associated only with the familiar family tabby. Further experience is necessary to extend the word to include the big cats in the big top. Still further experience involving knowledge of structure is necessary to build up a biologist's concept of "Felidae."

If it is difficult for a child to build up a meaning for concrete words which corresponds to the meaning in mature minds, it is much more difficult for him to get adequate meanings for abstract words. There is no sensible referent for an abstract word which he can fall off of or crack his shin against or to which others may point. There is in the minds of people only a concept which has been built up as a result of thinking. An example of this difficulty is found in Llewellyn's *How Green Was My Valley*. The author writes: "I remember well trying to think about mankind. I used to try to build up something that would look like mankind because Man I knew, and Kind I knew. And I thought at last that mankind was a very tall man with a beard who was very kind and always bending over people and being very good and polite." Another writer—Professor L. A. Sherman, I think—says that as a child he heard his father and the visiting minister use the theological word "grace." He had, of course, no idea of the meaning of the word, and it became associated in his mind with a shovelful of ashes which his father was taking from the stove during the conversation. Always afterward, even after he had learned the meaning of the word, it brought into his mind that early image....

Source: V. C. Coulter, "Does Your Conscience Hurt You?" in *College English*, Vol. 6, No. 5, February 1945, pp. 283–88.

Louis B. Salomon

In the following review, Salomon calls How Green Was My Valley *"a poetic novel from beginning to end."*

Here is the story of Huw Morgan, high-spirited son of a Welsh coal miner; the story, too, of his family, of the valley in which they lived, of the coming of hard times and industrial strife to mangle the peace of hard-working, Chapel-going folk whose consciences had for centuries done all the policing the community needed. Most of the action belongs to the years around the turn of the century, but it is told in nostalgic reminiscence as of the present time, when Huw, his old loves all dead or scattered to the ends of the world, is preparing to leave the valley forever.

Mr. Llewellyn (his full name is Richard D. V. Llewellyn Lloyd) is of course a native of Wales, who, though he has lived much more nomadically than his hero and has restlessly turned his hand to a dozen widely different arts and trades, is probably working a rich vein of personal recollection for many of his full-bodied people, with their intense national pride, in whom a fervent devotion to Queen Victoria as a symbol of the British Empire mingles strangely with a stubborn attachment to the spirit of old Owen Glendower: Wales for the Welsh, and to hell with the English and their heartless money-grubbing, and with all renegade Welshmen who shame their ancestors by aping English manners and trying to import the English tongue. Like all Celtic peoples, they love singing and a good fight, either physical or moral; and their quickness to avenge their honor with their fists is counterpoised by the purely aesthetic rivalry that culminates in the Eisteddfod.

Portrayal of national qualities and social changes, however, is only incidental to the extremely personal, subjective study of Huw Morgan's impassioned youth. A two-year period of invalid helplessness follows the fearful night in which his mother outfaced a mob of irate miners and he rescued her from a blizzard. A strong constitution and the adamant spirit of the Reverend Mr. Grufydd finally put him back on his feet; he attends the National School, runs afoul of his Welsh-English teacher, goes to work in the mines, sees his father killed by a cave-in. It is not an exciting life, not even a particularly happy one, except when measured in terms of what Huw remembers. How green the valley, indeed, when even in his childhood the slag heap beside the mine disfigured the hillside, and by the time he was a man this ugly mountain of refuse threatened to engulf the very cottages of the miners. But through the inverted telescope of thirty years those blots look like flyspecks on a windowpane,

and all that matters is the "lost lane-end into heaven, a stone, a leaf, an unfound door."

Without sugar-coating any part of the life it depicts, *How Green Was My Valley* leaves a good taste in the mouth. It is a poetic novel from beginning to end.

Source: Louis B. Salomon, "The Hills of Home," in *Nation*, Vol. 150, No. 6, February 10, 1940, pp. 221–22.

SOURCES

Davies, John, *A History of Wales*, rev. ed., Penguin Books, 2007, pp. 310–711.

Felton, Mick, "Richard Llewellyn," in *Dictionary of Literary Biography*, Vol. 15, *British Novelists, 1930-1959*, edited by Bernard Oldsey, Gale Research, 1983, p. 323.

Harris, John, "Popular Images," in *A Guide to Welsh Literature*, Vol. 7, *Welsh Writing in English*, edited by M. Wynn Thomas, University of Wales Press, 2003, pp. 207–208, 210.

Hopkins, Chris, "Depressed Pastorals? Documenting Wales in the 1930s," in *English Fiction in the 1930s: Language, Genre, History*, Continuum International Publishing Group, 2006, p. 74.

Jenkins, Geraint H., *A Concise History of Wales*, Cambridge University Press, 1984, pp. 173–306.

Jones, Glyn, *The Dragon Has Two Tongues: Essays on Anglo-Welsh Writers and Writing*, rev. ed., edited by Tony Brown, University of Wales Press, 2001, pp. 51, 53, 202.

Knight, Stephen, "'A New Enormous Music': Industrial Fiction in Wales," *A Guide to Welsh Literature*, Vol. 7, *Welsh Writing in English*, edited by M. Wynn Thomas, University of Wales Press, 2003, pp. 72–73.

———, "The Return of Romance: Richard Llewellyn," in *A Hundred Years of Fiction: Writing Wales in English*, University of Wales Press, 2004, p. 116.

Llewellyn, Richard, *How Green Was My Valley*, new ed., Michael Joseph, 1949.

Price, Derrick, "*How Green Was My Valley*: A Romance of Wales," in *The Progress of Romance: The Politics of Popular Fiction*, edited by Jean Radford, Routledge & Kegan Paul, 1986, pp. 73, 75, 79, 82–83, 93.

Smith, David, "Myth and Meaning in the Literature of the South Wales Coalfield—The 1930s," in the *Anglo-Welsh Review*, Vol. 25, No. 56, Spring 1976, pp. 29, 40.

Stephens, Meic, "Lloyd, Richard Dafydd Vivian Llewellyn," in *Oxford Dictionary of National Biography*, edited by H. C. G. Matthew and Brian Harrison, Vol. 34, Oxford University Press, 2004.

Williams, Gareth, *Valleys of Song: Music and Society in Wales, 1840-1914*, University of Wales Press, 1998.

FURTHER READING

Campbell, Joseph, *The Hero with a Thousand Faces*, Princeton University Press, 1968.

This is Campbell's classic text on the myth of the hero, drawing on examples from classical mythology.

Edwards, Wil Jon, *From the Valley I Came*, Angus & Robertson, 1956.

This is an autobiographical account by an actual miner of life in the mines and his involvement with Welsh nationalism and Socialism.

Herbert, Trevor, and Gareth Elwyn Jones, eds., *Wales, 1880-1914*, University of Wales Press, 1988.

This collection includes historical essays on the period during which *How Green Was My Valley* is set.

Smith, Dai, *Wales: A Question for History*, Seren, 1999.

Dai Smith (also known as David Smith), a Welsh historian and broadcaster, presents a number of essays on Welsh culture and history, including one that discusses *How Green Was My Valley*.

A Journal of the Plague Year

DANIEL DEFOE

1722

While Daniel Defoe is best known for *Robinson Crusoe*, the tale of a shipwrecked sailor, his novel *A Journal of the Plague Year* is counted among his literary masterpieces. The work was originally published in 1722 and recounts the horrific events that occurred in England in 1665 and 1666, when the bubonic plague devastated the country. A first-person narration, *A Journal of the Plague Year* is told from the point of view of a London tradesman who signs his account with the initials H. F. The plague was revisiting Europe at the time Defoe wrote and published his novel, and the book is often seen as the author's attempt to shape the politics of the management of another outbreak in England, should it occur. In this fictionalized account of the months of devastation and death, Defoe vividly details the particulars of how the plague attacked the body and decimated populations, and he also represents the terror and despair of individuals in particular and communities in general. Such descriptive realism is perhaps the most acclaimed feature of the work.

A Journal of the Plague Year was originally published in London in 1722 by E. Nutt and is available in a modern edition published by Dover Publications in 2001.

AUTHOR BIOGRAPHY

Little information about Defoe's early years is available. His given name was actually Daniel Foe (he altered his surname later in life), and the precise

Daniel Defoe (Library of Congress)

date and place of his birth are not recorded, although some scholars have theorized, based on circumstantial evidence, that Defoe was born in the fall of 1660 in the St. Giles Cripplegate parish of London. His parents, James and Alicia Foe, had two daughters before Defoe was born. James Foe was a member and officeholder of the Butcher's Company and also worked as an apprentice butcher, but many scholars believe that he worked primarily as a tradesman and merchant. Defoe was sent to schools operated by Dissenters, those members of the Church of England who opposed the rules of conformity created by the bishops of the Church. He lived through the plague that devoured London in 1665 and 1666. After completing his studies at an academy run by Dissenter Charles Morton, Defoe worked in London as a tradesman, merchant, and speculator. He married Mary Tuffley in January of 1684. The following year, Defoe joined the rebellion headed by the Duke of Monmouth against King James II of England, who had only recently ascended to the throne. Monmouth, who was the illegitimate son of James's father, King Charles II, and his followers feared the fate of English Protestantism under James's rule and objected to James's perceived partiality toward the Roman Catholic Church. At this time, Defoe had written numerous unpublished manuscripts, as well

as pamphlets that may have been published anonymously and not later acknowledged by Defoe. Scholars do not know where Defoe lived in exile following the unsuccessful rebellion. In 1689, William III and Mary became the ruling monarchs following James's flight from England. In 1691, the political pamphlet "A New Discovery of an Old Intreague" was published anonymously, but Defoe later acknowledged his authorship of the work, when he included it in a collection of poems and pamphlets titled *A True Collection of the Writings of the Author of The True-Born English-Man* (1703). Having been pardoned for his prior affiliation with the Monmouth rebellion, Defoe continued to produce countless political pamphlets, and was becoming increasingly renowned as a skilled poet. His business ventures at the time, however, were proving less than successful, as attested to by a variety of lawsuits filed against Defoe. By 1692, he had declared bankruptcy, having been sued numerous times. His first major work was published in 1697. *An Essay upon Projects* was a defense of invention and business opportunity as well as an extended social and political commentary. Other writings in a similar vein defended King William III and his policies. Defoe's pamphlets, in addition to providing political support for the king, also advocated social change, as in "The Poor Man's Plea for a Reformation of Manners, and Suppressing Immorality in the Nation" (1698). Another political pamphlet, in which Defoe again takes up the cause of the Dissenters ("The Shortest-Way with the Dissenters," 1702), resulted in Defoe's being arrested, despite his insistence that he had no treasonous intentions against the current monarch, Queen Anne, who had succeed to the throne in 1702 following William's death. The pamphlet, because of its satirical style, offended High Church officials as well as Dissenters. As part of his sentence, following his imprisonment, Defoe was asked to serve as a propagandist for the monarchy and as a government agent. On the income from this assignment, Defoe supported his large family (there are records for eight children, six of whom, it is documented, lived into adulthood). In 1714, changes in the monarchy—Queen Anne's death and the coronation of George I—altered Defoe's fortunes once again. No longer a paid agent of the government, he began pursuing his own writing in earnest. His convictions ran him afoul of the government once again, and attempting to keep himself out of prison, he agreed to a position as a domestic spy. His work as a journalist aided him in this capacity, and his writing at this time is largely political in temper. In 1719, he published something entirely different, however: a work of fiction titled *The Life and Strange Surprizing Adventures of Robinson Crusoe, of York, Mariner*. A fictitious adventure story, it is often regarded as the first English novel. In 1722, Defoe published *Moll Flanders*, an explicit story of the survival of a young woman struggling to make her way in the world, and *A Journal of the Plague Year*, a fictionalized account of the plague Defoe had lived through as a boy. Defoe continued to write prolifically, and his works included other novels and political writings. He died of a stroke in London on April 24, 1731, and was buried two days later.

PLOT SUMMARY

A Journal of the Plague Year is written as one man's recollection of the year 1665, during which the plague ravaged London, where most of the action of Defoe's novel takes place. The narrator is known only by the initials H. F., with which he signs the account upon its conclusion. The work reads at times like a detailed journalistic report, and as such has been criticized for having "no plot of any kind," according to critic Edward Wagenknecht in his 1943 study of the English novel, *Cavalcade of the English Novel*. Although it lacks a formal plot, the novel is structured around the spread of the plague from the western parishes to the east of London. (The narrator's geographic descriptions of London are based on the city's divisions into local church parishes.) The narrator tracks the progression of the disease through London using the bills of mortality, essentially a body count, produced by church parishes on a regular basis. The book opens with the narrator's observations about the first cases of the plague in England in September of 1664. After an isolated instance in Drury Lane, the narrator comments on the cases cropping up in the parishes of St. Giles-in-the-Fields and St. Andrews. Other reports follow.

During the winter, the number of deaths from the plague fluctuates, but there is no great explosion thus far. Still, the narrator observes that fearful people who remember previous outbreaks of the plague are fleeing the city, seeking to isolate themselves from the possibility of being contaminated through contact with the population of London. H. F. himself considers whether or not to join his brother, who is also secluding himself

MEDIA ADAPTATIONS

- An audio CD of *Journal of the Plague Year*, read by Tom Rapp, was published by Woronzow Records (2000).

and his family at their home in the Bedfordshire. The narrator's views on this decision change rapidly. After falling ill, though not with the plague, the narrator feels as though his decision has been made for him; his brother has already left, so he resolves to remain in London.

As the weather warms, the narrator notes that the plague, or distemper as he often calls it, begins to claim more victims. Yet the perception of many in London at the time is that the plague seems to be confined to the outlying parishes, which are poor, densely populated communities. There are attempts among inhabitants of the city to find divine explanations for the plague, and the narrator, as well, makes comments throughout the novel regarding whether or not the plague should be viewed as a punishment by God or a judgment on mankind. H. F. continues to trace the gradual spreading of the plague, repeatedly citing the parish bills of mortality. At the same time, the narrator includes anecdotes about individual experiences. He recounts how people discovered the signs of infection—spots of gangrene and swellings upon the neck and groin—upon their loved ones, and how panic spread as quickly as the infection.

The treatment of the infected and the dead are subjects of particular concern to the narrator. He tells of the way infected families are shut up in their homes and not allowed to leave, to prevent the spread of infection. Critical of this policy, H. F. discusses at length his views on why this practice is impractical and notes that this forced confinement leads to individuals being infected who might have otherwise escaped contamination. He also claims that it intensifies the sense of panic and desperation and therefore causes the confined people to find a way to flee their homes.

The plague is spread by these desperate people bursting out and either running away in secret or perpetrating violence on the watchmen assigned to keep them in their homes. H. F. advocates instead that healthy people either leave the city or procure supplies and voluntarily confine themselves to their homes in order to prevent contact with infected individuals. He also points out that many people do not know that they are contaminated and go about their business on city streets, unknowingly infecting others. Treatment of the dead is another topic the narrator discusses often. He speaks of the carts in which the dead are collected and the mass graves in which they are buried. His tone is one of objective, journalistic curiosity on the matter, and in general he praises the city officials for their efforts to collect the dead in a timely fashion, as it is believed that the disease can spread through contact with the bodies. The narrator also regards the plight of the poor with sympathy, since to avoid starvation they are forced to accept positions—such as handling the dead—that are laden with the risk of contamination.

As the plague spreads further into London, the narrator observes that many of the city's inhabitants are unprepared, having thought that the plague would confine itself to the outer reaches of the city. This is one of the primary reasons H. F. cites for the heavy toll the plague takes on the population of London. People are forced by a lack of provisions to intermingle with one another, and they cannot sequester themselves voluntarily while they are healthy. At this point in the narrative, it is early summer, and the number of plague deaths has increased dramatically. H. F. has just described in detail the horrors of the plague for pregnant women. He then begins an extended anecdote about three healthy men who decide to leave London and its miseries behind in the hope of preserving themselves against infection. The men are designated by their names and occupations, and like the unnamed individuals in shorter anecdotes, they represent any number of individuals who experienced similar fates. They are John, the biscuit maker or baker; his brother Thomas, the sail maker; and Richard, a joiner or builder. The three men join forces and finances and strike out into the countryside, avoiding areas where the plague has been rumored to have struck and struggling to make their way on roads sometimes blocked by officials attempting stop the spread of the disease by halting travel from town to town. They band with another group of plague-free individuals attempting to safeguard their health through escape and eventually set up a semipermanent campsite, where they remain for several weeks. Near the end of September, the group moves one final time, to an old house in disrepair that is made habitable by the efforts of the group. The narrator details the ways in which, with the cautious help of the townsfolk who live near the campsite and, later, the community near the farmhouse, the three men and their companions are able to survive.

Although the narrator functions primarily as a witness to the events in London, the reader does learn, throughout the novel, some of H. F.'s own experience. He discusses the way he secludes himself in his home at least for a time and later is appointed as an examiner (someone charged with visiting homes to determine whether or not they should be closed off and those inside sequestered). It is an appointment to which the narrator strenuously objects, and he admits that he was able to pay someone to do it for him and only served in the position for three weeks, rather than the requisite two months.

By the late fall of 1665, the plague has begun to loosen its grip on the city, the narrator observes. As fewer people become infected, and fewer infected people die from the plague, the narrator comments on whether the plague arose from natural causes, or whether it was visited on the people of London as some form of divine judgment. A case could be made, he asserts, for a view that incorporates both arguments. With the end of the epidemic in sight, the narrator summarizes some of his main observations. He is convinced that the best medicine is avoidance: running away from London or otherwise hiding oneself away from the plague. He criticizes individuals who, believing that they were protected by God against becoming infected, were not careful to protect themselves. He also discusses the effects of the epidemic on the local economy and on foreign trade. By February 1666, the narrator notes, the people of London "reckoned the distemper quite ceased."

CHARACTERS

Constable

The character known only as Constable appears after the group of three men (Richard, John, and Thomas) has joined forces with Ford and his people outside London. The group has traveled to the town of Walthamstow, where they are refused the right to pass through the town. The constable parleys (confers) with John, a former soldier turned baker. John has instructed Richard to fashion poles cut from trees into the shape of muskets, and additionally directs the rest of the group to make small campfires in the area, to make it look as if they are a larger company of armed individuals. The constable refuses to let the group pass through the town, determined as he is to keep the town safe from possible contamination. When John implies that his group is armed and willing to use force if necessary, the constable threatens to raise the county's own forces against the group. In the end, John secures from the constable the right to pass around the town and to be given some provisions as well.

Ford

The character known as Ford appears approximately midway through the novel, when the three men—Richard, John, and Thomas—who fled London hoping to escape the plague meet up with another group of people with the same goal. Ford appears to be the leader of this other, larger group. He encounters Richard, John, and Thomas when he and the others have approached a barn within which they hope to find a night of shelter. The group of three, however, has already set up camp there. Ford and Richard speak to one another, assessing the situations of each other's group, and upon finding that all members of both groups are plague-free, the men agree that they will shelter together in the barn. In the morning, it is agreed that they will join forces and travel together.

H. F.

H. F. is the designation the otherwise unnamed narrator gives himself at the conclusion of the novel. It has been speculated that H. F. was modeled after Defoe's uncle, Henry Foe, who was, like Defoe's narrator, a saddler (saddle maker) by trade. He is reluctant to leave his business and opts to not join his brother at a country house in Bedfordshire but to remain in London. Defoe's background in journalism serves him well in his use of H. F. as a source of detailed information about all manner of plague-related activities. H. F. reports on the physical symptoms of the plague; the experiences of individuals infected; the experiences of the uninfected who remain in their homes and the adventures of those who flee; and the way

city officials deal with quarantining infected people, distributing food to the poor, and burying the deceased. H. F.'s account ranges from an objective narration of events to an insistence that the practice of forced confinement of plague victims to their homes is a counterproductive measure. With respect to religion, H. F.'s views seem to vacillate, and the topic causes him a great deal of internal struggle. Repeatedly, the narrator speculates on whether or not the plague is a form of divine judgment. He criticizes individuals who interact freely with others, infected or not, in the conviction that God will either protect them or punish them based on his will, regardless of their own personal efforts to avoid the plague. At the same time, some of his own decisions, such as the choice to remain in London, are rooted in the same faith in God's protection. H. F. also speaks favorably of the religious group known as the Dissenters, a group with which Defoe identified himself, and praises their preaching at churches abandoned by Anglicans who fled the city. While Defoe depicts this practice in a positive light, other contemporary writers saw this as a symptom of the disorder brought on by the plague, according to critics such as Paula R. Backsheider in her 1989 biography, *Daniel Defoe: His Life*. Overall, H. F., in his assessment of the severity of the spread of the plague and the devastation it wrought, faults the attitudes, behaviors, and practices of both the rich and the poor, of the infected and healthy, of those who believed God would protect them and those who turned to superstition or medicine to protect them. The overriding tone of Defoe's narrator is a cautionary one, and H. F. focuses many of his comments throughout the narrative on the advocacy of what he views as the best practices for preventing the wildfire spread of the plague.

John

John is a former soldier and a biscuit maker, or baker. With the appearance of John, Defoe introduces an extended portion of the novel featuring dialogue among several characters, rather than the briefly recounted anecdotes of often-nameless individuals. In discussing his own situation and fears with his brother Thomas, John makes a case for leaving London, and he counters his brother's arguments about the difficulties they are likely to encounter with the insistence that fleeing the city is their best chance for survival. Their first discussion on this topic is in early July. Two weeks later, the brothers resolve to leave, as their employment has been terminated, and there is no work or wage to be

found anywhere. An acquaintance of Thomas, a
man named Richard, learns of their plan and
decides to accompany them. The three pool their
resources and set out. John is essentially the leader
of the group from the beginning. While it is
Richard who talks with Ford outside the barn
about the two groups sharing the shelter, it is at
John's suggestion that this be done. It is also John
who creates an elaborate scheme to fool the con-
stable outside the town of Walthamstow, where
the combined party of the three men and Ford's
group are denied passage. John instructs Richard,
a builder, to fashion tree branches into musket
shapes. He instructs members of the group to
build scattered campfires and has the tent set up
just outside the tree line, all so that the constable is
fooled into thinking John leads a group consider-
ably larger than their actual number, and one that
is also armed. Through this deception, the group is
allowed to camp outside the town. Through John's
efforts, through his ability to speak "rationally and
smoothly" to the townsmen, the group is also pro-
vided with food and other provisions during their
stay. The camp becomes a semipermanent one,
until it appears as though the plague is encroaching
ever closer. Near the end of September, the group
breaks camp and begins the search for a new safe
haven to wait out the worst of the plague. They are
given leave by a farmer to take up habitation in "an
old decayed house." Under John's direction, the
group makes the home livable and remains there
until December, at which point they return to
London.

Richard

Richard joins the brothers John and Thomas as
they set out from London. As a joiner (a builder or
woodworker), he proves to be a valuable member
of the group. He initially works with Thomas, a
sail maker, to construct a tent for the three men,
and later he helps build a variety of shelters for the
larger group when they camp outside Waltham-
stow. Richard is also instrumental in establishing a
relationship with Ford's group, assessing its status
and intentions and working out an agreement with
Ford about sharing the temporary lodging of the
barn. When the group moves to the old farm
house, Richard, who is described as ingenious,
helps to repair the building and make it habitable.

Thomas

Thomas is the brother of John and a former sailor
who, until the plague, was employed as a sail
maker. In his initial conversation with his brother

about whether or not to leave London, Thomas
expresses reluctance, and seems to accept his fate.
Although he says he is as willing as John to leave,
he despairs at not knowing where they will go, or
what they will do if they are turned away, town by
town. He points out that they have no friends or
relations to travel to or take up residence with.
Thomas says of London, "Here we were born,
and here we must die." He remains unconvinced
by John's arguments and only agrees to go when it
becomes clear that neither his nor John's situation
will improve. Once on the road, Thomas, with
Richard's help, refashions a sail into a tent to
provide temporary shelter for the men.

THEMES

Religion and Spirituality

Religion and spirituality play a central role in
Defoe's *A Journal of the Plague Year* and are of
primary personal significance to the narrator. His
personal sense of spirituality is revealed through
his revelation that he turns to biblical scripture to
aid in him in deciding whether to remain in Lon-
don or flee the city with his brother and his broth-
er's family and through his lament over the lack of
proper burial rites for the dead being deposited
into mass graves. Yet there are broader religious
issues at work in the narrative. Throughout the
novel, the narrator H. F. questions whether or not
the plague should be viewed as God's judgment on
or punishment of the people of London. As the
novel progresses, H. F. criticizes individuals who,
consoled by their belief in the idea that it is God's
will rather than their own actions that will deter-
mine whether or not they become infected, parade
freely around the city, regardless of their risk of
contamination. If they had fled from danger, the
narrator points out, they might have been able
to safeguard themselves. However, despite his
criticism of these individuals, the narrator uses
the same logic when determining his own course
of action. He argues with his brother on this very
point, asserting that he would put his trust in God
to protect his health and personal safety but that
he feared the loss of his business and possessions.
His brother tries to persuade him with the argu-
ment that it is "as reasonable that you should trust
God with the chance or risk of losing your trade"
as it is to presume to "trust Him with your life."
However, H. F. reports that every time he resolved
to go, some sort of "accident or other" would

TOPICS FOR FURTHER STUDY

- Samuel Pepys, who lived through the plague, writes about his experiences in his *Diary*, which was first published in 1825. Read the sections of this work that pertain to the plague year and study the similarities and differences between Pepys's recollections and Defoe's account. Do both authors present a similarly widespread epidemic? Are there any direct contradictions between the two accounts, or just differences in focus? Write an essay comparing the two works.

- *A Journal of the Plague Year* depicts the plague in London in 1665. As devastating as it was, the plague had previously ravaged Europe in the 1340s, leaving millions dead. Research the history of the plague in Europe. Where did the earlier epidemic begin? How quickly did it spread? Why do scientists think it was such a broad epidemic, compared with later outbreaks that were less widespread? Write a report on your findings.

- The concept of the plague as a highly contagious epidemic is treated in a number of modern horror films, in which the destruction wrought by a contagion is graphically portrayed in order to frighten audiences. Yet it has also been portrayed in a humorous light. *Monty Python and the Holy Grail*

  (1975) is a British film that includes a scene of a village beset by the plague. This scene is highly reminiscent of an episode in Defoe's *A Journal of the Plague Year*, in which a man who is "not quite dead" is thrown into the dead-cart. In an essay, compare the scene in the film (identified in the DVD chapter selections as "Plague Village") with Defoe's portrayal of this incident. What details in the scene are similar to Defoe's account? How does such a scene work to create comedy in both the film and in the novel? In your essay, present your opinion on the use of humor, in literature and film, to deal with serious topics.

- In *A Journal of the Plague Year*, Defoe traces the spread of the plague from London's western parishes through the eastern portions of the city. Research the geographic structure of London in Defoe's time (from the mid-seventeenth century to the mid-eighteenth century) and today. Draw a map of the city that includes the parish designations of the seventeenth century. Indicate on the map the spread of the plague by parish, using Defoe's novel as a guide. How might an epidemic spread differently in London today? Present your theory in a written or oral report.

---

prevent it, and he begins to read such events as divine signs that he should remain in London; if he remains there, he believes, God will be "able to effectually preserve [him] in the midst of all the death and danger that would surround [him]."

The narrator also brings up the politics of the Church of England and its rift with the group known as the Dissenters. After describing the split between the two parties, H. F. observes that people of both factions came together in the otherwise deserted churches to worship together, regardless of their differences. Such observations highlight Defoe's emphasis on the ability of spirituality to

unify and his disapproval of the way the religious regulations of the Church were used divisively. Although he refuses to belabor the point, H. F. does express his wish for a greater understanding between the two groups, while acknowledging that the setting aside of differences that occurred during the plague would not last once the epidemic had passed.

In the end, the narrator seems to come to the conclusion that the plague has both divine and natural causes and implications. As God has created nature and willed it to operate in a certain matter, H. F. explains, the plague may be viewed as having been ordained by God but "propagated by natural means." God's mercy or judgment, then, is carried out through such natural causes as the plague. On the last page of the novel, H. F. compares London during and at the end of the plague with "the children of Israel after being delivered from the host of the Pharaoh" and the way "they sang His praise, but soon forgot His works." Through this reference to the Old Testament story of Moses leading the Jews out of Egypt, the narrator expresses his belief that while the survivors of the plague may have believed that they had escaped God's judgment, they would nevertheless forget their risk of being judged and punished and would subsequently return to their former ways and "all manner of wickedness."

Social Politics of the Plague

Defoe's novel deviates from the historical sources about the plague in its emphasis on the plight of the poor and in its suggestion that the plague completely disrupted the lives of the entire population of London. Many critics have pointed out that for many citizens of London, life went on somewhat as usual and that the plague was confined largely to the extremely poor and overcrowded parishes of London. For those parishes, though, the plague was indeed an all-consuming problem, and Defoe is concerned with depicting the details of the daily challenges of poor individuals. He deals in particular with their economic existence, pointing out that in order to avoid death by starvation, many poor people had to face the risk of death from the plague. In order to provide for their families, they often took the worst jobs, such as retrieving the bodies of people who had died from the plague from their homes and burying them. The narrator also observes that many laborers were forced into poverty by the lack of work that resulted from the spread of the plague.

The efforts of local officials (the Lord Mayor, the sheriffs, the magistrates, and others) to avoid a city-wide famine, to contain the spread of the plague, and to "prevent the mob doing any mischief" are also subjects of the narrator's observations and often, but not always, objects of his praise. In particular, the narrator applauds the city's efforts to distribute food to the poor and to keep the city streets cleared of the bodies of individuals who have died from the plague. However, H. F. is critical about the city's policy of quarantining infected or possibly infected individuals and their families in their homes. Such a practice necessitates the use of a watchman to guard the homes

Death register, tallying victims of the Great Plague of London (Nicole Duplaix | Corbis)

and often leads to the panicked and desperate (and sometimes violent) escape of infected individuals, and consequently, to the further spread of the plague. Many times, because entire families are confined to the house, healthy people are needlessly infected. The narrator highlights the difficulty of assessing the need for confinement and enforcing that confinement. The narrator also observes that often the plague is spread by individuals who do not even know they are infected, and so would not have been shut up in their homes in any case. While acknowledging that in some instances the policy may have kept some infected individuals from running deliriously through the streets, the narrator sums up his opinion when he states that the policy of such confinement "seemed to have no manner of public good in it."

STYLE

First-Person Narrative

Defoe's novel is written as a first-person narrative, meaning that it is told from a single character's point of view and that the character refers to him- or herself as "I" throughout the novel. The narrator of this work is identified only by his initials, H. F. Furthermore, *A Journal of the Plague Year* also professes to be an eyewitness account of the year during which London was ravaged by the plague. However, the work is fictional; as J. R. Hammond explains in his 1993 study of Defoe's work (*A Defoe Companion*), the novel is not the contemporary account that it purports to be. Rather, it is "an imaginative reconstruction based partly on Defoe's memories, partly on accounts passed to him in later years by relatives and friends, and partly on written sources." Defoe was only a boy of about five when the plague struck, and scholars note that Defoe made use of a variety of historical sources when he was actually writing the work in the early 1720s (it was published in 1722). Incorporating official documents, such as the parish bills of plague-related deaths, bolsters the appearance of the work as a firsthand account. In addition, Defoe utilizes anecdotes—brief recountings of events—featuring various people who attest to the horrific details of life during this epidemic. The specifics mentioned by these individuals lend a tone of realism to the novel. For example, H. F. relates the story of a man who accompanies the dead-cart to a mass grave where his wife and children are about to be buried. The man's unimaginable grief is conveyed through his brave resolution to see his family buried, followed by his bursting into tears and then fainting when he sees that rather than the bodies being laid into the grave they are unceremoniously dumped from the cart. Another man is nearly buried alive, having been found drunk and passed out and subsequently loaded into the cart bearing the bodies to the mass grave. Even when the longer story of the three men (Richard, John, and Thomas) is related with ongoing dialogue among the characters, the narrator introduces the tale from his first-person point of view, and periodically interrupts the story, maintaining his presence as an observer throughout.

Historical Fiction

As a fictionalized account of events that occurred more than fifty years prior to its publication, Defoe's *A Journal of the Plague Year* may be categorized as historical fiction. Despite some early debate among critics who emphasized the veracity of the work's historical elements, it is now accepted among the majority of scholars that the novel is in fact a work of fiction. Just before publishing *A Journal of the Plague Year*, Defoe published *Due Preparations for the Plague*, a nonfiction work that details precautions that should be taken if another plague epidemic struck London. *A Journal of the Plague Year* drew on some of the same historical sources used to compile the work on plague preparations. This fact in some ways yokes the two works together and lends the fictitious novel a certain historical credibility. The novel contains stories that incorporate facts about the plague reported in other sources, yet Defoe conveys those stories through a fictional narrator. Defoe fleshes out the

reports from historical sources by creating fictionalized characters and situations that are paired with realistic details. The liberty Defoe takes with his historical sources has been noted by a number of critics, many of whom point to the fact that Defoe creates a London completely devastated by the plague, whereas historical sources indicate that even the most widespread effects were felt mainly by the city's poor. Maximillian E. Novak, in his 1983 work *Realism, Myth, and History in Defoe's Fiction*, uses quotations from the famous seventeenth-century diarist Samuel Pepys to support this contention. According to Pepys, for many Londoners, life went on as usual, despite some disruptions in the availability of goods and services. It may be argued that Defoe embellishes the scope of the plague, or at least that he chooses to portray the impact of the plague on the working class and poor in London rather than on the full spectrum of classes and on the entire country. In addition, H. F.'s own dimensions as a character with internal struggles emphasize the work's status as fiction.

HISTORICAL CONTEXT

The Plague in England

Defoe was around five years of age at the time that the plague he describes in *A Journal of the Plague Year* struck London. Given this young age, it was not possible for him to have been a true eyewitness who was able to report, some fifty-seven years later, on events with the level of detail found in *A Journal of the Plague Year*. Rather, writing about the event in the early 1720s, Defoe made use of a number of historical sources available to him at the time. According to J. R. Hammond's 1993 *A Defoe Companion*, these sources include "*The Weekly Bills of Mortality* and Nathaniel Hodge's contemporary report *Loimologia*." In Defoe's day, the manner by which the bubonic plague was spread was not known. The disease is characterized by fever, delirium, and inflamed and swollen lymph nodes known as buboes. As David Womersley explains in his 2005 work *"Cultures in Whiggism": New Essays on English Literature and Culture in the Long Eighteenth Century*, the plague was alternately believed to be spread by a contagion or "by a pestilential gas or miasma which seeped from the earth." Womersley further points out that in Defoe's view, as demonstrated in *A Journal of the Plague Year*, the plague was a

COMPARE & CONTRAST

- **1660s:** Dissenters are persecuted for religious beliefs and practices that run counter to the teachings of the Church of England. A number of acts designed to limit the ability of Dissenters to practice their faith are passed by Parliament from 1661 through 1665. Two such pieces of legislation are the Conformity Act (1661), which has the effect of barring Dissenters from holding public office, and the Act of Uniformity (1662), which requires Dissenters to sign oaths that contradict the tenets of their faith.

  1720s: New policies created during the rule of Queen Anne enforce old legislation that for a time have not been upheld by magistrates and other officials sympathetic to the Dissenters. Dissenters once again face fines, imprisonment, and denial of civil rights.

  Today: Modern Protestant denominations that have arisen out of the Dissenter tradition (also known as the Nonconformist tradition) include Presbyterians, Baptists, Quakers, Congregationalists, and Unitarian Universalists. Although the Church of England is still the established church in England, individuals of different faiths are free to practice their religions.

- **1660s:** From late 1664 through early 1665, London and some parts of England are hit by a bubonic plague epidemic. Approximately 70,000 Londoners die of the plague during this time.

  1720s: In 1720, the bubonic plague strikes Marseilles, France, and lasts until 1722. When word of this outbreak arrives in London, many fear a recurrence of the epidemic in England.

  Today: While the last major bubonic plague epidemic occurred in the 1920s in Los Angeles, California, it continues to appear in isolated outbreaks throughout the world, although it became a treatable disease with the development of antibiotic drugs in the 1940s. Deaths from plague occur primarily in Africa and Asia. The World Health Organization reports that in 2003, 98.9 percent of the 182 deaths from the plague are in Africa.

- **1660s:** England is ruled by a monarch and by the legislative body known as Parliament, which consists of the House of Lords and the House of Commons. The House of Commons is the elected branch of Parliament, whereas the House of Lords is filled through birthright, based on hereditary peerage, that is, rank as a duke, marquess, earl, viscount, or baron. Parliament during the 1660s seeks to shape the monarchy by designing legislation that will limit succession to Protestant royalty. Charles II, an Anglican with Roman Catholic leanings, is the ruling monarch from 1660 to 1685. He and his family flee London during the 1665 outbreak of the plague.

  1720s: Parliament continues to seek a balance of power between itself and the monarchy. After the death of Queen Anne in 1714, the crown passes to George I, the Protestant descendent of James I. The countries of England and Scotland are also now united under one monarch, following the passage of legislation in 1707 that created the United Kingdom of Great Britain.

  Today: Parliament is the ruling body of the United Kingdom. Admission to the House of Lords is no longer based on right of birth but rather on appointment. More political power rests in the hands of the Prime Minister, who leads the Cabinet of senior government ministers, than with the monarch, who is now merely a figurehead in the government of the United Kingdom.

contagious disease dependent on human contact for its continued spread. It is now known that the bubonic plague is transmitted via a bacteria carried by rat fleas. This fact helps explain why the plague in 1665 was often thought of as a disease of the poor; the crowded, unsanitary conditions found in many poor communities proved to be hospitable to the rapid transmission of the infection. There are several stages of plague infection. When a person is bitten by a flea infected with the bacteria, the organism infects the lymph nodes; this is the bubonic plague. Once the infection from the bacteria spreads to the blood, the disease is septicemic, and if it spreads to the lungs, it is pneumonic. Only the pneumonic form is considered contagious in that it may be transmitted from person to person through droplets in coughed fluids. Although the plague was not confined during this time (late 1664 through early 1666) to London alone, most estimates regarding the numbers of individuals who died from the plague pertain to London; a death toll of around 70,000 is typically cited. The number, while sobering, is small compared with the millions who died from the disease in Europe during the 1340s. The plague returned, sporadically, to Europe in the 1700s, and it has been suggested that Defoe's writings on the plague were occasioned by the reports of an outbreak in France in the 1720s.

Monarchy in Transition

From the time period during which Defoe's *A Journal of the Plague Year* takes place (September 1664 through February 1666) through the year in which it was published (1722), his country was ruled by a number of different monarchs, some who served England and some who served the newly united kingdoms of England and Scotland, known as the United Kingdom of Great Britain. Throughout this time period, Defoe's writings were at times offensive to the ruling monarch and at times used to support the legitimacy of the ruler. The politics of these years were heavily steeped in religious controversy, and Defoe touches on this controversy in his novel, referring to the Dissenters and to the Act of Uniformity, passed in 1662, a law that discriminated against Dissenters. In addition to passing legislation designed to punish Dissenters, Parliament often engaged in machinations geared toward eliminating the ability of Catholic heirs to claim the throne. Charles II was the king during Defoe's childhood, and he ruled from 1660 to 1685. This is the time period in which the events in *A Journal of the Plague Year* take place. Charles and his family fled London during the outbreak of the plague. The king later died of a stroke, in 1685. He had spent the last years of his life securing the claim of his brother James, a Catholic, to the throne. When Charles II died, his illegitimate son,

Man burying a body during the London Plague
(© Bettmann / Corbis)

James, Duke of Monmouth, who was a Protestant, attempted to capture the crown. Defoe participated in this thwarted rebellion and was forced into temporary exile as a consequence. It was James II rather than Monmouth who retained the throne, and the king had the would-be usurper beheaded. The rule of James II was short-lived, however. His eager appointment of Catholics to key posts and other unfavorable policies led to Parliament's inviting James's Protestant daughter Mary and her husband William to rule. James fled England, and Mary and William ascended the throne in 1689. Parliament worked during this time to ensure that Catholics would never rule England and attained the right to name the monarch's successor. Many of Defoe's writings from this time period show his support of William's reign. In 1694, Mary died of smallpox. William died several years later, in 1702, succumbing to pneumonia, a complication of injuries caused by being thrown from his horse. Following William's death, only the offspring of James II's Protestant marriage to Anne Hyde were eligible to rule, not those children who were the product of his

Catholic marriage to Mary of Modena. Therefore, James II's daughter Anne became the next queen. She married George, the prince of Denmark. The marriage failed to produce an heir to the throne. During Anne's reign, the Acts of Union were passed in 1707 by both the English and Scottish parliaments. The United Kingdom of Great Britain was the result of this legislation. Defoe ran afoul of Anne's supporters because of his support of the religious group the Dissenters. To regain his favor with the monarchy, Defoe agreed to work as a propagandist for the crown. Anne died of a blood disease in 1714. The crown then passed to George I, who was the great-grandson of James I. George was raised in the German province of Hanover and never learned English; he spent much of his time in Hanover during his reign. King George I was the ruler of Great Britain when Defoe published *A Journal of the Plague Year* in 1722, and he ruled until 1727.

CRITICAL OVERVIEW

When *A Journal of the Plague Year* was published in 1722, it was viewed in its relation to the recent outbreak of the plague in France, and was commonly held to be a political statement regarding Defoe's opposition to the possible quarantining of London. Paula R. Backsheider in her 1989 biography *Daniel Defoe: His Life* states that in *A Journal of the Plague Year*, Defoe "turned observations about the 1665 plague into a comprehensive plan for lessening the spread and suffering of future plagues." At the same time, its accuracy as a historical document was also accepted by many of the work's contemporary readers, as observed by J. R. Hammond in *A Defoe Companion* (1993), who states that because of Defoe's skill as a journalist, "many contemporary readers accepted the *Journal* at face value as an eyewitness account written at the time of the Great Plague." Hammond goes on to point out that many modern readers as well could easily make the same mistake because Defoe is an expert "literary counterfeiter." This observation highlights one of the central critical debates regarding Defoe's novel. The work's status as historical fiction is generally agreed upon, but some critics focus on its historical accuracy, Defoe's use of historical sources, and the way the work compares to other contemporary accounts of the plague, whereas other critics debate the work's success as a novel.

In Maximillian E. Novak's 1983 study of Defoe's fiction (*Realism, Myth, and History in Defoe's Fiction*), Novak concedes that while it is a somewhat "radical" notion, Defoe's novel may be seen as "history or historical fiction about 1665" as well as "government propaganda directed at England in 1722." Regardless of which stance is taken, Novak emphasizes the importance of ascertaining the work's historical accuracy by comparing *A Journal of the Plague Year* to other contemporary sources, such as the *Diary* of Samuel Pepys (1633–1703). His conclusion is that while Defoe fails to accurately present an overview of the plague's impact on the nation and on all social classes, Defoe avails himself of the medical details found in contemporary sources and offers a snapshot of the poor of London during the plague year. Backsheider similarly observes this discrepancy between Defoe's work and that of Pepys, and she adds to the list of sources whose facts present a picture different from Defoe's the work of John Dryden (1631–1700) and information found in the *London Gazette*. However, Backsheider praises Defoe's interest in and ability to relate "an alternate history," that is, his accounts and praise of the actions of the Dissenters, his reports of the quarantining policies implemented during the plague, and his criticism of those policies. Furthermore, Backsheider comments on Defoe's skills as a novelist, noting his achievement in constructing a novel "full of beautiful rhythms."

While Backsheider and Novak both note the ways in which Defoe's *A Journal of the Plague Year* differs from its historical sources, Everett Zimmerman, in the 1975 work *Defoe and the Novel*, contends that the work "follows historical sources almost scrupulously." Zimmerman then goes on to extol Defoe's use of the narrator H. F., maintaining that it is the narrator's personal spiritual experience that forms the central crisis of the book. The narrator seeks a guiding spiritual overlay in his attempt to comprehend the horrific epidemic he is witness to, yet his observation of the reality before him is such that "he cannot fully reconcile it with his religious assumptions." This discrepancy creates in the narrator a growing sense of conflict and anxiety, Zimmerman explains. Zimmerman stresses the significance of the narrator and his psychological tension to the work's being regarded as fiction. Other critics, however, find that as a character, the narrator tends to fade into the background of the events he is observing. Novak, for example, offers the view that London is the main focus of the work and that Defoe is most concerned not with H. F.'s having survived the plague or endured a crisis of faith but with the survival of the city and "the core of her people—the poor who remained."

CRITICISM

Catherine Dominic

Dominic is a novelist and a freelance writer and editor. In this essay, she explores the structure and relevance of the extended anecdote of the baker, the joiner, and the sail maker, found in the middle section of A Journal of the Plague Year, *and its relation to the novel as a whole.*

Midway through *A Journal of the Plague Year*, the narrator introduces a story of three men, a story whose significance is underscored by the narrator's comment that the account to follow "has a moral in every part of it" and that the conduct of the men and the other individuals with whom they join forces "is a pattern for all poor men to follow, or women either, if ever such a time comes again; and if there was no other end in recording it, I think this is a very just one, whether my account be exactly according to fact or no." As readers, we are given some very important instruction as to how the upcoming tale should be interpreted. We are told it will have a message of special significance, that it is designed to instruct individuals regarding the proper course of action in the event of future epidemics, and that it may not be historically accurate. Such an introduction sets the story apart from other, shorter anecdotes in the novel. With the other incidents and stories the narrator relates, there is no disclaimer regarding accuracy or preface underscoring the particular importance the reader should grasp. Structurally, the story of the three men differs from the other anecdotes in the work as well. The narrator does relate a few exchanges that feature dialogue, typically between himself and another individual, but such conversations are quite brief. Only in the story of the three men does the narrator tell the tale of several individuals, identified by name, with whom he himself does not converse, who share extended dialogue, and whose story consists of more than one scene or incident. The tale of the three men, then, is a story within a story, but it is seldom reviewed as such or at length by critics. The significance of this section of Defoe's novel may best be understood by examining the actions

WHAT DO I READ NEXT?

- Defoe's *Robinson Crusoe* was originally published in 1719. It is arguably his best-known work and is critically regarded as the first English novel. It is available in a 2001 edition published by Modern Library.

- *Of Captain Mission and His Crew* was published by Defoe in 1728 as part of the larger work *The History of the Pyrates*. Among Defoe's more neglected works, the story may be viewed as a satirical commentary on English politics and society. It was published by Hard Press in 2006.

- *The Great Plague: The Story of London's Most Deadly Year*, by A. Lloyd Moote and Dorothy C. Moote, offers a thorough history of the 1665 plague in London, discussing the epidemic from medical and social perspectives. The authors look to contemporary sources to help explain the experiences of both rich and poor people during the plague year. It was published by Johns Hopkins University Press in 2004.

- *Daniel Defoe: The Life and Strange Adventures*, by Richard West, is an accessible biography of Defoe that considers the author's life as an adventurer, a pamphleteer, a political spy, and a novelist. The book was published in 1999 by Da Capo Press.

- *The Plague*, written by Albert Camus in 1947, is a plague novel that scholars maintain was influenced by Defoe's work. It is set in Algeria, in northern Africa. A recent edition was published by Vintage in 1991.

of the group as a whole and of John in particular. An analysis of the tale of the three men reveals a moral and message, the presence of which is flagged by the narrator, of personal responsibility for one's salvation. This relates directly to the narrator's (and Defoe's) views on personal conduct during the plague and also to Defoe's own religious views as a Dissenter. (The term

> AN ANALYSIS OF THE TALE OF THE THREE MEN REVEALS A MORAL AND MESSAGE, THE PRESENCE OF WHICH IS FLAGGED BY THE NARRATOR, OF PERSONAL RESPONSIBILITY FOR ONE'S SALVATION."

"Dissenter" is used to describe various Protestant denominations that refused to accept basic principles of the Church of England as it existed in the mid-seventeenth century. Dissenters were often persecuted for their beliefs.)

The story of the three men serves a number of purposes in the novel and is viewed in a variety of ways by various critics. J. R. Hammond (in his 1993 study of Defoe's work *A Defoe Companion*) regards it within the context of Defoe's interest in survival narratives and likens it to Defoe's *Robinson Crusoe* in its focus on the use of "reason to overcome difficulties and escape from calamity." Maximillian E. Novak, in *Realism, Myth, and History in Defoe's Fiction* (1983) regards the excerpt in its political capacity, arguing that Defoe, as a "loyal Londoner" was not prepared "to see his city cut off from the rest of the country and left to die" and included the story as an objection to quarantine policies. Everett Zimmerman likens the adventures of the three men to the exodus of the Israelites from Egypt, finding that the story functions as a parable of "mankind seeking salvation" and that it emphasizes the "personal effort that, in addition to reliance on God, is necessary for salvation." All three critics touch on the meaning and appeal of this portion of Defoe's narrative, but none explore the unique qualities of this section of the novel and the way such qualities highlight the broader significance of the story.

In addition to the way the narrator prefaces the story of the men, as discussed above, this section of the story stands out immediately because of its structural differences from the rest of the book. As readers we are treated, with the appearance of John and his brother Thomas, to our first lengthy section of dialogue. Previous anecdotes included brief exchanges with the narrator and someone whom he encountered, or with people who related their own tales, but in this section of the novel, speaker names preface lines of speech, as in a play.

Visually, the ongoing, previously unbroken narrative is set off on the page in a manner that unmistakably tells the reader the next portion of the novel is different from all that preceded it. The characters speak at length to one another, not to the narrator. Two brothers are introduced to us, John, who is a former soldier and now a biscuit maker, or baker, and Thomas, a former sailor turned sail maker. The men discuss their present circumstances, the danger the plague poses for them, and the fact that they are both soon to be turned out of their lodgings. As they question the wisdom of leaving London, John asserts his right to travel the roads out of town, despite the reports of officials turning people back to their own parishes to prevent contamination. Thomas feels that as they have no friends or relatives to whom they could travel and with whom to stay, they are obliged to remain in London, where he acknowledges they will likely die. John vigorously disagrees, arguing that all of England is his birthright, not just the city in which he was born. As John counters all of his brother's arguments, it is plain that his instinct toward self-preservation is strong. Thomas presses him about where they would go if they left. "Anywhere," John replies, "to save our lives."

They make no preparations to leave, however, until two weeks later, when the situation in London has become more dire. A third man, a friend of Thomas named Richard, joins them just before departure. Defoe details their life on the road, explaining the shelter they make for themselves, and how they make decisions and keep watch. Through such details, Defoe calls to mind the tale of survival he had already published in 1719, *Robinson Crusoe*. Not only do such passages evoke Defoe's earlier novel, but they also serve to stress the difference between this section of *A Journal of the Plague Year* and the rest of the novel. These details of the men's survival, and other, similar details still to come, heighten the story's realism and increase the tension felt by the reader. We are placed, in a sense, on the road with three characters who are more well developed than those met in passing in the novel's other anecdotes. As John, Thomas, and Richard venture from London and encounter another band of people escaping the plague, they begin to lose their status as strangers to the reader, unlike their often unnamed counterparts in the shorter anecdotes of the novel.

Throughout the trio's travels, John increasingly stands out as the group's leader. His continued resourcefulness, demonstrated in the way he outwits the constable of the town of Walthamstow, aids him in preserving his own life, as well as the lives of all the members of the group. John secures safe passage, permission to set up camp outside town, and provisions for the company. When the plague ventures near, John leads the group to safety once again. He periodically makes reference to God's will, but his actions indicate his own unwillingness to be solely guided and protected by such a force. His sense of personal responsibility for the preservation of his own life is the force that leads him out of London and that protects him during the remainder of the plague year, not his faith in God's desire or ability to preserve him. At the end of the tale, Defoe points out that none of the group became infected and that they were all able to return to London in December.

Defoe's emphasis on personal responsibility like that exhibited by John and the others is reflected in other parts of the work but is nowhere so fully developed as in John's story. The narrator reiterates toward the end of the novel that "*the best physic [medicine] against the plague is to run away from it.*" Admitting that his own decisions ran counter to this advice, the narrator criticizes those individuals who believed that God would preserve them and who subsequently took no action to preserve themselves. Furthermore, the narrator throughout the novel comments on the policy of forced quarantining of infected individuals and their families in their homes, conceding that while sometimes this may have prevented loss of life, the policy ultimately did not benefit the population of London. What he seems to be suggesting as an alternative to forced quarantining is the notion of personal responsibility: the healthy should leave the city or remain in a home fortified for a lengthy stay, and the infected should sequester themselves voluntarily in the interest of sparing others from contamination. For example, the narrator admiringly describes the man who, suspecting himself contaminated, quarantines himself in one of the outbuildings on his property and "would not suffer his wife, nor children, nor servants to come up into the room, lest they should be infected." He died in that building but avoided being shut up in his house with his family members, whom he would have undoubtedly infected.

That *A Journal of the Plague Year* advocates a sense of personal responsibility for both saving one's own life and protecting the lives of others is evidenced by the many anecdotes in the novel that deal with this theme, but it is dramatically enacted in the story of John and his company. Arguably, Defoe's political stance against the quarantining of London is supported through the story of John and through other anecdotes in *A Journal of the Plague Year*. Yet the religious views for which Defoe was persecuted throughout his life are also reflected in the novel's theme of personal responsibility. The role of personal responsibility for one's spiritual salvation played a central role in the religious philosophy of the Dissenters. The dictates of one's individual conscience superseded the dictates of the Church of England for this group. Defoe's tale of the three men and its theme of personal responsibility is infused with social, political, and religious meaning, and its significance is highlighted by Defoe through the narrator's preface to it and through its unique structure within the larger framework of the novel.

Source: Catherine Dominic, Critical Essay on *A Journal of the Plague Year*, in *Novels for Students*, Gale, Cengage Learning, 2010.

Jeanne Guillemin

In the following review, Guillemin discusses how Defoe's account of the plague is not a deception, but rather a "brilliant reconstruction of the terrible impact of a real epidemic on ordinary urban people."

About 25 years ago, I picked up the 1948 Modern Library edition of Daniel Defoe's *A Journal of the Plague Year*. In his introduction, Louis Kronenberger described Defoe's account of the ravaging of London in 1664–65 as a literary "trick" and "the greatest fake document of its length in all literature." I thought otherwise. Rather than a deception, I saw a brilliant reconstruction of the terrible impact of a real epidemic on ordinary urban people, and on an insular country struggling with its relations to the outside world. For it was trade with that outside world that had contaminated London, through rats infected by lice—and throughout Defoe's account, although he was ignorant of the cause of the epidemic, trade is paramount.

To construct his narrative, published in 1722, Defoe used stories from his childhood and documents to tell a story of civic chaos and eventual survival. His account is both objective in its reporting of statistics and humane in its intent. "If I could but tell this part," he wrote of how people suffered, "in such moving accents as should alarm the very soul of the reader, I should rejoice that I recorded those things, however short and imperfect."

In 1992 I had the opportunity to investigate the largest outbreak of inhalational anthrax in recorded history, which occurred in 1979 in the Soviet city of Sverdlovsk. Through interviews with the families of the 68 people who died, I discovered that the cause of these deaths was an accidental release of spores from a nearby military facility. Anthrax is not contagious person to person, and the 1979 outbreak was small by comparison with anything recorded by Defoe. Yet I found myself, like Defoe, reconstructing an event that had taken place years before, and empathizing, as I am sure he did, with the complex civic response. The objective facts were there—on paper and on gravestones—and so were the tragic human accounts of sudden deaths that shocked and frightened the community. The great difference, of course, was that impersonal nature and ignorance had caused the plague of Defoe's journal, while a military-weapons program bent on attacking enemy civilians had caused the Sverdlovsk outbreak. The Soviets, of course, were not alone in this exploitation of microbiology. France, Japan, the United States, and Britain had preceded them with aggressive programs aimed at mass destruction.

Despite the end of such major programs, scenarios of indiscriminate lethal pandemics continue to preoccupy us centuries after Defoe's writing. Today the United States and other nations are concerned with the threat of bioterrorism. Meanwhile, terrible pandemics such as AIDS, drug-resistant tuberculosis, and malaria kill and debilitate millions each year in nonindustrialized parts of the globe that have as yet no Daniel Defoe to chronicle the chronic violence that these diseases exert on those ordinary lives—lives which, entirely contrary to logic and ethics, remain less valued than those in Western countries.

Source: Jeanne Guillemin, "An Account of the Plague," in *Chronicle of Higher Education*, Vol. 51, No. 23, February 11, 2005, p. B4.

Raymond Stephanson

In the following excerpt, Stephanson discusses Defoe's dramatic use of the restriction and imprisonment necessitated by the plague as a metaphor for imaginative confinement.

. . . Defoe expertly dramatizes imaginative restriction and paralysis through physical confinement—a "Neighbourhood of Walls." The words "confin'd" and "Confinement" are everywhere in the *Journal*, and the sense of imprisonment—both in anecdotes and in diction and imagery—is overwhelming. The reason is not hard to find: the threat of plague means the shutting up of houses, and in a world besieged by plague, "here were just so many Prisons in the Town, as there were Houses shut up . . . ." Many people have "lock'd themselves up" to avoid contagion, and those unfortunate victims in the agonies of swellings and fever are occasionally "ty'd in their Beds and Chairs, to prevent their doing themselves Hurt." Being "restrain'd" and "ty'd" by force is "counted a very cruel and Unchristian Method, and the poor People so confin'd made bitter Lamentations," but these domestic confinements are only part of a much larger, more appalling picture of stasis and constriction. When H. F. reports that "it was said, there was at one Time, ten thousand Houses shut up, and every House had two Watchmen to guard it," Defoe is suggesting a kind of physical confinement whose claustrophobic implications are staggering. Defoe describes a people who, at the height of the plague's mastery, are paralyzed and imprisoned in a city whose activities have been negated and confined by the plague's menacing void: trade and navigation are "at a full Stop"; "Employment ceased"; "The Inns-of-Court were all shut up"; "All the Plays and Interludes . . . were forbid to Act; the gaming Tables, publick dancing Rooms, and Music Houses . . . were shut up and suppress'd; and the Jack-puddings, Merry-andrews, Puppet-shows, Rope-dancers, and such like doings . . . shut up their Shops . . . ." What the imagination confronts is the specter of a city that has been captured, confined, and emptied by plague: "London was as it were entirely shut up." In response to this oppressive landscape, the imagination adopts a defensive posture, and its creative energies are quickly replaced by a fear of contagion.

Confinement is not limited to the intercourse of trade, commerce, and exchange. It also afflicts social relationships: "a vast Number of People lock'd themselves up, so as not to . . . suffer any . . . Company, to come into their Houses, or near them." Plague severs the normal bonds between people, who now confine themselves to their tiny window frames and maintain only a distant contact with a dying world: "I look'd thro' my Chamber Windows

AS PLAGUE DEVOURS THOSE IMAGINATIVE
AVENUES WE TAKE FOR GRANTED, OUR INITIAL
THRUST OF IMAGINATIVE ENERGY AGAINST THE
UNKNOWN IS QUICKLY CONFINED BY OUR FEAR OF
BODILY DISINTEGRATION, DEATH, AND
NOTHINGNESS."

(for I seldom opened the Casements) while I con-fin'd my self within Doors . . . "; "They had no way to converse with any of their Friends but out at their Windows, where they wou'd make such piteous Lamentations" (p. 155). Physical features and tableaux such as these offer an objective correlative for the centripetal movement of the imagination as it is hemmed in and threatened by the "acute penetrating Nature of the Disease." The sick are confined with the healthy, people fleeing London are confined in the spaces between towns, people are "imprisoned," houses are shut up, many have "*lock'd themselves up, and live on board*" ships (p. 107), neighbors are confined to their homes, the sick are tied down to beds and chairs, and there is, finally, the ultimate confinement in the Aldgate pit or in a pine box. While such diction and imagery refer literally to forms of social, economic, and physical imprisonment caused by the pestilence, they also provide an effective emblem of imaginative stasis and retreat: every imaginative avenue normally allowed by ordinary experience is either nonexistent or locked up. One cannot move; one cannot touch neighbors with the loving stuff of small talk; one cannot do business. One can only be shut up with the dying and the dead; the earlier flights of the imagination are now in thrall to plague.

These various kinds of restriction and imprisonment are the metaphorical vehicles in the *Journal* for imaginative immobility in the face of a threatening and incomprehensible void, and such structures of confinement are a feature in most of Defoe's anecdotes. One narrative sequence, for example, concerns "Another infected Person" who visits the family of a close friend to announce that he has "got the Sickness, and shall die to morrow":

The Women and the Man's Daughters which were but little Girls, were frighted almost to Death, and got up, one running out at one Door, and one at another, some down-Stairs and some up-Stairs, and getting together as well as they could, lock'd themselves into their Chambers, and screamed out at the Window for Help. . . . The Master . . . was going to lay Hands on him . . . but then considering a little the Condition of the Man and the Danger of touching him, Horror seiz'd his Mind, and he stood still like one astonished. . . . And so he [the infected friend] goes immediately down Stairs: The Servant that had let him in goes down after him with a Candle, but was afraid to go past him and open the Door . . . the Man went and open'd the Door, and went out and flung the Door after him.

What is noteworthy here and elsewhere in the *Journal* is the claustrophobic, almost pathological quality of the scene: the oppressive sense of futile flight, confinement, physical and social paralysis, fear of touch or movement, and the final sense of being shut up in one's own domain. This powerful sense of physical confinement is an effective way to illustrate how the plague shackles both physical and imaginative movement.

But Defoe ultimately is interested in re-creating in us a tangible experience of what this confinement is like. The ubiquitous presence of paralysis and confinement—in diction, imagery, anecdotes, and subject matter—profoundly influences our realization of the text. Like the Londoners faced with a diminishing physical and social world, we recoil from repeated accounts of inertia and decreasing possibility. The story of the soldier, sailor, and carpenter (the longest anecdote in the *Journal*) is paradigmatic in precisely this way. The preparations of the men as they ready themselves to escape London are the stuff of romance or adventure; what the narrative stresses is their excited voyaging forth into a realm of possibility that will test and reward their individual talents. This narrative formula, with its predictable resolutions and adventure plots, also presages a setting forth of the reader's imagination. The sudden possibility of imaginative excursion into the world of adventure and romance stands in sharp contrast to the typically claustrophobic events in the *Journal*. Having encouraged the imaginative flight that attends any adventure formula, Defoe then stifles and neuters that energy by concluding with confinement and stasis. What might have been escape and expansion for the three men becomes an entrapped, glum survival in an area between communities; what might have been imaginative flight for the reader becomes yet another exercise in imaginative entropy and narrative inertia.

This vicarious experience of imaginative confinement is evident even in the apparently unstructured shape of the plot itself. The traditional claims that the *Journal* is "an incoherent jumble" lacking a plan and that the structure of the narrative is "repetitive" and "undisciplined" fail to account for the way in which Defoe's organization of incident and anecdote contributes to the powerful feeling of confinement that the *Journal* evokes in its readers. The forward progress of the "journal" and its chronological advance in particular are frequently suspended; the ponderous movement of the daily and monthly account very often seems to give way to a more static representation of the plague year in which temporal and spatial features tend to recede altogether. This is true of many of Defoe's more striking anecdotes, which, although specific in detail, are characterized as without clear temporal or physical location. This paratactic or disjunctive narrative process can be attributed in part to H. F.'s use of the unique "case" to substantiate some general historical point. But the narrative structure can be accounted for in a different fashion as well.

As much as Defoe dramatizes temporal flux (however haltingly) in H. F.'s journalistic account of the events of 1664–65, he also restricts the reader's experience of the passage of time by developing a chronology of events in London only so far and then returning to issues that he already has handled. Numerous transitional sentences take the reader backward in time: "But I must go back again to the Beginning of this Surprizing Time, while the Fears of the People were young . . . "; "But I come back to the Case of Families infected, and shut up . . . "; "But I return to the shutting up of Houses"; "But I must go back here . . . to the Time of their shutting up Houses . . . ; "But to return to the Markets"; "But I return to the Coals as a Trade." This retrogressive, da capo movement creates an illusion of time stopping, of the normal experience of narrative duration being held in abeyance, and this structural feature effects another form of imaginative inertia for the reader—a sense that even the ordinary progress of time has been paralyzed. And the focus of the majority of these circular moves involves the reader's repeated confrontation with both the imaginative and spatial confinement that accompanies the shutting up of houses. Such movement is not

"incoherent" or "undisciplined"; it is rather an effective rhythm of closure, a re-creation of the imaginative paralysis brought by the plague . . . .

At its deepest and most threatening level, plague means the erasure of imaginative potential through a negation of those social and physical categories whose presence we need to maintain even a modicum of sanity. As plague devours those imaginative avenues we take for granted, our initial thrust of imaginative energy against the unknown is quickly confined by our fear of bodily disintegration, death, and nothingness.

If the threat of plague in part follows from its invisibility and lack of imaginative coordinates, then an equally unsettling implication is that once an image or symbol has been supplied, the imaginative structure finally fails to "contain" plague. Pestilence ultimately refuses to yield to the very act of imaginative appropriation it has precipitated and threatens to obliterate the self. We are left with our dwindling imaginative energy and with the realization that our apprehension of the world of others is like our experience of plague: the attempt to possess or neutralize through imaginative projection always will be met with that unknowable, irreducible essence that makes its own claims on us and that refuses to become a malleable figure in our psychological tableau.

Indeed, plague and the threat of infection force the drama of self and other to be played out at its most intimate and terrifying level. The site of confrontation is not some accidental place of contact, but within. The other has been literally internalized as a physiological presence, telling us that *we* are other. To be a victim of plague dramatizes an essential truth about our imaginative transactions with the other, namely, that our attempts to "know" or to translate the significance of the foreign entity are really about how we create a fictional second self, an alter ego, and locate it at arm's length, often forgetting that such an act is as much a measure of self as it is an understanding of other. Plague does not permit us to forget; its simultaneous invitation and impenetrability to the imagination, as well as its concurrent embodiment as abstract statistic and intimate physical presence, paradoxically suggest that to grapple with the unknowable other compels a better knowledge of self, however disquieting such insights may prove . . . .

Source: Raymond Stephanson, "The Plague Narratives of Defoe and Camus: Illness as Metaphor," in *Modern Language Quarterly*, Vol. 48, No. 3, September 1987, pp. 224–41.

SOURCES

Backsheider, Paula R., *Daniel Defoe: His Life*, Johns Hopkins University Press, 1989, pp. 3–21, 84–106, 412–36, 467–92, 493–528.

Cody, David, "Dissenters," in *Victorian Web*, http://www.victorianweb.org/religion/dissntrs.html (accessed October 27, 2008).

Defoe, Daniel, *A Journal of the Plague Year*, Dover Publications, 2001.

Giblin, James Cross, "The Black Death," in *When Plague Strikes: The Black Death, Smallpox, AIDS*, HarperCollins, 1995, pp. 11–53.

Hammond, J. R. "A Journal of the Plague Year," in *A Defoe Companion*, Macmillan, 1993, pp. 106–117.

Larsen, Timothy, "England, Victorian," in *Encyclopedia of Religious Freedom*, Routledge, 2003, pp. 108–112.

Marks, Geoffrey, and William K. Beatty, "Thomas Sydenham and the Epidemic Diseases of the Sixteenth and Seventeenth Centuries," and "Bubonic Plague—from London to San Francisco," in *Epidemics*, Charles Scribner's Sons, 1976, pp. 125–47, 248–61.

"Monarchs of Britain," in *Britannia.com*, http://www.britannia.com/history/h6f.html (accessed October 27, 2008).

Novak, Maximillian E., "History and Ideology in Defoe's Historical Fiction," in *Realism, Myth, and History in Defoe's Fiction*, University of Nebraska Press, 1983, pp. 47–70.

———, "Daniel Defoe," in *Dictionary of Literary Biography*, Vol. 39, *British Novelists, 1660–1800*, edited by Martin C. Battesin, Gale Research, 1985, pp. 143–66.

"Parishes in London and Westminster, outside the City of London," in *British History Online*, Institute of Historical Research and the History of Parliament Trust, http://www.british-history.ac.uk/report.aspx?compid = 38869 (accessed October 27, 2008).

"Plague," World Health Organization Web site, http://www.who.int/mediacentre/factsheets/fs267/en/index.html (accessed November 7, 2008).

Rosen, Alan, "Obscured Ends: Catastrophe, Narrative, and the Novel in Defoe's *Journal of the Plague Year*," in *Dislocating the End: Climax, Closure and the Invention of Genre*, Peter Lang, 2001, pp. 27–56.

Wagenknecht, Edward, "Defoe and His Contemporaries," in *Cavalcade of the English Novel*, Holt, Rinehart and Winston, 1943, pp. 31–45.

Womersley, David, "Confessional Politics in Defoe's *Journal of the Plague Year*," in *"Cultures in Whiggism": New Essays on English Literature and Culture in the Long Eighteenth Century*, edited by David Womersley, Associated University Press, 2005, pp. 237–56.

Zimmerman, Everett, "*A Journal of the Plague Year*: Fact and Fiction," in *Defoe and the Novel*, University of California Press, 1975, pp. 107–25.

FURTHER READING

Dryden, John, "Annus Mirabilis," in *Selected Poems*, Penguin, 2002, pp. 26–89.

> In this poem, the title of which translates to "year of miracles," Dryden reflects on the events that occurred during the plague year in London. Scholars note that Dryden himself escaped to the countryside when the plague struck London.

Hollis, Leo, *London Rising: The Men Who Made Modern London*, St. Martin's Press, 2008.

> Hollis provides a detailed social and political history of the city of London following the plague of 1665 and the great fire that swept London in 1666, detailing how the city and its sociopolitical structures were reimagined and rebuilt following the devastating events of the plague and fire.

Kickel, Katharine E., "Hearing Imagining: Rhetorical Discordance in Daniel Defoe's *A Journal of the Plague Year*," in *Novel Notions: Medical Discourse and the Mapping of the Imagination in Eighteenth-Century England*, Routledge, 2007, pp. 39–66.

> Kickel examines the rhetorical devices Defoe employs in *A Journal of the Plague Year*, focusing specifically on both the lack of spoken discourse and the insufficiency of the imagination as a tool for creating imagery within the novel.

Nicholson, Watson, *The Historical Sources of Defoe's "Journal of the Plague Year,"* Stratford, 1919.

> This volume includes commentary on Defoe's use of historical sources when writing *A Journal of the Plague Year*. It also includes excerpts from those sources.

Jude the Obscure

THOMAS HARDY

1895

Thomas Hardy confronted late Victorian England as a controversialist in an era when conformity and regimentation were the social norms. He was a pessimist in a society that prided itself on its industrial progress, its economic prowess, its imperial reach, and its military and naval might. Hardy was not a reformer but a storyteller; he was not an advocate but an anatomist. He examined and explored human lives in their complex psychological, social, and economic contexts. In *Jude the Obscure*, first published in 1895, Hardy examines the institution of marriage not as a philosopher or polemicist might but as a novelist, by means of placing complicated characters in difficult situations where they face conflicts between desire and duty and where self-fulfillment and social demands strongly contradict each other. In his consideration of marriage, Hardy, while never graphic or indelicate, focuses on the role of passion in determining how people behave and on the power of the severe grief and pain that can sometimes tragically result from compulsory marriage.

Hardy's moral views often put him at odds with his society, as did his scrupulous examination of aspects of human activity that many thought best left unmentioned. In order to show how the constraints of marriage can impinge destructively on human nature, Hardy established Jude and his beloved Sue Bridehead as figures whose sexual and intellectual aspects are in conflict with each other.

Thomas Hardy *(© Bettmann / Corbis)*

Written with Victorian reserve but an ancient Greek sense of the tragedy of life, and in the prose of the great poet that Hardy was, *Jude the Obscure* challenged and continues to challenge culturally received opinions. Hardy was aware of the delicacy of his undertaking, as he made clear in his 1895 preface to the novel:

> For a novel addressed by a man to men and women of full age, which attempts to deal unaffectedly with the fret and fever, derision and disaster, that may press in the wake of the strongest passion known to humanity, and to point, without a mincing of words, the tragedy of unfulfilled aims, I am not aware that there is anything in the handling to which exception can be taken.

In *Jude the Obscure* Hardy establishes the humanity of a set of characters whose humanity is sorely tried by the rules and conditions of late Victorian society and by their own inner conflicts. In consequence, the work stands not only as one of the great Victorian novels but as a historical document, grappling with one of the fundamental social issues of late nineteenth-century England. Considered a classic, *Jude the*

Obscure is widely available in paperback and hardcover, including a Modern Library edition published by Random House.

AUTHOR BIOGRAPHY

When Thomas Hardy was born in Dorset, England, on June 2, 1840, he appeared to be stillborn until the midwife realized he was alive. Hardy's father, also called Thomas, was a builder and stonemason. His mother, Jemima Hand, poor but literate, had been a domestic servant since the age of thirteen. Their unhappy marriage took place only because Jemima was pregnant. In December 1841, she gave birth to Hardy's sister, Mary. Jemima schooled young Thomas until he was eight; he then attended school until sixteen, when he was apprenticed to an architect. He continued to study architecture at King's College, in London, beginning in 1862, and he won prizes from the Royal Institute of British Architects and the Architectural Association.

Hardy also studied classical languages and literature. In 1862 he began writing poetry, and in 1867, while working as an architect, he began to write novels with *The Poor Man and the Lady*, which went unpublished and most of which he subsequently destroyed. In Cornwall, in 1870, while working on the restoration of a parish church, Hardy met Emma Gifford. They were married in 1874. That year, Hardy published *Far from the Madding Crowd*. In the preceding years he had already published, anonymously, *Desperate Remedies* (1871) and *Under the Greenwood Tree* (1872), as well as, under his own name, *A Pair of Blue Eyes* (1873). Although initially theirs was a loving marriage, with time, Hardy and Emma lived together estranged from one another. After Emma's death in 1912, Hardy experienced a rush of his first love for her and wrote a number of love poems in memory of her. They appeared in *Poems, 1912–13*. From the time of their marriage until he abandoned writing novels because of the scandalized reception that greeted *Tess of the D'Urbervilles* (1891) and *Jude the Obscure* (1895), his final novel, Hardy wrote some nine novels, including *The Return of the Native* and *The Mayor of Casterbridge*.

Hardy published his first volume of poetry, *Wessex Poems*, in 1898. In 1904, he published the first part of a three-part epic verse drama set in the era of Napoleon, *The Dynasts*. In 1910,

Hardy was awarded the Order of Merit. In 1914, two years after Emma's death, Hardy married Florence Dugdale, whom he had met and made his secretary in 1905. She was nearly forty years younger than he. Their marital happiness was dampened by his renewed devotion to his deceased wife. Hardy contracted pleurisy in 1927 and died on January 11, 1928. His ashes, despite his previously stated objection, were interred in the Poet's Corner of Westminster Abbey, but in partial compliance with his will, his heart was buried in Stinsford beside Emma's grave. In addition to novels and poetry, Hardy wrote several volumes of short stories, the drama *The Famous Tragedy of the Queen of Cornwall* (1923), and a two-volume autobiography, published after his death, with authorship attributed to his second wife, Florence. Nearly all of Hardy's notebooks and letters were burned by his executors after his death.

MEDIA ADAPTATIONS

- *Jude the Obscure* became a six-part British Broadcasting Corporation (BBC) television movie in 1971. Directed by Hugh Davis, it was released on video by BBC/Warner in 2000.

- Michael Winterbottom directed the BBC film adaptation *Jude*, starring Christopher Eccleston and Kate Winslet, in 1996.

- Recorded Books produced a reading of *Jude the Obscure* on CD and audiocassette in 2003.

PLOT SUMMARY

Part I: At Marygreen
Chapter 1

Schoolmaster Phillotson leaves the village of Marygreen to attend the university at Christminster. He tells his student Jude, eleven, an orphan, to be kind to animals and birds, to read, and to visit, which Jude longs to do.

Chapter 2

Jude's aunt, with whom he lives, reproaches him for being alive and for reading too much. His cousin Sue, she adds, also reads too much. She warns against marriage. Jude is working as a scarecrow in the farmer Troutham's fields. Feeling sympathy, he lets the birds feed. For this, Troutham paddles him. Jude begs for mercy but enrages Troutham by explaining that he wanted to be kind to the birds. Fired, Jude worries he is a burden to his aunt. Walking home, he avoids stepping on earthworms.

Chapter 3

Jude's days are filled with reveries about Christminster and conversations with others about that enchanting city.

Chapter 4

The salesman Vilbert promises to give Jude his old Latin and Greek grammars but forgets to. Phillotson sends for the piano he left in Jude's aunt's fuel house; Jude encloses a letter in the packing case asking Phillotson to send him used Latin and Greek grammars. When the books arrive, Jude is disheartened at the amount of work learning entails.

Chapter 5

Jude delivers baked goods for his aunt; along the way, he studies and trusts his horse to guide the wagon. Feeling too strongly influenced by pagan writers, Jude decides to study Christian texts. At sixteen, Jude apprentices himself to a church builder and becomes a stonecutter.

Chapter 6

Now aged nineteen, returning from work through the fields and daydreaming about his future as a scholar and churchman, Jude is hit by a pig joint that a farm girl named Arabella tosses at him. They talk; he asks to see her again.

Chapter 7

Jude and Arabella go walking, and sometimes their hands brush or he must support her. They wander far, such that it is late when they start for home. At a tavern they drink some beer. Jude thinks he is forward when he offers his arm, but Arabella thinks he is backward for not taking her round the waist. They kiss. Arabella invites

Jude in to the family's cottage, and visiting neighbors treat him like her intended. Jude is impatient to see Arabella again, while she schemes with her friends to catch him.

Chapter 8

Jude and Arabella chase loose pigs; overheated, Arabella drops beneath a tree and pulls Jude to her. He stands and tells her to do likewise: he wants to kiss her. Teasing, she rebuffs him, and Jude thinks he has offended her. A neighbor tells Arabella that Jude plans to go to Christminster. Arabella arranges to have the cottage to herself and lures Jude to her bedroom.

Chapter 9

Jude says he is leaving and wishes nothing had happened. Arabella, however, says she is pregnant. Despite his misgivings, they marry. Arabella wants Jude to abandon his studies and work as a stonecutter. When she tells him that she is not pregnant, Jude, angered, wonders why giving in to momentary sensuality should cause a lifetime of unhappiness in an unwanted marriage.

Chapter 10

When Jude slaughters their pig, his concern for its suffering disgusts Arabella. Jude overhears Arabella's friends talking about the pregnancy trick that she used to entrap him. He tells Arabella that their marriage is a torment to both of them.

Chapter 11

Arabella runs outside and tears her dress to show publicly that Jude mistreats her. Jude learns that his mother abandoned his father and him, as well as that his father's sister, his cousin Sue's mother, also made a bad marriage. Jude fails at a suicide attempt. He gets drunk. At home, a note from Arabella says she is going to Australia. Jude consents and encloses in his letter the little money he has. Arabella's family auctions all their possessions. Later, Jude finds in a pawn shop a framed picture of himself that he gave Arabella. He buys it, burns it, and resolves to go to Christminster.

Part II: At Christminster
Chapter 1

Three years later, in Christminster, Jude is seeking to enter the university. He hopes to meet Sue and to visit Phillotson.

Chapter 2

The walls of the colleges and his social class bar Jude from entering the university. He works as a stonecutter by day and studies by night. Seeing Sue working in a shop that makes religious statues, he resolves to introduce himself. He hesitates to allow his attraction, however, because he is married, she is his cousin, and marriages have not been happy in his family.

Chapter 3

Jude watches Sue in church, transported by the religious atmosphere and passionate desire. Sue buys busts of Venus and Apollo that she must hide even in the room at her residence because they are pagan deities. Jude studies the New Testament.

Chapter 4

Jude and Sue meet when she visits his workplace after hearing that he is in Christminster. She is leaving because her landlady destroyed the busts. They visit Phillotson, who does not remember Jude but invites them in. Jude suggests that Sue apply for an opening as an assistant teacher at Phillotson's school and remain in Christminster, and Phillotson agrees.

Chapter 5

Phillotson develops tender feelings for Sue. Jude is jealous seeing Sue and Phillotson together and imagines them happily married despite the fact that Phillotson is twenty years older than Sue.

Chapter 6

Jude's aunt discourages his affection for Sue. Jude writes to several heads of colleges about admission. Learning that Phillotson intends to open a school elsewhere, Jude wonders if Sue will go with him, perhaps to become his wife. The master of one college writes that Jude should remain a working man. Jude gets drunk and mocks his own learning.

Chapter 7

At Sue's house, Jude collapses and confesses his binge. She consoles him, and he falls asleep downstairs. In the morning, ashamed, he leaves before seeing Sue. In Marygreen, he speaks to the curate about his failed hopes of entering the church. The curate suggests that Jude become a curate.

Part III: At Melchester
Chapter 1

Sue enters a teacher-training college. Jude continues both his stonework and his study. Sue is alternately warm and chilly. She dislikes the school. Jude is contrite about his drunkenness; she forgives him but shows no sign of the kind of love he feels for her. She has promised to marry Phillotson in two years, and they will open a school together. Jude wishes her well.

Chapter 2

Jude and Sue miss the last train back after a day trip and stay the night in separate rooms at a cottage. Sue gives Jude her picture.

Chapter 3

At school, Sue is put in solitary for a week. She flees to Jude, and he gives her shelter.

Chapter 4

Jude and Sue discuss her lack of belief and her scorn for the academic medievalism of Christminster, as contrasted with his Christian faith and his love for Christminster and its academic tradition. Sue tells Jude about an undergraduate friend who loved her; she lived chastely with him. He died of consumption. Jude feels the hopelessness of loving Sue.

Chapter 5

Sue is expelled from teacher-training school and told she ought to marry Jude to keep her reputation. Jude has yet to tell Sue that he is married. Sue resolves to discuss her future with Phillotson. Jealous, Jude thinks about the discipline of renunciation, essential for a curate. Sue sends Jude a note asking him to meet her.

Chapter 6

Phillotson puzzles over Sue's letter expressing gratitude that he did not visit her often at school. He kisses her picture. When he visits the school, he learns of her expulsion. In the adjacent cathedral, he sees Jude repairing stonework. Jude acknowledges that he loves Sue but assures Phillotson of the innocence of their outing. Jude tells Sue that he is married.

Chapter 7

Jude consents to give Sue away. The morning of the wedding, Sue walks to church with Jude. They walk down the aisle together rehearsing the ceremony. Outside, they meet Phillotson, who is surprised to see Sue leaning on Jude's arm. Jude assumes that Sue's emotion, as he gives her away, is pity for Jude, not pain at making a marriage she would rather not. Parting, Sue begins to say something to Jude but leaves it unsaid.

Chapter 8

Jude gets work at Christminster. His aunt grows dangerously ill; he informs Sue and promises to meet her train there. Going for a drink with Tinker Taylor, Jude encounters Arabella working at the bar. They go to Aldbrickham, where no one knows them, to discuss what to do regarding their marriage. They spend the night together at an inn.

Chapter 9

Arabella tells Jude that she was remarried but has left her husband. Jude feels befouled, a victim of his own sensuality. He meets Sue a day late at his aunt's and makes an excuse but does not say that he saw Arabella. Sue says that it is better if he does not visit her again. Jude shows Sue where he and Arabella lived. Their aunt, recuperating, reproaches Sue for having married and says that Phillotson is a man who would repel any woman. Sue admits that she is repelled, but Phillotson is a considerate husband and allows her freedom. Jude tries to subdue his passion. Arabella writes that she and her husband have reconciled and she is going to London with him to keep a tavern.

Chapter 10

Jude joins a church choir. Moved by a hymn, he visits its composer, expecting to find spiritual nourishment, but finds him concerned with money, about to forsake composition for the wine business. Jude receives a letter from Sue, repenting her harshness and inviting him to visit.

Part IV: At Shaston
Chapter 1

Jude taps out the hymn on a piano. Sue places her hand upon his and plays the tune. They feel strong attraction; Sue tells Jude to leave. Jude misses his train. Wandering by Sue's house, through the window he sees her looking at a picture and wonders if it is his.

Chapter 2

Sue writes that she and Jude ought not meet. Jude writes that their aunt has died and that the funeral is Friday. After the funeral, Sue says that despite her regard for Phillotson, she is repelled by marital relations and has not engaged in them. Jude says he has seen Arabella. Sue lets Jude take her hand but says she will tell Phillotson. Jude embraces her; she recoils. After they have gone to sleep in their separate lodgings, Jude is roused by the sound of a rabbit suffering in a trap. Jude kills the rabbit. Sue, wakened, too, berates herself for not having understood what marriage entails. She sends Jude away with a kiss but prevents him from embracing her.

Chapter 3

Realizing that his desire makes him unfit to be a clergyman, Jude burns his theology books. Sue regrets their kiss, vows not to write to Jude, and is both glad at the suffering she will cause and pities him. Phillotson mistakes her sadness for grief at her aunt's death. Sue confesses her aversion to Phillotson, saying she ought not to have married him but did so to avoid scandal. She wishes to live apart, with Jude. Phillotson only consents to her living separately in the same house with himself.

Chapter 4

Phillotson mechanically enters Sue's bedroom instead of his own. She jumps out the window but is hardly injured. Phillotson tells his friend Gillingham that Sue loathes him as a wife, though she likes him as a friend, that she loves Jude, and that he will let her go. Gillingham says that all she needs is firm discipline, but Phillotson disagrees. Sue offers to remain friends, but he insists on a clean break.

Chapter 5

Jude joins Sue in the train at Melchester. They continue to Aldbrickham, where they are not known. Jude has consented to Arabella's request for a divorce. Sue says she wants to live with him but not as a lover. She admits that she feels passion for him but must be guarded. Sue refuses to stay at the hotel that Jude intended because he reserved only one room. Jude registers at a hotel he does not recognize, but a maid tells Sue that she has seen Jude there with Arabella. Sue is angry. Jude reveals that Arabella is divorcing him. Sue is mollified, and they go to their separate rooms.

Chapter 6

Scandalized, the school board demands that Phillotson resign. He refuses and is dismissed, then falls ill. Sue visits him. Her kindness leads him to ask her to return, but she refuses. Phillotson is left with the pain of her ambivalence and the image of her as Jude's lover. He decides to divorce her so that she can marry Jude.

Part V: At Aldbrickham & Elsewhere
Chapter 1

Jude wants to marry Sue, but she fears marriage will ruin their rapport. They wait.

Chapter 2

Arabella tells Sue that she is getting remarried in England to the man she had married and then left in Australia. She advises Sue to marry Jude.

Chapter 3

Jude and Sue still put off marrying for fear it will alienate them. Arabella informs Jude that a boy was born eight months after she left him. She wants Jude to take the boy, and Jude and Sue do so. The boy is sad and somber. Sue wishes to marry.

Chapter 4

At the municipal office, the dismal atmosphere and the depressing circumstances of other couples deter them from marrying. They stop in the local church and watch a marriage ceremony. They fear that the legal coercion of marriage would harm their love. They decide not to tell the boy that they have not married.

Chapter 5

Arabella sees Jude, Sue, and the boy at a fair. She buys a love potion from Vilbert. Sue tells Jude that she is happy. The boy is obsessed with death.

Chapter 6

Neighbors notice that Sue is pregnant. Jude and Sue go to London and say they were married there. Jude works in a cathedral repairing the letters of the Ten Commandments, while Sue repaints them. Townsfolk protest, and they are dismissed. Jude is forced to resign his position on a committee fostering education for workingmen. They auction their goods and leave Aldbrickham.

Chapter 7

At a fair, Arabella encounters Sue selling gingerbread that Jude baked. A widow, Arabella has become a teetotalist Christian. Sue is pregnant again. Jude is recovering from illness contracted while working in the rain.

Chapter 8

Arabella backslides and tells Anny that she wants Jude again. They give Phillotson a ride in their carriage. Arabella tells him that he was wrong to let Sue go, that she had not yet had adulterous relations with Jude, and that even had she, firm discipline would have tamed her. Hearing from Sue that Arabella has returned, Jude moves the family to Christminster.

Part VI: At Christminster Again
Chapter 1

Jude watches an academic procession and experiences a sense of failure. Sue sees Phillotson in the crowd and feels dread at having violated social rules despite not believing in them. Jude and Sue are refused lodgings. They find rooms for her and the children. While Jude is seeking a room, the landlady, after Sue explains they are not legally married, insists that she cannot stay after that night.

Chapter 2

Jude's first son, called Little Father Time, asks Sue if it were better he had not been born. He feels to blame for his parents' difficulties. Believing that having children is the cause of their woe, he gets angry when Sue tells him that she is pregnant once again. Little Father Time then hangs the two other children and himself and leaves a note explaining that they were too many. Sue blames herself for speaking to him about their trouble as if he were an adult. Jude cannot console her. She says their tragedy is a judgment for attempting to live happily outside social conventions. She becomes ill with grief, and the fetus she is carrying is stillborn.

Chapter 3

Jude says they ought to marry, but Sue feels that she is still married to Phillotson. She regrets pursuing her own desires and begins to believe in self-abnegation. Arabella offers condolences and learns that Jude and Sue never married. Jude finds Sue in church. She says that Jude is truly married to Arabella and that Arabella's son's killing her children signifies right killing wrong.

As a matter of conscience, not from dislike, Sue insists that they live apart.

Chapter 4

Arabella tells Phillotson that Sue and Jude never married and are living apart, and she gives him Sue's address. Phillotson writes to Sue and offers to take her back. At the cemetery, Sue tells Jude that she will marry Phillotson again, despite not loving him, to fulfill her duty, and she advises Jude to marry Arabella, for those are the consecrated unions, while theirs was a sin for which they paid with the death of their children.

Chapter 5

Phillotson realizes that Sue does not love him but accepts her obedience. Mrs. Edlin tells him that their marriage is wrong. Phillotson assures Sue that their relations can be nonsexual, as before.

Chapter 6

Arabella begs Jude for shelter. Jude's curiosity overwhelms him, and he allows Arabella to go to Marygreen to find out if Sue and Phillotson have actually married. They have. Arabella says that she feels married to Jude, but he brushes her off. He goes to a tavern and starts drinking. Arabella finds him, gets him drunk, and takes him to her father's cottage.

Chapter 7

Jude is sick in spirit and hungover. Arabella tends him, brings all his goods from his lodging, and schemes with her father to marry Jude again by keeping him drunk. After their remarriage, Jude is ironic and indifferent, hollowed out by the loss of Sue.

Chapter 8

Jude is consumptive, and Arabella is vexed at having to tend an ill husband. He asks her to write to Sue; she writes but does not send the letter. When Sue does not come, Jude goes to Sue through a rainstorm, to find her in the Marygreen church. He berates her for loving him badly and for sacrificing her critical intellect by remaking her marriage and approving his. She breaks down and in his arms confesses that although she has subdued her will, her marriage is not consummated. They confess their love, but Sue resists. Overcome by a sense of sin, she flees. Jude catches a chill.

Chapter 9

Arabella meets Jude at the station. He admits that the trip was suicidal. On the walk home, Jude feels the sprits of the dead scholars of Christminster. Consumed by guilt, Sue confesses that she has seen Jude, swears on the Bible never to see him again, and begs Phillotson to keep her as his wife as she steels herself against repulsion.

Chapter 10

Arabella offers to have Sue visit, but Jude refuses. Mrs. Edlin tells Jude that Sue and Phillotson have consummated their marriage. Vilbert attends Jude. Arabella flirts with Vilbert.

Chapter 11

Arabella leaves Jude's sickbed to see the town festivities. Delirious, Jude calls for water, talks to a phantom Sue, and regrets the day of his birth. Arabella returns to find Jude dead, but she wishes to go out again to watch the regatta. She tells her companions that Jude is sleeping. She flirts with Vilbert. Jude's body is laid out, and Arabella and Mrs. Edlin watch over it. Outside, the ceremonies of Christminster take place. Sue does not come. Mrs. Edlin says that she has found peace mortifying herself with Phillotson. Arabella says that Sue has not had peace since she abandoned Jude and will not until she is dead.

CHARACTERS

Anny

A minor character, Anny, a country girl, is a friend and confidant of Arabella's. She first gives Arabella the idea of becoming pregnant in order to get Jude to marry her.

Sue Bridehead

Sue is Jude's cousin and his beloved. She is physically delicate and emotionally complex. She demurs intellectually from many of the conventional values of her society but emotionally is often drawn to conformity. She is repulsed by duty but guilty in her defiance of it. She is more comfortable with the culture of ancient Greece than with the culture of Christianity, but she subdues her spirit and embraces asceticism. She marries Phillotson, admiring and respecting him and feeling under obligation to him for his help, but she does not love him, and they live in separate quarters in the same house until she asks him to release her so that she may go to Jude. With Jude, too, although she does love him and is attracted to him, she wishes to live in a nonsexual union. She knew a young man, a university student, before she met Jude, who had loved and desired her. She lived with him and was educated by him but refused to be his lover. He pined for her and died of consumption. She lives with Jude thus until they decide to alter their arrangement, and they do have children. After tragedy befalls their once hopeful union, torn by guilt and doubt, she returns to Phillotson and despite her revulsion lives with him as a wife. Her guilt arises not only because she has gone against convention; she feels responsible for the deaths of their three children because she spoke to Jude's boy about the burden of being alive openly, as if he were an adult, and consequently reinforced his feeling that Sue and Jude would be better off without children.

Mrs. Cartlett

See Arabella Donn

Mr. Challow

A minor character, Challow is the pig butcher who is late in coming to slaughter Jude and Arabella's pig, leaving it for Jude to do.

Arabella Donn

Arabella is a strong, healthy, coarse country girl who works as a barmaid. She has an earthy intelligence and a strong appetite for pleasure. She seduces Jude and tricks him into marrying her by saying that she is pregnant when she is not. Their incompatibility and his discovery of her trick cause them to separate soon after marriage. She goes to Australia with her parents, marries a tavern keeper there, and ultimately returns to London with him, where they run a tavern. She did, it turns out, have a child with Jude, and she gives the boy to his father to care for when she returns to London. She becomes a religious fanatic and a teetotaler for a brief time, but after she sees Jude with Sue, she reverts, desires to have Jude again, and sets about accomplishing this. She informs Phillotson that Jude and Sue have not married and that Sue is unhappy. Arabella remains a flirt and a tease and survives all the perplexities that beset Jude and Sue. She is selfish and wild rather than malicious. She is often the force that moves the plot forward. She is a good judge of character. When she is married to the tavern keeper, she is called Mrs. Cartlett.

Drusilla Fawley

Drusilla is the crotchety old aunt of both Sue and Jude. She takes Jude in when he is orphaned but often calls him useless and says he ought to have died, too. She strongly opposes marriage for him and for Sue whether to others or to each other because of the bad marriages that their parents made.

Jude Fawley

Orphaned, Jude is a delicate, tender-hearted boy who dreams of studying in the great university city of Christminster to become a scholar and a clergyman. He works on his own to study Latin and Greek. He is practical, too, and while he studies in Marygreen before setting out for Christminster, he also apprentices himself and becomes a stonemason, later loving the architecture of Christminster as well as its academicism. Jude's lower-class position makes entrance into the university impossible despite his efforts. He is determined in his goodness, sympathizing, for example, with the birds' need to peck at stored grain; he avoids stepping on earthworms when he walks. He is sensitive to beautiful music and moved by misty visions of devoting himself to ideals that he cherishes. He also has a tendency to seek solace in drink, although it never truly comforts him. His sensual nature overcomes him when he meets Arabella, who uses his weakness for alcohol to trap him into marriage. He ultimately gives his love to Sue and is guided by the constraints she puts on his love despite his sensuality. Loss of Sue leads to his complete deterioration. He remarries Arabella but exposes himself to inclement weather deliberately in order to see Sue a last time and to bring death upon himself.

Gillingham

Gillingham is Phillotson's friend and confidant. His role is to represent and to offer received social opinion; he advises Phillotson to exercise his authority as a husband over Sue and not give in to her wish to separate from him.

Little Father Time

The boy who is the fruit of Jude and Arabella's union is a pale, unhappy, morbid child, called "Little Father Time" because he is old even in his youth and sees the world as a place of pain and suffering. Feeling responsible for Jude and Sue's misfortune in a world where having children appears to be a burden, and confirmed in his grim vision by Sue, who shares her despair with him, the boy hangs his two siblings and himself. His action leaves Sue beset with guilt for having attempted to circumvent social rules. The boy's name seems to make him a figure who represents the consequences that develop in time for human actions that violate codes of conscience or morality.

Richard Phillotson

Phillotson was Jude's schoolteacher and his early role model. Phillotson leaves the small village of Marygreen to go to Christminster, a fictional version of Oxford University, to study there. He does not, however, enter the university but instead resumes his career as a schoolteacher. He develops tender feelings for Sue soon after she begins, at Jude's suggestion, to teach at his school. She accepts his proposal to marry even though she esteems but does not love him. When Phillotson discovers that Sue is repelled by him and loves Jude, Phillotson transcends his own interests and, despite conventional advice from a friend, releases Sue from her marriage bond. Phillotson endures social ostracism after his neighbors learn of his unconventional behavior, but he retains belief in the correctness of his behavior. When he learns that Sue is unhappy in her relationship with Jude because she is tormented by guilt, Phillotson marries her again; this time, although he does not insist on conjugal relations, he does behave with a more conventionally firm attitude than he had the first time.

Mr. Troutham

Troutham is a farmer. As a boy Jude works as a scarecrow in his fields, making noise with a clacker to keep the birds away. When Jude abandons his noisemaker, moved by a tender concern for the birds, and allows them to feed, Troutham catches him, whacks him with the clacker, gives him his wages, and dismisses him.

Vilbert

Vilbert is a quack doctor and snake oil salesman. He first meets Jude when Jude is a boy, promising to bring him Latin and Greek grammars if Jude canvases for him; Vilbert neglects to do so, however, even though Jude keeps his end of the bargain. Later he meets Arabella, sells her a love potion, and, after she tells him she has spiked his drink with his potion, begins to flirt with her. He will very likely become her husband after Jude dies.

THEMES

Faith and Charity versus Skepticism and Selfishness

Although Hardy does not directly take a stand on the question of faith versus skepticism in *Jude the Obscure*, it is one of the central concerns of the novel. Phillotson's initial response to Sue's distaste for him is one of openness and charity. He puts her happiness ahead of his will and releases her from her bond. He has faith in an ideal of goodness. By the time she returns to him, he has become cynical. His disposition is no longer charitable but disciplining. He has gone from faith in freedom to concern for its limits. As a youth, Jude is full of dreams. He hopes to become first a Christian scholar at the university in the distant city he longs for and then a clergyman. He is motivated by aspiration. He feeds birds and takes care not to step on earthworms. His religious faith is a faith of love. Jude's later encounters with several forms of actual love and his experience of social condemnation wipe away his capacity for faith. He is left with nothing to which to aspire, and only death can obliterate his losses. Jude loses his faith in life in stages: when he experiences his own animal nature; when he is excluded from the temple of learning owing to his lower-class birth; when Sue denies him her love and begins the process of self-mortification; and when, beaten down, he surrenders once more to a spiritless marriage with Arabella. Sue, who ends as a Christian penitent, chastising her own will and submerging herself faithfully in an eternal will, begins as an independent-minded young woman who feels the resonance of the classical pantheon more than that of the Christian one. She defies convention and sets her will against constrictions that violate her integrity. It is Arabella, however, who has the last word about the power of faith and the futility of ideals. She derides them when she contradicts Mrs. Edlin's report that Sue has found peace by saying what the reader must recognize as true—that Sue's faith will do nothing for her and she will have no peace until she is joined in death with Jude. Hardy's own attitude probably is expressed most clearly when he writes in part II, chapter 3, "It was a louring, mournful, still afternoon, when a religion of some sort seems a necessity to ordinary practical men, and not only a luxury of the emotional and leisured classes." He shows an ironically ambiguous attitude, accepting the psychological necessity for a sense of faith. For that very reason he seems to dismiss the sentiment's supposedly divine and absolute authority.

The Inevitability of Failure

A sense of the inevitability of failure hovers over the story and the characters in *Jude the Obscure*. No matter what they intend, there seems to be a

TOPICS FOR FURTHER STUDY

- The plot in *Jude the Obscure* is often set in motion through coincidences and accidents. Write a story in which the plot is both driven forward and resolved by coincidences and accidents.

- *Jude the Obscure* is in many ways a tragedy, a genre with roots in Greek drama. Research the conventions of Greek tragedy, and rewrite a compelling moment from the novel as a scene in a Greek tragedy. After your script has been approved by your teacher, enlist classmates to join you in performing the scene for the class.

- *Jude the Obscure* questions the rigid morality that governed behavior in England in Hardy's day. Research the concepts of moral relativism and moral absolutism. What philosophers are associated with each school of thought, and what are their ideas? What, in your opinion, are the positive and negative aspects of each position? Do you think society's morals are shown in *Jude the Obscure* to be absolutist or relativist? Why? Give an oral presentation on your findings.

- Research the history of divorce. How common was divorce and how was it viewed in different cultures throughout history? How common is it today and how is it viewed? Summarize your findings in a written report and present them in a talk before your class. Be sure to identify some high-profile divorces of the past and today and summarize public reaction to them.

Thomas Hardy's cottage *(© Andy Williams / Loop Images / Corbis)*

force at work, whether acting through character, fate, or society, intent upon subverting their efforts. Sue and Jude, after repeated struggles with themselves, each other, and the rules and customs of their society, strike out for a life of happiness with each other. In doing so, they violate social mores and seem to bring upon themselves the wrath of a fate that has determined beforehand that they will not succeed. Fate is a force that rules a person's destiny from without, a force that can overrule character, desire, and even effort. It is a force that is set against will.

This opposition between fate and will is presented, albeit in what seems to be a trivial matter, in the very first paragraph of *Jude the Obscure*. When Phillotson's departure from Christminster is described at the opening of the novel, the problem Hardy brings to the fore is the logistical problem of how to move his piano, which is too large for the cart that is transporting his goods.

Hardy informs the reader that Phillotson bought the piano but found himself unskilled at learning it and lost interest in it. Jude, on the other hand, despite the difficulties he encounters in learning Greek and Latin, persists in the endeavor, but he is fated to fail because of his lower-class status. Owing to his birth rather than his character, he is excluded from being able to enter the university at Christminster. Because of his voluptuous nature, which he cannot subdue but falls victim to through inebriation and active lust, he is repeatedly undone by Arabella. Sue, in turn, is undermined by her very dedication to her own will, whether she is intent on gratifying it, as in the first stages of the novel, or in subverting it, as in the last section. She fails in her attempts both to give herself to Jude and to withhold herself from him. Phillotson, despite his fundamental decency, cannot win Sue's love. When he does win her companionship, he becomes not her lover but the instrument of her penance. Even Arabella, who seems able to manipulate fate and who always seems to survive every obstacle set against her happiness, must adapt to failure, as she never truly succeeds in fulfilling her wishes. When she gets Jude back, for example, it is she who must care for him. She is only saved from what she finds to be a burdensome situation by his death.

The Unjust Power of Social Stratification and Conventional Morality

Although *Jude the Obscure* is not a polemic and does not have an overt social agenda so much as a bleak vision of life, nevertheless, the unjust power of social stratification and conventional morality is at the center of its plot. Jude is excluded from Christminster because of his class. Hardy emphasizes this factor in the letter that the head of one of the colleges writes to Jude in response to his quest for advice about gaining admission. The scholar-administrator advises Jude that since he is of the working class he ought to pursue his work as a stonemason and forgo ideas of scholarship. As well as class stratification, there is gender stratification. Despite her intellect and her unconventionality, or perhaps because of them, Sue is thwarted. She must rely on men, like the young man who loved her and died, for her education. Even Arabella is driven to her devious schemes regarding men, including Jude, because of her inferior position in the world—because she is a woman. The rules of social stratification are given authority in being sanctified by conventional morality, and their violation is punished by social ostracism. Perhaps Hardy's principal challenge to accepted ideas about morality is his probing examination of the human suffering that can result from too fastidious a regard for the institution of marriage and too little regard for the compatibility of the individual partners in a marriage.

STYLE

Accidents and Coincidences as Motivating Plot Devices

For a naturalistic story to advance, it is necessary for the characters to have motivations for their actions. Motivation is defined as the reason for a character's behavior. In *Jude the Obscure* there are two sorts of motivation. There is the primary assertion of a character's basic nature. Jude is a boy with the desire to learn, to be a part of Christminster,

and to treat all living things with respect and kindness. Sue is a young woman who sees beyond the social formulas that surround her. She is taken more by the classical sensibility of ancient Greece and Rome than by the rules of Christian society. She rebels against constraint, whether by purchasing the busts of Aphrodite and Apollo or by refusing to submit to the discipline of the teacher-training school. Phillotson is a gentle and somewhat ineffectual man whose accomplishments fall short of his ambitions, whether with regard to playing the piano, becoming a clergyman, or winning Sue's love. Arabella is motivated by her appetite for sensual gratification, whether with regard to procuring husbands or drinking intoxicating beverages. Once these fundamentals are established, what chiefly motivates Hardy's characters and advances the narrative of *Jude the Obscure* is a mixture of accidents and coincidences. It just so happens that there is space in Jude's aunt's fuel house for Phillotson's piano; that Jude passes by the hedge where Arabella can notice him; that he later overhears girls gossiping that Arabella set him up; that there is a fire in a nearby town when he and Arabella go walking; that he runs into Sue as he is moving stone; that a chambermaid recognizes him at a hotel where he stayed with Arabella and mentions it to Sue; that Arabella sees him at a fair after becoming devout and consequently reverts to her earthiness; that she meets Phillotson on the road and gives him a ride in her carriage and can, consequently, talk to him about Jude and Sue; that Christminster celebrations are occurring when Jude, Sue, and their children return there and when Jude is dying. These and more coincidences not only advance the plot but also help to give it an aspect of inevitability and seem to give what happens to the characters a sense of fate.

Naturalism

Hardy is a contemporary of the French novelist and social activist Emil Zola; both were born in 1840. Apart from his 1898 defense of the French captain Alfred Dreyfus against charges of treason motivated by anti-Semitism, Zola is best known for his novels. His subjects were lower- and working-class people whose lives were determined by the facts of their heredity and their social conditions. The manner of Zola's writing was called naturalism, as he sought to give an accurate sociological picture of characters' lives and circumstances. Naturalist writers seek to convey objective, detailed, unembellished, realistic accounts of human nature and social conditions. Hardy was himself a great

COMPARE
&
CONTRAST

- **1890s:** The 1893 Married Woman's Property Act is passed in England. This act extends the provisions of the 1882 Married Woman's Property Act, which allows married women to own and inherit property, a right that unmarried women already possess, and ensures their right to keep their own earnings.

  Today: In the United Kingdom, marriage legally invests both partners with equal rights regarding property and income.

- **1890s:** Oxford University, despite admitting women to colleges exclusively established for women in 1878, is rather restricted by class and by its educational focus on the classics, theology, and philosophy.

  Today: All of Oxford's colleges are coeducational, and the natural and applied sciences as well as medicine are taught.

- **1890s:** Though it is home to large, bustling cities like London, England is largely a country of rural villages and great amounts of green space.

  Today: After a great decline in the amount of green acreage in England, preservation efforts are paying off, and the BBC reports that not only has there been a halt to the disappearance of green space but there have been actual increases over previous years.

naturalist, and *Jude the Obscure* is one of the great naturalistic novels. Hardy shows Jude as a product of his heredity and of his environment. Early in the novel, Drusilla Fawley warns Jude against marriage and particularly against marriage to his cousin Sue because his parents' marriage and her parents' marriage both were plagued with animosity and misfortune. Jude's environment, too, is of primary importance in his fate. Being of a lower class, he is excluded from the intellectual pursuits of Christminster, subject to the corroding influences of alcohol, and beset by the problem of earning a living. He is ground down by the codes of social conformity regarding love and marriage as well; so is Phillotson, after he asserts his independent judgment and releases Sue from her marriage bond. Hardy's descriptions of landscapes and cities, of cathedrals, fields, railway stations, and fairs, also strive to be pictorially realistic, as if he were visually documenting a period in the later half of the nineteenth century in England.

Omniscient Narrator

In *Jude the Obscure*, Hardy functions as an omniscient narrator. An omniscient narrator is one who does not participate in the action of the story in any way, who knows everything about his characters and what happens to them, and whose knowledge is not accounted for. He is simply a reporting device. Hardy presents the reader with a series of settings, a cast of characters who function within those settings, and the consequences of their interactions. He even enters into their most private spaces, including their thoughts and feelings, and he knows all the public events that shape their lives, even ones of which they are unaware. Hardy's use of an omniscient narrator reinforces the sense that the characters' destinies are fated, predetermined by something outside their control.

HISTORICAL CONTEXT

Hebraism versus Hellenism

A tension between two sets of values runs through *Jude the Obscure*. The values may be called Hebraism, a term Matthew Arnold uses in *Culture and Anarchy* (1869), a discussion of class conflicts and the political forces shaping England at the time he was writing, and Hellenism. By Hebraism, Arnold refers to the fundamental tenets of Judeo-Christian culture; by Hellenism, he refers to classical Greek thought. Hebraism, Arnold argues, is defined by its dedication to "self-conquest . . . following not our own individual will but the will of God, *obedience*." An awareness of sin, Arnold observes, is of great importance to Hebraism. Whereas "strictness of conscience" defines Hebraism, Hellenism is characterized by "spontaneity of consciousness," by "an unclouded clearness of mind, an unimpeded play of thought," and by "seeing things in their essence and beauty." In *Jude the Obscure*, Jude attempts to unite his sense of duty with ideals of beauty and freedom of thought. Sue begins as a partisan of Hellenism in her choice of statues and in the way she chooses to live, following the ideals of her intellect rather than the dictates of convention. In the end, she is won over by Hebraism, as she concludes that she has sinned and imposes on herself a penitential regime of strict discipline and self-abnegation.

Medievalism

The traditions of scholarship and of architecture to which Jude is devoted reflect the penchant of the late Victorian era, in which Hardy wrote, for medievalism. Medievalism, for a number of late Victorian authors and painters, involved a celebration of workmanship and of workers' immediate connection with production for the glorification of both the spirit of God and the human spirit. In "The Nature of Gothic," a section of *The Stones of Venice*, the art and social critic John Ruskin details and praises the work patterns of men during the Middle Ages, especially with regard to the building of the great cathedrals. In *News from Nowhere*, William Morris celebrates the openness of thought and the delight in nature that he attributes to the English Middle Ages and contrasts those with the social rigidity and industrial decay that he finds in late Victorian England.

Oxford University

Hardy intended Christminster to represent the actual city of Oxford, seat of the great university bearing the city's name. Oxford University, founded in the late 1100s, long represented, and still does, a tradition in scholarship and architecture, Jude's two vocational passions. When Jude thinks of Christminster, of its learning and its buildings, he often thinks of intellectual and theological controversies, of which in real life Oxford was the center during the nineteenth century, and

Lovers' quarrel (Hulton Archive / Getty Images)

of some of the leading figures in those controversies, including John Henry Newman, who became Cardinal Newman after he defected from the Anglican Church and became a Roman Catholic. Complex arguments concerning the politics and doctrines of the Church of England led Oxford scholars to coalesce into what became known as the Oxford Movement, or Tractarianism. Its members addressed the issues that concerned them in a number of tracts put forth to challenge and break with the Anglican Church. For Jude, they symbolize the romance of the intellect in its resistance to convention.

The great walls of Christminster are both literal and symbolic barriers, preventing Jude from gaining entrance to the university. In 1899, four years after *Jude the Obscure* was published, Ruskin College was established at Oxford. While it is not a part of Oxford University, its students can share some of Oxford's facilities. What is special about Ruskin College, named for the great nineteenth-century art and social critic John Ruskin, is that its mission is to serve working people with little education—people like Jude.

CRITICAL OVERVIEW

When *Jude the Obscure* was published in its entirety in 1895, after first appearing serially and in censored form, it was met with wildly discrepant responses. Claire Tomalin reports in her biography *Thomas Hardy* that the Bishop of Wakefield announced in a letter to the *Yorkshire Post* that he had burned his copy and that he had persuaded the bookseller W. H. Smith not to carry the novel in its circulating library. Among other responses cited by Tomalin, *Jude the Obscure* was called "a titanically bad book," "a shameful nightmare," "Jude the Obscene," "dangerously near to farce," and "too deplorable a falling-off from Mr Hardy's former achievements to be reckoned with at all." However, there were supporters of the book who saw beyond the controversial content, beyond the skepticism about religion and conventional marriage. William Dean Howells, writing in *Harper's Weekly* (quoted in Tomalin), states, "All the characters... have the appealing quality of human creatures really doing what they must while seeming to do what they will. It is not a question of blaming them or praising them; they are in the necessity of what they do and what they suffer." Howells adds that the truly painful incidents "make us shiver with horror and grovel with shame, but we know that they are deeply founded in the condition, if not in the nature of humanity." In 1896, a writer in the British *Saturday Review* (quoted in Tomalin) argued that Hardy had captured "the voice of the educated proletarian, speaking more distinctly than it has ever spoken before in English literature." The poet A. C. Swinburne (quoted in Tomalin) wrote to Hardy himself, "The beauty, the terror, and the truth are all yours, and yours alone....The man who can do such work can hardly care about criticism or praise." Hardy did care, however, as Tomalin notes, and after *Jude the Obscure* he stopped writing novels. Public response to the novel was nevertheless enthusiastic, and the book sold extremely well.

Literary criticism of the novel has chiefly focused on Hardy's skill in creating characters and on their psychology. D. H. Lawrence was one of the earliest critics to see the fusion of the novel's ideas and the psychological complexity of its characters. In his book *Thomas Hardy*, arguing that Sue Bridehead "is a triumph of psychological portraiture," Irving Howe quotes Lawrence's analysis of her. Lawrence notes, "Here, then, was her difficulty: to find a man whose vitality could infuse her and make her live, and who would not, at the same time, demand of her a return of the female impulse into him." Howe adds, not contradicting Lawrence but attempting to achieve a less idiosyncratic view, that the "most important" thing that "must be said about Sue Bridehead" is that "as she appears in the novel itself, rather than in the grinder of analysis, she is an utterly charming and vibrant creature. We grasp directly, and not merely because we are told, why Jude finds himself unable to resist Sue. Hardy draws her with a marvelous plasticity." Robert B. Heilman, in "Hardy's Sue Bridehead" (1965), included in R. P. Draper's *Hardy: The Tragic Novels*, asserts that *Jude the Obscure* is "a novel in which skillful characterization eventually wins the day over laborious editorializing," connecting the psychology of a character with the stimuli of the environment. Heilman writes of Sue, "Hardy shows that her emotions cannot transcend the community which her mind endeavors to reject." Ian Gregor, in "A Series of Seemings" (1974), also included in Draper's volume, expands that insight:

> Far from the characters in *Jude* seeming fixed, they are seen in constantly shifting emphases and depths, taking themselves—and us— by surprise; the plot is less a narrative line made up of interlocking events, than a series of significant but isolated moments: the ideas debated seem integral to the characters rather than on loan from the author.

Philip M. Weinstein, in "'The Spirit Unappeased and Peregrine': *Jude the Obscure*" (1984), included in Dale Kramer's *Critical Essays on Thomas Hardy: The Novels*, extends still further a psychological analysis of Hardy's characters as they interact with their environment. He considers the psychological effect of the language of their environment as well as their own thought patterns as they create a tragedy from the interaction of those factors. Of the two main protagonists he notes, "They have not mastered the words they utter, making them their own, for Jude and Sue remain trapped within a linguistic world-view which holds that truth is external, universally applicable, and has already been uttered." That Hardy did not himself hold that view has been at the root of both condemnation and celebration of *Jude the Obscure*.

CRITICISM

Neil Heims

Neil Heims is a freelance writer and the author or editor of over two dozen books on literary subjects. In this essay, he explores the tragic dimension in Jude the Obscure *that leads each of the protagonists to despair.*

Jude the Obscure is a story of dashed hopes and broken dreams, of defeat and demoralization. Principally, whether the focus is Jude, Sue, or Phillotson, it is the story of a fall from idealism. It is a profoundly bitter work, one that brings together the forces of nature and society in a concerted attack upon idealism and endeavor. It is a book that seems grudgingly to say to every living creature, "Abandon hope and submit to fate, no matter how grim it may be, for fate is inevitable and any attempt to oppose it, control it, or alter it will only bring on worse fury and punishment. The power to choose is a myth. The forces of nature and society are so overwhelmingly strong that they constitute something like divine fate and contain the power to determine an individual's success or failure, no matter what his or her will or wish."

In order to convey what it is like to be alive in such a world, Hardy tells a tale of the forces that undo three characters: Jude, an idealistic young stonemason who dreams of becoming a learned man; Sue, a woman who tries to live by her intelligence and by her own heart's promptings rather than by convention; and Phillotson, a schoolteacher who attempts to live according to his own intuition of honorable decency and respect for others even when that means he must sacrifice his own happiness for someone else's. All three are driven in their aspirations and in their behavior by ideals that ought to define them as exemplary and heroic; yet they only seem heroic in their attempts to resist the calumny that they bring upon themselves by following their ideals. They seem to be examples only of ways of life that ought to be avoided for the sake of social acceptability and peace of mind. Each of them fails, renounces his or her noble vision, and surrenders in his or her own way to defeat and despair.

After a life of struggle to remain true to his dream of becoming a learned man and to live in domestic intimacy with his beloved Sue, Jude returns, in the first chapter of part VI, to the university city of Christminster with Sue, his

WHAT DO I READ NEXT?

- Hardy's novel *Tess of the D'Urbervilles* (subtitled *A Pure Woman Faithfully Presented*) appeared in 1891. Like *Jude the Obscure*, it presents a conflict between individual conduct and social disapprobation.

- William Morris's utopian novel *News from Nowhere* (1890), as it imagines a better future, offers a critique of the English society and politics reflected in *Jude the Obscure*.

- George Eliot, the pen name of Mary Ann Evans, published *Adam Bede* in 1859. One of the principal characters in this story, set in rural England and concerned with the role of religious values in ordinary life, Hetty Sorrel, is a model of a standard nineteenth-century type, the fallen woman, of which Sue Bridehead is a variation.

- Leo Tolstoy's classic novel *Anna Karenina*, serialized between 1873 and 1877, is a complex interweaving of the stories of a Russian society woman who falls from her position of social respectability and of a landowner who seeks to live according to ideals of social justice and Christian charity.

- The novel *Paul and Virginia* (1787), by Jacques-Henri Bernardin de Saint-Pierre, tells the story of a perfect love between the eponymous characters in a setting where the laws of nature are shown in general to be beneficent and more worth following than the laws and customs socially promulgated, which are seen to be antithetical to humanity.

wife in practice though not in law, and their children. Ironically, it is Remembrance Day in Christminster, an annual day of academic festivities celebrating the traditions of the university. The day emblematizes everything Jude wished for and did not achieve. As they await the procession, Jude explains the ceremony to a crowd of nonacademic townsfolk and is recognized and

THE TERRIBLE IRONY OF SUE'S STORY IS HOW
EXTREMELY BITTER A TASTE SOCIALLY DEFINED
VIRTUE CAN HAVE. SUCH IRONY CHALLENGES VALUES
THAT ARE SOCIALLY ACCEPTED AS THE RIGHT ONES
AND SUGGESTS THE VALIDITY OF VALUES THAT MAY
ELICIT SOCIAL DISAPPROVAL."

jeered at. Jude admits his failure. In his defense, Jude argues, "It was my poverty and not my will that consented to be beaten," although he concedes that "my impulses—affections—vices perhaps they should be called—were too strong not to hamper a man without advantages." To end his public confession, Jude exposes his innermost torment. He is, he proclaims, at a loss:

> What I appear, a sick and poor man, is not the worst of me. I am in a chaos of principles—groping in the dark.... I doubt if I have anything more for my present rule of life than following inclinations which do me and nobody else any harm, and actually give pleasure to those I love best.... I perceive there is something wrong somewhere in our social formulas.

It is this bewildered outcry that "there is something wrong somewhere in our social formulas," regarding the way that society has determined people must live and behave, that is at the root of what made, and for some still might make, *Jude the Obscure* a controversial novel—not simply because it is the story of a love realized out of wedlock, for that violation of the social order certainly does not go unpunished in the book. Moreover, Sue recants her apostasy and capitulates to society's rules. The actual quality of her apparent virtue, however, is subverted by Jude's indictment of society and by the depth of suffering Sue draws to herself and the misery she brings to Jude in her capitulation to the standards of social virtue. Even Phillotson, in whom much is to be admired because of his magnanimity, is lessened by his ultimate role as the disciplining husband of a submissive and self-abnegating wife.

Returning to Christminster highlights not only Jude's academic failure but also the failure of his unconventional relationship with Sue.

Since it is impossible for them to obtain lodgings together as a family because of their social unacceptability, the fruit of their love is blasted and wasted, for that is the immediate cause of Jude's son's desperate murder of his siblings and himself. Despite the addition of that bitter circumstance to his accumulated ill fortune, Jude is not beaten down to despair until Sue yields to defeat, leaves him to return to Phillotson, and urges that he marry Arabella again, arguing that Arabella is his true and only wife just as Phillotson is her real husband.

Sue is crippled and transformed by guilt and overcome by superstition after the death of the children. She tells Jude, "We must conform! All the ancient wrath of the Power above us has been vented upon us.... It is no use fighting against God!" When he objects, still prepared to assert his vision of what is right in opposition to society's, arguing that "it is only against man and senseless circumstance" that they have rebelled, Sue answers, "Whoever or whatever our foe may be, I am cowed into submission.... I am beaten, beaten!" In response, Jude takes the responsibility for their misfortunes upon himself, describing himself as a seducer, and suggests that they marry in order to escape further social scorn. But Sue responds according to her transformed conscience. She argues that it is good that they have not married, for to have done so would have been "insulting" to "the solemnity" of their previous marriages to Phillotson and Arabella. When Jude responds with surprise, she responds even more surprisingly that she has "a dreadful sense of my own insolence of action. I have thought—that *I* am still his [Phillotson's] wife!" When Sue does go back to Phillotson, submerging her will to be Jude's lover in what she believes, irrespective of her wishes, to be her duty—to be Phillotson's wife to the fullest despite her physical aversion to him—the reader is less inclined to see in it the victory of virtue and more apt to shudder at the awful rending of two spirits that seemed in harmony both with themselves and with each other and at the attendant pain and suffering. Describing their connection, Hardy writes of them that "when they talked on an indifferent subject... there was ever a second silent conversation passing between their emotions, so perfect was the reciprocity between them." After the children's deaths, Jude and Sue are each driving themselves and each other to discord and disintegration. Their reciprocity is not destroyed; it is simply disabled. The terrible irony of Sue's story is how extremely bitter a taste socially defined virtue can have. Such irony challenges values that are socially accepted as the right ones and suggests the validity of values that may elicit social disapproval. Jude says of such alternative values, "[They] do me and nobody else any harm, and actually give pleasure to those I love best."

If there were a normative figure in *Jude the Obscure* who could provide a moral compass, whom the reader might consider a surrogate for the author, it might have been Phillotson, who is a schoolmaster, after all. He is portrayed as the inspiration for Jude's behavior and for his aspirations. It is with Phillotson's removal from Marygreen and his pilgrimage to Christminster in search of a career as a university-trained clergyman that Jude's story begins. The reader's first insight into Jude's character comes in the episode in Farmer Troutham's fields when Jude, inspired by Phillotson's parting words about showing kindness to animals, allows the birds to feed upon the grain in the rick Jude has been employed to protect from them. Phillotson is authentic, not a hypocrite or a scoundrel, like Vilbert, who offers bogus remedies. Nor is he narrow or brutal, like his friend Gillingham, who thinks Sue "ought to be smacked and brought to her senses." Phillotson remains true to his compassionate creed even when it is painful to do so, until he is broken. When he realizes that Sue is physically repelled by him and loves Jude, Phillotson is calm and gracious. He tells Gillingham, over Gillingham's objections, that he will let Sue go to Jude, explaining, "I know I can't logically, or religiously, defend hers, or harmonize it with the doctrines I was brought up in. Only I know one thing: something within me tells me I am doing wrong in refusing her." He even concedes that the "right and proper and honorable" course socially prescribed "is to refuse it, and put her virtuously under lock and key, and murder her lover perhaps." But Phillotson, in his painful position, nevertheless has the character to argue against that code, rhetorically asking, "Is that essentially right and proper and honorable, or is it contemptibly mean and selfish?" He answers his own question by falling back on the promptings of his own instinct: "If a person who has blindly walked into a quagmire cries for help, I am inclined to give it."

But after he accidentally encounters Arabella and learns about Jude and Sue's misfortunes, discovers that they are not actually married, and digests Arabella's remonstrance that he ought not to have surrendered Sue, Phillotson is moved to rethink his values as he had not been in his conversation with Gillingham. Arabella laments to him, "*I* shouldn't have let her go! I should have kept her chained on—her spirit for kicking would have been broke soon enough! There's nothing like bondage and a stone-deaf task-master for taming us women." Phillotson can only reply submissively, "with biting sadness," that "cruelty is the law pervading all nature and society; and we can't get out of it if we would!" When Sue, in her guilt and despair, returns to him and even insists on submitting to the marital obligation, which he is ready to forgo, Phillotson accepts the world's cruelty as the proper model for his behavior. He turns what is actually a self-protective choice into a seeming imperative. He expresses his new view to Gillingham with the simple assertion, "I perceive it won't do to give way to impulse."

Unlike Jude, Sue, and Phillotson, Arabella does not grapple with problems of idealism or social virtue. Her one flirtation with idealism, evangelical teetotalism, is socially acceptable, as, paradoxically, is her life as a coquette and a barmaid. Significantly, religion hardly has a hold on her, for after once reencountering Jude, she renounces it and resumes her intemperate pursuit of pleasure, particularly regaining possession of Jude. Arabella neither rises nor falls in the novel, although she is a catalyst for the falls of the three main sufferers of the story. She activates Jude's earthly passions, his lust and his intemperance. She kindles the fire of self-assertion and severity in Phillotson. And she even draws from Sue the fatal assertion, regarding Jude, "I am not his wife." Arabella, by each of her diabolic interventions, pushes the plot forward and guides the other three to wretchedness. She is the embodiment of the undermining forces of the world, manipulating the weaknesses of the others for her own advantage. It is painfully ironic, too, that she is the wisest of them all in understanding human nature and human desire. While her subversion of the others' ideals can certainly be felt by readers to be cause for reprobation, her last attack on idealism—when in the last paragraphs of the novel she contradicts good Mrs. Edlin's consolatory belief that Sue has "found peace," saying, "She's never found peace since she left his arms, and never will again till she's" dead—is a truth whose implications challenge the social and self-imposed constraints that shape the plot of the novel and lead its protagonists to tragedy.

Source: Neil Heims, Critical Essay on *Jude the Obscure*, in *Novels for Students*, Gale, Cengage Learning, 2010.

Michelle Faubert

In the following essay, Faubert examines the character of Little Father Time in Jude the Obscure.

The name of the character Little Father Time, in Thomas Hardy's *Jude the Obscure*, attests to the contradictions that surround this mysterious figure. That is, the appellation "Little Father Time" clearly posits this character as a figure of allegory (Moore 278) and signifies that he represents something abstract or ideal—in this case, time. By extension, it would also seem that Little Father Time carries with him more than just his "ensigns," a key and a ticket (Moore 279), which further attest to his role as a symbolic character. Indeed, one can rightly expect this figure of allegory to convey a moral lesson, and according to his stepmother, Sue Bridehead, he does. She makes sense of Little Father Time's killing of her children by framing the events in moral terms, thereby casting the murderer as a manifestation of God's judgment on herself. She cries, "My children are dead—and it is right that they should be! [. . .] They were sin-begotten. They were sacrificed to teach me how to live!" Little Father Time's irrefutably allegorical name also draws attention to the similarly but more subtly symbolic names of most of the main characters in the novel. As a figure from allegory, Little Father Time is the locus of a fascinating contradiction in *Jude the Obscure*, for the novel's allegorical aspects are in direct contrast to the naturalistic details that Hardy's audience expects, given the author's place as a writer of naturalism par excellence. In allegory, the symbolic nature of the characters and the pat moral they convey circumscribe the narrative plot with an artificiality of which the novel of naturalism is supposed to be free, for it should reflect the unpredictable workings of natural law rather than the artifice of the writer's ordering imagination. Ironically though, as allegorical as Little Time is, he is also the harbinger of the workings of harsh reality in the novel. Hence, he establishes the novel as a work of naturalism, as well.

Little Time's unrealistic nature is partially revealed in his approach to time, which is very different from either that of his father, Jude, or of his natural mother, Arabella. Jude's life is guided by his love of the past, and this love is the very basis of his unfailing desire to be a scholar. As Moore puts it, "Jude takes to studying the outdated grammars of ancient languages. His books fall under the double rubric of the belated; they present dead mythologies for learning dead languages" (261). Jude's fascination with Christminster is also connected to his love of the past. Indeed, he lists as Christminster's most notable feature its history of having been home to the dead greats of old. By contrast, Little Time's mother, Arabella, is future oriented, so much so that she is practically prophetic. As the narrator puts it, she is "always imagining and waiting," concocting plans that will set her up for her future life. One of these plans is to lie to Jude about being pregnant so that he will marry her, thereby ensuring her future comfort. Her deception is eventually revealed, but as the existence of Little Time eventually shows, she correctly guessed the future in her lie. She looks out for the comfort of her future self through marriage later in the novel as well, deciding that she wants Jude back only six weeks after her other husband, Cartlett, dies and courting the attentions of Vilbert the physician while Jude is still warm in his deathbed. Furthermore, it is from this same doctor that Arabella buys future "immunity from the ravages of Time" in the form of pills. Unlike his parents, though, Little Father Time is not guided by his relationship to time, for he is time. He therefore approaches life without the usual limitations of time, "regarding his companions [on the train] as if he saw their whole rounded lives rather than their immediate figure." Supernaturally, Little Father Time represents all moments of time, being both aged, as he is called Father Time and "preternaturally old," and young, for he is a child.

Fantastic as this character seems to be in the terms outlined above, he is also presented as signifying a realism that contrasts with Jude and Sue's idealism. The harsh realism of Little Time is revealed in Hardy's first description of him: his "saucer eyes seemed mutely to say: 'All laughing comes from misapprehension. Rightly looked at there is no laughable thing under the sun.'" Moreover, the child's spoken words reveal his practicality, as his first complete sentences in the novel impart a harsh sense of imperative: he announces, "'I've got to go there'" and "'I must walk.'" He is a boy of few words, to be sure, and because of this characteristic, Jude and Sue are often "hardly conscious of him." Yet, Jude and Sue are not only unwitting of Little Time's person, but also of that which he represents. In short, Jude has the unrealistic dream of rising out of the lot into which he was born and redefining himself as a great scholar, or even a bishop. In his idealism he is similar to Sue, who tries to thwart one of society's most cherished contracts, marriage, without the expectation of retribution. For a while, Jude and Sue do live together in an unwedded state of "Greek joyousness," but Little Time eventually destroys their world after taking Sue's sad pronouncements on the state of their family too "literally," as one would expect of a realist. He kills himself, as well as Jude and Sue's two children, for a starkly practical reason, which he reveals in his note to be "because . . . [they] are too meny." Also significant is the fact that the idealists'—Jude and Sue's—two children die before they develop into distinct individuals, which is why Hardy neither mentions them separately nor describes them. It is as though the babies are abstract beings, or are merely embodiments of the idea of "child," who must be canceled out by reality in this novel of naturalism.

However shocking this murder scene is to readers, its consequences—the destruction of Jude and Sue's life together—might have been expected according to the dictates of naturalism. Indeed, "rightly looked at" as Little Father Time would say, it was only a matter of time before Jude and Sue's fantasy life would dissolve, and this collapse can literally be blamed on Time. Thus, we are reminded again of Little Father Time's allegorical associations. He is none other than stolid Time, "creep[ing] forward in a "steady mechanical" way heedless of the vain hopes and desires in the lives to which he brings change and careless of such particulars as individual people. In an ironic way, the same function of Little Father Time that follows from his allegorical identity—as Time—also emphasizes *Jude the Obscure*'s identity as a naturalistic novel.

Source: Michelle Faubert, "Hardy's *Jude the Obscure*," in *Explicator*, Vol. 60, No. 2, Winter 2002, pp. 76–79.

Sara Crangle

In the following excerpt, Crangle explores Hardy's use of the framed image throughout Jude the Obscure.

In *Jude the Obscure*, Hardy's framed images— be they photographs, windows, mirrors, or doorways—serve as "active signifiers" (Mast 85) that

"[carry] themes" (Berger 55). As a whole, Hardy's prolific use of the framed image throughout the novel reflects its most prominent theme, namely Sue Bridehead's and Jude Fawley's attempts to overcome the strictures/frames of social status and convention. As Elizabeth Langland writes, those strictures are exacerbated for Sue because of her sex: "Sue's is not simply a class conflict; it is a conflict of genders, a conflict finally between what woman can and is expected to do" (20). This distinction between male and female experience is symbolically represented in Hardy's framed images: while Sue's image is often encased, Jude consistently eludes almost all frames, both pictorial and social.

Sue's image is repeatedly framed in windows and photographs. Jude voyeuristically observes Sue through the window at her training school, at her house in Shaston, and at Marygreen, where she is staying with the Widow Edlin. On one occasion, Richard Phillotson and his friend Gillingham also engage in the same activity. Furthermore, photographs of Sue are much sought after and revered by the men with whom she is involved; Jude longs for, and eventually receives, Sue's photograph from their Aunt Drusilla, after which he "put the photograph on the mantelpiece, kissed it—he did not know why—and felt more at home." Jude is not the only man to possess and kiss Sue's image: Phillotson also keeps photographs of Sue as a girl and a young woman in his desk drawer, the latter being "a duplicate of the one she had given Jude, and would have given any man." Although Phillotson hesitates before kissing Sue's photograph, he "ultimately [kisses] the dead pasteboard with all the passionateness, and more than all the devotion, of a young man of eighteen." . . .

Sue is much more rigidly defined by society than Jude, who is a self-educated man who speaks in a more elevated language than the residents of Marygreen or the regular clientele at the public house in Christminster. As a stonemason, however, he can repair, but not enter, the frames of the colleges and universities he dreams of attending. He therefore exists in a space between societal frames, and his elusion of categorical definition is represented in Hardy's use of framed images: Jude's image is curiously lacking within the novel's window frames, looking-glasses, and photographs. Jude is never reflected in any surface, a fact evidenced in the first chapter, when young Jude looks down into the well at Marygreen, seeing "a long circular perspective ending in a shining disc of quivering water at a distance of a hundred feet down." The well, framed by stone, moss, and hart's tongue, is "as ancient as the village itself"; it is one of the hamlet's oldest surviving monuments. Here, where Jude might see himself, he sees only a distant light framed by stone; the image is evocative of Jude's search for a way of life that can fit within the established structures (the old stone wells) of his society.

When Jude is captured by frames he appears to be unrecognizable, as when he comes across his own framed portrait in a pawnshop. Arabella has discarded his picture with all of her other belongings in her haste to set out for Australia, and when Jude discovers it, he purchases it from the pawnbroker, who makes no mention of his resemblance to the framed image. And again, at the Great Wessex Agricultural Show, Arabella's friend Anny does not recognize Jude from the pictures of him that Arabella has shown her in the past. We know that Jude has given Sue pictures of himself because he wonders if it is his photograph she is looking at when he watches her through her window at Shaston, yet his portrait is conspicuously absent from the collection of photographs that Sue has in filigree and velvet on her dresser at the training school. All of this is in keeping with Jude's existence between frames—his bucking of the strictures of his class, his exclusion from the walled academy. But juxtaposed against the continual framing of Sue in the novel, the rationale cannot exclude considerations of gender: Sue is framed by a society that values her appearance and her body, whereas Jude exists in a masculine realm, freed from those constraints.

The world in which Sue and Jude live lacks parameters, or frames of reference, for the life they have generated. For Sue, this world cannot be sustained; she fulfills Jude's accusation that she is "'as enslaved to the social code as any woman [he knows]'" and comes to lead an enclosed life, pretending at real marriage with Phillotson. But to believe that Jude's brief life has been entirely for naught is to swallow completely the view that only formal institutions can impart the knowledge he sought. The text, in its undermining of Jude's idealization of the university town of Christminster (the rotting buildings; Sue's verbal dismantling of the academy), asserts the value of Jude's independent study. Furthermore, Jude acknowledges that in his own lifetime, the doors of the academy are slowly

creaking open to admit poor but determined men like himself. Thus Jude remains the true idealist because he has something to believe in: the progress of mankind. It is this certainty that strengthens the courage of his convictions. Ultimately, the only frame that completely and irreversibly encloses Jude's life is death.

Source: Sara Crangle, "Hard's *Jude the Obscure*," in *Explicator*, Vol. 60, No. 1, Fall 2001, pp. 24–27.

Anthony Kearney

In the following essay, Kearney discusses Hardy's use of the line "Save his own soul he hath no star" in Jude the Obscure.

Part 2 of Hardy's *Jude the Obscure* begins with an epigraph from Swinburne's prelude to *Songs Before Sunrise*: "Save his own soul he hath no star" (stanza 16). This was a favorite quotation of Hardy's, and he used it on another occasion to describe his own feelings of lively independence as a young man in London in the 1860s. Picturing himself as "an isolated student cast upon the billows of London with no protection but his brains", he added that he was then a "young man of whom it may be said more truly than perhaps of any, that 'save his own soul he hath no star'". Lacking social advantages and money, but with ability and determination in plenty, Hardy identified fully with Swinburne's call for self-reliance and with the spirit of an earlier assertion in the poem: "For what has he whose will sees clear / To do with doubt and faith and fear?" (stanza 4).

In his use of the line "Save his own soul he hath no star" in Jude, however, Hardy's intentions are not altogether clear. In what sense does the line apply to Jude? And in fact there is some uncertainty among commentators as to its precise bearing. Does it reinforce the parallel between the young Hardy and the young Jude as characters of talent and ambition? Is it there to suggest Jude's isolation and vulnerability as a young working-class protagonist? Or is it ambiguous, indicating either Jude's later freedom from outmoded ideas and codes, or—in stark contrast—an independence of thought and action that Jude signally fails to achieve? These are all possibilities put forward by various critics but not fully tested by relating the epigraph to a range of associated images in the novel. A further look at the line in context may help to clarity its application to Jude and his tragic destiny.

The quotation itself probably derives from some lines in a Beaumont and Fletcher play (the epilogue to *The Honest Man's Fortune*) which read: "Man is his own star, and the soul that can / Render an honest and a perfect man / Commands all light, all influence, all fate". Swinburn himself was a devoted reader of the Beaumont and Fletcher canon. The idea of man being his own star, controlling his own fate, was one that appealed as much to Victorian individualists as to Jacobean ones. In recycling the image, Swinburne provided Hardy with a familiar language for the handling of his own debate about the interaction of character and circumstance.

Jude, as soon becomes clear in the novel, is a contradictory individual. On the one hand, he is full of noble aspirations and keen to realize his Arnoldian best self; on the other, he is often passive and uncertain, the victim of his own desires and weaknesses. In one way, as Hardy indicates, Jude is the Tennysonian "gifted man" who "breaks his birth's invidious bar" and "breasts the blows of circumstances / And grapples with his evil star"—in fact we see Jude determined to "battle with his evil star" just before he sets out for Christminster in part 2. On the other hand, as the novel progresses, he increasingly flounders, and the lines from Swinburne that follow the epigraph seem to apply to him more: Man "sinks, except his own soul guide / Helmless in middle turn of tide". Potentially Jude would seem to be a heroic individual on the Swinburnian (or Tennysonian) model, but in practice he fails.

He fails partly because of his situation (as an aspirant to a status denied him by society on account of his background and poverty) but also because of his desperate need for, and failure to find, adequate guides through life. Far from being his own star, Jude comes under the influence of a succession of misleading, or otherwise problematic, guides—Phillotson, Christminster, Sue—before he finally sinks helmless in the tide. Sue, of course, is the key figure here and, significantly, Hardy attaches a number of star images to her. Having determined to battle with his "evil star" (his obscurity and poverty) at the close of part 1, Jude is quickly, and ironically, taken over by his idolization of Sue who, in effect, turns out to be another "evil star" for him. Sue, whose intellect "scintillated like a star"—in comparison to Jude, "like a star to a benzoline lamp"—exerts a power over Jude that makes him dependent on her to a fatal degree. Early on, he sees her as "a kindly star, an elevating power", but unfortunately for Jude she turns out to be a highly unstable guide, unsure of who she is and what she wants and in the end making Jude realize that—in words used by Sue herself—he will never know her "real star-pattern", only the multitude of confusing shapes that she presents to the world and to him. Finally Jude's "kindly star" abandons him, turning back to the Church and the husband she had earlier rejected for Jude, an action, as Jude tells her, designed "to save your own soul only!", a comment with a clear ironic echo of the Swinburnian epigraph at the beginning of part 2. Sue, as Jude sees it, has given the idea of self-determination hymned by the poets a wholly selfish twist.

This reading of the star/soul imagery of the novel supports the view that the Swinburne epigraph should be seen as having not a fixed but a changing relation to Jude and his fortunes. Jude, at the close of part 1, has rekindled "in his soul a spark of the old fire" and moves on to Christminster in hopes of fulfilling his ambitions. The novel is in one of its brief optimistic phases, a feeling reinforced by the stirring epigraph that immediately follows the report of Jude's new access of energy and enthusiasm. But as we have seen, the heroic self-sufficiency of Swinburne's poem is soon manifestly less and less applicable to Jude as he hitches his fate to Sue's star and both of them, victims of forces beyond their control, finally sink "helmless in middle turn of tide." The line, then, that Hardy applied self-flatteringly to himself in *Life of Thomas Hardy* takes on a sense of both pathos and irony when applied to Jude and Sue. Lives that started out with a Swinburnian promise of self-sufficiency and personal fulfillment, underscored by an inspiring epigraph, turn out to be doomed to a desperate search for a guidance that never arrives in a satisfactory form. In *Life of Thomas Hardy*, Hardy chronicles his own success story; in *Jude* he contemplates what might have been an alternative for himself—"a tragedy of unfulfilled aims" (preface to the first edition of *Jude*).

Source: Anthony Kearney, "Hardy's *Jude the Obscure*," in *Explicator*, Vol. 57, No. 3, Spring 1999, pp. 154–56.

James J. Snow

In the following excerpt, Snow discusses Jude the Obscure *in terms of Aristotle's views on friendship.*

. . . At the conclusion of *Jude the Obscure*, as Jude lies dying he whispers the words of the biblical Job: "Let the day perish wherein I was born, and the night in which it was said, There is a man child conceived." Jude's life ends with the

"

JUDE THE OBSCURE SEEMS IN NEGATIVE

FASHION TO BEAR OUT ARISTOTLE'S CONTENTION

THAT A GOOD LIFE IS NOT POSSIBLE WITHOUT THE

BENEFIT OF FINE FRIENDSHIPS."

realization that his life was a wasted life, a life that should not have been lived at all. He is ultimately crushed under the weight of a deep and profound regret, which is that he had to live at all. "Why died I not from the womb?" he asks; "Why did I not give up the ghost when I came out of the belly?" Arabella's prophecy at the end of the novel suggests that Sue, too, will find resolution and peace only in death, only when "she's as he is now." What, then, is the reason for Jude's misery? Who or what is responsible for his wretched existence?

Jude has a vision of a good life that strikes us as reasonable and right. It is a vision he pursues relentlessly. Throughout the story his aspiration is Christminster, the "city of light," "the heavenly Jerusalem," "a wonderful city for scholarship and religion." In Christminster, Jude thinks he can fulfill his dream of a life of scholarship.

> [H]e thought he might become even a bishop by leading a pure, energetic, wise, Christian life. And what an example he would set! If his income were 5000 pounds a year, he would give away 4500 pounds in one form or another, and live sumptuously (for him) on the remainder. Well, on second thought, a bishop was absurd. He would draw the line at an archdeacon. Perhaps a man could be as good and as learned and as useful in the capacity of archdeacon as in that of a bishop.

However much we realize that Jude idealizes the city of Christminster, his aspirations are admirable, lofty, good and pure. As Jean Brooks observes: "Jude Fawley differs from most antiheroes, to his credit, in knowing what he wants to escape from and where he wants to go to, in holding fast to his ideal of Christminster, and in refusing to demean his integrity in order to survive, Lucky Jim fashion, in the real defective world."

Aristotle recognizes that a good life is not entirely self-wrought. He says explicitly that "deprivation of certain [external] goods—e.g., good

birth, good children, beauty—mars our blessedness; for we do not altogether have the character of eudaimonia if we look utterly repulsive or are illborn, solitary or childless, and have it even less, presumably, if our children or friends are totally bad, or were good but have died" (NE1099b1-5). The most important external good, according to Aristotle, is friendship: "it is most necessary for our life" (1155a2); "friendship is not only necessary but also fine" (1155a29); furthermore, "no one would choose to live without friends even if he had all the other goods" (1155a5). It is Aristotle's view, then, that eudaimonia is not possible without benefit of external goods and that friendship is the most important of those goods. Friendship is both a necessary condition for living well and a major component of eudaimonia.

Jude the Obscure seems in negative fashion to bear out Aristotle's contention that a good life is not possible without the benefit of fine friendships. The characters in the novel are not the sort of friends that Aristotle deems necessary for eudaimonia. Rather than helping Jude realize his goals and aspirations, Arabella and Sue serve—sometimes maliciously, sometimes not— only to frustrate, to impede. As readers of the novel we suspect that if Jude had had other friends, better friends, his life might have turned out better than it did. Similarly, Jude is not the sort of friend who would make Sue's life more bearable. Jude is sometimes kindly tolerant of what he perceives as Sue's idiosyncracies, but he is conspicuously blind to her plight, to her otherness.

Both Sue and Jude lack the kind of friendships that Aristotle describes as essential to living well, that is, friendships that involve mutuality, respect, shared feeling and the like. Aristotle describes three kinds of friendships—friendships of pleasure, friendships of utility and friendships of good people—and it is the last mentioned that is so crucial to eudaimonia (NE1156a11ff.) He describes this kind of friendship in some detail, both in the Ethics and in the Rhetoric. Friendship cannot involve soulless things, Aristotle tells us, "since there is no mutual loving," and although friendship is not merely good will, to the extent that it involves good will "friendship is said to be reciprocated good will" (1155b28-34). Friendship is reciprocated trust and feelings of affection. Furthermore, friendship involves, as he says in the *Rhetoric*, "wish[ing] for someone what one thinks to be good, for that person's own sake and not for one's own..." (1381a1). Moreover, friends share feelings. "Your friend," he says, "is the sort of man who shares your pleasure in what is good and your pain in what is unpleasant... [and] this pleasure and pain of his will be the token of his good wishes for you..." (1381a5-6). Friendship involves doing things for the other. Friendship is caused by "doing kindnesses; doing them unasked; and not proclaiming the fact that they are done" (1381b35).

... Sue is far more complex than Arabella, both in her own right and in her relationship to Jude. At one level, she is merely the antithesis of Arabella. Jude envisions her as a "kindly star, an elevating power, a companion in Anglican worship, a tender friend." He is drawn to her virtues and talents, to her ecclesiastical manner; he "can see that she is exceptionally bright," and he is possessed with a "wish for intellectual sympathy, and a craving for loving-kindness in [his] solitude."

... Returning to the question of why the relationship between the seemingly like-minded Jude and Sue is such a bitter failure, we discover two answers. One answer returns us to Aristotle, the other does not. Neither Jude nor Sue approach the conditions of fine friendship discussed by Aristotle. Rarely does one act for the benefit of the other. Sue never wishes Jude well for his own sake; Jude never wishes Sue well for her own sake. Sue never does anything for Jude; nor Jude for Sue. Their relationship lacks those elements deemed essential by Aristotle. Jude's concern for Sue is always self-regarding. He says at one point:

> "Don't abandon me to them, Sue, to save your own soul only! They have been kept entirely at a distance since you became my guardian angel! Since I have had you I have been able to go out into any temptations of the sort without risk. Isn't my safety worth a little sacrifice of dogmatic principle? I am in terror lest, if you leave me, it will be with me another case of the pig that was washed turning back to his wallowing in the mire!"

Sue and Jude are blind to one another as Other. They are consumed with their own lives. The important elements of fine friendships all presuppose our ability to see the other as Other. Our ability to do kindnesses for another for his/her own sake presupposes that we can see another person as one with his/her own projects, aims, ambitions, aspirations and hopes, and not merely in terms of our own.

Aristotle acknowledges that fine friendships are as rare as they are beautiful. Fine friendships are between people of virtuous character. However, "these kinds of friendship are likely to be rare, since such people are few" (NE1156b25). Our reading of Aristotle suggests that if Jude had only found a better comrade than Sue (or Arabella), his life would have been better than it was. And similarly, if Sue had only found a better companion than Jude (or Phillotson), her life might not be as tragic as Jude's. Amidst the impersonal non-providential universe that is the backdrop to the story, we sense that two lives might have been considerably better than they were, if only each character had discovered a better sort of friend than either in fact did. We need, as Aristotle reminds us, the right friends if we are to live well; Jude and Sue, as luck would have it, are not at all well-suited to one another. In one sense, then, the story is a painful testimony supporting Aristotle's claims for both the rarity of fine friendships, and the importance of fine friendships for living well.

Hardy's novel, however, offers other perspectives on Jude's and Sue's relationship, and their miserable lives. One such perspective is the prophecy offered by Aunt Drucilla. She foretells Jude's ruin. Charged with raising the orphan, she tells her friends that "it would ha' been a blessing if Goddy-mighty had took thee too, wi' thy mother and father, poor useless boy!" Aunt Drucilla repeatedly warns Jude to stay away from Sue. Even after his arrival at Christminster, Jude "received a nervously anxious letter from his poor old aunt, on the subject which had previously distressed her—a fear that Jude would not be strong-minded enough to keep away from Sue Bridehead and her relations." Here the focus is on the particular character of Sue. The wise aunt, however, also suggests that it is not just Sue, and that there is something inherently devastating about human relationships themselves.

"The Fawleys were not made for wedlock," she tells Jude, for "it never seemed to sit well upon us. There's sommat in our blood that won't take kindly to the notion of being bound to do what we do readily enough if not bound." She cannot speak for the human condition—such would indeed sound strange coming from a rural Wessex woman—but the suggestion is clear that there exists something in our very nature—"sommat in our blood"—that is to blame. Aunt Drucilla appears to blame the Fawley family, but the implication is clear that the problem transcends the personalities of particular individuals.

Aunt Drucilla's prophecy takes us well beyond Aristotle. She warns us that there is something problematic about human relationships themselves. She does not tell us what; she only warns us, as it were, of something that we cannot ignore. That something seems to be that human beings want incompatible things: we want autonomy at the same time that we want the Other. Jude is drawn to the Other—both Arabella and Sue—almost against his will. Sue is drawn to the Other—both Phillotson and Jude—despite her desire for autonomy. Jude realizes that the Other may very well frustrate his ambitions but he pines for Sue with the same intensity that he aspires to Christminster. It is Jude's perception of the implications of this situation that constitutes his final realization and despair. . . .

Source: James J. Snow, "Two Different Ethics: Philosophy and Literature," in *Mosaic*, Vol. 27, No. 2, June 1994, pp. 75–94.

SOURCES

Arnold, Matthew, "Culture and Anarchy," in *The Portable Matthew Arnold*, edited by Lionel Trilling, Viking Press, 1966, pp. 560–64.

"A Brief History of the University," University of Oxford Web site, http://www.ox.ac.uk/about_the_university/introducing_oxford/a_brief_history_of_the_university/index.html (accessed November 24, 2008).

Digby, Kenelm Edward, *An Introduction to the History of the Law of Real Property: With Original Authorities*, 5th ed., Clarendon Press, 1897, reprint, Lawbook Exchange, 2005, p. 391.

"England Halts Green Space Decline," in *BBC News*, March 2, 2006, http://news.bbc.co.uk (accessed November 24, 2008).

Gregor, Ian, "A Series of Seemings," in *Hardy: The Tragic Novels*, edited by R. P. Draper, Macmillan, 1975, p. 228.

Hardy, Thomas, *Jude the Obscure*, Modern Library, 1923.

Heilman, Robert B., "Hardy's Sue Bridehead," in *Hardy: The Tragic Novels*, edited by R. P. Draper, Macmillan, 1975, pp. 209, 225.

Howe, Irving, *Thomas Hardy*, Macmillan, 1967, pp. 138, 143.

Sampson, George, and R. C. Churchill, *The Concise Cambridge History of English Literature*, Cambridge University Press, 1972, pp. 555–58.

Tomalin, Claire, *Thomas Hardy*, Penguin, 2007, pp. 259–60.

Weinstein, Philip M., "'The Spirit Unappeased and Peregrine': *Jude the Obscure*," in *Critical Essays on Thomas Hardy: The Novels*, edited by Dale Kramer, G. K. Hall, 1990, p. 233; originally published in *The Semantics of Desire: Changing Models of Identity from Dickens to Joyce*, Princeton University Press, 1984.

FURTHER READING

Adelman, Gary, Jude the Obscure: *A Paradise of Despair*, Twayne, 1992.
    Adelman provides an extensive and focused study of *Jude the Obscure*, offering a literary and historical context for the novel as well as a detailed, analytic reading of the work and discussions of particular critical methods that have been applied to the text.

Auerbach, Erich, "Odysseus' Scar," in *Mimesis: The Representation of Reality in Western Literature*, translated by Willard R. Trask, Princeton University Press, 2003.
    This is a great and seminal study of the differences in the way the author of the book of Genesis and the Greek epic poet Homer understand and represent reality in their literature.

Casagrande, Peter J., *Unity in Hardy's Novels: "Repetitive Symmetries,"* Regents Press of Kansas, 1982.
    Casagrande offers a detailed survey of Hardy's thought as it sprung from his experience and shaped his work.

Forster, E. M., *Howards End*, G. P. Putnam's Sons, 1910.
    Forster considers the problems of conventional morality, women's freedom, marriage, social class, and poverty in this novel written some fifteen years after Hardy's *Jude the Obscure*.

Pool, Daniel, *What Jane Austen Ate and Charles Dickens Knew: From Fox Hunting to Whist; The Facts of Daily Life in Nineteenth-Century England*, Touchstone, 1994.
    This social history details many of the customs and practices in Victorian England and includes chapters on marriage, occupations, and society.

The Little Prince

ANTOINE DE SAINT-EXUPÉRY

1943

The children's story *The Little Prince*, by the French author and aviation pioneer Antoine de Saint-Exupéry, was first published by Reynal & Hitchcock in the original French as *Le Petit Prince* in 1943. Also in 1943, the same publisher brought out an English-language version, translated by Katherine Woods, under the title *The Little Prince*. As of 2008, it is available in a 2000 edition published by Harvest Books, translated by Richard Howard.

The Little Prince tells the story of an encounter between an aviator whose airplane has crashed in the desert and an enigmatic visitor from another planet, the little prince of the title. The little prince's account of his journey to Earth via other planets and his impressions of the inhabitants becomes an allegory of human nature. An allegory is a representation of an abstract or spiritual meaning through concrete or material forms. The novel's themes include spiritual decay and the importance of establishing bonds of love and responsibility with other beings.

The novel is part of a French literary tradition of allegorical fantasies, of which the novel *Candide* (1759), by the eighteenth-century French author and philosopher Voltaire, is one of the best-known examples. In France, *The Little Prince* confirmed Saint-Exupéry's reputation as a great writer on aviation whose works have deep moral and spiritual significance.

Antoine de Saint-Exupéry

Elsewhere in the world, the novel was largely ignored by critics and academics in the decades following the author's death in 1944. However, this has not prevented the work becoming a great popular success with both adults and children across the world. It has become one of the most widely translated works of French literature.

AUTHOR BIOGRAPHY

The French author and aviator Antoine Jean Baptiste Marie Roger de Saint-Exupéry was born on June 29, 1900, in Lyon, France, into an aristocratic family. He was the third child of Count Jean de Saint-Exupéry, an insurance company executive, and his wife Marie de Fonscolombe de Saint-Exupéry. Count Jean died in 1904. In 1909, his widow moved with her children to live at the home of her aunt, the castle of Saint-Maurice-de-Rémens in Le Mans. Saint-Exupéry spent a happy childhood surrounded by his sisters and an extended family of aunts and cousins. His early interest in aviation was fuelled by family vacations taken near the airport at Bugey.

Saint-Exupéry was educated at Jesuit schools in Montgré and Le Mans and between 1915 and 1917 at a Catholic boarding school in Fribourg, Switzerland. He failed an examination to enter naval school and entered the École des Beaux-Arts to study architecture. After a short period of study he left in 1921 to begin military service. A turning point in Saint-Exupéry's life came when he was transferred to Strasbourg and later to Rabat in Morocco, as in both places he was able to take flying lessons. He received his pilot's license in 1922. During an assignment in Paris he had the first of a number of serious crashes.

Saint-Exupéry wanted to pursue a career in the air force, but objections were raised by the family of his fiancée, Louise de Vilmorin. He agreed to take a job that the family arranged for him in a tile manufacturing firm, but he continued to fly in his spare time. De Vilmorin broke the engagement in 1923, whereupon Saint-Exupéry left the tile firm and took a variety of jobs. He had begun to write, and his first published work was a story called "L'Aviateur" ("The Aviator"), which appeared in a magazine called *Le Navire d'Argent* in 1926. Some of Saint-Exupéry's favorite themes are already visible in the story, including the experience of flying and how it contrasts with the society left behind.

In 1926 Saint-Exupéry took a job flying the mail over North Africa for a commercial airline company, Aéropostale. Two years later he became the director of the remote Cap Juby airfield in the Spanish Sahara, where he lived in an isolated wooden shack. He developed a deep love of the desert, which later formed the setting for his novels *The Little Prince* (1943) and *Citadelle* (1948; translated into English as *The Wisdom of the Sands*, 1950). He improved relations between the Spaniards and the Moors in the region and also voluntarily engaged in dangerous rescue missions, accomplishing the rescue of downed pilots, the recovery of a plane, and the exchange of pilots being held for ransom. His courage was recognized in 1929, when he was awarded the French Legion of Honor Award. His experiences at Aéropostale and Cap Juby are reflected in his semiautobiographical novel *Courrier Sud* (1929; translated as *Southern Mail*, 1933).

Saint-Exupéry returned to France in 1928, and the following year he moved to South America to take up a post flying mail through the Andes for the Aeroposta Argentina Company. The occupation provided material for the novel that made his name, *Vol de Nuit* (1931; translated as *Night Flight*, 1932). The novel became an international bestseller, won the Prix Femina (a

French literary prize) in 1931, and was adapted for film two years later (*Night Flight*, 1933).

Saint-Exupéry traveled on leave to France in 1931, bringing with him a widowed Argentinian author and artist named Consuelo Gómez Carrillo, whom he married in Grasse. The marriage was stormy, as Saint-Exupéry was often absent and had affairs. In her memoir of their marriage, discovered in 1999 and published as *The Tale of the Rose*, Consuelo wrote that she was the model for the character of the rose in *The Little Prince*.

While Saint-Exupéry was in France, he heard that he was without a job, as the Aeroposta Argentina Company had collapsed. He took a position piloting hydroplanes in Africa but lost it after nearly drowning in a crash. In 1934, he began working as a journalist, traveling to Moscow and Spain to write reports. In 1935, he crashed his plane in the North African desert while trying to break a speed record in a contest and nearly died from dehydration before being saved by a Bedouin. The experience is reflected in *Le Petit Prince* (*The Little Prince*) and in his collection of anecdotes, meditations, and memoirs titled *Terre des Hommes* (1939; translated as *Wind, Sand and Stars*, 1939). Saint-Exupéry wrote *Terre des Hommes* while convalescing from severe injuries resulting from his crashing his plane in Guatemala. It was awarded the Grand Prix du Roman of the Académie Française and the National Book Award in the United States 1939.

World War II broke out in 1939. Saint-Exupéry enlisted for military service and took part in many dangerous flight missions. After France signed an armistice with Germany in 1940, he traveled to the United States, where Consuelo joined him. For the next two years the couple made their home between New York City, Long Island, and Quebec City, Canada. During this period of exile Saint-Exupéry wrote *Pilote de Guerre* (1942; translated as *Flight to Arras*, 1942), based on a reconnaissance mission he had flown over German territory in 1940 for which he received the Croix de Guerre. Other works written at this time were *Lettre à un Otage* (1943; translated as *Letter to a Hostage*, 1950), and *Le Petit Prince* (*The Little Prince*). Saint-Exupéry also worked on the manuscript for *Citadelle* (*The Wisdom of the Sands*). All these works convey his concern for the spiritual decay that he felt had overtaken Europe and the moral values that he believed were needed for its recovery.

In 1943 Saint-Exupéry sailed for North Africa to rejoin his old flying squadron, stationed at Laghouat, Algeria. At 43, he was told that he was too old for such duties, and he was frequently in pain as a result of his many injuries. He nevertheless insisted on flying high-risk reconnaissance missions from bases in Algeria and Sardinia. He set out from a base on Corsica on his final mission on July 29, 1944. He was reported missing two days later and is believed to have been shot down over Nazi-occupied southern France by a German fighter plane.

In 2004, a French team of underwater researchers found the remains of Saint-Exupéry's plane on the seabed off the coast of Marseille, France. No bullet holes were found, but this may be because the bullet-damaged parts of the plane are still missing.

PLOT SUMMARY

Chapters One–Three

The Little Prince opens with the narrator recalling a time when he was six years old. He draws a picture, called drawing No. 1. When he shows it to adults, they believe it to represent a hat, whereas the narrator means it to represent a boa constrictor digesting an elephant. He does another drawing, this time clearly showing the elephant inside the boa, but the adults are unimpressed. Discouraged, when he grows up, he learns to fly airplanes. He flies all over the world and meets many adults, but his opinion of them as people of poor understanding does not improve.

The narrator recalls a time six years ago, when his plane's engine failed and he crashed in the Sahara desert. The action jumps back six years. The narrator knows that he must repair the engine quickly, as he only has enough water for a week. On his first night in the desert, he is awakened by a voice asking him to draw a sheep. He is astonished to see a boy standing in front of him. He does not know how to draw a sheep, so repeats drawing No. 1. The boy knows what it is, but he rejects it because elephants and boas are unsuitable for the land where he comes from, where everything is small. The boy rejects the narrator's first three drawings of sheep because the sheep is too sick, has horns, or is old. Impatient to get on with his engine repair, the narrator draws a box with air holes in the side and tells the boy that the sheep is inside. The boy is

MEDIA ADAPTATIONS

- *The Little Prince* was adapted as a 1974 musical film of the same title with lyrics by Alan Jay Lerner and music by Frederick Loewe. The film, which was directed by Stanley Donen and starred Richard Kiley and Steven Warner, was distributed by Paramount Pictures. It was released on DVD in 2004.

- *The Adventures of The Little Prince—The Complete Animated Series* is a collection on DVD of a 1982 children's television cartoon series loosely based on Saint-Exupéry's novel. It stars the voices of Hal Smith and Julie McWhirter and was released in 2005 by Koch Vision.

- *The Little Prince* was adapted as an opera of the same title by the composer Rachel Portman, with a libretto by Nicholas Wright. A DVD of a staged version of the opera, directed by Francesca Zambello and produced by the BBC as part of its Concert Opera series, was released by Sony in 2005. The production starts Teddy Tahu Rhodes and Joseph McManners.

delighted. The narrator identifies the boy as the little prince of the novel's title.

The prince is amused to hear that, like him, the narrator dropped from the sky. The narrator discovers that the prince comes from another planet. The narrator offers to provide a rope and post to tie up the sheep, but the prince says that this is unnecessary, as his planet is so small that the sheep would have nowhere to go.

Chapters Four–Six
The prince's planet is an asteroid called B-612. The asteroid was identified by a Turkish astronomer, who announced his discovery at an international conference. But because the astronomer was dressed in Turkish attire, no one believed him. Years later, the astronomer repeated his discovery, this time dressed in a Western suit, and was believed.

The narrator says that he has given the name of the prince's planet only because it will make adults believe that the little prince existed. If he were to tell them the important things about the prince, such as that he laughed and wanted a drawing of a sheep, they would dismiss the story.

The narrative jumps forward in time to six years after the narrator and the prince have parted company. The narrator grieves the loss of his friend; he is writing this story so as not to forget him. He thinks he may make mistakes, as he is getting old and, unlike the prince, cannot see sheep through boxes.

The narrative jumps back to a time when the narrator and the prince are discussing the prince's planet. The prince is pleased that sheep eat shrubs, as his planet's soil is infested with the seeds of baobab trees. Each morning, the prince pulls out the shoots when they are still small, as otherwise they would take over the planet. The prince points out that some jobs are so important that they must not be put off.

The prince enjoys watching sunsets, especially when he is sad. His own planet is so small that he only needs to shift his chair a few inches to see a succession of sunsets.

Chapters Seven–Nine
The prince wants to know whether sheep eat flowers with thorns. The narrator replies that thorns are no defense against being eaten by sheep. He adds that flowers grow thorns out of spite but then admits that he said this only because he is preoccupied with repairing his engine: "I am busy with serious matters." The prince angrily accuses the narrator of being confused. He says that the question of whether sheep eat flowers is vital because on his planet is a flower that is unique, yet it may be destroyed by a sheep in one bite. He says that if someone loves a flower that lives on one star among millions, that is enough to make him happy when he looks at the stars. But if the sheep eats the flower, it is as if "all the stars went dark!" The prince is overcome with tears. The narrator comforts him with a promise to draw a muzzle for his sheep and a fence for his flower.

The prince tells the story of the rose that lives on his planet. As soon as she came into bloom the prince was struck by her beauty, though she was demanding and vain. He looked after her every need, watering her and shielding her from drafts. One day, he caught her telling a trivial lie and began to doubt her. However, the prince now feels that he was foolish to have taken her words seriously. He should have simply admired her and enjoyed her fragrance. He should have recognized the affection behind her tricks.

The narrator speculates that the prince escaped from his planet with the help of migrating birds.

At the beginning of chapter nine, the narrative point of view shifts to that of the prince. On the morning of his departure, the prince had cleaned out his volcanoes and torn out the baobab shoots. He believes he will not return. As he sadly says goodbye to the flower, she asks him to forgive her for having been silly. She tells him that she loves him, but that as he has decided to leave, he must do so immediately.

Chapters Ten–Twelve

The prince visits several different asteroids. The first is inhabited only by a king who is full of his own importance, in spite of the fact that he has no subjects to rule. He cannot accept that anything should happen unless it is as a result of his orders. The prince wants to leave, so he suggests that the king order him to do so. The prince reflects that grown-ups are odd.

The second planet that the prince visits is inhabited by a conceited man who cares only about being admired. However, as there is no one else on the planet, he never receives any admiration. To humor the man, the prince voices admiration, while thinking, again, that grown-ups are odd.

The third planet that the prince visits is inhabited by a drunkard. The man tells the prince that he drinks to forget that he is ashamed of drinking. The prince feels sad, and concludes once more that grown-ups are odd.

Chapters Thirteen–Fifteen

The fourth planet is inhabited by a businessman who, like the narrator when he meets the prince, is convinced that he is occupied with serious matters. He spends all his time counting the stars, which he thinks he owns. When the prince points out that the businessman cannot pick the stars as one can pick a flower, the businessman says he can put them in the bank. This means that he writes down the number of stars that he owns on a piece of paper and locks it in a drawer.

The prince feels that this is pointless. He himself owns a flower that he waters and volcanoes that he cleans out, so he is of use to the flower and the volcanoes. But the businessman's activities are of no use to the stars. The prince reflects that grown-ups are odd.

On the fifth planet lives a lamplighter whose sole occupation is to light a lamp at dusk and put it out at dawn. He is following orders to do this. Once, it was a reasonable job because the planet's rotation was slow enough to enable him to sleep for the hours between tasks. But now the planet's movement has sped up to one rotation per minute, yet the orders have not changed, so he gets no rest. The prince admires the lamplighter's faithfulness to orders. He reflects that of all the people he has met on his travels, he alone does not appear ridiculous, because he is not concerned only with himself.

The sixth planet is inhabited by a geographer who records in a book the location of the natural features of a land. He knows nothing at all about his own planet, which, the prince has noticed, is rich in natural features. The geographer feels that he is too important to leave his office and do any exploring. Instead, he relies on explorers to come and report their findings.

The prince tells the geographer that the most beautiful thing on his own planet is a flower, but the geographer discounts this as geographies take no account of ephemeral (temporary) things like flowers. The prince is shocked to realize that even though his flower is ephemeral, he has left her alone.

The geographer advises the prince to visit Earth.

Chapters Sixteen–Eighteen

At the beginning of chapter sixteen, the narrative point of view shifts back to the narrator as he gives some facts and figures (presumably for the benefit of those adults who like figures) about the numbers of lamplighters, drunkards, and so forth who live on the seventh planet that the prince visits, Earth.

The narrator says that even though people convince themselves that they take up a lot of space on Earth, if one were to collect them together, the space that they occupied would be tiny.

The narrative point of view shifts to the prince as he arrives on Earth. He lands in the desert. The first creature that he encounters is a snake. The snake says that he is so powerful that he can send a person back to the earth from whence they came simply with a touch. The snake is referring to his power to kill people with his venomous bite. He tells the prince that if he becomes homesick for his planet, he (the snake) can send him back there. The prince knows that the snake is offering to kill him and asks why he speaks in riddles. The snake replies that he also solves them.

The prince asks a flower where he can find people. She says that some passed several years ago. As they have no roots, the wind blows them around.

Chapters Nineteen–Twenty-one

The prince climbs a mountain and calls out a greeting, but hears only his echo in response. Feeling lonely, he fondly remembers that on his own planet, the flower was always the first to speak.

He walks through the desert and finds a garden of roses. He feels disappointed that his rose, contrary to her claim, is not unique.

Chapter twenty-one is the most important chapter in the novel. The prince meets a fox and invites him to play. The fox explains that he cannot, as he is not tame. To tame someone, the fox explains, means to establish ties. If the prince tames the fox, they will need one another and be unique to one another. The prince realizes that his flower has tamed him. The fox says that his life is monotonous, as it consists of hunting chickens and being hunted by men. All chickens are alike and all men are alike, but if the prince tames the fox, they will become unique to one another. The world will have meaning, because everything that reminds each of the other will be a source of joy. Men have no friends, says the fox, because they do not invest the necessary time. They prefer to buy ready-made things at stores.

The fox teaches the prince how to tame him. The prince must approach him gradually and without words, as "words are a source of misunderstandings." Each day the prince must sit a little closer to him, and he must come at the same time each day so that the fox begins to look forward to his visits and can prepare his heart. The fox says this regularity makes their meeting a rite, which he defines as something that makes one day different from all the other days.

The prince tames the fox, but he feels tearful when the time comes to depart. The fox says that this is the price of taming (establishing ties). The fox is glad that the prince tamed him, because

each time he sees a golden wheat field he will think of the prince, who has golden hair. He tells the prince to go and look again at the garden of roses. The prince does so and realizes that his rose is unique because he has tamed her by looking after her.

Before the prince leaves, the fox tells him, "It is only with one's heart that one can see clearly. What is essential is invisible to the eye." He adds that men have forgotten this truth: "For what you have tamed, you become responsible forever." The prince knows that he is responsible for his rose.

Chapters Twenty-two–Twenty-four

The prince meets a railway signalman who organizes the transport of thousands of travelers on trains. He observes that while the people travel this way and that, they are never satisfied with where they are. The prince reflects that only children know what they are looking for.

The prince meets a merchant who sells pills that take away people's thirst. Not having to drink saves them fifty-three minutes a week. The prince comments that if he had that amount of spare time, he would use it to drink fresh water from a spring.

The narrative point of view shifts to the narrator. He has not been able to repair his plane and has run out of water. The prince suggests that they look for a well. The narrator thinks there is no chance of finding one, but sets out with the prince. As they walk, the prince reflects that the stars are beautiful because of a flower that one cannot see, and that the desert is beautiful because of a hidden well. The prince falls asleep and the narrator carries him, musing that the prince's physical body is only a shell, and that what is important is invisible. He is moved by the thought of the prince's loyalty to a flower, and he feels that the image of the rose shines through his whole being. At daybreak, the narrator finds a well.

Chapters Twenty-five–Twenty-seven

The prince and the narrator drink water from the well. It tastes sweet and the narrator feels that it nourishes the heart. The prince says that men can grow thousands of roses yet not find what they are looking for. The narrator adds that they could find it in a single rose or a little water.

The prince reminds the narrator of his promise to provide a muzzle for the sheep. The narrator realizes sadly that the prince is planning to leave. The prince asks the narrator to go back to his plane and work on his engine, and to return tomorrow evening to meet him at the well. The narrator reflects that being tamed carries the risk of grief at the loss of the loved one.

By the following evening, the narrator has fixed his engine. He returns to the well to meet the prince and overhears him asking the snake whether his poison is so effective that he will not suffer for long. The narrator reaches for his gun, but the snake slips away. The narrator takes the prince in his arms. The prince says that he is going home, and that the narrator can go home, too. He comforts the narrator by telling him that from now on, whenever the narrator looks at the stars, he will love them all because one of them will be the prince's. The prince tells the narrator not to return tonight, as it will seem as if the prince is suffering and dying, but this will not be true. The narrator ignores this request and goes to meet the prince. The prince says that where he is going, he cannot take his body, as it is too heavy. It will look like an abandoned shell and is nothing to be upset about. The prince weeps as he explains that he is responsible for his flower. The snake bites him and he dies.

The action jumps forward six years to the time when the narrator is writing his story. He has partly recovered from his sorrow, but knows the prince returned to his planet because his body vanished by morning. The narrator loves to listen to the stars at night, as they sound to him like tinkling bells, which in turn are reminiscent of the prince's laughter. He worries that the prince will not be able to fasten the muzzle onto his sheep, as he forgot to draw the strap. He wonders if the sheep has eaten the flower.

In an epilogue, the narrator reflects that his drawing of the place where the prince appeared on Earth and disappeared is the most beautiful but the saddest landscape. He asks that if the reader ever travels through this landscape and meets a child with golden hair, he should write to the narrator to tell him that the prince has returned.

CHARACTERS

The Businessman

The businessman believes that he is a "serious" man. He spends all his time counting the stars, which he believes he owns. He writes down the figures and locks them in a drawer, an act that he thinks of as putting them in the bank. This, he believes, makes him a rich man.

The allegorical purpose of this character is to show the emptiness of the accumulation of wealth. It is shown as illusory, in that no one can truly own the stars. It is also shown as futile and selfish, in that money kept in the bank is merely figures on a piece of paper that do no good to anyone. The prince's idea of ownership, watering his flower and cleaning his volcanoes, is what is often called stewardship: taking care of the things and beings within one's sphere of responsibility, for the sake of the greater or common good.

The Conceited Man

The conceited man cares only about being admired. As there is no one else on his planet to admire him, this quality is made to look absurd. The allegorical message of this character is that pride and conceit are futile and foolish.

The Drunkard

The drunkard drinks in order to forget how ashamed he is of drinking; he is trapped in a vicious cycle of addiction. In his portrayal of the drunkard, Saint-Exupéry identifies an important truth about alcoholism and addiction in general.

The Fox

The fox is a wise character who teaches the prince about the importance of establishing ties of love and responsibility with another being, a process that he calls taming. He does this by inviting the prince to tame him. Once the prince has tamed the fox, they become unique to one another and lend meaning to the rest of the world, as different aspects of it remind each of the other. Significantly, the fox appears just as the prince is lamenting the fact that his rose is not unique as there are thousands of others like her. Through his relationship with the fox, the prince learns that his rose is unique to him because he has tamed her. The fox also points out the importance of ritual, which makes one day different from another and thus makes it special. He makes the prince observe a ritual (restricting their encounters to a set time each day) during the taming process.

It is worth noting that Saint-Exupéry makes this wise teacher of the prince a wild animal rather than a human being. This reinforces his message that humans have forgotten the most important things in life.

The Geographer

The geographer's allegorical role is to show the limitations of book learning. Shut up in his office, he is ignorant of the world's beauties because he is only interested in official reports from explorers of natural features that fit his criteria. He is not interested in the most beautiful aspect of the prince's planet, the flower, because it is ephemeral. The geographer is another example of how adults can ignore what is essential and restrict themselves to external matters that bring no joy or meaning to life.

The King

The king's role in the allegory is to show the absurdity of worldly pride, grandeur, and power. He thinks of himself as an absolute monarch, but this notion is exposed as absurd because he has no subjects to rule. He maintains his delusion of authority by ordering people to do what they would already do of their own accord. Another ruse he employs to maintain his sense of power is to ensure that he gives only reasonable orders that are within a person's capability to carry out, though he claims that his motive is kindness.

The allegorical message conveyed by the king may be that although people who find themselves in positions of authority may convince themselves that they are important and powerful, in reality they have little control over anything. Life would go on perfectly well without them.

The Lamplighter

The lamplighter is the only character the prince meets on his travels who he does not think is ridiculous, because he is not only concerned with himself. His lighting and putting out his lamp every minute shows his devotion to following orders correctly.

The allegorical purpose of this character may be to satirize bureaucracy, which can be so inflexible that it does not respond to changing circumstances. A rule that was once appropriate (when the planet's rotation was slower) is now inappropriate (because the planet's rotation has speeded up) and creates suffering for the man who is bound by the rule. The lamplighter himself is also a target of satire, as he faithfully but foolishly continues to follow an outdated rule.

The Little Prince

The prince is an enigmatic visitor to Earth from another planet, the asteroid B-612. While the narrator initially treats him rather dismissively as he is busy trying to repair his plane, he soon learns that the prince has a great deal to teach him and is, in fact, the wiser of the two about what is important in life—that is, matters of the heart. His purity of perception is shown by his ability to recognize what the narrator's drawing No. 1 represents. Innocent, joyful, and inquisitive, yet otherworldly, the prince can be seen as an idealized embodiment of childhood.

The prince is not, however, all-knowing, as is evidenced by his constant questioning of the narrator. He has to learn a lesson about his true feelings for the rose on his planet. While he was with her, he felt irritated, frustrated, and doubtful about her because he had caught her lying to him. Once he has left, he realizes that he should have appreciated her deeds and not focused on her words; he should have paid attention to her essence, rather than her superficial behavior. Thus the prince, like the narrator, has to learn the fox's lesson to the effect that "It is only with one's heart that one can see clearly. What is essential is invisible to the eye." The prince passes on what he has learned about love and life's priorities to the narrator. As a result of the fox's teaching, the prince recognizes that he has a lifelong responsibility to his rose and returns home to his planet, albeit through death.

The Merchant

The merchant sells pills intended to quench thirst, eliminating the need to drink. This saves a person fifty-three minutes per week. The prince comments that if he had that amount of spare time per week, he would choose to spend it drinking water from a spring. The allegorical purpose of the merchant is to satirize time-saving gadgets and technological quick fixes that cost money, add nothing of value to life, and in fact make it poorer.

The Narrator

The narrator is an aviator whose life is changed forever by his encounter with the prince six years before he writes the story. Because he makes the same mistakes as much of humanity, he is easier to relate to than the prince and serves as a kind of everyman in the story. He starts out as an imaginative and artistic child, but soon learns to curb his nature when he finds that adults do not understand his drawings. While his chosen profession of pilot may at first glance seem liberating, his life seems empty and lonely until he meets the prince. He has become trapped in the adult delusion of being "busy with serious matters," while he has lost touch with the profound values and matters of the heart represented by the prince. Just as when he was a child, his own imaginative nature was not understood by adults, now that he is an adult, he is slow to grasp the truths presented to him by the child prince. Whereas the prince learns his lessons instantly and without resistance, the narrator proves less open-hearted, driving the prince to tears of anger on one occasion. Eventually, the narrator learns from the prince that the most important thing in life is the bond of love and responsibility that binds people, creatures, and other beings together. The narrator's major bond of love is with the prince, whereas the prince's major bond is with his flower.

It is possible to interpret the narrator and the prince as two aspects of the narrator: the innocent and creative child on whom he turned his back and the adult who has entered the cage of materialistic and practical adult life.

The Railway Signalman

The railway signalman is responsible for organizing travelers on trains. He says that they are never happy with where they are but travel aimlessly. In the context of the allegory, the railway signalman draws attention to the dissatisfaction and lack of fulfillment that plagues humankind. The outward manifestation may be an internal spiritual restlessness or constant travel on the physical level.

The Rose

The rose is a traditional symbol of femininity and love in literature, and Saint-Exupéry's rose in *The Little Prince* fits firmly into this convention. The rose is vain, naïve, and demanding, expecting the prince to cater to her every whim. She displays inner strength when she realizes that the prince wants to leave, asking his forgiveness and telling him to go. Only when the prince has left does he realize that underneath her foolish ways is genuine love for him.

Although the rose seldom appears in the novel, her presence is felt throughout. The prince's annoyance at her follies prompts him to leave his planet, and she is also the reason he returns. As a result of the fox's teachings, the prince realizes that he loves the rose because of the time he has invested in caring for her and that he has a lifelong responsibility to her.

Many critics and biographers of Saint-Exupéry see the prince's relationship with his rose as based on the author's stormy relationship with his wife Consuelo. They are encouraged in this interpretation by Consuelo de Saint-Exupéry's memoir, *The Tale of the Rose* (2003), in which she writes that she was the model for the character of the rose.

The Snake

The snake is the most aware character in the novel. He needs nothing and nobody and is confident of his own role. He immediately recognizes the prince's innocence and correctly predicts that he will become homesick for his planet and want to return there.

In the context of the allegory, the snake represents death (recalling the Biblical symbol of the serpent in the Garden of Eden who brings death to Adam and Eve). He knows that he has the ultimate power over life and offers to kill the prince, enabling him to return to the earth from which he came. This seems to be the only way that the prince can return to his planet. The snake speaks in riddles, but says that he can also answer them all. This refers to the finality of death, which could be said to solve all problems by ending life.

THEMES

Freedom, Love, and Responsibility

The French author André Gide, in his Preface to Saint-Exupéry's novel *Vol de Nuit* (*Night Flight*), notes that Saint-Exupéry's writings express the "paradoxical truth" that an individual's happiness "lies not in freedom but in the acceptance of a duty." Although superficially, the narrator may appear to be free when he flies around the world unburdened by ties and responsibilities, it becomes clear when he meets the prince that he is actually restricted by his corrupted adult awareness. He is unable to hear the prince's serious question about whether the sheep will eat the

TOPICS FOR FURTHER STUDY

- Research the genre of allegory and read at least one allegorical work by another author. Compare and contrast that author's use of allegory with that of Saint-Exupéry in *The Little Prince*. Consider themes, symbolism, and the didactic (instructional) aspects of the works, along with any other aspects you think are relevant. Give an oral presentation on your findings.

- Write your own allegorical poem, story, or play and read or perform it to the class. End by reading aloud a brief paragraph analyzing the values or qualities you have highlighted in your work and say why they are important.

- Look at drawing No. 1 and drawing No. 2 in chapter one of *The Little Prince*. How do these drawings relate to the themes of the novel? Write an essay on your findings.

- The little prince rejects the narrator's first three drawings of a sheep, just as the adults rejected his drawing No. 1. What is the difference between these two rejections and what does it tell the reader? Lead a class discussion on the topic, first presenting your ideas.

- Consider the little prince's visit to the king (chapter ten), the conceited man (chapter eleven), and the businessman (chapter thirteen). What is the moral lesson of each of these chapters? How do these lessons relate to the rest of the novel? Write an essay on your findings.

- Read an allegorical work written before 1700 and another written in the twentieth or twenty-first century. Research the social, political, and cultural context of each work. Write an essay in which you (a) compare and contrast the values or lessons that each work attempts to inculcate in the reader, and (b) analyze the relevance of those values to the society of the time.

flower he loves because, as he says, "I am busy with serious matters," attempting to mend his plane. The prince accuses him of "confusing everything...mixing everything up." In other words, the prince says that the narrator has got his priorities wrong. The narrator forgets his true duty to another human being in pursuit of a perceived duty to practical matters. A matter of the heart that affects the prince deeply is swept aside, but it does not go away. There are emotional consequences to the narrator's warped priorities: the prince is very upset and the narrator has to comfort him.

As the narrator's affection for the prince grows, he finds that there is a price to pay for allowing love into his heart: he is grief-stricken when he has to part from his friend. This is foreshadowed by the prince's story of his meeting with the fox. The fox warns of the perils of taming, or establishing ties, with another being: "If you tame me, we shall need one another." When it comes time for the prince to leave, the fox says, "Oh!...I shall cry."

The process of taming brings a heavy responsibility. The fox tells the prince: "For what you have tamed, you become responsible forever." As the fox and the prince become responsible to each other forever (in that the happiness of each is dependent on the other), so the prince learns that he is responsible to his rose forever, and the narrator learns that he is responsible to the prince forever.

On the positive side, the fox tells the prince that their dependence on one another will lend meaning to their lives. They will look forward to seeing one another, and everything they see that reminds each of the other will evoke joy in their hearts. Thus, although the fox is wild and as free from ties as the narrator at the beginning of the novel, he longs to be tamed by the prince: "I beg of you...tame me!" Just as the fox will forever be reminded of the prince when he sees a field of golden corn because it is like the prince's golden hair, so the narrator will forever be reminded of the prince when he sees a sky filled with stars, because on one of the stars lives the prince. The moral lesson that can be extracted from the concept of taming is that the particular (the object of love, which is unique in the world) lends meaning to the general (the rest of the world). The loved one becomes a means of connecting the individual to the whole of creation. Establishing ties of love risks making the heart vulnerable to

*Le Petit Prince poster in Korcula, Croatia (© Ros
Drinkwater / Alamy)*

really is, as he has the ability to see beyond external forms to the essence within. He rejects the drawing for reasons that are so significant in his world that they are matters of life-and-death. A boa constrictor would be too dangerous, and an elephant too large to live on his planet. Thus his decision to reject the drawing is reasonable and sensible, whereas the adults' reaction is illogical and unwise.

Time and again in the novel, the typical adult perception is shown to be lacking, whereas the child's perception is shown to be clear. When the narrator impatiently tells the prince that flowers have thorns out of spite, because he is too preoccupied to pay attention properly to the subject of flowers and sheep, the prince accuses him of talking "just like grown-ups." He defines what he means: "You are confusing everything . . . mixing everything up." He tells the story of the man who has "never loved anybody" but "spent all his time adding up figures," all the while convincing himself that he is "busy with serious matters." Such inverted priorities, the prince points out, make a person less than human: "He is not a man, he is a mushroom."

pain and grief, but without such ties, life is bleak and bereft of meaning.

The Innocence of Childhood

From the novel's beginning, a line is drawn between the perception of adults and the perception of children. Adults, or "grown-ups," are portrayed as having a clouded perception that misses the essential aspects of things and warped priorities that convince them that superficial things are important while profound and significant things are irrelevant. This is shown in the adults' failure to see what the narrator's drawing No. 1 represents. Because the elephant is hidden inside the boa constrictor, the adults cannot see it. They see only the outside, superficial aspect of the form, and so mistake it for a hat and dismiss the drawing as insignificant.

The prince, on the other hand, represents an idealized embodiment of childhood. He instantly recognizes drawing No. 1 for what it

STYLE

Allegory

The Little Prince is an allegory. Allegory is a narrative technique in which characters represent things or abstract ideas and are used to convey a message or teach a lesson. Allegory is often used to teach moral, ethical, or religious lessons but is sometimes used for satiric or political purposes. Examples of allegorical works include the *Roman de la Rose* (a French poem about love that was originated by Guillaume de Lorris around 1230 and added to by Jean de Meun around 1275), Dante's *Divine Comedy* (written between 1306 and 1321 and first published in 1472) and John Bunyan's *The Pilgrim's Progress* (a Christian allegory published in 1678). The *Roman de la Rose* is linked to *The Little Prince* by the shared symbol of the rose. In the French poem, Rose is both the name of the beloved lady and a symbol of femininity. Similarly, in *The Little Prince*, the rose may be seen both as a character and as a symbol of feminine and romantic love.

In a typical feature of allegory, the characters that the prince meets on his travels each represent a particular human failing. The author's purpose in introducing them is to teach the reader to avoid those failings and to embrace a better way of being, often exemplified by the prince. For example, the character of the businessman shows the futility of accumulating wealth, in that his practice of counting the stars and keeping the records locked in a drawer is obviously a foolish and delusory activity. The function of literature to teach or instruct the reader (usually in moral or spiritual lessons) is called didacticism. The word has its root in the ancient Greek word meaning apt at teaching, *didaktikos*.

The most important teachings of the allegory of *The Little Prince* are voiced by the fox. He teaches the prince the importance of forming bonds of love and responsibility with others and shows him that his main bond of love and responsibility is with his rose, because he has taken care of her.

Symbolism

Fundamental to the allegory, symbolism is a literary device in which concrete objects represent ideas or concepts. Bonner Mitchell, in a 1960 essay for the *French Review* titled "*Le Petit Prince* and *Citadelle*: Two Experiments in the Didactic Style," notes that "virtually everything the hero does, e.g. his drinking from a well in the desert, is susceptible of symbolic interpretation; indeed, it obviously requires such interpretation" as otherwise it would have little significance in itself. Mitchell writes that the novel's events are far from realistic and its symbols are correspondingly "obscure in meaning," allowing for individual interpretation.

Prominent symbols in the novel include the well, the rose, the snake, and the prince himself. The episode (in chapter twenty-five) in which the narrator and the prince drink from the well after a long walk through the desert clearly has a symbolic meaning beyond its literal meaning. This is shown in the narrator's comment that the water was "good for the heart, like a gift," and his associated recollections of childhood Christmases. The water is portrayed as "something entirely different from ordinary nourishment." It is not merely sustenance for the narrator's physical body but is also nourishment for his emotional and spiritual being. The prince adds to the symbolic significance of the episode by commenting that people may grow thousands of roses yet not find that which they are seeking:

"And yet, what they are looking for could be found in a single rose or in a little water." He concludes, "But the eyes are blind. One must look with the heart." Thus, drinking from the well that was hidden in the desert becomes symbolic of seeing the invisible spiritual essence of things behind their superficial appearance. The importance of such true vision is one of the novel's central messages.

The rose can be seen as symbolic of love and the feminine. In his relationship with the rose, the prince has to learn to look beyond superficial appearances—her vain and irritating behaviors—to the love and ties of responsibility that, he finally recognizes, underlie them.

The snake is symbolic of death; it has undertones of the Biblical serpent that tempts Adam and Eve and brings death into the Garden of Eden.

The prince has symbolic undertones of Christ that are apparent in his purity and innocence and in the transcendental nature of his death. As with Christ, the prince's appearance on Earth is miraculous, and his departure is equally miraculous. No body is found after his death: it is as if it has been resurrected and accompanied his soul back to his planet.

HISTORICAL CONTEXT

World War II

Saint-Exupéry wrote *The Little Prince* while living in exile in the United States during World War II. However, attempts to draw parallels between the novel and historical events, such as the character of the snake and the evil of the Holocaust, are unconvincing. What can be said is that Saint-Exupéry's anguish over his exile from his homeland and his feelings about the events taking place appear to have influenced the novel's values. Catharine Savage Brosman, in her essay "Antoine de Saint-Exupéry" for the *Dictionary of Literary Biography*, notes that *The Little Prince* and the other works that the author wrote in exile all "reveal his concern for moral values that, he was persuaded, were essential for the rebuilding of Europe." The moral values exemplified in *The Little Prince* include people's responsibility to their fellows, a sense of the kinship of all humans, and the importance of moral and spiritual values over materialistic interests.

COMPARE & CONTRAST

- **1940s:** Saint-Exupéry's *The Little Prince* is written as an allegory of the traditional kind, expressing moral and spiritual certainties, at a time when allegory is out of favor.

  Today: Allegory, though a popular genre once more, often operates within the demands of realism and frequently expresses moral relativism (a school of thought that holds that morals do not reflect universal truths) or subverts institutions and ideologies.

- **1940s:** After World War II ends in 1945, shortages of basic supplies and consumer goods affect Europe, which may help to prompt an upsurge in materialism. The atrocities of the war lead artists, writers, and philosophers to question long-held beliefs about humanity, God, morality, and progress.

  Today: While materialism dominates Western culture, its future is in doubt due to financial and environmental crises. Some forms of religion and spirituality are undergoing a revival.

- **1940s:** The events of World War II lead to the formation of the United Nations in 1945 to facilitate progress toward world peace and social and economic progress.

  Today: The War on Terror, religious and ideological conflicts, and uncertainty about the sustainability of the economic system undermine the ideals of social unity and progress.

The Vichy Regime

The Vichy regime is the term used to describe the government of France during World War II between July 1940 and 1944. The government was formed by Marshal Philippe Pétain following the military defeat of France by Nazi Germany. Pétain and his government collaborated with the Nazis and even organized raids to capture Jews and other peoples designated by the Nazis to be sent to labor or death camps. The Vichy regime became a source of shame to many French nationals, who saw it as a betrayal of the French people, Jews, and other nations fighting the Nazis.

Saint-Exupéry's exile to the United States occurred later in the same year in which the Vichy regime was established. In 1942, he made a radio broadcast in which, according to Catharine Savage Brosman in her essay "Antoine de Saint-Exupéry" for the *Dictionary of Literary Biography*, he appealed to French nationals in exile "to go beyond the defeat and the Vichy regime and prepare the future together." The message of *The Little Prince* centers around just such bonds of responsibility and brotherhood.

The Allegory in the Twentieth and Twenty-first Centuries

At the time when Saint-Exupéry wrote *The Little Prince*, the literary genre of allegory was out of fashion. This may be because the didacticism (instructive quality) of allegory fell in popularity along with the acceptance of external and monolithic sources of authority such as the church and the state.

Ironically, World War II, the event that convinced Saint-Exupéry that a strong morality and value system was more needed than ever, played a large role in creating cynicism and loss of faith in the old sources of authority. Some states and churches were seen as creating and collaborating with Nazism and its attendant horrors such as the Holocaust.

With the decline in respect for established authorities came a rejection of organized religion and a corresponding rise in individualism, materialism, consumerism, and moral relativism. Moral relativism is a philosophical stance to the effect that moral or ethical values are not objective and universal truths but are instead dependent on changing factors such as social, cultural, or personal circumstances. In practice, this stance manifests as the assumption that an action that is morally right for one person in one situation and at one time may not be morally right for another person in another situation at a different time.

The rise of moral relativism had its counterpart in the field of literature. Allegories written after World War II take more account of the requirements of realism than traditional allegories. They are more likely to have well-developed characters who do not simply stand for a particular quality but have many facets. They are less likely to be dogmatic about what is right and wrong, with characters and situations that reflect moral complexities. In the latter half of the twentieth century, allegories that point to universal truths or uphold political or ideological institutions fell out of favor and were superseded by allegories that undermine these conventional authorities.

Twentieth-century allegorical works that fit the iconoclastic model include political allegories such as George Orwell's novel *Animal Farm* (1945), Hugh Leonard's play *The Au Pair Man* (1968), and J. M. Coetzee's novel *Waiting for the Barbarians* (1980). An allegory on religious and ideological themes is the Egyptian author Najib Mahfuz's novel *Awlad Haratina* (1959), English translations of which were published as *Children of Gebelawi* (1981) and *Children of the Alley* (1996).

Some allegories of this period, such as Paulo Coelho's popular novel *The Alchemist* (first published as *O Alquimista* in 1988 in a Portuguese-language version), do emphasize the importance of spiritual values. But unlike many allegories of the past, which pointed to an externalized set of spiritual or religious values, *The Alchemist* highlights a more modern, subjective, and individualistic type of spirituality that is perhaps best summarized as an injunction to follow one's dream.

In the first decade of the twenty-first century, attitudes appear to have come full circle. The collapse of financial institutions, a growing awareness of corruption in business and politics, and moral outrage at the human cost of military interventions across the globe have prompted intellectuals and politicians to call for a return to a universal system of morals and values.

CRITICAL OVERVIEW

The Little Prince is frequently termed a children's story for adults. This fanciful tale of an aviator meeting a prince from another planet in the desert may appeal to children, but other aspects of the story are more likely to appeal to an adult sensibility. These include the tale's moral and spiritual didacticism and the point of view from which it is written—that of an adult nostalgically looking back at the largely lost innocence and wonder of childhood.

The critic Philip A. Wadsworth, in his 1951 essay "Saint-Exupéry, Artist and Humanist" for *Modern Language Quarterly*, notes this dual aspect of the novel and links it, as many critics have done since, to Saint-Exupéry's own life and character. Saint-Exupéry, Wadsworth writes, "refused to turn into a 'grown-up.'" Inside the adult man was always the child, and the book that "most frankly expresses his personality," in Wadsworth's view, is *The Little Prince*, "with its mixture of gaiety and melancholy, of childish fancy and the wisdom of age."

Bonner Mitchell, in an essay for the *French Review* titled "*Le Petit Prince* and *Citadelle*: Two Experiments in the Didactic Style," places Saint-Exupéry's novel firmly in "an illustrious line of allegorical fairy tales which reached its French apogee in the eighteenth-century *conte philosophique* [philosophical tale]." The novel, writes Mitchell, fits less into a contemporary literary genre than into the literature of the past. Mitchell notes the novel's similarity to the *Divine Comedy*, an allegorical epic poem written by the Italian author Dante between 1306 and 1321 and first published in 1472. Mitchell points out that the novel's main message is not contained in the narrator's own remarks: instead, it "must be sought in the actual events and characters which he describes." The book's didacticism is thus "superficially covered over." Moreover, the hero, the prince, is not consciously instructive, although his remarks do indirectly teach the narrator. Similarly, Mitchell writes, the novel's symbolism is also obscure and open to interpretation.

Nona Balakian, in her 1970 review of a biography of Saint-Exupéry for the *New York Times* titled "Poet of the Air—and Earth," makes a general comment about the author that could apply to *The Little Prince*. Balakian writes that the author "breathed the romance of the air as no one had done before or has since." Nonetheless, she adds, the adventures he most prized were "those that had to do with the earth, with the world of men and their immutable link to each other."

Robert Gibson is one of many critics who explores the many correspondences between the novel and Saint-Exupéry's life and experiences. In his 1995 essay for the *Reference Guide to World Literature*, "Antoine de Saint-Exupéry: Overview," Gibson points out that Saint-Exupéry wrote the book when he was living in exile in the United States, "cut off from both the country and the people he most loved." In line with this period of the author's life, Gibson notes, the novel has been variously interpreted as "a hymn of exile and a lament for lost innocence."

The Little Prince has enjoyed great popularity with the public. Judy Quinn, in an article for *Publishers Weekly*, writes that as of 2000, the book had become available in sixty-two countries and had been translated into ninety-five languages, and it was still selling nearly 200,000 copies per year.

A key to its enduring popularity is suggested by Rachel Lynn Strongheart in an article for the *Reading Teacher* called "The Little Prince: My Ally from Asteroid B-612" (2001). Strongheart writes that of all the books she encountered as a child, "it best embodies and safeguards the magic I felt and believed in as a child." Strongheart sees strong correspondences between the trials of her own life and those of the stranded pilot in the novel. Always concerned with "matters of consequence," she feels trapped in "that self-imposed cage of practicality that ignores the heart and withers creativity." Only the wisdom of the little prince, she writes, "allows a smile or kind word to take precedence over my ever-present and ever-growing list of things to do."

WHAT DO I READ NEXT?

- Antoine de Saint-Exupéry's novel *Vol de Nuit* (1931; translated into English as *Night Flight*, 1932), is widely viewed as a classic of aviation. It tells the story of the men who risked their lives in pioneering the airmail service by flying planes over South America and the managers who gave the orders.

- The French philosopher and author Voltaire's *Candide* (1759) is an allegorical and satirical novel that tells the story of the trials of the young Candide and his mentor Dr. Pangloss. Voltaire's satirical targets include the naïve optimism promoted by the German philosopher Gottfried Wilhelm Leibniz, along with romantic love, science, philosophy, religion, and government.

- Allegory is not only a literary genre; it is also used in the visual arts. Matilde Battistini's *Symbols and Allegories in Art* (2005) is a fascinating book that breaks down various famous works of art into their component parts and explains the allegorical and symbolic meanings of each.

- Louis S. Rehr's *Marauder: Memoir of a B-26 Pilot in Europe in World War II* (2003) is a compelling account of Rehr's war experience from a Midwestern military academy in the United States, to pilot training, to joining a squadron in Europe, to the end of the war as commander of the squadron.

CRITICISM

Claire Robinson

Robinson has a master's degree in English and is a teacher of English literature and a freelance writer and editor. In the following essay, she examines the importance of true and mistaken vision in Antoine de Saint-Exupéry's The Little Prince.

In chapter twenty-one of Antoine de Saint-Exupéry's novel *The Little Prince*, the fox

teaches the prince that "it is only with one's heart that one can see clearly. What is essential is invisible to the eye." This is the central message of the novel. How the different characters see, and what they see, governs whether they grasp the truth about life or remain trapped in delusion. It is no coincidence that the narrator is a pilot, who has the potential of a godlike expanded perspective on creation. Nevertheless, throughout the course of the novel, he has to

> EVEN THE APPARENT HEAVINESS OF THE
> PRINCE'S PHYSICAL BODY HAS BEEN TRANSFORMED
> INTO SOMETHING WEIGHTLESS AND INTANGIBLE BY
> 'WHAT IS ESSENTIAL,' HIS INVISIBLE SPIRIT."

learn to see with different eyes from those that he uses to fly his plane.

As might be expected in a story in which seeing is central, the point of view from which the action of *The Little Prince* is told is also important. The narrative point of view shifts, and with it, the level of awareness. The novel's opening is told from the point of view of the narrator as a child, as remembered from the viewpoint of adulthood. At this point, the narrator still has the unclouded vision of a child, which enables him to pay more attention to the inward essence of things than the outward appearance. Thus he knows that his drawing No. 1 represents an elephant inside a boa, regardless of the fact that to superficially minded adults, it looks like a hat. At this point, adults are seen as an alien species, locked out of the child's world.

The point of view quickly changes to that of the narrator as an adult who has given up trying to make adults understand the truth of things. He is aware that he has had to bring himself down to the level of understanding of adults by learning to talk about things that he thinks are trivial, such as card games and golf. This is an ironic reversal of the assumed norm, whereby children are thought by adults to be preoccupied by trivial and senseless things and to be too foolish to understand significant things. In Saint-Exupéry's view, children are the wise beings who constantly have to indulge adults over their lack of understanding.

However, the narrator, who in childhood had to learn to indulge the foolishness of adults, in adulthood becomes tainted by their restricted view. Now "busy with serious matters," he has grown into, in part, one of the adults who previously earned his contempt. In his conversation with the prince about whether sheep eat flowers, in chapter seven, the narrator fails to see what truly matters. His own view, that sheep always

eat flowers, that the thorns of flowers are no defense against being eaten, and that flowers only grow thorns out of spite, all impatiently delivered while the narrator is "busy with serious matters," leads only to death and despair. As the tearful prince says of the one who loves the flower (himself), "If the sheep eats the flower, it is for him as if, all of a sudden, all the stars went dark! And you think that is not important!" The narrator is shocked by the prince's tears into realizing the truth about what is important in life. He has had to be taught by his child friend. The point is not that the prince knows everything—he himself has to be taught the importance of love and responsibility by the fox—but that crucially, his mind and heart are consistently open to learning. Unlike the narrator, he does not need to be shocked into realizing the truth.

Perhaps because the narrator's restricted adult viewpoint has been exposed as spiritually and emotionally redundant, the narrative point of view suddenly changes. At the beginning of chapter nine, the narrator's first-person narrative disappears until chapter sixteen, when the prince comes to Earth. For the interim, the point of view shifts to that of the prince and the reader sees events through his narrative. The child becomes the teacher of the adult and the novel's readers.

If Saint-Exupéry is eager to challenge the assumption of adult superiority when it comes to grasping the important things in life, he also challenges the assumption of human hegemony over the rest of creation. The prince is taught the truth about love not by a wise adult, but by an animal. If children's vision is less clouded than that of adults, the author seems to suggest, then animals' vision is closer than that of humans to the essence of truth. As if to drive home the notion of the corruption of adult human vision, Saint-Exupéry makes his wise animal a wild animal, that is, one without the influence of humans.

Nevertheless, humans can be redeemed, and the fox knows this. The fox longs to be tamed by a human, but only on his own terms. The fox chooses his tamer, the prince, carefully, insists that he approach him gradually and gently, and makes him observe the "rites" of only coming to visit him on certain days. Although it is superficially the fox who is being tamed, clearly it is the person doing the taming, the prince, who is being most radically educated (and as ever in this didactic novel, the readers along with him). The prince is encouraged to cultivate the respect, care, and consideration for others that is so often lacking in the busy and superficial adult world. The fox teaches the prince that the time and care invested in another being during this process of taming makes that being uniquely important.

The process of taming also makes the tamer forever responsible for the tamed being. These bonds of love and responsibility, once established, make the whole of creation meaningful, transforming the vision of the tamer. Thus the fox will be forever reminded of the prince whenever he sees a golden wheat field because the prince has golden hair, and he will feel the same joy in the presence of that wheat field as he felt in the presence of the prince. What was once just a wheat field becomes a profoundly nourishing experience felt in the heart. Similarly, for the narrator, the stars become forever associated with the laughter of the prince because he knows that one of those stars is the prince's home. The fox, after the prince's departure, cannot physically see the prince's hair, and the narrator cannot see the prince on his star, but they can feel his presence in their hearts. Also, when the narrator is suffering from thirst in the desert, the hidden well that he can not initially see and does not believe in turns out to exist and to give him sustenance on a level beyond the physical.

Even the mostly clear-sighted prince benefits from the fox's teaching that "what is essential is invisible to the eye." After the prince has abandoned his planet and his rose in frustration at the rose's behavior, he learns that he should not have paid attention to the superficial aspects of her behavior, her words and foolish tricks, but that he should have seen the love that lay behind them. Equally, he realizes that the time that he put into caring for her has bound him to her forever with invisible but powerful ties. These ties make her unique among all the thousands of other roses in the universe. Again, the invisible value is elevated above the visible surface. The message is underlined by the prince's conclusion that the garden of many roses, which superficially appears so impressive, is as nothing compared with the one rose that he loves. He tells the roses in the garden, "You are beautiful but you are empty.... One cannot die for you." Thus the love that cannot be seen but that lives in the heart invests the world with value.

This truth is hidden from the sad and deluded characters that the prince meets on his intergalactic travels. Their vision is clouded so that they miss the essence and the truth of life. The businessman who counts the stars and believes that he owns them focuses on external figures. Like the adult readers of the novel who will not believe in the prince unless they are told the number of the asteroid from which he comes, the businessman focuses on the superficial and visible yet empty and meaningless aspects of things. As a result, his life is without joy. Even the lamplighter, whom the prince concedes to be less selfish than the other deluded characters, makes the mistake of looking to external authorities (the outdated orders to light and put out his lamp at dusk and dawn) rather than the truth that he knows in his heart (that circumstances have changed and he should look to his own common sense as a guide).

The most important application of the fox's teaching that what is essential is invisible relates to the nature of death. Death is given unrivaled authority in the novel. It is represented by the one character who does not need to ask questions, as he already knows the answers: the snake. Also, the prince's final action is to die, so the novel's action leads to this point.

But death is revealed to be quite other than it superficially appears. First, it is portrayed as a return to the source. The snake says, "Whomever I touch I send back to the earth from which they came." For the prince, death is assumed to be the only way by which he can return home to his home planet. The prince tells the narrator not to believe what his eyes tell him with regard to his imminent death. He says, "I shall look as if I were dead and it will not be true." He explains that his body is "too heavy" to carry with him on his journey back to his planet and implies that there is another life that transcends the "old abandoned shell" of the physical body and that will continue on without it. However, when the narrator returns the next day to the place where the prince allowed himself to be killed by the snake, his body has vanished: "It wasn't such a heavy body, after all." Even the apparent heaviness of the prince's physical body has been transformed into something weightless and intangible by "what is essential," his invisible spirit.

Musing on the question of whether the sheep ate and destroyed the flower, the narrator's final message to readers is that they can transform reality simply by how they choose to perceive it: "Has the sheep eaten the flower, yes or no? And you will see how everything changes." Even that powerful force, death, can be transformed by an individual's quality of vision.

Source: Claire Robinson, Critical Essay on *The Little Prince*, in *Novels for Students*, Gale, Cengage Learning, 2010.

Rachel Lynn Strongheart

In the following essay, Strongheart discusses the impact of The Little Prince *on her life.*

The Little Prince by Antoine de Saint-Exupery (1943, Harcourt Brace Jovanovich) was not my first children's book. Of all the stories I read or was told, however, it best embodies and safeguards the magic I felt and believed in as a child. Over 20 years later, I still return to my little hero and companion when I lose touch with life's truths and wonders. The story and the ever-evolving meaning I construct from it have superseded the boundaries of a key literacy event or moment to become both a cloak of loving protection and the impetus for my professional endeavors. Although it would be misleading to credit one brief tale with being my sole emotional weathervane, no other story has had such a sustained and sustaining impact.

Oftentimes, I have felt like Saint-Exupery's stranded pilot in the desert, always concerned with "matters of consequence," that self-imposed cage of practicality that ignores the heart and withers creativity. It is only the wisdom of the little prince that allows a smile or kind word to take precedence over my ever-present and ever-growing list of things to do. As an adult and educator, joy and the need for constant growth and inquiry seem so easily obscured by the hunger for a rational and predictable formula for living. Fortunately, the little prince reminds me that the best in life often lies in the lap of the unexpected. He teaches me to see myself as a fellow traveler, perhaps not from the asteroids, but certainly on a mission larger than myself. Years after my first reading, he continues to speak to the part of me that marvels at sunsets, tends roses and vulnerable creatures, digs up baobabs, and can tame a fox. He whispers in my ear that it is always very important to care and be careful.

Like the pilot in this story, whose childhood drawings of an elephant being digested inside a boa constrictor were misconstrued by adults to be lopsided hats and taken to be indications of meager artistic aptitude, I was a child painfully aware of the gulf between school and life outside its confines. Early on, I became convinced that success in school required sacrificing my world of magic and imagination for one mired in facts and figures. Perhaps reading *The Little Prince* added fuel to the fires of my rebellion, pushing me to declare my opposition to fully participating in what felt like an alien process. Or perhaps my nature and upbringing would have necessitated such a stance under any circumstances. It is hard to be sure. What is clear is that those he meets on his journey—the pilot, the king, the conceited man, the tippler, the businessman, the lamplighter, and the geographer—seemed much like many of the adults I knew and a distant cry from the kind of grown-up I hoped to be. Ironically, as an adult, I have struggled to outgrow characteristics from each of these story characters in an attempt to awaken within myself the magical sight of a child and join it with the nurturing and guiding insight of a teacher.

As with all the landmarks and bookmarks in my life, large and small, this story's importance arose from within the realm and contest of my experience. That I cannot remember a single book discovered or read in school gives testimony to the fact that whatever texts we used were largely divorced from anything I considered meaningful. Literacy in my early education was narrowly defined by phonics and basal readers whose characters did not even faintly resemble people I knew or the lives they led. I knew that proficiency in reading and writing was the yardstick with which my intelligence and achievement were measured and the porthole through which I had to pass to enter the selectively enriched world of "gifted" students.

The Little Prince required nothing but curiosity and excitement as I entered into its private world alive with words and pictures. Its themes are like pages in a journal recounting some of my deepest musings and cataloguing my journey from childhood into a world vibrant with meaning and action. All of its characters and images remain with me as I continue to redefine "matters of consequence" in a more peaceful, heartfelt way. They remind me of eternal and difficult to achieve truisms: Love matters most; educating the mind without the heart isn't enough; and literacy must extend into the reaches of worlds real and imagined to be effective and meaningful. In Saint-Exupery's dedication he stated, "All grown-ups were once children—although few remember it . . . ." I believe that remembering is the key to teaching and learning for all of us.

Source: Rachel Lynn Strongheart, "The Little Prince: My Ally from Asteroid B-612," in *Reading Teacher*, Vol. 54, No. 5, February 2001, p. 498.

Helle Bering-Jensen

In the following essay, Bering-Jensen discusses the significance of airplanes in Saint-Exupéry's life and work, including The Little Prince.

If you disregard, for a moment, *Winnie the Pooh*, perhaps the most remarkable introduction in European children's literature goes like this: The pilot Antoine de Saint-Exupery has crashed his plane in the Sahara. "The first night, then, I went to sleep on the sand a thousand miles from any human habitation. I was more isolated than a shipwrecked sailor on a raft in the middle of the ocean. Thus one can imagine my amazement at sunrise when I was awakened by an odd little voice. It said: 'If you please—draw me a sheep.'"

As millions of children worldwide know, that odd little voice belongs to le Petit Prince, the remarkable visitor from Asteroid B612, where he owns three volcanoes and a flower in which he takes inordinate pride. The Little Prince is on a search throughout the universe for the true meaning of life.

As readers of Stacy Schiff's *Saint-Exupery: A Biography* (Knopf, 522 pp) will realize, the creator of the Little Prince was a remarkable fellow too—an impoverished aristocrat, an award-winning novelist and a pioneering aviator, as well as a stunningly disorganized individual of muddled political views and little ambition—but all in all, a man of great charm.

Saint-Exupery was born in Lyons in 1900, one of five children. His family was one of the oldest in France. (He could trace his roots back to the Crusades. His father died of a stroke when Saint-Exupery was 4; his mother, Marie, was forced to rely on the kindness of her in-laws.

Little Tonio, a gregarious and tirelessly enterprising child, soon found himself at odds with his rather stern grandfather. Where his indulgent mother saw him as a dreamer, the rest of the family tended to see him as a "first-rate devil," as an aunt put it. For his part, Saint-Exupery later had the Little Prince remark, "I have lived a great deal among grown-ups. I have seen them close. That has not much improved my opinion."

Almost from the start, airplanes were a part of Saint-Exupery's life. One of his own first inventions was a (nearly) flying bicycle. And in 1909, his mother moved the family to Le Mans, where Wilbur Wright had set up shop and made the place famous with his aeronautical exploits. Saint-Exupery received his own baptism by air at the age of 12, in a plane invented by the Polish brothers Wroblewski. The craft looked more like a bat than anything else but stayed in the air long enough to infect the young passenger with a passion for flying.

Later, as a student in Paris, Saint-Exupery found more passions to occupy him: galleries and the literary scene. At 15, he was writing epic poems that alternately impressed and exasperated his teachers. At 21, he entered the army, which sent him to Morocco for the start of his lifelong love affair with the desert, later celebrated in his memoir. It was in the army that he earned his pilot's license.

Saint-Exupery's marriage to Louise de Vilmorin—slightly handicapped by a hip ailment but an ethereal beauty and a great flirt—broke his heart. Their divorce plunged him into deep despair and set him on a journey throughout France. Among other things, he worked as a truck salesman, selling by his own count somewhere between one and no trucks at all during an entire year.

In 1926, he signed on with the literary magazine *Le Navire d'Argent*, which was a rather happier match, as was his connection with France's most ambitious mail airline, the Compagnie Latecoere in Toulouse. Here he began as a mechanic but soon rose to be a test pilot and a mail carrier, helping to establish routes over northwest Africa, South America and the South Atlantic. These were exploits on which he drew for his first novel, *Southern Mail*, published in 1929. While reviewers were respectful and encouraging of his first effort, they positively gushed over Saint-Exupery's second novel, *Night Flight*, published in 1931 and set in South America. With its dashing hero, the pilot Riviere, *Night Flight* would "relegate all novels of earthly chivalry to the nursery," according to Le Matin. Riviere even looked like Saint-Exupery—big, tan, with "black eyes that looked like radiant stars," as one admirer described him.

Later, as fascism closed in on Europe, Saint-Exupery's idealistic faith in progress and extravagant spirit was expressed in his memoir, *Terre des Hommes* (retitled *Wind, Sand, and Stars* in English) another huge hit. The American Booksellers Association voted it the best nonfiction book of 1939. It has been one of Saint-Exupery's problems ever since that everyone, from the existentialists to the Marxists, wanted to claim the book for their own. Tellingly, too, the book was as popular in Germany as it was in France and the United States.

In 1940, Saint-Exupery left German-occupied France for the United States, where he stayed two years in New York, bringing his second wife and his children. His second marriage also was unhappy, and he threw himself into numerous affairs with the fashionable ladies of Manhattan. But it was here that he oversaw the publication of *Le Petit Prince* just before embarking on the journey in April 1943 to join the Free French in Algiers.

Few reviewers at the time read *The Little Prince* as a children's tale, and many found it baffling. Among those who were deeply impressed was Orson Welles, who desperately tried to secure the screen rights for a combined live-action/animated feature.

Saint-Exupery spent more than a year flying reconnaissance missions out of North Africa and never set foot in France again before vanishing on June 31, 1944. His disappearance is the subject of as many theories and investigations in France as that of Amelia Earhart here. Exactly where his plane went after the radar lost track of him—whether the Alps, the Riviera or the Mediterranean—no one knows, but the search for clues never ends.

Meanwhile, *Le Petit Prince*, which many French critics sneered at as "boy-scoutish" and simpleminded, has been translated into 80 languages, more than any other book in the French language. It consistently sells some 125,000 copies a year in the United States alone.

Source: Helle Bering-Jensen, "Vive Antoine, le petit Prince," in *Insight on the News*, Vol. 11, No. 6, February 6, 1995, p. 27.

Philip Mooney

In the following essay, Mooney discusses Saint-Exupéry's death and legacy.

> VIRTUE, AS HE THEN DETAILED IT, MEANT SAVING THE SPIRITUAL AND CULTURAL HERITAGE OF FRANCE, AND DYING ON THE JOB, IF NECESSARY, TRUE TO ONE'S RESPONSIBILITY."

It is now 50 years since we saw the last of him, that lanky Frenchman with the doe eyes, turned-up nose and crow-foot of concern ever on his brow. The date was April 20, 1943, and Antoine Marie-Roger de Saint Exupery was heading home. As he passed the Statue of Liberty aboard the U.S. troop transport, he gazed up the East River beyond the throe nearer spans to the towers of the Queensboro Bridge shadowing his apartment, where he had said his adieu to his wife Consuelo several hours before. He thought back to that happy Monday morning in early August 1939, when Charles Lindbergh and he had gotten so caught up in conversation on that same bridge that the foremost American aviator had run out of gas! That weekend visit with the Lindberghs in their Huntington, Long Island, home just before the war had been such a peaceful time, and it had left its mark.

The French aviator-author had longed to recover a bit of that calm, so he and his wife had leased a house one bay over in Northport the previous autumn. It had become Antoine's haven of peace where he wrote *The Little Prince*. The stretch of sand out front and the roses that had bloomed through October had provided an inspiring setting for the Christmas story he had promised his publishers. But November's Allied landing in French North Africa had triggered Saint Ex's anxiousness to participate, prompting several trips to Washington. These interruptions prevented him from making his deadline; the publication of his Christmas story turned into an Easter event. In a profound sense, this date was much more appropriate for the symbolic tale, whose watercolor drawings the pilot did himself, tongue in teeth, with a little kit given him by movie producer Rene Clair.

Saint Exupery left his unfinished *Citadelle* with his wife and his manuscript of *Le Petit Prince* with his American friend Sylvia Hamilton.

Antoine had sensed that the parting present he gave to each was to be his final Easter adieu. He would never see either in this life again. He had more than once remarked that *Citadelle* would be his posthumous work, which it became, though still in need of his own meticulous kind of revision. But it is *The Little Prince*, the last book published in his lifetime, that remains the author's eternal carte de Noel.

The ship was picking up speed now. As Saint Ex took a long last look at the torch held high by the Alsatian Bartholdi's lady of freedom, it became the star the little prince had pointed out to the aviator: "You have your own star to follow." In his first wartime book, *Pilote de Guerre* [*Flight to Arras*], Saint Ex had insisted, "I cannot be myself unless I am participating," adding that personal knowledge is "not a matter of proof nor explanation but a vision one reaches only through participation." And in his tiny gem, *Letter to a Hostage*, put out by Brentano's in February, Antoine had acknowledged to his Jewish friend Leon Woerth that "when I go back to battle, it will be in the hopes of seeing your welcoming smile." He and Leon had shared a Paschal Pernod at the Cafe de la Marine near Tournus the Easter before the war. Saint Ex looked forward to that reunion where they could again toast their friendship "in the peace of a smile as bright as the dawn." Saint Exupery was sailing toward that meeting. He was following his star.

By heading home he was in a sense already there. The Manhattan skyline was now just lace on the afternoon ocean, Breezy Point a mere shadow on the water. The next sand Antoine would see would be Algerian. The sun caught the gold braid on the epaulets of his make-do French Air Force uniform. The brocade was not "regulation," but Saint Ex smiled in grateful appreciation at the extraordinary effort the Metropolitan Opera costumer had put into making him look the proper officer. Not bad on no notice! These were the Americans he remembered with a fond heart: nameless little people pitching in for a war effort that even now had gold stars saddening windows across the land. It was Antoine's turn now.

Why had he gone to so much trouble to go back to the war? He was overage for a combat pilot, seven years beyond the maximum age of 35. As a man of language, why had he made such fleeting efforts to learn English? Was it not to certify that he was first and always a Frenchman, not affiliated with any of the factions in the colony of French in the United States? Some of them had hectored him for not being an avowed Gaullist. The only touch of home he had felt in the United States was the nook in Northport whose strand of sand reminded him so of his sister Didi's house on the Cote d'Azur, where he had been married. It was after a morning stroll on that Long Island beach that he had inserted the lines in his *Letter to a Hostage*: "The presence of a friend who appears to be far away can be felt more deeply than physical presence. It is that of prayer. Never have I loved my home more than in the Sahara desert!" Never did he feel closer to his mother and family and friends in occupied France than during his Sahara saunter on Long Island Sound.

When he had said goodbye to his Northport retreat that last Dec. 8, Antoine de Saint Exupery knew his time had come. He had fulfilled his mission in the United States. The Americans were now making every sacrifice to free his people from Nazi tyranny while rolling back the tide of Japanese aggression in the Pacific. All his books were written, save *Citadelle*, which, like Mozart's *Requiem*, would find denouement only with his death. *The Little Prince* would be his testament, concluding almost like the New Testament with a plea for reunion with the prince: "Let me know he has come back!" Saint Ex's Christmas story also reveals the "secret" of his return to action: "I am responsible forever for my rose," the beloved for whom he was ready to give his life. Going back to sacrifice for his homeland was a matter of virtue for Antoine, as he wrote to a close friend the night before he died. Virtue, as he then detailed it, meant saving the spiritual and cultural heritage of France, and dying on the job, if necessary, true to one's responsibility.

Virtue was to fly in an unarmed airplane, a P-38, on reconnaissance missions. It was not easy for Saint Exupery to get airborne. He rejoined his group in North Africa soon after docking in Algiers, but had an accident in landing a P-38 because of bad brakes. The French air group was supplied with planes that had already logged thousands of miles in the South Pacific and were prone to break down. His friend Jules Hochede, whom he had praised in *Pilote de Guerre*, was killed in one of them six weeks after Saint Ex's arrival. Antoine was grounded by Aug. 16, 1943, and would not secure permission to fly again until the following June. He was all a-bubble when the O.K. finally came through from the headquarters of the American commander, General Ira Eakers: "See, my hair is growing back in. It's because I have the heart of a 20-year-old; it's because they are giving me a young man's job."

Saint Exupery was commended for the excellent photos he brought back from one of those missions. Then, on his 44th birthday, June 29, 1944, he almost "bought it" from a German Messerschmitt near Annecy after developing engine trouble. He had to cut another sortie short when his oxygen system failed. His commanding officer, Rene Gavoille was [wounded]. So he tried to share classified information with Saint Ex, which would have effectively grounded the aging pilot as a precaution against his being captured by the enemy. Antoine saw through his friend's ruse and would hear none of it.

Come July, his group II/33 was stationed in Corsica, with the Allied invasion of southern France only a few weeks away—though Antoine did not know this. He was in his tent writing what would be his last letter to his mother, which would not reach her until almost a year after his death. In closing, he shared the longing of his heart, "Oh, when will I be able to tell those who mean most, in person, how much they do!"

But, in a real sense, Antoine already had—in his book, *Pilote de Guerre*. Saint Ex would give his life for those close to him, those to whom he belonged. One particular person was the 14-year-old niece of the farmer in Champagne who had made him feel at home that evening at dinner back in 1939, when he was billeted there. Antoine caught her shy glance from the corner of his eye and detected the hint of the smile of welcome that blushed across her face. He would write, "I felt that I belonged here and no place else." Later, after surviving his bloody ordeal of May 22, 1940, Saint Ex became quite conscious of all those for whom he was ready to give his life. He saw them reflected in the Lalique-smile of the gift: "I returned from my mission over Arras, having formed my bond with my farmer's niece. Her smile became the crystal in which I could see my village and beyond my village, my homeland and beyond France all other nations." Antoine realized that he belonged only to those for whom he was ready to sacrifice,

those who had tendered him the welcoming smile of friendship.

One of those to whom he most belonged was Christian Antoine Gavoille, child of his friend the commandant. One week before his fatal day, Saint Ex flew over to Tunis to be Christian's godfather. He had earlier telegraphed to congratulate the mother and assure her that he would be the kindest godfather in all of France. He never had a chance to read anything to the child, or to make him paper helicopters and work magic tricks, as he did for other children. But he did leave Christian his Christmas story about the little prince who first appeared on earth under a star in the eastern Mediterranean, who was sent to his death by the serpent, and whose body was not found the next day. And the author had provided the key to his story and its practical wisdom in the secret of the fox: "One can only see clearly with the heart; what is essential is hidden from the eyes."

Saint Exupery's plane was never found. On the last day of July 1944, the feast of St. Ignatius Loyola, it plunged into the Bay of Angels off Nice. Later a friend received a letter from the pilot, whose final line read, "I have come simply to spend five minutes of eternity in friendship." Antoine Marie-Roger de Saint Exupery had devoted his brief time to those who were the rose of his heart, living out his understanding of virtue. He was that totally sincere friend who is "responsible forever for his rose."

Au revoir, Saint Ex.

Source: Philip Mooney, "Au Revoir, Saint Ex," in *America*, Vol. 169, No. 3, July 31–August 7, 1993, pp. 14–16.

Bonner Mitchell

In the following excerpt, Mitchell explores the didactic, or teaching, styles employed in Saint-Exupéry's The Little Prince *and* Citadelle, *arguing that "in both cases it is plainly ideas rather than plots which really matter."*

[It] is plain that Saint Exupery was venturing upon largely unbroken ground in choosing to write directly about "man's fate" while remaining in the realm of belles-lettres. Like [Andre] Malraux, [Jean-Paul] Sartre, and [Albert] Camus after him, he achieved his first successes in the novel, but his message fitted less and less well into that form.... Neither [*Le Petit Prince* nor *Citadelle*] is in the tradition of a major contemporary genre but each has

> THE LITTLE PRINCE DECLARES HIS SCORN FOR PEDESTRIAN ADULT LOGIC, AND HIS ATTITUDE IS REFLECTED BY CERTAIN QUALITIES OF THE BOOK ITSELF."

distinguished precedent in past literature. Thus, *Le Petit Prince* may be considered to descend from an illustrious line of allegorical fairy tales which reached its French apogee in the eighteenth century *conte philosophique. Citadelle* can be placed with some confidence in the formal tradition of Holy Scripture and of certain modern imitations such as [Friedrich] Nietszche's *Also sprach Zarathrustra* and [Andre] Gide's *Les Nourritures terrestres*. Despite the similarity of their ideological content, the two late works of Saint Exupery are thus cast in highly disparate literary molds. They exhibit great differences of tone and attitude which may reveal opposing sides of the author's character but which are also significant as parts of conscious stylistic exercises. These differences may be defined by the analysis of a number of stylistic details. We shall attempt to distinguish and contrast the two works for expository devices, for syntactical and logical transitions, and for symbols and imagery....

It seems more accurate to speak of expository devices than of narrative ones since in both cases it is plainly ideas rather than plots which really matter. Yet both works have elaborate fictional frameworks and their teaching is never done in an objective, impersonal style but is set either into personal monologues or into invented dialogues. *Le Petit Prince* is much more evidently a piece of creative literature than are *Pilote de guerre* or *Lettre a un otage* and its didacticism is correspondingly less frank. Expository devices are both more varied and more subtle. Like many marvelous and improbable tales, *e.g. Gulliver's Travels*, this one is put into the mouth of a normal, probable person, namely the real-life pilot Saint Exupery. He speaks in an intimate, down-to-earth way, addressing himself directly to the reader on numerous occasions and explaining with care the more realistic circumstances of his experience. This literary pose is not meant to fool anyone, but it has a definite esthetic and didactic purpose. The narrator's tone constitutes in effect an invitation to reflect along with him upon a series of events which, it is pretended, he does not entirely understand. This is an old procedure for writers of allegory, being found, for example, even in the opening of the *Divine Comedy*. The device of reflecting aloud upon personal experiences was not, moreover, new to Saint Exupery but had formed the very backbone of the autobiographical works already mentioned. This work's main message is not contained, however, in the narrator's own remarks, though he does begin to interpret near the end, but must be sought in the actual events and characters which he describes. The book's didacticism is thus superficially covered over. The hero of the tale is not, either, consciously instructive, however inadvertently revealing his remarks may be. He is ever reluctant to answer questions, and it is only near the end that he, too, starts to talk directly about the meaning of his experiences. The story does contain two avowed teachers but both are minor characters. One of these is the Snake, who tells the Prince about death. The other, considerably more prominent, is the Fox, whose imaginatively expressed lessons to the hero are transmitted to the narrator and thence to the reader. These lessons are so closely connected to the events of the story, however, that they would be almost incomprehensible out of context.

The weighty and solemn teachings of *Citadelle* are also set into a sort of fictional framework, and its instruction is conveyed largely through monologues and dialogues in which the character of the speaker—if not that of the hearer—is well-defined and individualized. Though Saint Exupery might have wished to fix the plot of this work more precisely in later revisions, it is clear even from the manuscript that the whole composition is to be regarded as a didactic testament left to his people by an old and wise ruler. This fictional author does not seek to establish any sort of intimacy between himself and his readers but addresses them *ex cathedra* with instruction as his sole aim. The prominence and individuality of his own character assure nevertheless that the work is a piece of literature and not one of pure exposition.... The book contains, besides the straightforward teaching of the narrator, several sorts of instructive dialogues. The first of these, both in order of chronology and in that of the book's arrangement, is a series of conversations which the Ruler recalls having had with his father. These are lessons in the art of government and, though there is a fair amount of exchange between the two speakers, the tone is overwhelmingly didactic. The Ruler also speaks on numerous occasions with various of his subjects. In such cases the questions or remarks of the subordinates usually give rise to elaborate harangues or reflections on the part of their chief. In many passages near the end of the book the Ruler's words are addressed to an anonymous "tu" who seems to represent his whole people. These sections, in which possible errors are brought forward and refuted, resemble superficially many passages of the *Carnets* in which Saint Exupery seems to be conversing with a more fallible *alter ego*, but there is between the two books an utter difference of tone. Indulgence is excluded from the reflections of *Citadelle* with almost shocking thoroughness....

Another sort of directed monologue, a much more original kind of expository device, is found in the narrator's prayers. In one passage ..., he tells of going to a mountaintop in search of God and of finding only a black rock. He had then concluded that prayers are not meant to be answered. The examples in *Citadelle* are striking demonstrations of this conception. . . . In *Tom Sawyer* Mark Twain has parodied the manner of rural Missouri prayer leaders who found it necessary to inform God of all that was going on on earth. It is impossible to escape the impression of a certain parallel in *Citadelle*, nor can one fail to notice that the tone adopted by the Ruler to address his "seigneur" is virtually the same as that used for instructing his subjects....

The Little Prince declares his scorn for pedestrian adult logic, and his attitude is reflected by certain qualities of the book itself. His remarks in conversations with the narrator often seem inconsequential, though his train of thought is, in another sense, unusually one-tracked. The occasional formal questions of *Pilote de guerre* and *Lettre a un otage*, followed by careful statements of opinion, are paralleled in *Le Petit Prince* by astonishing queries from the hero and the Fox. These questions are seldom answered right away, nor, indeed, are they answerable at all in objective terms. The events of the story, though not out of place in a fairy tale, are of course eminently unreasonable.

Yet even in telling of the strangest occurrences the narrator continues to speak the language of a reasonable and practical man, and he provides numerous practical and chronological details....

Citadelle appears upon first encounter to be a highly reasonable document. Its text is dense with the verbal apparatus of logic and dialectics. The very first sentence begins, astonishingly, with the word "car," and the extreme frequency and emphasis with which this term is used are largely responsible for the most salient impression left by any reading in *Citadelle*, the feeling that one has been subjected to a grueling scholastic lesson. It soon becomes apparent, however, that the content of chapters, paragraphs, and sentences introduced by this conjunction often have as enigmatic a causal relationship with what has preceded as does the first sentence with the void which it follows.... One notes also in *Citadelle* a general disregard for details of chronology and location. It is never quite clear when or where the events recounted have taken place. Some of this syntactical and logical obscurity is due to the book's unfinished state, but there is no reason to think that its essential character would have been changed by revisions, nor would it be at all true to say that even the manuscript is unintelligible.... All the stories and arguments of *Citadelle* are in a sense illustrations and justifications of the work's main thesis, which might be formulated broadly (and with some injustice) as the priority of the interests of civilization over personal ones. It is this general thesis, however difficult of expression, which lends to the book's apparent rambling and non-sequiturs a perceptible unity. There can be no doubt, on the other hand, that the striking illogicality of detail is deliberate and purposeful. It affords specific illustrations of Saint Exupery's conviction, expressed openly in *Citadelle* as in *Le Petit Prince*, that the power of human logic is limited, that some truths are discoverable only through other means, i.e. through experience and intuition. The Ruler's imperious man-handling of delicate logical processes and his scorn of most realistic details are meant to free his hearers from the fetters of narrow, unimaginative thinking and so to make it easier for them to be convinced intuitively of what he is teaching....

In all of Saint Exupery's works the figurative expression of ideas is extremely prominent and important. This is probably the best known single characteristic of his style. We shall discuss figurative expression in these works under two categories: narrative symbolism and imaginative language. In autobiographical compositions such as *Lettre a un otage* symbols were carefully developed from actual experiences.... *Le Petit Prince* is farther from real life and its symbols are accordingly both more in evidence and more obscure in meaning. The hero's planet, where he must live in constant relations with his volcanoes, his baobab trees, his rose and, later, with a sheep who may try to eat the rose, clearly represents social institutions, but the precise significance of all that is told about the planet is subject to interpretation. Besides grand symbols such as the planet and the serpent, the story has a host of symbolic details. Virtually everything the hero does, e.g. his drinking from a well in the desert, is susceptible of symbolic interpretation; indeed, it obviously requires such interpretation. The story itself, as distinguished from the narrator's "realistic" presentation, is almost pure allegory, much like that of *Le Roman de la rose*, with which it has in common a major symbol.

Though the setting and events of *Citadelle* are also wholly fictional, they are not unlikely in the same way as those of *Le Petit Prince*. Its symbolism is somewhat less striking and, at the same time, less obscure than that of the other book. The Ruler's citadel is an idealized but credible representation of human society. By sticking closer to objective reality than in the fairy tale, while still inventing his material, as he could not do in the autobiographical works, Saint Exupery is able to make his narrative symbolism both very clear and very specific in its application. The Ruler's observations about the events of his reign may be transferred very easily to modern social and political contexts. The symbolism of this work fits much better into the category of parable than into that of allegory.

An examination of all the author's works reveals not only that imagery is ubiquitous but also that the same image families or complexes are prominent everywhere. Just as he was obsessed all his life by certain humanistic conceptions and problems, so the images which embodied these problems and conceptions, *e.g.* *l'arbre* and *le navire*, were hardly ever out of his consciousness. It is scarcely rewarding, therefore, to search for different kinds of imagery in the two works, but there is more value in examining the function of the images and the manner of their presentation. The author of *Pilote de guerre* and *Lettre a un otage* reasons constantly in a language full of metaphors and similes, but neither the narrator nor the other characters of *Le Petit Prince* habitually talk in such a way. In this work where virtually the whole narrative is symbolic the language of reasoning is markedly down-to-earth. ...

The language of *Citadelle*'s arguments and harangues has an even greater density of figurative expressions than is found in the autobiographical works. Here all the author's imaginative themes are brought together to be taken up over and over again in the speech of the didactic personnages whom he has made his porte-paroles. Not just the Ruler and his father but even the subjects of the empire often express themselves figuratively with great skill, so that, apart from a few purely narrative passages, the book contains scarcely a paragraph of wholly literal language.... Some... expressions owe their meaning to special thematic development and one must undergo an apprenticeship in the reading of *Citadelle* in order to appreciate them. In this book such thematic developments of imaginative conceptions are often climaxed by the lifting up of a major symbol. Thus the many discussions of *liens, noeuds, relations* etc. Prepare for the book's final sentence... in which the Ruler makes the "noeud" a symbol of the God he has created. This looks very much like mystical symbolism, but it is of course highly contrived and literary....

Le Petit Prince and *Citadelle* are, in summary, two unusual and highly disparate exercises in the seductive exposition of their author's humanistic ideas. The first has an intimate tone and affects a superficial reasonableness, while the burden of its teaching is borne by an elaborate allegory which scorns logic and aims to charm instead of to convince by direct argument. *Citadelle* is imperious in tone rather than either intimate or reasonable, though it makes a great external show of logic. Its didactic message is entrusted mainly to parable and to imaginatively expressed lectures which seek more to overwhelm than to charm or to persuade by means of reason....

Source: Bonner Mitchell, "*Le Petit Prince* and *Citadelle*: Two Experiments in the Didactic Style," in *French Review*, April 1960, pp. 454–61.

SOURCES

Balakian, Nona, "Poet of the Air—and Earth," in the *New York Times*, December 5, 1970, p. 30.

Brosman, Catharine Savage, "Antoine de Saint-Exupéry," in *Dictionary of Literary Biography*, Vol. 72, *French Novelists, 1930–1960*, edited by Catharine Savage Brosman, Gale Research, 1988, pp. 314–30.

Gibson, Robert, "Antoine de Saint-Exupéry: Overview," in the *Reference Guide to World Literature*, 2nd ed., edited by Lesley Henderson, St. James Press, 1995.

Gide, André, "Preface," in *Vol de Nuit*, by Antoine de Saint-Exupéry, 1931, reprint, Ebooks Libres et Gratuits, May 2004, p. 5, http://www.scribd.com/doc/2324523/Vol-de-nuit?autodown = pdf (accessed November 29, 2008).

Mitchell, Bonner, "*Le Petit Prince* and *Citadelle*: Two Experiments in the Didactic Style," in the *French Review*, April 1960, pp. 454–61.

Quinn, Judy, "'Prince' and the Revolution," in *Publishers Weekly*, Vol. 247, No. 11, March 13, 2000, p. 26.

Saint-Exupéry, Antoine de, *The Little Prince*, translated by Irene Testot-Ferry, Wordsworth Classics, 1995.

Strongheart, Rachel Lynn, "The Little Prince: My Ally from Asteroid B-612," in the *Reading Teacher*, Vol. 54, No. 5, February 2001, p. 498.

Wadsworth, Philip A., "Saint-Exupéry, Artist and Humanist," in *Modern Language Quarterly*, March 1951, pp. 96–107.

FURTHER READING

Bloomfield, Morton W., ed., *Allegory, Myth, and Symbol*, Harvard University Press, 1981.
    This book is a useful collection of essays by different critics analyzing the use of allegory, myth, and symbol in a variety of works from the Anglo-Saxon era to the poetry of W. B. Yeats, Ezra Pound, and T. S. Eliot.

Grant, R. G., *Flight: 100 Years of Aviation*, DK, 2007.
    This large volume was produced in collaboration with the Smithsonian Institution's National Air and Space Museum. The book traces the history of aviation through its innovations, adventures, and pioneers and is lavishly illustrated with archival photographs.

Quilligan, Maureen, *The Language of Allegory: Defining the Genre*, Cornell University Press, 1992.
    This book provides a critical analysis of allegories both ancient and modern.

Robinson, Joy Marie, *Antoine de Saint-Exupéry*, Twayne's World Authors Series, Twayne Publishers, 1984.
    This book offers an accessible and concise critical introduction to the author's works along with biographical material and resources for further study.

Saint-Exupéry, Consuelo de, *The Tale of the Rose*, Random House, 2003.
    Saint-Exupéry's widow Consuelo wrote this compelling memoir of their tempestuous marriage in 1945, a year after his death. The manuscript languished in a trunk for decades until it was discovered in 1999. Consuelo describes how she was the model for the character of the rose in *The Little Prince*.

Schiff, Stacy, *Saint-Exupéry: A Biography*, Holt Paperbacks, 2006.
    This is a very readable biography by a Pulitzer Prize-winning author. Readers will enjoy spotting the many parallels between the otherworldly aviator Saint-Exupéry and the two protagonists of his novel *The Little Prince*.

The Once and Future King

T. H. WHITE

1958

T. H. White's *The Once and Future King*, published in 1958, is by far the best-known twentieth-century retelling of the legend of King Arthur and the Knights of the Round Table. The novel served as the basis for the Walt Disney animated movie *The Sword in the Stone* (1963), the 1960 Alan Jay Lerner and Frederic Lowe Broadway musical *Camelot*, and the 1967 movie *Camelot*, directed by Josh Logan.

In all, White published five books about King Arthur and his Knights, using medieval texts (notably those of Sir Thomas Malory) as his source material. The first, *The Sword in the Stone*, published in 1938, traces the boyhood of young Arthur. The second, *The Witch in the Wood*, published in 1939, is about the early days of Arthur's kingship and tells the story of Queen Morgause and her four sons. The third volume, *The Ill-Made Knight*, published in 1940, introduces Lancelot. In 1958, when White completed his fourth book of the series, *The Candle in the Wind*, he chose to republish the three earlier books along with the fourth in one volume titled *The Once and Future King*. His final Arthurian work, *The Book of Merlyn*, although written in 1941, was not published until 1977.

Readers of all ages find the stories of Arthur recounted in *The Once and Future King* fascinating and timeless. The novel is at once a humorous account of young Arthur's education, the chronicle of King Arthur's valor, the spiritual journey of

Terence H. White

knights in search of the Holy Grail, the tragic love triangle of Arthur, Guenever, and Lancelot, and a social commentary on the political events of White's own day. The novel asks readers to consider themes such as power, justice, love, and betrayal. Although more than a half-century has passed since the publication of *The Once and Future King*, the novel remains widely available and widely read, an important contribution to the cycle of stories of King Arthur and the Knights of the Round Table.

AUTHOR BIOGRAPHY

T. H. White was born Terence Hanbury White in Bombay, India, on May 29, 1906. His father, Garrick Hanbury White, was a police superintendent. His mother was Constance Edith Southcote Aston White. When White was just five he was sent to his grandparents in England to recover from a stomach infection. According to both Sylvia Warner Townsend in her biography of White and Elisabeth Brewer in her book *T. H. White's "The Once and Future King,"* White's father was an alcoholic, and the relationship between his parents was volatile. White's relationship with his mother was particularly troubled. Brewer notes that this was an important influence on *The Once and Future King*. Likewise, Hugh T. Keenan, in a biographical essay, "T. H. White," asserts that White's dysfunctional interaction with his mother accounted for his sadistic tendencies, a trait he gave to his character Lancelot.

In 1920, White was sent to Cheltenham College, a military-style boarding school. There he was subjected to ill treatment, as were all the students, by their upper-level peers. It was here, however, that he first learned about Sir Thomas Malory, the fifteenth-century English writer of *Le Morte D'Arthur*.

White finished at Cheltenham in 1923 and spent the next year tutoring, as he did not have the funds to start university immediately. He entered Queen's College, Cambridge, in 1925. In 1927, he contracted tuberculosis. According to Brewer and Keenan, White's mentor and teacher, L. J. Potts, along with other dons at Cambridge, gave him the money to go to Italy for his convalescence. While in Italy, he began his professional writing career.

White graduated from Cambridge in 1929 and taught for two years at a preparatory school. In 1932, he took a position at Stowe, an elite public school (or what would be termed a private school in the United States) in Buckinghamshire. He wrote several detective novels during the early 1930s, and then began publishing other types of fiction, nonfiction, and essays. In 1936, he published a book of memoirs and journal entries, *England Have My Bones*. This book met with popular success, and on the basis of his earnings from this volume, he was able to resign from teaching and move into a gamekeeper's cottage on the Stowe grounds in order to write full-time.

In 1938, White completed and published *The Sword in the Stone*, a book seemingly aimed at younger readers but one that found a wide readership among adults as well. In 1939, White moved to Ireland to wait out the conflict that became World War II. At the same time, he completed his second Arthurian novel, *The Witch in the Wood* (later drastically revised and titled *The Queen of Air and Darkness*). Several biographers suggest that White's depiction of the evil queen Morgause in this book was based on his own experiences with his mother.

White completed the third novel in his Arthurian series, *The Ill-Made Knight* in 1940, and the fourth, *The Candle in the Wind* in 1958. He did not publish the latter novel separately but instead chose to revise his earlier works and reissue them all under one title, *The Once and Future King*. This novel, published in 1958, met with immediate critical and popular success.

In addition to his Arthurian stories, White wrote a number of children's books and adult novels during the 1940s and 1950s, as well as several nonfiction books. By the time *The Once and Future King* appeared, he was financially sound and able to travel. During the early 1960s, he was in Italy before embarking on a speaking tour of the United States, where the musical *Camelot*, first produced in 1960 and based on *The Once and Future King*, was extraordinarily popular. While in the United States, he began a book titled *America at Last: The American Journal of T. H. White* (1965). He had been working on this book when he was found dead of a heart attack in his stateroom aboard an ocean liner in Athens, Greece, on January 17, 1964.

PLOT SUMMARY

The Sword in the Stone
Chapters 1–12

The Sword in the Stone, the first section of *The Once and Future King*, concerns the childhood of King Arthur, who is known only as Wart in this section. Humorous and often light-hearted, it also has a serious purpose: to demonstrate the qualities a king should cultivate and illustrate the knowledge a wise king must have.

The book opens with a description of the courses Wart and his foster brother, Kay, take in preparation for becoming knights. However, their education has been curtailed by the lack of a teacher. Sir Ector, Kay's father and Wart's foster father, begins a quest for a tutor to teach the boys.

Meanwhile, Kay decides to take a hawk named Cully out to hunt, against Wart's warnings that the hawk is not ready to go on a hunt. Kay disregards Wart's advice and quickly loses the bird. Kay loses patience with chasing the bird and returns to the castle. Wart, however, continues to track the bird's movements and ends up staying overnight in the forest, reluctant to return without the bird.

After spending the night out of doors, Wart awakens to a noise that turns out to have been made by Merlyn the magician. Merlyn announces that he is to be Wart's tutor. In addition, he reveals that because he lives backwards in time, he knows what will happen in the future. They capture Cully and make their way to Sir Ector's castle, located in the remote Forest Sauvage.

Wart's education soon begins in earnest. Merlyn turns himself and Wart into fish in the

MEDIA ADAPTATIONS

- In 1963, Walt Disney Productions released an animated film based on *The Sword in the Stone*, directed by Wolfgang Reitherman. The film featured the voices of Sebastian Cabot as Sir Ector and the narrator, Ricky Sorenson as Wart/Arthur, and Karl Swenson as Merlyn.

- The 1960 hit Broadway musical *Camelot* was based on *The Once and Future King*. Alan Jay Lerner wrote the book and lyrics, Frederic Lowe wrote the music, and Moss Hart directed the musical. Starring Richard Burton as King Arthur, Julie Andrews as Guenever, and Robert Goulet as Lancelot, *Camelot* went on to win four Tony awards and ran for over eight hundred performances. The original cast recording was the best-selling long-playing record in the United States for over a year.

- A film version of *Camelot*, directed by Josh Logan and starring Richard Harris, Vanessa Redgrave, and Franco Nero, was released in 1967.

- In 2008, Naxos Audio released CDs of all four sections of *The Once and Future King* as well as *The Book of Merlyn*, read by Neville Jason.

castle moat so that Wart can learn something about governance. While a fish, Wart meets a large pike, the king of the moat, who speaks to him about might and power. Wart narrowly escapes being eaten by the pike.

Merlyn next turns Wart into a small hawk and places him in the Mews, the place where the hunting hawks are kept. Wart encounters a militaristic, dangerous society with Cully, who has become psychopathic, in charge. In this section, White seems to be commenting on the dangers of fascism, a form of military dictatorship controlling Italy and Germany at the time of his writing of *The Sword in the Stone*. Wart again narrowly escapes with his life, having learned another important lesson.

In the next chapters, Wart and Kay have an adventure with a man called Robin Wood, although others call him Robin Hood. They also meet Maid Marian and Little John. They learn that Friar Tuck and Wat (one of Sir Ector's servants) have been abducted by Morgan le Fay, the Queen of the Fairies. Wart and Kay volunteer to help with the rescue. Morgan le Fay's castle is made entirely of butter and pork and guarded by a griffin, a mythological beast with the body of a lion, the head of a falcon, and the tail of a snake. The boys successfully free the prisoners; however, Wart is injured when the griffin falls on him, dead from Kay's arrow.

Chapters 13–24

While recovering from his injury, Wart asks Merlyn to change him into an ant. He discovers there a society where everything is regulated and communal. There are continual broadcasts of instructions and orders from some central command center. Here White seems to be commenting on Communism as a form of social order. The ant community is preparing to go to war with a neighboring group, and Merlyn changes Wart back into a boy just in time to avoid violence.

Wart has several more lessons in store in this section. First, Merlyn changes him into a bird, and Archimedes the owl teaches him to fly. Then Merlyn changes him into a goose. He meets a female goose named Lyo-lyok, who explains to him the details of goose society. She finds the idea of war utterly absurd. White seems to say that the rational, fair society of the geese is both admirable and worthy of emulation.

Six years pass between the close of chapter 19 and the opening of chapter 20. Kay and Wart have grown, but Kay has not matured. Although he is larger, he is both boorish and unpleasant. He fails to learn lessons in common decency. Wart is sad that Kay does not want him around anymore, and Merlyn tells him that the most important thing to do when one is sad is to learn something new.

Later, on the eve of Kay's knighting, King Pellinore returns to the Forest Sauvage to tell them that King Uther Pendragon is dead. A sword has been driven through an anvil in front of a church, and the words "Whoso Pulleth Out This Sword of this Stone and Anvil, is Rightwise King Born of All England" are written in gold letters on the sword. A tournament is scheduled for New Year's Day so that all the men in England can have a try at removing the sword from the stone.

On the day of the tournament, Wart accompanies Kay as his squire. However, Kay leaves his sword at the inn where they are staying. He sends Wart to retrieve it, but the inn is closed. In a rush to find a suitable sword, he attempts to remove the sword from the stone. On his third try, with the animals of the forest watching, he succeeds. When he hands the sword over to Kay, Kay immediately claims that he himself has pulled it out of the stone. Eventually he admits that he is lying and that Wart pulled it out. Sir Ector and Kay go down on their knees to Wart, who bursts into tears.

The Queen of Air and Darkness
Chapters 1–10

The second book of *The Once and Future King* is set primarily on Orkney, an island in the far north of Scotland. Four boys, Gawaine, Gaheris, Agravaine, and Gareth, tell themselves the story of their own heritage. Their grandmother Igraine had three daughters with her husband, Gorlois, the Earl of Cornwall: Elaine, Morgan, and Morgause, the boys' mother. King Uther Pendragon, besotted with Igraine, persuades Merlyn to change him into the likeness of Gorlois so that he is able to enter the castle. His men kill Gorlois, and Uther lies with Igraine, who believes that he is her husband. For the murder of their grandfather and the defilement of their grandmother, the four boys vow revenge on Uther and his heirs.

Back in Camelot, Arthur brags about his military victories to Merlyn, who tells him that he knows nothing about war. Merlyn warns him that a confederation of Gaelic kings is forming against him and that they will attack again. He particularly warns him about King Lot and explains to Arthur and to Kay how Uther killed Gorlois. Merlyn reveals that the hatred Queen Morgause and King Lot bear for Arthur is a result of this blood feud.

Arthur talks about the idea of chivalry with Kay, Ector, and Merlyn. He has come to understand that might does not equal right. However, he knows he must use force to put down the rebellion led by King Lot. Once accomplished, he promises to begin an order of knights who will fight only on the side of justice.

In Orkney, comic relief is provided by King Pellinore, Sir Palomides, and Sir Grummore, who are attempting a unicorn hunt. The four Orkney brothers decide to capture a unicorn to give to their mother with the help of a young kitchen servant who is a virgin. In a moment of hysteria, Agravaine beheads the unicorn, a cruel and wanton act.

Meanwhile, Arthur continues preparation for his order of knights, conceiving the idea of the Round Table. He also learns of Guenever. Merlyn tells him he will marry Guenever but that he must be careful of the relationship between Lancelot and Guenever. Merlyn is also troubled by something he cannot seem to remember to tell Arthur.

Chapters 11–14

More comic relief is provided by Pellinore, Palomides, Grummore, and the Questing Beast. Meanwhile, Arthur engages in the Battle of Bedegraine, a decisive moment in his kingship when he defeats the Gaelic forces of King Lot.

After the Gaels return home to Orkney with news of their defeat, Morgause plans a visit to Arthur's England, supposedly to plead for mercy for her husband and to attend King Pellinore's wedding. Meanwhile, Merlyn, now in an affair with the sorceress Nimue, suddenly remembers that he should have told Arthur that Morgause is Arthur's half-sister, but he is too far away to get word to Arthur. In the last four paragraphs of this section, readers learn that Morgause uses magic on Arthur and that nine months later, Morgause bears Arthur's child, a boy named Mordred.

The Ill-Made Knight
Chapters 1–10

This segment of *The Once and Future King* is drawn directly from Malory's *The Book of Sir Launcelot and Queen Guenevere* and traces the development of Lancelot, the son of King Bors. Oddly, White has chosen to make Lancelot incredibly ugly. The young knight demonstrates tremendous prowess as a fighter, and he trains with his Uncle Dap to be worthy of the Round Table. Merlyn next appears to Lancelot and tells him that he will be the greatest knight of the Round Table.

On the way to Camelot, Lancelot engages in a joust with an unknown knight, who turns out to be Arthur and who is very happy to see Lancelot. Back at Camelot, Arthur knights Lancelot. Lancelot has strong feelings for Arthur and finds himself jealous of young Queen Guenever. When he is cruel to her as a result, he hurts her feelings. Only when he realizes this does he find it possible to treat her as a human being. Their relationship grows, and rumors begin about the pair. Arthur refuses to believe any of them.

Arthur assembles a force, including Lancelot, to go to Europe to fight the Romans, who have demanded allegiance. They are gone for an extended period of time, with Arthur ultimately conquering most of Europe. Lancelot is his best knight. However, when they return to Camelot, Lancelot realizes that his feelings for Guenever will damage his relationship with Arthur, so he sets out on a series of quests.

Lancelot rescues Gawaine in one such quest and defeats many other knights, all of whom he sends to Camelot to bow before Guenever. When he returns, he finds that Guenever is in love with him and Arthur is distracted. The brothers from Orkney, in addition, are becoming very troublesome, although they are all now Knights of the Round Table. This situation is exacerbated by the fact that Arthur's friend King Pellinore has accidently killed their father, King Lot.

Chapters 11–20

After several weeks, Lancelot takes off on another quest. This time he finds his way to the castle of King Pelles, the Fisher King. He discovers that a young woman by the name of Elaine has been placed in a pot of boiling water by Morgan le Fay, and he immediately rescues her. Elaine falls in love with him, and with the help of her butler, tricks Lancelot into believing Guenever is waiting for him in a nearby castle. When Lancelot awakens in the morning, he finds himself in bed with Elaine. He is furious. He returns to Camelot and acts on his love for Guenever.

Arthur, meanwhile, goes off to France for a year to fight on behalf of King Ban. Lancelot stays at Camelot in charge of the kingdom, and the lovers enjoy their time while Arthur is away. Then, however, Guenever learns of Elaine and that she has born a child with Lancelot named Galahad. She is furious. Lancelot and Guenever finally make up, and when Elaine arrives at Camelot, Guenever is polite.

Once again, Elaine tricks Lancelot into her bed by pretending to be Guenever. The next day, Guenever confronts Elaine and Lancelot. Lancelot, suddenly realizing that he has once again been deceived, goes mad and jumps out the window.

Two years later, a wild man is seen near King Pelles' castle. The king believes the wild man to be Lancelot, although Lancelot will not answer when asked. Pelles locks him a stable until the servants, realizing that he is a nobleman, set him free.

Chapters 21–30
Meanwhile, Elaine is living in a convent. She comes across Lancelot and helps to heal him from madness. He stays with Elaine but asks that she not reveal his identity. At a tournament held several months later, Lancelot, using the name Chevalier Mal Fet, defeats all comers. Finally, hearing about the prowess of this knight, two of Arthur's knights come to the castle to fight with him. They realize that he is Lancelot. Still later, Uncle Dap arrives with all of Lancelot's gear. Lancelot decides to leave and go back to Camelot, but he promises Elaine that he will return.

Fifteen years pass. To the north, Queen Morgause has seduced young Sir Lamorak, King Pellinore's son. Pellinore has killed King Lot in a tournament by accident and was later killed himself. Arthur is horrified at this news, and even more horrified when he learns that Agravaine, finding his mother with Lamorak, has chopped off her head. Gawaine, Agravaine, and Mordred hunt down and kill Lamorak as well.

Arthur, troubled by the violence of the knights, knows that the Round Table is in danger. He decides to send the knights on a spiritual quest, the search for the Holy Grail. The Grail is the vessel from which Christ drank at the last supper. Meanwhile, Galahad is knighted and joins the quest.

After two years, the knights begin returning and telling their tales. Especially important is the contrast between Gawaine and Galahad. Gawaine's thirst for violence is not slaked by the quest, and he stands in stark contrast to the saintly Galahad. Later, Sir Lionel returns and tells the tale of his brother Sir Bors.

The final story of the Grail quest in this section concerns Sir Bors, Sir Galahad, and Sir Percival. These are the Grail knights, the holiest of all of Arthur's men.

Chapters 31–45
Lancelot finally returns to Camelot, much aged and unsuccessful in his search for the Grail. He tells a tale of meeting a knight who defeats him, and then discovers that the knight is his son, Galahad. Lancelot witnesses the three Grail knights achieve the holy object. This experience has changed Lancelot.

He vows to give up Guenever and finally leaves on another quest.

Camelot is crumbling. Mordred, Arthur's son with Morgause, has gained significant power. Guenever, in an attempt to make things as they were, holds a banquet. However, the blood feud between Pellinore's family and Gawaine's family continues. A poisoned apple is at the banquet, and all believe that Guenever tried to poison Gawaine. She must be defended by a champion in a trial by combat.

Lancelot returns to be Guenever's champion and wins the day. He is still torn between Elaine and Guenever, but he finally leaves Elaine for good. Elaine commits suicide; her body is put on a barge, and it sails down to Camelot. Guenever is terribly moved.

Lancelot and Guenever resume their affair, and Arthur continues to turn a blind eye. When Guenever is accused of adultery by Meliagrance, Lancelot again champions the queen and carries the day. The book closes with the arrival of Sir Urry, who has wounds that will not heal. Lancelot, who feels himself to be impure, nevertheless is able to heal Sir Urry.

The Candle in the Wind
Chapters 1–14
The final segment of *The Once and Future King* is also the shortest. Everyone is considerably older and the sheen has worn off Camelot. Agravaine and Mordred plot together to bring about Lancelot's downfall. Arthur has instituted courts of law, and they decide that the best way to defeat Lancelot is in the courtroom, not on the field of combat.

Gawaine is distraught when he learns of their plans and nearly kills Agravaine, who has drawn a knife on him. Arthur walks in and puts an end to their quarrel without knowing its source.

Guenever and Lancelot are still in love. They believe that Arthur must know, but they also realize that he will not do anything about it, because he loves both of them. When the three of them are together, Arthur tells them that Mordred is his son and that Arthur killed many children when Mordred was born in an attempt to avoid a fate prophesied by Merlyn, that Mordred would cause Arthur's destruction.

Mordred and Agravaine tell Arthur about the affair between Lancelot and Guenever. Arthur agrees sadly that if they provide proof, he will have to prosecute them in a court of law. While Arthur is away hunting, Mordred and Agravaine trap Lancelot in Guenever's room. Lancelot manages to escape, killing Agravaine and many others.

Later, Guenever is about to be burned at the stake for adultery. Lancelot arrives to save her but in the process kills Gareth and Gaheris, who are both unarmed. Without their colors, he does not recognize them.

Ultimately, the matter is settled by the Bishop of Rochester, who exiles Lancelot and returns Guenever to Arthur. Gawaine still wants revenge on Lancelot, however, and he and Arthur go to France to attack him. While they are gone, Mordred takes control of England and tells Guenever that she will now be his wife.

Arthur and Gawaine receive this news and know they must return to England. Gawaine, however, is sorely wounded. He writes a letter to Lancelot, forgiving him and asking for his forgiveness in return. He begs Lancelot to return to England to fight on the side of Arthur.

The last scene is of an aged Arthur the night before the final battle with Mordred. He thinks about what he has accomplished in his life. A young page, Thomas of Warwick (who becomes Sir Thomas Malory), receives the story from Arthur and vows that he will tell it far and wide. Arthur prepares himself for battle, and the book closes.

CHARACTERS

Agravaine

Agravaine is the son of King Lot of Lothian and Orkney and Queen Morgause. Among his four brothers, he is the cruelest and most violent. His feelings toward his mother are unnatural. As a boy, he kills a unicorn that he and his brothers have trapped as a gift for their mother. His relationship with his mother has the result that he both loves and hates women. He kills his mother by beheading her when he discovers her in bed with a young knight, an act that disgusts and horrifies his brothers, particularly Gareth. He, along with Mordred, plot against Guenever and Lancelot.

Arthur

King Arthur is the main character of *The Once and Future King*. Known only as Wart in the

opening section of the book, it is revealed that he is the son of Uther Pendragon when he pulls a sword out of a stone and an anvil. The lessons Arthur has learned from Merlyn as a boy help him become a good and wise ruler, although throughout the story he puzzles about the connections between right and might. Arthur creates the institution of the Round Table, a place where all knights can sit and none is superior to the other.

Although Arthur is successful in uniting Britain under one rule, he struggles with how to transition from a monarch who rules by force to one who rules by law. When he establishes peace in Britain, his knights become overly concerned with sport, and Arthur believes he must find another, more spiritual, undertaking to occupy their time. Consequently, he initiates the quest for the Holy Grail.

The seeds of Arthur's undoing and the destruction of the Round Table are sown when he allows himself to be seduced by Queen Morgause. He does not realize that she is his half-sister; the result of the incest is the conception of Mordred, a character who works against Arthur and all that he stands for.

By the end of the book, Arthur is old, tired, and heartsick, getting ready to fight his final battle. Nonetheless, he reaches an understanding of the good he has done, and he passes this story on to a young page attending him.

Ban

King Ban is from France and is Lancelot's father. He is a sworn ally of Arthur.

Bors

Bors is Lancelot's cousin and a sworn ally.

Ector

Sir Ector is Arthur's foster father and Kay's biological father.

Elaine

Elaine is the daughter of King Pelles. She is in love with Lancelot, who has rescued her from a vat of boiling water. She tricks him into sleeping with her by pretending to be Guenever, resulting in the conception of Galahad. Elaine is young and needy; she is not evil, although she does deceive Lancelot. When Elaine realizes that Lancelot will never return to her, she commits suicide. White has conflated two characters from Malory named Elaine into Elaine of Corbin.

Gaheris

Gaheris is one of the Orkneys, the son of King Lot and Queen Morgause and a brother to Gawaine, Agravaine, and Gareth.

Galahad

Galahad is the son of Lancelot and Elaine. He is the purest of all the knights and the one who finally achieves the Holy Grail. He is not well liked by the other knights.

Gareth

Gareth is the youngest of the Orkney clan, and he comes unannounced to Arthur's court, where he serves as a kitchen servant until he becomes a proficient knight. He worships Lancelot, who also greatly loves the young man. This is why it is so tragic that Lancelot ultimately kills Gareth in the fight for Guenever because he does not recognize him in the fray. Gareth's death has the result of turning Gawaine against Lancelot.

Gawaine

Gawaine (known as Gawain in most other sources) is historically one of the oldest of Arthur's knights. In *The Once and Future King*, he speaks in a Scottish dialect and is a rough-and-tumble sort of man. He is basically a good man, however, in spite of his heritage and upbringing. He is very emotional, nevertheless, and often acts out of passion rather than reason. He fights his brothers' attempts to betray Lancelot and Guenever and remains loyal to Lancelot because Lancelot has saved his life in the past. However, the death of Gareth turns him against Lancelot. Gawaine redeems himself at the end of the novel when, just before his death, he writes a long letter to Lancelot begging him to come to the aid of Arthur, who is fighting Mordred. He forgives Lancelot and begs his forgiveness as well.

Grummore Grummursum

Sir Grummore is a bumbling companion to King Pellinore, largely included in the book to provide comic relief.

Guenever

Queen Guenever is a beautiful and loving wife to King Arthur. Even when she falls deeply in love with Lancelot, she maintains her love for Arthur. White portrays her at times as foolish, selfish, and jealous; yet there is always a degree of sympathy for her. In addition, White allows her to age not always gracefully but somewhat realistically. Readers familiar with Malory know that eventually she will be separated from both Arthur and Lancelot to spend out her days repenting as a nun in a convent. This knowledge (and a future White includes in *The Book of Merlyn*) lends a sadness to Guenever's character throughout the entire novel.

Igraine

Igraine is initially the wife of the Gorlois, Duke of Cornwall, who is murdered by Uther Pendragon, who lusts for Igraine and becomes Igraine's second husband. She is the mother of Morgause and Morgan le Fay by Gorlois and of Arthur by Uther Pendragon.

Kay

Kay is Arthur's foster brother. He is portrayed as large, clumsy, and arrogant, often teasing the young Wart. In later books, he becomes the king's seneschal, or household administrator.

Lancelot

Lancelot is a young French knight who is devoted to Arthur. White depicts him as an incredibly ugly person with apelike features. He has a tendency toward cruelty, a characteristic he fights against constantly. Indeed, White tells the reader that he finds he can love Guenever only after he has hurt her. However, he is unable to kill opponents if they ask for mercy. Initially, he is so pure that he is able to work miracles, as in the case of Elaine of Corbin, whom he rescues from boiling water. After losing his virginity, however, he finds that his ability to work miracles is gone and he gives in to his passion for Guenever. Over the course of *The Once and Future King*, Lancelot goes mad several times and lives out in the woods. He is driven mad by his desire for Guenever, her rejection of him, and his loyalty to Arthur.

While Lancelot is unable to achieve the Grail himself, he witnesses the Grail knights Galahad, Bors, and Percival receive the holy vessel. In addition, his goodness is revealed when he is able to heal the wounds of Sir Urry, although he considered himself to be unworthy to do so.

King Lot

King Lot of Lothian and Orkney is the husband of Queen Morgause and the father of Agravaine, Gawaine, Gaheris, and Gareth.

Merlyn

Merlyn is a magician and sorcerer. He serves as Arthur's tutor when the king is a young man and is his mentor throughout his life. White makes Merlyn much more humorous than he is in Malory, although Merlyn can be quite daunting when crossed. Some critics suggest that White modeled Merlyn on himself: someone who values education and learning very highly but who is also eccentric and absentminded. Alone among the Arthurian sources, White makes Merlyn live backwards in time. Thus, he can tell the future because he has already lived it.

Mordred

Mordred is the son of Queen Morgause and her half brother Arthur. Born as a result of incest, Mordred is evil all the way through. White sees him almost as a young Nazi who gathers around him a mob of Fascist followers called the Thrashers. Mordred eventually brings down the Round Table by exposing the affair of Lancelot and Guenever and by trying to take control of England. In the final battle, both Arthur and Mordred are killed, a detail White does not describe in *The Once and Future King* but rather implies.

Morgan le Fay

Morgan le Fay is Morgause's sister and a sorceress.

Morgause

Morgause is the daughter of Igraine and Uther, the wife of King Lot, and the mother to Gawaine, Agravaine, Gareth, and Gaheris. There is no other character in *The Once and Future King* (except perhaps for Mordred) who is depicted viciously. She is beautiful, but also cunning. She uses magic and enchantments to manipulate Arthur and seduces him when he is in Orkney. Her upbringing of her sons leads to their psychological impairments and violent behavior.

The Narrator

While it is tempting to identify the voice telling the story of *The Once and Future King* with White, the narrator should be considered as a character as well. This voice passes judgment on the characters, the events, and the times. In addition, through the use of a narrator, White introduces his own political philosophy as well as many anachronisms. The narrator refers frequently to Malory, so the overall effect is of a garrulous grandfather retelling stories that he has read in a medieval text to the young people of the twentieth century.

Pellinore

King Pellinore is an old knight whose familial duty requires him to hunt the Questing Beast. He is a parody of a knight in shining armor.

Thomas of Warwick

At the end of the book, a young page named Thomas of Warwick listens to Arthur's tale of Camelot and vows to spread the story for the rest of his life. Arthur knights him, and the implication is that this is Sir Thomas Malory, who later in life wrote the book on which *The Once and Future King* is based. However, the historical Sir Thomas Malory lived during the fifteenth century and used as his sources texts that were far older than he. It is only in White's conceit that the young page grows into the chronicler of the Arthurian legend.

Uther Pendragon

Uther Pendragon is the king of England. White identifies him with William the Conqueror, a historical figure from Normandy who defeated the English at the Battle of Hastings in 1066. Clearly, White's depiction of Uther is a departure from historical fact. White paints Uther as a cruel man who takes what he wants when he wants it. When he lusts for the duchess of Cornwall, Igerne, he has her husband killed and uses magic to disguise himself as her dead husband. The result of this union is Arthur. When Arthur is born, Uther hands him over to Merlyn for fostering.

Wart

See Arthur

THEMES

Right and Might

One of the most important ideas that White follows throughout *The Once and Future King* is the relationship between right and might. That is, White explores the intertwining roles of justice, law, and power. Through Arthur, he traces a maturation of thought concerning what makes an action just, right, and lawful. White refers to rule by Fort Mayne several times in the novel; the words "Fort Mayne" mean force of arms. In such a rule, those who have the force of arms behind them have the ability to arbitrarily impose any laws or duties on the people under

TOPICS FOR FURTHER STUDY

- Create a timeline of British history from 1000 to 1500, marking the dates of the reigns of monarchs, famous battles, and other important events. On a parallel timeline, chart the major events in *The Once and Future King*. Illustrate your timeline with drawings and art. How has White used real events from history to frame his story? How does the legendary history White provides in *The Once and Future King* compare to the historical record?

- In *The Sword in the Stone*, Wart visits the animal kingdom on several occasions. Reread these sections carefully, and then construct a large poster that describes each of the systems of government Wart encounters in the animal world. What parallels can you draw between real human forms of government and the governments White creates for fish, falcons, ants, and geese?

- One of the most important texts in Middle English literature is *Sir Gawain and the Green Knight*, an Arthurian tale featuring Sir Gawain. Read a translation of this work. (An excellent one by Simon Armitage was published by W. W. Norton in 2008.) Write an essay in which you compare and contrast the character of Sir Gawaine in *The Once and Future King* and Sir Gawain in *Sir Gawain and the Green Knight*.

- Investigate King Arthur's family in a variety of sources, including Sir Thomas Malory's *Le Morte Darthur*, the writings of Geoffrey of Monmouth, the Arthurian romances of Chrétien de Troyes, Marion Zimmer Bradley's *The Mists of Avalon*, and other contemporary sources. After doing so, construct several poster-sized family trees for Arthur, demonstrating the differences among the sources you consulted. How do you account for the differences?

- Although *The Once and Future King* is essentially a novel about men, there are three very important female characters in the book: Guenever, Morgause, and Elaine. Additionally, White includes a brief section featuring Morgan le Fay. How does White characterize these women? Write an essay discussing White's depiction of women in *The Once and Future King*.

---

them. In such cases, it is the might or power that makes an action right because the powerful have the ability to impose their will on others. Thus, in one of Arthur's early lessons in political science he discovers that some believe that might makes right.

Arthur later understands that this system causes untold pain and suffering to many people. He decides that it is not a workable, fair, or just system of government. He next turns to the formulation "Might for Right." In this configuration, powerful people can use their strength of arms to fight for the good. For example, the Knights of the Round Table can use their prowess in battle to protect the weak. In so doing, he establishes a kind of justice.

Arthur discovers, however, that violence begets violence. Violence is still violence, even when used to accomplish a good deed. He decides that the only way to corral force is to set it on a spiritual journey. He thus devises the quest for the Holy Grail, believing that he is sending his knights on a quest that will curb their wickedness.

The Grail Quest does not accomplish anything, however. Those who are pure are lost to the world, while those who are wicked remain wicked. Finally, Arthur sets up courts of justice. Right is now defined not by force of arms but by force of law. This is the system in place in democratic countries. White seems to say that while it is not perfect, it is the best flawed humanity can manage.

*Roddy McDowell as Mordred, Julie Andrews as Guinever, and Robert Goulet as Lancelot in a
Broadway stage production of* Camelot *(© Bettmann / Corbis)*

Chivalry and Courtesy

The tension between chivalry and courtesy reso-
nates throughout *The Once and Future King* as
well as the entire Arthurian saga. The word *chivalry*
is derived from the French word for horseman,
chevalier. It originally described the conduct befit-
ting a warrior on horseback, generally an upper-
class man. Many of the virtues of chivalry had their
earliest expressions in the oaths of fealty a vassal
would swear to his lord. A chivalrous knight, there-
fore, would be loyal to his lord, act bravely, and put
his life before that of his lord. In addition, a chiv-
alrous knight would honor bravery and courage in
others as well as valuing it in himself.

The word *courtesy* had a significantly differ-
ent meaning in the Middle Ages than it has in
the twenty-first century. Now when someone is
called courteous, it simply means that he or she is
polite. However, in the Middle Ages, courtesy

was a much more comprehensive term, meaning
all of those forms of behavior that were fitting
for someone of courtly culture. This included
everything from dress, to food, to conversation.
In addition, by the twelfth century, the element
of courtly love had been conflated with courtesy.
Thus, interaction between men and women of
the court was dictated by the codes of courtesy.

In *The Once and Future King*, Lancelot is a
chivalric knight who is pledged to King Arthur.
His brave deeds reflect on his king, and he has
sworn an oath of loyalty to Arthur. At the same
time, he is in love with Guenever, to whom he
must display courtesy. In order to be courteous
to Guenever, however, he must betray his liege
lord, Arthur, and violate the codes of chivalry. In
order to behave according to the codes of chivalry,
he must forsake Guenever, thus violating the codes
of courtesy. (It is little wonder that he goes mad on
more than one occasion.)

STYLE

Anachronism

An anachronism is anything in a work of literature that is not placed in its proper historical time. *The Once and Future King* is famous for its many anachronisms. Some of them are included in the text as a result of the device of Merlyn's living backward in time. Therefore, he can say and do things that reference future times. Other anachronisms are rooted in the strange mix of real and fictional history White includes in the book. For example, most of the setting appears to be in the High Middle Ages, a period that extends roughly from 1000 to 1300. White refers to real English monarchs who ruled during that time, such as Edward I, who ruled from 1272 to 1307. At the same time, Pellinore states at Uther's death, "Uther the Conqueror, 1066 to 1216." The first anachronistic problem is that according to this reckoning, Uther would have been 150 years old at the time of his death. Secondly, White conflates Uther with the historical William the Conqueror, the Norman duke who invaded England and defeated the Anglo-Saxons at the Battle of Hastings. William ruled until his death in 1087. Likewise, if Arthur began his rule in 1216, as the text says, how then could he have made the acquaintance of the young Thomas Malory, who was not even born until about 1405? In effect, White compresses the entire Middle Ages, a period that lasted some four hundred years, into about twenty-five years. In so doing, he credits the shifts in culture and society that occur during the Middles Ages to Arthur's rule. The effect is both to root the story in reality and also firmly to establish *The Once and Future King* as fantasy.

White also engages in anachronistic language throughout the book. Often his characters will slip into Malory's language. For example, when Lancelot is caught in Guenever's room, he says, "Is there any armour in the chamber . . . that I might cover my body withal?" Malory, in the same scene, gives these words to Lancelot: "Madame . . . ys there here ony armoure within you that myght cover my body withall?" Clearly, the two passages are nearly identical. Yet only a few lines later, White puts these words in Lancelot's mouth: "If only I had my armour . . . it seems ridiculous to be caught like a rat in a trap." This is very modern language, right down to the cliché. In Malory, Lancelot says, "Alas! . . . in all my lyff thus was I never bestad that I shulde be thus shamefully slayne, for lake of myn armoure." This example illustrates White's continual shifting between the "high" language of Malory and the common language of the mid-twentieth century. Some readers find this shift disconcerting, while others find it both amusing and interesting. Regardless, the anachronistic language serves both to place *The Once and Future King* within the tradition of Arthurian literature and also to break with that tradition.

Aristotelian Tragedy

Aristotle was a famous Greek philosopher who lived between 384 and 322 BCE. One of his best known works is a treatise on literature called *Poetics*. In this work, he defines and describes tragedy. Aristotle writes that tragedy should cause the audience to experience both fear and pity, thereby allowing catharsis to take place. (Catharsis simply means a cleansing of emotion, in this case fear and pity.) Tragedy, in the Aristotelian sense, must include a tragic hero, who is someone of high standing and who suffers a fall due to some unexpected and catastrophic occurrence. The hero must be of high enough stature that his fall is very dramatic. In addition, for Aristotle, the hero must neither be too good or too bad. In either case, the audience would fail to identify with the hero, and therefore not experience catharsis.

White states directly in *The Once and Future King* that the story of Arthur is an Aristotelian tragedy. For this reason, he emphasizes all sides of Arthur's personality. He is not an overly virtuous person in that he allows himself to be seduced by Morgause and he subsequently kills a lot of baby boys in an attempt to cheat fate. But he is not a villain, either. He struggles with issues of right and wrong, in the same way that most humans do. Finally, because he successfully becomes King, unites all of Britain, and establishes the rule of law, he is in a very high position when the sins of his youth and his earlier errors of judgment catch up with him. His fall, then, is a mighty one, and one that provokes great fear and pity in its readers.

HISTORICAL CONTEXT

Fascism and Communism

When White was first writing the books that would be collected as *The Once and Future King*, fascism was growing in strength in Germany, Italy, and Japan while Communism was practiced in Russia, then known as the Soviet Union. Essentially, fascism is an ideology that favors a strong,

COMPARE
&
CONTRAST

- **1200s:** Feudalism is the most common political arrangement in western Europe, with land in control of local lords. Serfs produce all needed food and materials while the lords provide protection. China, on the other hand, has a strong centralized government with power resting in the emperor and his officials.

  1950s: Democracy, practiced in most countries of Europe and in the United States, and Communism, practiced in the Soviet Union and China, are the dominant political structures in the world.

  Today: While Communist governments continue to exist (most notably in China), most first-world nations are democratic.

- **1200s:** Songs and stories about King Arthur and his knights are popular throughout Europe, particularly in the royal courts of France.

  1950s: Writers as varied as T. H. White, John Steinbeck, and, slightly later, Mary Stewart keep the Arthurian tradition alive with their books. In 1960, White's book becomes the basis of the popular stage musical *Camelot*.

  Today: Arthur continues to be a popular subject for films, such as *King Arthur* (2004) and *First Knight* (1995), and books. Parodies of the Arthurian legend are also popular, including the stage musical *Spamalot*, based on the 1975 film *Monty Python and the Holy Grail*.

- **1200s:** In the Western world, tournaments and jousting are sporting events attended by common folk and royalty as well.

  1950s: Professional sports are gaining in popularity in the United States and Europe. Soccer, in particular, is widely viewed in Britain.

  Today: Professional sports are wildly popular around the world. Team colors, fans, and cheerleaders recall the medieval spectacle of the tournament.

---

nationalistic, central government headed by a single, autocratic ruler. Often, fascist states are also militaristic. In a fascist state, individual rights are denied, and the good of the state is put before the good of the individual. Communism, in its ideal form, is a socioeconomic system that strives for an egalitarian, classless society where all goods are held in common by all people. In the Soviet Union, however, Joseph Stalin established a dictatorial Communist rule in which all actions of all citizens were monitored and closely controlled. Individual freedoms were stringently curtailed.

White greatly opposed both fascism and Communism and used *The Once and Future King* as a way of expressing that opposition. The scene in which Wart is placed in the Mews, for example, illustrates a militaristic, dictatorial system where an insane ruler holds everyone's life in balance. Likewise, the scene in which Wart enters the world of the ants also demonstrates White's opposition to both fascism and Communism. White himself wrote that he saw Communism and fascism as essentially differing degrees of the same system, as reported by several of his biographers. While writing in the late 1930s and early 1940s, White saw the threat of Adolf Hitler in Germany and Benito Mussolini in Italy to be prime; however, by the time he revised these early books and wrote *The Candle in the Wind*, the cold war had begun and western Europe and the United States found themselves pitted against the Communist regime in the Soviet Union and its satellite nations. Thus, the experience with the ants seems almost like that described by George Orwell in *1984*, a book aimed at the growing power of the state in the Soviet Union.

Sir Thomas Malory

White borrowed heavily from Sir Thomas Malory's *Le Morte Darthur*, completed in 1469 or 1470 and

King Arthur *(Archive Photos. Reproduced by permission.)*

first published by William Caxton in 1485, one of the first books to be published in England. Indeed, White frequently refers to Malory in *The Once and Future King*. In discussing the Grail quest, for example, he writes, "If you want to read about the beginning of the Quest for the Gail, about the wonders of Galahad's arrival... and of the last supper at court, when the thunder came and the sunbeam and the covered vessel and the sweet smell through the Great Hall—if you want to read about these, you must seek them in Malory."

But who was Thomas Malory? Most scholars now agree that the writer of *Le Morte Darthur* must have been Sir Thomas Malory of Newbold Revel in Warwickshire, who lived from about 1416 to 1471. What is known of Malory comes mostly from legal records. He was a knight who served with the earl of Warwick. In 1450 to 1451, according to D. S. Brewer in the introduction to *Malory: The Morte Darthur*, he was charged and imprisoned for serious crimes, including cattle stealing, theft, and rape. After being pardoned, he served as a member of Parliament. Later, Malory found himself caught between contesting sides during the Wars of the Roses. Consequently, he was imprisoned for many years off and on as power shifted between the Houses of York and Lancaster, two families competing for the kingship of England. During this time, he took it upon himself to gather as many copies

of the Arthurian stories from as many different sources as he could. Notably, he drew from the French Vulgate (which he translated) as well as the English alliterative *Morte Arthure* as well as from other sources. His task was monumental; yet he successfully wove together the strands of the Arthurian legend as it had developed across Europe. Most scholars agree that Malory's work was largely responsible for the revival of interest in King Arthur and provides the link between medieval and contemporary renderings of the legend.

CRITICAL OVERVIEW

White was a writer who, while popular in his own day, has received less critical attention than one might expect, according to French literary critic François Gallix in his essay in *King Arthur: A Casebook* (edited and translated by Edward Donald Kennedy). Gallix suggests that White's broad interests may have worked against his acceptance by critics. At the time of White's death, a writer for the London *Times*, the leading newspaper in England, stated that White was "a writer of originality and distinction with an outlook which had more in common with the nineteenth than with the middle of the twentieth century."

The critical history of *The Once and Future King* extends over decades, as White released segments of the novel as stand-alone books in the late 1930s and early 1940s. *The Sword in the Stone*, published in 1938, received nearly universal praise, with minor reservations, from contemporary critics, who seemed to not know quite what to make of the volume. Beatrice Sherman, in a review appearing in the *New York Times* on January 1, 1939, writes, "It is an excellent book, a grand book. But since it is like no other book that one can think of, it is hard to hand it the highest honors in any class. Perhaps it would be safe to say that it is the most heartily enjoyable work on King Arthur's boyhood that ever was written." In another review appearing in the *New York Times* on January 2, 1939, critic Ralph Thompson writes, "The flavor of the book comes from the comedy and nonsense on page after page, some of it wearisome, perhaps, but most of it elegant and well sustained."

When White completed his fourth book in the series, *The Candle in the Wind*, he also chose to significantly revise his earlier Arthurian books, *The Sword in the Stone*, *The Witch in the Wood* (retitled *The Queen of Air and Darkness*), and *The Ill-Made Knight*. After completing this task, he combined the four volumes into one book, publishing it as *The Once and Future King*. Again, contemporary reviews were largely favorable, even if critics were at a loss as to how to describe the work. Orville Prescott, writing in the *New York Times*, calls it a "masterpiece." He continues, "How, then, to describe this indescribable book? . . . . [White's] book is vast, disorderly, neither one thing nor another, an artistic hodgepodge. But what an exhilarating hodgepodge!"

Critics since 1958 have been overall less charitable toward the book. In *Arthurian Romance: A Short Introduction* (2003), Derek Pearsall argues that the book exhibits "naive social idealism." He argues, "Anyone who got their history [from *The Once and Future King*] would need their brains unscrambled," concluding that "there is much for the grown-up reader to dislike in *The Once and Future King*—the cultivated quaintness, the conscious anachronisms that he means us to smile at and find charming . . . and the whole world of prep schools."

In spite of such negative criticism, virtually every academic scholar studying the Arthurian cycle comments on *The Once and Future King*, suggesting that its importance to literary studies is formidable. Novelist Anthony Burgess, for example, includes *The Once and Future King* in *99 Novels: The Best in English Since 1939*. It is likely that most readers and scholars will agree with Elisabeth Brewer, who writes in *T. H. White's "The Once and Future King"* (1993) that it is "the book by which T. H. White will be remembered. It reflects his own protean nature: it is the work of a sad man who also saw the funny side of things. . . . Our encounter with White's flamboyant personality and his total commitment to his story makes for a uniquely engaging Arthurian experience."

CRITICISM

Diane Andrews Henningfeld

Henningfeld is a professor emerita of English who holds a Ph.D. in medieval literature. In the following essay, she traces the changing conception of Arthur from early Welsh sources to T. H. White's The Once and Future King.

When T. H. White sat down to begin his saga of King Arthur and the Knights of the Round table during the dark days of the late 1930s, the

> **FOR WHITE, AS FOR MALORY, THE VALOR, GLAMOUR, AND ROMANCE OF THE ARTHURIAN COURT, AND THE PROMISE OF ARTHUR'S RETURN TO REDEEM HIS NATION, SERVED AS AN INSPIRATION IN DARK AND DIFFICULT TIMES."**

stories he was about to tell were already over one thousand years old. The first mention of Arthur dates back to anonymous Welsh sources as early as the year 600; there are other, even older, references to a hero who has been identified with Arthur dating from 547. Thus, White's conception of Arthur draws on not only the writer's imagination but also on the work of long-dead, often unnamed writers, who themselves drew on centuries of tradition. Indeed, the stories of Arthur exist widely in cultures and languages other than English. These stories are the result of centuries of reworking the Arthurian cycle to address cultural concerns and anxieties. The Arthurian legend seems particularly adaptable to a wide variety of circumstances, and for this reason, it continues to draw readers and writers alike. Tracing the origins of the legend and identifying crucial shifts in the characterizations of Arthur across the years can provide a clearer notion, then, of how and why White's depiction became the quintessential portrait of Arthur in the twentieth century.

The first question students raise about Arthur, as Norris J. Lacey and Geoffrey Ashe note in *The Arthurian Handbook*, is this: Was King Arthur a real person? Although Ashe and others have made a valiant effort to establish a historical record for a person named Arthur who was a ruler and a hero, the records are frustratingly hazy. What is certain, however, is that if Arthur existed, he was not the monarch contemporary readers picture him as. Rather, he would likely have been the leader of Romanized Celtic Britons, who fought against the waves of Saxon invaders that ultimately conquered the British Isles after the Roman Empire withdrew their troops in 410. There is evidence that the Britons were successful in holding off the Saxons for a period of time under a strong leader called Ambrosius Aurelianus, who may or may not have

WHAT DO I READ NEXT?

- *The Goshawk*, written by White in 1951, is a nonfiction account of his work training falcons, drawn primarily from journals he kept during the process.

- After his death, White's last novel concerning King Arthur, *The Book of Merlyn*, was published in 1977. A dark and brooding epilogue to *The Once and Future King*, it is of interest to those readers who want to understand how White envisioned tying up the loose ends of his previous novels.

- In *The Discovery of King Arthur* (1985; reprinted 2005), respected scholar Geoffrey Ashe examines the evidence for the historical reality of King Arthur. A fascinating, accessible study, this book is both controversial and entertaining.

- Marion Zimmer Bradley's *The Mists of Avalon* (1984) remains one of the most important retellings of the Arthurian story in the twentieth century. Told from the point of view of Morgaine, also known as Morgan le Fay, this novel offers a female perspective on Arthur and his court.

- In 1889, Mark Twain published *A Connecticut Yankee in King Arthur's Court*, a book that is at once a broad comedy and a biting social satire.

- The most important redaction of the Arthurian cycle in the nineteenth century was Alfred, Lord Tennyson's *Idylls of the King*. Written in verse and based on Malory, the book was published in segments between 1859 and 1885. A shorter poem, "The Lady of Shalott," published in 1832, is Tennyson's characterization of Elaine of Astolat, who dies for her love of Lancelot.

- One of the finest introductions to Arthurian romance for general readers is Derek Pearsall's *Arthurian Romance: A Short Introduction* (2003). Written in clear, concise language, this book is a wonderful starting point for any student interested in learning more about the literature of King Arthur.

- Joseph Goering's *The Virgin and the Grail: Origins of a Legend* (2005) is an excellent, credible introduction to the Grail legend that includes full-color prints of paintings and stained glass windows depicting the Grail.

been the model for the literary creation of Arthur. It should be remembered here that this period was nothing like the High Middle Ages with its royal courts, tournaments, chivalry, and courtly love. Rather, this was a rugged period of wars and battles fought by small bands of men.

The first mention of a hero by the name of Arthur occurs in a Welsh source dating from around 600 called the *Gododdin*, as noted by Ashe, Derek Pearsall in his *Arthurian Romance: A Short Introduction*, and James J. Wilhelm in *The Romance of Arthur*, among many other scholars. This hero circulates throughout early Welsh literature, most of it oral. This Arthur is the leader of a band of heroes who travel around doing great deeds of derring-do of a legendary and magical nature.

According to Pearsall, "In later Welsh legend, Arthur has the reputation of a warrior of superhuman powers, not particularly virtuous, in fact not virtuous at all, and certainly not a Christian." The Welsh Arthur bears more resemblance to White's depiction of the Orkney clan than to his conception of Arthur. Indeed, the names of the Welsh Arthur's companions include Kei, Bedwyr, and Gwalchmai, Welsh for Kay, Bedivere, and Gawain.

The first appearance of Arthur in a history text is in that by Geoffrey of Monmouth, written between 1130 and 1136. Pearsall writes that Geoffrey's Latin *Historia regum Britanniae* (History of the Kings of Britain) is "one of the most influential books ever written." This text exists in over two hundred manuscripts; given that only one in perhaps twenty manuscripts ever survive, this is a huge number of surviving copies, suggesting that the book was not only popular and widespread but also highly valued.

Geoffrey's book includes an extended section about Arthur, comprising about 25 percent of the entire book. Merlin is also included in the book, the first connection between Arthur and Merlin. Likewise, Gawain, Kay, Bedivere, and Mordred all figure in Geoffrey's account. Also included are the stories of Uther and Ygerna (Igraine in White), Arthur's marriage to Guenevere (Guenever in White), and descriptions of his battles. In Geoffrey, Arthur is depicted as a stalwart military commander who meets with great success on the field of battle. Arthur's campaign to Rome and Mordred's betrayal at home are also in the book, as are the details of Arthur's wounding and carrying away to Avalon.

It is difficult to overestimate how important Geoffrey is to the later redactions of the Arthurian legend. Wace, an Anglo-Norman writer, presented a copy of his French translation and adaptation of Geoffrey's book to Queen Eleanor of Aquitaine in 1155, thereby spreading the tales of Arthur to France and beyond. Wace's Arthur was similar to Geoffrey's, although there is a growing emphasis on chivalry and courtliness. Wace's work is more dramatic than Geoffrey's. Wilhelm opines that Wace is "weakest in scenes of violence and valor." although he "excels in dramatic episodes, such as King Uther's wooing of Igerna." In this regard, White can be more closely aligned with Wace's version of the story than with Geoffrey's.

In England, a lone monk named Layamon used Wace's version of Geoffrey as his source material for the first complete rendering of the story of Arthur in English, *Brut*. Layamon wrote in an English that was nearly archaic even in his own time, around 1190, and closer to Anglo-Saxon than other Middle English texts of the time. In addition, Laymon wrote in an outdated form, the alliterative verse of the Anglo-Saxons, similar to that found in texts such as *Beowulf*. In Laymon's version, Arthur is a strong and very English hero, known for his valor and his strength of arms. He has no interest in court or love, but is rather a poet of action, as Wilhelm argues. Because Layamon has no real interest in the internal lives of his characters, he is not much of a model for White, except that he is the first of the storytellers who includes the mystical accounting of Arthur's death.

After being wounded, Arthur states that he will go to Avalon to Morgan, who will heal his wounds. Layamon closes the poem stating that Britons continue to believe that Arthur lives with the faeries on Avalon and will one day return to save the British people. While *The Once and Future King* closes with Arthur just before the battle, White draws on the legend of the return of Arthur for his closing epitaph as well as for the book's title.

Back in France, a poet in the court of Marie de Champagne, Chrétien de Troyes (c. 1135–83), continued what Wace had started: the transformation of a story about a military commander and his men into a story about lovely ladies and the valiant knights who adored the lovely ladies. It is Chrétien who actually invented the Arthurian romance, the most significant shift in the story since Geoffrey. Lancelot first enters the saga in the romances of Chrétien and soon becomes the best of Arthur's knights, supplanting Gawain in that role. The love affair of Guenevere and Lancelot also has its roots in these romances. Arthur, on the other hand, is weaker than his earlier representations. He becomes a husband whose wife betrays him with his best friend. In addition, Arthur begins the movement away from actively participating in adventures to someone who listens to tales of adventures. White's novel owes much to Chrétien. White's Arthur demonstrates the weakening of Arthur as the book progresses. The longer the affair between Lancelot and Guenevere continues, the weaker Arthur becomes.

The stories of Arthur and his knights spread across Europe, based largely on the French romances. In England, however, according to Pearsall, by the "late fourteenth century there are two Arthurian traditions.... The one tradition represents Arthur as a national hero, a battle-leader, a historical king." Pearsall goes on to explain that the other tradition is the one that took root in France and then was reintroduced into England, that of the courtly Arthurian romance. Arthur is no longer a vital force in these new romances but rather serves only as the administrator of Camelot, someone who sends the knights out on quests and greets them when they return, ready to hear their stories. This tendency can be seen in *The Once and Future King*, especially after Arthur conceives of the Grail Quest. It seems that his major role is to listen to the returning knights tell of their adventures.

The most important event in the transmission of the Arthurian saga from the Middle Ages to modern times occurred in the fifteenth century.

Around 1469, Sir Thomas Malory completed a work he called *The Whole Book of King Arthur and of His Noble Knights of the Round Table*. The work is remarkable on many counts: In the first place, it is an amazingly comprehensive piece of work. Malory used sources from both the English and French, most notably the English alliterative *Morte Darthur* and the French Vulgate cycle. In the case of the former, Brewer notes, he "suppressed much of the heroic Gawain, and in turn exalted Lancelot, inventing new episodes to his glory." At the same time, Malory maintains Arthur as a strong and valiant king. Of note also is that Malory was a prisoner during the time he wrote his book, ending each section with pleas to the reader to pray for his deliverance. That White found Malory's vision of the Arthurian legend compelling goes without saying; he frequently refers directly to Malory in the pages of *The Once and Future King*, and often slips into the very language Malory uses.

Malory is slightly cagey about the legend of Arthur's return, however. He closes the *The Morte Darthur* with poignant words that reach out across the centuries:

> Yet som men say in many partys of Inglonde that kynge Arthure ys nat ded, but had by the wyll of oure Lorde Jesu into another place; and men say that he shall come agayne, and he shall wynne the Holy Crosse. Yet I woll nat say that hit shall be so, but rather I wolde sey: here in thys worlde he chaunged his lyff. And many men say that there ys wrytten uppon the tumbe thys: HIC IACET ARTHURUS, REX QUONDAM REXQUE FUTURUS.

> [Yet some men say in many parts of England that King Arthur is not dead, but has been taken to another place by the will of our lord Jesus; and men say that he shall come again, and he shall win the Holy Cross. Yet I will not say that it shall be so, but rather I would say: her in this world he changed his life. And many men say that there is written upon the tomb this: HERE LIES ARTHUR, FORMER KING, FUTURE KING]

White seems much more certain of Arthur's return, closing his book with the words "The Beginning." Most critics agree that Malory's work is the stronger of the two, although all agree that White's is a formidable achievement.

Why did T. H. White look to Malory when planning his own epic? Malory's work has remained an important force ever since its writing. D. S. Brewer writes in the introduction to *Malory: The Morte Darthur*,

The Arthurian tales, that mixture of myth, adventure, love-story, enchantment, and tragedy, live in [Malory's] work as the essence of medieval romance, yet always with a contemporary relevance. This combination of romantic remoteness with contemporary relevance was true even in his own day. He wrote in ... a period of sagging confidence, and bewildering change, when England's empire had been almost entirely lost.

Brewer could have been describing England at the close of World War II and during the years that White constructed his major work. For White, as for Malory, the valor, glamour, and romance of the Arthurian court, and the promise of Arthur's return to redeem his nation, served as an inspiration in dark and difficult times.

Source: Diane Andrews Henningfeld, Critical Essay on *The Once and Future King*, in *Novels for Students*, Gale, Cengage Learning, 2010.

Michael Cart
In the following essay, Cart discusses The Once and Future King *and the romantic ideal of Camelot.*

It's spring and, to paraphrase Tennyson, this young man's fancy has turned lightly to thoughts of ... housecleaning! For me, this means hiring a latter-day St. George to slay the evil dragon Grout that's taken over my bathroom tile. Meanwhile, I'm busy doing my part: cleaning up my files and dusting my bookshelves.

Rummaging in the stack of files, I happened on an article clipped from the November 5, 2005, *New York Times* headlined "Science and Religion Share Fascination in Things Unseen," by Lawrence M. Kraus. It contains the following paragraph, which I had highlighted on my first reading:

> "It seems that humans are hardwired to yearn for new realms well beyond the reach of our senses into which we can escape, if only with our minds. It is possible that we need to rely on such possibilities or the world of our experience would become intolerable."

Kraus may have been writing about religion, but has there ever been a more compelling argument for the importance of fantasy, science fiction, and that modern amalgam of the two that we've taken to calling "speculative fiction"? That is, books that specialize in "things unseen" and "new realms well beyond the reach of our senses."

Coincidentally, my rediscovery of this article comes on a day when I've been working my way through my collection of fairy tales and folklore. Frankly, I was never a big fan of either when I was a kid; I found Hans Christian Andersen depressing and thought the Brothers Grimm were downright scary, but this hasn't stopped me from assembling a wide-ranging collection of editions of their respective work along with half a dozen shelves of tales and lore from other hands (and lands). Poring over these books, I made an especially poignant discovery on the third shelf from the top: there was a long-neglected copy of a childhood favorite: Kenneth Grahame's *The Reluctant Dragon*, a wonderfully whimsical tale that first appeared as a chapter in the author's collection *Dream Days*. It's the story of a boy, an avid reader with a special fondness for natural history and fairy tales, who meets a dragon that is quite unlike the one that's laying waste to my modern-day plumbing. Grahame's is an affable, friendly dragon terrified by the prospect of having to duke it out with St. George. Of course, I had to take time off from dusting to reread the story, and, finishing it with a contented sigh, I placed it back on the shelf and then, on the next shelf down, my eyes fell on my rather ragtag collection of books about another knight in burnished armor, King Arthur.

Hot dog! I may not have cared much for fairy tales, but I absolutely adored the stories of the once and future king, his stalwart knights of the Round Table, and his shining court at Camelot. This was due, in large part, to my having discovered the Arthurian cycle not in the indecipherable words of Sir Thomas Malory ("Then were there no mo that durst be so hardy to set their hands thereto." Huh?) or in the poetry of Tennyson's *Idylls of the King* (what the heck were Idylls?) but, instead, in the four-volume retelling of author-artist Howard Pyle. Yet, even there, the lure wasn't the words but Pyle's amazing black-and-white drawings.

It wasn't until I was in high school that I finally found the version that completely captured my heart, my mind, and my imagination. It was, of course, T. H. White's incomparable *The Once and Future King*, his masterful reworking of his earlier four-volume novelization that included *The Sword in the Stone* (which I had discovered in junior-high school) and three additional volumes: *The Witch in the Wood*, *The Ill-Made Knight*, and *The Candle in the Wind*. Published in 1958 when I was a junior in high school, the resulting one-volume epic was, for me, an unforgettable reading experience.

My personal connection to White's great work goes beyond reading his words. For five years in the late 1960s and early '70s, my day job may have been director of the Logansport-Cass County (IN) Public Library, but my evenings (and weekends) belonged to the Logansport Civic Players. During that half-decade as an amateur actor, I played many parts, including Felix Unger in *The Odd Couple*, the title role in *Life with Father*, and many more. But the one I enjoyed the most, the one I think of as "the perfect part," was King Pellinore in *Camelot*, Lerner and Loewe's musical-comedy version of *The Once and Future King*. Playing that part is the principal reason I decided to give up the day job and move to California in hopes of becoming a professional actor. One of the first parts I reprised when I got to L.A. was, you guessed it, King Pellinore. I don't know how many evenings I stood in the wings during the final scene, crying like a baby as I waited to go onstage. Because my cue to enter stage right was Arthur's singing the words, "Don't let it be forgot / That once there was a spot / For one brief shining moment that was known / As Camelot."

Call me an incurable romantic, but I believe that Camelot—the place, the musical, the *idea* that has so captured the imagination since Malory wrote about it in the fifteenth century—represents the perfect fantasy, the quintessential new realm into which we can escape.

In White's version, especially, there is a quality of innocent delight that is irresistible, but surely any version of the timeless legend proves there is no better place—to borrow another phrase from Lerner and Loewe—for "happily ever-aftering" than there in Camelot.

Source: Michael Cart, "The Camelot Connection," in *Booklist*, May 15, 2006, p. 42.

Stephen P. Dunn

In the following excerpt, Dunn compares The Once and Future King *to the Arthurian poems by British poet Charles Williams.*

Among the recurring myths of Western man, adapted by each succeeding age to its own needs and tastes, one of the most persistent is the Arthurian cycle. Two of the more interesting current revivals of this cycle are T. H. White's *The Once and Future King* and the Arthurian poems by the British poet, novelist, and theologian Charles Williams (1886–1945).

"

Both White and Williams (to say nothing of other writers, like Eliot, who handle the same subject matter more tangentially), despite their differences, show a profound distaste for the modern world, its values, preoccupations, and achievements. Neither White nor Williams says, as many modern thinkers do, that our age is a bad one because it has failed to realize its own ideals; on this score, no age was any better. On the contrary, both say in very different ways that the ideals themselves are all wrong. Neither White nor Williams seems, as do most of the Beats and Angry Young Men, to be complaining nihilistically or out of cosmic pique. Each makes his critique on a firm philosophical basis: in Williams' case radically Christian, in both senses of the word "radical"; in White's, for want of a better term, Stoic; but in both cases basically hardheaded, humane, and broadly inclusive—indeed, omnivorous.

On several counts, White and Williams might seem an odd pair to yoke together. *The Once and Future King* is a novel or series of novels, though far from conventional in form or matter; Williams' "Arthuriad" is a cycle of separate poems, mostly short, some narrative, others lyrico-philosophical, quite various in form, and neither written nor published in consecutive order relative to the story they collectively tell. Furthermore, Williams left his work incomplete at his death; the corpus consists of two books of verse—*Taliessin through Logres* (1938) and *The Region of the Summer Stars* (1944)—and the posthumous prose fragment "The Figure of Arthur." This is part literary history of the Arthurian cycle, and part imaginative reconstruction of the actual circumstances on which it may have been based. "The Figure of Arthur" was published, together with a quite elaborate commentary on the poems, by C. S. Lewis as *The Arthurian Torso* (1946).

White and Williams, then, were not by any means trying to do the same thing, even assuming that both of them had been able to carry out their intentions fully. Still, starting from viewpoints which might seem diametrically opposed, both reach closely similar conclusions—White's expressed in terms of quite down-to-earth politics, Williams' in terms of a complex and highly personal poetic symbolism. Finally, the two writers handle the myth in entirely different ways and show sharply contrasting attitudes toward history.

The Once and Future King is one of those books which is a world, in which almost every reader can find something to his taste. Its locale is a generalized, idealized medieval Britain, which the author obviously does not intend to be taken as a picture of any actual country in any actual historical epoch. Yet despite the idealization White's Britain is firmly grounded in physical and social reality. Those elements of the marvellous and romantic which were so prominent in Arthurian literature from Malory to Tennyson and even beyond are here scaled down to human, and humorous, terms. Where fantasy enters, it is not taken seriously, but put in with an indulgent chuckle and a dig in the reader's ribs. White's humor is arch, whimsical, peculiarly British—a little like Lewis Carroll, but without his faintly horrifying surrealism. The first appearance of Merlyn, in fact, bears a marked resemblance to the entrance of the White Rabbit:

> There was a well in front of the cottage, and the metallic noise which the Wart had heard was caused by a very old gentleman who was drawing water out of it by means of a handle and chain.
>
> Clank, clank, clank, went the chain, until the bucket hit the lip of the well, and "Drat the whole thing!" said the old gentleman. "You would think that after all these years of study you could do better for yourself than a by-our-lady well with a by-our-lady bucket, whatever the by-our-lady cost.
>
> "By this and by that," added the old gentleman, heaving his bucket out of the well with a malevolent glance, "why can't they get us the electric light and company's water?"

(Merlyn, it should be explained, lives backwards, so that he knows what, in our terms, is going to happen, but not what has happened. "The Wart" is Arthur's nickname as a small boy.) The old-fashioned knights—like the fox-huntin' Sir Grummore Grummursum, the dim-witted King Pellinore, who spends his life pursuing the amorous and complicated Questing

Beast, and Arthur's foster-father Sir Ector—talk like upper-class Dorothy Sayers characters; Sir Palomides, the Saracen knight, speaks the lotus-flavored English of a Bengali *baby* out of Kipling. At times, White does not disdain even the frankly Walt Disney touch, as in the scene where the Wart is turned, at his own request, into a fish—the first phase of his formal education:

> Merlyn took off his hat, raising his staff of lignum vitae politely in the air, and said slowly, "Snylrem stnemilpmoc ot enutpen dna lliw eh yldnik tpecca siht yob sa a hsif?"

> Immediately there was a loud blowing of sea-shells, conches and so forth, and a stout, jolly-looking gentleman appeared seated on a well-blown-up cloud above the battlements. He had an anchor tattoed on his stomach and a handsome mermaid with Mabel written under her on his chest. He ejected a quid of tobacco, nodded affably to Merlyn, and pointed his trident at the Wart.

White said in an interview when *The Once and Future King* was first published that the humor was put in to make the moral and philosophical pill—which, in all conscience, is a fairly bitter one—slide down more easily. If this is true, so much the worse for the book as a work of art. But, with all respect to the learned and cantankerous author, I think he is kidding us—if not himself—at this point. I do not think he is really a sermonizer, and I think he means something more, and something less obvious, by his innocent-seeming and rather Edwardian japes. Laughter is the voice of the freely-working intellect, and its first message is proportion: when we laugh, we limit the extent to which our passions can be involved—or at least the extent to which they control our actions. By poking consistent, gentle fun at his story, White puts the reader on notice that this is not high tragedy, or even high romance; that he is giving us the world and life as they are—grubby, seedy, inconclusive, with the best intentions usually yielding the worst results—and not as some tragedian or romancer with an eschatological turn of mind (such as Charles Williams, for instance) would like them to be. He indicates as much when he says that there were dragons in the forest around Sir Ector's castle, where Arthur grew up, but "these were small ones, which lived under rocks and could hiss like a kettle."

White's selection of material—and his handling of material which he finds embarrassing or repugnant, but in the nature of his story cannot avoid—is highly revealing, both of his powers and of his limitations. The whole Tristram-Iseult affair is barely mentioned, and then only at third hand, as a tawdry and distressing scandal. In fact, like most modern writers, White seems ill-at-ease with sex, at least in its more "normal" and straightforward aspects. With courtly love, which he regards as an institutionalized neurosis, he does quite well, up to a point. The Lancelot-Guenevere story, for example, is treated with discretion and sympathy, but remains peripheral to the action as a whole (whereas Williams makes it metaphysically central, while actually saying almost nothing about it).

The essential limitations of White's method appear most strongly in his version of the Grail Quest. He presents this as what we would call a kind of propaganda operation—a device invented by Arthur to hold his Round Table together and keep it functioning at a time when its original objective, the establishment of an order of temporal justice, had already been achieved, and the energies of its members were finding no adequate outlet and turning sour as a result. As White describes it, this attempt to do the impossible failed like all the others.

This notion of a sort of spiritual W.P.A. may seem ridiculous, if not sacrilegious, to many people, but it is quite in keeping. White's message (if he has one), his vision, and his imagery are all essentially political, and essentially negative—that is, incomplete or lopsided. The Round Table, he says through Arthur's mouth, was founded "'to dig a channel for Might, so that it would flow usefully. The idea was that all the people who enjoyed fighting should be headed off, so that they fought for justice, and I hoped that this would solve the problem.'" The enterprise failed because, again in Arthur's words, "'Unfortunately we have tried to establish Right by Might, and you can't do that,'" and because "'We have achieved what we were fighting for, and now we still have the fighters on our hands.'" The attempt to control force by force, in other words, is self-defeating. The Grail Quest likewise failed in its earthly purpose, White implies, because those who succeeded in it disappeared from the earth—either by being actually translated to another level of existence, directly into the Divine Presence, like Galahad (the only completely successful Grail-seeker), or by more or less withdrawing from worldly concerns, like Lancelot, Bors, or Percivale—leaving it in as poor shape as ever. All of this, of course, indicates a profoundly pessimistic view of human nature, and at the very end of the story this is spelled out. The aged Arthur, before his last battle, reflects on the teachings of Merlyn—here rather startlingly represented as a Shavian liberal of pre-1914 vintage:

He had been taught . . . to believe that man was perfectible: that he was on the whole more decent than beastly: that good is worth trying: that there was no such thing as original sin. He had been forged as a weapon for the aid of man, on the assumption that men were good.

But,

if there was such a thing as original sin, if man was on the whole a villain, if the Bible was right in saying that the heart of men was deceitful above all things and desperately wicked, then the purpose of his life had been a vain one. Chivalry and justice became a child's illusions, if the stock on which he had tried to graft them was to be the Thrasher, was to be *Homo ferox* instead of *Homo sapiens*.

For all of White's exuberant though sharply limited imagination, his delicious, dancing humor, his encyclopedic learning and superb sense of history, his ultimate outlook is bleak and cheerless. As a convinced though eccentric and highly sophisticated Christian, Charles Williams would no doubt have agreed with White's implied assessment of the nature of man, but he would certainly have drawn radically different conclusions. The reader who finishes White and plunges straight into Williams, as I have just done, finds a shocking change in mood and atmosphere. White's world, despite the medieval costumes and armor, the details of manners and mores, and the occasional use of the high chivalric style, is still the world as we, unfortunately, know it—or perhaps rather the world we knew before 1939; this is made clear by Merlyn's playful parallel between medieval war and Victorian fox hunting. Williams deals in archetypes; his locale refuses to be pinned down with any precision. Almost all we can say about it, sociologically speaking, is that it contains an ideal of civil polity and civilization, embodied in the Byzantine Roman Empire, and an ideal of universal religion embodied in monastic Christianity. . . .

Source: Stephen P. Dunn, "Mr. White, Mr. Williams, and the Matter of Britain," in *Kenyon Review*, Vol. 24, No. 2, Spring 1962, pp. 363–71.

SOURCES

Brewer, D. S., ed., "Introduction," in *Malory: The Morte Darthur*, Northwestern University Press, 1970, pp. 1–19.

Brewer, Elisabeth, *T. H. White's "The Once and Future King,"* Boydell and Brewer, 1993, pp. 1–4, 8–9.

———, "The Figure of Guenevere in Modern Drama and Fiction," in *Arthurian Women: A Casebook*, edited by Thelma S. Fenster, Garland Publishing, 1996, pp. 310–17.

Burgess, Anthony, *99 Novels: The Best in English Since 1939*, Summit Books, 1984.

Chrétien de Troyes, *Arthurian Romances*, edited, translated, and introduced by William W. Kibler, Penguin Books, 1991, pp. 1–22.

Gallix, François, "T. H. White and the Legend of King Arthur: From Animal Fantasy to Political Morality," translated by Edward Donald Kennedy, in *King Arthur: A Casebook*, edited by Edward Donald Kennedy, Garland Publishing, 1996, pp. 281–98.

Goering, Joseph, *The Virgin and the Grail: Origins of a Legend*, Yale University Press, 2005, p. 1.

Kennedy, Edward Donald, ed., *King Arthur: A Casebook*, Garland Publishing, 1996, pp. xiii–xl.

Lacey, Norris J., and Geoffrey Ashe with Debra N. Mancoff, "Modern Arthurian Literature," in *The Arthurian Handbook*, Garland, 1997, pp. 137–96.

Malory, Thomas, *Malory: Works*, edited by Eugène Vinaver, Oxford University Press, 1971.

"Mr. T. H. White," Obituary in the *Times* (London), January 18, 1964, p. F15.

Pearsall, Derek, *Arthurian Romance: A Short Introduction*, Blackwell Publishing, 2003, pp. 3, 7, 60, 150, 153.

Prescott, Orville, Review of *The Once and Future King*, in *New York Times*, August 25, 1958, p. 19.

Sherman, Beatrice, Review of *The Sword in the Stone*, in *New York Times*, January 1, 1939, p. 72.

Thompson, Ralph, Review of *The Sword in the Stone*, in *New York Times*, January 2, 1939, p. 28.

"T. H. White Dead; Novelist Was 57," in *New York Times*, January 18, 1964, p. 21.

Warner, Sylvia Townsend, *T. H. White: A Biography*, The Viking Press, 1967.

White, T. H., *The Once and Future King*, Ace Books, 1987.

Wilhelm, James J., ed., *The Romance of Arthur: An Anthology of Medieval Texts in Translation*, expanded ed., Garland, 1994, pp. 3–10, 95–120, 529–30.

FURTHER READING

Chaucer, Geoffrey, *The Wife of Bath*, edited by Peter G. Beidler, Bedford Books, 1996.

> This book includes a well annotated edition of Chaucer's only Arthurian tale, along with several critical articles and essays on the historical and social contexts of Chaucer's work.

Geoffrey of Monmouth, *The History of the Kings of Britain*, translated and introduced by Lewis Thorpe, Penguin, 1966.

> Written in 1136 in Latin, this book is the first extended recording of Arthur. Thorpe's translation into English of the original text remains

the standard; newer editions continue to include his work.

Stewart, Mary, *The Crystal Cave*, Morrow, 1970.
This book is first in British writer Mary Stewart's four-volume retelling of the Arthurian story from the perspective of Merlin, an excellent example of a twentieth-century treatment.

Wace and Layamon, *Arthurian Chronicles*, introduced by Gwn Jones, translated by Eugene Mason, Dent, 1962.

This accessible translation of the Arthurian materials of Wace and Layamon provides the means for students to compare and contrast the English course of the Arthurian legends with the more courtly French path of the same stories.

White, T. H., *England Have My Bones*, 1936, reprint, Putnam Publishing Group, 1982.
This book is White's autobiographical account of his life in the 1930s, drawn from journals that he kept at the time.

To Sir, With Love

E. R. BRAITHWAITE

1959

An autobiographical novel, *To Sir, With Love* is E. R. Braithwaite's account of his years as a schoolteacher in postwar England, in the rough, working-class neighborhood of London's East End. Originally published in 1959, the novel was adapted into a film in 1966. The novel was Braithwaite's first and is his best-known work. Throughout the course of the novel, the relationship between the narrator (Braithwaite)—who happens to be a citizen of British Guiana and of African descent—and his students is explored. (British Guiana, now Guyana, was until 1966 a British colony. The country is located along the northeastern coast of South America.) Initially, Braithwaite focuses on his status as an outsider (as a black man from another continent) in a country in which he has always felt he belonged due to his British citizenship. Through the examination of the relationship between Braithwaite and the students, the issues of racial and class prejudices are exposed. The best-selling work was a critical success and launched a writing career Braithwaite, as a man of science who had originally pursued a career in physics, had not actively sought. The work continues to be reprinted and remains a valued resource, not only as an engaging work of literature and as a study of the racism in postwar England but also as a relevant tool for the exploration of educational methods and modern race relations.

To Sir, With Love was originally published in 1959 by Bodley Head and is available in a

E. R. Braithwaite (The Library of Congress)

University of London. In 1950, after a number of disappointing interviews for positions in the science and technology sector, Braithwaite secured employment as a teacher in London's East End. He worked at St. George-in-the-East Secondary School until 1957, and his experiences contributed to the content of his first published work, the autobiographical novel *To Sir, With Love*, published in 1959. Following his departure from the educational field, Braithwaite was employed as a welfare officer and a consultant for the London County Council Department of Child Welfare, where he worked from 1958 through 1960. This was followed by a move to Paris, where Braithwaite served as a human rights officer for the World Veteran's Foundation until 1963. Remaining in Paris for several more years, Braithwaite served as an educational consultant and lecturer from 1963 through 1966 for the United Nations Educational, Scientific and Cultural Organization (UNESCO). From 1967 to 1968, he served the United Nations in another capacity in New York as a permanent representative from Guyana. Additionally, he worked on behalf of Guyana as an ambassador to Venezuela from 1968 to 1969. Braithwaite later worked as a professor of English at New York University and in 2002 served as writer in residence at Howard University in Washington, D.C.

number of more recent editions, including the 1977 Jove (a division of the Berkley Publishing Group) publication.

AUTHOR BIOGRAPHY

Braithwaite was born Eustace Edward Ricardo Braithwaite in 1920, in Georgetown, British Guiana, to Charles Edwardo and Elizabeth Martha (Greene) Braithwaite. Ricardo, or Ricky, Braithwaite was well educated, having attended Queen's College in British Guiana. He then went on to City College (now the City University of New York), where he received a bachelor of science degree in 1940. With his educational plans temporarily suspended by World War II (1939–1945), Braithwaite enlisted in the Royal Air Force, serving as a fighter pilot from 1941 through 1945. Following his desire to be a physicist, Braithwaite then went on to University of Cambridge's Gonville and Caius College, where he received his master's degree in physics in 1949. He also studied at the Institute of Education at the

PLOT SUMMARY

Chapter 1

As the novel opens, the narrator, who is later identified as Ricardo, or Ricky Braithwaite, is riding a bus in London. He observes the middle-class working women, and eavesdrops on their sometimes lewd chatter. He describes himself as a Negro and the only male on the bus other than the bus driver. When a "smartly dressed" woman steps onto the bus and silently refuses to sit next to him, Braithwaite becomes angry at her "undisguised prejudice." Nevertheless, he notices the street name through the window and realizes that the next stop is his. He rises and prepares to disembark, and the woman takes his vacated seat. Braithwaite walks through London's East End, depressed that the scene before him of rundown buildings and littered streets conflicts with the images he has created in his mind about London, images taken from works of literature and history books. Entering the Greenslade Secondary School, Braithwaite finds

MEDIA ADAPTATIONS

- *To Sir, With Love*, adapted as a film and directed by James Clavell and starring Sidney Poitier, was produced and distributed by Columbia Pictures in 1967.
- *To Sir, With Love*, adapted as a television movie by James Clavell and directed by Jay Sandrich, was produced by David Gerber Productions in 1974.
- *To Sir, With Love 2* was based on the characters in Braithwaite's novel and was a television movie sequel to the 1967 film *To Sir, With Love*. This sequel was written by Philip Rosenberg, starred Sidney Poitier, was directed by Peter Bogdanovich, and was produced by TriStar Television in 1996.

the headmaster, Alex Florian, and the two discuss a possible teaching position. Florian invites Braithwaite to explore the school before the job offer is finalized.

Chapter 2

Braithwaite passes a classroom in chaos, a class of about forty older students, boys and girls. No teacher is present. The students inform Braithwaite that the teacher, Hackman, has left the class, telling them he will return when they are ready to behave, and that Hackman may be found in the staff room. After proceeding to the staff room, Braithwaite finds another teacher there, who tells Braithwaite that Hackman has left. Mrs. Grace Dale-Evans, another teacher, enters and greets Braithwaite. He then continues to explore the school and grounds. When he returns to the staff room, he finds Mrs. Dale-Evans preparing tea. Other teachers begin to file in during this break period, and Braithwaite is introduced to Miss Josy Dawes, Miss Euphemia Phillips, Mr. Theo Weston, Mrs. Selma Drew, Miss Vivienne Clintridge, who is often called "Clinty," and Miss Gillian Blanchard, whom Braithwaite finds very attractive. A bell sounds and all the teachers except Miss Blanchard depart. Miss Blanchard

and Braithwaite discuss the school's reputation as a dumping ground for delinquent students, as well as its uncommon practices of fostering independence and self-expression and forbidding corporal punishment.

Chapter 3

After some further exploration of the school and discussions with the other teachers, Braithwaite agrees to accept the teaching position at Greenslade. He will be assigned to the senior class at the school. Florian launches into an explanation of the philosophy and methods employed at the school, expressing at the same time great sympathy for the often challenging domestic situations of the students. Despite some reservations about the challenges he will face, Braithwaite's thoughts reveal his elation at simply being employed.

Chapter 4

This chapter opens with Braithwaite's recollections about his life during his service for the Royal Air Force during the early to mid-1940s and directly following. He maintains that as a serviceman, he experienced no discrimination. Braithwaite also discusses his education and expertise in science, his college degrees, and his experience in the field of engineering technology. Despite these qualifications, he is rejected because a prospective employer refuses to place him in a position of authority over white workers. He becomes very aware of the color of his skin. In looking back on his formative years, Braithwaite examines what the "British Way of Life" meant to him as a British citizen in the colony of British Guiana, and how his understanding of the concept of Britishness changed once he was living in Britain as a private citizen.

Chapter 5

Braithwaite's look into the past continues as he recounts his many efforts to secure employment, efforts that are repeatedly thwarted by the prejudices of those with whom he is interviewing. He finds that his disillusionment and disappointment are turning to anger and hatred. At his most bitter point, he happens to sit next to a stranger on a park bench. The man succeeds in engaging Braithwaite in conversation and suggests to him that he attempt to find employment as a schoolteacher. Initially disdainful of this idea, Braithwaite argues that if his race has been a barrier in the science and industry sector, it most certainly will be in education as well. The stranger counters with the insistence that the need for teachers, especially in a rough area such as the East End of London, is great. They discuss the matter further, and Braithwaite is impressed with the man's kindness and insight, so much so that he follows the man's advice. It is this course of events, he explains, that leads him to Greenslade school.

Chapter 6

Braithwaite arrives for his first day of teaching, recalling his departure from home, a house he lives in with an elderly couple, Mr. and Mrs. Belmont, who had befriended him following his demobilization from the Royal Air Force. Before entering the classroom, Braithwaite stops at the staff room and asks the other teachers about the children's usage of foul language, some of which he has overheard on his way into school. Receiving encouragement from Mrs. Drew, Miss Clintridge, and Miss Blanchard, Braithwaite heads off to his class. After taking role, he assesses the lot of them disapprovingly, finding them dirty, ill-kempt, course, and rude. The morning is occupied with Braithwaite's efforts to determine the students' reading abilities. Overall, he is extremely disappointed with the children's skill level and frustrated by the distractions some in the group are causing. One student, Pamela Dare, volunteers to demonstrate that not everyone in the class is an atrocious reader. As Pamela stands to read, Braithwaite notices that "unlike most of the class she was clean and neat." At the morning break, Miss Clintridge brings Braithwaite a cup of tea and suggests ways in which he might reach the class. Braithwaite attempts, with some success, to engage the class in a lesson on weights and measures but finds they are easily distracted. He scolds them loudly, then turns to sarcasm to goad them into behaving better.

Chapter 7

As he has lunch in the staff room, Braithwaite and the other teachers discuss his students. While opinions about best approaches to the challenging group of children vary, Braithwaite feels that most of the teachers are hoping for the best for him. The day's lessons continue, and Braithwaite notices that not all the children are determined to be unfriendly to him.

Chapter 8

Braithwaite discusses his efforts to reach the students. He is aware of how much many of them resist his attempts to teach them and is concerned and frustrated by their continued animosity. Braithwaite details three stages of his initial relationship with the

students, the first being the "silent treatment," in which they refuse to verbally respond to or converse with him. The next is the "noisy treatment," in which loud distractions, such as the slamming of desktops, are used to disrupt his lessons. The third stage Braithwaite refers to as the "bawdy" stage, in which many of the students use foul language in front of him and to him. Through it all, Braithwaite attempts to calmly continue his instruction, but one incident in particular results in a much stronger reaction. Walking into class, Braithwaite finds a group of students clustered around the classroom fireplace. He describes being "horrified to see that someone had thrown a used sanitary napkin into the grate and made an abortive attempt to burn it." Finding that he can no longer control his temper, he orders the boys to leave the room and launches into an angry lecture directed at the girls, condemning their lack of decency and self-respect. He leaves the room to collect his thoughts. When he returns, he finds the fireplace has been cleaned and all the students are sitting quietly. Braithwaite is surprised to find that the girls actually seemed ashamed.

Chapter 9

The next day, Braithwaite explains clearly and deliberately what he will be expecting of the children and why. In order for him to teach and for the students to learn, he explains, an atmosphere of mutual respect will be instituted. Everyone will have the opportunity to express his or her views without interruption. The boys will address the girls as "Miss," followed by their surname (last name) and the boys will all be addressed by their last name. He insists on being addressed as "Mr. Braithwaite" or "Sir" at all times, and informs them of the need to come to school dressed and groomed appropriately.

Chapter 10

Braithwaite observes his class attending to their Weekly Review. This assignment is a requirement, insisted upon by Florian, in which the children assess the events of the week. Reading through the reviews, Braithwaite finds that despite some criticism of his measures, the children in general are pleased to be treated as adults. However, Braithwaite identifies a group of boys, led by one named Denham, who continue to resist his authority, while the rest of the students are becoming increasingly absorbed in classroom discussions. In one such lesson, about the history of clothing in Britain, the idea for a field trip to a museum is brought up, and Braithwaite promises to look into it. Braithwaite has a conflict with Denham about the inappropriate magazine in the boy's desk. Denham is furious when the offensive material is confiscated.

Chapter 11

During the next gym class, or P.T. (physical training), Braithwaite senses some excitement in the students. Denham requests that the boys be allowed to practice boxing first, a sport at which he has previously noted his expertise. Braithwaite allows it, and the boys pair themselves off, with Denham being left without a partner. Beginning to realize the whole thing has been orchestrated, he denies Denham's request to partner with him. Seeing the disgust and disappointment on the faces of the onlooking boys, and guessing that they think he is afraid to box Denham, Braithwaite agrees to the matchup. Gloves on, the two begin to box, and Braithwaite acknowledges how stupid it is for him to have allowed himself to be lured into this situation. Denham strikes him in the face, drawing blood. Braithwaite lands a blow designed to knock the wind out of Denham. Winded but unhurt, Denham sinks to the floor, and when others rush to help him, Braithwaite instructs them to line up for another activity instead. He himself helps Denham to a bench, where the boy recovers from the blow. At the end of the lesson, Braithwaite speaks with Denham lightly, dismissing the affair and telling the boy to give his head a quick soak in some cold water to revive himself. Denham answers politely, and Braithwaite recognizes the moment as a turning point in his relationship with Denham in particular and the class as a whole. Braithwaite next describes the way this shift changes the dynamic in the classroom. As the students demonstrate their respect and acceptance of him, as well as their obedience to his rules, Braithwaite finds himself liking them as individuals and seeking to learn more about them. He approaches Florian about the idea of the field trip to the museum, and the headmaster gives his consent, provided Braithwaite takes with him one other teacher. Discussing the upcoming field trip in the staff room, Braithwaite asks Miss Blanchard to accompany the class with him.

Chapter 12

The field trip to the museum is executed without any trouble. Back in the staff room after the trip, Miss Blanchard and Braithwaite discuss the trip, and Pamela. Miss Blanchard is convinced Pamela has a crush on Braithwaite and alludes to the fact that it is understandable due to Braithwaite's attractiveness. Flustered with her attention, he leaves. Miss Blanchard approaches him once more, and the two teachers confess that they both have feelings for one another. The next morning, Braithwaite finds that the students have gathered flowers for him as a thank you for the field trip.

Chapter 13

In this chapter, Braithwaite discusses the course his instruction with the students is taking, noting that the lessons have covered biology (involving the examination of a human skeleton), as well as geography (in which the British colonies, including that of British Guiana, are discussed). Braithwaite also comments on the progression of his relationship with Miss Blanchard, whom he now refers to as Gillian.

Chapter 14

After the August holiday, when the children return to school, Braithwaite notices that Pamela seems different, more serious. He also begins to learn more about the children's personal lives and families. Pamela remains behind at recess, asking to help him, and she scolds the others when she perceives them to not be properly respectful of Braithwaite. The other students accuse her of having a crush on Braithwaite. She ignores the accusation but appears less brooding in the days following.

Chapter 15

This chapter opens with Braithwaite learning that one of his students, Patrick Fernman, is in police custody after seriously injuring someone. Braithwaite and Gillian speak to the boy's family and learn that he had been taking a knife to be sharpened, an errand his grandmother sent him on. He had encountered another boy to whom he had showed the knife, but Fernman would not let the other boy touch it. The two argued and the other boy attempted to take the knife from Fernman. In his effort to prevent this from happening, Fernman accidentally stabbed the other boy. Braithwaite attends Fernman's hearing at the Juvenile Court, where Fernman is released with probation and a stern warning.

Chapter 16

Pamela's mother has requested to speak with Braithwaite, and when Braithwaite agrees, Mrs. Dare tells him about her worries concerning Pamela, and about how Pamela has been staying out late and not telling Mrs. Dare where she is going. Mrs. Dare asks that Braithwaite speak to Pamela, which he does, somewhat reluctantly. The conversation reveals that Pamela is feeling cut off from her mother, who has recently begun dating (Pamela's father has been dead for some time). Braithwaite consents to Pamela's request that he speak to her mother. Reluctantly, he visits the Dares in their home, feeling as if he has made a mistake in coming. Braithwaite's conversation with Mrs. Dare is awkward and concludes with Braithwaite admonishing Pamela to respect her mother.

Chapter 17

In this chapter, Braithwaite recounts the half-yearly report of the Students Council, in which the students of the school report to the faculty and other students on what they have been studying thus far. Braithwaite's class representatives speak knowledgeably about their coursework and place a considerable amount of emphasis on how much they have learned about different peoples, cultures, customs, and the importance of international and interracial cooperation.

Chapter 18

Shortly after the students' report, Braithwaite and Gillian Blanchard go out to celebrate Gillian's birthday. At an expensive restaurant, Braithwaite is treated rudely. Gillian grows angry and storms out of the restaurant. When the couple has returned to Gillian's home, she verbally and physically attacks Braithwaite, enraged that he did not put up any kind of a fight at the restaurant. Braithwaite calms her and attempts to explain himself, becoming surprised by her ignorance of how pervasive such racist attitudes are. During the course of their conversation, they admit their love for one another.

Chapter 19

Following a summary of the progress all his students have made, Braithwaite turns to the subject of the school's new P.T. teacher, Mr. Bell. Bell's unkind treatment of the male students is revealed, and his particular disdain for the overweight Buckley is observed. During one P.T. session, Bell goads Buckley into performing a vault maneuver in which Buckley is injured. Another student (Potter), enraged at Bell, comes at him with the broken metal leg of the vault, yelling at him for his treatment of Buckley and threatening him with the improvised weapon. Tich Jackson, having taken in Buckley's injury and Potter's rage, runs to tell

Braithwaite, who appears on the scene before Potter injures his teacher. Buckley is taken to Mrs. Dale-Evans, while Braithwaite instructs his students to return to his classroom. He finds Bell in the staff room. Before this incident, Florian has already spoken to Bell about derogatory statements he has made to several students. Bell is therefore now uneasy about telling the headmaster what has happened, but Braithwaite presses upon him the importance of doing so. In discussing the matter with his students, Braithwaite expresses his disappointment with Potter for his response. He stresses the importance of being able to control one's temper once the students are out in the working world. Potter is shocked at being reprimanded and told by Braithwaite that he must apologize to Bell. When another student comments that it is easy for Braithwaite to be so calm, as no one pushes him around, Braithwaite responds, with some emotion, "I've been pushed around until I began to hate people so much that I wanted to hurt them, really hurt them." Potter concedes the necessity of an apology, and after seeking Bell in the staff room, returns to the class and is shortly followed by Bell, who offers his own apology to the students.

Chapter 20

Because the school has often been the object of criticism for its unique approach to education, one which does not involve physical punishment and one in which individuality and self-expression are encouraged, Florian agrees to allow the school to be the subject of a newspaper article. Students and teachers are interviewed and photographed, although Braithwaite objects to being held up as any sort of example of the school's uniqueness. He maintains that he does not want to be viewed as an oddity and that his success as a teacher has nothing to do with the color of his skin. When the article appears, it has turned into another criticism of the school rather than an attempt to explain its educational goals. Later in the chapter, Lawrence Seales, a student of mixed race, announces that his mother has died. The class takes up a collection for flowers to be taken to the mother's funeral, but the students all balk at the notion of actually taking them to the Seales' home. The explanation for this behavior is the fear of "what people would say if they saw us going to a colored person's home." Braithwaite's reaction is one of shocked disbelief. He walks out of the room and attempts to discuss the matter with Florian, but the headmaster tries to justify the children's attitude by commenting on the prejudices the children have inherited. Braithwaite's disbelief turns to anger. When Braithwaite returns to the classroom, Pamela Dare announces that she will take the flowers to Mrs. Seales's funeral. On his way to the funeral the following Saturday, Braithwaite's anger at his students and their hypocrisy, as well as his sense of betrayal, are all utmost in his mind until he feels the anger turning to hate. Yet as he approaches the Seales' home, he spots just beyond the hearse nearly all of the students in his class. He is overcome with love for them.

Chapter 21

Braithwaite describes the last days of the term as poignant ones. He expresses his happiness with the progress of his students as well as the deepening of his relationship with Gillian. Meeting her parents, Braithwaite is prepared to defend his relationship with Gillian. Her mother and father seem to like him and are concerned about the challenges Gillian will face. Despite some tense moments, the parents' overall attitude is one of openness and friendship.

Chapter 22

During the last days of the term, Braithwaite's students ready themselves for their lives outside of the classroom. Many of them have jobs awaiting them already. The end of the term is celebrated with a Christmas dinner and dance. Braithwaite emphasizes the adult appearance and attitudes of his students at the celebration. He and Gillian hold hands and dance often, allowing the students and faculty to see that the two of them are a couple. Braithwaite summarizes the abilities and growth of many of his students. They express their gratitude to him with a speech, given by Moira Joseph, and with a gift addressed, "To Sir, with love," presented to him by Pamela and signed by all of them.

CHARACTERS

Bell

Mr. Bell is referred to as a "supply" teacher at the school. This is the British term for a substitute teacher. He is enlisted to help out with P.T. (physical training, or gym) classes and appears toward the novel's end. Bell has negative opinions about the students, opinions he expresses to the students and to other teachers. After a conflict with one of the students and a discussion with Braithwaite on the matter, he apologizes to the class for his behavior.

Bob Belmont

Bob Belmont and Jess Belmont are the elderly couple with whom Braithwaite lives. Mr. Belmont is called "Dad" by Braithwaite, and the gentleman offers advice to Braithwaite.

Jess Belmont

Jess Belmont is the wife of Bob Belmont. Braithwaite resides with the Belmonts and refers to Mrs. Belmont as "Mom." She exhibits a maternal attitude toward Braithwaite and even packs him lunches to take to school.

Jacqueline Bender

Jacqueline Bender is a student of Braithwaite's. Near the novel's end, it is Jacqueline who attempts to explain to Braithwaite the students' reluctance to bring flowers to Lawrence Seales's house after the death of Lawrence's mother.

Gillian Blanchard

Gillian Blanchard is a new teacher at Greenslade. She started only a few days before Braithwaite. Upon being introduced to her, Braithwaite instantly finds her attractive. Throughout the course of the novel, a romantic relationship between Miss Blanchard and Braithwaite develops. She periodically offers advice and sometimes disagrees with Braithwaite's methods or decisions. When faced with the difficulties a relationship with Braithwaite will present, Miss Blanchard becomes angry at her society's prejudices, but nevertheless she chooses to remain romantically involved with Braithwaite.

Ricardo Braithwaite

Ricardo Braithwaite is the narrator of the novel and its main character. The extent to which the author Braithwaite fictionalized the novel version of himself cannot be known for certain, although according to Michael Fielding (in a 2005 issue of the educational journal *Forum*), Braithwaite has indicated in recent interviews that the book is not a work of fiction. It may be assumed, therefore, that Braithwaite the author intended the character Braithwaite to be viewed as an accurate portrayal of himself. A British citizen born and raised in the colony of British Guiana, Braithwaite describes himself as well educated and largely unaware of the prejudices inherent in British society in the 1940s. He claims to not have been aware of racial prejudice while he served in the Royal Air Force, but after he was demobilized and attempting to seek employment in the private sector, the injustice of the attitudes of white British society became apparent. He lives with Mr. and Mrs. Belmont, who treat him as a son. After repeatedly being turned down for employment for which he is more than qualified, Braithwaite begins to grow angry and comments several times on the feeling of that anger turning to hatred. He also perceives that he is quick to anger, a habit he strives to control. When he acquires the teaching position at Greenslade, Braithwaite's attitude is shaped by the racism he has dealt with daily for so long. He feels little sympathy for the experiences of the white children in the school as Florian describes the difficulties the children encounter at home and at school. Braithwaite remains certain that no matter how challenging their personal situations, "they were white," and as far as he is concerned, "that fact alone made the only difference between the haves and the have-nots." Entering into the school and his teaching position with his own prejudices, Braithwaite initially has little tolerance for the children's behavior, dress, and attitudes. Through his firm handling of them and through his insistence on mutual respect, Braithwaite gradually begins to see the children as individuals interested in learning and maturing into young adults. As they offer him their obedience, and however slowly it is given, their trust as well, Braithwaite finds himself liking them as people. He becomes personally involved in their lives and their problems, often against his better judgment, but by the novel's end, they are able to view him not as their black teacher but simply as their teacher and friend. He finds that his affection for them as individuals has blossomed, as has his understanding that he has as much to learn from them as they from him.

Buckley

Buckley is a heavy student of Braithwaite who finds himself the object of Mr. Bell's reproach. Buckley is injured after performing a vault Bell has ordered him to do. The injury is mild and he shortly returns to class.

Vivienne Clintridge

Vivienne Clintridge, nicknamed Clinty by the other teachers, is the art and drama teacher. Miss Clintridge is kind and welcoming in her attitude toward Braithwaite, who finds her immediately friendly. She is described as a plump brunette of about thirty years of age. Periodically throughout the novel, she offers encouragement and advice to Braithwaite.

Clinty

See Vivienne Clintridge

Grace Dale-Evans

Mrs. Grace Dale-Evans is Greenslade's "Domestic Science," or home economics, teacher. Braithwaite describes her as an attractive blond woman who is often found making tea or tidying up the staff room. Early in the novel, she introduces Braithwaite to the other teachers.

Pamela Dare

Pamela Dare is one of Braithwaite's students. She is often described as attractive and grown-up for her age. She is intelligent and well spoken, and she is the first of the students to impress Braithwaite with her clean and tidy appearance as well as with her educational accomplishments. She defends Braithwaite when he is whispered about on the bus on the way to the field trip, is eager to help around the classroom, and is accused of having a crush on Braithwaite, although she never admits the truth of this accusation. Pamela is depicted both as a child and as a young woman. Hurt and confused by her mother's behavior, she asks Braithwaite to speak to her mother, unable to appreciate the inappropriateness of this request and the delicacy of the matter. Yet she demonstrates her fair-mindedness and courage when she alone volunteers to bring flowers to the home of Lawrence Seales, the son of a white mother and a black father, when Lawrence's mother dies. At the novel's end, at the Christmas celebration, Braithwaite observes how womanly Pamela has become in her appearance and her bearing, particularly when she dances with him.

Josephine "Josy" Dawes

Miss Josy Dawes is a teacher at the school with whom Braithwaite has only a little interaction. Upon being introduced to her, he comments on her somewhat plain appearance. Braithwaite occasionally observes Miss Dawes engaged in private conversation with another teacher, Miss Euphemia Phillips. Later in the novel, Miss Blanchard expresses her suspicion that Josy Dawes and Euphemia Phillips are girlfriends.

Denham

Denham is a student in Braithwaite's class. His first name is never given; he is referred to throughout the novel by his surname, Denham. When he and Braithwaite first interact in the class, Denham demonstrates his desire to challenge his teacher and entertain his classmates. Denham is among the last students Braithwaite wins over. Refusing to submit to Braithwaite's authority, Denham arranges a boxing match between himself and Braithwaite, a match in which Braithwaite knocks the wind out of Denham. Following that encounter, Denham becomes cooperative and helpful.

Selma Drew

Mrs. Drew is the school's deputy headmistress. An elderly woman, Mrs. Drew is portrayed as kindly, elegant, and reliable.

Patrick Fernman

Patrick Fernman is a student in Braithwaite's class. He is one of the few students who does not seem interested in resisting or challenging Braithwaite's authority. Later in the novel, Fernman accidentally stabs another boy. Braithwaite attends Fernman's hearing and is relieved when Fernman is sentenced only to a year's probation.

Alex Florian

Alex Florian is the headmaster at Greenslade school. The character is based on radical educationalist Alex Bloom, who was the headmaster at St. George-in-the-East, the school at which Braithwaite actually taught. Braithwaite describes Florian as small and hunchbacked in stature, with white hair but a youthful face and eyes that "seemed filled with a kind of wonder, as if he were on the verge of some new and exciting discovery." This sense of excitement the headmaster possesses appears to stem from his feelings toward his students and from the unique educational experience he seeks to offer them. From Braithwaite's first interview with Florian, the headmaster's devotion to and personal interest in the students at his school is apparent. He professes an understanding of their domestic circumstances and the financial challenges their working-class parents face; this understanding is accompanied by a deep sense of compassion for the children. In describing the philosophy of the school to Braithwaite, Florian states that the children are viewed as young adults immersed in the "process of development" and that this development should never be "forced or restricted at the arbitrary whim" of any person who happens to be in a position of authority. Florian approves of the progress Braithwaite makes with the children. He is depicted as a sympathetic defender of the children and their interests.

Hackman

Hackman is the teacher who has fled his classroom just before Braithwaite's arrival at the school. By the time Braithwaite makes it to the staff room, Hackman has gathered his belongings and fled entirely. It is Hackman's class that Braithwaite takes over.

Tich Jackson

Tich Jackson is a student in Braithwaite's class, who, along with Fernman, is from the beginning cooperative and in general not deliberately disruptive.

Moira Joseph

Moira Joseph is one of Braithwaite's students. Braithwaite identifies her as one of the leaders in the class, a tall girl with a charisma that draws others to her. Moira is the student who makes the speech on behalf of the class at the end of the novel in which she thanks Braithwaite for teaching them.

Monica Page

Monica Page is a student in Braithwaite's class who participates in the "noisy" treatment by slamming her desk repeatedly during class. Her later rude comments usher in what Braithwaite refers to as the "bawdy" stage of the class's treatment of him.

Palmer

Palmer, identified only by his last name, is the first student Braithwaite calls upon to read. The unflattering description of the boy refers to his blotchy complexion, his thick neck, and his large head. Braithwaite notes that his reading is surprisingly bad.

Barbara Pegg

Barbara Pegg is a student in Braithwaite's class "whose eyes always held a smile." Barbara is the student who initially suggests the field trip to the museum.

Euphemia Phillips

Euphemia Phillips is a teacher at the school whom Braithwaite initially finds young and immature-looking. He occasionally comments about how

Miss Phillips and Miss Dawes converse privately in the staff room. Miss Blanchard informs Braithwaite that she suspects the two young women are girlfriends. While Braithwaite wonders early on in the novel how such a small, young-looking woman could handle the often coarse and rough students, he later expresses admiration for her cool confidence in dealing with the students.

Potter

Potter is a student in Braithwaite's class and a friend of Denham's. The boy is described as tall and overweight. Braithwaite eventually finds Potter to be intelligent, though he remains hotheaded throughout the novel. Potter threatens to attack Bell after the P.T. teacher has instructed Buckley to perform a maneuver that ends up injuring Buckley. After Braithwaite lectures the boy, Potter apologizes to Bell.

Jane Purcell

Jane Purcell is a student in Braithwaite's class whose dress habits are described as sloppy and whom Braithwaite initially finds quite rude.

Sapiano

Sapiano, another student of Braithwaite's, is identified as Denham's friend.

Lawrence Seales

Lawrence Seales is a student in Braithwaite's class. On their first meeting, Braithwaite identifies him as a student "obviously of mixed parentage." Lawrence remains uninvolved in much of the mischief the other students create but also maintains for a time an unfriendly stance toward Braithwaite. Like the other students, he eventually warms to Braithwaite's methods and forthright manner.

Theo Weston

Theo Weston is one of the first teachers Braithwaite encounters at the school. Weston is described as somewhat untidy, and from the start he is rude and disdainful toward Braithwaite. His sarcastic comments occasionally have a racial slur imbedded within them, as when he joking calls Braithwaite a "black sheep" or "our sunburned friend," although he attempts an air of levity. The students periodically express their dislike of him, and the other teachers at the school are known to tease, ignore, or openly disagree with Weston. He is generally not well liked at the school.

THEMES

Prejudice and Racism

The racism prevalent in Great Britain during the mid-1940s, the time period during which *To Sir, With Love* takes place, is of primary significance in the novel. The narrator cites repeated incidents in which he experiences the racism of white Britons, including encounters on the bus, at job interviews, at Greenslade school, when searching for housing, at a restaurant with his girlfriend. Braithwaite is initially struck by the unexpectedness of such prejudice. Growing up in British Guiana, he viewed himself as a British citizen, not as a black British citizen in a British colony. When he served Great Britain in the Royal Air Force, his uniform, he came to understand later, insulated him from racism. He was treated with respect due to the service he was rendering Great Britain. Divested of this symbol of duty, sacrifice, and loyalty to the nation, he finds he is perceived as an outsider, yet he also notes the subtlety with which white Britons display their prejudices. He maintains that while Americans were rather blatant in their racism, in Great Britain, people do not actually admit to "anti-Negro prejudice." Blacks are free to ride any bus or train and sit anywhere on it. The fact that people choose to avoid sitting next to a black person on such transportation is "casually overlooked." Any accommodation in a hotel or boardinghouse is allowed to be sought, although the "courteous refusal" that often results from such a quest is "never ascribed to prejudice." Braithwaite's extensive experience and education count for nothing in job interviews, where he is repeatedly told that the position has already been filled or that he is overqualified. The "charm and courtesy" with which the racism is perpetrated heightens Braithwaite's sense of betrayal. His response to the racism he experiences is varied. He never lashes out physically and only rarely does he do so verbally. He exhibits patient endurance at times, and at others he describes the way the rage inside him is transforming into a hatred so strong that he desires to hurt those who treat him unfairly. As a result of such experiences, Braithwaite finds that when he begins teaching at Greenslade school, no matter what difficulties the students there might face personally and however disadvantaged they may be in terms of income or education, they are white, which he believes gives them an automatic advantage in the world. This advantage initially impedes Braithwaite's ability to see the students as individuals, as people with their own

TOPICS FOR FURTHER STUDY

- *To Sir, With Love* was adapted into a motion picture by James Clavell in 1967. In a 2005 article for the educational journal *Forum*, Michael Fielding states of the film: "Despite its status as a cinema classic, my own view, and, more importantly, the view of E. R. Braithwaite, is that it is a betrayal of the book." Watch the 1967 film (available on DVD through Sony Pictures), and compare the film with the book. In what ways do the two works differ? What are the similarities? Does the movie, in your opinion, "betray" the book? Write an essay in which you compare the two works and consider why events or people in the book may have been altered for the film.

- In *To Sir, With Love*, Braithwaite's class, along with Braithwaite and Miss Blanchard, take a field trip to a museum. A comment in the classroom discussion led to a discussion of the way clothing in Britain had changed throughout history, and an exhibit at a local museum provides an opportunity for the class to further research this process. Continue the study. Research the same topic from postwar Britain, where Braithwaite's class would have stopped, to the present day. Create a visual display using images found in books or from your Internet research to chart the history of British fashion. Be sure to discuss the developments and changes you observe. How did the clothing of the time reflect current social attitudes or historical events? Accompany your display with an oral or written report on your findings.

- The topic of racial prejudice and discrimination is a prevalent one in *To Sir, With Love*. In both Great Britain and the United States, racism was intense and widespread, and discrimination was legal for many years. Research and compare the developments in the civil rights movements in Great Britain and the United States from the postwar period (the mid-1940s) through the 1960s. What major pieces of legislation were passed in both countries and when? What events led to the passage of civil rights legislation in both countries? Who were the prominent civil rights leaders of the time in both countries? Write a report on your findings.

- Braithwaite was born in British Guiana, a colony of Great Britain until 1966. In his novel, Braithwaite discusses his youth there and how his education differed from what he was now witnessing at the school in London's East End. Prepare a multimedia presentation on the cultural history of British Guiana. Examine what would it have been like to grow up there in the 1920s and 1930s as Braithwaite did. Consider such questions as the following: What were the schools like, and how does your research compare with Braithwaite's reflections in the novel? What was the racial makeup of the country during this time period? What holidays did citizens of British Guiana celebrate? How "British" were their customs?

seemingly insurmountable problems. It appears as though the students and Braithwaite, throughout the course of the novel, make a considerable amount of progress in terms of their mutual ability to view one another fairly. Yet when tested, upon the death of Lawrence Seales's mother, both parties fail one another, at least temporarily. When the students express their unwillingness to bring flowers to the house of the grieving family because Seales is black, Braithwaite is stunned by the way the students cling to their old notions of race, despite all the growth they have previously exhibited. Even though one student, Pamela Dare, has volunteered to bring the flowers, claiming she cares not what people say about her, as Braithwaite rides the bus to the funeral he lumps the whole group of students

Sidney Poitier as Mark Thackeray and Lulu as herself in the 1967 film version of To Sir, With Love
(Columbia | The Kobal Collection)

together in his mind, making them all the object of a "throbbing hate" so powerful it makes him feel light-headed. Moments later, however, he forgives them when he finds that most of the class have indeed looked past their old prejudices and have come to the funeral after all. Not only does he forgive the students but he asks God to forgive him for his "hateful thoughts" because he loves the children after all.

Education

In *To Sir, With Love*, the educational program offered by the Greenslade school is presented as somewhat radical compared to what is provided by most other public schools in Great Britain. The headmaster, Alex Florian, initially describes the school by saying that "Things are done here somewhat differently from the usual run, and many teachers have found it, shall we say, disquieting." Braithwaite learns more about the school by

observation and from information provided by other faculty members. He witnesses children casually and often sloppily dressed, running through the halls, smoking, and speaking about the staff and to one another disrespectfully. Miss Blanchard explains in a little more detail the unique rules of the school, telling Braithwaite that the school does not have a punishment or discipline policy and that the students are always encouraged to speak their minds. Florian elaborates, delineating the economic difficulties the children face, how they are often ill clothed and ill fed, and emphasizing that the role of the teachers is to provide them with "affection, confidence and guidance, more or less in that order, because experience has shown us that those are their most immediate needs." Florian goes on to discuss the school's discipline policy, stating that it is wrong to describe the school's practice as "free discipline." Rather, he clarifies, they attempt to create an atmosphere of "disciplined freedom," creating a situation in which children feel safe and comfortable enough to learn and express themselves. Florian acknowledges that all teachers are not suited to this type of educational environment but stresses that he will not interfere in Braithwaite's classroom so long as the broad guidelines are respected. He is true to his word. Throughout the novel, examples of how such aims are pursued are presented, as when Braithwaite discusses the students' Weekly Reports, or the school-wide Students Council report, both of which are shown to be opportunities for the children to comment not only on what they are learning but on how they are being taught. Additionally, references are made throughout the course of the novel regarding the outside perception of the school, as when the newspaper article is published and the children and school are painted in a negative manner. As the novel ends in an uplifting way, with both Braithwaite and the students growing and learning from one another, the methods of Greenslade are meant to be taken as valuable alternatives to traditional educational models.

As Michael Fielding discusses in his 2005 article "Alex Bloom, Pioneer of Radical State Education," published in *Forum*, the educational practices and events Braithwaite discusses in *To Sir, With Love* reflect the influence of Alex Bloom on Braithwaite. Bloom opened the secondary modern school St. George-in-the-East (where Braithwaite taught) in 1945 and served as its headmaster from 1945 through 1955. The novel represents the innovations in education being achieved during that time period.

STYLE

First-Person Narrative

As a first-person narrative, *To Sir, With Love* is written from one character's point of view, that of Ricardo Braithwaite, who refers to himself as "I" throughout the work. By employing this point of view, the author sets certain limits on the way the action of the book is perceived by the reader. All information the reader ascertains passes through the filter of the narrator, and therefore the reader of the novel must consider the narrator's observational accuracy and potential biases when assessing information the narrator provides about other characters and events. As a highly educated, worldly individual, who

has himself been discriminated against because of his race, Braithwaite often provides less-than-flattering portraits of many of the working-class or poor men, women, and youngsters he encounters. Considering the racism he has experienced firsthand, and at the same time weighing the fact that he is a representative of the educated, professional class, it is reasonable to ask whether Braithwaite's observations are objective ones or are tinged with the anger he admits to or the sense of social superiority he occasionally demonstrates. For example, in describing the charwomen, or cleaning ladies, he encounters on the bus in the opening scene of the novel, Braithwaite describes the sturdy physiques of the women as "bovine" (cowlike). He further reflects that the women remind him "somehow of the peasants in a book by Steinbeck: they were of the city, but they dressed like peasants, they looked like peasants, and they talked like peasants." Although he admits the women possess their "own kind of dignity," he nevertheless has offered a somewhat derogatory depiction of the gainfully employed women by describing them as both animal-like and impoverished. At the same time, similar comments made about the students at Greenslade school may seem unkind but are more likely to be accurate. Braithwaite makes several observations regarding the children's often untidy or grubby appearance. These comments, however, are often backed up by statements Braithwaite shares with the reader, statements made by other teachers at the school. Even characters such as Florian, whom Braithwaite acknowledges has genuine affection and respect for the children, concedes that their appearance is often substandard. As understanding as they may be, several other teaches provide the same assessment. Braithwaite as a first-person narrator is often reliable but is not completely free from bias.

Autobiographical Novel

To Sir, With Love is typically described as an autobiographical novel. The autobiographical novel genre is a slightly ambiguous one, as it is difficult for the reader to assess where autobiography ends and fiction begins. In a 2005 article in the educational journal *Forum*, Michael Fielding maintains that in phone interviews from the same year, Braithwaite has insisted that *To Sir, With Love* is not a work of fiction but rather a "selection from his [Braithwaite's] own notes and reflections that he wrote every day." At the same time, as an author Braithwaite fictionalizes the framework of the events of the book to some degree. While the school-related incidents he describes may have all actually happened, as an author Braithwaite does compress the time frame of real events to suit the needs of his novel. As Fielding and others have noted, following the end of World War II, Braithwaite returned to Cambridge University to complete his postgraduate studies before entering the job market. Yet in *To Sir, With Love*, the narrator Braithwaite talks about returning from the demobilization center (where he met with career advisors, underwent a medical exam, and turned in service equipment) to live with the Belmonts, vacationing with the couple, and immediately beginning a search for employment. Through such selection and revision, Braithwaite's work as a whole may accurately be viewed as a fictionalized account of a period of his life, a true autobiographical novel exhibiting elements of autobiography and fiction, despite the author's insistence on the accuracy of his reflections regarding his time spent at the school.

HISTORICAL CONTEXT

Postwar British Colonialism

Following World War II, a war in which Braithwaite fought as a fighter pilot in the Royal Air Force from 1941 until 1945, Britain still held colonies all over the world. However, anticolonial movements in India, Africa, and elsewhere were on the rise. Clement Attlee presided over the British government as prime minister from 1945 through 1951, and under his leadership India was granted independence. The struggles of other British colonies to gain their independence went on for some time, with waves of success in the 1950s and 1960s, largely because of the support of Prime Minister Harold Macmillan, who governed from 1957 through 1963. Seeking to avoid costly, violent insurrections, the British government often granted peaceful transfers of power to many of their colonies that sought independence and were establishing stable, non-Communist governments, although in some instances, civil unrest resulted in civilian casualties as borders were redrawn and some people were forced to relocate. The colony of British Guiana, where Braithwaite was born, was not granted independence until 1966. In his novel, Braithwaite recounts growing up in British Guiana

and the way he embraced his British citizenship. He speaks at some length about the pride many colonial people feel in their British citizenship. In fact, Braithwaite does not appear to harbor any anticolonial sentiments until he is in Britain and is exposed to the racial prejudices of white Londoners. Once he is faced with the discrimination he encounters in the job market, he observes that "it is wonderful to be British—until one comes to Britain."

Race Relations in Postwar England

England during the immediate postwar period during which Braithwaite's novel is set and in the subsequent decade, at the end of which the novel was published, saw an intensification of racial discrimination. A postwar economic boom in the 1950s began to bring migrant workers from the colonies of the British West Indies to industrial jobs in London. Racial tensions between British whites and black immigrants resulted in the Notting Hill Race Riots in 1958. Until 1965, discrimination on the basis of skin color was not illegal, and Braithwaite writes in his novel of the prejudice that left him unemployed and of the way racism was overlooked and unacknowledged. In 1965, the first Race Relations Act was passed, outlawing discrimination on the basis of race and establishing the Race Relations Board (RRB). The RRB was designed to investigate complaints. The 1965 act was strengthened by further provisions set up in 1968, including the Community Relations Commission, which was designed to enforce the new race laws. The Race Relations Act of 1976 was a much more comprehensive piece of legislation that broadened the understanding of discrimination and further restricted the practice of racial discrimination and victimization. At the same time that the Race Relations Act of 1968 was passed, Home Secretary James Callaghan was also responsible for the passage of the Commonwealth Immigration Act, a piece of legislation that restricted the flow of migrant workers, such as those from the West Indies, who flooded London just prior to the riots in 1958. At the time the two acts were passed, Callaghan explained that the purpose of the legislation was to create a society in which all citizens were treated with equality, even though the government exercised control of who was allowed into that society. The institutionalized racism and pervasive prejudices Braithwaite describes were a long time in being overcome.

COMPARE & CONTRAST

- **1940s:** Education in England is undergoing a number of changes. The Butler Education Act is passed in 1944, introducing an educational system known as the Tripartite System, in which children are funneled into one of three "tracks" based on academic test scores: grammar school (the most academic school), technical school, or modern school (focusing on practical skills and basic education). Greenslade Secondary School, the institution depicted in Braithwaite's novel, is an example of a modern school. In 1947, education is made compulsory for children through the age of fifteen.

  1950s: Despite a considerable amount of debate regarding the Tripartite System, this educational model is upheld and supported by the Conservative government of the 1950s.

  Today: The Tripartite System, abolished in 1976, has been replaced by the Comprehensive System, in which schools educate children of all academic aptitudes. Additionally, the Education Reform Act of 1988 instituted a National Curriculum and assessments based on this curriculum for students at the ages of seven, eleven, fourteen, and sixteen. A number of agendas and programs, including Every Child Matters and the Children Act of 2004, are implemented to promote the health, well-being, and proper education of all children in the United Kingdom.

- **1940s:** In 1945, Alex Bloom opens the St. George-in-the-East Secondary Modern School, where Braithwaite taught. Bloom revolutionizes state education by refusing to use corporal punishment on his students and by encouraging individuality and self-expression over traditional educational regimentation. Braithwaite bases the character of Headmaster Alex Florian, in *To Sir, With Love*, on Alex Bloom.

  1950s: Bloom's school remains unique in its individualistic approach to education, despite its being a part of a system (the Tripartite System) that generalizes students' academic abilities and forces them into a narrowly defined track based on this general assessment. Alex Bloom dies on September 20, 1955.

  Today: While some efforts have been made to focus on students as individuals and to respect each student's particular learning needs, critics of the modern British state educational system find that many students are not receiving the high-quality education they deserve. Advocates of Bloom's philosophy in particular are harshly critical of the efforts of the U.K. Department for Children, Schools, and Families to improve educational opportunities for children in the United Kingdom. They believe that Bloom's legacy has not yet been fulfilled.

- **1940s:** Following World War II, the United Kingdom struggles to transform its economy from war production to peacetime productivity. The economy has been severely weakened by the war. Food rationing begun during the war increases in the immediate postwar period. The government attempts to regulate industries, wages, and prices; to reduce the number of goods imported to the country; and to boost exports. Times are difficult, particularly for working-class families such as those Braithwaite depicts in his novel.

  1950s: Postwar food rationing finally ends in 1954, and the economic controls of the previous years have begun to strengthen the war-weakened British economy. The standard of living increases, unemployment is low, and more consumer goods are available and affordable.

  Today: Although for much of the twentieth and early twenty-first centuries the United Kingdom is among the world's leading industrialized nations, it is not immune to the worldwide economic crisis of 2008 and 2009. The government is faced with staggering budget deficits and failing economic institutions.

British actress/singer Lulu (© *Bettmann / Corbis*)

CRITICAL OVERVIEW

While there is not an abundance of critical examinations of *To Sir, With Love*, the critical and popular responses to the work have been largely favorable since the work's original 1959 publication. In a 1960 review in the *New York Times Book Review*, John Wain describes the book as a "moving and inspiring record of Mr. Braithwaite's struggle." Braithwaite, Wain finds, "is not a literary giant," but Wain does go on to state that Braithwaite "writes well enough to tell his story clearly, swiftly and without wasting words." More recent assessments view Braithwaite's novel within the larger context of postwar black British writing. James Procter, for example, in *Writing Black Britain, 1948–1998: An Interdisciplinary Anthology* (2000), views Braithwaite's work as the product of the "pioneering black settlers of the 1950s and early 1960s" who appear to be "struggling to 'fit in', or assimilate." Other assessments of the work are made on the basis of the teaching methods Braithwaite describes in the novel. In Michael Fielding's article on the British educator Alex Bloom, which appeared in a 2005 issue of *Forum*, Fielding states his desire to not "diminish the

artistic merits of the book," but focuses on the community Braithwaite discusses in his work as well as on Braithwaite's discussion of the students' ability to express their opinions to the school's teaching staff. Caryl Phillips, in a 2005 article in the United Kingdom periodical the *Observer*, praises Braithwaite's keen insights and bravery in directly addressing the racism inherent in postwar British society.

CRITICISM

Catherine Dominic

Catherine Dominic is a novelist and a freelance writer and editor. In this essay, she studies the relationships among the teachers at the school depicted in Braithwaite's To Sir, With Love. *She maintains that in recounting the interactions of the teaching staff, Braithwaite seeks to emphasize the integral nature of professional support among colleagues to his success as a teacher and to the achievements of the students.*

Braithwaite's *To Sir, With Love* recounts the author's first year as a teacher in a unique school in London's East End. The novel is in many ways an exploration of the value of the school's educational methodology, which was a revolutionary one at the time. Children were not subjected to corporal punishment or really disciplined in any way. They were encouraged to speak their minds and given regular opportunities to comment on what they were being taught and how their lessons were administered. The overt message of the book emphasizes the equal exchange that occurs between Braithwaite and his students. He learns as much from them as they do from him. Yet a more subtle, but equally important, commerce of ideas occurs among the teachers. They freely offer one another advice and discuss their personal teaching experiences. With the exception of Theo Weston, the teachers are for the most part a supportive group of professionals who learn from one another. Braithwaite, focusing in particular on Mrs. Drew, Mrs. Dale-Evans, Miss Clintridge, and Miss Blanchard, presents the faculty interactions as integral to Greenslade's educational program and sense of community as well as to the students' and his own success.

Braithwaite's initial contact with the faculty of Greenslade Secondary School is with the headmaster, Alex Florian. Florian's greeting is warm and he expresses his pleasure at having Braithwaite

WHAT DO I READ NEXT?

- *Paid Servant* is Braithwaite's second novel, published in 1962 by Bodley Head. In this work, which has been described as a sequel to *To Sir, With Love*, Braithwaite recounts his experiences as a social worker for the London County Council Department of Child Welfare.

- *Honorary White*, published in 1975 by Bodley Head, is inspired by Braithwaite's trip to South Africa. In the book, Braithwaite discusses South African apartheid (legalized segregation and discrimination). The title of the book refers to the official status given to him by the government, so that he would be admitted to restricted hotels and various public venues.

- *An East End Story*, an autobiography written by Alfred Gardner and published in 2002, provides another version of the events occurring in the East End school where Braithwaite taught.

- *The Blackboard Jungle*, written by Evan Hunter, originally published in 1954 and reprinted in 2004 by Simon and Schuster, is based on Hunter's experiences as a teacher at a vocational high school in the Bronx. Like *To Sir, With Love*, it portrays the challenges of educating "tough," working-class children with less-than-ideal home lives. Also like *To Sir, With Love*, the novel was adapted into a film version, which was released in 1955 by MGM.

- *Our Hidden Lives: The Remarkable Diaries of Post-War Britain*, was edited by Simon Garfield and published in 2005 by Ebury Press. The book offers a glimpse of daily life in Britain during the time frame in which Braithwaite's novel is set. It is a collection of actual diary entries written by British citizens in the years immediately following World War II.

- *The Middle Passage*, a book-length work of nonfiction by V. S. Naipaul, was written in 1962 (published by A. Deutsch) and reprinted in 2002 by Vintage. Like Braithwaite, Naipaul is a British colonial citizen. In this book Naipaul recounts his travels through British West Indian colonies, commenting on the impact of slavery and colonialism on the nations he explores.

consider a teaching position at the school. The first teacher Braithwaite speaks with is Theo Weston, who provides a less-than-flattering portrait of what the school has to offer Braithwaite. Upon encountering Braithwaite, Weston comments that Braithwaite is "another lamb to the slaughter," and, unable to restrain himself from commenting on Braithwaite's race, adds "or shall we say black sheep?" Rather put off by Weston's unfriendly demeanor, Braithwaite hopes that upon getting to know Weston better, he will find that Weston is in fact better natured than he appears. Most of the other teachers Braithwaite next encounters offer a warmer and more encouraging greeting. Their enthusiasm toward him and admiration for one another put Braithwaite a bit more at ease. Grace Dale-Evans introduces herself to Braithwaite and, shortly thereafter, introduces him to the other teachers. She quietly comments on some of the teachers to Braithwaite during this process. Mrs. Dale-Evans notes that Miss Vivienne Clintridge, the arts and drama teacher, is "an excellent artist." Mrs. Dale-Evans praises the deputy headmistress, Mrs. Drew, as "one of the best." In addition to chastising Weston for his discouraging attitude, Mrs. Dale-Evans expresses her desire that the other teachers help encourage Braithwaite to accept the position at Greenslade. As for Miss Blanchard, the reader learns that she has only been at the school for a few days and that while she does find it to be a "frightening" place, she also seems intrigued by the challenges it offers. Miss Blanchard also offers an

> THE OVERT MESSAGE OF THE BOOK
>
> EMPHASIZES THE EQUAL EXCHANGE THAT OCCURS
>
> BETWEEN BRAITHWAITE AND HIS STUDENTS. HE
>
> LEARNS AS MUCH FROM THEM AS THEY DO FROM HIM.
>
> YET A MORE SUBTLE, BUT EQUALLY IMPORTANT,
>
> COMMERCE OF IDEAS OCCURS AMONG THE
>
> TEACHERS."

honest description of the general atmosphere of the school to Braithwaite. She admits to not having teaching experience and to being a bit intimidated by the children, who seem quite grown up to her.

The next day, on Braithwaite's first day of teaching, more helpful advice from some of the teachers is offered. Mrs. Dale-Evans answers Braithwaite's questions about the children's use of foul language and comments on her own methods for dealing with the issue. Miss Clintridge brings Braithwaite a cup of tea during a break period and says she has come to see how his first day is going. Miss Clintridge then expresses her support of Florian's views on the children, on how they are deserving of sympathy and compassion, and how they should be encouraged to speak for themselves. She suggests that an attempt be made to see the world from the children's point of view if one is to understand them better. At the same time, Miss Clintridge insists that teachers have to consider themselves as well and to do what they can to make their challenging jobs "bearable." She advises Braithwaite to find a way, as they have all had to do, of letting the children know who the boss is. Hackman, the teacher whose job Braithwaite has taken over, attempted to be popular with the children, Miss Clintridge informs him, and that was a mistake.

Later, in the staff room, the teachers are gathered and they ask Braithwaite about how things are going in his classroom. He tells Miss Blanchard that he thinks he will take Miss Clintridge's advice about being an authority figure for the children rather than trying to be popular with them. Mrs. Drew chimes in, cautioning Braithwaite to not be too hard on the students, as they are "not bad when you get to know them." Here Weston makes a comment either suggestive of his own frustrations

as a teacher or indicative of his interest in advising Braithwaite as well. Responding to Mrs. Drew's comment, Weston tells Braithwaite that the "trick" of it is actually getting to know the students. His statement is made, unlike some of his other comments, without a snide remark attached and may be viewed as an attempt at solidarity with his fellow teachers. Miss Clintridge responds sarcastically to Weston, as she typically does, emphasizing the animosity the two seem to have for one another. Weston thereafter reverts to his former habit of making thinly veiled taunts and insinuations, all with a smile or sneer. In this one instance, however, it seems as though Weston made an honest effort at fitting in, or even at mentoring the school's new teacher.

Following this exchange, Braithwaite makes a significant discovery about his fellow teachers. He states that "this much was clear, most of my colleagues wanted me to make good; they had accepted me unconditionally as one of them. And that was the most important thing of all." Braithwaite here acknowledges the deep significance of their support and advice and seems almost surprised at how much such things mean to him. As the novel progresses, Braithwaite comments in several places that the advice of his colleagues was employed or considered in decisions he makes in relation to his own students. Determined to establish order in his continually unruly class, Braithwaite recalls Miss Clintridge's advice about being "the teacher in charge—the boss—as Clinty had said." When sharing with Miss Blanchard his ideas about implementing social order and the use of formal addresses in the class, Braithwaite finds that Miss Blanchard is uncertain if this is the best decision, but she nevertheless supports his judgment and hopes that the idea will work. Later Weston also questions Braithwaite's insistence on the students' formality with Braithwaite and their fellow students. To Braithwaite's surprise, Miss Dawes, a teacher with whom he has previously had few exchanges, defends Braithwaite's methods against Weston's criticisms.

When Bell arrives at the school and has his own difficulties in controlling the children, Braithwaite steps into the role of mentor. Bell's problems with the students mirror those Braithwaite faced when he first started teaching at Greenslade. Bell objects to the often sloppy appearance of the children and also to their odor, as many of them are unable to wash properly because of inadequate plumbing in their homes. Like Braithwaite initially was, Bell is dismayed by the students' apparent lack of an understanding of basic hygiene. After making insulting comments to the children, Bell is spoken to by Florian, who explains to Bell some of the same things he explained to Braithwaite at the beginning of the novel. The domestic situations of the children is often substandard, and new teachers are often unaware of the consequences of such circumstances to the children's general appearance. Additionally, Bell feels strongly, as did Braithwaite, that he must demonstrate his authority over the children. In Bell's case, he refuses to let a student opt out of attempting a maneuver in gym class. The child is subsequently injured, and when another student threatens Bell for "making" the child attempt the activity, Braithwaite intervenes. He avoids judging Bell's motives or methods, but he does ask Bell about why he insisted that the student attempt the vault maneuver. "I had to, don't you see," Bell responds. He goes on to say, "he just stood there refusing to obey and the others were watching me; I just had to do something." Braithwaite speaks in an understanding way to Bell, saying that he is not criticizing, merely asking. He goes on to explain the affection the students have for one another, and urges Bell to report the incident to the headmaster, which Bell does. Bell, after hearing an apology from the student who threatened to attack him, offers his own apology to Braithwaite's students. When Miss Clintridge and Braithwaite are later discussing the incident, she notes that Bell is in fact a good teacher and says she hopes he "hasn't had too much of a fright." Bell attempts to insist, just as Braithwaite had, upon being an authority figure to the children, and just as Braithwaite does, he makes mistakes along the way but is encouraged by the support of his colleagues.

This last episode underscores Braithwaite's message. The support of other teachers is vital to the continuance of Greenslade. The teachers aid one another in understanding the approach of the school and the value of this approach. They provide one another with advice on how to reach the students and how to maintain their own dignity and sanity in such a challenging atmosphere. Braithwaite quite naturally reaches out to Bell with compassion and empathy in the same way that Mrs. Drew, Mrs. Dale-Evans, Miss Clintridge, and Miss Blanchard aided him. The sense of comradeship and acceptance, mutual respect, and mentoring is, as Braithwaite himself says, "the most important thing of all," as it enriches their personal

> HERE IS A LEAP THAT TAKES US INTO A QUITE DIFFERENT WORLD OF RICH AND VIBRANT EXCHANGE BETWEEN YOUNG PEOPLE AND ADULTS AS EQUAL PARTNERS IN THE PROCESSES OF LEARNING IN A SHARED, VERY PUBLIC PLACE."

and professional lives and enables all of them to better serve the students of Greenslade.

Source: Catherine Dominic, Critical Essay on *To Sir, With Love*, in *Novels for Students*, Gale, Cengage Learning, 2010.

Michael Fielding

In the following excerpt, Fielding considers To Sir, With Love *as a "rich testament" to radical English educator Alex Bloom.*

...Immediately prior to World War Two, Braithwaite studied at Cambridge University and on the outbreak of hostilities he joined the RAF as a pilot. Having returned to Cambridge at the end of the war and completed his studies he then tried to get a job that would utilise his engineering skills and qualifications, but the racial prejudice he encountered in civilian life, though not in the RAF, resulted in no engineering job and his eventual arrival, without any formal teacher training, at St George-in-the-East. The origins of *To Sir With Love* lie in his daily struggle to learn how to teach in a way that engaged young people respectfully, creatively and demandingly in a school that, as we have seen, took these matters very seriously indeed. In recent interviews Braithwaite has insisted that *To Sir With Love* is not a novel, not fiction; rather it is a selection from his own notes and reflections that he wrote every day when he got home as a way of learning how to teach better. This is not, of course, to diminish the artistic merits of the book. What is pertinent to this study of Bloom's work is Braithwaite's firm insistence that all that is contained in *To Sir With Love* actually happened and as such it is a legitimate additional source of insight into the kind of community that St George-in-the-East was just after the War.

To Sir With Love is indeed a rich testament not only to Braithwaite's courage and creativity as a teacher, but also to the work of Alex Bloom....

STUDENT VOICE AS IT MIGHT BE

Chapter 17 of *To Sir With Love* opens with an air of excitement: 'The half yearly report of the Students' Council... was one of the most important days in the calendar of (the) school' and Braithwaite admits to 'being as excited as the children as the day approached'. The proceedings begin with Bloom speaking 'at length, re-iterating the aims and policy of the school and of the important contribution each child could make to the furtherance of those aims'. Bloom is then followed by the Head Girl explaining the purpose of the Council and its activities prior to each class, through its chosen reps for each subject, reporting on their half-year's work with 'the emphasis... on what they understood rather than what they were expected to learn'. What then transpires is a truly remarkable process in which students move beyond reportage and appreciation to a reciprocally demanding, sometimes critical, dialogue with three randomly chosen members of staff who, with varying degrees of skill and conviction, seek to justify and, in some cases defend, the basis of the school curriculum on which the student body had communally reflected in such detail. In this instance, one of the older boys challenged the nature of PE that the school offered:

> He complained that the PT was ill-conceived and pointless, and the routine monotonous; he could see no advantage in doing it; a jolly good game was far better. Apparently, he was voicing the opinion of all the boys, for they cheered him loudly.

There then follows a series of impassioned, thought-provoking exchanges between students and staff about the nature and possible justification of compulsion, the necessity of recognising differences in need and capacity, the importance of thinking about and helping others, and the relationship between school and wider society, particularly with regard to preparation for adult life.

This is student voice as it might be. This is student voice making a quantum leap from our current attempts at carefully circumscribed, often rather timid encounters of small consequence and little learning. Here is a leap that takes us into a quite different world of rich and vibrant exchange between young people and adults as equal partners in the processes of learning in a shared, very public place. Here we transcend the cautious compartmentalisation of student voice and staff voice and create new, publicly shared, common spaces that are brave, exploratory, vibrant in their willingness to challenge, to listen, to laugh, to risk adventure and to do so together in ways which affirm our shared humanity.

WEEKLY REVIEWS

Whilst this exhilarating articulation of an early version of the School Council adds a lived dimension to other more deliberately analytic accounts of student voice at St George-in-the-East, it is also important to understand that Bloom's development of student voice was expressed as much through daily encounter as it was through the development of a richly democratic, public realm. Some of the most moving parts of Braithwaite's book draw on ways in which young people's felt experience of teaching and learning at the school were affirmed, legitimated and made significant through the simple mechanism of each student's 'Weekly Review'. In these Reviews

> Each child would review the events of his school work in his own words, in his own way; he was free to comment, to criticise, to agree or disagree, with any person, subject or method, as long as it was in some way associated with the school.

Bloom not only insisted on the necessity of Weekly Reviews, he staunchly supported the right of young people to say what they thought and felt 'without reprisal'. What better way to draw this section on radical student voice to a close than with Braithwaite's account of Bloom's defence of a practice that speaks to us, quietly and wisely, on the 50th anniversary of his death. In reading it we gain courage and hope and come to understand our spiritual debt to teachers like Alex Bloom, E. R. Braithwaite and those amongst our contemporaries... 'who', in Stephen Spender's memorable words, 'are truly great. Who from the womb remember the soul's history... Who in their lives fight for life, who wear at their hearts the fire's centre' (Spender, 1964).

> 'Look at it this way', (Mr Bloom) had said. 'It is of advantage to both pupil and teacher. If a child wants to write about something which matters to him, he will take some pains to set it down as carefully and with as much detail as possible; that must in some way improve his written English in terms of spelling, construction and style. Week by week we are able, through his reviews, to follow and observe his

progress in such things. As for the teachers, we soon get a pretty good idea what the children think of us and whether or not we are getting close to them. It may sometimes be rather deflating to discover that a well-prepared lesson did not really excite Johnny Smith's interest, but, after all, the lesson was intended to benefit Johnny Smith, not his teacher; if it was uninteresting to him then the teacher must think again. You will discover that these children are reasonably fair, even when they comment on us. If we are careless about our clothing, manners or person they will soon notice it, and it would be pointless to be angry with them for pointing such things out. Finally, from the reviews, the sensible teacher will observe the trend of individual and collective interests and plan his work accordingly.'

Whilst the words are not Bloom's the integrity of the advocacy and the substance of the argument are entirely true to the spirit and practice of his life's work.

'HE IS EDUCATED WHO IS ABLE TO RECOGNISE RELATIONSHIPS BETWEEN THINGS AND TO EXPERIENCE JUST RELATIONSHIPS WITH PERSONS'

Student voice is important because education is essentially about relationships. As Bloom has it: 'He is educated who is able to recognise relationships between things and to experience just relationships with persons' (Bloom, 1952, p. 136) It is through certain kinds of relationships that we come to understand and change the world. Whilst the organisational arrangements that have featured so prominently in the latter half of this paper are without doubt among the most impressive features of St George-in-the-East, they are not, however, the most important. The communitarian strand of radical democratic progressive schooling which Bloom's work exemplifies regards relationships, our encounters with others, as both the end and the means of our fulfilment. Organisational arrangements, democratic or otherwise, are a necessary, but not a sufficient condition of our well-being together. They should be expressive of just and caring human relationships and the degree to which they achieve this is a measure of their legitimacy and their creative capacity to sustain and encourage a better world.

Fundamental to the success of any attempt to realise a community in which human beings can be and become good persons is the establishment of certain kinds of relationships amongst those involved. The capacity to become aware of the thoughts and feelings of young people

and the adults who learn and work with them through the structures of daily encounter must rest not only on the energy and imagination with which individual, group and community share their work together, but also on the way these encounters are conducted, the honesty and openness of their touch, the courage of their engagement with conflict, and the firmness of their desire to value difference as well as confront what should be opposed....

Source: Michael Fielding, "Alex Bloom, Pioneer of Radical State Education," in *FORUM*, Vol. 47, No. 2–3, 2005, pp. 119–34.

Bruce King

In the following excerpt, King discusses the portrayal of discrimination against black West Indians in London in To Sir, With Love.

...Whereas the Indian prose writers, many of whom were birds of passage, were mostly concerned with differences between the cultures of Asia and Europe, the West Indians, who came to settle in England, faced problems of what was to be their identity and home along with racial discrimination. Un-British behaviour was thought savage or exotic, but to behave British was to be one of the *Mimic Men* (the title of V. S. Naipaul's novel about the deracinated, British-educated, colonial middle class who inherited power in the new nations). Much of the literature for decades will be concerned with making a transition and with the need for England to be remade.

The most popular West Indian author of the period was E. R. Braithwaite. An RAF fighter pilot during the war, he took a further degree at Cambridge after demobilization, then spent eighteen months unsuccessfully seeking appropriate employment before teaching at a school in the East End of London, the first year of which provided material for *To Sir, With Love* (1959). Anyone questioning whether the educated black West Indian faced discrimination in England only need read *To Sir, With Love*, one of several auto-biographies in which West Indians describe being teachers in England. The portrayal of Braithwaite's first interview for a position as a manager in the electronics industry, a field in which be was well qualified, revealed he was unlikely ever to use his qualifications in England. The refusal by white working-class landlords to rent him a room fills in the other end of the social spectrum. England then was often a place of colour prejudice. A particularly telling example occurs late in the book with the death of the father of the one black student in his class, actually someone of mixed blood. The class pitches in to purchase flowers which no one is willing to take to the boy as they do not want to be seen going to the house of a 'darkie'.

To Sir, With Love is about overcoming prejudice, class and educational as well as racial. Braithwaite, one of the first black teachers in the British school system, was the missionary bringing civilization to the native savages. His students are from a notoriously impoverished and tough part of London, often themselves the children of European immigrants and the unemployed; their families have little money and the places in which they live are overcrowded, damp, without mod cons. They speak and dress poorly, seldom wash, have few academic skills, and have been sent to this particular school because of discipline problems. Braithwaite at first looks down on his students as do many other new teachers. As the students discover he is human and not just a 'darkie', he learns that they are intelligent, in many ways mature, and will be interested in topics if treated with respect. Thus the parallel between Braithwaite and his students.

The effectiveness of *To Sir, With Love* results from understatement and economy. Braithwaite writes in a confidet, clear, concise, explanatory manner. There is, however, a tense ambivalence in the prose, reflecting self-control as if the reader were not being told all that is felt. Braithwaite seems too insistent on proclaiming his abilities, attractiveness, intelligence, judgement, and unassertiveness.

Paid Servant (1962) recounts a frustrating period after teaching when Braithwaite, in another first, became a child-welfare officer expected to locate homes for black children, while *A Kind of Homecoming* (1962) describes travels in four West African nations. This was followed by a novel, *A Choice of Straws* (1967), about white working-class racial violence in London told from the perspective of a white hooligan who after killing a 'spade' falls in love with one. Braithwaite portrays the white sympathetically and with understanding. *Honorary White* (1975) tells of six weeks in South Africa when as a distinguished visitors he was temporarily unblackballed. Braithwaite was one of the many West Indians who either returned to the Caribbean or eventually settled in the United States or Canada. Like Sam Selvon's work, their writings can be seen as transitional; they were late colonials who

were legally British and regarded themselves as such until racial discrimination made them self-consciously Other . . . .

Source: Bruce King, "Prose: Culture Conflict and Lonely Londoners," in *The Internationalization of English Literature*, in *Oxford English Literary History, 1948-2000*, Vol. 13, Oxford University Press, 2004, pp. 32–61.

Philip Butcher

In the following review, Butcher discusses the success of To Sir, With Love *in the United States.*

Edward Ricardo Braithwaite, born and reared in Georgetown, British Guiana, spent two years as a communications engineer in Venezuela and arrived in England, planning graduate study, in time to enlist in the RAF for the defense of the land he loved. As an airman he was accepted; but, once the war was over, as a black man he was automatically ineligible for all the jobs he sought. His mounting bitterness was mitigated by occasional kindnesses and the steady encouragement of the elderly white couple, "Mom" and "Pop," with whom he lived. Finally he was appointed as a teacher in London.

The children of the East End school to which he was assigned were products of degrading slums and postwar disillusionment. These Cockney "Teddy boys" and tarts had driven away many a teacher unable either to control or instruct them, and Braithwaite, hindered by his race and his inexperience, promised to be an easy victim. The school did not permit corporal punishment. Its idealistic headmaster blamed society for the problems his charges presented, and he insisted that his teachers do everything possible to help these underpriviledged pupils become respectable citizens and as enlightened adults as their capacities would permit.

Braithwaite's victory over the tormenting youngsters began when he found that he really liked them, collectively and singly. He adopted a rule requiring that they address one another in formal fashion and that they call him "Sir." This acceptance of the students as worthwhile young adults and the demand that they conform to certain simple social graces worked wonders. Despite unpleasant episodes in the classroom and the community, even in London as a whole, Braithwaite's success as a teacher was established. His students' regard for him was demonstrated in a climactic moment when they attended, in a body, a funeral at the home of a colored classmate, for the one thing Braithwaite struggled hardest to teach them was tolerance, and in this difficult act they showed they had mastered the lesson. When the school year ended they expressed their affection with a present marked "*To Sir, With Love.*"

The girls in Braithwaite's class, adolescents about to take on adult responsibilities, show their maturity in part by the devotion they bestow on him, but it is a fellow teacher, Miss Blanchard, who wins him. Their engagement, reluctantly but decently accepted by her well-to-do parents, brings the book to a close.

Braithwaite studied for a time at an unidentified institution in America and hence can claim some authority for his analyses of racial prejudice in England and in the United States. First published in England, where it was a minor literary sensation, *To Sir, With Love* has enjoyed a similar and quite deserved success here. It lacks the psychological penetration the modern reader has come to expect in autobiography, and in its endorsement of tolerance and the platitudes of progressive education the book seems sometimes to report what should have happened rather than what did happen. Braithwaite's conversion of his students from sinners to saints is too easy and too complete to be convincing. His genteel love affair seems contrived to illustrate the theme and does not engage the reader's emotions. But the book has a solid sociological validity unblemished by professional jargon and a sturdy directness which makes it a memorable and rewarding narrative.

Source: Philip Butcher, "Teaching Tolerance in London," in *Journal of Negro Education*, Vol. 29, No. 4, Autumn 1960, pp. 463–64.

SOURCES

"Bank Shares Fall Despite Bail-out," in *BBC News*, October 13, 2008, http://news.bbc.co.uk (accessed December 2, 2008).

Braithwaite, E. R., *To Sir, With Love*, Jove Books, 1977.

"The Children Act and Report," Web site of the Department for Children, Schools, and Families, http://www.dcsf.gov.uk/publications/childrenactreport/ (accessed December 2, 2008).

"Clement Attlee (1883–1967)," in *BBC History*, http://www.bbc.co.uk/history/historic_figures/attlee_clement.shtml (accessed November 25, 2008).

"E. R. Braithwaite," Web site of the Guyana Folk Festival and the Guyana Cultural Association of New York,

http://www.guyfolkfest.org/2007_ERBrathwaite.htm (accessed November 20, 2008).

"Economy Boost May Mean Pain Later," in *BBC News*, November 21, 2008, http://news.bbc.co.uk (accessed December 2, 2008).

"Education Act of 1944," in *NationMaster Encyclopedia*, http://www.nationmaster.com/encyclopedia/Education-Act-1944 (accessed December 2, 2008).

Fielding, Michael, "Alex Bloom, Pioneer of Radical State Education," in *Forum*, Vol. 47, Nos. 2 and 3, 2005, pp. 119–34.

"Guyana: Historic Events," in *Guyana News and Information*, http://www.guyana.org/history.html (accessed November 19, 2008).

"Harold Macmillan (1894–1986)," in *BBC History*, http://www.bbc.co.uk/history/historic_figures/macmillan_harold.shtml (accessed November 25, 2008).

Phillips, Caryl, "To Ricky with Love," in the *Observer*, July 23, 2005, Features and Reviews section, p. 28.

"Postwar British Economy," in *MSN Encarta*, http://uk.encarta.msn.com/encyclopedia_781539317/post-war_britain.html (accessed December 2, 2008).

Procter, James, "Introduction: 1948 to late 1960s," in *Writing Black Britain, 1948–1998: An Interdisciplinary Anthology*, Manchester University Press, 2000, pp. 13–16.

"Race Relations Acts, 1965 to 1976," Web site of the Museum of London, http://www.museumoflondon.org.uk/English/Collections/OnlineResources/X20L/Themes/1380/1203/ (accessed November 25, 2008).

"*To Sir, With Love*: A Dialogue with E R Braithwaite," in *Doctoral School NETwork*, Institute of Education, University of London, http://doctoralschool.ioe.ac.uk/index.php?option = com_content&task = view&id = 86 (accessed December 1, 2008).

"UK October Budget Deficit Widens," in *BBC News*, November 20, 2008, http://news.bbc.co.uk (accessed December 2, 2008).

Wain, John, "Outlander Among Savages," in the *New York Times Book Review*, May 1, 1960, p. BR6.

FURTHER READING

Fenwick, I. G. K., *The Comprehensive School, 1944–1970: The Politics of Secondary School Reorganization*, Methuen, 1976, reprinted by Routledge, 2007.

Fenwick discusses the movement toward the comprehensive school system and away from the educational tracking of the Tripartite system (of which Braithwaite's school was a part) in England. Fenwick's focus is on the question of which groups (for example, teachers, counselors, and government officials) exerted the most influence in the reformation of the educational system.

Mohanram, Radhika, *Imperial White: Race, Diaspora, and the British Empire*, University of Minnesota Press, 2007.

Mohanram explores the overlapping ideas of racism and colonialism by examining what it means to be both white and British in Great Britain and in its colonies. Her study includes a discussion of the literary texts that contributed to the racialization of the notion of Britishness.

Phillips, Lawrence, *London Narratives: Post-war Fiction and the City*, Continuum International Publishing, 2006.

In this analysis of the fictional representations of post–World War II London, Phillips maintains that through the fictional narratives set in postwar London, the very idea of the city and its history was transformed, and that this shift paralleled the physical transformation the city underwent during the rebuilding process.

Wambu, Onyekachi, ed., *Hurricane Hits England: An Anthology of Writing about Black Britain*, Continuum International Publishing, 2000.

This collection of writing by and about black Britons writing during the postwar period of decolonization includes a preface by E. R. Braithwaite. The works anthologized here reveal the attitudes of Great Britain to native-born blacks and to newly arriving black immigrants from British colonies.

Typical American

GISH JEN

1991

Typical American is a novel by Gish Jen, published in 1991. Jen is the daughter of Chinese immigrants to the United States, and the novel follows the story of three Chinese people who come to the United States in 1947 and become U.S. citizens in the 1950s. The novel covers a twenty-year period, up to the mid-1960s, and shows how Ralph Chang, his wife, Helen, and his sister Theresa gradually adapt to life in their new country and become "typical Americans." *Typical American* raises many thought-provoking questions about the nature of U.S. society and culture. Is it too materialistic? Is it racist? The book also explores the nature and extent of personal freedom. To what extent do people really have the opportunity to become everything they wish to be and attain the American dream? The Changs seem to attain their dream and become "typical Americans," but they are subject to a reversal of fortunes that makes them question their values and the dominant ethos of the society in which they live. Reviewers hailed *Typical American* as an outstanding contribution to the literature that describes the immigrant experience in the United States. The novel was praised for its humor, graceful style, insight into the way immigrants view the United States, and blend of comedy and tragedy.

Gish Jen *(Steve Liss | Time Life Pictures | Getty Images)*

AUTHOR BIOGRAPHY

Gish Jen was born Lillian Jen on August 12, 1955, in Long Island, New York, the daughter of Chinese immigrants Norman and Agnes Jen, who had met in the United States in the 1940s. Both her parents expected to return to China, but were prevented from doing so (like Ralph Chang in *Typical American*) by the Communist takeover of China in 1949.

As a child Jen lived in Yonkers, New York, but the family later moved to the Jewish suburb of Scarsdale, where Jen went to high school and acquired the nickname, Gish. Jen attended Harvard University, graduating with a degree in English in 1977. At that time she had no ambition to be a writer. Her family expected her either to go into business or become a doctor or a lawyer. So even though, as she told interviewer Rachel Lee, she "really had never had any interest in . . . business," Jen attended business school at Stanford University from 1979 to 1980, dropping out in her second year of study and then making a trip to China. On her return, she decided to enroll in an M.F.A. program at the University of Iowa in 1981. Her parents opposed her decision, but she persevered and graduated in 1983.

Jen married David O'Connor and moved to Silicon Valley in California. In 1985 the couple moved to Cambridge, Massachusetts, where Jen was awarded a fellowship at the Bunting Institute at Radcliffe College. This enabled her to start work on her first novel, *Typical American*, a tale of Chinese immigrants to the United States, which was published in 1991. The novel was hailed by reviewers as a remarkable contribution to Asian American literature and was named "Notable Book of the Year" by the *New York Times*. It was also a finalist for the 1991 National Book Critics Circle Award. Jen's second novel, *Mona in the Promised Land* (1996) continued the story of the Chang family from *Typical American*. *Mona in the Promised Land* was named one of the ten best books of the year by the *Los Angeles Times*. A collection of eight short stories, *Who's Irish?*, followed in 1999, and in 2004 Jen published her third novel, *The Love Wife* (2004), also a contribution to literature about Chinese immigrants to the United States and issues such as cultural diversity.

As of 2008 Jen lives with her husband and children in Cambridge, Massachusetts.

PLOT SUMMARY

Part I: Sweet Rebellion

Typical American begins in Jiangsu Province, near Shanghai, China, with a glimpse of six-year-old Yifeng (Ralph Chang), who fails to please his demanding father. In 1947 Yifeng leaves China for graduate study in engineering in the United States. Soon after he arrives in New York, he develops a crush on Cammy, a secretary in the Foreign Student Affairs Office. Cammy gives him an English name, Ralph. Ralph studies hard and tries to adapt to life in the United States. He falls in love with Cammy, but his attempts to get closer to her end when she is fired from her job.

After the Communists take over China in 1949, Ralph's father asks him to return to China, but the U.S. government refuses to let Chinese students return. After this, Ralph loses touch with his family. He also forgets to renew his visa and is too fearful of going to the Foreign Student Affairs Office, because he thinks the man in charge, Mr. Fitt, does not like him. He lives a quiet existence, hoping that the lack of a visa will not matter, but then he starts to receive letters from the Department of Immigration. He moves to a different building, trying to elude detection.

Within a few months, he moves nine times, losing touch with his Chinese student friends, except for Little Lou. Ralph sees no future for himself. He stops studying and takes a job at a Chinese restaurant, where he kills and plucks chickens in the basement. After some time, he approaches Pinkus, the head of the engineering department, saying he wants to resume his doctoral studies. Pinkus agrees to help him, but weeks go by and nothing happens. Ralph alienates Pinkus by following him in the streets and also following his daughter home. When he finally meets Pinkus in a bar, the professor calls him a liar.

Ralph moves again. He stops going to work and sinks into despair. Then one day he is sitting on a bench on the street when to his surprise, his older sister, Theresa, passes by. Theresa, who is in New York studying medicine, has been searching for Ralph. Now chance brings them together. Ralph also meets Theresa's Chinese friend Helen, who accompanied her to the United States. Ralph's fortunes improve, and he finds a job as a draftsman. He normalizes his immigration status, returns to his Ph.D. studies, and marries Helen.

Part II: The House Holds

Ralph, Helen, and Theresa live together in a run-down apartment in a poor neighborhood. Ralph and Helen fight a lot. Ralph is also critical of Theresa and generally morose. Helen adapts well to life in America; she is the practical one in the family.

Helen becomes friends with Janis Chao, the wife of a Chinese man and old acquaintance of Ralph's, Old Chao. Janis decides it is time for Theresa to get married, and she and Helen arrange for Theresa to meet Janis's landlord, an American-born Chinese man named Grover Ding. They all meet for supper at Old Chao's house. Theresa takes a dislike to Grover, but Ralph likes him because he is a sharp businessman. When the men go outside to look at Old Chao's new car, Old Chao shows Grover how to drive it, but he is astonished when Grover drives off with Ralph in the passenger seat. Grover drives for hours, and late in the evening they pull into a diner and eat a huge meal. Ralph is excited to be on this adventure. Grover turns out to be the owner of many buildings and restaurants and claims to be a self-made millionaire. Ralph is impressed. It also transpires that Grover owns the diner they are eating in, so there is no bill to pay. The two men spend hours at the diner.

Then, as Old Chao's car is out of gas, Grover orders a taxi, and Ralph is driven home.

In the meantime, Janis, Old Chao, Theresa, and Helen worry about what has happened to Ralph. At dawn they hear the car has been found abandoned at a diner in Pennsylvania. When Ralph finally shows up, he blames Grover for what happened. Later, he tries unsuccessfully to get in touch with Grover, while Helen secretly nourishes affection for the charming, handsome rogue she believes Grover to be. Helen gives birth to a baby girl, Callie, and then another girl, Mona. Ralph graduates with a Ph.D., Theresa acquires her M.D., and the family moves to a larger house.

Part III: This New Life

Several years go by, and Ralph, Helen, and Theresa are settled and optimistic about the future. Ralph is now an assistant professor. As a sign of their rise in the world, Ralph buys a car from Old Chao, although he fails his driving test several times before he manages to acquire a license. He drives his family to Connecticut, where they see many suburban houses and long to acquire one for themselves.

Helen becomes an expert on different kinds of houses. They need help in coming up with a down payment, so Ralph thinks about getting in touch with Grover. Meanwhile, Theresa works long hours in an emergency room. She develops a friendship with Old Chao, while Ralph hopes to get tenure in the engineering department.

Theresa and Old Chao get closer, and Helen finds the perfect house in the suburbs. They manage to get a bank loan to buy it, even though it costs more than they can really afford. They are thrilled by their new house, and Ralph and Helen get along better than they have for years. Ralph sees Theresa and Old Chao together and tells Helen they are having an affair. Ralph gets tenure, although he decides he would sooner be almost anything other than a professor. He and Helen are short with Theresa, and she realizes they think she is having an affair. Old Chao tells her not to worry about it, and their involvement with each other deepens.

Part IV: Structural Weakening

Ralph takes his family on a vacation, but he is already bored with his new position as a professor. He feels that life offers more for him if he makes up his mind to seek it. He calls Grover, and they meet in a deli. Grover says they can do business together but asks Ralph for five thousand dollars. Ralph later mails him a check, and Grover arranges for him to buy a fried chicken take-out restaurant from a man who is to testify against Grover in a court case. Ralph is overjoyed to get this no-money-down deal. Ralph and Grover plan to have Ralph buy the business in his own name, sell it back to Grover, and then buy it back from Grover out of the profits.

Ralph takes a leave of absence from his teaching job. Grover becomes a friend of the family, but Theresa remains in her room when he visits. Ralph reads self-help books, hoping to learn how to become rich. The chicken business flourishes, and Ralph learns from Grover how to rig the cash register so he can cheat on taxes. The family becomes respectable, buying lots of consumer items. Everyone is happy except for Theresa, who feels she has lost her place in the family. She continues her affair with Old Chao, but Ralph becomes hostile to her, and as a result, Theresa moves out of the house.

Grover turns his romantic attentions to Helen, and she is charmed by him. Ralph does not notice. With Theresa gone, he must find a way of making his business more profitable. He has an idea to build an addition to the building, on top of the roof, but Grover will not help him. Grover and Helen continue their discreet affair, and Grover tries to persuade Helen to leave her husband.

Ralph becomes suspicious, and he and Helen are cool toward each other. Ralph finally convinces Grover to agree to the addition, and construction begins. When it is complete, Ralph's Chicken Palace, as it is called, flourishes. Then Chuck, Grover's assistant, tells them that Grover is in jail for tax evasion. Ralph decides they should start paying their taxes in full, and Helen goes to work as a cashier at the restaurant to help them meet their expenses.

The walls in the new addition crack, and soon it is clear that the building will fall down. Ralph discovers that Grover is not really in jail, and that he has taken advantage of them. Grover built the original building and sold it to them knowing that it rested on soil full of rotting logs and was therefore unstable.

Part V: A Man to Sit at Supper and Never Eat

Ralph closes the store, while Helen tries to find a job as a shop girl and debates whether to tell Ralph of her affair with Grover. Ralph says they must sell the house, and he and Helen start to quarrel. During one fight, Ralph pushes her through a window, but she is not seriously injured. They invite Theresa to return to live with them, and she arrives with her two cats. She tells Helen that Old Chao wants to marry her; he has told his wife, Janis, about their affair. Theresa refused Old Chao's proposal. When Old Chao comes to visit, Ralph either hides out in his bedroom or takes the dog for a walk. One day he encounters Grover and Chuck, and Grover makes a nasty allusion to having an affair with Helen.

Ralph is furious and forces Helen to go for a drive with him. He drives recklessly, demanding that she tell him what went on between her and Grover. Meanwhile, Theresa is feeding the dog when it lunges at her. She throws the food can at it and runs for the garage just as Ralph and Helen return. Ralph is driving too fast and is unable to avoid hitting Theresa as she runs in front of the car.

Ralph drives Theresa to the emergency room. She is badly injured and falls into a coma. The family keeps a vigil. The Changs sell their house and move into an apartment. One day, Theresa makes a groaning noise, and she slowly begins to recover. She blinks, then opens her eyes, and identifies Ralph and Helen's children, Callie and Mona, by name. The novel ends with Ralph driving to the hospital to visit Theresa, his thoughts a mixture of elation and sadness.

CHARACTERS

Cammy

Cammy is the secretary in the Foreign Student Affairs Office at the university Ralph attends. She hates her job and her boss, Mr. Fitt, and does not even like the idea of having to work. However, she takes a liking to Ralph and even chooses his English name. Ralph becomes infatuated with her, and they go on a few innocuous dates together. Their relationship ends when Cammy is fired by Mr. Fitt.

Callie Chang

Callie Chang is the older daughter of Ralph and Helen Chang. The Changs decide that she will be raised as an American, speaking English and learning Chinese later in life.

Helen Chang

Helen is a Chinese woman originally from Shanghai. Her Chinese name is Hailan. She met Theresa when Theresa was sent by her parents to keep Helen company in Shanghai for a few months. At the time, Helen was sickly and considered an invalid, never allowed to do anything for herself. She and Theresa became close friends and traveled together to the United States on student visas.

Helen adapts quickly to life in the United States, and soon marries her friend's brother, Ralph. She quits school after acquiring permanent residency in the United States. Helen does not appear to have any ambition to work outside the home, but she develops practical domestic skills, such as cooking and making curtains and bedspreads. She finds this kind of work enjoyable, although she also enjoys having periods of sheer idleness. Helen becomes materialistic, coveting a large new house and all the material comforts that she sees Americans enjoying. When they move into the house, she becomes quite the suburban homemaker, joining the neighborhood bridge club and cultivating their garden. Eventually, however, she finds it necessary to work as a cashier at Ralph's Chicken Palace in order to boost the family income.

Helen is a quiet but resilient woman. She attempts to weather the ups and downs of her marriage, learning how to be assertive with Ralph when she needs to be. However, she has a brief affair with Grover Ding. This affair leads indirectly to the catastrophe that befalls Theresa, as the accident occurs in part as a result of Ralph's reckless driving after he learns of the affair.

Mona Chang

Mona Chang is the younger daughter of Ralph and Helen Chang. Like her sister, she grows up speaking English.

Ralph Chang

Ralph Chang is the central character in the novel. His Chinese name is Yifeng, and as a boy growing up in China, he incurs the displeasure of his father, a former government official who expects high standards from his son, because Yifeng does not appear to be learning well at school. Yifeng goes to the United States for graduate study in engineering and takes the name Ralph. He is determined to study hard and

avoid girls. The latter resolution is broken when he develops a crush on Cammy, a secretary in the Foreign Student Affairs Office. After the Communists take over China in 1949, Ralph's father implores him to return home, but the U.S. government will not allow Chinese students to leave. After this event, Ralph never hears from his family again. He is now alone in a foreign land and somehow has to make his way. His troubles begin when he forgets to renew his visa. Too nervous to make the appropriate actions to rectify the situation, he drops out of school, moves around from place to place to escape detection by the immigration authorities, and ends up working in a Chinese restaurant, slaughtering chickens in the basement. He gets so depressed that at one point he even contemplates suicide.

Ralph is at least temporarily saved when he meets his sister, Theresa, on the street. He marries Helen, a friend of Theresa, and soon they have two daughters. He normalizes his immigration status, completes his Ph.D., and eventually gets a tenured position in the engineering department at the university where he studied. However, he decides that he is not suited to the life of a professor. He has absorbed the American idea that a man can become anything he wants to be if he only puts his mind to it. He meets Grover Ding and gets obsessed with becoming a successful businessman. Not astute enough to realize that Grover is cheating him, Ralph conceives big plans for the chicken restaurant he buys from Grover. He wants to become financially successful and tries to expand the business. Ralph gets greedy, cheating on his taxes, while he and his family live beyond their means in a big suburban house. Ralph is so preoccupied by business matters he fails to notice that his wife is having an affair with Grover in his own house. Ralph's marriage deteriorates, and he becomes violent toward Helen. He is at least partly responsible for the tragic car accident that leaves Theresa with devastating injuries.

Theresa Chang

Theresa is Ralph's older sister. In China, she went to a convent school where she played baseball. Ralph's father encouraged Ralph to study Theresa, since she was studious and clever, doing everything right while he did everything wrong. As a result, Ralph called her "Know-It-All." Not considered beautiful, Theresa was briefly engaged to a banker's son, but the match was arranged by a go-between and the two young people had never met. The man insisted on meeting her but broke off the engagement as soon as he saw her.

Theresa, who at five foot seven inches, is tall for a Chinese woman, comes to the United States to study medicine. She and Ralph meet unexpectedly, and when Ralph and Theresa's close friend Helen marry, the three of them live together. Theresa does not marry. When Janis and Helen try to set her up with Grover Ding, she takes an immediate dislike to him. But she becomes angry about her solitary situation and allows herself to slip into an affair with Old Chao. The affair causes a rift in the Chang family, and Theresa decides to move out of the family home and into her own apartment. She refuses to marry Old Chao when he suggests it.

She works very hard as a student, especially when she spends long hours in the emergency room as part of her medical training. She eventually begins specialty training in obstetrics and starts practicing at a clinic. Theresa returns to live with Ralph and Helen, but Ralph resents her presence in the house. Her story ends in tragedy when she is hit by Ralph's car as it enters the driveway. She remains in a coma for a long time, and although she shows some signs of progress, her recovery is uncertain at the end of the book.

Yifeng Chang
See Ralph Chang

Henry Chao
See Old Chao

Janis Chao
Janis Chao is the wife of Old Chao who becomes friends with Helen. Janis grew up in China. After the early death of her father, her mother made a living by selling jewelry, and as a result, Janis saw "more of Chinese society than a nice girl should." Janis is a confident, capable, sociable woman who is easy to get along with. She starts a career in real estate and helps the Changs find a house. She has a son, Alexander. Old Chao eventually tells her that he is having an affair with Theresa, and Janis attempts to adjust to the situation.

Old Chao
Old Chao is one of Ralph's fellow Chinese students studying in the United States. He is older than Ralph, which is why his nickname is Old

Chao, meaning "Old Something-or-another," a common way in which younger classmates refer to older classmates. Old Chao, who marries Janis, is a complete contrast to Ralph. He is successful from the beginning and always seems to have good luck, as is shown when he wins a car in a church drawing. His career follows a rapid upward curve; he quickly gets tenure in the engineering department and becomes acting chairman of the department and then full professor within a year. Then he goes to work in the space program. Many years later, Old Chao has settled down in life and is more willing to take it easy. Old Chao has an affair with Theresa and wants to marry her, but she refuses.

Chuck
Chuck is Grover Ding's overconfident and arrogant assistant. He deceives the Changs by telling them that Grover is in jail for tax evasion.

Grover Ding
Grover Ding is an American-born Chinese man. Janis Chao thinks he would make a good husband for Theresa, but when they meet, Theresa cannot stand him. Grover has a lot of self-confidence and can be very charming. He is a slick, unscrupulous businessman and is quite wealthy, owning a number of buildings and restaurants; he calls himself a self-made millionaire, a "can-do type." Ralph likes him and tries to emulate him. Grover appears to befriend Ralph, arranging for Ralph to buy a small business, but in reality he is only using Ralph to serve his own ends. However, years pass before Ralph and Helen find this out, during which time the smooth-talking Grover seduces Helen and tries to persuade her to leave Ralph. It eventually transpires that Grover is a con artist and a liar. He cannot be trusted on any matter, and he has no sense of ethics, fairness, or morality. Grover is willing to ruin Ralph financially so he can steal his wife.

Mr. Fitt
Mr. Fitt is Cammy's boss in the Foreign Student Affairs Office. He is a severe, impatient man who often argues with Cammy. Ralph thinks he is a bully.

Little Lou
Little Lou is a Chinese student at the university that Ralph attended. He is a loyal friend to Ralph, even when Ralph is not successful. Little

Lou, a quiet young man, continues to visit Ralph when Ralph's other friends have forgotten about him. He later commits suicide.

Pete

Pete is the supervisor at the building in which Ralph and Helen make their first home. He is a self-important kind of man, and Ralph and Helen make fun of him.

Professor Rodney S. Pierce

Professor Rodney S. Pierce succeeds Pinkus as head of the engineering department. He is helpful to Ralph, giving him a book called *The Power of Positive Thinking.*

Pinkus

Pinkus is a Jewish professor who supervises Ralph's graduate studies until he is succeeded by Professor Pierce. He likes Ralph, but he refuses to lie on Ralph's behalf when Ralph allows his visa to lapse. He says he has to be careful of his own reputation.

Arthur Smith

Arthur Smith is one of the Changs' neighbors when they move into their big suburban house. He watches what they do from his window.

THEMES

Materialism, Consumerism, and the American Dream

Ralph, Helen, and Theresa immigrate to the United States from a traditional, hierarchical Chinese society in which people know their station in life and the rules for social interactions are clear and understood by all. They soon discover that American society is completely different, embodying what Theresa calls a "wilderness of freedoms." As strangers in a foreign land they must find their own ways of dealing with an unfamiliar culture. Ralph's initial goal is to cultivate virtue and bring honor to his family, a traditional aspiration in Chinese culture. But as he starts to absorb American culture, he finds that its dominant values are rather different from virtue and honor.

Unable to return to China, Ralph wanders aimlessly throughout his new country until he meets his sister, Theresa; the family connection provides stability in his life that he had lost. At

TOPICS FOR FURTHER STUDY

- Write a paragraph describing what you think a "typical American" is. Then read it to your class and explain how you reached your conclusions. Incorporate answers to the following questions in your writing. What qualities define an American, aside from U.S. citizenship? In such a large and diverse nation, what does it mean to be a "typical American?" Why do you think Jen chose this title for her novel?

- Conduct interviews with some first- or second-generation Americans in your school or community. Ask them about their experiences in the United States. Have they faced discrimination? Do they identify themselves primarily as Americans? Do they retain allegiance to their nations of origin? Give a class presentation in which you discuss your findings.

- Read Jen's sequel to *Typical American, Mona in the Promised Land.* Write an essay in which you describe the challenges that the Changs' daughters, Mona and Callie, face as they grow up as second-generation Americans. Contrast the challenges Mona and Callie face with those their parents face in *Typical American.*

- Write a short story based on a day in the life of a new immigrant to the United States. Make the story center on one or two incidents and the person's reaction to them. Try to capture the unfamiliarity, to the immigrant, of his or her new environment, and the ways in which cultural misunderstandings or misperceptions might occur.

first, Ralph, Theresa, and Ralph's wife, Helen, have a negative view of Americans and their culture, but this gradually changes, and they eventually become "typical Americans."

Ralph's first encounter with a core notion that Americans cherish about their society is through the building supervisor, the otherwise uninspiring Pete. For Pete, "A man . . . was what he made up his mind to be." At the time, Ralph does not take this notion seriously, but he will learn that it is the essence of the American spirit, the idea that there are no limitations to what a person can achieve with hard work and determination. Ralph begins to realize that although in China a person's place in society is largely assigned, in the United States one is free to create his or her own place, to achieve unlimited success and material prosperity. This idea is often referred to as the American dream and is sometimes associated with a strain of self-help, individualistic philosophy that aims to cultivate the right attitude to gaining success. The moment Ralph starts on his new path is when his professor gives him a copy of a new book, *The Power of Positive Thinking*. Written by Norman Vincent Peale, this book was first published in 1952 and has sold millions of copies over the years. It teaches mental techniques designed to cultivate unshakable optimism, faith, and self-confidence. Ralph studies this book in detail; he starts to become an "imagineer," imagining the future he envisions for himself. He posts inspirational quotations in his office, such as "WHAT YOU CAN CONCEIVE, YOU CAN ACHIEVE," and develops ambitions of a truly American scale. When he meets Grover Ding, a self-described self-made millionaire who seems to embody an American success story, Ralph goes into business too, wanting to get rich. He becomes materialistic, apparently equating the success of his life with how much money he can make. Helen, too, absorbs the American spirit, consumed with her desire for a nice large house in the suburbs, which she equips with all the consumer items that she believes belong in a prosperous American home.

Like an enterprising American, Ralph is willing to take a financial risk in order to expand his business. He also becomes dishonest, cheating on his taxes. Unfortunately for Ralph and Helen, their newfound acquisitive natures almost bring them to financial ruin when their business collapses and they are forced to sell their home. Over the course of nearly two decades, they become authentic Americans—rising fast, accumulating possessions, taking risks, but also falling and having to pick themselves up again. They have found out, as Ralph sensed at the very beginning of the story, that "anything could happen, this was America."

Love, Friendship, and Betrayal

Ralph, Helen, and Theresa not only have to adapt to a new culture but they must also work out their relationships with one another. This proves to not be easy. Soon after their marriage, Ralph and Helen begin quarreling. Ralph, not very successful in his career at first, tries to compensate by asserting himself as the head of the household, but he succeeds only in being a bully. In frustration, he admits to himself that "He had never dreamed a person could be so powerless in his power." He and Helen go through various phases in their marriage. Sometimes they attain a precarious harmony, before the marriage finally disintegrates in a flurry of resentment and violence following the collapse of their business and the revelation of Helen's affair with Grover Ding. For her part, Helen succumbs to Grover's seduction, because she is able to manipulate Grover, who desires her, giving her a sense of power that as a quiet, unassertive, shy woman, she never experienced before. She feels like a "commanding presence" in his company, and her betrayal of her husband does not seem to weigh too heavily on her conscience.

Theresa's difficulties also center around relationships. She never comes close to marriage, and she feels angry and ashamed about it. Her heart is a "fist," closed up and clenched. It is because of this frustration that she eventually has an affair with Old Chao, even though the situation is ironic, given that she "had always been nice about her morals." The affair causes a rift with Helen, her closest friend, and is also a betrayal of her friend Janis, Old Chao's wife. Theresa and Helen are like sisters, but once the estrangement takes place and Theresa moves out of the family home, it is difficult to heal: "There was too much face to be lost."

Theresa's relationship with Ralph is also fraught with a difficulty that simmers under a seemingly affectionate surface. Ralph resents her as he did when they were both children and he was told to copy his older sister because she was intelligent and diligent. This pattern continues in their adult life in the United States. Ralph begrudges the fact that Theresa's medical studies go smoothly for her. She is a hard worker, while he can only work in fits and starts. When Theresa gets a state scholarship, he ridicules her. Theresa, who feels a sense of duty toward her brother, pretends that the scholarship has been cancelled, just so that he does not feel bad.

Family at a meal *(© Camelot | amanaimages | Corbis)*

When Theresa returns to live with Ralph and Helen, Ralph blames her for his feeling like an outsider in his own home. His continuing resentment of Theresa may also be partly responsible for the final tragedy that befalls her. When she runs in front of Ralph's car, he sees not only her but also her "second self" a "stark shadow.... He saw its blackness growing, running, a creature waving monstrous, tentacled arms. It reached the ceiling. It had no face." Ralph asks himself whether his foot hit the brake instantly, but he knows that even if it did, his heart was cold toward his sister and that mattered just as much.

STYLE

House as Metaphor

Much emphasis is placed on houses and buildings in *Typical American* as Ralph, Helen, and Theresa struggle to create a home for themselves in a new country. "Could this place ever be a home?" Helen wonders when after her marriage to Ralph, they move into an apartment in a run-down townhouse. The gradual transition from old, unsavory accommodations to the large, split-level suburban home that they eventually buy reflects their increasing sense of being at home in the United States, of being "typical Americans," since home ownership has always been considered an essential part of the American dream. Houses also serve as a metaphor for the relative strength or weakness of the family. When they move into their big house, their family life seems to improve, and they feel so much more alive. Helen wonders, "Could a house give life to a family?" She is skeptical about her own idea, and yet it seems as if, at least for a while, she is right. They seem liberated, free to be themselves. Several of the titles of the book's section suggest a link between the quality of family life and the state of the building in which it takes place. Part II is called "The House Holds," which cleverly combines the sense of a household (a family) and the fact that the house in which they live literally, at the level of bricks and mortar, is held together. Part II ends with the family moving from their apartment in a building full of leaks and cracks to a newer house with "solid ceilings"; they are relieved that the old "house had held," at least until they moved out of it, and "now they were moving on." As the house holds, so does the family. Similarly, part IV is titled "Structural Weakening," which refers both to the fact that the family structure is weakened by quarreling and Theresa's departure from the home to her own apartment, and to the cracks that appear in the new addition to Ralph's Chicken Palace. As the family crumbles, so does the building that houses the family business, and as a result, the Changs must move out of their beloved home.

Multiple Languages and Nonstandard English

The language in which the characters speak reflects the transition they are making from China to the United States. Jen uses many Chinese phrases, especially in the first part of the novel. This aspect of the book reflects the fact that Ralph is new to the United States and still thinks in his native tongue. When he is in a difficult position, for example, he thinks "*Xiang banfa,*" a Chinese expression that means "think of a way." Ralph's English is poor; he mispronounces words, saying "tank you" instead of "thank you," and makes grammatical errors, as when he says to Cammy, "You are like star in sky," in which he omits the indefinite article *a* before the noun. In another instance, he states, "This building falling down," omitting the verb. It appears that he never masters standard English; he "invented his grammar on the fly." When Ralph has been in the United States for many years, he still forgets English-language conventions. On one occasion, he says, "On top of roof," and Grover Ding (who was born in the United States and only speaks English) corrects him, saying, "On top of *the* roof." In contrast, Old Chao, who is older and more successful than Ralph, speaks perfect grammatical English, as can be seen in the scene when Grover comes to dinner. Since Grover does not speak Chinese, they all must speak English at dinner.

When Ralph, Helen, Theresa, and other Chinese American characters in the book talk amongst themselves, they speak Chinese. In these occurrences, dialogue is italicized, indicating to the reader that although the words are printed in English, the characters are in fact speaking in their native tongue. Gradually, however, English becomes more prominent in their speech, and they find themselves thinking in English: "There were things they did not know how to say in Chinese." Indeed, Ralph and Helen's children, Callie and Mona, are raised speaking English, and so their parents speak English when the children are present (as shown by the absence of italics in the dialogue). However, even at the end of the novel, when the Chinese characters in the book have lived in the United States for nearly twenty years, they still speak to one another in Chinese, an indication of the limits placed on their assimilation into the United States.

HISTORICAL CONTEXT

Communism Comes to China

One of the two short scenes that take place at the beginning of *Typical American* is set in China in 1947, two years after the end of the "Anti-Japanese War." This appellation refers to the war fought between Japan and China, from 1937 to 1945 as part of World War II. After the defeat of Japan, a civil war occurred in China between the Nationalist government and the Communists. This revolution is the historical event referred to in part I of the novel. In 1949 the Communists succeeded in pushing the Nationalists out of mainland China. Nationalist leader Chiang Kai-shek fled to the island of Taiwan under American protection. The Communists under Mao Zedong proclaimed the country the People's Republic of China. It was modeled on the Soviet Union, with a strong central government and a socialist economy. In the novel, Ralph hopes that the Communists will be unable to stay in power, especially since the Americans do not recognize the new Chinese government. However, the Communists retained control of China, and the United States eventually recognized the People's Republic of China in 1979.

From McCarthyism to the Civil Rights Movement

Typical American alludes to events that took place in the United States and abroad during the 1950s and 1960s. Soon after Ralph inadvertently lets his visa expire, he appeals to his adviser, Pinkus, to help him. Pinkus, however,

COMPARE
&
CONTRAST

- **1950s:** Chinese American literature is not widely known and is not considered part of mainstream American literature. Two Chinese American works that attain some popularity are the novels *Chinatown Family* (1948) by Lin Yutang and *Flower Drum Song* (1957) by Chin Yang Lee.

  1990s: Following the success of Chinese American Amy Tan's bestselling novel *The Joy Luck Club* (1989), the mainstream media starts to pay more attention to Asian American literature. Gus Lee publishes *China Boy* (1991), about Chinese immigrants to the United States, and Frank Chin, who came to prominence as a new voice in Chinese American literature during the 1960s and 1970s, publishes the novels *Donald Duk* (1991) and *Gunga Din Highway* (1994).

  Today: Amy Tan's fourth novel, *The Bonesetter's Daughter* (2001), and Ha Jin's novel, *War Trash* (2004), which wins the PEN/Faulkner Award and is a finalist for the Pulitzer Prize, reflect the continuing success of Chinese American writers.

- **1950s:** The number of Chinese immigrants in the United States increases because of the repeal of the Chinese Exclusion Acts in 1943. However, there are still restrictions on Chinese immigration. By the end of the decade, there are 99,735 foreign-born Chinese

  people living in the United States, according to the U.S. Census Bureau.

  1990s: In 1990 there are 676,968 foreign-born Chinese people in the United States, which represents 3.4 percent of the foreign-born population. The Chinese are the sixth-largest foreign-born immigrant group in the United States.

  Today: In 2006 the number of foreign-born Chinese immigrants in the United States rises to 1,551,316, or 4.1 percent of the foreign-born population. The Chinese are the third-largest foreign-born immigrant group in the United States.

- **1950s:** Chinese immigrants to the United States are concentrated mainly in New York and California, in specific neighborhoods, known as Chinatowns, in large cities.

  1990s: Although Chinatowns still flourish, Chinese immigrants settle across a wider geographic area. Their choice of where to live is frequently dictated by the location of their jobs and sometimes also by the quality of school districts.

  Today: Second-generation Chinese Americans live in widely dispersed areas. Within New York City, for example, many second-generation Chinese Americans live in South Brooklyn, and Corona, Elmhurst, and Flushing in the borough of Queens.

is wary of doing anything that might harm his reputation. He says, "The way things are going, pretty soon everyone's going to be a spy or a Commie or both." Pinkus references the fear of Communism that swept through the United States at the beginning of the cold war (an ideological conflict between the United States and the Soviet Union) in the 1950s. The anti-Communism culminated in the witch hunts of the McCarthy years, named after the Wisconsin Republican U.S.

senator Joseph McCarthy, who made unsubstantiated allegations that the federal government was being infiltrated by Communists and their sympathizers.

To show the passage of time and indicate the kinds of issues that people in the United States were talking about at the time, *Typical American* makes reference to the Korean War. When Theresa and Helen chat about "whether the United States was doing the right thing in

Couple standing in front of red convertible *(© Camelot | amanaimages | Corbis)*

Korea," they are referring to the war that lasted from 1950 to 1953, in which South Korea, aided by the United States and other powers, fought against North Korean and Chinese forces.

The 1950s also witnessed the so-called space race, in which the Soviet Union and the United States vied against each other in the field of space exploration. In 1957 the Soviet Union launched Sputnik I, the first artificial satellite to orbit the earth, and in 1958, the United States responded by launching the satellite Explorer I; *Typical American* alludes to both of these events. As Ralph reviews his tenure application, he makes a list of how many members of the committee "were working feverishly on space. Sputnik! What trouble the Russians had made for him." Ralph also alludes to the fact that "everyone was in love with the moon. Moon rockets!" Various missions involved exploring the moon, beginning with a Soviet lunar probe in 1959 and culminating in the Apollo 11 mission, the successful

U.S. moon landing in 1969 in which humans walked on the moon for the first time.

Typical American also makes passing reference, after Ralph gets tenure, to the administration of President John F. Kennedy, which lasted from 1961 to Kennedy's assassination on November 24, 1963. Jen's note of "an invasion failed" refers to the Bay of Pigs Invasion in 1961, a U.S.-backed invasion of Communist Cuba by Cuban exiles that failed dismally. The final contemporary reference in the novel is to the U.S. civil rights movement: "Troops had turned their muzzles on the marchers down South." The civil rights movement was prominent from the mid-1950s to the late 1960s. The reference in the novel may be to an incident that took place on a civil rights march from Selma to Montgomery, Alabama, in March 1965, in which marchers were attacked by state and local police.

Jen's historical allusions throughout the text give a wider context to the Changs' lives as they adapt to living in the United States.

CRITICAL OVERVIEW

Typical American has been praised as an original, cleverly written contribution to the literature that tells the story of immigrants in the United States. Sybil Steinberg writes in *Publishers Weekly*, "A wry but compassionate voice and distinctive sensibility animate this accomplished first novel." Steinberg also comments that "the view of this country through the eyes of outsiders attempting to preserve their own language and traditions while tapping into the American dream of success and riches is the piquant motif that binds the novel." Phoebe-Lou Adams, writing in *Atlantic Monthly*, calls *Typical American* a "tragicomic novel," noting that Jen's style "is deftly adjusted to that mixture, shifting unobtrusively from mischievous gaiety in the opening pages to cool sobriety in the final chapters."

Writing in the *New York Times Book Review*, A. G. Mojtabai offers high praise for Jen's use of language and her style, writing of "the intelligence of Gish Jen's prose, its epigrammatic sweep and swiftness. There's no pause, no underlining, no winking aside to the reader to signal how clever this is, how humorous that is. The author just keeps coming at you, line after stunning line." Mojtabai confesses that he was so engrossed in and appreciative of the book that he wanted to know in more depth why Helen and Ralph succumb so easily to the lure of American greed and consumerism. Mojtabai wonders, "Were there no contending forces? No dim remembrance of Confucian harmonies or Buddhist detachment before Ralph's obsession gained full sway?"

For Richard Eder, a *Los Angeles Times Book Review* critic, "Jen has done much more than tell an immigrant story.... Or rather, she has done it more and in some ways better than it has ever been done." Eder attributes much of the success of the novel to Jen's skillful characterization of Ralph and Helen. Also, like Mojtabai, Eder admires the quality of Jen's writing, which is so good that "the language itself becomes the narrative and the characters. Hers is percussive; it detonates and sizzles like a sausage over a hardwood blaze."

CRITICISM

Bryan Aubrey

Aubrey holds a Ph.D. in English. In this essay on Typical American, *he discusses the extent to*

WHAT DO I READ NEXT?

- *Mona in the Promised Land* (1996) is Jen's sequel to *Typical American*. Set in the late 1960s and early 1970s, it focuses on Callie and Mona, the daughters of Ralph and Helen Chang. Unlike their parents, the children were born in the United States and possess a dual cultural heritage.

- Like Jen's *Typical American*, Mei Ng's first novel, *Eating Chinese Food Naked* (1997), is an exploration of the Chinese American experience in New York. The main character, Ruby Lee, returns from college to live with her parents next to the family laundry business. She must learn to forge an identity as she straddles two worlds, the American and the Chinese.

- *New York City's Chinese Community* (2007), by Chinese American author Josephine Tsui Yueh Lee, presents a history of Chinese immigration to New York City since the late nineteenth century. The book contains many historic photographs and describes people, culture, businesses, significant events, and neighborhoods.

- *Native Speaker* (1995), a well-received first novel by Chang-Rae Lee, centers around the life of Henry Park, a second generation Korean American in New York City who works as an undercover agent for a nongovernmental intelligence agency. Park is separated from his American wife and struggles with issues of family and cultural identity.

which Ralph Chang's views of the nature of American society represent reality.

"It's an American story," states the narrator in the very first words of the novel, a story of how three immigrants from the other side of the world gradually become "typical Americans." But how typical are the Changs? And what does their story say about the United States, its ideals, and its self-image? Is "typical American"

" LIKE IMMIGRANTS EVERYWHERE, THE
CHANGS SEE THE UNFAMILIAR CULTURE WITH FRESH
EYES AND THEREFORE NOTICE THINGS ABOUT IT THAT
THOSE WHO HAVE BEEN RAISED WITHIN IT ARE
UNABLE TO SEE. BUT THEY ALSO MAKE MISJUDG-
MENTS DUE TO A LACK OF UNDERSTANDING."

a complimentary term, or is it used with pejorative intent?

Traditionally, many immigrants who come to the United States lack economic opportunities in their home countries or seek to escape repressive political systems. They view the United States as a land of opportunity where they can achieve status and material prosperity. The Changs do not really fall into this category, since Ralph and Theresa, and Helen, come from quite well-to-do families near Shanghai, China. They come to the United States initially to study, without intending to stay permanently. It is only when they are denied permission to return to China after the Communists take over the country in 1949 that the Changs face the prospect of remaining in the United States for the rest of their lives.

When Ralph arrives in this unfamiliar land, his first perceptions of America are quite ambivalent. As he nears the West Coast by boat, he imagines the Golden Gate Bridge in San Francisco, California: "That splendor! That radiance! True, it wasn't the Statue of Liberty, but still in his mind its span glowed bright, an image of freedom, and hope, and relief for the seasick." This passage ends in what is called *bathos*—the sudden descent from the exalted to the trivial or commonplace, usually unintentional but in this case deliberately intended. It is an example of the humor that is liberally spread throughout this highly entertaining novel. When Ralph's ship actually arrives in the harbor, he can barely see the Golden Gate Bridge until he is almost under it, because of the dense fog, and all he can hear are foghorns. Thus, at the beginning of the novel two images of America are presented, one of freedom, splendor, and hope, the other of hope

lost in a fog. Which image will prove to be the most appropriate for Ralph's experience in his adopted country?

Naturally enough, when Ralph, Helen, and Theresa first arrive in the United States, they prefer their Chinese culture, because they are used to it. When Ralph first goes to Theresa's room in a women's residence, he sees "around her, China." Everything about the way the room is equipped suggests her homeland. As the three immigrants settle down together as a family and are still more familiar with China than the United States, they indulge in a kind of lighthearted but seriously felt prejudice against Americans. Every time an American does something of which they disapprove, they use the epithet, "typical American" to describe it. If a clerk shortchanges them, for example, they declare "typical American no-morals!" Like immigrants everywhere, the Changs see the unfamiliar culture with fresh eyes and therefore notice things about it that those who have been raised within it are unable to see. But they also make misjudgments due to a lack of understanding. Certainly, the Changs' contemptuous attitude toward Americans does not last for long. Theresa remarks that they should stop using the phrase "typical American" and regard people as individuals. From this point on they adapt handily to life in the United States and show no particularly strong desire to hang on to their Chinese heritage. They celebrate Christmas as well as the Chinese New Year, Ralph buys a Davy Crockett hat, and Helen learns the lyrics of popular songs from American musicals. They do face some racism, notably when they attend a Yankees baseball game and people are abusive toward them, telling them to "go back to their laundry." Even so, the Changs do not allow racism to become the dominant feature of their experience in the United States. They happily stay at home and watch the Yankees' games on television, calling themselves, in a witty acknowledgement of their dual cultural status, the "Chang-kees." Ralph is determined to rise above racism and prejudice by achieving material success, which he knows will give him and his family a higher status in American society.

With prosperity in mind, Ralph soon becomes imprinted with the American spirit. When his academic adviser presents him with a copy of *The Power of Positive Thinking*, he starts to absorb the characteristically American, individualistic idea that he can become whatever he sets his mind to. As Ralph embraces this idea, he thinks of himself as an "imagineer" who can create the reality that he wants for himself, believing that "he could do anything!" However, this very American ideal is undercut by reality. Out of a sense of duty, Ralph readily agrees to attend a supper at Old Chao's house, but on the day of the dinner he is stung by a bee on the street. He can barely see, and he has to go to the dinner with a swollen face. As with the earlier incident at the foggy harbor, a positive characteristic of American spirit—hope, freedom, the idea that Ralph can control the way his life unfolds—is immediately undercut by something that seems to invalidate it. The lesson of the latter incident appears to be that people can imagine all they want, but random events in the universe may nullify all their efforts. Perhaps the American dream is not all that it seems.

Yet another of these double-edged incidents occurs soon after Ralph gets tenure in the engineering department. Everything is going well for him, and as he drives home he thinks, "The greatness of America!. . . . Freedom and justice for all!" But then he looks more closely at the people on the streets, and many of them appear "bedraggled"; one man slumps down in a doorway. Ralph thinks, "A man living in a country sending satellites into space could still land up a heap in a doorway. How was that?" Theresa also notices some of the disparities in the great land of wealth, especially as it relates to medical care of the poor at the hospital; "they died waiting."

These occurrences function like little parables that foreshadow the later plot development in which the Changs' apparent fulfillment of the American dream (with their large suburban home) is soon undercut by the collapse of the building which houses their business. The dream may reach up to heaven, giving the Changs the impression that the United States is indeed "a paradise," but the building that allows this dream to manifest literally crumbles.

In the America of *Typical American*, there appears to be a large gap between the ideal and the real. Is the United States in fact a country in which greed, selfishness, and materialism triumph, with firm limits on what an immigrant like Ralph can achieve? The answer, perhaps, is yes and no. A consideration of Grover Ding, one of the major characters in the novel, reveals the darker side of the American dream. It is unfortunate for Ralph, a man who is lucky and unlucky by turns, that the con artist Grover is in

a sense the most American man he meets, one who appears to be living the dream. Born in the United States, Grover is Chinese in ethnicity but thoroughly American in spirit. He is a self-made man who is involved in many capitalistic business ventures. He knows how to exploit any business situation to his own advantage and has no qualms about taking advantage of the trusting Ralph, who as an emerging American, admires people who make money. Americans, Ralph seems to realize, do not so much admire academics and scholars, which is why, as he becomes a "typical American," he leaves the steady if unexciting life of a university professor to become a successful businessperson. Regrettably, his mentor turns out to be an unscrupulous, amoral man who uses the freedom afforded by capitalism to cheat his way to success. Is Grover a "typical American," too? The novel leaves this question open, but it does suggest that freedom not only provides the opportunity to create wealth but also involves choosing how to live one's life. Grover chooses to live corruptly and take advantage of others.

Ralph also makes choices—not all of them good—including his selection of the sleazy Grover as a role model. In his disappointment at how things have worked out for him and his family, Ralph becomes disillusioned with America and the philosophy he associates with it: "He was not what he made up his mind to be. A man was the sum of his limits; freedom only made him see how much so. America was no America."

One could argue that Ralph's view of the United States was unrealistic in the first place, not because of any fault in the country but because of Ralph's intoxication with an idea carried beyond its limits. It seems that the entire Chang family becomes carried away with the freedoms of the United States, which is so different from the "terraced society" they knew in China; they have forgotten that all human life takes place within limitations. Their unrealistic expectations are apparent in the reflections of Ralph and Helen as Theresa lies in a coma in the hospital: "Was death possible in this bright country? It was, they knew. Of course. And yet they began to realize that in the fiber of their beings they had almost believed it a thing they had left behind, like rickshaws." Whether in the United States or anywhere else, only sober reflection can save people from their own folly, ignorance, and naïveté. This may at first seem a "bleak understanding," but it is the beginning of wisdom, and Ralph Chang, U.S. citizen, typical American, has his adopted country to thank for it.

Source: Bryan Aubrey, Critical Essay on *Typical American*, in *Novels for Students*, Gale, Cengage Learning, 2010.

A. Robert Lee

In the following excerpt, Lee discusses the nature of the humor in Typical American.

... '*Bu yao fa feng* [...] stop acting crazy'. An apter working gloss would be hard to come by for the world of Gish Jen's *Typical American*. For Helen Chang's reprimand to her children, Callie (Kailan or 'Open Orchid' in Chinese) and Mona (Mengna or 'Dream Graceful'), applies in equal part to all the Changs and their immigrant circle. Ralph Chang, the jug-eared Yifeng as was, who leaves 1940s China to become an engineering Ph.D in New York and who progresses from one kind of self-bewildering American close encounter to the next, is temporarily seized by a fantasy to make millionaire bucks from a fast-food chicken restaurant. Theresa Chang MD, the sister he once called *Bai Xiao* or Know-It-All, and whose affair with Ralph's married Head of Department amounts to a parody of the American hospital romance, herself suffers near fatal injury in a Gatsbyesque car-accident brought on by Ralph's own bad driving and the dog the Changs have bought to certify their credentials as *bona fide* American suburbanites. Grover Ding, raised Chinese-American, and as practised, and mysterious, an adept in Yankee double-dealing as Bellow's Dr Tamkin in *Seize The Day* (1956), plays...courtier to Helen at the same time as seducing Ralph with prospects of instantaneous, and to be sure shady, all-American wealth. Each, throughout Jen's novel, suggests Americanization as a comedy of errors, a process startlingly funny the one moment, yet wry, even bitter, the next.

For in *Typical American* Jen has written a kind of ethnic fantasia in which displacement, if not otherness itself, is put under the deftest ironic scrutiny. Which otherness is the greater, for instance, China as 'enormous circumspection', a 'terraced society', or America as 'a wilderness of freedoms', 'spread-out'? How to reconcile, at another reach, the Chinese-Confucian goal of 'reunification' with the American-Franklinesque goal of 'the self-made man'? This sense of cultural divide, and of the spaces between, the novel

FOR IN *TYPICAL AMERICAN* JEN HAS WRITTEN A KIND OF ETHNIC FANTASIA IN WHICH DISPLACEMENT, IF NOT OTHERNESS ITSELF, IS PUT UNDER THE DEFTEST IRONIC SCRUTINY."

especially locates in the Changs' acquisition of English—not least the family's relish in thinking themselves 'Chang-kees' as against 'Yankees'. Helen contrasts her Chinese-language and American-language worlds as follows: 'In China [...] the world [...] was like a skating rink, a finite space, walled. Words inevitably rebounded. Here the world was enormous, all endless horizon; her words arced and disappeared as though into a wind-chopped ocean'. Theresa, for her part, struggles:

> to put her Chinese thoughts into English. But now she had English thoughts too—that was true also. They all did. There were things they did not know how to say in Chinese. The language of *outside the house* had seeped well inside—Cadillac, Pyrex, subway, Coney Island, Ringling Brothers and Barnum & Bailey Circus. Transistor radio. Theresa and Helen and Ralph slipped from tongue to tongue like turtles taking to land, taking to sea; though one remained their more natural element, both had become essential.

Ralph's reaction to workaday Manhattan perhaps summarizes the contrast even more succinctly. 'The very air smelled of oil', he observes, 'Nothing was made of bamboo'.

'It's an American story' assures the opening sentence. But however so, it is also one whose comic dividends lie in Jen's play of Chinese and American discrepancies. Confucius vies with Franklin. More terrestrially, the small (and so unprivate) dynastic home in Jiangsu Province, near Shanghai, contrasts with the Changs' eventual tract home in Tarrytown, New York, complete with its accoutrements of lawn, fitted kitchen, garage, central heating, and 'family' and other separate rooms ('All bespoke bounty, and peace, and a world never ending'). Prophetically, and in preparing for America, Ralph learns the gap between Chinese and English verbs to be more than simply grammatical ('What's taken for granted in English [. . .] is spelled out in Chinese [. . .]; there's even a verb construction for this purpose. *Ting de jian* in Mandarin means, one listens and hears. *Ting bu jian* means, one listens but fails to hear'. If, too, his father cites Confucian lore ('*Opposites begin in one another*'), Yifeng-Ralph on his way to America sets himself a Franklin-cum-Gatsby schedule ('I will do five minutes of calisthenics daily' etc.).

Further disjunctures crowd in on him. To get to New York he travels cross-country from the Golden Gate Bridge and thus at the same time both east to west and west to east. If he can ponder world-historical movements in the light of the Fall of Manchuria ('Kingdoms rise up, kingdoms collapse'), he can also fall for the big-breasted Cammy, the University's 'Foreign Student Office' secretary, with whom he fantasizes American love and a honeymoon in Paris. Instead of Yifeng ('Intent on the Peak'), she selects the homespun Ralph as a name for him. Where once he has learned Grammar Book English, he learns a slew of Americanisms in a bar— 'dames' and 'dough' early among them. Heir, too, to fables of The Three Kingdoms, he also quickly hears from a would-be landlady 'I don't rent to Chinks. So far's I'm concerned they bring bugs'.

'This is America you're in', George Fitt, the antagonistic Foreign Student Adviser, tells Ralph. But which America? On marrying the very Chinese, very docile, Helen, formerly Hailan or Sea-Blue, he finds her the readiest American housewife (to his patriarchal amazement she fixes the boiler in their apartment). 'Typical American' becomes his (and his family's) mantra for each acquired new reality or phrase, whether they have the matter right or not. New York, '*the* American city' as he thinks it, compels yet distorts him as though beyond the reach of all 'Chinese' criteria—'So clangorous— such screeching, rumbling, blaring, banging! Such hiss! Everything buzzed. [. . .] No equation could begin to describe it all.' If engineering palls for him, 'imagineering', as he calls it, does not ('Was death possible,' he asks himself, 'in this bright country?'). Even his 'unlife' in the blood-splattered abattoir where he is forced to work to pay for his studies fails to give him a working hold on American reality.

For Ralph 'imagines' himself at one with the dream so Faustianly dangled before him by Grover Ding as fixer, charmer, and villain, and by his exhilarated reading of self-promotional manuals such as Norman Vincent Peale's *The Power of Positive Thinking*, or *Making Money, Be Your Own Boss!*, and *Ninety Days to Power and Success*. He even lines his office with Babbitry, 'inspirational quotes' of the kind 'ALL RICHES BEGIN IN AN IDEA' or 'WHAT YOU CAN CONCEIVE, YOU CAN ACHIEVE'. The upshot of his urge to American well-being, satiety, is 'Ralph's Chicken Palace', the deflationary irony of whose name escapes him—and, in preparation for which, he practises endlessly on a cash-register even as Helen betrays him in the room above with Grover ('Ralph [. . .] all blind focus, saw nothing but the register'). That the whole restaurant scheme has Grover's wheeler-dealing in it, literally collapses (the diners, absurdly, moved to ever more lower-level tables), involves yet other scams and half-baked schemes, and, finally, reduces the Changs to bankruptcy, signals a matching betrayal.

Each of Ralph's reeling, comic pratfalls, however, together with Helen's dalliance, Grover's dubiously supposed imprisonment for tax-evasion (has he or has he not been doing time for his finagling?) and, above all, Theresa's accident, bring him to a hard-won acknowledgement of illusion, the snares built into desire. He sees, accordingly, that China has become a 'thing recalled', that America as he has believed it is 'no America', and that he himself cannot be the fantasy-success 'he made up his mind to be'. China and America thus offer him a new, if chastening, synthesis: 'A man was the sum of his limits; freedom only made him see how much so.' But against this winter-time 'bleak understanding', he also calls to mind a 'heartening' summer's day in which Theresa has been frolicking with Old Chao, her lover. It points him to the world he still has, animated, intimate, wholly deserving of acceptance, none other than his and the family's 'house' of Chinese-America. For in showing how the Changs of China become the Changs of America, *Typical American* tells a Cautionary Tale, as contemplative as it is witty. . . .

Source: A. Robert Lee, "Eat a Bowl of Tea: Asian America in the Novels of Gish Jen, Cynthia Kadohata, Kim Ronyoung, Jessica Hagedorn, and Tran Van Dinh," in *Yearbook of English Studies*, Vol. 24, 1994, pp. 263–80.

Scarlet Cheng

In the following review, Cheng identifies Typical American *as an "adeptly crafted novel," despite the fact that, in Cheng's view, its characters "tend to remain emotionally remote."*

The last year brought a bloom of books from Chinese American writers, including the long-awaited second novel from Amy Tan, whose beautifully written bestseller, *The Joy Luck Club*, triggered the current fascination with Chinese American Literature.

Several distinctive first novels are among the offerings. All treat the Chinese American experience with a certain comic sensibility, but *Typical American* is by far the most adeptly crafted.

Jen signals that this is going to be a story about the immigrant experience from her first line: "It's an American story: Before he was a thinker, or a doer, or an engineer, much less an imagineer like his self-made-millionaire friend Grover Ding, Ralph Chang was just a small boy in China, struggling to grow up his father's son." The story begins in 1947 when Yifeng, the only son of the Chang family in Jiangsu province, is dispatched by his father to study engineering in the United States. Dutifully Yifeng goes, "his stomach burbling with fool hope."

Upon arrival he changes his name to Ralph, falls in love with the school secretary, who has "Orange hair, pink face, blue eyes." With the Communist takeover of China in 1949, Ralph can't go home again. Because this new country is so strange and incomprehensible, he bumbles his way through the days.

Fortunately his sister Theresa, also unmoored from the motherland, finds him one day in a public park. She introduces Ralph to her friend Helen, a fellow Chinese expatriate, the two are drawn to one another, "And she [Helen] married Ralph, officially accepting what seemed already true—that she had indeed crossed a violent, black ocean; and that it was time to make herself as home in her exile as she could." Eventually, Ralph finishes his university degree and gets a tenure-track teaching job. "They celebrated Christmas in addition to Chinese New Year," writes Jen, "and were regulars at Radio City Music Hall. Ralph owned a Davy Crockett hat. Helen knew most of the words to most of the songs in *The King and I* and *South Pacific*." With a house in the suburbs and two daughters,

Ralph and Helen Chang seem cozily settled into the American middle-class way of life.

But into their lives walls Grover Ding, a clever assimilated Chinese American in starched shirts and expensive suits. He is the temptation of the New World incarnate. He charms them all with his self-confidence, his savoir faire, and his pie-in-the-sky talk of bigger and better things. He explains his "break" in life to Ralph like this: "We happened to get to talking, just like we're talking now, and the next thing—bang—I'm a millionaire. A self-made man. What do you think of that?...In America, anything is possible."

Ralph adores Grover, lends him money that he never gets back, then goes into partnership with him to run a fast-food joint that begins to fall apart at the foundations. Helen is falling for Grover in a different way. Meanwhile, Theresa is having an affair with a married Chinese man, Old Chao. The American Dream tailspins into chaos.

Unfortunately, Jen's characters tend to remain emotionally remote. They seem too much like figures in a morality play, and we never really get under their skin, feel their angst, or experience their joy. The narrative style has an edgy self-consciousness that noticeably strains as it reaches for comic effect.

Still, Jen writes well and wryly, and her subject is serious. As she said to me in an interview, "Every single group that has come here from the time of the Pilgrims has tried to hold onto their Old World identity, and they've inevitably been changed by being here." Through this satiric, cautionary tale, Jen shows us that the road to cultural assimilation is often paved with misguided intentions.

Source: Scarlet Cheng, "The Typical American Comes to Town," in *Belles Lettres*, Vol. 7, No. 2, Winter 1991–1992, p. 21, 23.

Vivian Gornick

In the following review, Gornick discusses Typical American *as a conservative immigrant novel.*

The immigrant novel is a staple in American Literature. It is always with us, always its own spare self, always telling its same, allegorical tale. It has an unerring ear for the inner sound of the time in which it finds itself. Repeatedly, the story of displacement is told anew in a tone of voice sympathetic to the contemporary reader. A

> **THE VIRTUES OF *TYPICAL AMERICAN* ARE ABUNDANT, BUT ITS PREMISE IS A PIECE OF RECEIVED WISDOM THAT REMAINS REGRETFULLY UNTRANSFORMED BY ITS GLORIOUS SENTENCE MAKING."**

hundred years ago, the typical immigrant was a Jewish tailor, and his story (pronoun intended) was self-consciously earnest and romantic. Today, he is a Chinese engineer, and his story is told with tempered irony. It's the tone of voice that does it. Tone of voice makes new language. New language seems to mean the experience has not yet run its course. But the operative word is "seems." The genre is problematic.

The situation in Gish Jen's *Typical American* is simplicity itself. Ralph Chang is sent to the United States in 1947 to get a Ph.D. in mechanical engineering. Within the year China is plunged into communist revolution. Ralph is cut off from the family. He becomes confused, his visa expires, he wanders around New York in fear and poverty. At last he is rescued by his sister Theresa—nicknamed Know-It-All—who has also made her way to the States and is living with Helen, a friend from China. Ralph and Helen marry and the three of them settle down together. Ralph completes his education, and Theresa becomes a doctor. After a while, Ralph and Helen have two little girls, Ralph gets tenure, Helen longs for a house in the suburbs, Theresa falls into an affair with a married man.

Ralph begins to hunger for the friendship of Grover Deng, a Chinese-American hustler he thinks will make him rich. Sure enough, Grover cheats and cuckolds him. At the same time he, Ralph, remains a moralizing prig who forces his sister to leave the house. Everything begins to fall apart. He gets hysterical over Helen's affair with Grover, and in a frenzy of self-pity accidentally runs down his sister in his car. Theresa falls into a coma that traumatizes them all. By the time she emerges from it Ralph has seen the light: to lose sympathy with the family is indeed to lose one's soul.

Typical American is remarkable for its pacing, and for its sentence structure. The pacing—

really lovely—produces a rhythm on the page that keeps Ralph a most sympathetic creature. Sometimes we're at eye level with him (his adventure so familiar it's painful). Sometimes he's floating above us, sort of lying on the air (we call to him, Hang on!). Sometimes he shoots away and we cry out (Stop, you fool!). But he's always there, dancing through a marvelous manipulation of syntax for which Gish Jen has a real talent. The sentences themselves achieve a jazzy American sound alternating throughout with a tinkly Chinese-into-English sound that makes us feel America bobbing around Ralph at the same time that we feel the emptiness inside him as he gets lost in the deracination of his New York life. The scene in which Ralph—broke, frightened, without a visa, living in a fleabag—wanders out into the street and is found by Theresa, illustrates perfectly the virtuosity of the novel. Here it is in part:

Time spun on. Ralph slept.

Time spooled itself fat. Still Ralph slept. The sky cracked. Dust rained in his eyes.

He turned over.

Dust rained in his hair.

He turned on his side. Dust rained in his ear. . . .

He looked for his black shoes, found them plaster-dust white . . .

And outside, white. A conspiracy. He trudged through the streets, studiously ignoring the broad blue sky, the winking sun.

He was not to be mocked. . . .

From an open door, the smell of hot dogs . . .

The first he gulped down, the second, savored. Sweet, salty, juicy, soft, warm. Squish of the frank. Tang of the sauerkraut. Bun—here juice soaked, here toast rough. His stomach gurgled. Twenty cents each, he couldn't afford it. Still he had another. Another.

His stomach started to heave.

Eighty cents! He swallowed manfully, and as the man behind the counter gave him an alarmed look—not here, please, not here—Ralph made his way into the street. . . .

A park. He cleared the wet snow from a bench. . . .

Why him? That's what he really wanted to know. Why, of all people, him, From up the path, a black coat migrated his way, like an answer slow in coming. He squinted at it . . .

Was miracle. This was Ralph's version of the story. "Miracle!" And even so many years later, anyone could still hear in his voice all that the word meant to him—rocks burst into blossom, the black rinsed from the night sky. Life itself unfurled. As he apparently, finally, deserved. How else could it be, that he should find himself lying in coin-spangled ice slosh, in America, embracing—of all people—his sister? Saved! Know-It-All in his arms! Impossible! So he would have thought; so anyone would have thought. But, heart burning, there he was just the same—hugging her, by Someone's ironic grace, as though to never let her go.

Yet *Typical American* is a most conservative novel. Emotionally, the characters remain unformed. Psychologically, they hardly exist at all. From beginning to end they are only the sum of their immigrant circumstances. America, in this book, is still an allegorical corruption into which people fall from some original grace with which they seem to have crossed the ocean. Here—inevitably—they will pursue acquisition and appetite; their souls will be forged in the smithy of a weakened moral system, and in the end they will learn anew that family loyalty is to be equated with first values. Somehow, in 1991, this does not seem an adequate perspective from which a serious novel can move forward.

At the top of the last page of *Typical American*, when Ralph is out in the street trying to hail a taxi in the suburbs to get to Theresa's bedside, Gish Jen writes: "It seemed to him at that moment, as he stood waiting and waiting, trapped in his coat, that a man was as doomed here as he was in China. *Kan bu jian. Ting bu jian.* He could not always see, he could not always hear. He was not what he made up his mind to be. A man was the sum of his limits; freedom only made him see how much so. America was no America." Now there, I thought, is a novel about Ralph Chang I'd like to read; the one that would illuminate that paragraph.

In 1937 Delmore Schwartz published *In Dreams Begin Responsibilities*, the first of his brilliant stories about immigrant parents and their intellectual children. A decade later Saul Bellow wrote *The Adventures of Augie March*, a tour-de-force of Jewish-American hustling. After that came Bernard Malamud's great work of neo-realist fiction, *The Assistant*. Each of these writers took the immigrant experience deeper into metaphor. Each of them produced a fractured and inventive English that enriched the prose, extended the characters and widened the original context so that it became something

other than its own narrow, already familiar self. Their books changed the American language forever; without them Gish Jen would not have found her way into the delicious syntax of *Typical American*.

They also made it difficult to tell again the immigrant's tale as it had been told for half a century or more. *Augie March* embodied a wildness of hunger that went to the limit; corruption of the soul became its subject. *The Assistant* moved so deeply into "not belonging" that it achieved an equation between deracination and profound despair. *In Dreams Begin Responsibilities* was a modernist parable. Surely, one could not write again a simple old-fashioned recital of the uprooted innocent cast down on the greedy, indifferent streets of New York.

A reader always thinks originality of language will mean originality of thought, but we have arrive at a peculiar moment in American writing, one in which language ensures skill not insight, voice not point of view. The virtues of *Typical American* are abundant, but its premise is a piece of received wisdom that remains regretfully untransformed by its glorious sentence making.

Source: Vivian Gornick, "Innocents Abroad," in *Women's Review of Books*, Vol. 8, No. 10–11, July 1991, p. 14.

SOURCES

Adams, Phoebe-Lou, Review of *Typical American*, in *Atlantic Monthly*, Vol. 267, No. 4, April 1991, p. 108.

Eder, Richard, "The Americanization of Chang," in *Los Angeles Times Book Review*, March 17, 1991, pp. 3, 9.

Jen, Gish, *Typical American*, Vintage Books, 2008.

Kasinitz, Philip, John Mollenkopf, Mary C. Waters, and Jennifer Holdaway, "Becoming American/Becoming New Yorkers: The Second Generation in a Majority Minority City," in *Migration Information Source*, http://www.migrationinformation.org/Feature/display.cfm?ID=440 (accessed October 24, 2008).

Kim, Elaine H., *Asian American Literature: An Introduction to the Writings and Their Social Context*, Temple University Press, 1982.

Lee, Rachel, "Gish Jen: Interview by Rachel Lee," in *Words Matter: Conversations with Asian Writers*, edited by King-Kok Cheung, University of Hawaii Press, 2000, p. 217.

Mojtabai, A. G., "The Complete Other Side of the World," in *New York Times Book Review*, March 31, 1991, pp. 9–10.

National Aeronautics and Space Administration (NASA), "Past Missions," http://www.nasa.gov/missions/past/index.html (accessed October 22, 2008).

Simal, Begoña, "Gish Jen," in *Dictionary of Literary Biography*, Vol. 312, *Asian American Writers*, edited by Deborah L. Madsen, Thomson Gale, 2005, pp. 142–54.

Steinberg, Sybil, Review of *Typical American*, in *Publishers Weekly*, Vol. 238, No. 3, January 18, 1991, p. 46.

Terrazas, Aaron Matteo, and Bhavna Devani, "Chinese Immigrants in the United States," in *Migration Information Source*, http://www.migrationinformation.org/USfocus/display.cfm?id = 685 (accessed October 24, 2008).

U.S. Census Bureau, "Region and Country or Area of Birth of the Foreign-Born Population: 1960 to 1990," http://www.census.gov (accessed October 24, 2008).

Wong, Sau-ling Cynthia, "Chinese American Literature," in *An Interethnic Companion to Asian American Literature*, edited by King-Kok Cheung, Cambridge University Press, 1997, pp. 39–61.

FURTHER READING

Chang, Iris, *The Chinese in America: A Narrative History*, Viking, 2003.
> Chang tells the story of Chinese immigration to the United States from the early nineteenth century to the end of the twentieth century.

Grice, Helena, *Negotiating Identities: An Introduction to Asian American Women's Writing*, Manchester University Press, 2002, pp. 202–206.
> Grice discusses the importance of home ownership in ethnic fiction in general and *Typical American* in particular.

Lee, Rachel C., *The Americas of Asian American Literature: Gendered Fictions of Nation and Transnation*, Princeton University Press, 1999, pp. 44–72.
> Lee examines the question of whether the Changs can be considered typical Americans, focusing on the author's critiques of the exclusion of Asians as a group and the violence revealed in the Asian American family. She concludes that the novel reveals inequities in American society based on race and gender.

Li, David Leiwei, *Imagining the Nation: Asian American Literature and Cultural Consent*, Stanford University Press, 1998, pp. 102–107.
> Li examines *Typical American* in terms of the discrimination the Changs face and the materialism of American society. He sees the ending of the novel, when Theresa returns to the family, as a hopeful sign of the possibility of harmonious family life overcoming the desire for money.

Glossary of Literary Terms

A

Abstract: As an adjective applied to writing or literary works, abstract refers to words or phrases that name things not knowable through the five senses.

Aestheticism: A literary and artistic movement of the nineteenth century. Followers of the movement believed that art should not be mixed with social, political, or moral teaching. The statement "art for art's sake" is a good summary of aestheticism. The movement had its roots in France, but it gained widespread importance in England in the last half of the nineteenth century, where it helped change the Victorian practice of including moral lessons in literature.

Allegory: A narrative technique in which characters representing things or abstract ideas are used to convey a message or teach a lesson. Allegory is typically used to teach moral, ethical, or religious lessons but is sometimes used for satiric or political purposes.

Allusion: A reference to a familiar literary or historical person or event, used to make an idea more easily understood.

Analogy: A comparison of two things made to explain something unfamiliar through its similarities to something familiar, or to prove one point based on the acceptedness of another. Similes and metaphors are types of analogies.

Antagonist: The major character in a narrative or drama who works against the hero or protagonist.

Anthropomorphism: The presentation of animals or objects in human shape or with human characteristics. The term is derived from the Greek word for "human form."

Anti-hero: A central character in a work of literature who lacks traditional heroic qualities such as courage, physical prowess, and fortitude. Anti-heroes typically distrust conventional values and are unable to commit themselves to any ideals. They generally feel helpless in a world over which they have no control. Anti-heroes usually accept, and often celebrate, their positions as social outcasts.

Apprenticeship Novel: See *Bildungsroman*

Archetype: The word archetype is commonly used to describe an original pattern or model from which all other things of the same kind are made. This term was introduced to literary criticism from the psychology of Carl Jung. It expresses Jung's theory that behind every person's "unconscious," or repressed memories of the past, lies the "collective unconscious" of the human race: memories of the countless typical experiences of our ancestors. These memories are said to prompt illogical associations that trigger powerful emotions in the reader. Often, the emotional process is primitive, even primordial. Archetypes are the literary images that grow out of the "collective unconscious." They appear in literature as incidents and plots that repeat basic patterns of life. They may also appear as stereotyped characters.

Avant-garde: French term meaning "vanguard." It is used in literary criticism to describe new writing that rejects traditional approaches to literature in favor of innovations in style or content.

B

Beat Movement: A period featuring a group of American poets and novelists of the 1950s and 1960s—including Jack Kerouac, Allen Ginsberg, Gregory Corso, William S. Burroughs, and Lawrence Ferlinghetti—who rejected established social and literary values. Using such techniques as stream of consciousness writing and jazz-influenced free verse and focusing on unusual or abnormal states of mind—generated by religious ecstasy or the use of drugs—the Beat writers aimed to create works that were unconventional in both form and subject matter.

Bildungsroman: A German word meaning "novel of development." The *bildungsroman* is a study of the maturation of a youthful character, typically brought about through a series of social or sexual encounters that lead to self-awareness. *Bildungsroman* is used interchangeably with *erziehungsroman*, a novel of initiation and education. When a *bildungsroman* is concerned with the development of an artist (as in James Joyce's *A Portrait of the Artist as a Young Man*), it is often termed a *kunstlerroman*.

Black Aesthetic Movement: A period of artistic and literary development among African Americans in the 1960s and early 1970s. This was the first major African-American artistic movement since the Harlem Renaissance and was closely paralleled by the civil rights and black power movements. The black aesthetic writers attempted to produce works of art that would be meaningful to the black masses. Key figures in black aesthetics included one of its founders, poet and playwright Amiri Baraka, formerly known as LeRoi Jones; poet

and essayist Haki R. Madhubuti, formerly Don L. Lee; poet and playwright Sonia Sanchez; and dramatist Ed Bullins.

Black Humor: Writing that places grotesque elements side by side with humorous ones in an attempt to shock the reader, forcing him or her to laugh at the horrifying reality of a disordered world.

Burlesque: Any literary work that uses exaggeration to make its subject appear ridiculous, either by treating a trivial subject with profound seriousness or by treating a dignified subject frivolously. The word "burlesque" may also be used as an adjective, as in "burlesque show," to mean "striptease act."

C

Character: Broadly speaking, a person in a literary work. The actions of characters are what constitute the plot of a story, novel, or poem. There are numerous types of characters, ranging from simple, stereotypical figures to intricate, multifaceted ones. In the techniques of anthropomorphism and personification, animals—and even places or things—can assume aspects of character. "Characterization" is the process by which an author creates vivid, believable characters in a work of art. This may be done in a variety of ways, including (1) direct description of the character by the narrator; (2) the direct presentation of the speech, thoughts, or actions of the character; and (3) the responses of other characters to the character. The term "character" also refers to a form originated by the ancient Greek writer Theophrastus that later became popular in the seventeenth and eighteenth centuries. It is a short essay or sketch of a person who prominently displays a specific attribute or quality, such as miserliness or ambition.

Climax: The turning point in a narrative, the moment when the conflict is at its most intense. Typically, the structure of stories, novels, and plays is one of rising action, in which tension builds to the climax, followed by falling action, in which tension lessens as the story moves to its conclusion.

Colloquialism: A word, phrase, or form of pronunciation that is acceptable in casual conversation but not in formal, written communication. It is considered more acceptable than slang.

Coming of Age Novel: See *Bildungsroman*

Concrete: Concrete is the opposite of abstract, and refers to a thing that actually exists or a description that allows the reader to experience an object or concept with the senses.

Connotation: The impression that a word gives beyond its defined meaning. Connotations may be universally understood or may be significant only to a certain group.

Convention: Any widely accepted literary device, style, or form.

D

Denotation: The definition of a word, apart from the impressions or feelings it creates (connotations) in the reader.

Denouement: A French word meaning "the unknotting." In literary criticism, it denotes the resolution of conflict in fiction or drama. The *denouement* follows the climax and provides an outcome to the primary plot situation as well as an explanation of secondary plot complications. The *denouement* often involves a character's recognition of his or her state of mind or moral condition.

Description: Descriptive writing is intended to allow a reader to picture the scene or setting in which the action of a story takes place. The form this description takes often evokes an intended emotional response— a dark, spooky graveyard will evoke fear, and a peaceful, sunny meadow will evoke calmness.

Dialogue: In its widest sense, dialogue is simply conversation between people in a literary work; in its most restricted sense, it refers specifically to the speech of characters in a drama. As a specific literary genre, a "dialogue" is a composition in which characters debate an issue or idea.

Diction: The selection and arrangement of words in a literary work. Either or both may vary depending on the desired effect. There are four general types of diction: "formal," used in scholarly or lofty writing; "informal," used in relaxed but educated conversation; "colloquial," used in everyday speech; and "slang," containing newly coined words and other terms not accepted in formal usage.

Didactic: A term used to describe works of literature that aim to teach some moral, religious, political, or practical lesson. Although didactic elements are often found in artistically pleasing works, the term "didactic" usually refers to literature in which the message is more important than the form. The term may also be used to criticize a work that the critic finds "overly didactic," that is, heavy-handed in its delivery of a lesson.

Doppelganger: A literary technique by which a character is duplicated (usually in the form of an alter ego, though sometimes as a ghostly counterpart) or divided into two distinct, usually opposite personalities. The use of this character device is widespread in nineteenth- and twentieth-century literature, and indicates a growing awareness among authors that the "self" is really a composite of many "selves."

Double Entendre: A corruption of a French phrase meaning "double meaning." The term is used to indicate a word or phrase that is deliberately ambiguous, especially when one of the meanings is risqué or improper.

Dramatic Irony: Occurs when the audience of a play or the reader of a work of literature knows something that a character in the work itself does not know. The irony is in the contrast between the intended meaning of the statements or actions of a character and the additional information understood by the audience.

Dystopia: An imaginary place in a work of fiction where the characters lead dehumanized, fearful lives.

E

Edwardian: Describes cultural conventions identified with the period of the reign of Edward VII of England (1901-1910). Writers of the Edwardian Age typically displayed a strong reaction against the propriety and conservatism of the Victorian Age. Their work often exhibits distrust of authority in religion, politics, and art and expresses strong doubts about the soundness of conventional values.

Empathy: A sense of shared experience, including emotional and physical feelings, with someone or something other than oneself. Empathy is often used to describe the response of a reader to a literary character.

Enlightenment, The: An eighteenth-century philosophical movement. It began in France but had a wide impact throughout Europe and America. Thinkers of the Enlightenment valued reason and believed that both the individual and society could achieve a state of perfection. Corresponding to this essentially humanist vision was a resistance to religious authority.

Epigram: A saying that makes the speaker's point quickly and concisely. Often used to preface a novel.

Epilogue: A concluding statement or section of a literary work. In dramas, particularly those of the seventeenth and eighteenth centuries, the epilogue is a closing speech, often in verse, delivered by an actor at the end of a play and spoken directly to the audience.

Epiphany: A sudden revelation of truth inspired by a seemingly trivial incident.

Episode: An incident that forms part of a story and is significantly related to it. Episodes may be either self-contained narratives or events that depend on a larger context for their sense and importance.

Epistolary Novel: A novel in the form of letters. The form was particularly popular in the eighteenth century.

Epithet: A word or phrase, often disparaging or abusive, that expresses a character trait of someone or something.

Existentialism: A predominantly twentieth-century philosophy concerned with the nature and perception of human existence. There are two major strains of existentialist thought: atheistic and Christian. Followers of atheistic existentialism believe that the individual is alone in a godless universe and that the basic human condition is one of suffering and loneliness. Nevertheless, because there are no fixed values, individuals can create their own characters—indeed, they can shape themselves—through the exercise of free will. The atheistic strain culminates in and is popularly associated with the works of Jean-Paul Sartre. The Christian existentialists, on the other hand, believe that only in God may people find freedom from life's anguish. The two strains hold certain beliefs in common: that existence cannot be fully understood or described through empirical effort; that anguish is a universal element of life; that individuals must bear responsibility for their actions;

and that there is no common standard of behavior or perception for religious and ethical matters.

Expatriates: See *Expatriatism*

Expatriatism: The practice of leaving one's country to live for an extended period in another country.

Exposition: Writing intended to explain the nature of an idea, thing, or theme. Expository writing is often combined with description, narration, or argument. In dramatic writing, the exposition is the introductory material which presents the characters, setting, and tone of the play.

Expressionism: An indistinct literary term, originally used to describe an early twentieth-century school of German painting. The term applies to almost any mode of unconventional, highly subjective writing that distorts reality in some way.

F

Fable: A prose or verse narrative intended to convey a moral. Animals or inanimate objects with human characteristics often serve as characters in fables.

Falling Action: See *Denouement*

Fantasy: A literary form related to mythology and folklore. Fantasy literature is typically set in non-existent realms and features supernatural beings.

Farce: A type of comedy characterized by broad humor, outlandish incidents, and often vulgar subject matter.

Femme fatale: A French phrase with the literal translation "fatal woman." A *femme fatale* is a sensuous, alluring woman who often leads men into danger or trouble.

Fiction: Any story that is the product of imagination rather than a documentation of fact. characters and events in such narratives may be based in real life but their ultimate form and configuration is a creation of the author.

Figurative Language: A technique in writing in which the author temporarily interrupts the order, construction, or meaning of the writing for a particular effect. This interruption takes the form of one or more figures of speech such as hyperbole, irony, or simile. Figurative language is the opposite of literal language, in which every word is truthful, accurate, and free of exaggeration or embellishment.

Figures of Speech: Writing that differs from customary conventions for construction, meaning, order, or significance for the purpose of a special meaning or effect. There are two major types of figures of speech: rhetorical figures, which do not make changes in the meaning of the words, and tropes, which do.

Fin de siecle: A French term meaning "end of the century." The term is used to denote the last decade of the nineteenth century, a transition period when writers and other artists abandoned old conventions and looked for new techniques and objectives.

First Person: See *Point of View*

Flashback: A device used in literature to present action that occurred before the beginning of the story. Flashbacks are often introduced as the dreams or recollections of one or more characters.

Foil: A character in a work of literature whose physical or psychological qualities contrast strongly with, and therefore highlight, the corresponding qualities of another character.

Folklore: Traditions and myths preserved in a culture or group of people. Typically, these are passed on by word of mouth in various forms—such as legends, songs, and proverbs—or preserved in customs and ceremonies. This term was first used by W. J. Thoms in 1846.

Folktale: A story originating in oral tradition. Folktales fall into a variety of categories, including legends, ghost stories, fairy tales, fables, and anecdotes based on historical figures and events.

Foreshadowing: A device used in literature to create expectation or to set up an explanation of later developments.

Form: The pattern or construction of a work which identifies its genre and distinguishes it from other genres.

G

Genre: A category of literary work. In critical theory, genre may refer to both the content of a given work—tragedy, comedy, pastoral—and to its form, such as poetry, novel, or drama.

Gilded Age: A period in American history during the 1870s characterized by political corruption and materialism. A number of important novels of social and political criticism were written during this time.

Gothicism: In literary criticism, works characterized by a taste for the medieval or morbidly attractive. A gothic novel prominently features elements of horror, the supernatural, gloom, and violence: clanking chains, terror, charnel houses, ghosts, medieval castles, and mysteriously slamming doors. The term "gothic novel" is also applied to novels that lack elements of the traditional Gothic setting but that create a similar atmosphere of terror or dread.

Grotesque: In literary criticism, the subject matter of a work or a style of expression characterized by exaggeration, deformity, freakishness, and disorder. The grotesque often includes an element of comic absurdity.

H

Harlem Renaissance: The Harlem Renaissance of the 1920s is generally considered the first significant movement of black writers and artists in the United States. During this period, new and established black writers published more fiction and poetry than ever before, the first influential black literary journals were established, and black authors and artists received their first widespread recognition and serious critical appraisal. Among the major writers associated with this period are Claude McKay, Jean Toomer, Countee Cullen, Langston Hughes, Arna Bontemps, Nella Larsen, and Zora Neale Hurston.

Hero/Heroine: The principal sympathetic character (male or female) in a literary work. Heroes and heroines typically exhibit admirable traits: idealism, courage, and integrity, for example.

Holocaust Literature: Literature influenced by or written about the Holocaust of World War II. Such literature includes true stories of survival in concentration camps, escape, and life after the war, as well as fictional works and poetry.

Humanism: A philosophy that places faith in the dignity of humankind and rejects the medieval perception of the individual as a weak, fallen creature. "Humanists" typically believe in the perfectibility of human nature and view reason and education as the means to that end.

Hyperbole: In literary criticism, deliberate exaggeration used to achieve an effect.

I

Idiom: A word construction or verbal expression closely associated with a given language.

Image: A concrete representation of an object or sensory experience. Typically, such a representation helps evoke the feelings associated with the object or experience itself. Images are either "literal" or "figurative." Literal images are especially concrete and involve little or no extension of the obvious meaning of the words used to express them. Figurative images do not follow the literal meaning of the words exactly. Images in literature are usually visual, but the term "image" can also refer to the representation of any sensory experience.

Imagery: The array of images in a literary work. Also, figurative language.

In medias res: A Latin term meaning "in the middle of things." It refers to the technique of beginning a story at its midpoint and then using various flashback devices to reveal previous action.

Interior Monologue: A narrative technique in which characters' thoughts are revealed in a way that appears to be uncontrolled by the author. The interior monologue typically aims to reveal the inner self of a character. It portrays emotional experiences as they occur at both a conscious and unconscious level. images are often used to represent sensations or emotions.

Irony: In literary criticism, the effect of language in which the intended meaning is the opposite of what is stated.

J

Jargon: Language that is used or understood only by a select group of people. Jargon may refer to terminology used in a certain profession, such as computer jargon, or it may refer to any nonsensical language that is not understood by most people.

L

Leitmotiv: See *Motif*

Literal Language: An author uses literal language when he or she writes without exaggerating or embellishing the subject matter and without any tools of figurative language.

Lost Generation: A term first used by Gertrude Stein to describe the post-World War I generation of American writers: men and women haunted by a sense of betrayal and emptiness brought about by the destructiveness of the war.

M

Mannerism: Exaggerated, artificial adherence to a literary manner or style. Also, a popular style of the visual arts of late sixteenth-century Europe that was marked by elongation of the human form and by intentional spatial distortion. Literary works that are self-consciously high-toned and artistic are often said to be "mannered."

Metaphor: A figure of speech that expresses an idea through the image of another object. Metaphors suggest the essence of the first object by identifying it with certain qualities of the second object.

Modernism: Modern literary practices. Also, the principles of a literary school that lasted from roughly the beginning of the twentieth century until the end of World War II. Modernism is defined by its rejection of the literary conventions of the nineteenth century and by its opposition to conventional morality, taste, traditions, and economic values.

Mood: The prevailing emotions of a work or of the author in his or her creation of the work. The mood of a work is not always what might be expected based on its subject matter.

Motif: A theme, character type, image, metaphor, or other verbal element that recurs throughout a single work of literature or occurs in a number of different works over a period of time.

Myth: An anonymous tale emerging from the traditional beliefs of a culture or social unit. Myths use supernatural explanations for natural phenomena. They may also explain cosmic issues like creation and death. Collections of myths, known as mythologies, are common to all cultures and nations, but the best-known myths belong to the Norse, Roman, and Greek mythologies.

N

Narration: The telling of a series of events, real or invented. A narration may be either a simple narrative, in which the events are recounted chronologically, or a narrative with a plot, in which the account is given in a style reflecting the author's artistic concept of the story. Narration is sometimes used as a synonym for "storyline."

Narrative: A verse or prose accounting of an event or sequence of events, real or invented. The term is also used as an adjective in the sense "method of narration." For example, in literary criticism, the expression "narrative technique" usually refers to the way the author structures and presents his or her story.

Narrator: The teller of a story. The narrator may be the author or a character in the story through whom the author speaks.

Naturalism: A literary movement of the late nineteenth and early twentieth centuries. The movement's major theorist, French novelist Emile Zola, envisioned a type of fiction that would examine human life with the objectivity of scientific inquiry. The Naturalists typically viewed human beings as either the products of "biological determinism," ruled by hereditary instincts and engaged in an endless struggle for survival, or as the products of "socioeconomic determinism," ruled by social and economic forces beyond their control. In their works, the Naturalists generally ignored the highest levels of society and focused on degradation: poverty, alcoholism, prostitution, insanity, and disease.

Noble Savage: The idea that primitive man is noble and good but becomes evil and corrupted as he becomes civilized. The concept of the noble savage originated in the Renaissance period but is more closely identified with such later writers as Jean-Jacques Rousseau and Aphra Behn.

Novel: A long fictional narrative written in prose, which developed from the novella and other early forms of narrative. A novel is usually organized under a plot or theme with a focus on character development and action.

Novel of Ideas: A novel in which the examination of intellectual issues and concepts takes precedence over characterization or a traditional storyline.

Novel of Manners: A novel that examines the customs and mores of a cultural group.

Novella: An Italian term meaning "story." This term has been especially used to describe fourteenth-century Italian tales, but it also refers to modern short novels.

O

Objective Correlative: An outward set of objects, a situation, or a chain of events corresponding to an inward experience and evoking this experience in the reader. The term frequently appears in modern criticism in discussions of authors' intended effects on the emotional responses of readers.

Objectivity: A quality in writing characterized by the absence of the author's opinion or feeling about the subject matter. Objectivity is an important factor in criticism.

Oedipus Complex: A son's amorous obsession with his mother. The phrase is derived from the story of the ancient Theban hero Oedipus, who unknowingly killed his father and married his mother.

Omniscience: See *Point of View*

Onomatopoeia: The use of words whose sounds express or suggest their meaning. In its simplest sense, onomatopoeia may be represented by words that mimic the sounds they denote such as "hiss" or "meow." At a more subtle level, the pattern and rhythm of sounds and rhymes of a line or poem may be onomatopoeic.

Oxymoron: A phrase combining two contradictory terms. Oxymorons may be intentional or unintentional.

P

Parable: A story intended to teach a moral lesson or answer an ethical question.

Paradox: A statement that appears illogical or contradictory at first, but may actually point to an underlying truth.

Parallelism: A method of comparison of two ideas in which each is developed in the same grammatical structure.

Parody: In literary criticism, this term refers to an imitation of a serious literary work or the signature style of a particular author in a ridiculous manner. A typical parody adopts the style of the original and applies it to an inappropriate subject for humorous effect. Parody is a form of satire and could be considered the literary equivalent of a caricature or cartoon.

Pastoral: A term derived from the Latin word "pastor," meaning shepherd. A pastoral is a literary composition on a rural theme. The conventions of the pastoral were originated by the third-century Greek poet Theocritus, who wrote about the experiences, love affairs, and pastimes of Sicilian shepherds. In a pastoral, characters and language of a courtly nature are often placed in a simple setting. The term pastoral is also used to classify dramas, elegies, and lyrics that exhibit the use of country settings and shepherd characters.

Pen Name: See *Pseudonym*

Persona: A Latin term meaning "mask." *Personae* are the characters in a fictional work of literature. The *persona* generally functions as a mask through which the author tells a story in a voice other than his or her own. A *persona* is usually either a character in a story who acts as a narrator or an "implied author," a voice created by the author to act as the narrator for himself or herself.

Personification: A figure of speech that gives human qualities to abstract ideas, animals, and inanimate objects.

Picaresque Novel: Episodic fiction depicting the adventures of a roguish central character ("picaro" is Spanish for "rogue"). The picaresque hero is commonly a low-born but clever individual who wanders into and out of various affairs of love, danger, and farcical intrigue. These involvements may take place at all social levels and typically present a humorous and wide-ranging satire of a given society.

Plagiarism: Claiming another person's written material as one's own. Plagiarism can take the form of direct, word-for-word copying or the theft of the substance or idea of the work.

Plot: In literary criticism, this term refers to the pattern of events in a narrative or drama. In its simplest sense, the plot guides the author in composing the work and helps the reader follow the work. Typically, plots exhibit causality and unity and have a beginning, a middle, and an end. Sometimes, however, a plot may consist of a series of disconnected events, in which case it is known as an "episodic plot."

Poetic Justice: An outcome in a literary work, not necessarily a poem, in which the good are rewarded and the evil are punished, especially in ways that particularly fit their virtues or crimes.

Poetic License: Distortions of fact and literary convention made by a writer—not always a poet—for the sake of the effect gained. Poetic license is closely related to the concept of "artistic freedom."

Poetics: This term has two closely related meanings. It denotes (1) an aesthetic theory in literary criticism about the essence of poetry or (2) rules prescribing the proper methods, content, style, or diction of poetry. The term poetics may also refer to theories about literature in general, not just poetry.

Point of View: The narrative perspective from which a literary work is presented to the reader. There are four traditional points of view. The "third person omniscient" gives the reader a "godlike" perspective, unrestricted by time or place, from which to see actions and look into the minds of characters. This allows the author to comment openly on characters and events in the work. The "third person" point of view presents the events of the story from outside of any single character's perception, much like the omniscient point of view, but the reader must understand the action as it takes place and without any special insight into characters' minds or motivations. The "first person" or "personal" point of view relates events as they are perceived by a single character. The main character "tells" the story and may offer opinions about the action and characters which differ from those of the author. Much less common than omniscient, third person, and first person is the "second person" point of view, wherein the author tells the story as if it is happening to the reader.

Polemic: A work in which the author takes a stand on a controversial subject, such as abortion or religion. Such works are often extremely argumentative or provocative.

Pornography: Writing intended to provoke feelings of lust in the reader. Such works are often condemned by critics and teachers, but those which can be shown to have literary value are viewed less harshly.

Post-Aesthetic Movement: An artistic response made by African Americans to the black aesthetic movement of the 1960s and early '70s. Writers since that time have adopted a somewhat different tone in their work, with less emphasis placed on the disparity between black and white in the United States. In the words of post-aesthetic authors such as Toni Morrison, John Edgar Wideman, and Kristin Hunter, African Americans are portrayed as looking inward for answers to their own questions, rather than always looking to the outside world.

Postmodernism: Writing from the 1960s forward characterized by experimentation and continuing to apply some of the fundamentals of modernism, which included existentialism and alienation. Postmodernists have gone a step further in the rejection of tradition begun with the modernists by also rejecting traditional forms, preferring the anti-novel over the novel and the anti-hero over the hero.

Primitivism: The belief that primitive peoples were nobler and less flawed than civilized peoples because they had not been subjected to the tainting influence of society.

Prologue: An introductory section of a literary work. It often contains information establishing the situation of the characters or presents information about the setting, time period, or action. In drama, the prologue is spoken by a chorus or by one of the principal characters.

Prose: A literary medium that attempts to mirror the language of everyday speech. It is distinguished from poetry by its use of unmetered, unrhymed language consisting of logically related sentences. Prose is usually grouped into paragraphs that form a cohesive whole such as an essay or a novel.

Prosopopoeia: See *Personification*

Protagonist: The central character of a story who serves as a focus for its themes and incidents and as the principal rationale for its development. The protagonist is sometimes referred to in discussions of modern literature as the hero or anti-hero.

Protest Fiction: Protest fiction has as its primary purpose the protesting of some social injustice, such as racism or discrimination.

Proverb: A brief, sage saying that expresses a truth about life in a striking manner.

Pseudonym: A name assumed by a writer, most often intended to prevent his or her identification as the author of a work. Two or more authors may work together under one pseudonym, or an author may use a different name for each genre he or she publishes in. Some publishing companies maintain "house pseudonyms," under which any number of authors may write installments in a series. Some authors also choose a pseudonym over their real names the way an actor may use a stage name.

Pun: A play on words that have similar sounds but different meanings.

R

Realism: A nineteenth-century European literary movement that sought to portray familiar characters, situations, and settings in a realistic manner. This was done primarily by using an objective narrative point of view and through the buildup of accurate detail. The standard for success of any realistic work depends on how faithfully it transfers common experience into fictional forms. The realistic method may be altered or extended, as in stream of consciousness writing, to record highly subjective experience.

Repartee: Conversation featuring snappy retorts and witticisms.

Resolution: The portion of a story following the climax, in which the conflict is resolved.

Rhetoric: In literary criticism, this term denotes the art of ethical persuasion. In its strictest sense, rhetoric adheres to various principles developed since classical times for arranging facts and ideas in a clear, persuasive, appealing manner. The term is also used to refer to effective prose in general and theories of or methods for composing effective prose.

Rhetorical Question: A question intended to provoke thought, but not an expressed answer, in the reader. It is most commonly used in oratory and other persuasive genres.

Rising Action: The part of a drama where the plot becomes increasingly complicated. Rising action leads up to the climax, or turning point, of a drama.

Roman à clef: A French phrase meaning "novel with a key." It refers to a narrative in which real persons are portrayed under fictitious names.

Romance: A broad term, usually denoting a narrative with exotic, exaggerated, often idealized characters, scenes, and themes.

Romanticism: This term has two widely accepted meanings. In historical criticism, it refers to a European intellectual and artistic movement of the late eighteenth and early nineteenth centuries that sought greater freedom of personal expression than that allowed by the strict rules of literary form and logic of the eighteenth-century neoclassicists. The Romantics preferred emotional and imaginative expression to rational analysis. They considered the individual to be at the center of all experience and so placed him or her at the center of their art. The Romantics believed that the creative imagination reveals nobler truths—unique feelings and attitudes—than those that could be discovered by logic or by scientific examination. Both the natural world and the state of childhood were important sources for revelations of "eternal truths." "Romanticism" is also used as a general term to refer to a type of sensibility found in all periods of literary history and usually considered to be in opposition to the principles of classicism. In this sense, Romanticism signifies any work or philosophy in which the exotic or dreamlike figure strongly, or that is devoted to individualistic expression, self-analysis, or a pursuit of a higher realm of knowledge than can be discovered by human reason.

Romantics: See *Romanticism*

S

Satire: A work that uses ridicule, humor, and wit to criticize and provoke change in human nature and institutions. There are two major types of satire: "formal" or "direct" satire speaks directly to the reader or to a character in the work; "indirect" satire relies upon the ridiculous behavior of its characters to make its point. Formal satire is

further divided into two manners: the "Horatian," which ridicules gently, and the "Juvenalian," which derides its subjects harshly and bitterly.

Science Fiction: A type of narrative about or based upon real or imagined scientific theories and technology. Science fiction is often peopled with alien creatures and set on other planets or in different dimensions.

Second Person: See *Point of View*

Setting: The time, place, and culture in which the action of a narrative takes place. The elements of setting may include geographic location, characters' physical and mental environments, prevailing cultural attitudes, or the historical time in which the action takes place.

Simile: A comparison, usually using "like" or "as," of two essentially dissimilar things, as in "coffee as cold as ice" or "He sounded like a broken record."

Slang: A type of informal verbal communication that is generally unacceptable for formal writing. Slang words and phrases are often colorful exaggerations used to emphasize the speaker's point; they may also be shortened versions of an often-used word or phrase.

Slave Narrative: Autobiographical accounts of American slave life as told by escaped slaves. These works first appeared during the abolition movement of the 1830s through the 1850s.

Socialist Realism: The Socialist Realism school of literary theory was proposed by Maxim Gorky and established as a dogma by the first Soviet Congress of Writers. It demanded adherence to a communist worldview in works of literature. Its doctrines required an objective viewpoint comprehensible to the working classes and themes of social struggle featuring strong proletarian heroes.

Stereotype: A stereotype was originally the name for a duplication made during the printing process; this led to its modern definition as a person or thing that is (or is assumed to be) the same as all others of its type.

Stream of Consciousness: A narrative technique for rendering the inward experience of a character. This technique is designed to give the impression of an ever-changing series of thoughts, emotions, images, and memories in the spontaneous and seemingly illogical order that they occur in life.

Structure: The form taken by a piece of literature. The structure may be made obvious for ease of understanding, as in nonfiction works, or may obscured for artistic purposes, as in some poetry or seemingly "unstructured" prose.

Sturm und Drang: A German term meaning "storm and stress." It refers to a German literary movement of the 1770s and 1780s that reacted against the order and rationalism of the enlightenment, focusing instead on the intense experience of extraordinary individuals.

Style: A writer's distinctive manner of arranging words to suit his or her ideas and purpose in writing. The unique imprint of the author's personality upon his or her writing, style is the product of an author's way of arranging ideas and his or her use of diction, different sentence structures, rhythm, figures of speech, rhetorical principles, and other elements of composition.

Subjectivity: Writing that expresses the author's personal feelings about his subject, and which may or may not include factual information about the subject.

Subplot: A secondary story in a narrative. A subplot may serve as a motivating or complicating force for the main plot of the work, or it may provide emphasis for, or relief from, the main plot.

Surrealism: A term introduced to criticism by Guillaume Apollinaire and later adopted by Andre Breton. It refers to a French literary and artistic movement founded in the 1920s. The Surrealists sought to express unconscious thoughts and feelings in their works. The best-known technique used for achieving this aim was automatic writing—transcriptions of spontaneous outpourings from the unconscious. The Surrealists proposed to unify the contrary levels of conscious and unconscious, dream and reality, objectivity and subjectivity into a new level of "super-realism."

Suspense: A literary device in which the author maintains the audience's attention through the buildup of events, the outcome of which will soon be revealed.

Symbol: Something that suggests or stands for something else without losing its original identity. In literature, symbols combine their literal meaning with the suggestion of an abstract concept. Literary symbols are of two types: those that carry complex associations of meaning no matter what their contexts, and those that derive their suggestive meaning from their functions in specific literary works.

Symbolism: This term has two widely accepted meanings. In historical criticism, it denotes an early modernist literary movement initiated in France during the nineteenth century that reacted against the prevailing standards of realism. Writers in this movement aimed to evoke, indirectly and symbolically, an order of being beyond the material world of the five senses. Poetic expression of personal emotion figured strongly in the movement, typically by means of a private set of symbols uniquely identifiable with the individual poet. The principal aim of the Symbolists was to express in words the highly complex feelings that grew out of everyday contact with the world. In a broader sense, the term "symbolism" refers to the use of one object to represent another.

T

Tall Tale: A humorous tale told in a straightforward, credible tone but relating absolutely impossible events or feats of the characters. Such tales were commonly told of frontier adventures during the settlement of the west in the United States.

Theme: The main point of a work of literature. The term is used interchangeably with thesis.

Thesis: A thesis is both an essay and the point argued in the essay. Thesis novels and thesis plays share the quality of containing a thesis which is supported through the action of the story.

Third Person: See *Point of View*

Tone: The author's attitude toward his or her audience may be deduced from the tone of the work. A formal tone may create distance or convey politeness, while an informal tone may encourage a friendly, intimate, or intrusive feeling in the reader. The author's attitude tward his or her subject matter may also be deduced from the tone of the words he or she uses in discussing it.

Transcendentalism: An American philosophical and religious movement, based in New England from around 1835 until the Civil War. Transcendentalism was a form of American romanticism that had its roots abroad in the works of Thomas Carlyle, Samuel Coleridge, and Johann Wolfgang von Goethe. The Transcendentalists stressed the importance of intuition and subjective experience in communication with God. They rejected religious dogma and texts in favor of mysticism and scientific naturalism. They pursued truths that lie beyond the "colorless" realms perceived by reason and the senses and were active social reformers in public education, women's rights, and the abolition of slavery.

U

Urban Realism: A branch of realist writing that attempts to accurately reflect the often harsh facts of modern urban existence.

Utopia: A fictional perfect place, such as "paradise" or "heaven."

V

Verisimilitude: Literally, the appearance of truth. In literary criticism, the term refers to aspects of a work of literature that seem true to the reader.

Victorian: Refers broadly to the reign of Queen Victoria of England (1837-1901) and to anything with qualities typical of that era. For example, the qualities of smug narrowmindedness, bourgeois materialism, faith in social progress, and priggish morality are often considered Victorian. This stereotype is contradicted by such dramatic intellectual developments as the theories of Charles Darwin, Karl Marx, and Sigmund Freud (which stirred strong debates in England) and the critical attitudes of serious Victorian writers like Charles Dickens and George Eliot. In literature, the Victorian Period was the great age of the English novel, and the latter part of the era saw the rise of movements such as decadence and symbolism.

W

Weltanschauung: A German term referring to a person's worldview or philosophy.

Weltschmerz: A German term meaning "world pain." It describes a sense of anguish about the nature of existence, usually associated with a melancholy, pessimistic attitude.

Z

Zeitgeist: A German term meaning "spirit of the time." It refers to the moral and intellectual trends of a given era.

Cumulative Author/Title Index

Cumulative Nationality/Ethnicity Index

Japanese

Abe, Kobo
The Woman in the Dunes: V22
Ishiguro, Kazuo
The Remains of the Day: V13
Mori, Kyoko
Shizuko's Daughter: V15
Watkins, Yoko Kawashima
So Far from the Bamboo Grove: V28
Yoshimoto, Banana
Kitchen: V7

Jewish

Asimov, Isaac
I, Robot: V29
Bellow, Saul
Herzog: V14
Humboldt's Gift: V26
Seize the Day: V4
Kafka, Franz
The Trial: V7
Kertész, Imre
Kaddish for a Child Not Born: V23
Malamud, Bernard
The Assistant: V27
The Fixer: V9
The Natural: V4
Roth, Philip
American Pastoral: V25
Salinger, J. D.
The Catcher in the Rye: V1
Franny and Zooey: V30
West, Nathanael
The Day of the Locust: V16
Wiesel, Eliezer
Night: V4
Yezierska, Anzia
Bread Givers: V29
Yolen, Jane
Briar Rose: V30

Korean

Choi, Sook Nyul
Year of Impossible Goodbyes: V29

Mexican

Esquivel, Laura
Like Water for Chocolate: V5
Fuentes, Carlos
The Old Gringo: V8

Native American

Alexie, Sherman
The Lone Ranger and Tonto
Fistfight in Heaven: V17
Dorris, Michael
A Yellow Raft in Blue Water: V3
Erdrich, Louise
Love Medicine: V5

Momaday, N. Scott
House Made of Dawn: V10
Silko, Leslie Marmon
Ceremony: V4
Welch, James
Winter in the Blood: V23

New Zealander

Hulme, Keri
The Bone People: V24

Nigerian

Achebe, Chinua
Things Fall Apart: V3
Emecheta, Buchi
The Bride Price: V12
The Wrestling Match: V14

Norwegian

Rölvaag, O. E.
Giants in the Earth: V5

Polish

Conrad, Joseph
Heart of Darkness: V2
Lord Jim: V16
Kosinski, Jerzy
The Painted Bird: V12

Portuguese

Saramago, José
Blindness: V27

Romanian

Wiesel, Eliezer
Night: V4

Russian

Asimov, Isaac
I, Robot: V29
Bulgakov, Mikhail
The Master and Margarita: V8
Dostoyevsky, Fyodor
The Brothers Karamazon: V8
Crime and Punishment: V3
Notes from Underground: V28
Nabokov, Vladimir
Lolita: V9
Pasternak, Boris
Doctor Zhivago: V26
Rand, Ayn
Anthem: V29
Atlas Shrugged: V10
The Fountainhead: V16
Solzhenitsyn, Aleksandr
One Day in the Life of Ivan
Denisovich: V6

Tolstoy, Leo
Anna Karenina: V28
War and Peace: V10
Turgenev, Ivan
Fathers and Sons: V16
Yezierska, Anzia
Bread Givers: V29

Scottish

Grahame, Kenneth
The Wind in the Willows: V20
Spark, Muriel
The Prime of Miss Jean Brodie: V22
Stevenson, Robert Louis
Treasure Island: V20

South African

Coetzee, J. M.
Dusklands: V21
Gordimer, Nadine
July's People: V4
Paton, Alan
Cry, the Beloved Country: V3
Too Late the Phalarope: V12

Spanish

de Cervantes Saavedra, Miguel
Don Quixote: V8

Sri Lankan

Ondaatje, Michael
The English Patient: V23

Swiss

Hesse, Hermann
Demian: V15
Siddhartha: V6
Steppenwolf: V24

Turkish

Pamuk, Orhan
My Name is Red: V27

Uruguayan

Bridal, Tessa
The Tree of Red Stars: V17

Vietnamese

Duong Thu Huong
Paradise of the Blind: V23

West Indian

Kincaid, Jamaica
Annie John: V3

Zimbabwean

Dangarembga, Tsitsi
Nervous Conditions: V28

Subject/Theme Index